MAIN CURRENTS
OF MARXISM

MAIN CURRENTS OF MARXISM

ITS ORIGIN, GROWTH, AND DISSOLUTION

by
Leszek Kołakowski

VOLUME III
THE BREAKDOWN

Translated from the Polish
by
P. S. Falla

CLARENDON PRESS · OXFORD
1978

Oxford University Press, Walton Street, Oxford OX2 6DP

OXFORD LONDON GLASGOW
NEW YORK TORONTO MELBOURNE WELLINGTON
IBADAN NAIROBI DAR ES SALAAM LUSAKA CAPE TOWN
KUALA LUMPUR SINGAPORE JAKARTA HONG KONG TOKYO
DELHI BOMBAY CALCUTTA MADRAS KARACHI

© *Oxford University Press 1978*

British Library Cataloguing in Publication Data
Kolakowski, Leszek
  Main currents of Marxism.
  Vol. 3: The breakdown.
  1. Communism—History
  I. Title   II. Falla, Paul Stephen
  335.4′09′034   HX21   78–40082
  ISBN 0–19–824570–X

*Filmset in Great Britain by
Northumberland Press Ltd, Gateshead, Tyne and Wear
and printed by
Fletcher and Son Ltd, Norwich*

PREFACE

THE present volume deals with the evolution of Marxism in the last half-century. Writing it has involved especial difficulties, one of which is the sheer bulk of the available literature: no historian can be fully acquainted with it, and it is therefore, so to speak, impossible to do everyone justice. Another difficulty is that I am not able to treat the subject with the desirable detachment. Many of the people mentioned in this volume I know or have known personally, and some of them are or were my friends. Moreover, in describing the controversies and political struggles in Eastern Europe in the later 1950s I am writing about events and issues in which I myself took part, so that I appear in the invidious role of a judge in my own cause. At the same time, I could not pass over these matters in silence. The upshot is that the most recent period, which is the one I know best from my own experience, is treated less fully than any other. The last chapter, which deals with this period, could be expanded into a further volume; but, setting aside the difficulties already mentioned, I am not convinced that the subject is intrinsically worthy of treatment at such length.

CONTENTS

Contents

BIBLIOGRAPHICAL NOTE

Sources of quotations used in the text:

ADORNO, THEODOR W., *Negative Dialectics*, The Seabury Press, New York, 1972; Routledge & Kegan Paul, London, 1973.

GOLDMANN, L., *The Hidden God*, trans. Thody (International Library of Philosophy), Routledge & Kegan Paul, London, 1974.

HORKHEIMER, MAX and THEODOR W. ADORNO, *Dialectic of Enlightenment*, trans. John Cummings, The Seabury Press, New York, 1972; Allen Lane, The Penguin Press, London, 1973.

KORSCH, KARL, *Marxism and Philosophy*, trans. F. Halliday, New Left Books, London, 1970.

LUKÁCS, GEORGE, *The Meaning of Contemporary Realism*, The Merlin Press, London, 1970.

MAO TSE-TUNG, *Anthology of His Writings*, ed. Anne Fremantle, Mentor Books, New American Library, New York, 1962.

— — *Four Essays on Philosophy*, Peking, 1966; Collet's, London, 1967.

— — *Quotations From Chairman Mao Tse-tung*, ed. Stuart Schram, Pall Mall Press, London, 1968.

— — *Mao Tse-tung Unrehearsed*, ed. and trans. Stuart Schram, Pelican Books, London, 1974, and as *Chairman Mao Talks to the People*, Pantheon Books, New York, 1975.

MARCUSE, HERBERT, *One-Dimensional Man*, Routledge & Kegan Paul, London, 1964.

— — *Five Lectures*, Allen Lane, The Penguin Press, London, 1970.

13 vols., Lawrence & Wishart, London, 1953–5.

SNOW, EDGAR, *The Long Revolution*, Hutchinson, London, 1973.

STALIN, JOSEPH, *Collected Works*, vols. 7 and 8, English ed., 13 vols., Lawrence & Wishart, London, 1953–5.

TROTSKY, LEON, *Their Morals and Ours*, ed. George Novack, Pathfinder Press, New York, 1969.

—— *In Defense of Marxism*, New Park Publications, London, 1971; Pathfinder Press, New York, 1971.

—— *Writings of Leon Trotsky, 1929–1940*, 12 vols., Pathfinder Press, New York, 1971–7.

WOLFF, ROBERT P., BARRINGTON MOORE, JR., and HERBERT MARCUSE, *Critique of Pure Tolerance*, Jonathan Cape, London, 1969.

ZHDANOV, A. A., *On Literature, Music, and Philosophy*, Lawrence & Wishart, London, 1950.

CHAPTER I

The first phase of Soviet Marxism.
The Beginnings of Stalinism

1. What was Stalinism?

THERE is no general agreement as to what the term 'Stalinism' connotes. It has never been used by the official ideologists of the Soviet state, as it would seem to imply the existence of a self-contained social system. Since Khrushchev's time the accepted formula for what went on in Stalin's day has been 'the cult of personality', and this phrase is invariably associated with two presuppositions. The first is that throughout the existence of the Soviet Union the party's policy was 'in principle' right and salutary, but that occasional errors were committed, the most serious of which was the neglect of 'collective leadership', i.e. the concentration of unlimited power in Stalin's hands. The second assumption is that the main source of 'errors and distortions' lay in Stalin's own faults of character, his thirst for power, despotic inclinations, and so on. After Stalin's death all these deviations were immediately cured: the party once more conformed to proper democratic principles, and that was the end of the matter. As to Stalin's errors, the most serious was the mass liquidation of Communists and especially of the higher party bureaucracy. In short, Stalin's rule was a monstrous but accidental phenomenon: there was never such a thing as 'Stalinism' or a 'Stalinist system', and in any case the 'negative manifestations' of the 'personality cult' fade into insignificance beside the glorious achievements of the Soviet system.

Although this version of events is doubtless not taken seriously by its authors or by anyone else, controversy still prevails as to the meaning and scope of the term 'Stalinism', which is in current use outside the Soviet Union even among Communists.

The latter, however, whether critical or orthodox in their views, restrict its meaning to the period of Stalin's personal tyranny from the early 1930s to his death in 1953, and they blame the 'errors' of the time less on Stalin's own wickedness than on regrettable but unalterable historical circumstances: the industrial and cultural backwardness of Russia before and after 1917, the failure of the hoped-for European revolution, external threats to the Soviet state, and political exhaustion after the Civil War. (The same reasons, incidentally, are regularly advanced by Trotskyists to explain the degeneration of Russia's post-Revolutionary government.)

Those, on the other hand, who are not committed to defending the Soviet system, Leninism, or any Marxist historical schema generally regard Stalinism as a more or less coherent political, economic, and ideological system, which worked in pursuit of its own aims and made few 'errors' from its own point of view. Even on this basis, however, it may be debated how far and in what sense Stalinism was 'historically inevitable': i.e. was the political, economic, and ideological complexion of Soviet Russia already determined before Stalin's rise to power, so that Stalinism was only the full development of Leninism? The question also remains, how far and in what sense have all these characteristic features of the Soviet state persisted to the present day?

From the point of view of terminology it is of no special importance whether we confine the meaning of 'Stalinism' to the last twenty-five years of the dictator's life or extend it to cover the political system prevailing at the present time. But it is more than a purely verbal question whether the basic features of the system that took shape under Stalin have altered in the last twenty years, and there is also room for argument as to what its essential features were.

Many observers, including the present author, believe that the Soviet system as it developed under Stalin was a continuation of Leninism, and that the state founded on Lenin's political and ideological principles could only have maintained itself in a Stalinist form; such critics hold, moreover, that 'Stalinism' in the narrow sense, i.e. the system that prevailed until 1953, has not been affected in any essential way by the changes of the post-Stalinist era. The first of these points has been to some extent established in previous chapters, where Lenin was shown to be

BIBLIOGRAPHICAL NOTE

Sources of quotations used in the text:

ADORNO, THEODOR W., *Negative Dialectics*, The Seabury Press, New York, 1972; Routledge & Kegan Paul, London, 1973.

GOLDMANN, L., *The Hidden God*, trans. Thody (International Library of Philosophy), Routledge & Kegan Paul, London, 1974.

HORKHEIMER, MAX and THEODOR W. ADORNO, *Dialectic of Enlightenment*, trans. John Cummings, The Seabury Press, New York, 1972; Allen Lane, The Penguin Press, London, 1973.

KORSCH, KARL, *Marxism and Philosophy*, trans. F. Halliday, New Left Books, London, 1970.

LUKÁCS, GEORGE, *The Meaning of Contemporary Realism*, The Merlin Press, London, 1970.

MAO TSE-TUNG, *Anthology of His Writings*, ed. Anne Fremantle, Mentor Books, New American Library, New York, 1962.

—— *Four Essays on Philosophy*, Peking, 1966; Collet's, London, 1967.

—— *Quotations From Chairman Mao Tse-tung*, ed. Stuart Schram, Pall Mall Press, London, 1968.

—— *Mao Tse-tung Unrehearsed*, ed. and trans. Stuart Schram, Pelican Books, London, 1974, and as *Chairman Mao Talks to the People*, Pantheon Books, New York, 1975.

MARCUSE, HERBERT, *One-Dimensional Man*, Routledge & Kegan Paul, London, 1964.

—— *Five Lectures*, Allen Lane, The Penguin Press, London, 1970.

13 vols., Lawrence & Wishart, London, 1953-5.

SNOW, EDGAR, *The Long Revolution*, Hutchinson, London, 1973.

STALIN, JOSEPH, *Collected Works*, vols. 7 and 8, English ed., 13 vols., Lawrence & Wishart, London, 1953-5.

TROTSKY, LEON, *Their Morals and Ours*, ed. George Novack, Pathfinder Press, New York, 1969.

—— *In Defense of Marxism*, New Park Publications, London, 1971; Pathfinder Press, New York, 1971.

—— *Writings of Leon Trotsky, 1929–1940*, 12 vols., Pathfinder Press, New York, 1971–7.

WOLFF, ROBERT P., BARRINGTON MOORE, JR., and HERBERT MARCUSE, *Critique of Pure Tolerance*, Jonathan Cape, London, 1969.

ZHDANOV, A. A., *On Literature, Music, and Philosophy*, Lawrence & Wishart, London, 1950.

the creator of totalitarian doctrine and of the totalitarian state in embryo. Of course many events in the Stalin era can be attributed to chance or to Stalin's own peculiarities: careerism, lust for power, vindictiveness, jealousy, and paranoid suspicion. The mass slaughter of Communists in 1936–9 cannot be called a 'historical necessity', and we may suppose that it would not have taken place under a tyrant other than Stalin himself. But if, as in the typical Communist view, that slaughter is regarded as the true, 'negative' significance of Stalinism, it follows that the whole of Stalinism was a deplorable accident—the implication being that everything is always for the best under Communist rule until prominent Communists start being murdered. This is hard for the historian to accept, not only because he is interested in the fate of millions who were not party leaders or even party members, but also because the sanguinary terror on a huge scale which occurred in the Soviet Union at certain periods is not a permanent or essential feature of totalitarian despotism. The despotic system remains in force irrespective of whether, in a particular year, official murders are counted in millions or only in tens of thousands, whether torture is used as a matter of routine or only occasionally, and whether the victims are only workers, peasants, and intellectuals or include party bureaucrats as well.

The history of Stalinism, despite arguments over points of detail, is generally known and is adequately described in many books. As in the previous two volumes of this work, the main theme is the history of doctrine: political history will be dealt with cursorily, so far as is necessary to indicate the broad framework within which ideological life developed. In the Stalin era, however, the link between the history of doctrine and political events is much closer than before, since the phenomenon we have to study is the absolute institutionalization of Marxism as an instrument of power. This process, it is true, began earlier on: it goes back to Lenin's view that Marxism must be 'the party's world-outlook', i.e. that its content must be governed by the needs of the struggle for power at a particular moment. None the less, Lenin's political opportunism was to some extent restrained by doctrinal considerations; whereas in Stalin's day, from the early thirties onwards, doctrine was absolutely subordinated to the purpose of legitimizing and glorifying the Soviet government and everything it did. Marxism under Stalin cannot be defined by any collection of statements, ideas, or concepts: it was not a question of propositions as such but of the fact that there existed an all-powerful authority competent to declare at any given moment what Marxism was and what it was not. 'Marxism' meant nothing more or less than the current pronouncement of the authority in question, i.e. Stalin himself. For instance, up to June 1950 to be a Marxist meant, among other things, accepting the philological theories of N. Y. Marr, while after that date it meant rejecting them utterly. You were a Marxist not because you regarded any particular ideas—Marx's, Lenin's, or even Stalin's—as true, but because you were prepared to accept whatever the supreme authority might proclaim today, tomorrow, or in a year's time. This degree of institutionalization and dogmatization had never been seen before and did not reach its acme until the thirties, but its roots can be clearly traced in Lenin's doctrine: since Marxism is the world-view and instrument of the proletarian party, it is for the latter to decide what is Marxism and what is not, regardless of any objections 'from outside'. When the party is identified with the state and the apparatus of power, and when it achieves perfect unity in the shape of a one-man tyranny, doctrine becomes a matter of state and the tyrant is proclaimed infallible. Indeed, he really *is* infallible as far as the content of Marxism is concerned, for there is no Marxism but that which the party asserts in its capacity as the mouthpiece of the proletariat, and the party, having once achieved unity, expresses its will and its doctrine through the leadership embodied in the dictator's person. In this way the doctrine that the proletariat is historically the leading class and, in contrast to all other classes, the possessor of objective truth is transformed into the principle that 'Stalin is always right'. This, in fact, is not too grave a distortion of Marx's epistemology combined with Lenin's notion of the party as the advance guard of the workers' movement. The equation: truth = the proletarian world-view = Marxism = the party's world-view = the pronouncements of the party leadership = those of the supreme leader is wholly in accordance with Lenin's version of Marxism. We shall endeavour to trace the process by which this equation found final expression in the Soviet ideology which Stalin christened Marxism–Leninism. It is gnificant that he chose this term rather than speaking of Marxism *and* Leninism, which would have suggested two separate doctrines. The compound expression signified that Leninism was not a distinct trend within Marxism—as though there might be other forms of Marxism that were not Leninist—but was Marxism *par excellence*, the sole doctrine in which Marxism was developed and adapted to the new historical era. In actual fact Marxism–Leninism consisted of Stalin's own doctrine plus quotations selected by him from the works of Marx, Lenin, and Engels. It should not be supposed that anyone was free, in Stalin's day, to quote at will from Marx, Lenin, or even Stalin himself: Marxism–Leninism comprised only the quotations currently authorized by the dictator, in conformity with the doctrine he was currently promulgating.

In arguing that Stalinism was a true development of Leninism I do not mean to belittle Stalin's historical importance. After Lenin, and alongside Hitler, he certainly did more to shape the present-day world than any other individual since the First World War. Nevertheless, the fact that it was Stalin and not any other Bolshevik leader who became sole ruler of the party and state can be accounted for by the nature of the Soviet system. The view that his personal qualities, while they had a great deal to do with his victory over his rivals, did not themselves determine the main lines of the development of Soviet society is supported by the fact that throughout his earlier career he did not belong to the extremist wing of the Bolshevik party. On the contrary, he was something of a moderate, and in intra-party disputes he often stood on the side of common sense and prudence. In short, Stalin as a despot was much more the party's creation than its creator: he was the personification of a system which irresistibly sought to be personified.

2. *The stages of Stalinism*

It is a mania of Soviet historians to divide all epochs into stages; but the procedure is justified in some cases, especially where the delimitation is based on ideological grounds.

Since Stalinism was an international and not merely a Soviet phenomenon, its variations must be considered not only from the point of view of Russian internal policy and sectional strife, but also from that of the Comintern and international Bolshevism.

There are, however, difficulties of correlating the respectiv
periods, and also of nomenclature. Trotskyists and ex-
Communists are in the habit of distinguishing 'leftist' and
'rightist' stages of Soviet history. The period immediately after
1917, dominated by the Civil War and by hopes of world
revolution, is referred to as 'leftist' and is followed by the 'rightist'
period of the N.E.P., when the party acknowledged the 'temporary stabilization of capitalism' in the world at large. Then
comes a 'swing to the left' in 1928–9, when the party declared
that this stabilization was at an end; the 'tide of revolution' set
in once more, social democracy was denounced and combated
as 'social Fascism', and Russia witnessed the beginning of mass
collectivization and forced industrialization. This stage is supposed to have ended in 1935, when a 'rightist' policy was once
more adopted under the slogan of a popular front against
Fascism. These successive shifts of policy are associated with
sectional and personal in-fighting among the Russian leaders.
The rule of Stalin, Zinovyev, and Kamenev led to the political
elimination of Trotsky; then Zinovyev and Kamenev were
ousted in favour of Bukharin, Rykov, and Tomsky; then, in 1929,
Bukharin was cast out and effective dissidence within the
Bolshevik party came to an end.

This chronology is full of difficulties, however, even apart from
the vague and arbitrary use of the terms 'left' and 'right'. As
to the latter point, it is not clear why the slogan of 'social
Fascism' was 'leftist' while the attempt to compromise with
Chiang Kai-shek was 'rightist'; or why it was 'leftist' to persecute
peasants on a vast scale but 'rightist' to use economic methods
for political ends. It can of course be laid down that the more
a policy involves terror, the more 'leftist' it is—this principle
is frequently applied at the present day, and not only in Communist publications, but it is hard to see what it has to do with
the traditional idea of 'leftism'. Apart from this, there is no
clear correlation between changes in Comintern policy and the
different phases of Soviet internal policy and ideology. The
so-called 'leftist' assertion that European social democracy was
a branch of Fascism was coined by Zinovyev and was current
at least as early as 1924; the Comintern's fight against social
democracy was intensified in 1927, long before the forced
collectivization of the Russian peasantry was thought of. In 1935,

when the campaign against social democracy was called off and clumsy efforts were made to patch up an alliance, there had already been a wave of mass political repression in the Soviet Union and another, more terrible one was about to commence.

In short, it makes no sense to present the history of the Soviet Union in terms of artificial criteria of 'left' and 'right', which in some cases lead to absurd results. Nor is it correct to interpret changes in the Politburo as historical turning-points. During the period after Lenin's death certain political and ideological features became steadily more prominent, while others fluctuated in importance according to circumstances. The totalitarian character of the regime—i.e. the progressive destruction of civil society and absorption of all forms of social life by the state—increased almost without interruption between 1924 and 1953 and was certainly not diminished by the N.E.P., despite concessions to private ownership and trade. The N.E.P., as we saw, was a retreat from the policy of running the whole economy by means of the army and police, and was necessitated by the imminent prospect of economic ruin. But the use of terror against political opponents, the increased severity and intimidation within the party, the suppression of independence and enforcement of servility in philosophy, literature, art, and science—all this continued to be accentuated during the whole period of the N.E.P. From this point of view the thirties were only an intensification and consolidation of the process which began in Lenin's lifetime and under his direction. The collectivization of agriculture, with its countless victims, indeed constituted a turning-point; but this was not because it involved a change in the character of the regime or a 'swing to the left', but because it enforced the basic political and economic principle of totalitarianism in a single sector of key importance. It completely dispossessed the most numerous social class in Russia, established state control of farming once and for all, annihilated the last section of the community that was in any degree independent of the state, laid the basis for the oriental cult of the satrap with unlimited power, and, by means of famine, mass terror, and the death of millions, destroyed the spirit of the population and broke down the last vestiges of resistance. This was undoubtedly a milestone in the history of the Soviet Union, but it was no more than the continuation or extension of its basic principle, namely the extermination of all forms of political, economic, and cultural life that are not imposed and regulated by the state.

The Comintern, meanwhile, had been transformed in a few years into an instrument of Soviet foreign policy and espionage. Its policy twisted and turned in accordance with Moscow's assessment, correct or otherwise, of the international situation; but these changes had nothing to do with ideology, doctrine, or the difference between 'left' and 'right'. Similarly, it would be naïve to inquire whether, for instance, the Soviet Union's pact with Chiang Kai-shek or Hitler, the massacre of Polish Communists by Stalin, or Soviet participation in the Spanish Civil War, were in accordance with Marxism or betokened a 'leftist' or 'rightist' policy. All these moves can be judged in the light of how far they served to strengthen the Soviet state and increase its influence, but any ideological grounds adduced to defend them were invented for the purpose and have no bearing on the history of ideology, beyond showing how completely it was degraded to the role of an instrument of Soviet *raison d'état*.

Having said this, we may divide the history of the Soviet Union since Lenin's death into three periods. The first, from 1924 to 1929, is that of the N.E.P. During this time there was considerable freedom of private trading; political life no longer existed outside the party, but there were genuine disputes and controversies within the leadership; culture was officially controlled, but different trends of opinion and discussions were allowed within the bounds of Marxism and of political obedience. It was still possible to debate the nature of 'true' Marxism; one-man despotism was not yet an institution, and a fair proportion of society—the peasantry, and 'Nepmen' of all kinds— was not yet wholly dependent on the state from the economic point of view. The second period, from 1930 to Stalin's death in 1953, is marked by personal despotism, the almost complete liquidation of civil society, the subordination of culture to arbitrary official directives, and the regimentation of philosophy and ideology. The third period, from 1953 to the present, has features of its own which we shall consider in due course. As to which particular Bolshevik leader is in power, this is in general of minor importance. The Trotskyists, and of course Trotsky himself, regarded his removal from power as a historical turning-point; but there is no reason to agree with them and, as we shall see, it can well be maintained that 'Trotskyism' never existed, but was a figment invented by Stalin. The disagreements between Stalin and Trotsky were real to a certain extent, but they were grossly inflated by the struggle for personal power and never amounted to two independent and coherent theories. This is even more true of the disputes between Zinovyev and Trotsky, and the later conflict between Zinovyev and Trotsky on the one hand and Stalin on the other. Stalin's conflict with Bukharin and 'right-wing deviationism' was more substantial, but even this was not a dispute over principles but only as to the method and timetable for putting them into effect. The debate on industrialization in the twenties was certainly of great importance as regards practical decisions in industry and agri-culture, and consequently the lives of millions of Soviet people, but it would be an exaggeration to see it as a basic doctrinal dispute or as involving the 'correct' interpretation of Marxism or Leninism. All the Bolshevik leaders without exception changed their attitude to the question so radically that it is pointless to speak of Trotskyism, Stalinism, or Bukharinism as coherent bodies of theory or variations of basic Marxist doctrine. (In this matter the historian of ideologies is interested in aspects that are, in themselves, secondary: doctrinal standpoints are of more significance to him than the fate of millions of people. This, however, is not a question of objective importance, but merely of professional concern.)

3. Stalin's early life and rise to power

Unlike the great majority of Bolshevik leaders, the future Com-munist ruler of All the Russias was, if not a proletarian, at any rate a man of the people. Joseph (Yosif) Dzhugashvili was born on 9 December 1879 in the small Georgian town of Gori. His father, Vissarion, was a shoemaker and drunkard, his mother illiterate. Vissarion moved to Tiflis, where he took a job in a shoe factory, and died there in 1890. His son attended the parish school at Gori for five years and was admitted in 1894 to the Theological Seminary at Tiflis—the only school in the Caucasus at which an able youth of his social condition could, in practice, receive further education. The Orthodox seminary was at the same time an organ of Russification, but, like many

Russian schools, it was also a hotbed of political unrest, where Georgian patriotism flourished and socialist ideas were disseminated by many exiles from Russia proper. Dzhugashvili joined a socialist group, lost any interest he may have had in theology, and, in the spring of 1899, was expelled for failing to attend an examination. Traces of his seminary background can be discerned in his later writings, with their biblical tags and fondness for a catechetical style that lends itself well to propaganda. In articles and speeches he was in the habit of posing questions which he would then repeat verbatim in his answers: he also made his articles more assimilable by numbering each separate concept and statement.

From his seminary days onwards Stalin was associated with various rudimentary socialist groups in Georgia: the Russian Social Democratic party did not yet exist, though a formal decision to establish it was taken at the Minsk gathering in March 1898. For some months in 1899–1900 he worked as a clerk at the Tiflis geophysical observatory, after which he devoted himself entirely to political and propaganda activities, both legal and illegal. From 1901 he wrote articles for the clandestine Georgian socialist paper *Brdzola* (*The Struggle*) and spread propaganda among workers. Towards the end of that year he became a member of a committee to direct party work in Tiflis. In April 1902 he was arrested for organizing a workers' demonstration in Batum. He was sentenced to exile in Siberia, but escaped from his place of detention (or while on the way there) and was again in the Caucasus at the beginning of 1904, living as a member of the underground with forged papers. Meanwhile the Social Democratic party had held its second congress and had split into the Bolshevik and Menshevik factions. Stalin soon declared for the Bolsheviks and wrote pamphlets and articles supporting Lenin's idea of the party. The Georgian Social Democrats were nearly all Mensheviks: their leader was Noakh Zhordania, the most prominent Caucasian Marxist. During and after the 1905 Revolution Stalin worked for a time at Baku as a party activist with duties covering the whole Caucasus area.

It was some years, however, before he played a part in Bolshevik activities in Russia proper. He attended the party conference at Tammerfors in December 1905, and in April 1906 he was the only Bolshevik to attend the 'unity' congress at Stockholm (his credentials for so doing were disputed by the Mensheviks). However, until 1912 the real scene of his activity was the Caucasus. At Tammerfors he had his first meeting with Lenin, whose doctrine and leadership he never seriously challenged. At Stockholm, however, while siding with Lenin on all other questions, he took the line that the party programme should advocate the division of land among the peasants, and not its nationalization as Lenin contended.

Stalin's writings at this period contain nothing original or worthy of note: they are popular propaganda articles reproducing Lenin's slogans on current topics. Much space is given to attacking the Mensheviks, and there is of course criticism of the Kadets, the 'recallists' (otzovists), 'liquidators', anarchists, etc. The only article of any length, 'Anarchism or Socialism?', appeared in Georgian in 1906 (from 1905 onwards Stalin also wrote articles in Russian): it is a rather clumsy exposition of the Social Democratic world-view and its philosophical premises.

In 1906–7 Stalin is known to have been one of the organizers of 'expropriations', i.e. armed raids for the purpose of filling the party coffers. This activity was forbidden and condemned, despite Lenin's opposition, at the party's Fifth Congress in London in April 1907; but the Bolsheviks continued to practise it until it gave rise to a major scandal some months later.

In recent years several historians have examined allegations made originally by Zhordania and, after Stalin's death, by Orlov, a former high official of Soviet intelligence, to the effect that Stalin was in the service of the Okhrana (the Tsarist secret police) for some years after 1905. But the evidence for this charge is slight, and it is rejected by most historians, including Adam Ulam and Roy Medvedyev.

Between 1908 and the February Revolution Stalin spent most of his time in prison and exile, from which he escaped on every occasion except the last (1913–17). He acquired the reputation of a skilful, stubborn, and indefatigable revolutionary, and did his best to salvage the party's Caucasian organization during the calamitous years after 1907. Like many other leaders inside Russia he did not take a keen interest in the theoretical debates and squabbles among the *émigrés*. There is some evidence that he took a sceptical view of Lenin's *Materialism and Empirio-criticism* (which he afterwards extolled as the supreme achieve-ment of philosophical thought), and that in the darkest days of 1910 he made genuine efforts to restore unity with the Mensheviks. In January 1912, when Lenin called an all-Bolshevik conference at Prague to set the seal on the breach with the Mensheviks, Stalin was in exile at Vologda. The conference elected a Central Committee of the party, to which Stalin was later co-opted at Lenin's suggestion, thus making his début on the all-Russian political scene.

After escaping from Vologda, Stalin was once more arrested and deported, and escaped again. In November 1912 he travelled outside Russia for the first time in his life, spending a few days at Cracow in Austrian Poland, where he met Lenin. He returned to Russia but in December went abroad again, this time to Vienna for six weeks—the longest period he was ever to spend on foreign soil. In Vienna he wrote for Lenin an article on 'Marxism and the National Question' which appeared in 1913 in the journal *Prosveshchenie* (*Enlightenment*), and which constitutes his earliest claim, and one of his principal ones, to celebrity as a theoretician. It does not add anything to what Lenin had said on the question, except for defining a nation as a community possessing a single language, territory, culture, and economic life—thus excluding, for example, the Swiss and the Jews. The article was written as an attack on the Austro-Marxists, especially Springer (Renner) and Bauer, and on the Bund (the General Jewish Workers' Union of Russia). As Stalin could read only Russian and Georgian he was probably helped by Bukharin, then in Vienna, to select quotations from the Austro-Marxist writers. In opposition to the latter's ideas of national cultural autonomy based on self-determination by the individual, Stalin argued for the right of national self-determination and political separation on a territorial basis. However, like Lenin, he emphasized that while the social demo-crats recognized the right of every people to form a state of its own, this did not mean that they would support separatism in every case; the deciding factor was the interest of the working class, and it must be remembered that separatism was often used as a reactionary slogan by the bourgeoisie. The whole debate was of course conducted on the assumption of a 'bourgeois revolution'. Like all socialists at that time, except Trotsky and Parvus, Stalin expected Russia to undergo a democratic revolution, followed by many years of bourgeois republican rule; but he held that the proletariat must take a leading part in bringing the revolution about, and not play second fiddle to the bourgeoisie or act merely as a servant of its interests.

The article on nationality was the last that Stalin wrote before the February Revolution. Soon after his return from Vienna, in February 1913, he was again arrested and sentenced to four years' deportation. This time he did not try to escape but remained in Siberia, reappearing in Petrograd in March 1917. For some weeks, until Lenin arrived, he was effectively in charge of the party in the capital city. Together with Kamenev he took over the editorship of *Pravda*. His attitude towards both the Provisional Government and the Mensheviks was a good deal more conciliatory than Lenin's, and he incurred the latter's censure by toning down the articles that Lenin was sending from Switzerland. However, after Lenin's return to Russia and the presentation of his 'April Theses' Stalin, with some hesitation, accepted the policy of working for a 'socialist revolution' and government by the Soviets. By contrast, during the first few weeks in Petrograd he was still writing in terms of a 'bourgeois revolution', peace with the Central Powers, confiscation of the big estates, and a policy of exerting pressure on the Provisional Government but not attempting its overthrow. Only after the July crisis, at the conference of the party organization in Petrograd, did Stalin speak clearly of transferring power to the proletariat and the poor peasantry; at this time the slogan 'All power to the Soviets' was abandoned, as the latter were dominated by Mensheviks and S.R.s. By the time of the October revolution Stalin was unquestionably among the chief party leaders, alongside Lenin, Trotsky (who joined the Bolsheviks in July 1917), Zinovyev, Kamenev, Sverdlov, and Lunacharsky. As far as we know he did not take part in the military organization of the uprising, but in Lenin's first Soviet government he was made Commissar for Nationalities. During the party crisis over the Treaty of Brest-Litovsk he supported Lenin against the 'left-wing Bolsheviks' who were pressing for a revolutionary war with Germany. However, he believed, as Lenin did, that the European revolution would break out any day, and that accepting the German peace terms was no more than a temporary tactical retreat.

As an expert on nationality affairs Stalin at this time made speeches to the effect that self-determination must be understood 'dialectically' (in other words, used as a slogan when it suited the party but not otherwise). At the Third Congress of Soviets at the beginning of 1918 he explained that self-determination, properly speaking, was for the 'masses' and not the bourgeoisie, and must be subordinated to the fight for socialism. In articles published in that year he emphasized that the secession of Poland and the Baltic States was a counter-revolutionary move and played into the hands of the imperialists, as these countries would form a barrier between revolutionary Russia and the revolutionary West; on the other hand, the struggle of Egypt, Morocco, or India for independence was a progressive phenomenon as it tended to weaken imperialism. All this was fully in accord with Lenin's doctrine and with party ideology. Separatist movements are progressive when directed against bourgeois governments, but once the 'proletariat' is in power national separatism automatically and dialectically changes its significance, since it is a threat to the proletarian state, socialism, and world revolution. Socialism, by definition, cannot practise national oppression, and thus what appear to be invasions are in fact acts of liberation —as, for instance, when the Red Army under Stalin's orders marched into Georgia, which at the time (1921) had a Menshevik government on a basis of representative democracy. Notwithstanding this, the slogan of national self-determination, which was never revoked, contributed largely to the Bolshevik victory in the Civil War, as the White commanders made no secret of the fact that their purpose was to restore Russia, one and indivisible, without any loss of her pre-Revolutionary territory.

Stalin played an important part in the Civil War, though his achievements were overshadowed by Trotsky's. The roots of the conflict between the two men no doubt go back to this period with its personal jealousies and recriminations—who did most to bring about victory at Tsaritsyn, whose fault was the defeat before Warsaw, etc.

In 1919 Stalin became Commissar for the Workers' and Peasants' Inspectorate. This institution, as we have seen, represented a desperate and hopeless attempt by Lenin to protect the Soviet system from the inroads of bureaucracy: the Inspectorate, composed of 'genuine' workers and peasants, had unlimited powers of supervision over all other branches of the state administration. Far from curing the situation it made things worse, since in the absence of any democratic institutions the Inspectorate became simply an additional tier of the bureaucratic edifice. Stalin, however, was able to make use of it to strengthen his control of the apparatus, and his tenure of the Commissarship was undoubtedly a factor that helped him in his rise to supreme power.

At this stage an important, though not original, observation should be made. In later years, when the whole history of the party was rewritten under Stalin's orders and for his own glorification, he was presented, or rather presented himself, as having been Lenin's 'second in command' from his early youth. In every field of action he was the leader, the chief organizer, the inspiration of his comrades, and so forth. (In a party questionnaire he claimed to have been expelled from the seminary for carrying on revolutionary activity; no doubt he discussed forbidden subjects while there, but in fact he was expelled for failing to attend an examination.) According to this fantastic version he was Lenin's closest confidant and helper from the very moment the party was founded; the infant socialist movement in the Caucasus had thriven under his brilliant leadership; later on, the whole party regarded him without question as the rightful and natural successor to Lenin, and so on. He was the brains of the Revolution, the architect of victory in the Civil War, the organizer of the Soviet state. In the hagiography composed by Beriya the year 1912 is singled out as the turning-point in the history of the Russian party, and therefore in the history of mankind, as it was then that Stalin became a member of the Central Committee.

On the other hand, Trotsky and the many other Communists who had reason to hate Stalin were at pains to belittle his role in the history of Bolshevism and to depict him as a second-rate *apparatchik* who, by a mixture of cunning and good fortune, managed in due course to climb on to a pedestal from which it proved impossible to dislodge him.

Neither of these versions can be accepted as the truth. Certainly, before 1905 Stalin was an obscure local figure and there were many in his own area who were more esteemed and played a more important part than he. None the less, by 1912 he had made himself one of the six or seven most prominent Bolshevik leaders, and in Lenin's last years—although less well known than Trotsky, Zinovyev, or Kamenev, and certainly regarded by no one as Lenin's 'natural' successor—he was one of a small group ruling over the party and Russia; and at the time of Lenin's death, in practice although not in theory he enjoyed greater power than anyone else in the country.

From the documents now available we know that even before the Revolution Stalin's comrades noticed qualities that later turned him into a pathological despot. Some were mentioned in Lenin's 'Testament': he was known to be brutal, disloyal, arbitrary, ambitious, envious, intolerant of opposition, a tyrant to his subordinates. Until he had wiped out the whole of the Bolshevik 'old guard', no one in the party took him seriously as a philosopher or theoretician: from this point of view he was outclassed not only by Trotsky and Bukharin but by a host of party ideologists. Everyone knew that Stalin's articles, pamphlets, and speeches contained nothing original and showed no sign that they were intended to: he was not a 'Marxist theoretician', but a party propagandist like hundreds of others. Later, of course, in the delirium of the 'personality cult', any scrap of paper he had ever written became an immortal contribution to the treasury of Marxism–Leninism; but it is perfectly clear that his whole reputation as a theoretician was nothing but a part of the ordained ritual and was forgotten within a short time of his death. If his ideological writings had been those of a man with no political claim to fame, they would scarcely deserve mention in a history of Marxism. But since, during his years of power, there was scarcely any other brand of Marxism than his, and since the Marxism of those days can hardly be defined except in relation to his authority, it is not only true but is actually a tautology to say that for a quarter of a century he was the greatest Marxist theoretician.

In any case, Stalin had many qualities that were useful to the party, and it was not only due to chance that he made his way to the top and eliminated his rivals. He was a tireless, shrewd, and efficient worker. In practical matters he knew how to disregard doctrinal considerations and discern clearly the relative importance of issues. He neither panicked (except in the first days of Hitler's invasion) nor lost his head from success. He was adept at distinguishing real from apparent power. He was a poor speaker and a dull writer, but he could say things in a plain way so that the ordinary party member could grasp them, and his pedantic habits of repetition and the numbering of points gave his exposés an appearance of force and clarity. He bullied subordinates, but he could use them as well. He knew how to adapt his style to different interlocutors, whether party members, foreign journalists, or Western states-men, and could at will play the part of a strategist, an intrepid fighter for the proletarian cause, or the no-nonsense 'boss' of his country. He had the rare skill of contriving to receive the credit for all successes and to blame all failures upon others. The system he helped to establish enabled him to become a tyrant, but it must also be said that he worked long and hard to achieve that result.

Lenin undoubtedly valued Stalin's efficiency and powers of organization. Although Stalin occasionally disagreed with Lenin, he was always behind him at times of crisis. Unlike most of the front-rank Bolsheviks he had no 'intellectual' leanings, which Lenin could not endure. He was a matter-of-fact character who did not mind taking on hard and ungrateful tasks. And, although in a belated moment of vision Lenin realized what a dangerous man he had raised to the summit of power, there is some truth in Stalin's retort to his opponents when they at last decided to drag Lenin's 'Testament' out of the archives and in-voke it against him. Yes, said Stalin, Lenin did accuse me of brutality, and I *am* brutal where the revolution is concerned—but did Lenin ever say that my policy was wrong? To this the opposition had no answer.

There is no reason to doubt that Stalin was Lenin's personal choice for Secretary-General of the party in April 1922, and there is no evidence that any of the other leaders objected to his nomination. It is quite true, as Trotsky afterwards pointed out, that nobody regarded the creation of this post and Stalin's appointment to it as signifying that he was to be Lenin's heir, or that the holder of the secretary-generalship would in practice be the supreme ruler of the Soviet party and state. All important decisions were still taken by the Politburo or the Central Committee, which ran the country through the intermediary of the Council of People's Commissars. The new office was not the highest individual post in the party hierarchy, and there was indeed no such post. The Secretary-General's function was to supervise the current work of the party bureaucracy, ensure co-ordination within the machine, control senior appointments, etc. With hindsight it is possible to see clearly that when all other forms of political life have been destroyed and the party is the only organized force in the country, the individual in charge of the party machine must become all-powerful. This is what actually happened, but no one perceived it at the time: the Soviet state was without precedent in history, and it is not astonishing that the actors on the political stage did not foresee the dénouement of the play. Stalin as Secretary-General was able to put his own men in the majority of local party posts and even central ones, except those of the highest rank, and his power was enhanced by the function of organizing conferences and congresses. This, of course, was a gradual process: the first few years still witnessed intra-party disputes and the formation of rival groups and opposition platforms, but as time went on these became more infrequent and tended to be confined to the very highest level.

As we have seen, during Lenin's lifetime there were opposition groups within the party, reflecting the discontent of some Communists at the increase in despotic and bureaucratic methods of government. The 'Workers' Opposition', whose best-known spokesmen were Aleksandr Shlyapnikov and Aleksandra Kollontay, believed in a literal 'dictatorship of the proletariat', i.e. that power should actually be exercised by the whole working class and not only by the party. They did not by any means advocate a return to state democracy, but they fondly imagined that the Soviet system could preserve democratic forms of life for the privileged minority, i.e. the proletariat, after having abolished such forms as far as the great majority were concerned, especially the peasants and intellectuals. Other opposition groups wanted to restore democracy within the party, though not for those outside it: they protested at the growing power of the bureaucracy, the system of nomination to all posts, and the reduction of intra-party discussions and elections to an empty ritual.

Such brands of utopian criticism to some extent anticipated the 'critical' trends which made themselves felt within the Communist system after Stalin's death: the demand that democracy should prevail within the party although not outside it, or that power should be wielded by the whole proletariat or by workers' councils, though not, of course, by the rest of society. Apart from these ideas, however, there appeared in the early years a new version of Communism which in a sense prefigured Maoism, reflecting as it did the needs and interests of Asiatic peasant peoples. The author of this trend was Mir Sayit Sultan-Galiyev, a Bashkir by nationality and a teacher by profession. He became a Bolshevik soon after the October Revolution, and was one of the few intellectuals from the Muslim area of the Soviet Union who secured early recognition as an expert on the affairs of the Central Asian peoples. His conviction was, however, that the Soviet system did not solve any of the Muslims' problems but merely subjected them to a different form of oppression. The urban proletariat which had assumed dictatorial power in Russia was no less European than the bourgeoisie, and equally alien to the Muslim peoples. The basic conflict of the age was not between the proletariat and bourgeoisie of the developed countries, but between colonial or semi-colonial peoples and the whole industrialized world. Not only could Soviet power in Russia do nothing to liberate those peoples, but it would instantly begin to oppress them and pursue an imperialist policy under the red flag. The colonial peoples must unite against the hegemony of Europe as a whole, create their own parties and an International independent of the Bolshevik one, and combat Western colonizers as well as Russian Communists. They must combine anti-colonial ideology with Islamic tradition, and create one-party systems and state organizations backed by armed force. In accordance with this programme Sultan-Galiyev tried to form a Muslim party separate from the Russian one, and even an independent Tatar-Bashkir state. His movement was soon suppressed, conflicting as it did with both Lenin's ideology and the interests of the Bolshevik party and the Soviet state. Sultan-Galiyev was expelled from the party in 1923 and imprisoned as an agent of foreign intelligence: perhaps the first occasion on which this charge, which afterwards became a matter of routine in such cases, was levelled against a prominent party member. He was executed many years later, during the great purges, and his cause was soon forgotten. In a speech in June 1923 Stalin said that he had been arrested less because of his pan-Islamic and pan-Turkic views than because he had conspired against the party with the Basmach rebels of Turkestan. The episode is worth remembering on account of the striking resemblance between Sultan-Galiyev's ideas and subsequent Maoist doctrine, or some ideologies of the 'Muslim socialist' type.

As to those opposition groups which advocated democracy for the party or the proletariat, they were speedily and unanimously crushed by the leaders including Lenin, Trotsky, Stalin, Zinovyev, and Kamenev. The prohibition of splinter groups, and the right of the Central Committee to expel party members who joined them, were proclaimed at the Tenth Congress in 1921. It was indeed clear, as the defenders of party unity pointed out, that under a one-party system separate groups within the party were bound to become the mouthpieces of all social forces which would in the old days have formed parties of their own: hence, if 'factions' were allowed, there would virtually be a multi-party system. The inevitable conclusion was that a party ruling despotically must itself be despotically ruled, and that, having destroyed democratic institutions in society at large, it was idle to think of preserving them within the party, let alone for the benefit of the whole working class.

None the less, the process of transforming the party into a passive instrument in the hands of the bureaucracy took longer than the destruction of democratic institutions within the state, and was not completed until the late twenties. In 1922–3 there were strong currents of rebellion against the growing tyranny within the party, and no one was so skilful in repressing them as Stalin. Having successfully achieved control over the information that reached Lenin, who was ill and infirm, Stalin ruled the party with the aid of Zinovyev and Kamenev and systematically excluded Trotsky from power. The latter was in a losing position from an early stage, despite his oratorical skill and his prestige as the architect of victory in the Civil War. He did not dare to appeal to opinion outside the party, as this would have conflicted with the principle of Soviet power; and it proved easy to mobilize against him the party bureaucracy, which was the only active force in political life. Trotsky had joined the Bolsheviks at a late stage and was distrusted by the old-timers, who also disliked his excess of rhetoric and his haughty, arrogant manners. Stalin, Zinovyev, and Kamenev skilfully exploited all Trotsky's weaknesses: his Menshevik past, his hankering after the militarization of labour (a policy which Stalin never formulated in such despotic terms), his criticism of the N.E.P., his old quarrels with Lenin, and the charges that Lenin had trumped up against him in former times. As Commissar for the Armed Forces and a member of the Politburo he still appeared powerful, but by 1923 he was isolated and helpless. All his former tergiversations were turned against him. When he came to realize his situation he attacked the bureaucratization of the party and the stifling of intra-party democracy: like all overthrown Communist leaders he became a democrat as soon as he was ousted from power. However, it was easy for Stalin and Zinovyev to show not only that Trotsky's democratic sentiments and indignation at party bureaucracy were of recent date, but that he himself, when in power, had been a more extreme autocrat than anyone else: he had supported or initiated every move to protect party 'unity', had wanted—contrary to Lenin's policy—to place the trade unions under state control and to subject the whole economy to the coercive power of the police, and so on. In later years Trotsky claimed that the policy, which he had supported, of prohibiting 'fractions' was envisaged as an exceptional measure and not a permanent principle. But there is no proof that this was so, and nothing in the policy itself suggests that it was meant to be temporary. It may be noted that Zinovyev showed more zeal than Stalin in condemning Trotsky—at one stage he was in favour of arresting him—and thus supplied Stalin with useful ammunition when the two ousted leaders tried, belatedly and hopelessly, to join forces against their triumphant rival.

4. *Socialism in one country*

The doctrine of 'socialism in one country', formulated towards the end of 1924 against Trotsky and his idea of 'permanent revolution', was for a long time regarded as a major contribution of Stalin's to Marxist theory, with the corollary that Trotskyism constituted a rival body of coherent dogma—a view that Trotsky himself apparently came to share. In reality, however, there was no basic political opposition between the two men, let alone any theoretical disagreement.

As we have seen, the leaders of the October uprising believed that the revolutionary process would soon spread to the principal European countries, and that the Russian revolution had no hope of permanent success except as the prelude to world revolution. None of the Bolshevik leaders in the early days held or expressed any view other than this: some of Lenin's statements on the subject were so unequivocal that Stalin later had them expunged from his works. However, as hopes of a world revolution receded and the Communists failed in their desperate efforts to bring about an uprising in Europe, they also agreed that the task immediately before them was to build a socialist society, though no one knew exactly in what this ought to consist. Two basic principles continued to be accepted: that Russia had begun a process which, by the laws of history, must finally embrace the whole world, and that, as long as the West was in no hurry to start its own revolution, it was for the Russians to set about the socialist transformation of their own country. The question whether socialism could in fact be built once and for all was not seriously considered, as no practical consequences depended on the answer. When Lenin perceived, after the Civil War, that you could not make corn grow by issuing decrees or even by shooting peasants, and when he accordingly instituted the N.E.P., he was certainly concerned with 'building socialism' and was more interested in the internal organization of the state than in stirring up revolution abroad.

When Stalin, in the spring of 1924, published his article 'The Foundations of Leninism'—his first attempt to codify Lenin's doctrine after his own fashion—he reiterated points that were generally accepted, and attacked Trotsky for 'underestimating' the revolutionary role of the peasantry and holding that the revolution could originate in one-class rule by the proletariat. Leninism, he argued, was the Marxism of the age of imperialism and proletarian revolution; Russia had become the native country of Leninism because it was ripe for revolution owing to its relative backwardness and the many forms of oppression from which it suffered; and Lenin had foreseen the transformation of the bourgeois revolution into a socialist one.

However, Stalin emphasized, the proletariat of a single country could not bring about final victory. In the autumn of the same year Trotsky published a collection of his own writings dating from 1917, with a preface designed to prove that he was the only statesman faithful to Leninist principles, and to discredit the then leaders, especially Zinovyev and Kamenev, for having shown a hesitant and even hostile attitude towards Lenin's insurrectionary plan. He also attacked the Comintern, of which Zinovyev was then the chief, for the defeat of the uprisings in Germany and for failing to exploit the revolutionary situation. Trotsky's criticism provoked a collective answer by Stalin, Zinovyev, Kamenev, Bukharin, Rykov, Krupskaya, and others, blaming him for all past errors and defeats, accusing him of arrogance and of quarrelling with Lenin, and belittling his services to the revolution.

It was at this time that Stalin constructed the doctrine of 'Trotskyism'. The idea of 'permanent revolution', formulated by Trotsky before 1917, presupposed that the Russian revolution would pass continuously into a socialist phase, but that its fate would depend on the world revolution which would also result from it; moreover, in a country with a huge peasant majority, the working class would suffer political destruction unless it were supported by the international proletariat, whose victory alone could consolidate that of the Russian workers. As the question of the 'transformation of the bourgeois revolution into a socialist one' had meanwhile lost its application, Stalin represented Trotskyism as signifying that socialism could not be definitively built in one country—thus suggesting to his readers that Trotsky's real design was to restore capitalism in Russia. In the autumn of 1924 Stalin declared that Trotskyism rested on three principles. Firstly, it did not recognize the poorest class of peasants as an ally of the proletariat; secondly, it accepted peaceful coexistence between revolutionaries and opportunists; and thirdly, it slandered the Bolshevik leaders. Later on, the essential feature of Trotskyism was declared to be the contention that, while it is possible to set about building socialism in one country, it is not possible to bring it to completion. In *Concerning Questions of Leninism* (1926) Stalin criticized his own theory of the spring of 1924, saying that a distinction must be drawn between the possibility of finally building socialism in one country and the possibility of finally protecting oneself against capitalist intervention. In conditions of capitalist encirclement there could be no absolute guarantee against intervention, but a fully socialist society could nevertheless be constructed.

The point of the controversy about whether socialism could be finally built in one country or not resided, as Deutscher well observes in his life of Stalin, in the latter's desire to transform the psychology of party workers. In proclaiming that the Russian revolution was self-sufficient he was less concerned with theory than with countering the demoralization produced by the failure of world communism. He wished to assure party members that they need not be troubled as regards the uncertain support of the 'world proletariat', since their own success did not depend on it; he wanted, in short, to create an atmosphere of optimism, without, of course, abandoning the consecrated principle that the Russian revolution was the prelude to a worldwide one.

It is possible that if Trotsky had been in charge of Soviet foreign policy and the Comintern in the 1920s he would have taken more interest than Stalin did in organizing Communist risings abroad, but there is no reason to think his efforts would have had any success. Naturally he used every defeat of Communists in the world to accuse Stalin of neglecting the revolutionary cause. But it is not at all clear what Stalin could have done if he had been actuated by the internationalist zeal which Trotsky accused him of lacking. Russia had no means of ensuring a German Communist victory in 1923 or a Chinese one in 1926. Trotsky's later charge that the Comintern failed to exploit revolutionary opportunities because of Stalin's doctrine of socialism in one country is completely devoid of substance.

Thus there is no question of two 'essentially opposite' theories, one asserting and the other denying that socialism could be built in one country. In theory everyone accepted the need to support world revolution and also the need to build a socialist society in Russia. Stalin and Trotsky differed to some extent as to the proportion of energy that ought to be devoted to one task or the other, and both men did their share to inflate these differences into an imaginary theoretical antithesis.

Still less is it possible to believe the assertion frequently made by Trotskyists that intra-party democracy was of the essence of their system. Trotsky's attacks on bureaucratic rule within the party began, as we have seen, when he himself was effectually deprived of power over the party apparatus; as long as he was still in power, he was one of the most autocratic champions of bureaucracy and of military or police control over the whole political and economic system. The 'bureaucratization' against which he later inveighed was the natural and inevitable result of destroying all democratic institutions in the state, a process into which Trotsky threw himself with zeal and which he never afterwards repudiated.

5. Bukharin and the N.E.P. ideology. The economic controversy of the 1920s

The controversy over Soviet economic policy in the 1920s was much more genuine than the issue of 'socialism in one country', which was rather a disguise for faction than a key to the solution of any practical or theoretical problem. Even the famous debate on industrialization, however, does not deserve to be presented as a clash between two opposite principles. All agreed that Russia must be industrialized: the point in dispute was the speed of the process and the connected issue, fraught with doom, of Soviet agriculture and the government's relations with the peasantry. These matters, however, were of fundamental practical importance, and different points of view concerning them led to different political decisions of great importance to the whole country.

Bukharin, the chief ideologist of the N.E.P. (inaugurated in 1921), enjoyed great popularity in party circles and was regarded as a first-class theoretician. After the fall of Zinovyev and Kamenev in 1927 he became the most important man in the party after Stalin.

Nikolay Ivanovich Bukharin (b. 1888, d. 13 or 14 March 1938) belonged to the generation that entered the socialist movement during or shortly after the 1905 Revolution. Born and brought up in Moscow, a member of the intellectual class (his parents were teachers), he joined a socialist group while still at school and was a Bolshevik from the outset of his political career. He joined the party when just over eighteen, at the end of 1906, and carried out propaganda work in Moscow. In 1907 he enrolled at the University as a student of economics, but politics took up most of his time and he never completed the course.

In 1908 he was already in charge of the small Bolshevik organization in Moscow. Arrested in autumn 1910 and sentenced to
deportation, he escaped and spent the next six years as an
émigré in Germany, Austria, and the Scandinavian countries,
where his writings gained him the reputation of an expert
Bolshevik theorist in the sphere of political economy. In 1914
he finished a work entitled *The Economics of the Rentier Class: the
Austrian School's Theory of Value and Profit*: this was first published
in full in Moscow in 1919, and an English version, *The Economic
Theory of the Leisure Class*, appeared in 1927. The book is a defence
of Marxian doctrine and an attack on the theory of value of
the marginalists, especially Böhm-Bawerk. As the title suggests,
Bukharin argued that the Austrian school of economic theory
was an ideological expression of the mentality of the parasitic
dividend-drawing bourgeoisie; as far as the defence of Marx goes,
his work added nothing to Hilferding's earlier criticism. On
the outbreak of war in 1914 he was deported from Vienna to
Switzerland, where he worked on the economic theory of
imperialism. At this time he was involved in controversy with
Lenin, who accused him of 'Luxemburgist' errors over the
national and peasant questions. Bukharin held, in the light of
classic Marxist schemata, that the national question was becoming less and less important and that the purity of socialist class
policies should not be sullied by doctrines of national self-
determination, which was both utopian and contrary to
Marxism. In the same way he disapproved of the party bidding
for peasant support in its revolutionary policy, as Marxism
taught that the class of small farmers was doomed to disappear
anyway and that the peasantry was historically a reactionary
class. (In the future, however, Bukharin was to be noted chiefly
as an exponent of precisely the opposite 'deviation'.)

In Switzerland and afterwards in Sweden Bukharin wrote
Imperialism and World Economy, first published in full in Petrograd
in 1918; Lenin saw the manuscript and used it freely for his
Imperialism, the Highest Stage of Capitalism. Bukharin himself made
much use of Hilferding's analysis, but he also emphasized that
as capitalism develops the economic role of the state grows in
importance and leads to a new social form, that of state capitalism, i.e. an economy centrally planned and regulated on the
scale of a national state. This meant the extension of state control

to ever wider areas of civil society and the intensification of human slavery. The Moloch of the state was capable of functioning without internal crises, but only by encroaching on more and more aspects of private life. Bukharin, however, disagreed with Kautsky's and Hilferding's expectation of an 'ultra-imperialist' phase in which the necessity of war would be obviated by a centralized organization of the world economy: state capitalism, he thought, was feasible on a national scale but not on a global basis. Hence competition, anarchy, and crises would continue, but would take on increasingly international forms. It followed also—and here Bukharin agreed with Lenin, though for slightly different reasons—that the cause of the proletarian revolution must now be envisaged in the context of the international situation.

At a somewhat later date Lenin criticized the young Bukharin for his 'semi-anarchist' view that the proletariat would have no need of state power after the revolution—a utopian idea very similar to that expounded in Lenin's *State and Revolution* in 1917.

Towards the end of 1916 Bukharin went to the United States, where he held discussions with Trotsky and endeavoured to persuade the American Left of the rightness of the Bolshevik view on questions of war and peace. Returning to Russia after the February Revolution, he soon took his place among the party leaders and gave whole-hearted support to Lenin's 'April Theses'. During the crucial months before and after October he was chiefly active in Moscow as an organizer and propagandist. Soon after the Revolution he became editor-in-chief of *Pravda*, a position he held until 1929. Sharing the general view that the fate of the Russian revolution depended on whether it could set fire to the West, Bukharin stoutly opposed Lenin's policy of a separate peace with Germany. During the first dramatic months of 1918 he was one of the leaders of the 'Left Communists' who pressed for a continuance of the revolutionary war, despite Lenin's sober appraisal of the technical and moral condition of the army. Once peace was concluded, however, he stood by Lenin in all important economic and administrative questions. He did not support the left opposition's protest against the employment of 'bourgeois' specialists and experts in industry, or against the organization of the army on a basis of professional competence and traditional discipline.

During the period of 'War Communism' (a misleading term, as we have seen) Bukharin was the chief theoretical advocate of an economic policy based on coercion, requisitions, and the hope that the new-born state could manage without a market or a monetary system and would organize socialist production in no time. During the years before N.E.P., in addition to his work *Historical Materialism* which we shall discuss presently, he published two books expounding the party's economic policy: *The Economics of the Transition Period* (1920) and, with E. Preobrazhensky, *The ABC of Communism* (1919, English trans. 1922). These works enjoyed semi-official status as an authoritative account of Bolshevik policies at the time. Not only did Bukharin, like Lenin, jettison his utopian doctrine that the state would vanish immediately after the revolution, but he insisted on the necessity of an economic as well as a political dictatorship of the proletariat. He also reiterated his view regarding the evolution of 'state capitalism' in the advanced countries. (Lenin used this term to refer to private industry in socialist Russia, a fact which gave rise to some verbal misunderstanding.) Bukharin stressed the notion of 'equilibrium' as a key to the understanding of social processes. He argued that once the capitalist system of production has lost its equilibrium—as evidenced by the revolutionary process with its inevitable destructive consequences—this can only be restored by the organized will of the new state. Hence the state apparatus must take over all functions connected with the social organization of production, exchange, and distribution. In practice this means the 'statization' of all economic activity, the militarization of labour, and a general rationing system, in short the application of coercion throughout the economy. Under Communism there can be no question of the spontaneous working of the market; the law of value ceases to operate, as do all economic laws independent of human volition. Everything is subject to the planning power of the state, and political economy in the old sense ceases to exist. And, although the organization of society is essentially based on coercion *vis-à-vis* the peasants (compulsory requisition) and the workers (militarization of labour), there is clearly no exploitation of the working class, as it is impossible by definition for that class to exploit itself.

Bukharin, like Lenin, regarded the system of basing economic life on mass terror not as a transient necessity but as a permanent principle of socialist organization. He did not shrink from justifying all means of coercion and held, like Trotsky at the same period, that the new system called essentially for the militarization of labour—i.e. the use of police and military force to compel the whole population to work in such places and conditions as the state might arbitrarily decree. Indeed, once the market is abolished there is no longer any free sale of labour or competition between workers, and police coercion is therefore the only means of allocating 'human resources'. If hired labour is eliminated, only compulsory labour remains. In other words, socialism—as conceived by both Trotsky and Bukharin at this time—is a permanent, nation-wide labour camp.

Trotsky, it is true, had doubts for a time in 1920 as to the efficacy of an economy based on nothing but terror, and proposed that the requisition of grain should be replaced by a tax in kind. But he soon changed his mind, and during the N.E.P. period he was one of the chief opponents of a 'loose' economy with substantial concessions to the peasantry and with free trade as the principal mode of exchange between town and countryside.

Bukharin's views, on the other hand, evolved in the opposite direction. In 1920 the idea of a planned economy belonged to the realm of fantasy: Russia's industry lay in ruins, there was barely any transport, and the one pressing problem was how to save the towns from imminent starvation, not how to bring about a Communist millennium. When Lenin, in this catastrophic situation, beat a retreat from his economic doctrine and made up his mind to a long period of coexistence with a peasant economy, free trade in farm products, and the toleration of small-scale private industry, Bukharin likewise abandoned his earlier stand and became a fervent advocate and ideologist of the N.E.P., in opposition first to Trotsky and then to Zinovyev, Kamenev, and Preobrazhensky. From 1925 onwards he was Stalin's chief ideological supporter against the opposition. Like Lenin, he had come to recognize that the whole programme set out in *The Economics of the Transition Period* was a delusion; he did not concern himself with the millions of victims who had paid with their lives for the leaders' brief moment of frenzy.

Bukharin's arguments for returning to a market economy—

while, of course, maintaining state ownership of the banks and main industries—were chiefly economic but to some extent also political. Throughout the N.E.P. period (1921–8) his economic utterances expressed the views of a substantial majority of the political leadership, including Stalin.

The main issue was how the state could influence the commodity market by economic means so as to achieve the desired level of accumulation and develop industry, in a situation where agriculture was almost entirely in the hands of small farmers. To obtain the necessary quantity of grain from the peasants under market conditions it was necessary to supply the countryside with an equivalent value of producer and consumer goods. In the ruined state of industry this was difficult if not impossible, but if it were not done the peasants would refuse to sell their produce, as there would be nothing they could buy with the proceeds. In addition it was a question how the 'proletariat', i.e. the Bolshevik party, could maintain its dominant position if the state economy was at the mercy of the peasants: as the market developed, their position would become stronger and they might in the end threaten the 'proletarian dictatorship'.

Preobrazhensky, who was regarded as a Trotskyist in economic affairs and who led the theoretical opposition to Stalin's and Bukharin's policy of concessions to the peasants, argued as follows. The principal task of a socialist state in its initial phase is to create a strong industrial base and ensure the necessary degree of accumulation. All other economic aims must be subordinated to the development of industry, and particularly the manufacture of industrial equipment. Capitalist accumulation was facilitated by plundering colonies; the socialist state has no colonies and must achieve industrialization from its own resources. State industry, however, cannot of itself create a sufficient basis of accumulation but must draw upon the resources of small producers, i.e. in practice the peasantry. Private holdings must be the object of internal colonization: Preobrazhensky admitted frankly that it was a matter of exploiting the peasant, extracting the maximum amount of surplus value from his labour to increase investment in industry. The 'colonization' process was to be achieved mainly by fixing the price of industrial products at a high level in relation to the prices paid by the state for farm produce. This must be reinforced by other forms of economic pressure on the peasantry, so as to extort the maximum aid to industry in the shortest possible time. The party leaders, on the other hand, were pursuing a policy which encouraged accumulation on the part of small producers and neglected industry, especially heavy industry, for the sake of the peasants' well-being. Moreover, the chief beneficiaries of this policy were the kulaks, the class of rural exploiters: for, as everything was being done to increase agricultural productivity regardless of the claims of industry, the relative strength of classes, and the dictatorship of the proletariat, naturally credits and facilities went by preference to those peasants who promised the biggest deliveries. This was bound to strengthen the kulaks, who, economically at first and soon politically too, would start to undermine the power of the proletariat. There could be no compromise between the two rival policies. Those who, like the existing government, wished to satisfy all the peasants' economic demands to induce them to sell grain would have to pursue a corresponding foreign trade policy and import consumer goods for the peasants instead of producer goods for industry. The whole trend of development would be distorted in the interest of a class other than the proletariat, and the result would be a threat to the existence of the socialist state.

Arguing on these lines, Preobrazhensky and the whole Left Opposition pressed for the collectivization of agriculture, though they did not explain clearly by what means it was to be achieved.

Trotsky argued on similar lines. As he wrote in 1925, if state industry developed at a slower rate than agriculture, the restoration of capitalism was inevitable. Agriculture must be mechanized and electrified so that it could be transformed into a branch of state industry: only thus could socialism purge the economy of alien elements and liquidate class divisions. But all this depended on industry being adequately developed. In the last resort, the triumph of a new form of society was a function of the productivity of labour in that society: socialism would win because it had the power eventually to achieve greater productivity than capitalism and a more efficient development of productive forces. Thus the victory of socialism depended on socialist industrialization. Socialism, indeed, had all the advantages on its side: technical advances could be brought into immediate and universal application, unhampered by the obstacles that private ownership created. The centralization of the economy prevented the waste which was due to competition; industry was not at the mercy of consumers' whims, and nation-wide norms ensured a higher level of productivity. The complaint that centralization and standardization killed initiative and meant more monotonous work was nothing but a reactionary hankering for pre-industrial production. The whole economy must be transformed into a 'single, uniform, automatic mechanism', and for this purpose there must be an unremitting campaign against capitalist elements, i.e. small peasant producers: to abandon the fight was to acquiesce in the return of capitalism. Trotsky did not, like Preobrazhensky, speak of the 'objective law of socialist accumulation' and the need to extort the maximum amount of surplus value from the peasants for the sake of industrial investment, but his call for an economic offensive against capitalist elements came to the same thing. The opposition accused Bukharin of being basically in favour of a wealthy kulak class and a 'Thermidorean reaction': his policy, they claimed, would strengthen classes hostile to socialism and increase the specific gravity of capitalist elements in the economy. In reply Stalin, Bukharin, and their supporters declared that the call for 'super-industrialization' was unrealistic and that the opposition's policy would turn the bulk of the middle peasantry, not only the kulaks, against the regime; this would violate Lenin's sacred canon of an 'alliance between the proletariat and the poor and middle peasants' and would threaten the existence of the Soviet state. The opposition were constantly demanding that capitalist elements should be kept in check, but they did not say what should be done if increased government pressure— albeit economic only—deprived the peasantry of incentive, and how the state could then ensure food production and deliveries by any other method than a return to police coercion.

Bukharin's argument, supported at this time by Stalin, was that an out-and-out war by the state against the peasantry would be economically ineffective and politically disastrous, as the period of War Communism had sufficiently proved. The economic development of the country should depend not on the maximum exploitation of the peasantry but on preserving the market as a link between the state and rural economies and hence between the working class and the peasants. The rate of

accumulation depended on the efficiency and rapidity of circulation, and it was to this that efforts should be directed. If the
peasant were deprived of all his surpluses by coercion or economic
means, he would produce no more than he could eat himself;
hence to coerce the peasantry was against the manifest interest
of the state and proletariat. The only way to increase farm
production was to provide material incentives. Certainly, this
would be to the kulaks' advantage; but the development of
commercial co-operatives would make it possible to bring the
whole peasantry, including kulaks, into a state-controlled system
that would promote the growth of the economy as a whole.

The development of industry depended on the rural market;
accumulation by the peasants meant increased demand for
industrial products, and it was therefore in the whole country's
interest to permit accumulation by peasants of all categories.
Hence Bukharin's appeal to the peasants in 1925, 'Get rich!'
—a slogan that was often quoted later as a glaring proof of his
unorthodoxy. In his view the policy of declaring war on the
better-off peasants and stirring up class conflict in the countryside would ruin not only agriculture but the whole economy.
Poor peasants and farm labourers must be helped not by ruining
the kulaks but by the state using the latter's resources, which
it must first allow them to accumulate. Consumers' and marketing co-operatives would in time lead naturally to the development of producer co-operatives. The Trotskyist policy, on the
other hand, would mean disaster in both agriculture and
industry; it would alienate the whole peasantry from the state,
and thus destroy the dictatorship of the proletariat. Moreover,
the artificial raising of the price of industrial goods to a high
level in order to exploit the countryside, as proposed by Preobrazhensky and Pyatakov, would not only hit the peasants but
the workers as well, since the bulk of these goods were consumed
by the urban population. As for the opposition's attacks on
bureaucratic degeneration in the government machine, this
danger indeed existed, but it would be a hundred times worse
if their policy towards the peasants were adopted. A return to
the methods of War Communism would mean creating a whole
class of privileged functionaries for the main purpose of coercing
the countryside, and this huge apparatus would be far more
expensive than all the losses resulting from a lack of organ-

ization in agriculture. The cure for bureaucracy was to encourage
the population to form voluntary social organizations in various
spheres of life; the remedy proposed by the opposition was the
exact reverse of this, and would be worse than the disease.

In this controversy with the Left Opposition Bukharin did not
advocate any steps that would have led to an extension of
democracy within the state or party. On the contrary, he
attacked Trotsky, Zinovyev, and Kamenev as leaders of faction
and splitters of party unity. It was, he reminded them, the ABC
of Leninism that the dictatorship of the proletariat entailed the
existence of a single ruling party and that that party must be
united and not permit the existence of 'fractions', which must
lead to the development of separate parties. All the oppositionists
had been well aware of this until recently, and no one would
be deceived by their sudden transformation into democrats.

In the debate on industrialization both sets of adversaries,
of course, claimed that 'objectively' their opponents' policy
would lead to the restoration of capitalism. According to
Bukharin, Preobrazhensky wanted the socialist state to imitate
capitalism in achieving accumulation by exploiting and ruining
small-scale producers. The dictatorship of the proletariat would
be destroyed if its basis, an alliance with the peasantry and
especially the middle peasantry, was undermined; meanwhile
'internal colonization' meant an attack not only on the kulaks
but on the whole countryside, if only because all sections of the
peasantry were equally affected by the ratio between industrial
and agricultural prices. Against this, the Left contended that
the Stalin–Bukharin policy would steadily increase the economic
power of private owners, especially the kulaks, and that the
weakening of socialist industry and the working class could only
end by destroying the dictatorship of the proletariat. The
opposition also held that industry, and especially heavy industry,
was the key to socialist development. Bukharin maintained, on
the other hand, that the exchange of goods between town and
country was the main lever, that production was not an end
in itself but a means to consumption, and that the opposition
were echoing Tugan-Baranovsky's theory (in relation to the
capitalist system) that there could be an economy in which
production goes on creating an ever-increasing market for itself
regardless of the volume of demand. As things then were in

Russia, rural accumulation was by no means contrary to the workers' interest but coincided with it. To this the opposition replied that there could be no identity of interest between exploiters and the exploited, and that since the kulak was an exploiter by definition, to assist him to accumulate wealth was to foster the class enemy.

In this way there took shape, as it were, two variants of Bolshevism, both, of course, constantly appealing to pronouncements by Lenin. Lenin had said that there must be an alliance with the middle peasantry, but he had also spoken of the danger presented by the kulaks. Roughly speaking, Bukharin's case was that the kulaks could not be abolished without at the same time destroying the middle peasants, while the opposition held that the middle peasants could not be aided without also aiding the kulaks: these were two ways of expressing the same fact, with opposite political intentions. The opposition looked for support among the many Communists who were indignant at the rise of a class of well-to-do 'Nepmen' while the workers were in a state of misery, and who took seriously and literally the slogans of egalitarianism and the dictatorship of the proletariat (so that it was natural for the Trotsky–Zinovyev group to make common cause eventually with the remnants of the old 'Workers' Opposition'). They were chiefly interested in the question of power, dictatorship, and heavy industry as an index of power; Bukharin, on the other hand, was concerned with effectively increasing welfare, and was prepared to tolerate the class of materially privileged Nepmen if their activity meant a better deal for the whole population, including the working class.

Throughout the debate, which was to decide the fate of millions of individuals, Stalin supported Bukharin's position but did not commit himself too completely, leaving it to Bukharin or Rykov to make the ideological declarations. He took note of Bukharin's blunder in inviting the peasants to 'get rich'— an expression that touched many Communists on the raw—but treated it as a slip of the tongue, not to be compared with the monstrous crimes of the opposition. Stalin never advanced too far in discussion, but it could be seen that up to 1928 there was no disagreement in economic policy between him and Bukharin: Stalin too repeated Lenin's words concerning the need for a lasting alliance with the middle peasants and attacked the 'ultra-Left' opposition for its 'revolutionary adventurism' and the shocking notion of 'internal colonization'. He got the upper hand in the political and organizational dispute with the opposition, not only thanks to his dominant position in the party machine but because it was easy to show how all the opposition-ists were violating principles that they had recently been shouting from the house-tops. It was no trouble to prove that Trotsky's love of democracy was of extremely recent date, and when he and Zinovyev conspired together against Stalin the latter had only to quote the insults they had been hurling at each other the day before. As for democracy within the party, none of those who were now defending it could refer to his own past without embarrassment. As Stalin put it at the Fourteenth Congress in December 1925, 'Are not the comrades of the opposition aware that for us Bolsheviks formal democracy is an empty shell, but the real interests of the party are everything?' (*Works*, English ed, vol. 7, 1954, p. 394). A few months later he gave a more exact definition of party democracy: 'What does inner-Party democracy mean? Inner-Party democracy means raising the activity of the Party masses and strengthening the unity of the Party, strengthening conscious proletarian discipline in the Party' (Report to Leningrad party organization, 13 Apr. 1926; *Works*, English ed., vol. 8, 1954, p. 153). Stalin, however, was not so incautious as to speak of a 'party dictatorship', though neither Lenin nor, apparently, Bukharin shrank from this: instead he referred to the 'dictatorship of the proletariat under the party's leadership'. At a session of the Executive Committee of the Comintern of 7 December 1926, and on other occasions, he declared that Trotsky, by maintaining that socialism could not be built in one country, was inviting the party to relinquish power.

Trotskyist historians still brood regretfully over the events of the 1920s and speculate as to how Trotsky might have avoided various false moves and regained power by this or that political alliance or combination. It does not seem, however, that this was a real possibility at any time after 1923. Trotsky might indeed have made timely use, in public, of Lenin's 'Testament' to discredit Stalin; he not only failed to do so, but afterwards deprived himself of the possibility by denying the authenticity of the 'Testament' when it was published abroad. Possibly Stalin might have been overthrown in 1924, but this would have been of little benefit to Trotsky, as he was detested by the other leaders, who only showed readiness to conspire with him after they themselves were dislodged from power.

Economic and fiscal policy did not in fact remain unaltered during the N.E.P. period, but moved in the direction of increased pressure on the peasantry. Apart from Bukharin the advocates of N.E.P. in the top ranks of the party were Rykov, who succeeded Lenin as Premier, and Tomsky, in charge of the trade unions. Both these were prominent Bolsheviks in their own right and were by no means puppets of Stalin; however, from an early date Stalin brought into the leadership men like Molotov, Voroshilov, Kalinin, and Kaganovich, who signified nothing in themselves and showed him unquestioning obedience. The uncertainty and ambiguity of economic policy (even N.E.P. enthusiasts could not, in the last resort, altogether give up the idea of a 'class struggle in the countryside') led to an impasse from which there was no satisfactory way out. Substantial concessions to the peasants in 1925 led to an increase in farm production, but by 1927 the output of grain had still not reached its pre-1914 level, while the demand for food was increasing with the progress of industry and urbanization. Smallholders had little grain to dispose of, and the kulaks were not in a hurry to sell either, as there was nothing to buy with the money they received. Hence, in 1927, Stalin made up his mind to adopt extreme measures of confiscation and coercion. Bukharin at the outset approved this policy and revised his own programme in the direction of more planning, more investment in heavy industry, a greater degree of state interference with the market, and, finally, an 'offensive' against the kulaks. This was not enough to satisfy the Left Opposition, but the fact was of little consequence as their positions had meanwhile been destroyed.

The increased economic and administrative pressure on the peasants led to a drastic fall in deliveries and a worsening of the already serious food situation. Stalin talked more and more of the kulak danger and the growing strength of the class enemy, but in February 1928 he was still insisting that rumours of the abandonment of N.E.P. and the liquidation of the kulaks were counter-revolutionary twaddle. Barely four months later, however, he announced that the 'time was ripe' for the mass organization of collective farms. At the plenum of the Central Committee in July he endorsed all the theses of Preobrazhensky that he had till then violently attacked. Russia could only achieve industrialization by means of internal accumulation; the only solution was to fix prices at a level that would make the peasants pay through the nose for industrial goods. At the same time he continued to uphold the principle of a 'lasting alliance with the middle peasants' and averred that small-scale agricultural production was still a necessity. None the less, Bukharin, Rykov, and Tomsky rebelled against the new policy, whereupon Stalin branded them as a new, right-wing opposition: he informed the Politburo of this sad development at the beginning of 1929, and the world at large soon afterwards. (In the autumn of 1928 he had referred in speeches to the 'rightist danger' but declared that unanimity reigned in the Politburo.) The right-wing deviation consisted, it was explained, of slowing up industrialization, deferring collectivization to an indefinite future, re-establishing complete freedom of trade, and repudiating the use of 'extraordinary measures'—i.e. requisitions, arrests, and police pressure—against the kulaks. It soon appeared also that the 'Rightists' were in error concerning the international situation: they still believed in the stabilization of world capitalism, and refused to fight against the social democratic Left.

At this time also, Stalin made a number of speeches (the first in July 1928) in which he announced a new principle that was to add to his fame as a theoretician. This was that as Communism continued to advance, the class struggle and the resistance of the exploiters would become more and more violent. For the next twenty-five years this discovery served as the basis for wholesale repressions, persecutions, and massacres in the Soviet Union and the countries subjected to its rule.

Such was the setting for the mass collectivization of Soviet agriculture—probably the most massive warlike operation ever conducted by a state against its own citizens. Attempts to use coercion in moderation having proved fruitless, Stalin decided at the end of 1929 to embark at once on full collectivization, accompanied by the mass 'liquidation of the kulaks as a class'. A few months later, in March 1930, when this policy had already led to catastrophic results—the peasants destroyed grain and slaughtered livestock on a huge scale—Stalin decreed a temporary lull and, in an article 'Dizzy with Success', blamed the excessive zeal and haste of some party officials and the violation of the 'voluntary principle'. This caused the party and police apparatus to hesitate, with the result that numerous collective farms disbanded of their own accord. There was nothing for it but to revert to the policy of coercion, which turned the country into an inferno. Hundreds of thousands, and finally millions, of peasants, arbitrarily labelled 'kulaks', were deported to Siberia or other desolate areas; desperate revolts in the villages were bloodily suppressed by the army and police, and the country sank into chaos, starvation, and misery. In some cases the inhabitants of whole villages were deported or starved to death; in the mass convoys, hastily organized, thousands were done to death or succumbed to cold and privation; half-dead victims roamed the countryside vainly pleading for succour, and there were cases of cannibalism. To prevent the starving peasants from fleeing to the towns an internal passport system was introduced and unauthorized change of residence was made punishable with imprisonment. Peasants were not allowed passports at all, and were therefore tied to the soil as in the worst days of feudal-serfdom: this state of things was not altered until the 1970s. The concentration camps filled with new hordes of prisoners sentenced to hard labour. The object of destroying the peasants' independence and herding them into collective farms was to create a population of slaves, the benefit of whose labour would accrue to industry. The immediate effect was to reduce Soviet agriculture to a state of decline from which it has not yet recovered, despite innumerable measures of reorganization and reform. At the time of Stalin's death, almost a quarter of a century after mass collectivization was initiated, the output of grain per head of population was still below the 1913 level; yet throughout this period, despite misery and starvation, large quantities of farm produce were exported all over the world for the sake of Soviet industry. The terror and oppression of those years cannot be expressed merely by the figures for loss of human life, enormous as these are; perhaps the most vivid picture of what collectivization meant is in Vasily Grossman's posthumous novel, *Forever Flowing*.

It is widely held that in adopting the 'new course' and the policy of forced collectivization Stalin was simply taking over the Trotsky–Preobrazhensky programme after first eliminating its authors. This was Bukharin's charge from the outset, and it was believed by many of the former opposition who hastened to beg Stalin to pardon them on the ground that there was no longer any fundamental clash of policy. Those, such as Radek, who succeeded in this were able to serve the state for a few years longer, though they did not escape final destruction. Several Marxist thinkers have seen the situation in the same light, from Lukács to Roy Medvedyev. Trotsky, however (who was expelled from the Politburo in autumn 1926 and from the party a year later, deported to Alma Ata at the beginning of 1928, and exiled to Turkey with the consent of the Turkish Government in February 1929), did not share the view that Stalin's policy was identical with his own. The Stalinist bureaucracy, he wrote, had indeed been forced by opposition pressure to adopt left-wing objectives, but it had put them into effect in a ruthless and opportunist way. The opposition believed in collectivization, but not in mass coercion; the kulaks should have been checked and combated 'by economic means'. This was also the line subsequently taken by all Trotsky's followers.

Their contention, however, is a very weak one. Trotsky, it is true, never spoke of forced collectivization, but then neither did Stalin. Anyone who knew the history of those years only from Stalin's speeches and articles would unquestionably suppose that the peasants flocked into the collective farms for the sake of a better life, that the 'revolution from above' was greeted with unbridled joy, and that the only sufferers from stern measures were a handful of incorrigible saboteurs, enemies of the working people and of the government that infallibly expressed that people's interests. What is true is that Stalin put the opposition's programme into effect by the only possible means. All the economic inducements they suggested were tried before Stalin resorted to out-and-out coercion. Tax and price incentives, and a policy of limited terror, had been applied in the previous two years, but the only effect had been that grain deliveries fell and were likely to fall still further. No further means of economic pressure remained, and there were only two alternatives: either to go back to the N.E.P. in its full form and permit free trade, relying on the market to ensure food production and delivery, or to pursue the course already embarked on and eliminate the whole independent peasantry by the mass use of troops and police terror. In choosing the latter policy Stalin gave effect to the demands of the Left in the only feasible way.

Why did he do so? The first alternative was not excluded by any 'laws of history', and there was no fatal compulsion to take the second road. None the less, there was a logic in the Soviet system which operated strongly in the direction that was actually chosen. The ideology in force was far more consonant with a slave economy based on terror than with the return to market conditions, even under state control. As long as the bulk of the population was economically more or less independent of the state, and even kept the state in some degree of dependence on itself, the ideal of an indivisible dictatorship could not be fully realized. Marxist–Leninist doctrine taught, however, that social-ism could only be built up by a completely centralized political and economic power. The abolition of private ownership of the means of production was the supreme task of humanity and the main obligation of the most progressive system in the world. Marxism held out the prospect of the merging or unification of civil society with the state through the dictatorship of the proletariat; and the only way to such unity was by liquidating all spontaneous forms of political, economic, and cultural life and replacing them by forms imposed by the state. Stalin thus realized Marxism–Leninism in the only possible way by con-solidating his dictatorship over society, destroying all social ties that were not state-imposed and all classes, including the working class itself. This process, of course, did not take place overnight. It required, first, the political subjugation of the working class and then of the party: all possible nuclei of resistance had to be crushed, and the proletariat deprived of all means of self-defence. The party was able to do this because at the outset of its power it was supported by a large part of the proletariat. It was not simply that, as Deutscher emphasizes, the old working class, politically conscious and seasoned in battle, was decimated by the Civil War, and that post-war ruin and misery brought about a mood of apathy and fatigue. The party's success was also due to its using the period of proletarian support in two ways. In the first place, it systematically promoted the ablest members of the working class to privileged positions in the state service, thus turning them into a new ruling class; and secondly, it destroyed all existing forms of working-class organization, especially other socialist parties and trade unions, and saw to it that the material means of reviving such organizations were kept out of the workers' reach. All this was done at an early stage and quite efficiently. The working class was thus paralysed, and not only fatigue but the rapid progress of totalitarianism prevented it from subsequently taking effective action, in spite of occasional desperate attempts. In this sense it may be said that the Russian working class created its own despots, regardless of their individual class origins. In the same way the intelligentsia for many years laboured unconsciously to destroy itself by hesitancy and submission in the face of unremitting blackmail from the extreme left.

Thus was fulfilled the prophecy of the Mensheviks, who in 1920 compared the brave new world announced by Trotsky to the building of the Pyramids by Egyptian slaves. Trotsky, for many reasons, was ill suited to carry out his own programme; Stalin was Trotsky *in actu*.

The new policy meant the political downfall of Bukharin and his allies. At the outset of the controversy the Right still had firm political positions and fairly widespread support in the party; but it soon appeared that all their assets were nothing compared to the power of the Secretary-General. 'Rightist deviation' became the main target of attack by Stalin and his henchmen. The Bukharinites—the last opposition group in the party who fought for principles of government and not merely for personal power—were, in the course of 1929, thrust out of all the posts they occupied in the state bureaucracy. This did not signify by any means that the Left Opposition were restored to favour. None of them were brought back into their old posts, though Stalin took on a few for minor duties: the capable Radek was kept on for a few years as government panegyrist. The Bukharinites did not dare appeal to opinion outside the party, any more than the Leftists had done (though in their time there was more possibility of doing so). Nor did the Bukharinites even dare to organize 'fractional' activity: it was only a short time, after all, since the struggle with Trotsky and Zinovyev, in which they had inveighed against fractionalism and exalted party unity. As for one-party rule, it was questioned neither by the Left

Opposition nor by the Right. All were prisoners of their own doctrine and their own past: all had worked with a will to create the apparatus of violence that crushed them. Bukharin's hopeless attempt to form a league with Kamenev was no more than a pitiful epilogue to his career. In November 1929 the deviation-ists performed a public act of penance, but even this did not save them. Stalin's victory was complete; the collapse of the Bukharinite opposition meant the triumph of autocracy in the party and in the country. In December 1929 Stalin's fiftieth birthday was celebrated as a major historical event, and from this point we may date the 'cult of personality'. Trotsky's prophecy of 1903 had come true: party rule had become Central Committee rule, and this in turn had become the personal tyranny of a dictator.

The destruction of the Soviet peasantry, who formed three-quarters of the population, was not only an economic but a moral disaster for the entire country. Tens of millions were driven into semi-servitude, and millions more were employed as executants of the process. The whole party became an organization of torturers and oppressors: no one was innocent, and all Com-munists were accomplices in the coercion of society. Thus the party acquired a new species of moral unity, and embarked on a course from which there was no turning back.

At this time also, what remained of independent Soviet culture and the intelligentsia was systematically destroyed: the regime was entering the phase of final consolidation.

Bukharin's personal fate from 1929 to his judicial murder in 1938 was of no consequence to the history of the Soviet Union or of Marxism. After his downfall he worked for a time as director of research under the Supreme Economic Council and published occasional articles in which he tried—as Stephen F. Cohen points out in his excellent biography—to voice an occasional, muted note of criticism. He remained a member of the Central Com-mittee and, after a further public recantation, became editor of *Izvestiya* in 1934. At the Writers' Congress in August of that year he made a speech which was 'liberal' for the times, and in 1935 he was effective chairman of the commission which drafted the new Soviet Constitution: this document, promul-gated in 1936 and in force until 1977, is mainly if not wholly Bukharin's work. Arrested in February 1937, Bukharin was sentenced to death in the last of the series of monster show trials. His biographer calls him 'the last Bolshevik', a description which is true or false according to the meaning we attach to it. It is true if we mean by a Bolshevik one who accepted all the principles of the new order—the unlimited power of a single party, 'unity' within the party, an ideology excluding all others, the economic dictatorship of the state—and who also believed that it was possible, within this framework, to avoid despotism by an oligarchy or an individual, to govern without the use of terror, and to preserve the values that the Bolsheviks had championed during the struggle for power: namely, government by the work-ing people or the proletariat, free cultural development, and respect for art, science, and national traditions. But if 'Bolshevik' means all this, it simply means a man incapable of drawing logical conclusions from his own premisses. If, on the other hand, Bolshevik ideology is not just a matter of generalities but involves accepting the inevitable consequences of one's own principles, then Stalin was right to boast himself the most consistent of all Bolsheviks and Leninists.

CHAPTER II

Theoretical controversies in Soviet Marxism in the 1920s

1. The intellectual and political climate

As we have seen, the N.E.P. years from 1921 to 1929 were by no means a period of freedom in the intellectual sphere. On the contrary, independent art, literature, philosophy, and the humane sciences were subjected to ever-increasing pressure. Nevertheless, in these fields too the subsequent years of collectivization mark a turning-point, which may be defined as follows. During the N.E.P. period writers and artists were required to show loyalty to the regime and were not allowed to produce anti-Soviet work, but within these limits various trends were permitted and in fact existed. There were no exclusive canons of art and literature; experimentation was allowed, and direct glorification of the regime or its leader was not a *sine qua non* of publication. In philosophy Marxism reigned supreme, but it was not yet codified, and it was by no means universally clear in what 'true' Marxism consisted. Accordingly, controversies continued, and there were convinced Marxists who genuinely sought to discover what was or was not consonant with Marxism. Moreover, the philosophers of the 1920s, although they left no works of particular importance, were men of 'normal' intellectual background and, while loyal to the regime, did not trouble themselves as to how it might react to their speculations.

For some years, too, private publishing firms were in operation. In 1918–20 non-Marxist works were still published—for example, those of Berdyayev, Frank, Lossky, Novgorodtsev, and Askoldov—and one or two non-Marxist periodicals appeared, such as *Mysl i slovo* and *Mysl*. This shows how baseless was the later argument that increased repression was necessary because of the acute threat to Soviet power. The years of relative cultural freedom were those of the Civil War, when the threat to the regime was much greater than subsequently (and, in the same way, a certain degree of relaxation in cultural matters took place in 1941 and after, when the country's fate hung in the balance). In 1920, however, the university chairs of philosophy were suppressed, and in 1922 all non-Marxist philosophers, including those mentioned above, were expelled from the country.

In art and literature the 1920s were marked by many valuable achievements. Outstanding writers who identified with the Revolution gave it a kind of authenticity by their work: these included Babel, the young Fadeyev, Pilnyak, Mayakovsky, Yesenin, Artem Vesyoly, and Leonov. Their creativity is proof of the fact that the Revolution was not a mere *coup d'état* but an explosion of forces truly present in Russian society. But other writers who by no means favoured the Soviet system were also active at this time, for example, Pasternak, Akhmatova, and Zamyatin. In the thirties all this came to an end. Indeed, it is hard to say whether it was safer in that period to identify with the Revolution or to be a 'bourgeois survival'. Many of the former class of writers were murdered (Babel, Pilnyak, Vesyoly) or committed suicide (Mayakovsky, Yesenin); of the second category some, such as Mandelshtam, died in labour camps, but others survived the years of persecution and heartbreak (Akhmatova, Pasternak) or managed to emigrate (Zamyatin). Those who chose to become panegyrists of Stalin's tyranny (Fadeyev, Sholokhov, Olesha, Gorky) generally sacrificed their talent in the process.

The first years after the Civil War witnessed an upsurge in all forms of culture. The names of the great producers and directors—Meyerhold, Pudovkin, Eisenstein—belong to the world history of theatre and the cinema. Current Western fashions, especially of a more or less *avant-garde* type, were embraced eagerly and without fear of the consequences. Soviet adherents of Freud, such as I.D. Yermakov, stressed the materialist and determinist aspects of psychoanalysis; Trotsky himself showed a favourable interest in Freudianism. J. B. Watson's works on behaviourism appeared in Russian translation. As yet there were no ideological attacks on new developments in natural science. The theory of relativity was received with favour by commentators who argued that it confirmed dialectical materialism by asserting that time and space are forms of the existence of matter. 'Progressive' trends in education were also welcomed, especially Dewey's emphasis on the 'free school' as opposed to discipline and authority; at the same time Viktor M. Shulgin, for example, held out the prospect that schools would 'wither away' under Communism. It was indeed not incongruous with Marx's doctrine that all old-world institutions should be doomed to wither away: the state, the army, the school, nationality, and the family. Views such as these expressed a naïve *avant-garde* spirit of Communism which itself was destined soon to 'wither away' for good and all. Its adherents believed that a new world was coming into existence in which effete institutions and traditions, sanctities and taboos, cults and idols would collapse into dust before the triumphant power of Reason; the world proletariat, like another Prometheus, would create a new age of humanism. This iconoclastic fervour attracted many Western intellectuals of the literary or artistic *avant-garde*, such as the French surrealists, who saw in Communism the political embodiment of their own struggle against tradition, academism, authority, and the past in general. The cultural atmosphere of Russia in those years had an adolescent quality, common to all periods of revolution: the belief that life is just beginning, that the future is unlimited, and that mankind is no longer bound by the shackles of history.

The new regime made a strong effort to abolish illiteracy and promote education. The schools were soon used for ideological indoctrination, and the whole educational system was greatly expanded. Universities were founded right and left, but many did not last long, as the figures show: before the war Russia had 97 places of higher learning, in 1922 there were 278, but in 1926 there were again only half as many (138). At the same time 'Workers' Faculties' (*rabfaki*) were founded, providing crash courses to prepare workers for higher education. Initially, Soviet cultural policy under Lunacharsky was content with limited objectives. It was impossible to remove all 'bourgeois' scholars and teachers from academic institutions at a stroke, as this would have virtually put an end to learning and education. The universities, from the outset, were more subjected to political pressure than the Academy and research institutes, as is still the case today: there is naturally less strict control over bodies that are not engaged in teaching the young. In the 1920s the Academy of Sciences retained a considerable measure of autonomy, while the universities lost it at an early date, their governing bodies being packed with representatives of the Commissariat for Education and party activists from the Workers' Faculties. Professorial chairs were assigned to politically reliable individuals without academic qualifications; the enrolment of students was subjected to class criteria so as to exclude 'bourgeois' applicants, i.e. children of the old intelligentsia or the middle class. Stress was laid on 'vocational' education, in opposition to the old idea of a 'liberal' university with a fairly flexible curriculum: the object was to prevent the creation of an intelligentsia in the old sense, i.e. a class of people who wished not only to be skilled in their own profession but to enlarge their horizons, to acquire an all-round culture and form their own opinions on general topics. The education of the 'new intelligentsia' was to be confined as far as possible to strictly professional qualifications. The principles that still hold good today were introduced at an early date; however, the intensity of political pressure varied in different fields. At the outset there was practically no coercion as far as the content of natural science was concerned; in the humanities it was strongest in ideologically sensitive areas, namely philosophy, sociology, law, and modern history. Works by non-Marxists on the history of the ancient world, Byzantium, or old Russia were still allowed to appear in the 1920s.

As to the non-Russian peoples of the Soviet state, while their 'right of self-determination' soon proved to be a mere scrap of paper (as Lenin had predicted), they received the benefits of universal education through the medium of their own tongue, and Russification was not at first a significant factor. To sum up, although the general level of education inevitably suffered a good deal, the new regime did succeed in establishing a generally accessible school system for the first time in Russia's history.

For the first decade of Soviet power the universities were to a large extent influenced by academics of the old type, even though some faculties—especially history, philosophy, and law were completely 'reformed' or closed down. To form new teaching cadres and encourage the spread of orthodox learning the authorities created two party-based institutions: the Red Professors' Institute (1921) to train up replacements for the old intelligentsia in the universities, and, at an earlier date, the Communist Academy in Moscow. Both these bodies were supported by Bukharin as long as he remained in power, and were several times purged of 'left-wing' or 'right-wing' deviationists; they were disbanded in due course, when the party was in full control of all academic institutions and no longer needed a special training-ground to fill them with reliable staff. Another creation of this time was the Marx–Engels Institute, which studied the history of Communism and inaugurated a first-class critical edition of the works of Marx and Engels (the *M.E.G.A.* edition). Its director, D. B. Ryazanov, was dismissed from his post in the 1930s, like practically all genuine Marxist intellectuals, and probably fell a victim to the purge, though some say that he died a natural death at Saratov in 1938.

The principal Marxist historian of the 1920s was Mikhail N. Pokrovsky, an eminent scholar and a friend of Bukharin. He was for some years Deputy Commissar for Education under Lunacharsky, and was the first director of the Red Professors' Institute. He taught history in the classic Marxist style, endeavouring to show that detailed analysis invariably confirmed the general tenets of Marxism: the decisive role of technology and class conflicts, the subordinate importance of individuality in the historical process, and the doctrine that all nations went through essentially the same phases of evolution. Pokrovsky wrote a history of Russia that was much admired by Lenin, and had the good fortune to die in 1932, before the great purges. Subsequently, his views were branded as incorrect and he was accused of denying the 'objectivity' of historical science, for instance in the often-quoted statement that history is nothing but politics projected into the past. He was, however, a genuine historian and a conscientious sifter of evidence, unlike the party champions of 'scientific objectivity'. The accusations against him and his school were mainly connected with the growing influence of nationalism in state ideology and the cult of Stalin as the supreme authority on history: Pokrovsky, it was said, showed 'lack of patriotism' and his researches underestimated the role of Lenin and Stalin. The charge was true in so far as Pokrovsky did not glorify the conquests of Tsarist

Russia, as became *de rigueur* in later years, or extol the virtues and general superiority of the Russian people.

Party history was naturally subject to the strictest control from the very beginning. Nevertheless, there was no single authoritative version for many years, indeed not until the publication of the *Short Course* in 1938, and, as long as fractional strife continued, each group presented party history in the light most favourable to itself. Trotsky put about one version of the Revolution, Zinovyev another. Various manuals appeared, all of course written by party activists or historians under orders (for example, A. S. Bubnov, V. I. Nevsky, N. N. Popov), but not precisely the same in content. For some time the most authoritative version was that by E. Yaroslavsky, first published in 1923 and revised several times in accordance with power shifts among the leaders. Eventually it was replaced by a collective work with Yaroslavsky as editor, but despite all his efforts it was found to be marred by 'serious errors', i.e. it was not sufficiently laudatory of Stalin. Party history, in fact, was degraded to the status of a political weapon at an earlier date than any other branch of learning: from the outset, manuals of party history were nothing but manuals of self-praise. None the less, valuable material in this domain was also published in the twenties, chiefly in the form of memoirs and contributions to specialized journals.

The best-known Soviet expert on legal and constitutional theory in the 1920s was Yevgeny B. Pashukanis (1890–1938), who perished in the great purge like so many others. He was head of the department of legal studies in the Communist Academy, and his *General Theory of Law and Marxism* (published in a German translation in 1929) is regarded as typical of Soviet ideology of the period. His argument was that not only particular changing systems of legal norms, but the very form of law itself, i.e. the phenomenon of law as a whole, is a product of fetishistic social relationships and therefore, in its developed form, is a historical manifestation of the age of commercial production. Law was created as an instrument for the regulation of trade and was then extended to other types of personal relationship. It is therefore in accordance with Marxist theory to hold that in a Communist society law must wither away in the same manner as the state and other creations of commodity fetishism. Soviet law, currently in force, shows by its very existence that we are in a transitional period in which classes have not yet been abolished and survivals of capitalism are inevitably still present. There can be no such thing as a form of law peculiar to Communist society, as personal relationships in that society will not be mediated by juridical categories.

Pashukanis's theory was indeed strongly rooted in Marx's teaching and was in accordance with the interpretation of Marx advanced at the time by Lukács and Korsch; social democrats, on the other hand, such as Renner and Kautsky, regarded law as a permanent instrument for the regulation of relations between individuals. According to Lukács's argument in his analysis of reification, it follows from Marx's social philosophy that law is a form of the reified and fetishistic character of personal relations in a society dominated by commodity exchange. When social life returns to its unmediated form, human beings will not be obliged, or even able, to conduct their relationships through abstract legal rules; as Pashukanis emphasized, legal associations reduce individuals to abstract juridical categories. Law is therefore an aspect of bourgeois society, in which all personal associations take on a reified form, and individuals are only the puppets of impersonal forces—those of exchange-value in the economic process, or abstract legal rules in political society.

Similar conclusions were drawn from Marxist theory by another legal theoretician of the 1920s, Petr I. Stuchka, who contended that law as such is an instrument of the class struggle and must therefore exist as long as class antagonism continues: in socialist society it is an instrument for suppressing the resistance of hostile classes, and in a classless society there can be no further need for it. Stuchka, who represented Latvia in the Comintern, was for many years an officer in the Soviet secret police.

In literature and other areas less sensitive politically than party history, the state and party leaders for the most part saw no harm in allowing a certain pluralism within the limits of general loyalty to the regime. Neither Lenin, Trotsky, nor Bukharin sought to impose a strait-jacket on literature. Lenin and Trotsky were old-fashioned in their personal tastes and had no time for *avant-garde* literature or for Proletkult; Bukharin had some sympathy for the latter, but Trotsky, who published several articles on literary topics, stated flatly that there was not and could not be any 'proletarian culture'. The proletariat, he argued, could not produce any culture at the present time because it was not educated, and, as for the future, socialist society would not create a class culture of any sort but would raise the whole of human culture to new levels. The dictatorship of the proletariat was only a short, transient phase after which the glorious classless society would set in—a society of supermen, any one of whom could become the intellectual equal of Aristotle, Goethe, or Marx. In Trotsky's view it was wrong to canonize any particular literary style, or label creative forms as progressive or reactionary regardless of their content.

The imposition of a uniform pattern on art and literature and their transformation into media for the glorification of the state, the party, and Stalin was a natural effect of the development of totalitarianism; but the creative intelligentsia, or at least large sections of it, helped considerably in the process. During the time when various literary and artistic schools were in competition and were tolerated on condition of general loyalty to the regime, almost every one of them canvassed the party for support against its rivals: this applied especially to literature and the theatre. In this way writers and others seeking a monopoly for their views accepted and encouraged the baneful principle that it was for the party and state authorities to permit or prohibit this or that form of art. The destruction of Soviet culture was in part the work of its own representatives. There were, however, exceptions. For instance, the 'formalist' school of literary criticism flourished in the 1920s and was respected as an important humanistic trend; it was condemned at the end of the decade, but several of its members refused to bow to political pressure and police sanctions and had to be forced into silence. It is noteworthy that, as a result of this tenacity, formalism continued to exist as an underground current and reappeared twenty-five years later, during the partial thaw after Stalin's death, as a strong, untarnished intellectual movement, though of course some of its leaders had meanwhile died of natural causes or otherwise.

The twenties were also the period of the 'new proletarian morality'—a term which stands for a number of planned or spontaneous changes, not all in the same direction. On the one

hand there was a continuing struggle against 'bourgeois prejudices': this was not specifically Marxist, but reflected the old
Russian revolutionary tradition. It was seen, for instance, in
the relaxation of legal forms concerning the family: marriage
and divorce became rubber-stamp operations, discrimination
between legitimate and bastard children was abolished, no
restriction was placed on abortion. Sexual freedom was the rule
among revolutionaries, as Alexandra Kollontay had long
advocated as a matter of theory and as may be seen from
Soviet novels of the period. The government was interested in
these changes in so far as they tended to weaken parental
influence and facilitate a state monopoly of education. Official
propaganda encouraged all forms of collective education of
even the youngest children, and family ties were often represented as simply another 'bourgeois survival': children were
taught to spy on their parents and inform against them, and
were rewarded when they did so. However, in this as in other
aspects of life, such as schooling and the army, later years
brought a marked change in the official outlook. Of the radical
and iconoclastic ideals preached in the early years of the revolution, all were discarded except those which helped the state to
exert absolute control over the individual. Hence the idea of
collective education and reduction of parental authority to the
minimum continued to hold sway, but an end was put to
'progressive' educational methods designed to promote initiative
and independence. Strict discipline became once more the rule,
and in this respect Soviet schools differed from Tsarist ones only
in the immensely increased emphasis on indoctrination. In due
course, puritanical sexual ethics were restored to favour. The
first slogans to go were, of course, those relating to the democratization of the army. Trotsky, at the time of the Civil War, was
well aware that an efficient army needs absolute discipline, a
strict hierarchy, and a professional officer corps: dreams of a
people's army based on brotherhood, equality, and revolutionary zeal were soon recognized to be utopian.

   The state also set out from the beginning to destroy the
influence of the Church and religion: this was manifestly in
accord with Marxist doctrine and also with the state's object
of destroying all independent education. We have already seen
that, although the Soviet regime proclaimed the separation of

Church and State, it has never succeeded, and cannot succeed, in making this principle a reality; for it would mean that the state took no interest in the religious views of its citizens and assured them all of equal rights whether they belonged to any denomination or none, while the Church or Churches would be recognized as subjects of private law. Once the state had become an apanage of the party with its anti-religious philosophy, this separation was impossible. The party's ideology became that of the state, and all forms of religious life perforce became anti-state activity. The separation of Church and State means that believers and non-believers have equal rights and that the former have as much chance of exercising power as atheistic party members. It is sufficient to state this principle to realize how absurd it is in Soviet conditions. A state which from the outset professed adherence to a basic philosophy or ideology from which its legitimacy was derived could not be neutral *vis-à-vis* religion. Accordingly, throughout the twenties the Church was persecuted and prevented from preaching Christianity, though the intensity of the process varied at different times. The regime succeeded in persuading part of the hierarchy to give ground—it made no concessions on its own part, so one can hardly speak of a compromise—and in the later twenties, after many recalcitrant priests had been murdered, a fair proportion of those who remained professed loyalty and instituted prayers for the Soviet state and government. By then, after innumerable executions, the dissolution of monasteries and convents, expropriations and deprivation of civil rights, the Church was only a shadow of what it had been. Nevertheless, anti-religious propaganda has remained to this day an important element in party education. The League of Militant Atheists, set up in 1925 under Yaroslavsky's leadership, harried and persecuted Christians and other believers in every possible way, and was supported by the state in doing so.

The most powerful educative force in the new society was, however, the system of police repression. Although this fluctuated in intensity, it was always the case that any citizen, at any time, could be subjected to repressive measures at the will of the authorities. Lenin had laid down that law in the new society must have nothing to do with law in the traditional sense, i.e. it must not be allowed to limit government power in any way. On the contrary, since law under any regime was 'nothing but' an instrument of class oppression, so the new order adopted a corresponding principle of 'revolutionary legality' which meant that the authorities did not have to bother with legal forms, rules of evidence, the rights of accused persons, etc., but could simply arrest, imprison, and do to death anyone who might seem to present even a potential danger to the 'dictatorship of the proletariat'. The Cheka, forerunner of the K.G.B., was empowered from the beginning to imprison anyone without the sanction of the judiciary, and decrees were issued immediately after the Revolution to the effect that various loosely defined categories of people—speculators, counter-revolutionary agitators, agents of foreign powers, etc.—were to be 'shot without mercy'. (It was not stated what categories were to be shot mercifully.) This meant in practice that local police authorities had absolute powers of life and death over every citizen. Concentration camps (the term was actually used) were set up in 1918, under the authority of Lenin and Trotsky, for various types of 'class enemy'. Initially these camps were used as places of punishment for political adversaries—Kadets, Mensheviks, and S.R.s, later Trotskyists and other deviationists, priests, former Tsarist officials and officers, and members of the property-owning classes, common criminals, workers who committed breaches of labour discipline, and recalcitrants of all kinds. Only after some years did the camps become an important factor in the Soviet economy by virtue of providing slave-labour on a massive scale. At different times the terror was directed especially against one or another social group, according to what the party chose to regard as the 'chief danger' of the moment; but from the outset the system of repression was completely above the law, and all decrees and penal codes served merely to authorize the use of arbitrary power by those who already possessed it. Show trials began at an early stage, for example, those of S.R.s and priests; a grim warning of things to come was the trial at Shakhty in May 1928 of some dozens of engineers working in the Donets coal basin, in which the evidence was trumped up from beginning to end and was based on extorted confessions. The victims, accused of sabotage and 'economic counter-revolution', were convenient scapegoats for the regime's economic set-backs, its organizational blunders, and the wretched state of the population. Eleven were sentenced to death and many to long terms of imprisonment. The trial was meant to serve as a warning to all members of the old intelligentsia that they could not expect indulgent treatment from the state. The record of the proceedings has been admirably analysed by Solzhenitsyn and presents a picture of the absolute degradation of legal concepts under the Soviet regime.

There is no evidence that any of the party leaders at any time protested or attempted to prevent repressions or obviously faked trials, as long as none of the victims was a Bolshevik. The opposition groups only began to complain when the terror affected their own members, who were devoted party activists; but by that time complaints were of no avail. The police apparatus was completely in the hands of Stalin and his helpers, and on the lower levels it took precedence of the party bureaucracy. It cannot be said, however, that the police ever controlled the party as a whole, for Stalin ruled supreme throughout the period as head of the party, not of the police; it was through the police, however, that he governed the party.

2. *Bukharin as a philosopher*

One of the distinguishing features of Communism was the conviction of the importance of philosophy in political life. From the very beginning, i.e. from Plekhanov's early writings, Russian Marxism showed the tendency to develop into an integral 'system', embracing and answering all questions of philosophy, sociology, and politics. Although individuals differed as to what the 'true' philosophy consisted in, they were all agreed that the party must and did have a clearly defined philosophical outlook, and that this outlook could tolerate no rival. There was virtually no counterpart in Russia to the philosophic 'neutralism' of so many German Marxists, which expressed itself in two logically independent propositions. The first of these was that Marxism, as a scientific theory of social phenomena, had no more need of philosophical premises than any other science; the second, that the party was bound by a political programme and a historico-social doctrine, but that its members were free to adhere to any religion or philosophy they liked. Lenin violently attacked both these principles, and in so doing he was entirely representative of Russian Marxism.

Accordingly, the party authorities lost no time after the Revolution in concerning themselves with philosophical education. There was, however, as yet no codified philosophy. Apart from Marx and Engels, Plekhanov was regarded as the main authority; Lenin's work on empiriocriticism by no means enjoyed the status of a canonical text to which all were obliged to refer.

Bukharin was the first of the party leaders after Lenin who attempted a systematic exposition of the party's general philosophy and social doctrine. He was better equipped for the task than most others, as during the years in emigration he had studied non-Marxist sociological works such as those of Weber, Pareto, Stammler, and others. In 1921 he published *The Theory of Historical Materialism: a popular manual of Marxist sociology* (English translation, 1926). Unlike Lenin's *Empiriocriticism*, which was an attack on one particular heresy, Bukharin's work purported to give a general account of Marxist doctrine. For many years it was used as a basic text in the theoretical training of party cadres, and its importance lies in this fact rather than in its intrinsic merits.

Bukharin holds that Marxism is a strictly scientific, and the only scientific, comprehensive theory of social phenomena, and that it treats these phenomena as 'objectively' as any other science treats its proper subject-matter; hence Marxists are able correctly to foresee historical processes, which no one else can do. True, Marxism is also a class theory, as are all social theories; but it is a theory entrusted to the proletariat, which has wider mental horizons than the bourgeoisie, because its aim is to change society and it is therefore able to look into the future. Thus only the proletariat can produce, and has in fact produced, a 'true science' of social phenomena. This science is historical materialism, or Marxist sociology. (The term 'sociology' was not approved of by Marxists, and Lenin rejected it on the ground that 'sociology' as such—not merely this or that theory—was a bourgeois invention. However, Bukharin evidently wished to acclimatize a term already in use to denote a particular field of scientific inquiry.)

Historical materialism, Bukharin argues, is based on the premiss that there is no difference between the social and natural sciences in either methods of investigation or the causal approach to the object. All social processes are subject to invariable causal laws; despite the objections of such theorists as Stammler, the fact of human purpose makes no difference to this, as will and purpose are themselves conditioned like everything else. Theories of purposive action in either the natural or the social field, and all indeterminist theories, lead straight to the postulate of a Deity. Man does not have free will: all his actions are causally determined. There is no such thing as chance in any 'objective' sense. What we call chance is the intersection of two chains of causation, only one of which is known to us: the category of 'chance' is merely an expression of our ignorance.

As the law of necessity applies to all social phenomena, it is possible to predict the course of history. Such predictions are 'not yet' so exact that we can foretell the dates of particular events, but this is only because of the imperfectness of our knowledge.

The conflict between materialism and idealism in sociology is a particular instance of a basic philosophical controversy. Materialism asserts that man is a part of nature, that mind is a function of matter and thought an activity of the physical brain. All this is contradicted by idealism, which is nothing but a form of religion and has been effectively refuted by science. For who could take seriously the crazy theory of solipsism, or Plato's notion that there are no such things as people or pears, but only 'ideas' of them?

In the social sphere, then, the same question arises as to the primacy of spirit or matter. From the point of view of science, that is of historical materialism, material phenomena, namely productive activities, determine spiritual phenomena such as ideas, religion, art, law, etc. We must, however, take care to observe the way in which general laws operate in the social context, and not simply transpose the laws of natural science into social terms.

Dialectical materialism teaches that there is nothing permanent in the universe, but that all things are interconnected and affect one another. This is denied by bourgeois historians, who are at pains to argue that private property, capitalism, and the state are eternal. Changes in fact arise from internal conflicts and struggles, for, in society as everywhere else, all equilibrium is unstable and is eventually overthrown, and the new equilibrium must be based on new principles. These changes are effected by qualitative leaps resulting from the accumulation of quantitative changes. For instance, water is heated and, at a given movement, reaches boiling-point and turns into steam—a qualitative change. (We may note in passing that none of the 'classic Marxist writers', from Engels to Stalin, who repeated this example observed that water does not have to reach a temperature of 100° centigrade to evaporate.) Social revolution is a change of the same sort, and this is why the bourgeoisie rejects the dialectical law of change by qualitative leaps.

Specifically social forms of change and development depend on the interchange of energy between man and nature, that is to say on labour. Social life is conditioned by production, and social evolution by the increasing productivity of labour. The relations of production determine thought, but, as human beings produce commodities in mutual dependence on one another, society is not merely a collection of individuals but a true aggregate, every unit of which affects every other. Technology determines social development; every other factor is secondary. Geography, for instance, can at most affect the rate at which peoples evolve, but does not explain evolution itself; demographic changes depend on technology and not the other way about. As for racial theories of evolution, they were decisively refuted by Plekhanov.

'In the last resort' all aspects of human culture can be explained by technological change. The organization of society evolves according to the condition of productive forces. The state is an instrument of the ruling class and serves to maintain its privileges. How, for example, did religion come into being? Very simply: in primitive society there was a ruler of the tribe, and people transferred this concept to their own selves, thus arriving at the idea of a soul that rules the body; then they transferred the soul to the whole of nature and endowed the universe with spiritual qualities. Finally these fantasies were used to justify class divisions. Again, the idea of God as an unknown power 'reflects' the dependence of capitalists on fate, which they cannot control. Art is likewise a product of technical development and social conditions: savages, Bukharin explains, cannot play the piano, for if there is no piano one cannot play on it or compose works for it. Decadent modern art—impressionism, futurism, expressionism—expresses the decline of the bourgeoisie.

Despite all this the superstructure is not without importance: the bourgeois state, after all, is a condition of capitalist production. The superstructure affects the base, but at any given moment it is 'in the last resort' conditioned by the forces of production.

As for ethics, they are a product of the fetishism of class society and will vanish with it. The proletariat has no need of ethics, and the norms of behaviour that it creates in its own interest are technical in character. Just as a carpenter making a chair conforms to certain technical rules, so the proletariat builds communism on the basis of knowledge concerning the interdependence of members of society; but this has nothing to do with ethics.

In general, the whole dialectic may be reduced to an unending process of the disturbance and restoration of equilibrium. There is no longer any purpose in opposing the 'dialectical' to the 'mechanistic' view of phenomena, as in modern times mechanics has itself become dialectical: do we not learn from physics that everything affects everything else, and nothing in nature is isolated? All social phenomena can be explained by the conflict of opposing forces because of man's struggle with nature. (Bukharin seems to believe, nevertheless, that when communism is finally built, social equilibrium will be established once and for all. At present, however, we are in a revolutionary era, which inevitably involves a regression in technical matters.) Production relations are simply the co-ordination of human beings, considered as 'living machines', in the labour process. The fact that people think and feel while engaged in this process does not mean that production relations are spiritual in character: everything spiritual owes its existence to material needs and is subservient to production and the class struggle. It is not the case, for instance, as Cunow and Tugan-Baranovsky assert, that the bourgeois state performs functions that are for the benefit of all classes. True, the bourgeoisie is compelled in its own interest to organize activities in the sphere of public utility, for example, to build roads, maintain schools, and promote scientific knowledge; but all this is done purely from the point of view of the capitalist class-interest, and thus the state is nothing but an instrument of class domination.

Besides the 'law of equilibrium' Bukharin formulated in *Historical Materialism* several other laws of social life. One of these, the 'law of the materialization of social phenomena', was to the effect that ideologies and the various forms of spiritual life are embodied in things—books, libraries, art galleries, etc. —which have an existence of their own and become a point of departure for further evolution.

Bukharin's book is of an extremely simplistic kind, in some ways even more so than Lenin's *Empiriocriticism*. Lenin at least tried to argue, though his arguments were logically valueless, but Bukharin has not even this to his credit. The work is a series of 'principles' and 'fundamental points', enunciated dogmatically and uncritically, without any attempt to analyse the concepts used or to refute the objections to historical materialism that occur as soon as the doctrine is formulated and have repeatedly been advanced by critics. Bukharin's examples illustrate the level of his reasoning, as when he tells us that the dependence of art on social conditions is proved by the fact that no one can play the piano if there are no pianos. Other instances of primitive thought are the childish belief that science in the future will be able 'objectively' to predict the date of social revolutions in the light of technological development, or the 'scientific law' that people write books, or baseless fantasies on the origin of religion, etc. The characteristic feature of this 'manual', as of much subsequent Marxist literature, is its incessant use of the term 'scientific', and the insistent claim that its own statements possess this quality in an exceptional degree.

The mediocrity of Bukharin's book did not escape the notice of intelligent Marxist critics such as Gramsci and Lukács, who drew attention in particular to its 'mechanistic' tendency. Bukharin thought of society as a connected whole in which everything that happens can be explained by the current state of technology; people's thoughts and feelings, the culture in which they express them, and the social institutions they create, are all brought into being by the forces of production with the unalterable regularity of natural law. Bukharin does not explain clearly what he means by the 'law of equilibrium': we are told that equilibrium in society is constantly being disturbed and having to be restored, and that this equilibrium depends on

the 'accordance' of production relations with the level of technology, but there is no indication of the criteria to be used in
determining whether this accord exists at a given time. In
practice, Bukharin seems to equate the disturbance of equilibrium with revolution or social upheaval of any kind. The
'law of equilibrium' thus appears to mean that crises and
revolutions have occurred in history and will no doubt do so
again. It did not enter Bukharin's head that the study of social
phenomena is itself a social phenomenon and, as such, helps
to bring about historical change: he believed that the 'proletarian
science' of the future would be able to analyse and predict
historical events in the same way as astronomy informs us of
planetary movements.

Thanks to his political position Bukharin's standardized
version of Marxism was long regarded as the most authoritative
statement of the party's 'world-outlook', though it never became
binding on the faithful in the way that Stalin's works were to
do. *Historical Materialism* in fact contains almost everything that
Stalin put into his own manual. Stalin did not mention the
'law of equilibrium', but he took over Bukharin's 'laws of the
dialectic' (numbering them for good measure) and explained
historical materialism as an 'application' or special case of the
general principles of philosophical materialism. This approach,
for which a basis can be found in Engels and especially
Plekhanov, was presented by Bukharin as the essence of
canonical Marxism.

Later, when Bukharin fell from grace and 'mechanism' was
officially condemned, it became the task of party philosophers
to show that there was a close connection between his
'mechanistic' errors and his right-wing deviation in politics, and
that his ignorance of dialectic, which Lenin had justly blamed,
was the root cause of his defence of the kulaks and opposition
to collectivization. This kind of link between philosophy and
politics, however, is quite baseless and artificial. The vague
generalities in Bukharin's work do not provide any ground for
specific political conclusions, except for such propositions as no
one disputed then or later: for example, that the socialist
revolution of the proletariat must eventually conquer the world,
that religion must be combated, and that the proletarian state
must foster the growth of industry. As for more precise con-

clusions, the most contradictory aims could be and were deduced with equal logic from the same theoretical formulas; doctrine, in fact, was ancillary to politics. If 'on the one hand' the base determined the superstructure, but 'on the other hand' the super-structure reacted upon the base, then to whatever extent and by whatever means the 'proletarian state' endeavoured to regulate economic processes, it would always be acting in accordance with the doctrine. Bukharin accused Stalin of disturbing the economic balance between town and countryside, but his 'law of equilibrium' supplied no clue as to when and in what conditions the existing equilibrium should be maintained or overthrown. Until final stabilization is attained under Communism, equilibrium will remain subject to disturbance, and such policies as Stalin's 'revolution from above', i.e. the forced expropriation of the peasantry, may be perfectly in accordance with the thesis of the general trend of society towards equilibrium: for the object of that policy was to eliminate 'contradictions' between state industry and private agriculture, and hence to remove factors of imbalance. Cohen rightly observes that Bukharin wrote his handbook at a time when he himself exemplified what was called in party language an extremely 'voluntaristic' attitude to economic phenomena: i.e. he believed that the whole of economic life could be perfectly well regulated by administrative and coercive means, and that after the victory of the proletariat all economic laws would be dialectically superseded. Later he abandoned his War Communism outlook and became the ideologist of the N.E.P.; but he made no alteration to the thesis of *Historical Materialism*, and it was therefore absurd to detect in that work the inspiration of his policy in 1929. Nor, for that matter, can the ideas of War Communism be deduced from it either: we can only say once again that such vague philosophical statements can be used to justify any policy or, which comes to the same thing, that they do not justify one more than another.

3. *Philosophical controversies: Deborin versus the mechanists*

Independently of Bukharin's intention, his book contributed to a lively dispute in the 1920s between two opposed camps, the 'dialecticians' and the 'mechanists'. The controversy was reflected in the pages of the monthly *Pod znamenem Marksizma*

(*Under the banner of Marxism*): this journal, founded in 1922, played an important part in the history of Soviet philosophy and was one of the party's theoretical organs. (The first issue contained a letter from Trotsky, which, however, consisted merely of generalities.) The articles published were all by professed Marxists, but in the first few years readers were given sound information on contemporary philosophy outside Russia, for example, that of Husserl, and the general level of exposition was a great deal higher than in the standard philosophical writings of later years.

If the gist of the controversy were to be expressed in a single sentence, one might say that the mechanists represented the opposition of the natural sciences to philosophic interference, while the dialecticians stood for the supremacy of philosophy over the sciences and thus reflected the characteristic tendency of Soviet ideological development. The mechanists' outlook might be called negative, while the dialecticians ascribed immense importance to philosophy and regarded themselves as specialists. The mechanists, however, had a much better idea of what science was about. The dialecticians were ignoramuses in this sphere and confined themselves to general formulas about the philosophical need to 'generalize' and unify the sciences; on the other hand, they knew more than the mechanists about the history of philosophy. (Eventually the party condemned both camps, and created a dialectical synthesis of both forms of ignorance.)

The mechanists accepted Marxism but maintained that the scientific world-view had no need of a philosophy, as it merely represented the sum total of all the natural and social sciences. In one of the journal's first numbers there appeared an article by O. Minin, of whom nothing else is known, which was often quoted thereafter as an extreme example of the mechanists' anti-philosophical prejudice. The view expressed by Minin in a highly simplistic form was that feudal lords had used religion to further their class-interests and the bourgeoisie had similarly used philosophy; the proletariat, on the other hand, rejected both and drew all its strength from science.

In a more or less acute form, dislike of philosophy as such was typical of the whole mechanist camp. Its best-known adherents were Ivan I. Skvortsov-Stepanov (1870–1928) and

Arkady K. Timiryazev (1880–1955), son of an eminent physiologist. Lyubov A. Akselrod, whose views we have discussed elsewhere, also professed a 'mechanist world-view', but, as a disciple of Plekhanov, she adopted a less extreme position than others of the group.

The mechanists, with some support from Engels's works, held that from the Marxist point of view there was no such thing as a 'science of sciences' which would dictate to particular sciences or claim a right to judge their findings. The dialectic as understood by the opposing camp was not only superfluous but contrary to scientific investigation: it consisted of introducing into the world-picture entities and categories unknown to science, a Hegelian inheritance that was equally alien to the scientific revolutionary spirit of Marxism and to the interests of socialist society. The natural aim of science was to explain all phenomena more and more precisely by reducing them to physical and chemical processes, whereas the dialecticians with their qualitative leaps, inner contradictions, etc. were doing the opposite: they were in effect confirming the alleged qualitative differences between various spheres of reality, by borrowing fictitious entities from the idealists. All changes could be finally reduced to quantitative terms, and the view that this did not apply, for example, to living phenomena was no more than idealistic vitalism. True, it was possible to speak of a struggle between contraries, but not in Hegel's sense of the internal disjunction of concepts: the struggle was between conflicting forces, as could be seen in physics, biology, or the social sciences without having to resort to any particular dialectical logic. Scientific investigation must be wholly based on experience, and all Hegel's dialectical 'categories' were irreducible to empirical data. The position of the dialecticians was clearly being undermined by the progress of natural science, which was proving slowly but surely that all processes in the universe could be expressed in physical and chemical terms. The belief in irreducible qualitative differences and the discontinuity of natural processes was nothing short of reactionary, as was the dialecticians' claim that 'chance' was something objective and not merely a term for our ignorance of particular causes.

The dialecticians' hand was much strengthened in 1925 by the publication of Engels's *Dialectics of Nature*, which provided ample ammunition against mechanism and philosophical nihilism and in favour of the demand for a philosophical and dialectical interpretation of the sciences. Even stronger support came in 1929 with the publication of Lenin's *Philosophical Notes*, which emphasized the need for a materialistic version of the Hegelian dialectic, enumerated a long list of dialectical 'categories', and declared that the principle of unity and the conflict between opposites was central to Marxism.

Of the two rival groups, the dialecticians were more numerous and better furnished with scientific institutions. Their leader and most active writer was Abram Moiseyevich Deborin (1881–1963). Born in Kovno, he joined the social democratic movement as a youth and was an *émigré* in Switzerland from 1903; he was at first a Bolshevik but afterwards joined the Menshevik group. After the Revolution he was for some years a non-party Marxist, but re-entered the party in 1928. In 1907 he wrote an *Introduction to the Philosophy of Dialectical Materialism*, which was not published until 1915; many times reprinted, it was a staple of Russian philosophical education in the 1920s. Although not a party member he lectured at the Communist Academy and the Red Professors' Institute and published several works. From 1926 he was chief editor of *Pod znamenem Marksizma*; from this time on the journal ceased to publish articles by the mechanists and became purely an organ of the dialecticians.

Although not an original writer, Deborin was well versed in philosophy. He expresses few ideas that cannot be found, for example, in Plekhanov, but compared to later Soviet philosophers he and his followers had a fair knowledge of the history of philosophy and were well able to turn it to polemical use.

Deborin's *Introduction* is a typical product of the Plekhanov school of Marxism. It contains no analysis of concepts but only a string of unsupported assertions, which are supposed finally to resolve all the problems that beset pre-Marxian philosophy. However, Deborin, like Plekhanov, emphasizes the link between Marxism and the whole of past philosophy, exalting the importance of Bacon, Hobbes, Spinoza, Locke, Kant, and especially Hegel in paving the way for dialectical materialism. He criticizes idealism, empiricism, agnosticism, and phenomen-

alism on the lines laid down by Engels and Plekhanov, as may
be seen from the following extract.

If, then, from the metaphysicians' point of view, everything is but
nothing becomes, from the point of view of phenomenalism everything becomes but nothing is, i.e. nothing really exists. The dialectic
teaches us that the unity of being and non-being is becoming. In
concrete materialistic terms this means that the basis of everything is
matter in a state of constant development. Thus changes are real and
concrete, and, on the other hand, what is real and concrete is
changeable. The subject of the process is absolutely real being, the
'substantive All' as opposed to the phenomenalistic Nothing ... The
contradiction between the quality-less, unchanging substance of the
metaphysicians on the one hand, and, on the other, the subjective
and changing states that are supposed to exclude the reality of
substance, is resolved by dialectical materialism in the sense that
substance, matter, is in a perpetual state of motion and change, that
qualities or states have objective significance and that matter is the
cause and the foundation, the 'subject' of qualitative changes and
states. (*Introduction to the Philosophy of Dialectical Materialism*, 4th edn.,
1925, pp. 226–7)

This passage is typical of Deborin's style in the book quoted
and in his other works. 'Dialectical materialism teaches that...';
'dialectical materialism takes over the correct portions' of this
or that philosophy; subjective idealists are wrong because they
do not recognize matter; objective idealists are wrong because
they do not realize that matter is primary and mind secondary,
and so forth. In every case a particular conclusion is stated,
usually in extremely vague terms, and there is no attempt to
support it by argument. It is not explained how we know that
the phenomenalists are wrong, rather than their opponents;
dialectical materialism tells us so, and that is all there is to it.

The opposition between the dialectic and 'metaphysics' is that
the former teaches us that all things are connected and nothing
is isolated; everything is in a state of constant change and
development; this development is the result of real contradictions' inherent in reality itself, and takes the form of
qualitative 'leaps'. Dialectical materialism states that everything
is knowable, that there are no 'things in themselves' beyond
our knowledge, that man comes to know the world by acting

upon it, and that our concepts are 'objective' and comprehend 'the essence of things'. Our impressions are 'objective' too, that is to say they 'reflect' objects, although (here Deborin follows Plekhanov in the error denounced by Lenin) they do not resemble them; the congruity between impressions and objects lies in the fact that identities and differences in objects are matched by identities and differences in their subjective 'reflections'. This is what Mach and his Russian followers Bogdanov and Valentinov deny: according to them only psychic phenomena are real, so that the world 'outside us' does not exist. But in that case there are no laws of nature, and therefore nothing can be predicted.

Although their writings were dogmatic, simplistic, and of poor quality, Deborin and his followers had the merit of emphasizing historical studies and training up a generation of philosophers with a fair knowledge of classical literature; moreover, while stressing the 'qualitative' novelty of Marxism they also drew attention to its roots in tradition, especially the link with Hegel's dialectic. According to Deborin, dialectical materialism was a 'synthesis' of the Hegelian dialectic and the materialism of Feuerbach, wherein both these elements were transformed and 'raised to a higher level'. Marxism was an 'integral world-view' which comprised dialectical materialism as a general method-ology of knowledge and also two more specific aspects, the dialectic of nature and the dialectic of history, otherwise historical materialism. As Engels had stated, the term 'dialectic' could be used in a three-fold sense. The 'objective' dialectic was the same thing as the laws or dialectical 'forms' of reality; 'dialectic' could also mean a description of those laws or, thirdly, a way of observing the universe, i.e. 'logic' in a broad sense. Changes were subject to a general regularity which applied equally to nature and to human history, and the study of this regularity, i.e. philosophy, was therefore a synthesis of all science. In order for scientists to be correctly oriented from the methodological point of view and to understand the meaning of their own observations they must recognize the primacy of philosophy, to which they supplied material for 'generalizations'. Thus Marxism called for a constant exchange between philos-ophy and the exact sciences: philosophy was empty without the 'material' provided by the natural and social sciences, but the sciences were blind without philosophy to lead them.

The purpose of this double requirement was clear enough. For philosophy to make use of the results of science meant, roughly speaking, that natural scientists must look for examples showing how natural objects undergo qualitative changes, and thus confirming the 'laws of the dialectic'. For philosophy to awaken the sciences to their own nature and preserve them from blindness meant that it was entitled to supervise their content and ensure that it conformed to dialectical materialism. Since the latter was synonymous with the party's world-view, Deborin and his school provided a justification for the party's supervision of the content of all sciences, natural as well as social.

Deborin claimed that all crises in natural science were due to the fact that physicists were not acquainted with Marxism and did not know how to apply dialectical formulas. He also believed, like Lenin, that the development of science would, spontaneously and continuously, lead to the emergence of Marxist philosophy.

For these reasons Deborin and his followers accused the mechanists of falling into pernicious error when they insisted on the autonomy of science and its independence of any philosophical premisses. Materialism, thus conceived, had more in common with empiricist neutralism than with any ontological doctrine, and recalled Engels's remarks about the kind of materialism that is nothing more than the observation of nature without any outside element whatever. Natural science, Deborin maintained, must recognize a philosophical basis of some kind, and therefore any attempt to deprive philosophy of its guiding role, or to ignore it altogether, would mean in practice subjection to bourgeois and idealist doctrines. All philosophical ideas were class-based, either bourgeois or pro-letarian, and so by attacking philosophy the mechanists were supporting the enemies of socialism and the working class. As for denying the existence of 'qualitative leaps' and maintaining that all development is continuous, did not this amount to rejecting the idea of revolution, which was a leap *par excellence*? In short, the mechanists were not only wrong philosophically but were political revisionists as well.

The 'dialecticians' endowed Soviet Marxism with a stock of basic terms, statements, and dogmas which, even though their authors were later condemned, passed into the canon of state ideology and remained binding for decades. Part of their legacy was the attack on formal logic, which went far to bring about the collapse of logical studies in Russia. The dialecticians had no notion of what logic was concerned with or what its statements signified. They imagined, however, that as logic 'abstracts from the content of concepts' it must be contrary to the dialectic, for the latter requires us to study phenomena 'in the concrete' and 'in their mutual relations' (whereas logic isolates them) and also 'in motion' (which formal logic does not recognize). These absurdities were partly due to ignorance, but were partly based on some remarks by Engels. In an article of 1925 on Lenin, Deborin wrote that formal logic could not take account of the fact that the world was both uniform and manifold, and in *Dialectical Materialism and Natural Science* in the same year he declared that formal logic served only to build 'metaphysical systems' and had been put out of court by Marxism, since the dialectic taught that form and content must 'interpenetrate each other'. The sciences could not advance on the basis of formal logic, as each of them was only a 'collection of facts' and only Marxist dialectic could link these facts into a systematic whole. If the physicists would read Hegel instead of sticking to their 'crawling empiricism' they would soon see how the dialectic helped them to make progress and to overcome their various 'crises'. Engels, the creator of 'theoretical natural science', had, all along, absorbed the dialectic from Hegel.

Holding as he did that it was for philosophy to rule the sciences, Deborin was naturally incensed by Lukács's *History and Class-Consciousness*, which questioned the possibility of a dialectic of nature on the ground that the dialectic was an interaction of subject and object in progress towards unity. By taking this line, Deborin argued, Lukács had unmasked himself as an idealist who thought that cognition was the 'substance of reality'. In an article published in 1924 in the Austrian journal *Arbeiterliteratur* Deborin denounced Lukács's errors and his disrespectful attitude to Engels and therefore to Marx. What was more, Lukács had stated that Marxist orthodoxy consisted merely in acknowledging Marx's methods, whereas method, for a Marxist, was 'inseparably bound up with content'. As for Lukács's 'identity of subject and object', this was rank idealism and contrary to the express statements of Engels, Lenin, and Plekhanov. All the subject did was to 'reflect' the object, and to hold otherwise was to jettison 'objective reality'.

In attacking mechanism, 'crawling empiricism', and the autonomy of the sciences, and defending Hegel, 'qualitative leaps', and 'real contradictions', Deborin was supported by a large group of like-minded scholars and co-religionists. The most active of these were G. S. Tymyansky, who translated and commented on Spinoza's works (the commentary, though very schematic, was instructive and useful from the factual point of view); I. K. Luppol, an aesthetic philosopher and historian of philosophy; V. F. Asmus; N. A. Karev; I. I. Agol; and Y. E. Sten. Sten, as Medvedyev states in his book on Stalinism, gave Stalin lessons in philosophy in 1925–8 and tried to get him to understand the Hegelian dialectic. Most of the group, though not all, perished in the great purges of the 1930s.

In the later twenties, however, the dialecticians held the field and obtained complete control over Soviet philosophical institutions. At a conference of teachers of Marxism–Leninism in April 1929 Deborin presented his philosophical programme and repeated his denunciation of the heretics; the Communist Academy fully supported him and issued a decree condemning mechanism. Previously the conference itself, at Deborin's instance, had passed a resolution which confirmed the role of Marxism–Leninism as the theoretical weapon of the dictatorship of the proletariat, called for the application of Marxist methods in natural science, and condemned the mechanists for 'revisionism', 'positivism', and 'vulgar evolutionism'. The custom of deciding philosophical questions by voting at party assemblies, or gatherings subject to party control, was by this time well established and surprised nobody. The mechanists defended themselves in the discussion and even counter-attacked, charging their opponents with cultivating an 'idealist dialectic', seeking to impose imaginary schemata on nature, directing their fire against mechanism only and ignoring the problems raised by idealism, and diverting attention from the practical tasks imposed by the party. This defence was of no avail, however, and the mechanists were branded not only as schismatics but as representatives, in the philosophical field, of the 'right-wing deviation' which was just then being attacked by Stalin.

After this victory the Deborinists held sway in all institutions connected with teaching and popularizing philosophy or publishing philosophical works; but their triumph did not last for long. Despite all their efforts the 'dialecticians', it appeared, had not measured up to the party's expectations in philosophical matters. In April 1930, at a second philosophical conference in Moscow, Deborin and his group were attacked by a band of younger party activists from the Red Professors' Institute, who accused them of showing insufficient party spirit. This criticism was repeated in June in an article by M. B. Mitin, P. F. Yudin, and V. N. Raltsevich, which appeared in *Pravda* and was endorsed editorially, i.e. by the party authorities. The new critics called for a 'fight on two fronts' in philosophy as in party life, and accused the current philosophical leaders of being 'formalists' who overrated Plekhanov at Lenin's expense and sought to detach philosophy from party objectives. The dialecticians disputed the charge in vain. In December the party executive of the Red Professors' Institute had an interview with Stalin, who coined the expression 'Menshevizing idealism' to describe the Deborinist view. This label was officially applied from then on, and the executive passed a long resolution condemning, on the one hand, the mechanist and 'often Menshevizing' revisionism of Timiryazev, Akselrod, Sarabianov, and Varyash, and, on the other, the idealist revisionism of Deborin, Karev, Sten, Luppol, Frankurt, and others. The resolution stated that 'The whole theoretical and political outlook of the Deborinist group amounts essentially to a Menshevizing idealism, based on a non-Marxist, non-Leninist methodology and expressing a petty bourgeois ideology, as well as reflecting the pressure of hostile class forces surrounding the proletariat.' The group had 'distorted' the teaching of Lenin's article 'The Significance of Militant Materialism', 'separated theory from practice', and deformed and rejected 'the Leninist principle of party philosophy'; they had failed to recognize Leninism as a new stage in dialectical materialism, and in many ways made common cause with the mechanists while pretending to criticize them. Their publications contained 'Kautskyist' errors concerning the dictatorship of the proletariat, right-wing opportunist errors in cultural matters, Bogdanovist errors as regards collectivism and individualism, Menshevik errors as to the conception of productive forces and production relations, semi-Trotskyist errors concerning the class struggle, and idealist errors as to the interpretation of the dialectic. The Deborinists had unduly glorified Hegel; they had dissociated method from world-view, the logical from the historical, and had belittled Lenin's importance in questions of natural science. True, the chief danger of the moment was mechanist revisionism, as it furnished a theoretical basis for the right-wing deviation that sought to defend kulak interests within the party; but the struggle must be conducted unflinchingly on both fronts, as the two forms of revisionism really constituted a single block.

All these criticisms were further developed in a lecture at the Communist Academy by Mitin, who himself aspired at this time to become the leader of the 'philosophical front'. The lecture referred repeatedly to the links between 'Menshevizing idealism' and Trotskyism: to be sure, as the mechanists supplied a philosophical front for Bukharin and his pro-kulak deviation, it was natural to infer that the Deborinists, while pretending to be orthodox, were supporting the left-wing deviation of Trotskyism. According to Mitin, both groups had put about the vicious slander that in philosophical and theoretical matters Lenin merely echoed what Marx and Engels had said—as though Stalin had not proved that Lenin represented a qualitatively new stage in the history of Marxist theory by 'developing it, making it deeper and more concrete'! The deviationists had also neglected Lenin's principle that philosophy and all the sciences, including natural science, must be imbued with party spirit. Mitin quoted an article by Karev to the effect that while Plekhanov had made many political and philosophical mistakes his writings, as Lenin had testified, were among the best works of Marxist literature. This, said Mitin, showed that the Deborinists were taking up the cudgels for 'the whole Plekhanov, Plekhanov as a Menshevik'. They even dared to assert that Lenin was a pupil of Plekhanov in philosophy, whereas in reality he was the most consistent and orthodox Marxist after Marx and Engels. Plekhanov, on the other hand, did not understand the dialectic correctly, he was sunk in formalism, inclined to agnosticism, and influenced by Feuerbach, Chernyshevsky, and formal logic. The root of the Deborinists' errors, however, lay in 'separating theory from practice'. Their battle against the mechanists was a sham fight, as was shown by the fact that, although it had continued for years, not a single mechanist had admitted that he was mistaken! In fact there was little to choose between the two groups, as both the Menshevizing idealists and the Menshevizing mechanists took a disparaging view of Lenin's philosophy.

The purging of Soviet philosophy was completed by a decree of the party's Central Committee published in *Pravda* on 25 January 1931, which condemned the errors of *Pod znamenem Marksizma* and briefly summarized the criticisms already formulated.

Deborin, Luppol, and some other members of the group hastened to perform self-criticism and to thank the party for helping them to see the light. Sten, Luppol, Karev, Tymyansky, and many others perished in the purges of the 1930s. Deborin survived, though he was dismissed from the editorship of *Pod znamenem Marksizma* (the editorial board was in fact completely changed). He was not expelled from the party, and in subsequent years published many articles of irreproachable Stalinist ortho-doxy. He survived into the Khrushchev era, and in the last years of his life worked for the rehabilitation of his many pupils and colleagues who had fallen victim to the purges. Asmus also survived into the post-war period (he died in 1975), and was subjected to further attack in the 1940s.

From 1931 onwards the history of Soviet philosophy under Stalin is largely a history of party ukases. In the next two decades a younger generation of careerists, informers, and ignoramuses monopolized the philosophical life of the country, or rather completed the extinction of philosophical studies. Those who made a career in this field generally did so by betraying their colleagues or parroting the party slogans of the moment. As a rule they knew no foreign languages and had no idea of Western philosophy, but they were more or less word-perfect in the works of Lenin and Stalin, from which their knowledge of the outside world was mainly derived.

The condemnation of 'Menshevizing idealists' and mechanists led to a flood of articles and dissertations whose authors echoed the party decrees and vied with one another in expressing indignation at the insidious plots of the philosophical saboteurs.

What was the real point of the whole discussion (if that is

the right name for it)? Obviously it had nothing to do with any particular philosophical or even political outlook. The association of 'mechanism' with Bukharin's policy or of 'Menshevizing idealism' with Trotsky's was a fabrication of the most arbitrary kind: the condemned philosophers did not belong to any opposition groups, and there was no logical connection between their views and those of the oppositionists. (The accusers' argument ran that the mechanists 'absolutized the continuity of development' by denying 'qualitative leaps', and were therefore on the side of Bukharin, while the Deborinists overemphasized 'leaps' and thus represented the 'revolutionary adventurism' of the Trotskyists; but this is based on such flimsy analogies as not to be worth discussing.) The mechanists, it is true, invited condemnation by insisting on the independence of science *vis-à-vis* philosophy, which meant in practice denying the right of an infallible party to pronounce on the correctness of scientific theories and tell scientists what subjects they should investigate and what their results should be. No such charge, however, could be levelled against the Deborinists, who appeared to be Leninists of the purest type: Deborin at an early date recanted his Plekhanovian error concerning 'hieroglyphs' and attacked the mechanists for holding this doctrine, which contradicted the theory of reflection. The Deborinists paid due homage to Lenin, and the party spokesmen had the greatest trouble finding quotations to buttress their attacks, which therefore consisted almost entirely of vague, incoherent generalities: the Deborinists 'underestimated' Lenin, 'overestimated' Plekhanov, 'did not understand' the dialectic, lapsed into 'Kautskyism', 'Menshevism', etc. The point was not simply that the party proclaimed at this stage that such and such philosophical views were right and that the Deborinists had expressed views different from them. It was not the substance of any doctrine that was at issue: the official, canonical version of dialectical materialism that was later adopted was virtually indistinguishable from Deborin's. What counted, as indeed the accusations made plain, was the principle of 'party-mindedness', or rather its application —since, of course, the Deborinists accepted the principle itself. Feeble as the Deborinists' writings were from the intellectual point of view, they were genuinely interested in philosophy and did their best to prove the validity of the specific principles of

Marxism and Leninism. They believed that their philosophy would help to build socialism, and for this reason they developed it to the best of their ability as a philosophy. But 'party-mindedness' under Stalin meant something quite different. Despite constant assurances, there was no thought of letting philosophy work out its own principles or discover truths that could be used or applied in politics. Philosophy's service to the party was to consist purely and simply in glorifying its successive decisions. Philosophy was not an intellectual process but a means of justifying and inculcating the state ideology in whatever form it might assume. This indeed was true of all the humane sciences, but the fall of philosophy was greater. The pillars on which all philosophical culture is based—logic and the history of philosophy—were swept away: philosophy was deprived of even the humblest technical support, in a way that did not apply altogether to the historical sciences, despite the extent of their corruption. The significance of Stalinism for philosophy does not lie in any particular conclusions that were forced upon it, but in the fact that servility became practically its whole *raison d'être*.

CHAPTER III

Marxism as the ideology of the Soviet state

1. The ideological significance of the great purges

THE 1930s in the Soviet Union witnessed the crystallization of a new version of Marxism as the official and canonical ideology of the totalitarian socialist state.

In the years following collectivization the Stalinist state went through a series of defeats and misadventures, while the population was subjected to one wave of repression after another. The enforcement of collectivization coincided with the beginning of the first five-year plan, which was officially dated from 1928 although not actually approved till the following year. According to the ideas formulated by Trotsky and Preobrazhensky and taken over by Stalin, the function of the enslaved peasantry was to supply surplus value for the rapid development of industry. From then on, the dogma of the primacy of heavy industry became a permanent part of the state ideology. The initial objectives were laid down arbitrarily, without any serious calculation, on the presumption that everything could be done by force and that 'there were no fortresses that Bolsheviks could not storm'. None the less, Stalin was constantly dissatisfied with production targets and kept boosting them to still greater heights. Most of the aims, of course, proved unattainable: even in heavy industry, to which the maximum human and financial effort was devoted, the results were sometimes half, a quarter, or an eighth of what they were supposed to be. The cure for this was to arrest and shoot statisticians and falsify their findings. In 1928–30 Stalin closed down almost all economic and statistical journals, and most statisticians of importance, including N. D. Kondratyev, were executed or thrown into gaol. It also became customary from this time on to calculate the national income in such a way as to count the same products two or three times, at different stages of manufacture, thus producing meaningless totals which were periodically vaunted as proof of the superiority of socialism. Figures for agriculture were systematically faked, as collectivization wrought more and more havoc in the countryside. How far Stalin or the other leaders were aware of the true state of the economy is not clear. Meanwhile the ranks of industrial workers were rapidly swelled by recruits from the rural sector. To compensate for the sufferings of society there were constant arrests and trials of engineers or agricultural experts on grounds of sabotage, i.e. failing to achieve impracticable norms. In 1932–3 there ensued a famine in which millions perished; by comparison the famine of 1891–2, which turned a whole generation of the intelligentsia into radicals and did much to foster the growth of Marxism, was a set-back of insignificant proportions. Stalinist propaganda repeated without ceasing that the country was full of wreckers and saboteurs, crypto-kulaks, disloyal intellectuals of the pre-war type, Trotskyists, and agents of the imperialist Powers. Starving peasants could be and were sentenced to concentration camps for stealing a handful of grain from the collective farm. The slave-labour camps proliferated and became an important factor in the state economy, especially in regions where conditions were most arduous, as in the mines and forests of Siberia.

Nevertheless, at the cost of indescribable suffering, exploitation, and oppression, amid the chaos of fictitious planning and the flood of official lies, Soviet industry did in fact progress, and the second five-year plan (1933–7) was much more realistic than the first. The fact that in those years the Soviet Union laid the basis of its present-day industrial power is still invoked by Communists as a historical justification of Stalinism, and many non-Communists take a similar view, believing that Stalinist socialism was necessary to enable backward Russia to modernize its industry with speed. Anticipating our argument to some extent, this may be answered as follows. The Soviet Union did indeed build up a considerable industrial base, especially in heavy industry and armaments, during the 1930s. It did so by methods of mass coercion and complete or partial enslavement, which had as side-effects the ruin of the nation's culture and the perpetuation of a police regime. In these ways Soviet industrialization was probably the most wasteful process of its kind in history, and there is no proof at all that progress could not have been achieved without human and material sacrifices on this scale. History records various methods of successful industrialization, all of which have been costly in social terms, but it is hard to point to any case in which the cost was as heavy as in socialist Russia. The further argument, often adduced, that the course followed by Western Europe could not have been repeated on the periphery of the industrial world because the big capitalist centres had already consolidated their position, is refuted by the example of 'peripheral' countries such as Japan, Brazil, and most recently Iran, which have all succeeded in industrializing themselves by means different from Russia's, albeit with considerable sacrifice. Russia before 1917 was a country of rapid and intensive industrialization, a process which the Revolution delayed for many years. The graph of industrial development rose markedly in the last two decades of Tsarist rule; it fell catastrophically after the Revolution, and it was a long time before the various indices (some recovering faster than others) once again reached their pre-war levels and continued to rise. The intervening period was one of social disintegration and the destruction of millions of lives, and it is mere fantasy to suggest that all this sacrifice was necessary to enable the country to resume its pre-Revolutionary development.

If one takes the view that historical processes have an immanent purpose independent of human intention, or a hidden meaning that is only discernible with hindsight, it must be said that the meaning of the Russian revolution did not consist in industrialization, but rather in the coherence and expansive energy of the Russian Empire: for in this respect the new regime has indeed been more efficient than the old.

After the resistance of all social classes—proletariat, peasantry, and intelligentsia—had been successively overcome, after all forms of social life not ordained by the state had been crushed out of existence, and the opposition within the party destroyed, it was time to subdue the last element that might—though it did not in practice—threaten the completeness of totalitarian rule under a single despot: namely the party itself, the instrument which had been used to stifle and destroy every other rival force in the community. The destruction of the party was achieved during the years 1935–9, and established a new record in the conflict between the Soviet regime and its own subjects.

In 1934 Stalin was at the height of his power. The party's Seventeenth Congress at the beginning of the year was an orgy of flattery and worship. There was no active opposition to the adored dictator, but there were many in the party, especially Old Bolsheviks, who paid him due honour but were not bound to him heart and soul. They had risen by their own efforts, not merely by his favour, and might therefore be a dangerous source of unrest or revolt in time of crisis. Hence, as a potential opposition, they must be destroyed. The first pretext for their extermination was the murder, on 1 December 1934, of Sergey Kirov, a secretary of the Central Committee and head of the party organization in Leningrad. Most historians, though not all, agree that the real author of the crime was Stalin, who at one stroke got rid of a possible rival and created a pretext for mass repression. The witch-hunt that followed was aimed in the first place at former oppositionists within the party, but soon also at the dictator's faithful servants. Zinovyev and Kamenev were arrested and sentenced to prison; mass executions took place in larger cities throughout the country, but especially in Leningrad and Moscow. The terror reached a paroxysm in 1937, the first year of the 'great purge'. August 1936 saw the first of the major show trials, at which Zinovyev, Kamenev, Smirnov, and others were sentenced to death; a second trial in January 1937 brought to light the 'treason' of Radek, Pyatakov, Sokolnikov, and others. In March 1938 the accused included Bukharin, Rykov, Krestinsky, Rakovsky, and Yagoda, the last-named having been head of the N.K.V.D. (security service) in 1934–6 and organizer of the earlier purges. Shortly before, in 1937, Marshal Tukhachevsky and several other top army leaders were tried in secret and shot. The accused in all the public trials confessed to fantastic crimes, describing one after another how they had intrigued with foreign intelligence services, conspired to murder party leaders, offered parts of Soviet territory to the imperialist Powers, murdered and poisoned their fellow citizens, sabotaged industry, deliberately caused famines, etc. Almost all were sentenced to death and executed out of hand; a few who, like Radek, only received prison sentences were done to death soon after their trial.

The inferno of the great purges has often been described by

historians, novelists, and memoir-writers. The show trials were only the visible fragment of a mass operation of genocide, with the party as its principal victim. Millions were arrested, hundreds of thousands executed. Torture, previously used sporadically and, as a rule, for the purpose of getting at the truth, now became a routine method of extracting thousands of false confessions to the most improbable crimes. (Torture had ceased to be a part of Russian judicial procedure in the eighteenth century, though it was afterwards used in exceptional circumstances such as the Polish insurrections or the 1905 Revolution.) Investigating officers were free to devise and inflict all manner of physical and mental suffering to induce people to admit to crimes which the persecutors well knew to be totally imaginary. Those few who did not succumb to such measures generally broke down when told that if they refused to confess their wives and children would be killed—a threat which was sometimes carried out. No one felt safe, for no degree of subservience to the tyrant was a guarantee of immunity. In some cases the party committees of whole regions were slaughtered and were followed into the grave by their own successors in office, whose hands still reeked from the execution. Among the victims were almost all the Old Bolsheviks, all Lenin's closest associates, former members of government and of the Politburo and the party secretariat, activists of every rank, scholars, artists, writers, economists, military men, lawyers, engineers, doctors, and—in due course, when they had done their stint—the agents of the purge themselves, whether senior officers of the security service or especially zealous party members. The officers' corps of the army and navy was decimated, a major cause of Soviet defeats in the first two years of the war with Germany. Quotas of arrests and executions were assigned to particular areas by the party authorities; if the police did not fulfil these they were liable to be executed themselves, if they did they might in time be brought to account for exterminating party cadres. (With a macabre humour typical of Stalin this charge was brought against some, such as Postyshev, who had distinguished themselves in the campaign of mass murder.) Those who performed their task badly might be shot for sabotage; those who did it too well might be suspected of showing zeal to cover up their own disaffection. (In a speech in 1937 Stalin said that many wreckers were doing precisely this.) The purport of the trials and investigations was to show that almost the whole original nucleus of the party, including Lenin's closest collaborators, were a band of spies, imperialist agents, and enemies of the people, whose one idea was and had always been to destroy the Soviet state. Before an astonished world, every imaginable crime was confessed to by the accused themselves at the great show trials. Of all the Grand Guignol victims Bukharin was the only one who, though he admitted general responsibility for the alleged crimes of the mythical counter-revolutionary organization, refused to confess to such damning charges as espionage and plotting to assassinate Lenin. While expressing penitence for all his misdeeds he added, in a phrase epitomizing the atmosphere of the trials, 'We rebelled by criminal methods against the joyfulness of the new life.' (Apparently Bukharin was not physically tortured, but was threatened with the murder of his wife and small son.)

The first effect of the purges was to create a desolation, not only in the party but in every aspect of life in the Soviet Union. The blood-bath accounted for a large majority of the delegates, for the most part loyal Stalinists, who had attended the Seventeenth Congress, which had done little but vote adulatory addresses to the leader. A whole series of eminent artists perished, and over a third of all Soviet writers. The whole country was in the grip of a monstrous fit of madness, induced apparently—but the appearance was deceptive—by the will of a single despot.

Foreign Communists in Russia fell victim to the purges also. The Poles suffered most: in 1938 a resolution of the Comintern dissolved the Polish Communist party (which was illegal in Poland) on the ground that it was a hotbed of Trotskyists and other enemies, and its cadres in the Soviet Union were decimated by arrests and executions. Almost all the leaders were imprisoned, and only a few regained their liberty some years later. The fortunate ones were those who could not make their way to Russia when summoned, as they were in prison in Poland. The few who actually disobeyed the summons were publicly declared to be agents of the Polish police, and were thus delivered into the latter's hands—a device frequently used in the thirties against 'deviationist' members of underground Communist parties in other countries. Besides Poles, victims of the purges were many Hungarian Communists (including Béla Kun), Yugoslavs, Bulgarians, and Germans; some of the latter who survived till 1939 were, in due course, handed over by Stalin to the Gestapo.

The concentration camps were full to bursting. Every Soviet citizen had got used to the fact that being arrested and sentenced to death or to an arbitrary and indefinite term of imprisonment had nothing to do with whether a man's work was good or bad, whether he did or did not belong to any kind of opposition, or even whether he did or did not love Stalin. The climate of atrocity brought about a kind of universal paranoia, a monstrous but unreal world in which all previous criteria, even those of 'ordinary' despotism, had ceased to be applicable.

Historians and others who, in later years, have sought to account for this unparalleled orgy of bloodshed and hypocrisy have posed questions that are not at all easy to answer.

In the first place, what could be the reason for such destructive frenzy when, to all appearances, there was no real threat to Stalin or the regime, and every possible source of revolt within the party could easily have been wiped out without mass slaughter? In particular, how could this be explained when it seemed obvious that the wholesale destruction of senior cadres would fatally weaken the state, both militarily and economically?

Secondly, why was there a complete lack of resistance when all members of the population were threatened, even those who carried out the atrocities most devotedly? Many Soviet citizens had displayed military courage and had risked their lives in battle: why did no one raise a hand against the tyrant, why did all go willingly to the slaughter?

Thirdly, granted that the victims of show trials were made to confess to non-existent crimes for propaganda reasons, why were such confessions extorted from hundreds of thousands or millions of lesser people of whom no one would ever hear? Why the tremendous effort to induce unknown victims to sign fantastic admissions which would be buried in police files and not used for any public purpose?

Fourthly, how was it that in those very years Stalin was able to raise the cult of his own personality to unprecedented heights? Why, in particular, did so many Western intellectuals, on whom there was no personal pressure, fall for Stalinism at this period

and meekly swallow, or actively applaud, the Moscow chamber°
of horrors and the official explanation of it, whereas the lies
and cruelty of the performance should have been obvious to
everyone?

All these questions are relevant to an understanding of the
peculiar function that Marxist-socialist ideology was beginning
to exercise in the new system.

As to the first question, most historians believe that the main
purpose of the great purges was to eliminate the party as a
potential focus of political life, a force that might in some
circumstances acquire a life of its own and not be merely an
instrument in the ruler's hands. Isaac Deutscher, in his first book
on the Moscow trials (published in Polish), advanced the
remarkable theory that they were an act of revenge by the
Mensheviks against the Bolsheviks!—this because the victims
were nearly all Old Bolsheviks, while Vyshinsky, the chief
prosecutor, was an ex-Menshevik, and the main party propagandist of those days, David Zaslavsky, had been a member
of the Jewish Bund. This is as fanciful as the explanation that
Deutscher afterwards put forward in the third volume of his
life of Trotsky (*The Prophet Outcast*, 1963, pp. 306–7), namely
that the higher Soviet bureaucracy were not content with their
privileges, great though these were, because they could not
accumulate wealth or bequeath it to their children, and there
was therefore a risk, as Trotsky feared, that they would seek
to destroy the system of social ownership. Stalin, according to
Deutscher, was aware of this danger and used terror to prevent
the new privileged class from consolidating itself and ruining
the system. This, in effect, is a paraphrase of the Stalinist
version that the victims intended to restore capitalism in Russia.
However, in his life of Stalin (1949) Deutscher adopted what
is more or less the general view of historians. Stalin wanted
to destroy all possible alternative governments or party leaders;
there was no longer an active opposition, but a sudden crisis
might bring one to life, and he must therefore crush any possibility of a rival centre of power within the party.

This explanation may fit the Moscow trials, but it is less clear
how it accounts for the mass character of the purge, affecting
millions of unknown people who had no chance whatever of
becoming alternative party leaders. The same objection applies

to other theories sometimes advanced, such as Stalin's need to find scapegoats for economic failures, or his personal vengefulness and sadism—which certainly account for a great many individual cases, but hardly for the massacre of millions.

It may be said that the great purges were a macabre irrelevancy, in the sense that the purpose they served could quite well have been attained by other means. Yet they were, so to speak, part of the natural logic of the system. It was a question not only of destroying any actual or potential rivals but of wiping out the sole organism in which there were still any remnants, however faint and impotent, of loyalty to any cause other than the state and its leader—in particular, remnants of a belief in Communist ideology as a frame of reference and an object of worship, independent of the leader and the party's current directives. The object of a totalitarian system is to destroy all forms of communal life that are not imposed by the state and closely controlled by it, so that individuals are isolated from one another and become mere instruments in the hands of the state. The citizen belongs to the state and must have no other loyalty, not even to the state ideology. This may seem paradoxical, but it is not surprising to anyone who knows a system of this type from within. All forms of revolt against the ruling party, all 'deviations' and 'revisionism', fractions, cliques, rebellions—all alike had appealed to the ideology of which the party was the custodian. Consequently, that ideology had to be revised so as to make it clear to all that they were not entitled to appeal to it independently—just as in the Middle Ages unauthorized persons were not allowed to comment on the Scriptures, and the Bible itself was at all times *liber haereticorum*. The party was essentially an ideological body, that is to say one whose members were linked by a common faith and shared values. But, as always happens when ideologies are turned into institutions, that faith had to be vague and indefinite enough to be used to justify any political move while maintaining that there was no 'real' change of doctrine. Inevitably, those who took the faith seriously wanted to interpret it for themselves and to consider whether this or that political step was in accordance with Stalin's version of Marxism–Leninism. But this made them potential critics and rebels against the government, even if they swore fealty to Stalin; for they might always invoke yesterday's Stalin against today's and quote the leader's words against himself. The purge, therefore, was designed to destroy such ideological links as still existed within the party, to convince its members that they had no ideology or loyalty except to the latest order from on high, and to reduce them, like the rest of society, to a powerless, disintegrated mass. This was a continuation of the same logic that began with liquidating the liberal and socialist parties, the independent Press and cultural institutions, religion, philosophy, and art, and finally fractions within the party itself. Wherever there was any ideological link other than loyalty to the ruler, there was a possibility of fractionalism even if it did not actually exist. The object of the purge was to eradicate this possibility, and in that object it was successful; but the principles which dictated the hecatomb of the 1930s are still in force and have never been abandoned. Loyalty to Marxist ideology as such is still a crime and a source of deviations of all kinds.

Even so, the fact that the holocaust was not resisted by the Soviet public or even by the party seems to suggest that a purge was not necessary, at all events on that scale. The party, it would seem, was already close enough to the ideal condition of a 'sack of potatoes' (as Marx said of the French peasants), and was neither desirous nor capable of producing any centre of independent thought. On the other hand, we do not know whether, but for the purge, it might not have done so at a time of crisis, for example, in the most dangerous moments of the war with Germany.

This brings us to the second question: how is it that Soviet society was quite incapable of resistance? The answer seems to be that the party, outside the top leadership, was already incapable of organizing itself in any way independently of the apparatus. Like the rest of the population, it was reduced to a collection of isolated individuals; in the context of repression, as in every other sphere of life, the omnipotent state on the one hand confronted the lone citizen on the other. The paralysis of the individual was complete; and, at the same time, it could not be denied that the party was acting in accordance with the principles that had obtained since the beginning. All its members had taken part in mass acts of violence against the public, and when they themselves became victims of lawlessness there was nothing to which they could appeal. None of them had objected to fake trials and executions as long as the sufferers were not party members; all of them accepted, actively or passively, that 'in principle' there was nothing wrong in judicial murder. They all agreed, too, that at any given moment it was for the party leaders to decide who was a class enemy, a friend of the kulaks, or an imperialist agent. The rules of the game, which they had accepted, were being brought to bear against them, and they had no moral principles that might have fostered a spirit of resistance.

During the war, in one of Stalin's prisons, the Polish poet Aleksander Wat encountered an Old Bolshevik, the historian I. M. Stetlov, and asked him why all the protagonists of the Moscow trials had confessed to the most ludicrous charges. Stetlov replied simply: 'We were all of us up to the elbows in blood.'

As to the third question, it may at first seem that we have to do with collective hallucination. Even supposing Stalin had good reasons for massacring Communists, why was it necessary to make countless insignificant people confess under torture that they had plotted to sell Uzbekistan to the British, or been agents of Pilsudski, or tried to murder Stalin? But there was a grain of method even in this madness. The victims had to be not only destroyed physically or rendered harmless, but morally annihilated as well. It might have been thought that the N.K.V.D. agents could have signed the false confessions themselves and then finished off their tortured victims or sent them to camps on the ground of their 'admitted' guilt—except, of course, for the show-trial defendants who had to proclaim their crimes to the whole world; but these were only a tiny percentage of the whole. In fact, however, the police insisted on people signing their own confessions, and as far as is known they did not forge signatures. The effect was that the victims became accessories to the crimes committed against themselves, and participants in the universal campaign of falsification. Almost anyone can be forced by torture to confess to anything, but as a rule, in the twentieth century at least, torture is used to obtain true information. In the Stalinist system both the torturers and their victims knew perfectly well that the information was false; but they insisted on the fiction, as in this way everyone helped to build an unreal 'ideological' world, in which universal fiction took on the guise of truth.

A similar regime of organized make-believe prevailed in many other fields, for example, in the system of general 'elections'. It might have been thought that the government could have spared itself the trouble and expense of these performances, the absurdity of which was obvious to all; but they were important because they turned every citizen into a participant and co-author of the same fiction, the official 'reality' which, by that very fact, ceased to be completely spurious.

The fourth question again presents us with a baffling phenomenon. The information that reached the West from the Soviet Union was, of course, fragmentary and uncertain; the regime had done a thorough job of restricting contacts and limiting the flow of news in either direction; foreign travel by Soviet citizens was strictly controlled in the state interest, and any unauthorized communication to foreigners was treated as espionage or treason. Nevertheless, the Soviet state could not cut itself off entirely from the world. Some information about the police terror filtered through to the West, though nobody realized its scope. Moreover, the Moscow trials were prepared hastily and clumsily, and the contradictions and absurdities that emerged were pointed out in some Western newspapers. What, then, was the explanation for the indulgent attitude that Western intellectuals took up towards Stalinism, when they did not actively support it? The honest and incorruptible British socialists, Sidney and Beatrice Webb, visited the Soviet Union more than once during the height of the terror and produced an enormous book on the 'new civilization'. The Soviet system, they declared, was the embodiment of man's dearest longing for justice and happiness, in glaring contrast with Britain's corrupt and crumbling pseudo-democracy; they saw no reason to doubt the genuineness of the Moscow trials or the perfection of Russia's first 'democratic' government. Others who belauded the system and swallowed the fiction of the trials were Leon Feuchtwanger, Romain Rolland, and Henri Barbusse. Among the few who did not join in the chorus was André Gide, who visited the U.S.S.R. in 1936 and described his impressions. Naturally he saw nothing of the atrocities: he was surrounded by flattery and was only shown delusive achievements of the regime, but he realized that the façade concealed a system of universal mendacity. Some Polish writers also saw through the make-believe, as did the British journalist Malcolm Muggeridge (*Winter in Moscow*, 1934).

The reaction of Western intellectuals was a remarkable triumph of doctrinaire ideology over common sense and the critical instinct. True, the years of the purges were also those of the Nazi threat, and this may explain up to a point how many thinkers and artists brought up in a left-wing or liberal tradition saw in Russia the only hope of saving civilization from the menace that hung over it; they were prepared to forgive the 'proletarian state' a great deal if it could be relied on to provide a bulwark against Fascist barbarism. They were the more readily bamboozled because Nazism, unlike Stalinism, scarcely bothered to conceal its evil face from the world: it proclaimed openly that its intention was to create an all-powerful German giant, grinding other nations into the dust and reducing 'inferior races' to slavery. Stalin, on the other hand, continued to preach the socialist gospel of peace and equality, liberation of the oppressed, internationalism, and friendship among peoples. Westerners whose profession was to think critically found this verbiage more convincing than any facts: ideology and wishful thinking were stronger than the most manifest reality.

It is important to notice, in considering the purges, that Stalin's Russia was at no time governed by the police, nor was the police ever 'above the party': this was an alibi used by would-be reformers after Stalin's death, who maintained that their task was to restore party supremacy. True, the police under Stalin could arrest and murder party members at will, but not on the highest level, where all such procedures had to be ordered or approved by the top party authorities and in particular by Stalin himself. Stalin used the police to rule the party, but he himself ruled both party and state in his capacity as party leader, not as a security chief: this point is well brought out by Jan Jaroslawski in his study of the party's functions in the Soviet system. The party, embodied in Stalin, did not abandon supreme power for a single moment. When the post-Stalin reformers demanded that the party should be above the police, they meant only that party members should not be arrested without the approval of the party authorities. But this had always been so, since even if the police at a certain level arrested party leaders of equal seniority, they did so under the eye of party leaders of a still higher grade. The police were an instrument in the party's hands. A police system in the strict sense, i.e. one in which the police have a completely free hand, did not and could not prevail in the Soviet state, as it would have meant that the party had lost power, and this could not happen without causing the whole system to collapse.

This also explains the special part played by ideology, both under Stalin and at the present day. Ideology is not simply an aid or adjunct to the system but an absolute condition of its existence, irrespective of whether people actually believe in it or not. Stalinist socialism created an empire ruled from Moscow, the basis of whose legality is entirely derived from ideology: in particular, from the doctrine that the Soviet Union embodies the interests of all working people and especially the working class everywhere, that it represents their desires and aspirations, and that it is the first step towards a world revolution that will liberate the toiling masses wherever they may be. The Soviet system could not do without this ideology, which is the sole *raison d'être* for the existing apparatus of power. The apparatus is essentially ideological and internationalist in character and could not be replaced by the police, the army, or any other institution.

This is not to say that the policy of the Soviet state at any given moment is determined by ideology; but the ideology must be there to justify it when required. Ideology is built into the system and consequently plays a quite different part in the Soviet Union as compared to states where the basic principle of legitimacy is derived from popular elections or the charisma of a hereditary monarchy.

A system of the Soviet kind enjoys the advantage that it does not have to justify its actions to the public: by definition, it represents their interests and desires, and nothing can alter this ideological fact. However, it is also exposed to a risk from which democratic structures are immune: namely, it is extremely sensitive to ideological criticism. This means, among other things, that the intelligentsia plays a part that is not paralleled elsewhere. A threat to the intellectual validity of the system, or the advocacy of a different ideology, represents a mortal danger. The totalitarian state can never become completely invulnerable or stamp out critical thought altogether. It may appear all-powerful, as it dominates all aspects of life, but it is also weak inasmuch as any crack in the ideological monolith is a threat to its existence.

It is hard, moreover, to maintain a system in which ideology is deprived of its own inertial movement and reduced to nothing more or less than the actual dictates of the state authority. The logic of Stalinism is that truth is what the party, i.e. Stalin, says at any given moment, and the effect of this is to empty ideology of its substance altogether. On the other hand, ideology must be presented as a general theory with a consistency of its own, and as long as this is done there is no guarantee that it may not acquire a momentum of its own and be used—as actually happened in the post-Stalinist period—against its chief spokesmen and sole authorized interpreters.

In the late 1930s, however, this danger appeared highly remote. The system had been brought to an almost ideal state of perfection, in which civil society hardly existed any more and the population seemed to have no other purpose than to obey the behests of the state personified in Stalin.

An essential instrument for the destruction of social ties was the universal system of spying on one's neighbour. Every citizen was under a legal and moral obligation to do so, and tale-bearing was the chief method of getting on in life. The continuing slaughter made room for many who aspired to join the privileged ruling class, and were prepared to demonstrate their fitness by destroying others. In this way, too, huge numbers of people became accessories to crime for the sake of personal advancement. The ideal of Stalinist socialism appeared to be a situation where everyone in the country (except Stalin) was an inmate of a concentration camp and also an agent of the secret police. It was hard to achieve this ultimate perfection, but the trend towards it in the 1930s was very strong.

2. Stalin's codification of Marxism

In the thirties every branch of culture in the Soviet Union was strictly regimented, and independent intellectual life practically ceased to exist. Belles-lettres were gradually but effectively reduced to an adjunct of politics and propaganda, with the sole purpose of glorifying the system and its leader and unmasking 'class enemies'. In 1932, talking to a group of writers at Gorky's home, Stalin described authors in general as 'engineers of men's souls'; this flattering term duly became the official formula. Films and the theatre were treated in the same way, though the latter suffered less. A traditional repertoire of plays was allowed to subsist in so far as the authors, mostly classical Russian dramatists, could be described as 'progressive' or even 'partially progressive': this let in Gogol, Ostrovsky, Saltykov-Shchedrin, Tolstoy, and Chekhov, and even in the worst years excellent productions could be seen on the Russian stage. Novelists, poets, and film directors vied with one another in Byzantine adulation of Stalin: this reached its peak in the post-war years, but was already highly developed in the period we are considering.

However, repression and regimentation affected different spheres of intellectual life in different degrees. In the thirties there was a strong trend towards Marxist orientation in certain branches of science, especially theoretical physics and genetics, but this did not reach a climax until the late forties. Other subjects, however, which were particularly sensitive from the ideological point of view, such as philosophy, social theory, and history—especially the history of the party and of modern times generally—were not merely strait-jacketed in the thirties but were codified into completely Stalinist terms.

An important stage in the subjection of Soviet historiography was marked in 1931 by a letter from Stalin to the journal _Proletarian Revolution,_ which the editorial board printed with an appropriate self-criticism. The letter upbraided them for publishing an article by Slutsky on relations between the Bolsheviks and the German social democrats before 1914, in which Lenin was criticized for failing to appreciate the danger of 'centrism' and opportunism in the Second International. After trouncing the journal for the 'rotten liberalism' of suggesting that Lenin 'failed to appreciate' anything, i.e. that he ever made a mistake, Stalin gave a complete history in outline of the Second International, which thereafter became a canonical text. His main concern was with the non-Bolshevik left wing of the International and with Trotsky. According to Stalin, while the socialist Left had done some service in the battle against opportunism, it had also made grievous mistakes. Rosa Luxemburg and Parvus had several times sided with the Mensheviks in party disputes, for example, over the party Rules, and in 1905 had devised the 'semi-Menshevik scheme of permanent revolution' that Trotsky later adopted, the fatal error of which was to reject the idea of an alliance between the proletariat and the peasantry. As for Trotskyism, it had long ceased to be part of the Communist movement and had become the 'advanced detachment of the counter-revolutionary bourgeoisie'. It was a monstrous lie to suggest that Lenin before the war did not understand that the bourgeois-democratic revolution was bound to develop into a socialist one, and that he afterwards picked up this idea from Trotsky. Stalin's letter (*Works*, English edn., vol. 13, 1955, pp. 86 ff.) laid down the rules of Soviet historiography once and for all: Lenin had always been right, the Bolshevik party was and had always been infallible, even though at times enemies crept into the fold and tried unsuccessfully to divert it from the correct path. All non-Bolshevik groups in the socialist movement had always been hotbeds of treason or, at best, breeding-grounds of pernicious error.

This judgement set the seal on Rosa Luxemburg's historical reputation, and also disposed finally of Trotsky. It was a few years longer, however, before all problems of history, philosophy, and the social sciences were settled once and for all. This was done in 1938 by the *History of the Communist Party of the Soviet Union (Bolsheviks)*, a *Short Course* edited by an anonymous commission: Stalin was identified at the time only as the author of the celebrated section on 'Dialectical and Historical Materialism' (ch. IV), setting out the approved version of the party's world-view. After the war, however, it was officially stated that the whole book was by Stalin, and it was to have been republished as a volume in the series of his collected works, had not this been discontinued after his death. The exact genesis of the *Short Course* is not known: it was probably compiled in the main by a team of official writers and then revised by Stalin. His distinctive style is evident in several places, especially where he speaks of various traitors and deviationists as 'White Guard pygmies', 'contemptible lackeys of the Fascists', etc.

The fortunes of the *Short Course* are a remarkable episode in the history of the printed word. Published in millions of copies

in the Soviet Union, it served for fifteen years as a manual of
ideology completely binding on all citizens. The size of the
editions could no doubt be compared only with those of the
Bible in Western countries. It was published and taught everywhere without ceasing. In the upper forms of secondary schools,
in all places of higher learning, party courses, etc., wherever
anything was taught, the *Short Course* was the Soviet citizen's
main intellectual pabulum. For any literate person it would have
been an unusual feat to remain ignorant of it; most people were
obliged to read it time and again, and party propagandists and
lecturers knew it virtually by heart.

The *Short Course* set up a world record in another respect also.
Among books with historical pretensions there is probably none
that contains so high a proportion of lies and suppressions. As
the title indicates, the book is a history of the Bolshevik party
from its inception, but Chapter IV also introduces the reader
to general questions of world history and expounds the 'correct'
version of Marxist philosophy and social theory. Morals are
drawn liberally from historical events and shown to have formed
the basis of the actions of the Bolshevik party and the world
Communist movement. The historical conclusions are simple:
the Bolshevik party, under the brilliant leadership of Lenin and
Stalin, unswervingly pursued from the outset the faultless policy
which was crowned by the success of the October Revolution.
Lenin is always depicted in the forefront of history, and Stalin
directly after him. A few individuals of the second or third rank
who were lucky enough to die before the great purges are briefly
mentioned at appropriate points in the story. As for the leaders
who actually helped Lenin to create the party, carry out the
Revolution, and found the Soviet state, they are either not
mentioned at all or are shown as double-dyed traitors and
wreckers who crept into the party and whose whole career
consisted of sabotage and conspiracy. Stalin, on the other hand,
was from the beginning an infallible leader, Lenin's best pupil,
his truest helper and closest friend. Lenin himself, the reader
is given to understand, formed a plan for the development of
humanity while he was still a youth, and each successive act
of his life was a deliberate step in furtherance of that plan.

The *Short Course* not only established a whole pattern of
Bolshevik mythology linked to the cult of Lenin and Stalin, but

prescribed a detailed ritual and liturgy. From the time of its publication party writers, historians, and propagandists who touched on any part of its subject-matter were obliged to adhere to every canonical formula and to repeat every relevant phrase verbatim. The *Short Course* was not merely a work of falsified history but a powerful social institution—one of the party's most important instruments of mind control, a device for the destruction both of critical thought and of society's recollections of its own past.

From this point of view the book belongs squarely within the pattern of the totalitarian state created by Stalin. To bring the system to perfection and reduce civil society to a cipher it was necessary to root out all forms of life that were not state-controlled and might constitute a threat of any kind. It was also necessary to devise means of destroying independent thought and memory—an extremely difficult but important task. A totalitarian system cannot survive without constantly rewriting history, eliminating past events, personalities, and ideas and substituting false ones in their place. It was unthinkable in terms of Soviet ideology to say that a particular leader who had fallen a victim to the purge had once been a true servant of the party but had subsequently fallen from grace: anyone who was proclaimed a traitor in the end must have been one from the beginning. Those who were simply done to death without being branded as traitors became unpersons and were never heard of again. Soviet readers became used to seeing editions of books that were still on sale but from which the editor's or translator's name had been carefully erased. If, however, the author himself was a traitor, then the book disappeared completely from circulation and only a few copies remained in the 'prohibited' sections of libraries. This was so even if the book's content was irreproachably Stalinist: as in all magical thinking, an object connected in any way with the evil spirit was contaminated for ever and must be cast out and blotted from memory. Soviet citizens were allowed to remember the existence of a few traitors mentioned in the *Short Course* so as to include them in ritual comminations, but the rest of the satanic crew were supposed to be forgotten and no one dared to speak their names. Old newspapers and journals became unclean overnight if they contained photographs of traitors or articles written by them. Not only was the past constantly revised but—an important feature of Stalinism—everybody was supposed, on the one hand, to be aware of this and of the fairly simple way in which it was done, but, on the other, to say nothing about it on pain of the direst consequences. There were in the Soviet Union many other pseudo-secrets of this kind, i.e. matters that the whole population was intended to know about but never to mention. The labour camps were never spoken of in the newspapers, but it was an unwritten law that the citizen should know about them: not simply because such things could not be kept secret anyway, but because the government wanted people to be aware of certain facts of Soviet life while pretending to one another that no such facts existed. The object of the system was to create a dual consciousness. At public meetings, and even in private conversations, citizens were obliged to repeat in ritual fashion grotesque falsehoods about themselves, the world, and the Soviet Union, and at the same time to keep silent about things they knew very well, not only because they were terrorized but because the incessant repetition of falsehoods which they knew to be such made them accomplices in the campaign of lies inculcated by the party and state. It was not the regime's intention that people should literally believe the absurdities that were put about: if any were so naïve as to do so and to forget reality completely, they would be in a state of innocence *vis-à-vis* their own consciences and would be prone to accept Communist ideology as valid in its own right. Perfect obedience required, however, that they should realize that the current ideology meant nothing in itself: any aspect of it could be altered or annulled by the supreme leader at any moment as he might see fit, and it would be everyone's duty to pretend that nothing had changed and that the ideology had been the same from everlasting. (Stalin took care to emphasize that he himself, like Lenin, had not 'added' anything to Marxism but only developed it.) In order to realize that the party ideology at any given time was neither more nor less than what the leader said it was, the citizen had to possess a dual consciousness: in public he professed adherence to the ideology as an unchanging catechism, while in private or semi-consciously he knew that it was a completely adaptable instrument in the party's hands, i.e. Stalin's. He thus had to 'believe without believing', and it was this state of mind that the party sought to create and maintain in its own members and, as far as possible, in the whole population. Half-starved people, lacking the bare necessities of life, attended meetings at which they repeated the government's lies about how well off they were, and in a bizarre way they half-believed what they were saying. They all knew what it was 'right' to say, i.e. what was demanded of them, and in a curious way they confused this 'rightness' with truth. Truth, they knew, was a party matter, and therefore lies became true even if they contradicted the plain facts of experience. The condition of thus living in two separate worlds at once was one of the most remarkable achievements of the Stalinist system.

The *Short Course* was a perfect manual of false history and doublethink. Its lies and suppressions were too obvious to be overlooked by readers who had witnessed the events in question: all but the youngest party members knew who Trotsky was and how collectivization had taken place in Russia, but, obliged as they were to parrot the official version, they became co-authors of the new past and believers in it as party-inspired truth. If anyone challenged this truth on the basis of manifest experience, the indignation of the faithful was perfectly sincere. In this way Stalinism really produced the 'new Soviet man': an ideological schizophrenic, a liar who believed what he was saying, a man capable of incessant, voluntary acts of intellectual self-mutilation.

As we have mentioned, the *Short Course* contained a new exposition of dialectical and historical materialism—a complete Marxist catechism for a whole generation. This work of Stalin's did not really add anything to the simplified account of Marxism that might be found, for example, in Bukharin's manual, but it had the merit that everything was numbered and set out systematically: the exposé of Marxism, like the rest of the book, had a didactic purpose, and it was easy to assimilate and remember.

The passage begins by stating that dialectical materialism, the philosophy of Marxism, consists of two elements: a materialistic view of the world, and a dialectical method. The latter is distinguished by four principal features or laws. The first is that all phenomena are interlinked and that the universe must be studied as a whole. Second, everything in nature is in a state of change, movement, and development. Third, in all spheres of reality qualitative changes result from an accumulation of quantitative changes. Fourth, the law of the 'unity and struggle of opposites' states that all natural phenomena embody internal contradictions and that the 'content' of development is the conflict between those contradictions. This is seen in the fact that all phenomena have a positive and a negative aspect, a past and a future, so that the struggle takes the form of a conflict between new and old.

This account, it may be noticed, does not include the 'negation of the negation' of which Engels wrote, as did Lenin in his *Philosophical Notes*. The reason for the omission is not explained, but, at all events, the dialectic henceforth comprises four laws and no more. The contrary of dialectics is 'metaphysics'. Metaphysicians are bourgeois philosophers and scholars who deny one or more of the laws in question: thus they claim to judge phenomena in isolation and not in their mutual relations, they maintain that nothing develops, they do not recognize that qualitative changes arise from quantitative ones, and they reject the idea of internal contradictions.

The materialistic interpretation of nature embodies three principles. The first is that the world is by its nature material, and all phenomena are forms of matter in motion; the second, that matter or being is an 'objective reality' existing outside and independent of our mind; and the third, that everything in the world is knowable.

Historical materialism is presented as the logical consequence of dialectical materialism, a view for which support can be found in some statements by Engels, Plekhanov, and Bukharin. Since 'the material world is primary and mind is secondary', it follows that 'the material life of society' i.e. production and the relations of production, is also primary and is an 'objective reality', while the spiritual life of society is a secondary 'reflection' of it. The logical basis of this deduction is not explained. Stalin then quotes Marxist formulas concerning the base and superstructure, classes and the class struggle, the dependence of ideology (and all other forms of superstructure) on production relations, the wrongness of attributing social changes simply to geographical or demographic conditions, and the fact that history depends primarily on technological development. Then comes an account of the five main socio-economic systems: primitive-communal, slave-owning, feudal, capitalist, and socialist. The order in which these succeed one another is described as historically inevitable. Nothing is said about Marx's 'Asiatic mode of production': the probable reasons for this have been discussed elsewhere (vol. I, ch. XIV, pp. 350–1).

The enumeration of the five types of society and their application to the history of every country in the world presented Soviet historians with a major problem. It was no easy matter to discern the existence of a slave or feudal society among populations that had never heard of such phenomena. Moreover, as capitalism had been established by a bourgeois revolution and socialism by a socialist one, it was natural to suppose that previous transitions had taken place in a similar way. Stalin indeed wrote (or 'proved': in Soviet philosophy the two terms mean the same thing where the classics of Marxism–Leninism are concerned) that the feudal system emerged from the slave-owning one as the result of a slave revolution. He had in fact made the same point in an address on 19 February 1933: the slave-owning system was overthrown by a slave revolution, as a result of which feudal lords took the place of the old exploiters. This gave historians the additional problem of identifying the 'slave revolution' in every case of transition from slave-owning to feudalism.

Stalin's work was greeted by a chorus of ideologists as the supreme achievement of Marxist theory and a milestone in philosophical history. For the next fifteen years Soviet philosophy consisted of little but variations on the theme of its superlative merit. Every philosophical article and manual dutifully enumerated the four 'marks' of the dialectic and the three principles of materialism. Philosophers had little to do but to find examples showing that different phenomena were interrelated (a proof of Stalin's first law), or that things changed (a proof of the second), and so on. In this way philosophy was degraded to the status of a medium for incessant flattery of the supreme leader. Everyone wrote in exactly the same style; no writer could be distinguished from another by the form or content of his work. The same soporific clichés were repeated endlessly, with no attempt at independent thought: any such attempt, however timid and obsequious, would have exposed the author to immediate attack. To say anything of one's own in philosophy could only signify that one was accusing Stalin of having omitted something important; to write in a style of one's own was to show dangerous presumption by suggesting that one could express something better than he. Thus Soviet philosophical literature came to consist of heaps of waste paper reproducing in diluted form Chapter IV, Section 2 of the *Short Course*. Compared with this, even the polemics of the 'dialecticians' and 'mechanists' were an example of bold, creative, and independent thought. As for the history of philosophy, it became an almost forgotten subject. In the thirties a few translations of philosophical classics still appeared, but only of such authors as were classed, rightly or wrongly, as 'materialists' or had written against religion: the Soviet reader might thus occasionally see an anticlerical pamphlet by Holbach or Voltaire or, if he was lucky, something by Bacon or Spinoza. Hegel's works were also published, as he belonged to the canon of 'dialectical' writers. But for about forty years there was no chance of reading Plato, not to mention any more dangerous idealist. Professional philosophers quoted only the 'classics of Marxism–Leninism', namely Marx, Engels, Lenin, and Stalin: the chronological sequence was, of course, observed when the names were cited together, but in terms of frequency of quotation the order was precisely the reverse.

It might have seemed that the ideological situation resulting from the publication of the *Short Course* was one of final perfection; but the post-war years showed that it could still be improved upon.

It should not be supposed, however, that Marxism as codified by Stalin differed in any essential way from Leninism. It was a bald, primitive version, but contained scarcely anything new. Indeed, very little that is original can be found in any of Stalin's works before 1950, with two exceptions. The first, of which we have considered the import, was that socialism could be built in one country. The second was that the class struggle must become fiercer as the building of socialism progressed. This principle remained officially valid even after Stalin declared that there were no longer any antagonistic classes in the Soviet Union—there were no classes, but the class struggle was acuter than ever. A third principle, which Stalin seems first to have enunciated at a plenum of the Central Committee on 12 January 1933, was that before the state 'withered away' under Communism it must, for dialectical reasons, first develop to a point of maximum strength; but this idea had already been formulated by Trotsky during the Civil War. The second and third principles, in any case, were of no significance except as a justification of the system of police terror.

However, it should be emphasized once again that what mattered about Stalinist ideology was not its content—even though it was expressed in catechetical form—but the fact that there was a supreme authority from whose judgement on ideological matters there was no appeal. Ideology was thus completely institutionalized, and virtually the whole of intellectual life was subordinated to it. The 'unity of theory and practice' was expressed by the concentration of doctrinal, political, and police authority in Stalin's person.

Dialectical and historical materialism as expounded by Stalin amounted to an unimaginative, schematic version of Marxism according to Plekhanov, Lenin, and Bukharin: a philosophy with cosmic ambitions, proclaiming that the dialectic expressed universal 'laws' which governed every aspect of reality, and that human history was a special case of the application of these laws. This philosophy claimed to be 'scientific' in the same way as astronomy, and declared that social processes were as 'objective' and predictable as any other. In this respect it departed radically from the Marxian viewpoint as reconstructed by Lukács and Korsch, according to which, in the particular case of the proletarian consciousness, the social process and awareness of that process became one and the same, and knowledge of society coincided with the revolutionary praxis that transformed it. Stalin took over the popular naturalism which prevailed among Marxists of the Second International, and in which there was no room for the peculiar Marxian view of the 'unity of theory and practice'. True, this formula was acknowledged and emphasized at every opportunity by Stalin and his attendant philosophers; but its meaning was in effect reduced to the proposition that practice was superior to theory and that theory was ancillary to practice. In accordance with this view pressure was put on scholars—especially after the ideological reconstruction of the Academy of Sciences in the early thirties—to confine themselves to fields that might be of immediate profit to industry. This pressure applied to all the natural sciences and even, though less severely, to mathematics. (Mathematical studies were scarcely ever 'supervised' ideologically in the Soviet Union, as even the omniscient high priests of Marxism did not pretend to understand them; consequently, standards were upheld and Russian mathematical science was saved from temporary destruction.) The 'unity of theory and practice', of course, applied to the humane sciences also, but in a slightly different sense. Broadly speaking, the natural sciences were harnessed to the demands of industry, and the humanistic sciences to those of party propaganda. History, philosophy, and the history of literature and art were supposed to 'serve the party and state', i.e. to buttress the party line and provide theoretical support for current decisions.

The demand that natural science should confine itself to subjects of immediate technical use was highly damaging to important branches of research, and this very soon made itself felt in technology as well. Even more pernicious, however, were attempts to exercise ideological control over the actual results of scientific investigation, in the name of Marxist 'correctness'. In the thirties the 'idealist' theory of relativity came under fire from a band of philosophers and half-baked physicists, led by A. A. Maksimov. The same period saw the rise of Trofim D. Lysenko, whose mission was to revolutionize Soviet biological science in accordance with Marxism–Leninism and to explode the 'bourgeois' theories of Mendel and T. H. Morgan. Lysenko, an agronomist, had explored various techniques of plant breeding and decided, early in his career, to develop them into a universal theory of Marxist genetics. After 1935, together with his assistant I. I. Prezent, he attacked the modern genetic theory and claimed that hereditary influences could be almost completely eliminated by appropriate changes in environment: genes were a bourgeois invention, as was the distinction between genotype and phenotype. It was not hard to convince the party leaders and Stalin himself that a theory which rejected the 'immortal substance of heredity' and proclaimed that living organisms could be altered to any desired extent by environmental changes was in accordance with Marxism–Leninism ('everything changes') and was admirably suited to the ideology which maintained that human beings, especially 'Soviet man', could transform nature in any way they had a mind to. So Lysenko rapidly secured party support and exercised a growing influence on research institutes, academicians, journals, etc., until, as we shall see, his revolutionary theory achieved a complete triumph in 1948. Party propaganda extolled his discoveries incessantly from about 1935 onwards, and those who objected that his experiments were scientifically worthless were soon put to silence. The eminent genetician Nikolay I. Vavilov, who refused to subscribe to the new theory, was arrested in 1940 and perished in the Kolyma concentration camp. Most Soviet philosophers, as was to be expected, joined in acclaiming Lysenko's views.

Today no one has any doubt that Lysenko was an ignoramus and a charlatan, and his career is an instructive example of how the Soviet system functions, not only with respect to science and culture but also in the economic and administrative sphere. The self-destructive features that were to become still more evident later on were already visible. As the party exercises unlimited authority in every area of life, and the whole system is organized hierarchically with a one-way chain of command, it follows that the career of any individual depends on his obedience to authority and proficiency in the arts of flattery and denunciation. It is fatal, on the other hand, to display initiative, a mind of one's own, or even a minimal respect for truth. When the main object of those in authority is to maintain and increase their power it is inevitable that the wrong people will come to the top, both in science (especially if it is ideologically controlled) and in economic administration. Inefficiency and waste are built-in features of the Soviet system; economic development is hampered by both the promotion of the unfit and the wholesale restriction of information on grounds of politics and 'security'. Later attempts at rationalizing the economy have had some success, but only in so far as they departed from the totalitarian principle or the ideal of 'unity' which the Stalinist system brought to such perfection.

Another important feature of Soviet culture in the 1930s was the growth of Russian nationalism. This too is a phenomenon that reached its peak later on, but it was already discernible in the early thirties, when Stalin's speeches began to strike the

note of a 'strong Russia' which could and must be created by
socialism. The patriotic theme was stressed increasingly in
propaganda, and Soviet and Russian patriotism coincided more
and more. The glories of Russian history were revived in an
appeal to national pride and self-sufficiency. Some nations, such
as the Uzbeks, who had formerly written their language in Arabic
script and were then given a Latin alphabet by the Soviet
authorities, were now compelled to adopt a form of Cyrillic,
so that three alphabets were used in a single generation. The
idea of 'national cadres' exercising power in the non-Russian
republics of the Union soon proved to be a fiction: in practice
though not in theory, the top posts in the party and state
administration were usually held by Russians appointed from
Moscow. The ideology of state power became by degrees
indistinguishable from that of Russian imperialism.

Marxism as the ideology of the Soviet state very soon ceased
to be an independent factor in the determination of policy. Of
necessity, its content had to be so vague and general as to justify
any particular move in home or foreign affairs: N.E.P. or
collectivization, friendship with Hitler or war with Hitler, any
toughening or relaxation of the internal regime, and so on.
And indeed, since the theory states that 'on the one hand' the
superstructure is a creation and instrument of the base, but 'on
the other' it also affects the base, it can be shown that any
imaginable government policy for the regulation of the economy,
or for controlling culture in a greater or less degree, is in
accordance with Marxism. If 'on the one hand' individuals do
not make history, but 'on the other' exceptional individuals who
understand historical necessity do play an important part (and
both points of view can be supported by quotations from Marx
and Engels), then it is equally in accordance with Marxism to
pay divine honours to the socialist despot or to condemn this
practice as a 'deviation'. If 'on the one hand' all nations are
entitled to self-determination, but 'on the other hand' the cause
of world socialist revolution is paramount, then any policy,
whether mild or severe, with the object of discouraging the
national aspirations of the non-Russian inhabitants of the empire
will be indubitably Marxist. Such in fact was the ambivalent
basis of Stalin's Marxism, and its vague and contradictory
tenets were alike put down to the 'dialectic'. From this point

of view both the function and the content of official Soviet Marxism have remained the same since Stalin's death. Marxism has become simply a rhetorical dressing for the Realpolitik of the Soviet empire.

The rationale of this change was very simple: since the Soviet Union is by definition the bastion of human progress, whatever serves Soviet interests is progressive and whatever does not is reactionary. Tsarist Russia, like most other Powers in history, supported the aspirations of smaller peoples in order to weaken its own rivals, and the Soviet Union pursued this policy from the outset, but under a different guise. Even 'feudal' sheikhs and Asiatic princes, according to Stalin, played an 'objectively' progressive role in so far as they undermined the imperialist front. This was fully in accordance with Lenin's theory of world revolution, which admitted and even required the participation of non-socialist, non-proletarian, and, in Marxist terms, 'reactionary' forces. From a dialectical point of view the reactionaries immediately and dialectically became progressive if their efforts were hostile to the interests of other world Powers. In the same way it became axiomatic after 1917 that, as the Soviet Union was by definition the mainstay of the worldwide liberation movement, any armed incursion or seizure of foreign territory on its part was not an invasion but an act of liberation. Marxism thus provided the Soviet state with a repertoire of arguments that were far more useful as tools of imperialism than the clumsy and even absurd principles with which Tsarist Russia sought to justify its rule over alien peoples.

3. The Comintern and the ideological transformation of international Communism

In the natural course of things, Stalinization spread throughout the world Communist movement. For the first decade of its existence the Third International was still a forum of discussion and conflict between different forms of Communist ideology, but thereafter it lost all independence and became an instrument of Soviet foreign policy, completely subordinated to Stalin's authority.

The various left-wing groups and fractions that emerged within social democratic parties during the First World War were not all pure Leninists, but all agreed in condemning the betrayal of the movement by the leaders of the Second International; they all rejected reformism, and sought to revive the traditional internationalist spirit. The October Revolution had created a new revolutionary stronghold, and most of these left-wingers believed that the world Communist revolution was imminent. In 1918 Communist parties were formed in Poland, Germany, Finland, Latvia, Austria, Hungary, Greece, and Holland. In the next three years larger or smaller revolutionary parties, representing various minority groups, came into existence in all European countries. Despite many complicated disputes and schisms, there took shape in this way an international Communist movement inspired by Leninist principles.

In January 1919 the Bolshevik party issued a manifesto drafted by Trotsky and calling for the creation of a new International. A congress was held at Moscow in March, at which the project was approved by delegates of certain Communist parties and left-wing social democratic groups. The Third International was not actually set up until the Second Congress, in July–August 1920. From the beginning various parties developed internal divisions and departures from the Leninist norm. On the one hand were 'rightist' groups who hankered after a reconciliation with the social democrats from whom they had recently split off; on the other were 'leftist' or 'sectarian' deviationists who, as a rule, rejected compromise tactics or association with parliamentary politics. It was against this school of thought that Lenin wrote *'Left-Wing' Communism: an Infantile Disorder*. Given the belief prevalent among Communists that within a year the whole world, or at least Europe, would become a Soviet republic, 'leftist' tendencies were much stronger and more in evidence than 'reformist' ones.

The statutes of the Comintern marked a radical departure from the principles of the Second International, but harked back to the tradition of the First. They provided that the International was to be a single centralized party, of which the national parties were sections, and that its purpose was to use every means, including armed force, to bring about an international republic of Soviets, which, as the political form of the dictatorship of the proletariat, was the historically ordained prelude to the abolition of the state. The International was to hold annual congresses (biennial after 1924) and be governed in between times by its Executive Committee, which could expel 'sections' that disregarded its instructions and could require them to cast out groups or individuals for breaches of discipline. The theses adopted at the 1920 Congress included a firm rejection of parliamentarianism as a suitable form of the society of the future. Parliaments and all other bourgeois political institutions must be used only in order to destroy them; Communists must take part in elections for this purpose alone, and Communist deputies were responsible to the party alone and not to the anonymous mass of voters. The theses on colonial questions, drafted by Lenin, instructed Communists in colonial and backward countries to enter into temporary alliances with national revolutionary movements; at the same time Communists must remain independent, not allowing the national bourgeoisie to get hold of the revolutionary movement, but fighting from the outset for a Soviet republic; under their leadership the backward countries would achieve Communism without having to go through a capitalist stage.

The congress also issued a manifesto demanding unconditional support for the cause of the Soviet Union as being the cause of the whole International.

Another important document was a list of 'Twenty-One Conditions' which must be fulfilled by parties joining the Comintern, and which extended Leninist forms of organization to the whole Communist movement. The 'Conditions' provided that Communist parties must wholly subordinate their propaganda activities to decisions of the Comintern. The Communist Press was to be completely under party control. The 'sections' must resolutely combat reformist tendencies and, whenever possible, remove reformists and centralists from workers' organizations. They must also—this was specially emphasized—carry out systematic propaganda within their countries' armed forces. They must combat pacifism, support colonial liberation movements, be active in workers' organizations and especially trade unions, and make efforts to win peasant support. In Parliament, Communist deputies must subordinate their whole activity to revolutionary propaganda. Parties must be centralized to the maximum, observe iron discipline, and periodically purge their ranks of petty-bourgeois elements. They must unquestioningly support all existing Soviet republics. Each party's programme must be endorsed by a congress of the International or by its Executive Committee, and all decisions of congresses or the Executive Committee were binding on all sections. All parties must call themselves 'Communist', and those that were allowed by the laws of their country to function openly must, in addition, set up clandestine organizations for action 'at the decisive moment'.

In this way a centralized party operating on military lines became the prescribed mode of organization of the world Communist movement. However, Lenin and Trotsky, the creators of the International, did not envisage it as an instrument of Soviet state policy. The idea that the Bolshevik party itself was no more than a 'section' or branch of the world revolutionary movement was, at the outset, taken quite seriously. But the way in which the Comintern was organized, and the historical circumstances of its creation, soon dispelled such illusions. The Bolshevik party naturally enjoyed great prestige as the agent of the first successful revolution, and Lenin's personal authority was unshakeable. From the beginning Russia had a deciding voice in the Executive Committee, and the permanent representatives of other parties, residing in Moscow, gradually became Soviet functionaries. Internal struggles within the Soviet leadership were not only reflected in the International but eventually became its main concern. Each of the Bolshevik oligarchs who contended for power after Lenin's death naturally sought support among the leaders of fraternal parties, and the victories or defeats of international Communism were in turn exploited in fractional struggles in Moscow.

The first congresses of the International were held regularly in accordance with the statutes. The third took place in June–July 1921, the fourth in November 1922, and the fifth in June–July 1924. By this time Russia had been through the Civil War, the N.E.P. had entered its first phase, and Lenin had died. In accordance with Lenin's precepts, the International busied itself from the outset with revolutionary agitation in colonial and undeveloped countries. The Indian Communist Nath Roy argued that revolution in Asia should be the main objective of world Communism: the stability of capitalism depended on profits from colonial territories and it was there, not in Europe, that the future of humanity would be decided.

A majority of the International, however, thought that Europe should still be the main focus of activity. The defeat of the Soviet armies before Warsaw in 1920 caused hopes of an early revolution to recede, but they did not fade completely. However, in March 1921 an attempt at revolution in Germany ended in fiasco, and the resolutions of the Third Comintern Congress in June were less optimistic as to the prospect of a world Soviet republic. The German uprising was condemned by Lenin and Trotsky and duly criticized by the congress. However, Paul Levi, the German communist leader, who had himself opposed the rising and was therefore expelled from the party shortly before the congress opened, was not rehabilitated; he was again condemned and his expulsion ratified. The new 'Leninist' style was clearly in full operation.

As the world revolution was hanging fire the Comintern leaders decided, against strong opposition from the 'leftist' minority, to adopt a 'united front' policy of co-operation with the socialists. Conversations were begun before the Fourth Congress in 1922, but came to nothing: the socialists suspected, with good reason, that the 'united front' was a ploy aimed at their destruction. A further abortive rising took place in Germany in October 1923; this time Heinrich Brandler, the new party leader, was made the scapegoat for a plan that had been wholly organized and initiated by the Comintern and the Bolshevik party. In 1924 Trotsky accused the Comintern, then under Zinovyev's direction, of failing to exploit the revolutionary situation by seizing power in Germany.

The Fifth Comintern Congress, held in mid-1924 at a time when the ruling triumvirate of Stalin, Zinovyev, and Kamenev was engaged in a crucial struggle with Trotsky, passed a resolution calling for the 'Bolshevization' of all member parties. This meant in theory that they should adopt the methods and style of the Russian party, but in practice that they should accept its authority in all matters. The congress itself showed that 'Bolshevization' was already well advanced: the Communists of all countries unanimously condemned Trotsky at the bidding of Stalin and his associates. In the following year there was a demonstration at the congress of the German Communist party of what Bolshevization meant, when the Soviet delegate Manuilsky, one of Stalin's chief henchmen in the Comintern, attempted to lay down the law as regards the membership of the Central Committee. As the German delegates refused to comply, Zinovyev, chairman of the Executive Committee, summoned them to Moscow and ordered them to get rid of their 'leftist' leaders, Ruth Fischer and Arkady Maslow, who had tried to maintain some semblance of autonomy *vis-à-vis* the Bolsheviks.

Another resolution of the Fifth Congress assessed the position of the social democrats, stating that their role, in collusion with the bourgeoisie, was to instil democratic and pacifist illusions in the working class. As capitalism decayed, social democracy came closer and closer to Fascism: the two were in fact aspects of a single weapon in the hands of capital. This was the genesis of the theory of 'social Fascism', which a few years later became the principal guideline of Comintern policy.

Four years elapsed between the Fifth and Sixth Comintern Congresses: Stalin was probably unwilling to call one until he had finally achieved victory over Trotsky and also Zinovyev, Kamenev, and their associates. Meanwhile the Comintern, in spite of its doctrine concerning 'social Fascism', made advances to the British trade unions which resulted in the formation, in 1925, of an Anglo-Russian committee to promote the unification of the world trade union movement. This, however, was short lived and unsuccessful. In 1926–7 the Comintern suffered a more serious set-back in China, where the small Communist party, on Moscow's instructions, had supported the revolutionary Kuomintang in its efforts to unify and modernize China and free it from Western domination. This, in Stalin's opinion, was a bourgeois nationalist movement and was not destined to lead at once at a dictatorship of the proletariat. The Soviet Union helped with arms and military and political advisers, and in the spring of 1926 the Kuomintang was even admitted to the Comintern as a 'sympathizing' party. However, when Chiang Kai-shek formed his government he excluded the Communists from any share in power, and in April 1927 he put down a Communist rising in Shanghai with many arrests and executions. Stalin, realizing too late that Chiang had anticipated the intentions of his 'allies' by getting his blow in first, attempted to save the situation by ordering an insurrection in Canton; this took place in December, but was quelled by another massacre. Trotsky blamed Stalin for these defeats, declaring that instead of accepting Chiang's leadership the Chinese Communists should have aimed at setting up a Soviet republic from the outset—though he did not explain how they could have prevailed against Chiang in the then state of their forces. However, the Comintern laid the blame on the Chinese party for pursuing a 'false policy', and its leader, Chen Tu-hsiu, was condemned and later expelled.

The Sixth Comintern Congress, in August 1928, put a final stop to attempts at co-operating with the socialists, which in any case had been feeble and unsuccessful. The congress declared that international social democracy and the trade unions under its control were the mainstay of capitalism, and Communist parties were ordered to concentrate all their efforts against the 'social Fascists'. The temporary stabilization of capitalism, it was proclaimed, had now come to an end, and a new revolutionary period was beginning. The Communist parties in various countries duly expelled 'Rightists' and 'conciliators' from the ranks, and the new purge claimed many victims among the leaders in Germany, Spain, the U.S.A. and elsewhere.

The fact that the German Communists, who represented a powerful political force, turned their fire against the socialists was a major cause of Hitler's accession to power. The party line was that Nazism could only be a transient episode and that by radicalizing the masses it would pave the way for Communism. Even after Hitler came to power, for a whole year the German Communists treated the socialists as their chief enemy; by the time they changed their minds, the party was already broken and helpless.

By the end of 1929, after the downfall of Bukharin (who had succeeded Zinovyev as chairman of the Executive Committee in 1926), Stalin was the unquestioned owner of the Bolshevik party and, through it, of international Communism. The Comintern lost all significance of its own and was merely a channel for the transmission of the Kremlin's orders to other parties. Its staff consisted exclusively of people loyal to Stalin and controlled by the Soviet police; among their tasks was to recruit intelligence agents for the Soviet Union. All the fraternal parties, after repeated purges, accepted without demur Moscow's changing directives, which for the most part were dictated by Soviet foreign policy. Stalin financed the parties generously and thus increased their dependence on himself. By the mid-thirties the Comintern was a mere façade, as it was no longer needed even for the purpose of securing obedience from foreign parties.

The Seventh and last Comintern Congress, held in Moscow in July–August 1935, proclaimed a new policy which had been foreshadowed for a year or more, that of the 'popular front' against Fascism. What had recently been condemned as 'rightist opportunism' now became the official line. All democratic forces, especially the socialists (the 'social Fascists' of two years earlier), as well as liberals and even conservatives if need be, were to rally under Communist leadership against the Fascist threat. Stalin's reason for this policy seems to have been his fear that France and the other Western countries would remain neutral if Hitler attacked Russia. France, in any case, was the main target of the 'popular front' policy: as far as Germany was concerned it could only apply to powerless *émigré* groups, and the Communist parties in other countries were too weak to affect events. In France the popular front was victorious at the election in May 1936, but the Communists refused to enter Léon Blum's government. In general the policy did not last long and produced few results. Although not officially revoked, it became a dead letter when Stalin decided to seek a *rapprochement* with Nazi Germany. Meanwhile the German Communist party, which had been smashed and driven underground, belatedly adopted Hitler's slogans of the unity of all Germans and the liquidation of the Polish Corridor.

The true character of the 'popular front' policy was shown up by the Civil War in Spain. Some months after Franco's rebellion, Stalin decided to intervene in defence of the republic. International brigades were formed, and besides military advisers the Soviet Union sent an army of political agents who purged the republican forces of Trotskyists, anarchists, and deviationists of all kinds.

International Communism was by now completely 'Bolshevized', and in any case non-Bolshevik forms of Communism had long ceased to signify. In the twenties individuals or groups who had been expelled from their parties or had seceded in protest against Comintern policy tried from time to time to organize a non-Soviet Communist movement, but these attempts never came to anything. The Trotskyists vegetated in small groups, appealing impotently to the 'internationalist conscience' of the world proletariat. The authority of the Bolshevik party, and the organizational principles accepted by all Communists, were such that until the 1950s no dissident group achieved any support or influence. World Communism marched obediently along the route prescribed by Stalin. The dissolution of the Comintern in May 1943 was a mere gesture to persuade Western public opinion of Soviet good will and democratic intentions. It had no other significance, as the Communist parties were so well trained and so dependent on the Soviet Union for their organization and finances that no special institution was necessary to keep them in line.

One effect of Stalin's dictatorship over world Communism was the gradual decline of Marxist studies. In the twenties, during the process of 'Bolshevization', the parties were dominated by various fractional and personal quarrels: these usually took the form of disputes over the correct interpretation of Lenin's political testament, but they had no permanent effect on doctrine apart from the gradual codification of Soviet-type orthodoxy. None the less, the revolutionary mood of the early twenties gave rise to several theoretical documents in which Marxist doctrine as transmitted by the orthodox thinkers of the Second International was subjected to a thorough revision. The most important of these are the writings of Lukács and Korsch, both of whom were stigmatized as 'ultra-leftist' by the Comintern. In different ways they attempted to reconstruct Marx's philosophy from the beginning, putting fresh life into the idea of the 'unity of theory and practice' and combating the scientistic outlook that prevailed among both the orthodox and the neo-Kantians. In various countries stalwarts of the previous generation still carried on traditions of undogmatic Marxism outside the Communist movement: Adler and Bauer in Austria, Krzywicki in Poland, Kautsky and Hilferding in Germany. Their activity in those years did not, however, have much effect on the evolution of doctrine: some of them were content to repeat ideas and themes that had already been worked out, while others gradually fell away from Marxist tradition. Meanwhile theoretical work was paralysed by the Comintern's policy of polarizing the socialist movement by combating the social democrats. The latter became largely divorced from Marxism and lost the need for a single binding ideology; Marxism was practically monopolized by Soviet ideologists, and became more barren with every year that passed.

Only in Germany was there an important Marxist centre that did not identify with Communism: the Institut für Sozialforschung, founded at Frankfurt in 1923. Its members were at first strongly influenced by Marxist tradition, but the links weakened by degrees, and a pattern took shape which was later increasingly evident. On the one hand, Marxism became ossified as an institutionalized party ideology and, while politically effective, lost all philosophical value; on the other, it combined with quite different traditions to the point where it ceased to present a clear outline and became only one of many contributions to intellectual history.

Around the middle thirties, however, the Marxist movement in France revived to some extent. Among its leaders were scientists, sociologists, and philosophers, not all of whom were Communists: Henri Wallon, Paul Langevin, Frédéric Joliot-Curie, Marcel Prenant, Armand Cuvillier, and Georges Friedmann. These men were to play an important part in French intellectual life after the war, either as scholars who were politically committed to Communism (but not necessarily Marxist theoreticians) or as continuers of certain aspects of traditional Marxist theory, which had ceased to form a system but had penetrated intellectual life in a piecemeal fashion. The best-known orthodox Marxist in France between the wars was Georges Politzer, who was put to death during the occupation; he wrote a ferocious critique of Bergson and a popular handbook of Leninist dialectical materialism. In Britain J. B. S. Haldane, the well-known biologist and author of books on the origins of life on earth, endeavoured to prove the affinity of Marxism with modern science. Another Marxist was the American geneticist H. J. Muller. In both these cases, however, Marxism figured in aspects that were not specifically Marxist: in biology it appeared chiefly in the form of a general opposition to vitalism and finalism. Maurice Dobb, also in Britain, defended Marxist economic theory, especially in relation to the trade cycle.

On the left wing of the Labour party Harold J. Laski expounded in Marxist terms the theory of the state, the nature of authority, and the history of political ideas. In the later thirties he adopted the classic Marxist theory of the state as an instrument which 'in the last resort' serves to enable one class to coerce another. He attacked contemporary liberalism as an ideology whose main purpose was to keep the exploited from being heard, and asserted that if the vital interests of the property-owning classes were threatened they would increasingly reject liberal forms of government and resort to naked force. The growth of Fascism in Europe was a natural result of the development of the bourgeois state; bourgeois democracy was in a state of decline, and the only alternative to Fascism was socialism. None the less, Laski was attached to traditional democratic liberties and believed that the proletarian revolution would leave them intact. The key to social development lay, he declared, in the attitude of the middle classes. John Strachey, at this time a Communist (he later became a social democrat), discussed the same problems from an orthodox Leninist viewpoint.

A gifted author, Christopher Caudwell (pseudonym of Christopher St. John Sprigg, 1907–37), was briefly prominent in British Marxism. His career as a Marxist and Communist lasted barely two years—he was killed fighting in the International Brigade in Spain—but in 1936 he produced a notable work entitled *Illusion and Reality: a Study of the Sources of Poetry*. Before becoming a Communist he wrote some detective stories and popular books on aviation. His poems were published posthumously, as were *Studies in a Dying Culture* (1938), a collection of essays on contemporary British literature and 'bourgeois culture' in general, and an unfinished work *The Crisis in Physics* (1939), a Leninist attack on idealism, empiricism, and indeterminism in modern scientific theory. In *Illusion and Reality*, the best known of his Marxist works, he attempted to correlate the history of poetry, including metrical changes, with different stages of social and technical evolution. At the same time he attacked the bourgeois idea which envisaged freedom as independence of necessity, whereas Engels had shown that freedom meant exploiting natural inevitability for human ends. The book devotes particular attention to English poetry from the sixteenth century onwards: Marlowe and Shakespeare stand for the heroic era of primary accumulation, Pope for mercantilism, and so on. Caudwell took the view (which is not specifically

Marxist and can be found in earlier anthropological works) that poetry was originally only an element in the agricultural rites of primitive society, with the purpose of increasing production. Later on, in class societies, poetry, music, and the dance were disjoined from production, which meant the alienation of art; the function of socialism was to reverse this process and restore the unity of productive and artistic activities.

The intellectual life of Western Europe, and to some extent of the U.S.A., in the later thirties presented a curious picture. On the one hand, Stalinism was in full career, and some of its most repulsive features were laid bare for all the world to see; but, on the other, many intellectuals were attracted by Communism as the only alternative to Fascism and as a defence against it. All other political groupings appeared weak, irresolute, and helpless before the threat of Nazi aggression. Marxism seemed to many to uphold the tradition of rationalism, humanism, and all the old liberal ideals, while Communism was the political embodiment of Marxism and the best hope of containing the Fascist onslaught. Left-wing intellectuals were drawn towards Marxism by features that had indeed been present in it from the beginning but were not specifically Marxist. As long as Soviet Russia seemed to be the main force opposed to Fascism, these intellectuals endeavoured to identify Soviet Communism with Marxism as they understood it. In so doing they deliberately blinded themselves to the realities of Communist policy. Those who, like George Orwell, formed an idea of Communism in action from empirical facts instead of from doctrinaire assumptions met with hatred and indignation. Hypocrisy and self-delusion had become the permanent climate of the intellectual Left.

CHAPTER IV

The crystallization of Marxism–Leninism after the Second World War

1. The wartime interlude

By the end of the 1930s Marxism had taken on a clearly defined form as the doctrine of the Soviet party and state. Its official name was Marxism–Leninism, which, as we have explained, meant nothing more or less than Stalin's personal ideology: it included bits of theory from Marx, Engels, and Lenin, but purported to be a single doctrine which the four 'classical' teachers had successively 'developed' and 'enriched'. In this way Marx was promoted to the rank of a 'classic of Marxism–Leninism' and a forerunner of Stalin. The true content of Marxism–Leninism was expounded in Stalin's writings, more particularly in the *Short Course*.

As we have seen, the characteristic feature of this ideology, which pre-eminently reflected the interests of the governing stratum of a totalitarian state, was its combination of extreme rigidity and extreme flexibility. These seemingly opposite qualities reinforced each other perfectly. The ideology was rigid in the sense that it was expressed in a collection of unchanging, cut-and-dried formulas which all were obliged to repeat without the slightest deviation; but the content of those formulas was so vague that they could be used to justify any state policy whatsoever, in all its phases and variations.

The most paradoxical effect of this function of Soviet Marxism was its partial self-liquidation during the Second World War.

In the second half of the thirties Europe was paralysed by the menace of Nazi aggression. During the crises which preceded the outbreak of war, the Soviet Union with Stalin at the helm pursued a skilful and subtle policy aimed at securing its position against threats from every side. The Western Powers' pusillanimous policy of appeasement made it difficult to foresee what would happen if Germany should attack her Eastern or Western neighbours. After the Anschluss and the subjugation of Czechoslovakia it was clear to most people that war was unavoidable. The German–Soviet non-aggression pact of August 1939 contained a secret protocol providing for the partition of Poland between the signatories and assigning Finland, Estonia, and Latvia to the Soviet sphere of interest (Lithuania was added to these in a modification of the agreement on 28 September). Germany invaded Poland on 1 September, the day after the Soviet Union ratified the pact, and on 17 September the Red Army marched in to 'liberate' the Polish Eastern territories, while the Soviet and German governments proclaimed that Poland had been annihilated once and for all. The aggressors concluded a secret agreement to aid each other in stamping out underground activity in the occupied territories. (During the period of Nazi–Soviet co-operation the Russians handed over some German Communists who were imprisoned in the U.S.S.R., including the physicist Alexander Weissberg: he survived the war, however, and was thus able to write one of the first documentary accounts of Stalin's purges.) The pact with Hitler brought about a transformation of Soviet state ideology. Attacks on Fascism, and the word 'Fascism' itself, disappeared from Soviet propaganda. The Western Communist parties, especially the British and French, were ordered to direct their whole propaganda against the war effort and to blame Western imperialism for the fight against Nazi Germany. The unsuccessful invasion of Finland revealed Russia's military weakness to the world and not least to Hitler, whose object from the beginning was to destroy his Soviet 'ally'. Still more catastrophic was the disarray of the Soviet Union immediately after the German invasion on 21 June 1941. Historians still debate the causes of its astonishing unpreparedness. The purging of the best army cadres, Stalin's military incompetence and refusal to heed warnings of an early attack, and the complete psychological disarmament of the Soviet people—a week before the invasion, the government publicly condemned rumours of war as 'absurd' —are among the reasons advanced for the series of defeats that brought the Soviet state to the brink of destruction.

The German–Soviet war brought about further ideological

changes in the Soviet Union and the whole Communist world. The Western Communists no longer had to direct their fire against the anti-Nazi forces, but were free to treat Fascism as a 'natural' enemy. The Polish Communists, who until June 1941 had obediently accepted the abolition of the Polish state, re-established their party and combated the Nazi invader, partly in the U.S.S.R. but mainly as an underground movement in German-occupied Poland. Apart from 'normal' cruelty and destruction, the war in Russia brought 'ideological' atrocities of its own: the mass deportation and murder of Poles, especially the intelligentsia, from Poland's Eastern territories; the massacre of Polish officers taken captive by the Russians; the resettlement *en masse*, while the struggle with Germany was still going on, of eight minority peoples of the U.S.S.R. and the dissolution of four autonomous national republics—those of the Volga Germans, the Crimean Tatars, the Kalmyks, and the Chechens and Ingushes. Countless lives were lost in these deportations, and the evacuated peoples were never to return to their native homes.

On the other hand, the war did much to relax the grip of ideology in Russia. With the nation struggling for dear life, Marxism proved worthless as a psychological weapon; it virtually disappeared from official propaganda, and Stalin appealed instead to Russian patriotism and the memory of such heroes as Alexander Nevsky, Suvorov, and Kutuzov. The Internationale ceased to be the Soviet anthem and was replaced by a hymn glorifying Russia. Anti-religious agitation was stopped, and the League of Militant Atheists was actually dissolved, while the clergy were invited to help maintain the spirit of patriotism.

Soviet propaganda since 1945 has represented the victory over Hitler as a triumph of socialist ideology, alive in the hearts of fighting men and of the whole Soviet people. The opposite would be closer to the truth: it was a necessary condition of victory, though of course not a sufficient one, that the nation should forget about Marxist ideology and be imbued with national and patriotic sentiments. Apart from the efforts of the Soviet state and people, other factors played their part, including the vast quantity of U.S. military aid and the 'ideological' folly of Hitler, who, dazzled by his overwhelming success in the first months of the war, subjected the conquered territories to the full rigour of Nazi doctrine: instead of posing as a liberator in Byelorussia and the Ukraine, he brandished the scourge of racialism and treated the inhabitants as sub-men to be exterminated or enslaved for ever. (The Germans did not even disband the collective farms in conquered territory, as the system made it easier for them to commandeer produce.) The bestial cruelty of the Nazis convinced the whole population that there could be no greater evil than Hitlerism. The Red Army soldiers, who, after the first reverses, showed outstanding courage and devotion, fought for their country's existence and not for Marxism–Leninism. Many in Russia hoped that the war would not only bring final victory over Nazism but also internal freedom or at least a relaxation of tyranny. It was natural to think so when ideological controls had been loosened so that every effort might be devoted to winning the war, but very soon after victory it was clear that such hopes were an illusion.

In spite of everything, various Marxist institutions continued to function throughout the war. The only important event in the sphere of Soviet philosophy was a decree of the party's Central Committee condemning errors in the third volume of a collective *History of Philosophy* edited by G. F. Aleksandrov: the authors, failing to keep abreast of the times, had over-praised Hegel's role as a philosopher and forerunner of Marxism–Leninism, without taking account of his German chauvinism. This condemnation was only one of many wartime acts of anti-German propaganda, but it helped to destroy Hegel's standing in the annals of Marxist–Leninist orthodoxy. In an interview with Soviet philosophers Stalin described Hegel as an ideologist of the aristocratic reaction to the French Revolution and French materialism, and from then on this assessment became obligatory in philosophical circles.

As the prospect of victory became a virtual certainty Stalin's policy, motivated throughout by the desire for conquest and territorial expansion, concerned itself with the post-war order in Europe and the world. By the Tehran and Yalta agreements the Western Allies gave the Soviet Union, in practice, a free hand in Eastern Europe. In addition to the outright annexation of the three Baltic States and the acquisition of territory from nearly all its neighbours, the Soviet Union, with the acquiescence of Churchill and Roosevelt, enjoyed a dominant position in

Poland, Czechoslovakia, Hungary, Romania, Bulgaria, and, to a lesser extent, Yugoslavia. It was some years before Communist rule in these countries, and also in East Germany, was finally consolidated, but the result was a foregone conclusion.

Some historians argue that both the annexations and the imposition of Communism on countries occupied by the Red Army were not due to imperialist designs but to a concern for security which required the Soviet Union to surround itself as far as possible with 'friendly', or rather subservient, states. But this is a distinction without a difference, since as long as any states are not wholly subjected to the Soviet Union there can be no absolute guarantee of its security: to be perfectly effective, the 'defensive' process must continue until the whole world is under Soviet rule.

2. The new ideological offensive

At the end of the war Soviet Russia had suffered immense casualties and was in a state of economic ruin; yet its position in the world, and consequently Stalin's personal prestige, had risen enormously. Stalin emerged from the turmoil of war as a great statesman, a brilliant strategist, and the destroyer of Fascism. Once the war was over and the Soviet conquests in Europe were assured, the dictator launched a new ideological offensive to reverse the pernicious effects of wartime 'liberalism', to teach the Russian people that the government had no intention of abating its power, and to compel those who, thanks to the war, had seen countries other than the homeland of the world proletariat to forget about such sights as quickly as possible. (A particularly drastic instance of this policy was the wholesale banishment to concentration camps of Soviet prisoners of war who had been freed and handed over by the Western Allies.) The terror and 'authenticity' of war, together with the relaxation of Marxist ideological criteria, had led to a certain cultural revival marked by the appearance of outstanding novels, for example, those of V. P. Nekrasov and A. A. Bek, as well as poems, films, and other works.

The remorseless ideological campaign that set in from 1946 onwards might be summed up in the maxim once used by Alexander II to the Poles: 'Point de rêveries!' The object was not only to restore ideological purity but to raise it to fresh heights, at the same time isolating Soviet culture from all contact with the outside world. Every form of intellectual life was affected in turn: literature, philosophy, music, history, economics, natural science, painting, architecture. The theme was the same in each case: to stop 'kowtowing to the West', to destroy every vestige of independence in thought and art, and to harness all forms of culture to the glorification of Stalin, the party, and the Soviet state.

The chief agent of this policy in 1946–8 was A. A. Zhdanov, a secretary of the Central Committee and a veteran of the war against cultural independence. It was he who, on behalf of the party, informed the All-Union Writers' Congress in August 1934 that Soviet literature was not only the greatest in the world but was the only creative and developing literature, while the whole of bourgeois culture was in a state of decay and corruption. Bourgeois novels were full of pessimism, their authors had sold out to capitalism and their heroes were mostly thieves, prostitutes, spies, and hooligans. 'The great body of Soviet authors is now fused with the Soviet power and the Party, having the aid of Party guidance and the care and daily assistance of the Central Committee and the unceasing support of Comrade Stalin.' Soviet literature must be optimistic, it must be 'forward-looking', and must serve the cause of the workers and collective farmers.

Zhdanov's first important move after the war was to attack two Leningrad literary journals, *Zvezda* (*Star*) and *Leningrad*. A resolution condemning these journals was passed by the Central Committee in August 1946. The main victims were the eminent poetess Anna Akhmatova and the humorist Mikhail Zoshchenko. Zhdanov made a speech at Leningrad in which he violently attacked both writers. Zoshchenko was a malevolent slanderer of the Soviet people: he had written a story about a monkey deciding that it would rather stay in its cage in the zoo than live at large in Leningrad, and this obviously meant that Zoshchenko wanted to reduce humanity to the level of monkeys. Even in the 1920s he had turned out unpolitical art devoid of party spirit, and had wanted nothing to do with the building of socialism: he was and remained 'a literary slum-rat, un-principled and consciousless'. As for Akhmatova, she was a sex-crazed mystic longing for 'Catherine's good old days . . . It would be hard to say whether she is a nun or a fallen woman; better perhaps say she is a bit of each, her desires and her prayers intertwined.' The fact that Leningrad journals printed such stuff showed that literary life was in a bad way. Many writers were imitating corrupt bourgeois literature, others were using history to escape from present-day themes, and one had even dared to parody Pushkin. The business of literature was to inspire young people with patriotism and revolutionary zeal. As Lenin had laid down, it should be political and imbued with party spirit: it should unmask the rottenness of bourgeois culture and show the greatness of Soviet man and the Soviet people, not only as they were today but as they would be in the future.

Zhdanov's clear injunctions set the course of Soviet literature for the next few years. Writers who were ideologically off-colour were forced to silence, if not worse. Even the most orthodox, like Fadeyev, revised their work to the new specifications. To be 'forward-looking' literature had, in practice, to describe the Soviet system not as it was but as ideology required it to be. This resulted in a flood of saccharine literature glorifying the party and extolling the beauties of Soviet life. The printed word was abandoned almost completely to time-servers and syco-phants.

Music was not spared either. In January 1948 Zhdanov made a speech to a conference of composers, conductors, and critics, attacking the corruption of bourgeois music and calling for more of the patriotic Soviet variety. The immediate occasion was afforded by the opera *The Great Friendship* by the Georgian composer Muradeli. This work, with the best intentions, had shown the Caucasian peoples—Georgians, Lezgians, and Ossetes —as having fought the Russians directly after the Revolution, but soon becoming reconciled to the Soviet regime. Nothing of the kind, said Zhdanov: all these peoples had fought for Soviet power from the very beginning, shoulder to shoulder with the Russians. The only ones who had not were the Chechens and Ingushes, who—as Zhdanov did not mention on this occasion, but as everyone was well aware—had been deported *en masse* during the Nazi–Soviet war, while their autonomous republic was razed from the map. Not content with this example, Zhdanov launched a general attack on composers who sought inspiration in Western novelties instead of continuing the great

Russian tradition of Glinka, Tchaikovsky, and Mussorgsky. Soviet music was 'lagging behind' other forms of ideology; composers were succumbing to 'formalism', departing from 'musical truth' and 'socialist realism'. Bourgeois music was anti-people, being either formalistic or naturalistic, but in any case 'idealistic'. Soviet music must serve the people: there was a need for operas, songs, and choral works, which some composers, tainted with formalism, looked down on as unimportant. Such composers looked askance at programme music, yet classical Russian music was mostly of this species. The party had already overcome reactionary and formalistic tendencies in painting and had re-established the healthy tradition of Vereshchagin and Repin, but music was still backward. The classic Russian heritage was unsurpassed, and composers must have a more sensitive 'political ear' as well as a musical one.

The results of this admonition were felt without delay. It suffices to compare Khachaturian's piano concerto, composed before Zhdanov's speech, with his violin concerto. Shostakovich, criticized for his Ninth Symphony among other works, made amends by composing an ode in praise of Stalin's forestry plan, and many other musicians repaired their ideological fences; the most favoured form of composition at this time was an oratorio in honour of the party, the state, and Stalin.

The campaign against literature and music reflected the general principles of Stalin's policy at the time, which was one of ideological intimidation and physical and moral rearmament against the eventuality of war. The doctrine was founded on a division of humanity into two camps: the corrupt and decadent world of imperialism, destined soon to collapse under the weight of its own contradictions, and the 'camp of peace and socialism', the bulwark of progress. Bourgeois culture was by definition reactionary and decadent, and anyone who looked for positive values in it was committing high treason and serving the interests of the class enemy.

3. The philosophical controversy of 1947

After literature, it was the turn of philosophy to be disciplined. The occasion of the campaign was *History of West European Philosophy* by G. F. Aleksandrov, published in 1946. This was wholly orthodox in intent, full of quotations from the Marxist–

Leninist classics and written in a spirit of true devotion to the party. It was a popular exposition of scant historical value, but paid ample attention to the 'class content' of the doctrines it described. The party, however, was incensed by the fact that it covered only Western philosophy and ended its survey in 1848, thus precluding a demonstration of the incomparable superiority of Russian philosophy. In June 1947 the Central Committee organized a large-scale discussion at which Zhdanov formulated directives for the benefit of philosophical writers. In the part of his speech devoted to Aleksandrov's book he declared that it showed a lack of party spirit; the author had failed to point out that Marxism represented a 'qualitative leap' in the history of philosophy and the beginning of a new era in which philosophy was a weapon of the proletariat in the struggle against capitalism. Aleksandrov suffered from corrupt 'objectivism': he had merely recorded the views of various bourgeois thinkers in a neutral spirit, instead of fighting ruthlessly for the victory of the one true, progressive Marxist–Leninist philosophy. The omission of Russian philosophy was itself a sign of deference to bourgeois tendencies. The fact that Aleksandrov's fellow philosophers had not themselves criticized these glaring defects, which were only revealed thanks to the personal intervention of Comrade Stalin, was a clear indication that all was not well on the 'philosophical front' and that philosophers were losing their Bolshevik fighting spirit.

The rules laid down by Zhdanov for future philosophical work in the Soviet Union may be reduced to three. In the first place, it must be remembered once and for all that the history of philosophy was the history of the birth and development of scientific materialism, and of its conflict with idealism in so far as the latter had obstructed its development. Secondly, Marxism was a philosophical revolution: it had taken philosophy out of the hands of the élite and made it the property of the masses. Bourgeois philosophy had been in a state of decline and dissolution since the rise of Marxism, and was incapable of producing anything of value. The history of philosophy for the past hundred years was the history of Marxism. The compass to steer by in combating bourgeois philosophy was Lenin's *Materialism and Empiriocriticism*. Aleksandrov's book showed a spirit of 'toothless vegetarianism', as though the issue were not the class struggle but some kind of universal culture. Thirdly, the 'question of Hegel' had already been settled by Marxism and there was no need to return to it. In general, instead of digging about in the past philosophers should attend to the problems of socialist society and concern themselves with contemporary issues. In the new society there was no longer any class struggle, but there was still a fight of the old against the new; the form of this battle, and thus the motive force of progress and the chosen instrument of the party, was criticism and self-criticism. Such was the new 'dialectical law of development' of progressive society.

All the chief members of the 'philosophical front' took part in the debate, echoing the party directives and thanking Comrade Stalin for his creative contribution to Marxism and for correcting the errors of Soviet philosophy. Aleksandrov performed the ritual self-criticism, acknowledging that his work contained serious mistakes, but consoled by the fact that his colleagues had supported Comrade Zhdanov's criticism; he vowed unshakeable fidelity to the party, and promised to mend his ways.

During the debate Zhdanov opposed the idea of a special journal for philosophy (*Under the Banner of Marxism* had ceased publication three years before), arguing that the party monthly *Bolshevik* covered the ground perfectly well. Finally, however, he relented and agreed to the creation of *Problems of Philosophy*, the first number of which appeared shortly afterwards and contained a stenographic report of the debate. The first editor was V. M. Kedrov, who specialized in the philosophy of natural science and was a man of deeper culture than most Soviet philosophers. However, he committed the grave error of publishing in the second number of the journal an article by the eminent theoretical physicist M. A. Markov entitled 'The Nature of Physical Cognition', which defended the views of the Copenhagen school on the epistemological aspects of quantum physics. The article was attacked by Maksimov in the official weekly *Literary Gazette*, and Kedrov lost his post in consequence.

The 1947 debate left no room for doubt as to what Soviet philosophers were to write about and in what manner: the style of Soviet philosophy was thus fixed for many years. Zhdanov did not confine himself to repeating Engels's formula, which had long been paramount in Stalin's Russia, that the 'content' of the history of philosophy was the conflict between material-ism and idealism. Under the new doctrine, its true content was the history of Marxism, i.e. the works of Marx, Engels, Lenin, and Stalin. In other words, it was not the business of historians of philosophy to analyse bygone theories or even elucidate their class origins: their studies must be teleological and wholly devoted to proving the superiority of Marxism–Leninism over all that had gone before, while 'unmasking' the reactionary functions of idealism. In writing about Aristotle, for instance, they had to show that he had 'failed to understand' this or that (for example, the individual and universal dialectic) or had 'wavered' reprehensibly between idealism and materialism. The effect of Zhdanov's formula was virtually to eliminate all differ-ences between philosophers. There were materialists and ideal-ists and those who 'wavered' or were 'inconsistent', and that was the end of it. Anyone who read the philosophical publi-cations of those years would get the firm impression that the whole of philosophy consisted of the two rival assertions 'matter is primary' and 'spirit is primary', the former view being pro-gressive and the latter reactionary and superstitious. St. Augustine was an idealist and so was Bruno Bauer, and the reader was left to suppose that their philosophies were more or less identical. Without quoting long extracts it would be hard to bring home the incredible primitiveness of the Soviet philo-sophical output of those years to anyone who has not examined it. In general historical studies went to the wall: scarcely any books on the history of philosophy were published, nor were translations of philosophical classics, except for Aristotle's *Analytics* and Lucretius' *De Rerum Natura*. The only history that was acceptable was that of Marxism or of Russian philosophy. The former consisted of diluted expositions of the four classics, while the latter was concerned with the 'progressive contribu-tion' of Russian philosophy and its superiority to the Western brand: thus there were articles and booklets showing how Chernyshevsky outclassed Feuerbach and extolling Hertsen's dialectic, Radishchev's progressive aesthetics, Dobrolyubov's materialism, etc.

The ideological purge did not, of course, spare the study of logic, the position of which in Marxism–Leninism had been doubtful from the beginning. On the one hand, Engels and Plekhanov had spoken of the 'contradictions' inherent in all movement and development, and it appeared from their formulas that the principle of contradiction, and hence formal logic in general, could not claim universal validity. On the other hand, none of the classics had condemned logic unequivocally, and Lenin had enjoined that it be taught at the elementary level. Most philosophers took it for granted that 'dialectical logic' was a higher form of thought and that formal logic 'did not apply' to phenomena of movement; it was not clear, however, in what way and to what extent this 'restricted' logic was admissible. Philosophical writers unanimously condemned 'logical formalism', but none of them could explain the exact difference between this and 'formal logic', which was tolerated within narrow limits. In the late forties elementary logic was taught in the higher forms of secondary schools and in philosophical faculties; some textbooks also appeared, one by the jurist Strogovich and another by the philosopher Asmus. Apart from the ideological trimmings these were old-fashioned manuals, which scarcely went beyond Aristotelian syllogistics and ignored modern symbolic logic: they resembled the textbooks used in nineteenth-century high schools. Asmus's work, however, was violently attacked for lack of party spirit and for being apolitical, formalistic, and deficient in ideology: these criticisms were made in a debate organized by the Ministry of Higher Education in Moscow in 1948. The chief ground for the charge of neglecting politics was that in giving examples of syllogistic reasoning Asmus chose 'neutral' propositions devoid of militant ideological content.

Modern logic was a sealed book to the philosophers; it was not completely ignored, however, thanks to a small group of mathematicians, who concentrated on technical problems and took care not to get involved in philosophical discussions, which could only have spelt disaster to them. Thanks to their efforts translations of two excellent books on symbolic logic were published in 1948: Alfred Tarski's *Introduction to Mathematical Logic* and *The Foundations of Theoretical Logic* by Hilbert and Ackermann. Articles in *Problems of Philosophy* by otherwise unknown authors denounced these works as an 'ideological diversion'. Some improvement in this sphere was brought in

1950 by Stalin's essay on philology, as the defenders of logic invoked it to support their view that logic, like language, was classless, i.e. there was not a bourgeois and a socialist form of logic but a single one valid for all mankind. The status of formal logic and its relation to dialectical logic was debated several times in and after the Stalin era. Some maintained that there were two kinds of logic, formal and dialectical, which applied to different circumstances, the former representing a 'lower level of cognition'; others held that only formal logic was logic in the true sense and that it did not conflict with the dialectic, which provided other, non-formal rules of scientific method. As a whole, the attacks on 'formalism' contributed to depressing the general level of logical studies in the U.S.S.R., which was already extremely low.

Soviet philosophy reached its nadir in the last years of Stalin's rule. Philosophical institutions and periodicals were run by people whose only qualifications were servility, tale-bearing, and similar services to the party. The textbooks of dialectical and historical materialism that saw the light during those years are lamentable in their intellectual poverty. Typical examples are *Historical Materialism*, edited by F. V. Konstantinov (1951) and *An Outline of Dialectical Materialism* by M. A. Leonov (1948): Leonov disappeared from circulation when it was discovered that his book was largely cribbed from the unpublished manuscript of another philosopher, F. I. Khaskhachikh, who was killed in the war. Other members of the 'philosophical front' besides those mentioned earlier were D. Chesnokov, P. Fedoseyev, M. T. Yovchuk, M. D. Kammari, M. E. Omelyanovsky (who, like Maksimov, was especially on the look-out for idealism in physics), S. A. Stepanyan, P. Yudin, and M. M. Rozental: these last two writers compiled an authoritative *Concise Dictionary of Philosophy* which ran through several editions and revisions.

It is safe to say that throughout the Stalin era there did not appear in the Soviet Union a single book on philosophy worth mentioning for its own sake and not merely as a pointer to the state of intellectual culture at the time, nor is there any philosophical writer whose name deserves to be recorded.

It should be added that in this period there were institutional mechanisms that cleansed philosophical works of all original ideas and all individuality of style. Most books were discussed before publication by one philosophical group or another, and it was the participants' duty to show party vigilance by pouncing on even the most timid attempts to exceed the bounds of the catechism in force. Sometimes several such operations were practised on the same text, and the result was that all the books were virtually identical. Leonov's case, mentioned above, is remarkable inasmuch as it might be thought that plagiarism could never have been detected, so closely did the authors' styles resemble one another.

4. *The economic debate*

At the same time as Zhdanov was dealing with the philosophers, economic science also underwent an ideological purge. The occasion was afforded in this case by Varga's book, published in 1946, on the effects of the Second World War on the capitalist economy. Jenő Varga (1879–1964), an eminent economist of Hungarian origin, had lived in the Soviet Union since the fall of Béla Kun's short-lived Communist republic and was the director of the Institute for World Economy, the purpose of which was to observe trends and predict crises in the capitalist system. In his book he sought to examine the permanent changes that the war had brought to the capitalist economy. It had obliged the bourgeois states to introduce a degree of economic planning and had vastly increased the functions of the state, especially in Britain and the U.S.A. The question of outlets for production had ceased to be decisive, and the struggle for markets was no longer a key factor in international affairs; the export of capital, however, had taken on greater importance. It was to be expected that overproduction in the U.S.A. and wartime destruction in Western Europe would combine to bring about a crisis situation which capitalism would seek to cure by the large-scale export of American capital to Europe. Varga's theories were debated in May 1947 and again in October 1948. His critics, and particularly K. V. Ostrovityanov, the chief economist of the Stalin era, accused him of believing that planning was possible under capitalism, of divorcing economics from politics, and of ignoring the class struggle. He had failed to perceive the general crisis of capitalism and, instead of emphasizing the power of capital over the bourgeois state, had made the mistake of supposing that the state was in control of capital. In addition Varga was accused of cosmopolitanism, kowtowing to Western science, reformism, objectivism, and underestimation of Lenin. The string of accusations was a conventional one, but the gist of Varga's book was indeed inimical to Stalinist ideology. His conclusion that capitalism had at its disposal more and more ways of remedying crisis situations, instead of fewer and fewer, was manifestly contrary to Lenin's teaching and to the party line for the past three decades, which held that the contradictions of capitalism were becoming more acute every day and that the universal crisis was more and more intense. Varga did not perform self-criticism after the first debate, but he finally did so in 1949; he was dismissed from his main functions, and the journal he edited was closed down. He was rehabilitated after Stalin's death, however, and repeated and developed his theses in a book published in 1964, in which he criticized Stalin and the dogmatic inability of Stalin's ideologists to recognize facts that conflicted with preconceived schemata. In a manuscript that was not published in Russia but reached the West after his death he went further still, maintaining that Lenin's plan of building socialism in Russia had proved a failure and that the bureaucratization of the Soviet system was in part due to Lenin's false prognoses.

5. Marxism–Leninism in physics and cosmology

A particularly blatant example of aggressive Stalinism was the ideological invasion of the natural sciences. Apart from mathematics, which was left unscathed, the campaign of Marxist regimentation affected all branches of science in some degree: theoretical physics, cosmology, chemistry, genetics, medicine, psychology, and cybernetics were all ravaged by the interference which reached its peak in 1948–53.

Soviet physicists, for the most part, were not anxious to engage in philosophical discussions, but in some spheres they were unavoidable: neither the quantum theory nor the theory of relativity could be fully expounded without bringing out certain epistemological assumptions. The question of determinism, and that of the effect of observation on the object observed, obviously had philosophical bearings, and this was recognized in discussions throughout the world.

Soviet Russia and Nazi Germany were the two countries in

which the theory of relativity was attacked and proscribed as contrary to official ideology. In the Soviet Union, as we have seen, the campaign started before the Second World War, but it was intensified in the post-war years. In Germany the indisputable argument against it was that Einstein was a Jew. In Russia this point was not raised, and the critics based their opposition on the teaching of Marxism–Leninism that time, space, and motion were objective and that the universe was infinite. Zhdanov in his address to the philosophers in 1947 inveighed against the disciples of Einstein who declared that the universe was finite. The philosophical critics also argued that, since time was objective, the relation of simultaneity must be absolute and not dependent on the frame of reference as the special theory of relativity maintained. In the same way motion was an objective property of matter, and therefore the path of a moving body could not be partly determined by the system of co-ordinates (an argument that of course applied against Galileo as well as Einstein). In general, since Einstein made temporal relations and movement dependent on the 'observer', i.e. on the human subject, he must be a subjectivist and thus an idealist. The philosophers who took part in these debates (A. A. Maksimov, G. I. Naan, M. E. Omelyanovsky, and others) did not confine their criticism to Einstein but attacked the whole of 'bourgeois science', their favourite targets being Eddington, Jeans, Heisenberg, Schrödinger, and all known methodologists of the physical sciences. Had not Einstein, moreover, admitted that he got his first ideas about relativity from Mach, whose obscurantist philosophy had been demolished by Lenin?

However, the essential point of the debate (which also touched, but only in a secondary fashion, on the general theory of relativity and the question of the homogeneity of space) did not reside in any 'contradiction' between the content of Einstein's theory and Marxism–Leninism. Marxist doctrine on time, space, and motion was not so precise that it could not be reconciled with Einsteinian physics without any special logical difficulty. It was even possible to contend that the relativity theory was a confirmation of dialectical materialism: this line of defence was adopted, in particular, by V. A. Fock, an eminent theoretical physicist, who at the same time produced scientific arguments for thinking that Einstein's theory was of limited validity. The campaign against Einstein—and indeed against most of the main achievements of modern science—had, however, two basic motives. In the first place, 'bourgeois versus socialist' meant practically the same as 'Western versus Soviet'. The state doctrine of Stalinism embraced Soviet chauvinism and demanded the systematic rejection of all the important achievements of 'bourgeois' culture, especially those dating from after 1917 when only one country in the world was the source of progress, while capitalism was in a state of decay and disruption. In addition to Soviet chauvinism there was a second motive. The simplistic doctrine of Marxism–Leninism coincided at many points with the common-sense everyday ideas of uneducated people: it was to these, for instance, that Lenin chiefly appealed in his attack on empiriocriticism. The theory of relativity, on the other hand, was undeniably to some extent an assault on common sense. The absoluteness of simultaneity, extension and motion, and the uniformity of space, are assumptions of everyday life that we accept as a matter of course, and Einstein's theory violated these in the same way as Galileo's paradoxical assertion that the earth revolves round the sun. Thus Einstein's critics were not only speaking for Soviet chauvinism but also for the ordinary conservatism that rejects theories inconsistent with the plain evidence of our senses.

The fight against 'idealism in physics' was also waged, with similar motives, against the quantum theory. The epistemological interpretation of quantum mechanics accepted by the Copenhagen school found favour with some Soviet physicists. The debate was triggered off by M. A. Markov's article of 1947, already mentioned. Markov followed Bohr and Heisenberg on two basic points which aroused the hostility of Marxist–Leninist philosophers. In the first place, as it is impossible simultaneously to measure the position and the momentum of microparticles, it is meaningless to say that a particle *has* a definite position and a definite momentum and that only a defect of observational technique prevents our measuring both at once. This point of view was in accord with the general empiric attitude of many physicists: the only real properties of objects are those that are empirically detectable, and to say that an object has a certain property but that there is no possibility of ascertaining it is either self-contradictory or meaningless. It must therefore be accepted that the particle does not have, simultaneously, a definite position and momentum, but that one or the other of these is attributed to it in the process of measurement. The second point of disagreement concerned the possibility of a literal description of the behaviour of micro-objects, which have different properties from macro-objects and therefore cannot be characterized in language evolved to describe the latter. Thus, according to Markov, theories describing microphysical phenomena are inevitably a translation into macrophysical terms: so that the microphysical reality that we know and can speak of meaningfully is partly constituted by processes of measurement and the language used to describe them. It followed that physical theories could not be spoken of as furnishing a copy of the universe under observation, and also, though Markov did not expressly say this, that the whole concept of reality, at least as far as microphysics was concerned, was inescapably relativized in respect of cognitive activity—which was manifestly contrary to Lenin's theory of reflection. Markov, therefore, was denounced by the new editors of *Problems of Philosophy* as an idealist, an agnostic, and a follower of Plekhanov's theory of 'hieroglyphs', refuted by Lenin.

It should be emphasized that, unlike the theory of relativity, quantum mechanics really were hard to reconcile with materialism and determinism in the Marxist–Leninist sense. If it is meaningless to say that particles have certain unascertainable physical parameters which define their status, the doctrine of determinism seems untenable; if the very presence of certain physical properties presupposes the presence of measuring devices used to detect them, it becomes impossible to apply meaningfully the concept of an 'objective' world observed by physics. These problems are by no means imaginary: they were and are discussed by physicists quite irrespective of Marxism–Leninism. In the Soviet Union they were debated rationally by D. I. Blokhintsev and V. A. Fock, among others, and the discussion continued into the post-Stalinist era. In the sixties, when party ideologists had less say in determining the 'correctness' of scientific theories, it became clear that most Soviet physicists took the indeterminist view, including Blokhintsev, who had previously held out for latent parameters.

In general the so-called discussions of the Stalin period on the philosophical aspects of physics and other sciences were destructive and anti-scientific not because they treated of unreal problems but because in the confrontation—as was usually the case—of scholars on the one hand and party ideologists on the other, the latter were assured of victory by the support of the state and its police apparatus. Charges of advancing theories inconsistent, or suspected of inconsistency, with Marxism–Leninism could and sometimes did turn into charges under the criminal code. The great majority of ideologists were ignorant of the points at issue and skilled only in ferreting out statements at variance with the words of Lenin or Stalin. Scientists who did not believe that Lenin was the greatest authority in physics and all other subjects were 'unmasked' in the popular press as enemies of the party, the state, and the Russian people. The 'debate' often degenerated into a political witch-hunt; the police were brought into play, and the resulting condemnations had nothing to do with rational argument. Almost all branches of modern knowledge underwent this treatment, and the party authorities regularly backed the noisy ignoramuses against scholars and scientists. If the term 'reactionary' has any meaning, it is hard to think of a more reactionary phenomenon than Marxism–Leninism in the Stalin era, which forcibly suppressed everything new and creative in science and in every other form of civilization.

Chemistry was not spared either. The years 1949–52 witnessed attacks in philosophical journals, and also in *Pravda*, against structural chemistry and the resonance theory, propounded in the 1930s by Pauling and Wheland and accepted by some Soviet chemists, but now denounced as idealistic, Machist, mechanistic, reactionary, etc.

Still more sensitive ideological themes were involved in debates on the philosophical aspects of modern theories of cosmology and cosmogony, from which it appeared that all existing answers to the basic questions were unfavourable to Marxism–Leninism. Various theories of an expanding universe were hard to accept because they inevitably involved the question 'How did it start?' and suggested that the universe as we know it was finite and had a beginning in time. This in turn gave support to creationism (an inference accepted by many

Western authors), and nothing worse could be imagined from the point of view of Marxism–Leninism. The supplementary theory that, while the universe went on expanding, the density of matter remained the same because new particles kept on coming into existence involved a process of constant creation *ex nihilo* and was thus contrary to the 'dialectic of nature'. Hence Western physicists and astronomers who argued for either of these two hypotheses were automatically written off as defenders of religion. The alternative theory of a pulsating universe, according to which the cosmos passes through alternative phases of expansion and contraction, was free from troublesome implications as regards a beginning in time, but it conflicted with the Marxist–Leninist doctrine of the unidirectional evolution of matter. A pulsating universe was a 'cyclic' one and could not be said to 'develop' or 'progress', as the 'second law of the dialectic' required. The dilemma was a difficult one: the unidirectional principle seemed to involve the idea of creation, while the opposite theory was contrary to the principle of 'endless development'. Those who took part in the cosmological discussions were, on the one hand, astronomers and astrophysicists (V. A. Ambartsumian, O. Y. Schmidt), who arrived at their conclusions by scientific methods and then tried to show that they were consonant with dialectical materialism, and, on the other, philosophers who judged the issue in terms of ideological orthodoxy. That the universe was unlimited by time and space, and that it must 'develop' eternally, were philosophical dogmas from which Marxism–Leninism could not possibly depart. In this way Soviet philosophers under the party's aegis dragooned men of learning in every field and did enormous harm to the cause of Soviet science.

6. *Marxist–Leninist genetics*

Of all the battles between Marxism–Leninism and modern science, the dispute over genetics attracted most attention in the outside world. The way in which the official state doctrine was used to solve the problem of heredity, and the destructive effect of the 'debate' generally, were indeed especially blatant. In the case of relativity and the quantum theory the champions of orthodoxy succeeded in holding up research and in obtaining certain condemnations, but they did not bring about the complete destruction of the opposition and the official and absolute prohibition of the theories complained of, as happened in the case of genetics.

We have already mentioned the pre-war phase of Lysenko's activity. The matter came to a climax in August 1948, at a debate in the Lenin Academy of Agricultural Sciences in Moscow. Here the 'Mendelist–Morganist–Weissmannists' were finally condemned and Lysenko's view endorsed by the party's Central Committee, as he himself announced to the meeting. His doctrine, which the party declared to be the only one consistent with Marxism–Leninism, was that heredity was 'ultimately' determined by environmental influences, so that in certain conditions traits acquired by individual organisms in the course of their lives could be inherited by their progeny. There were no genes, no 'unchanging substance of heredity', no 'fixed unalterable species', and there was in principle nothing to prevent science, especially Soviet science, from transforming existing species and creating new ones. Heredity, according to Lysenko, was merely a property of an organism consisting in the fact that it needed particular conditions in which to live and reacted in a particular way to its environment. An individual organism in the course of its life interacted with environmental conditions and turned them into characteristics of its own that could be transmitted to its progeny—which might in turn lose those characters or acquire new ones transmissible by heredity, as external conditions might determine. The adversaries of progressive science, who believed in an immortal hereditary substance, claimed in opposition to Marxism that mutations were subject to uncontrollable accident; but, as Lysenko argued at the Academy session, 'science is the enemy of chance' and is bound to assume that all processes of life are subject to rule and can be governed by human intervention. Organisms formed a 'unity with their environment', and therefore there was no limit in principle to the possibility of influencing an organism through its environment.

Lysenko presented his theory in the first place as a development of the ideas and experiments of the agronomist Michurin (1855–1935), and secondly as an example of 'creative Darwinism'. Darwin had gone wrong in so far as he did not recognize 'qualitative leaps' in nature and regarded the intra-species struggle (survival of the fittest) as the main factor in evolution; but he had explained evolution in purely causal terms, not resorting to teleological interpretations, and had brought out the 'progressive' character of evolutionary processes.

As to the empirical basis of Lysenko's theory, biologists today have no doubt that his experiments were scientifically worthless and were either faultily conducted or interpreted in a purely arbitrary manner. This, of course, did not affect the debate in the slightest. Lysenko emerged from the 1948 session as the unquestioned leader of Soviet biological sciences: the few disciples of idealistic, mystic, scholastic, metaphysical, bourgeois, formal genetics were irrevocably crushed. All institutions, journals, and publishing enterprises concerned with biology were put under the authority of Lysenko and his helpers, and for many years there was no question of any defender of the chromosome theory of heredity (*ex hypothesi* a Fascist, racist, metaphysician, etc.) being allowed to speak in public or appear in print. 'Creative Michurinist biology' reigned supreme, and the press was flooded with propaganda extolling Lysenko and denouncing the wicked plots of the Mendelist–Morganists. The glorious triumph of Soviet science was celebrated at innumerable meetings and congresses. The philosophers, of course, at once joined in the campaign, organizing sessions and passing resolutions against bourgeois genetics and writing a multitude of articles hailing the victory of progress over reaction. Humorous journals pilloried the adherents of idealistic genetics, and a song was written in praise of Lysenko, 'marching firmly in Michurin's traces and foiling the deceits of the Mendelist–Morganists'.

Lysenko's career continued for some years after 1948. Meanwhile, under his direction, some steppe areas were planted with forest belts to protect the fields against erosion, but the experiment proved a complete failure. In 1956, during the partial ideological thaw after Stalin's death, as a result of pressure from scientists he was removed from the presidency of the Academy of Agricultural Sciences. Some years later he was restored to his various posts owing to Khrushchev's favour, but not long afterwards, to the general relief, he finally disappeared from the scene. The losses that Soviet biology suffered from his ascendancy are incalculable.

7. General effect on Soviet science

The Lysenko affair illustrates the considerable degree of for-
tuitousness in the history of the regime's battle with culture.
It is easy to see that ideology was much more clearly involved
in questions of cosmogony than in the matter of the inheritance
of acquired characters. The theory that the universe had a
beginning in time is hard to reconcile with dialectical materialism, but this is not obviously the case with the chromosome
theory of heredity, and one can easily imagine Marxism–
Leninism triumphantly proclaiming that this theory resound-
ingly confirmed the immortal ideas of Marx–Engels–Lenin–
Stalin. Yet in fact the ideological struggle was especially acute
in the case of genetics, and it was here that the party's intervention took its most brutal form, whereas the agitation over
cosmogony was much milder. It is hard to find any logical
explanation of the difference: much depended on accident, on
who was in charge of the campaign, whether Stalin was interested
in the point at issue, and so on.

Nevertheless, if we take a panoramic view of the history of
those years we may perceive a certain gradation of ideological
pressure, corresponding roughly to the hierarchy of the sciences
established by Comte and Engels. Pressure was almost zero in
mathematics, fairly strong in cosmology and physics, stronger
still in the biological sciences, and all-powerful in the social and
human sciences. The chronological order roughly reflected these
degrees of importance: the social sciences were regimented from
the outset, while biology and physics were not controlled until
the last phase of Stalinism. In the post-Stalin era it was physics
that first regained its independence; biology followed after a
certain time, while the humanistic sciences remained under fairly
strict control.

The fortuitous element in ideological supervision can also be
seen in the case of psychology and the physiology of the higher
nervous functions. The special feature here was that Russia was
the birthplace of Ivan P. Pavlov, a scientist of world repute.
Pavlov, who died in 1936, had several pupils who continued
his experiments and were allowed to develop his theories
independently of ideological pressure. Typically, the regime went
to the opposite extreme and erected his theory into an official

dogma from which physiologists and psychologists were forbidden to deviate. It is safe to say that if Pavlov had been British or American his ideas would have been sternly condemned by Soviet philosophers as mechanistic on the ground that they explained mental functions by conditioned reflexes: he would have been accused of 'reducing' the human mind to the lowest forms of nervous activity, ignoring the 'qualitative difference' between men and animals, and so forth. As it was, Pavlov's theory officially represented Marxism–Leninism in the field of neurophysiology, and the ideological invasion in this field was less devastating than elsewhere. None the less, the very fact that a theory, albeit based on serious scientific experiment, was erected into a state and party dogma inevitably had a cramping effect on further research.

A particularly astonishing example of ideology running counter to the interests of the Soviet state was the attack on cybernetics, the science of systems of control of dynamic processes. Cybernetic studies had made a major contribution to the development of automation in all technical fields and especially in military technology, economic planning, etc., yet the champions of Marxist–Leninist purity were able for a time completely to hold up the progress of automation in the Soviet Union. In 1952–3 a campaign was mounted against the imperialist 'pseudo-science' of cybernetics. There were indeed real philosophical or semi-philosophical problems involved: whether and how far social life could be described in cybernetic categories, in what sense mental activities were 'reducible' to cybernetic schemata, or, conversely, in what sense certain functions of artificial mechanisms could be equated with thought, and so on. But the real ideological danger was that cybernetics was a discipline of wide scope, developed in the West and claiming, rightly or wrongly, to be a *mathesis universalis*, a general all-embracing theory of dynamic phenomena: for this was precisely what Marxism–Leninism claimed to be. According to unofficial reports (not, of course, confirmed by any public information), it was the military who finally put a stop to the campaign against cybernetics, as they realized the practical importance of the subject and were strong enough to combat the obscurantist attacks which were damaging the fundamental interests of the Soviet state.

8. Stalin on philology

In the first few days of the Korean War, when international tension was at its height, Stalin added to his existing titles as the leader of progressive humanity, the supreme philosopher, scientist, strategist, etc., the further distinction of being the world's greatest philologist. (As far as is known, his linguistic attainments were confined to Russian and his native Georgian.) In May 1950 *Pravda* had published a symposium on the theoretical problems of linguistics and especially the theories of Nikolay Y. Marr (1864–1934). Marr, a specialist in the Caucasian languages, had endeavoured towards the end of his life to construct a system of Marxist linguistics and was regarded in the Soviet Union as the supreme authority in this field: linguists who rejected his fantasies were harassed and persecuted. His theory was that language was a form of 'ideology' and, as such, belonged to the superstructure and was part of the class system. The evolution of language took place by 'qualitative leaps' corresponding to qualitative changes in social formations. Before mankind developed spoken language it used the language of gesture, corresponding to the primitive classless society. Spoken language was a feature of class societies, and in the class-less community of the future it would be replaced by a universal thought-language (of which, to be sure, Marr was unable to give much account). The whole theory showed signs of paranoid delusion, and the fact that it ranked for years as linguistic science *par excellence* and the only 'progressive' philological theory is eloquent testimony to the state of Soviet culture.

Stalin intervened in the debate with an article published in *Pravda* on 29 June, followed by four explanatory answers to readers' letters. He roundly condemned Marr's theory, declaring that language was not part of the superstructure and was not ideological in character. It was not part of the base either, but was directly 'linked' with creative forces. It belonged to society as a whole and not to particular classes: class-determined expressions were only a small fraction of the general vocabulary. Nor was it true that language developed by 'qualitative leaps' or 'explosions': it changed gradually, as some features died out and new ones came into being. When two languages competed the result was not a new composite language but the victory

of one or other. As to the future 'withering-away' of language
and its replacement by thought, Marr was fundamentally wrong:
thought was linked with language and could not exist without
it. People thought in words. Stalin took occasion to repeat the
Marxist theory of the base and superstructure, making clear,
firstly, that the base does not consist of productive forces but
of relations of production, and secondly, that the superstructure
'serves' the base as its instrument. He went on to condemn in
strong terms the monopoly position that Marrism had acquired
by the suppression of free discussion and criticism—an 'Arak-
cheyev regime' (alluding to the despotic minister of Alexander I's
reign) under which learning obviously could not develop
properly.

The proposition that language was not a class matter and
not part of the superstructure meant simply that French capitalists and French workers both speak French, and that the Russians
went on speaking Russian after the Revolution. This discovery
was hailed as a historic breakthrough in the history of philology
and of other sciences. A wave of academic sessions and debates
swept through the country, glorifying the new work of genius.
In reality, although Stalin's remarks were no more than sensible
truisms they served a useful purpose by clearing away Marr's
absurdities, and they were of some benefit to the study of formal
logic and semantics: advocates of these subjects could claim that
they too were not part of the superstructure and that pursuing
them did not necessarily turn one into a class enemy. As for
Stalin's remarks about the 'auxiliary function' of the superstructure in relation to the base, these were a repetition of the
basic doctrine, already well known to all, that culture in socialist
countries was the handmaiden of 'political objectives' and must
not lay claim to independence. It need hardly be said that
Stalin's call for free discussion and criticism had no effect
whatever in other cultural fields. The Marrists were ousted from
the domain of linguistics (though it is not known that they
suffered police repression), while elsewhere things remained as
before.

9. *Stalin on the Soviet economy*

Stalin's last theoretical work was an article in the party journal
Bolshevik in September 1952, entitled 'Economic Problems of

Socialism in the U.S.S.R.' and intended as a basic document for the forthcoming Nineteenth Congress. Its main theoretical argument was that socialism too was subject to the 'objective laws of economics', of which advantage should be taken in planning and which could not be arbitrarily set aside. In particular the law of value applied under socialism—a statement which probably meant that money was in use in the Soviet Union, and that in running the economy account should be taken of profitability and the balancing of revenue and expenditure. The principle of the 'objectivity of the economic laws of socialism' was an implied condemnation of Nikolay Voznesensky, who was head of the State Planning Commission before the war and afterwards deputy Premier and a member of the Politburo. He had been shot as a traitor in 1950, and his book on the Soviet economy during the war with Germany was withdrawn from circulation. By implication it denied that socialism was subject to objective economic laws, maintaining instead that all economic processes were subordinate to the state's planning power. Stalin, however, in his defence of the law of value assured his readers that whereas capitalism was governed by the principle of maximum profit, the guiding rule of the socialist economy was the maximum satisfaction of human needs. (It was not clear how, as Stalin contended, the beneficent effect of socialism could be an 'objective law' independent of the will of the state planning authorities, and in particular how this 'law' could operate simultaneously with the 'law of value'.) Stalin's article also outlined a programme for the transition of the Soviet Union to the communist stage: for this it would be necessary to do away with the opposition between town and country and between physical and mental work, to raise collective farm property to the status of national property (i.e., in effect, to turn the collective farms into state farms), and to increase production and the general level of culture.

Stalin's thoughts on the perfect communist society of the future were a repetition of traditional Marxist motifs. As to the 'objective laws of economics', the only practical message that could be derived from the article was, apparently, that while those responsible for the economy endeavoured to satisfy the population's needs to the maximum, they should not lose sight of economic accountability.

10. General features of Soviet culture in Stalin's last years

The peculiarities of Soviet cultural life at this period were not simply due to Stalin's idiosyncrasies. They might be summed up in a word by saying that the nation's culture was that of a parvenu—its every feature expressing almost to perfection the mentality, beliefs, and tastes of someone enjoying power for the first time. Stalin himself exemplified these peculiarities in a high degree, but they were also characteristic of the whole governing apparatus, which, while he reduced it to serfdom, continued to support him and maintain his supreme authority.

After successive purges and the extermination of the Bolshevik old guard and the former intelligentsia, the Soviet governing class consisted mainly of individuals of worker and peasant origin, very poorly educated and with no cultural background, athirst for privilege and filled with hatred and envy towards genuine 'hereditary' intellectuals. The essential trait of the parvenu is his incessant urge to 'make a show', and accordingly his culture is one of make-believe and window-dressing. A parvenu has no peace of mind as long as he sees about him representatives of the intellectual culture of the former privileged classes, which he hates because he is shut out from it, and which he therefore decries as bourgeois or aristocratic. The parvenu is a fanatical nationalist, wedded to the notion that his native country or milieu is superior to all others. His language is, in his eyes, 'language' *par excellence* (he generally knows no other), and he endeavours to convince himself and everyone else that his meagre cultural resources are the finest in the world. He detests anything that smacks of the *avant-garde*, cultural experimentation, or creative novelty. He lives by a restricted set of 'common-sense' maxims and is furious when they are challenged by anyone.

These features of the parvenu mentality can be recognized in the essential traits of Stalinist culture: its nationalism, the aesthetics of 'socialist realism', and even the system of power itself. The parvenu combines a peasant-like subservience to authority with an overmastering desire to share in it; once raised to a certain level in the hierarchy he will grovel to his superiors and trample on those beneath him. Stalin was the idol of parvenu Russia, the incarnation of its dreams of glory. The parvenu state must have a pyramid of power and a leader who is worshipped even while he scourges his subordinates.

As we have seen, Stalinist cultural nationalism developed gradually in the pre-war years, and after victory it took on gigantic proportions. In 1949 the Press launched a campaign against 'cosmopolitanism', a vice that was not defined but evidently entailed being anti-patriotic and glorifying the West. As the campaign developed, it was intimated more and more clearly that a cosmopolitan was much the same thing as a Jew. When individuals were pilloried and had previously borne Jewish-sounding names, these were generally mentioned. 'Soviet patriotism' was indistinguishable from Russian chauvinism and became an official mania. Propaganda declared incessantly that all important technical inventions and discoveries had been made by Russians, and to mention foreigners in this context was to be guilty of cosmopolitanism and kowtowing to the West. The *Great Soviet Encyclopedia*, published from the end of 1949 onwards, is an unsurpassed example of this half-comical and half-macabre megalomania. The historical section of the article on 'Motor Cars', for example, starts by saying that 'In 1751–2 Leonty Shamshugenkov (q.v.), a peasant in the Nizhny Novgorod province, constructed a self-propelling vehicle operated by two men.' 'Bourgeois', i.e. Western, culture was constantly attacked as a hotbed of corruption and decadence. Here, for example, is an extract from the entry on Bergson.

French bourgeois philosopher—idealist, reactionary in politics and philosophy. B.'s philosophy of intuitionism, disparaging the role of reason and science, and his mystical theory of society serve as a basis for imperialist policies. His views present a glaring picture of the decay of bourgeois ideology in the imperialist age, the growing aggressiveness of the bourgeoisie in the face of increasing class contradictions and its fear of the intensified class struggle of the proletariat ... In the period of the incipient general crisis of capitalism and the intensification of all its contradictions B. appeared as a rabid enemy of materialism, atheism and scientific knowledge, an enemy of democracy and the liberation of the toiling masses from class oppression, disguising his philosophy with pseudo-scientific trimmings ... B. sought to present as a 'new' justification of idealism the view of ancient mystics and medieval theologians, long since disproved by life, practice and science, concerning cognition by 'inner vision' ... Dialectical materialism refutes the idealist theory of intuition by the indisputable fact that

knowledge of the world and reality does not take place by some kind
of supersensual means but through the socio-historical practice of
humanity ... B.'s intuitionism expresses the fear of the imperialist
bourgeoisie before the inevitably looming collapse of capitalism, the
urge to escape from the irrefutable implications of the scientific
knowledge of reality and especially the laws of social development
discovered by Marxist–Leninist science ... An enemy of national
sovereignty, B. advocated bourgeois cosmopolitanism, the rule of world
capitalism, bourgeois religion and morality. B. favoured the cruel
bourgeois dictatorship and terrorist method of stifling the workers.
Between the First and Second World Wars this militant obscurantist
argued that imperialist wars were 'necessary' and 'beneficial'...

Here, again, is a portion of the entry on 'Impressionism':

Decadent trend in bourgeois art in the second half of the 19th century.
I. was the result of the incipient decay of bourgeois art (see *Decadence*)
and the break with progressive national traditions. The adherents of I.
advocated an empty, anti-popular programme of 'art for art's sake',
rejected the truthful, realistic depiction of objective reality and claimed
that the artist should record only his primary subjective impressions....
The subjective-idealist attitude of I. is related to the principles of
contemporaneous reactionary trends in philosophy—neo-Kantianism,
Machism (q.v.) etc., which denied objectivity and the reliability of
knowledge, divorced perception from reality and reason from impressions ... Rejecting the criterion of objective truthfulness, indifferent
to mankind, social phenomena and the social functions of art, the
adherents of I. inevitably produced works in which the picture of
reality disintegrated and artistic form was lost...

The isolation of the Soviet Union from world culture was
almost complete. Apart from a few propaganda works by
Western Communists the Soviet reader was kept in total ignorance of what the West was producing in the way of novels,
poetry, plays, films, not to speak of philosophy and the social
sciences. The rich stores of twentieth-century painting in the
Hermitage at Leningrad were kept in cellars so as not to corrupt
the honest citizen. Soviet films and plays unmasked bourgeois
scholars who served the cause of war and imperialism, and
praised the unexampled joys of Soviet life. 'Socialist realism'
reigned supreme: not, of course, in the sense of presenting Soviet
reality as it actually was—that would have been crude naturalism and a kind of formalism—but in the sense of educating Soviet
people to love their country and Stalin. The 'socialist realist'

architecture of the period is the most permanent monument to Stalinist ideology. Here too the ruling principle was the 'primacy of content over form', though no one could explain how these were distinguished in architecture. The effect, in any case, was to produce pompous façades in a style of exaggerated Byzantinism. At a time when scarcely any dwellings were being built and millions of people in large and small towns were living in crowded squalor, Moscow and other cities were adorned with huge new palaces full of false columns and spurious ornament, of a size proportionate to the 'magnificence of the Stalin era'. This again was a typical parvenu style of architecture, which could be summed up in the motto: 'Big is beautiful.'

The keystone of the whole ideology was the cult of the Leader, which took on grotesque and monstrous forms at this period and has probably never been surpassed in history except by the later cult of Mao Tse-tung. Poems, novels, and films glorifying Stalin poured out in a constant stream; pictures and monuments of him decorated all public places. Writers, poets, and philosophers vied with one another in inventing new forms of dithyrambic worship. Children in crèches and kindergartens expressed heartfelt thanks to Stalin for their happy childhood. All the forms of popular religiosity were revived in a distorted shape: icons, processions, prayers recited in chorus, confession of sins (under the name of self-criticism), the cult of relics. Marxism in this way became a parody of religion, but one devoid of content. Here, chosen at random, is a typical exordium from a philosophical work of the time:

Comrade Stalin, the great master of the sciences, has given a systematic exposition of the foundations of dialectical and historical materialism as the theoretical basis of Communism, in a study unsurpassed for its depth, clarity and vigour. The theoretical works of Comrade Stalin were admirably described by the Central Committee of the All-Union Communist Party (Bolsheviks) and the Council of Ministers of the USSR in an address to Comrade Stalin on his seventieth birthday: 'Great leader of science! Your classic works developing the theory of Marxism–Leninism in relation to the new age of imperialism, proletarian revolution and socialist victory in our country are a tremendous achievement of humanity, an encyclopedia of revolutionary Marxism. From these works Soviet men and women and leading representatives of the working people of all countries derive knowledge and confidence and new strength in the battle for the victory of the cause of the working class, finding in them answers to the most burning problems of the contemporary struggle for Communism.' Comrade Stalin's brilliant philosophical work on *Dialectical and Historical Materialism* is a powerful means of knowledge and revolutionary transformation of the world and an irresistible ideological weapon against the enemies of materialism and the decaying ideology and culture of the capitalist world, doomed to inevitable overthrow. It is a new, supreme stage in the development of the Marxist–Leninist world-view ... In his work Comrade Stalin has with unsurpassed clarity and conciseness expounded the basic features of the Marxist dialectical method and indicated their importance for the understand-ing of the regular development of nature and society. With the same depth, force, conciseness and party-political determination Comrade Stalin formulates in his work the basic features of Marxist philosophical materialism ... (V. M. Pozner, *J. V. Stalin on the Basic Features of Marxist Philosophical Materialism*, 1950)

Stalin was extolled indirectly as well, through the great heroes of Russian history. Films and novels about Peter the Great, Ivan the Terrible, and Alexander Nevsky were made into tributes to his glory. (However, Eisenstein's film praising Ivan the Terrible and, at Stalin's express order, his *oprichnina* or secret police was not screened during Stalin's lifetime because it showed how the Tsar was obliged, albeit with a heavy heart, to cut off the heads of the most inveterate conspirators—even though the spectator is left in no doubt that they were double-dyed villains who merited no less, and that Ivan did the very least that could be expected of a prudent statesman.) Stalin, who was of low stature, was shown in films and plays as a tall, handsome man, considerably taller than Lenin.

The hierarchical structure of Soviet bureaucracy was seen in the fact that the cult of Stalin cast its shadow on lesser mortals. In many fields of life, though not in all, there was an individual who was known to be officially the 'greatest' in his line. Apart from the many instances in which Stalin himself held the top position—as philosopher, theoretician, statesman, strategist, economist, etc.—it was known, for example, who was the greatest painter, biologist, or circus clown. (The circus, incidentally had been ideologically reformed in 1949 by an article in *Pravda* which condemned bourgeois formalism in this domain. There were, it appeared, some performers who lapsed into cosmopolitan forms of humour, without ideological content, and tried simply to make people laugh instead of educating them to deal with the class enemy.)

During this period the falsification of history and pressure on the historical sciences reached a climax. It became the task of historians to show that the foreign policy of Tsarist Russia was essentially progressive, especially its conquests, which brought the blessings of Russian civilization to other peoples. The fourth edition of Lenin's works contained some new documents but suppressed others, including some unduly categorical remarks about the impossibility of building socialism in one country, and an enthusiastic preface to John Reed's *Ten Days That Shook the World*. Reed, who was in Petrograd during the October Revolution, had much to say about Lenin and Trotsky but did not mention Stalin at all, so that it was an unpardonable *gaffe* of Lenin's to commend his book to the world. The new edition also omitted, almost in their entirety, some very valuable historical comments and notes whose authors had perished in the purges. (This method of re-editing the past did not come to an end on Stalin's death: a few months later, when Beriya was put to death by the new leaders, subscribers to the *Great Soviet Encyclopedia* found a note in the next volume telling them to excise certain earlier pages with a razor blade and insert the new pages that accompanied the note. On turning up the place referred to, the reader found that it was the article on Beriya; the substitute pages, however, were not about Beriya at all but contained additional photographs of the Bering Sea.) Historical archives, without exception, were in the hands of the police, and access to them was strictly regulated, as it still is today. This often proved to be a wise measure: for instance, a woman journalist once discovered in old parish archives that Lenin's mother was of Jewish extraction, and even had the naïvety to attempt to publish this information in the Soviet Press.

This atmosphere naturally bred all kinds of scientific impostors who proclaimed their achievements in suitably patriotic language. Lysenko was the most famous, but there were many others. A biologist named Olga Lepeshinskaya announced in 1950 that she had succeeded in producing live cells from inanimate organic substances, and this was acclaimed by the Press as a proof of the superiority of Soviet science over the bourgeois kind. Soon, however, all her experiments turned out to be valueless. After Stalin's death a still more sensational article appeared in *Pravda* to the effect that a machine had been constructed in a Saratov factory which gave out more energy than it consumed—thus finally disposing of the second law of thermodynamics and at the same time confirming Engels's statement that the energy dispersed in the universe must also be concentrated somewhere (in the Saratov factory, to be specific). Soon afterwards, however, *Pravda* had to publish a shamefaced recantation—a sign that the intellectual atmosphere had already changed.

The written and spoken word faithfully reflected the atmosphere of Stalin's day. The purpose of public utterances was not to inform, but to instruct and edify. The Press contained only reports glorifying the Soviet system or discrediting the imperialists. The Soviet Union was immune not only from crime but from natural disasters: both were the unhappy prerogative of the imperialist countries. Virtually no statistics were published. Newspaper readers were used to gaining information from a special code that was known to all though never openly formulated: for instance, the order in which party dignitaries were named on this or that occasion was an index of how high they stood in Stalin's favour at that moment. On the face of things it might seem that 'Let us fight against cosmopolitanism and nationalism' was the same as 'Let us fight against nationalism and cosmopolitanism'; but as soon as the Soviet reader came across the latter formulation after Stalin's death he realized that 'the line had changed' and that nationalism was now the principal enemy. The language of Soviet ideology was composed of hints and not of direct statements: readers of leading articles in *Pravda* knew that their gist was usually contained in a single throwaway sentence amid the flood of clichés. It was not the content of particular statements that conveyed the meaning, but the order of words and the structure of the whole text. Bureaucratic monotony of language, an impersonal deadness, and an impoverished vocabulary became fixed canons of socialist culture. Many set phrases recurred automatically, so that from each word one could predict the next: 'the bestial face of imperialism', 'the glorious achievements of the Soviet people', 'the unshakeable friendship of the socialist nations', 'the immortal works of the classic authors of Marxism–Leninism'—countless stereotypes of this sort became the intellectual diet of millions of Soviet people.

Stalin's philosophy was admirably suited to the parvenu bureaucratic mentality, in both form and content. Thanks to his exposition anyone could become a philosopher in half an hour, not only in full possession of the truth but aware of all the absurd and nonsensical ideas of bourgeois philosophers. Kant, for instance, said it was impossible to know anything, but we Soviet people know lots of things, and so much for Kant. Hegel said that the world changes, but he thought the world consisted of ideas, whereas anyone can see that what we have around us are not ideas but things. The Machists said that the desk I am sitting at is in my head; but obviously my head is in one place and the desk in another. On these lines philosophy became the playground of every petty official, who had the satisfaction of knowing that by repeating a few common-sense truisms he had disposed of all philosophical problems.

11. *The cognitive status of dialectical materialism*

The social function of 'diamat' and 'histmat', as they are familiarly called, and of Soviet Marxism–Leninism in general, consists in the fact that it is an ideology used by the governing bureaucracy to glorify itself and justify its policies, including those of imperialist expansion. All the philosophical and historical principles of which Marxism–Leninism is composed reach their culmination and final meaning in a few simple propositions. Socialism, defined as state ownership of the means of production, is historically the highest form of social order and represents the interests of all working people; the Soviet system is therefore the embodiment of progress and, as such, is automatically right against any adversary. The official philosophy and social theory are merely the self-praising rhetoric of the privileged Soviet ruling class.

We may, however, disregard the social aspect for a moment and consider dialectical materialism in its Stalinist form as a corpus of statements about the universe. Concentrating on the main aspects of 'diamat' and leaving aside the many critical remarks we have already made in connection with the views of Marx, Engels, and Lenin, we may make the following observations.

'Diamat' consists of assertions of different kinds. Some are truisms with no specific Marxist content, while others are philosophical dogmas that cannot be proved by scientific means. Others again are nonsense, while a fourth category consists of propositions that can be interpreted in different ways and, according to their interpretation, fall into one or other of the first three classes.

Among the truisms are such 'laws of dialectic' as the statement that everything in the universe is somehow related, or that everything changes. No one denies these propositions, but they are of very little cognitive or scientific value. The former statement has, it is true, a certain philosophical bearing in other contexts, for example, the metaphysics of Leibniz or Spinoza, but in Marxism–Leninism it does not lead to any consequences of cognitive or practical importance. Everyone knows that phenomena are interconnected, but the problem of scientific analysis is not how to take account of the universal interconnection, since this is what we cannot do, but how to determine which connections are important and which can be disregarded. All that Marxism–Leninism can tell us here is that in the chain of phenomena there is always a 'main link' to be grasped. This seems to mean only that in practice certain connections are important in view of the end pursued, and others less important or negligible. But this is a commonplace of no cognitive value, as we cannot derive from it any rule for establishing the hierarchy of importance in any particular case. The same is true of the proposition that 'everything changes': cognitive value attaches only to empirical descriptions of particular changes, their nature, tempo, etc. Heraclitus' aphorism had a philosophical meaning in his day, but it soon sank into the category of common-sense, everyday wisdom.

The fact that truisms like these are represented as profound discoveries, known from no other source, led the adherents of Marxism–Leninism to proclaim that Marxism was confirmed by 'science'. Since the empirical and historical sciences are concerned generally with the fact that something changes or that it is connected with something else, it is safe to assume that each new scientific discovery will confirm the truth of 'Marxism' as thus understood.

Turning to the category of unprovable dogmas, the first of

these is the main thesis of materialism itself. The analytical
standard of Marxism philosophy is so low that this thesis is seldom
clearly formulated, but its general implication is plain enough.
As we have pointed out, the statement that 'the world is material
by nature' loses all meaning if matter is defined, after Lenin's
fashion, as mere 'objectivity' in abstraction from its physical
properties, or, as Lenin also put it, as 'being, independent of
consciousness'. For, leaving aside the fact that the concept of
consciousness is thus included in the very concept of matter,
the statement that 'the world is material' turns out to mean
only that the world is independent of consciousness. But this,
if applied to the whole universe, is manifestly false—since some
phenomena, as Marxism–Leninism itself admits, are dependent
on consciousness—and anyway it does not make the case for
materialism, since, for example, according to religious ideas God,
the angels, and devils are likewise independent of human
consciousness. If, on the other hand, matter is defined by
physical properties—extension, impenetrability, etc.—there is
reason to think that some of these may not apply to micro-
objects, which would thus prove not to be 'material'. In its
earliest versions materialism assumed that all existent objects
had the same properties as those of everyday life. Basically,
however, its thesis was a negative one, namely that there was
no reality essentially different from that which we perceive
directly, and that the world was not created by a rational being.
This was Engels's own formulation: the point at issue in materialism was whether or not God created the world. Clearly there
can be no empirical proof that he either did or did not, and
no scientific arguments can prove that God does not exist.
Rationalism rejects the existence of God on the principle of the
economy of thought (a principle which Lenin denied), not on
the strength of any empirical information. This doctrine presupposes that we are only entitled to accept that something
exists if experience compels us to do so. But this stipulation is
itself debatable and rests on assumptions that are far from
obvious. Without going into the issue here we may take note
that the principle of materialism, thus reformulated, is not a
scientific but a dogmatic statement. The same applies to 'spiritual
substance' and the 'non-materiality of human consciousness'.
Men have always known that consciousness is affected by physical

processes: it did not take much scientific observation, for instance, to discover that a man could be stunned by clubbing him over the head, and subsequent research into the mind's dependence on the body has added nothing essential to our knowledge on the point. Those who believe in a non-material substratum of consciousness do not maintain that there is no link between consciousness and the body (if they do, like Descartes, Leibniz, or Malebranche, they have to devise complicated and artificial ways of accounting for the facts of experience): they assert only that while bodily processes can suspend the operation of the human spirit, they cannot destroy it—the body is a medium through which consciousness functions, but is not an essential condition of its functioning. This assertion cannot be proved empirically, but it cannot be disproved either. Nor is it the case, as Marxists claim, that the theory of evolution has refuted the argument for a non-material soul. If the human organism has evolved by mutation from lower forms of life, it does not logically follow that the soul does not exist. If it were so, there could not be such a thing as a consistent theory combing, on the one hand, a modern view of evolution and, on the other, a non-material substratum of consciousness, or even a teleological view of the world. But there have been several such theories, from Frohschammer through Bergson to Teilhard de Chardin, and it is far from clear that they involve any inconsistency. Christian philosophers have also found various ways of immunizing dogma from the theory of evolution, and while these may be open to objection it cannot be said that they are self-contradictory. Judged by the criteria of validity that are applied in scientific work, the materialist thesis is no less arbitrary in this respect than its opposite.

Among what I have called the nonsensical assertions of 'diamat' is the statement that impressions 'reflect' things in the sense of resembling them, as Lenin contended against Plekhanov. It is not clear what can be meant by asserting that a process taking place in the nerve-cells, or even the 'subjective' awareness of such a process, bears a 'resemblance' to those objects or processes in the outside world which, the theory informs us, are the cause of such changes in the nerve-cells. Another non-sensical statement (never specifically endorsed by Stalin, but advanced by Plekhanov and regularly repeated in expositions of Marxism) is that formal logic 'applies' to phenomena at rest, and dialectical logic to changes. This absurdity, which is not worth discussing, is simply the result of the Marxist–Leninists' ignorance and failure to understand the terms of formal logic.

Other assertions, as stated above, belong to one or other of the first three categories according to how one interprets them. Among these is the 'dialectical law' concerning 'contradictions'. If, as many Soviet textbooks inform us, this means that motion and change can be 'explained' by 'inner contradictions', it belongs to the class of meaningless statements, since 'contradiction' is a logical category denoting a relation between propositions, and it is impossible to say what is meant by 'contradictory phenomena'. (Impossible, at least, from the materialist point of view; in the metaphysics of Hegel, Spinoza, and some others who identify logical and ontological connections, the idea of Being involving a contradiction is not meaningless.) If, on the other hand, we interpret the statement as meaning that reality must be apprehended as a system of tensions and opposing tendencies, this seems to be no more than a truism with no specific consequences for scientific investigation or practical action. That many phenomena affect one another, that human societies are divided by conflict and discordant interests, that people's acts often bring about results they did not intend— these are all commonplaces, and to extol them as a 'dialectical method', the profundity of which contrasts with 'metaphysical' thinking, is only one more instance of the typical Marxist boastfulness which presents time-honoured truisms as momentous scientific discoveries imparted to the world by Marx or Lenin.

To this category also belongs the assertion, discussed in an earlier part of this work, that truth is relative. If this is no more than to say, as Engels noted, that in the history of science received opinions are often not abandoned altogether as a result of later research but that their validity is recognized as limited, there is no reason to dispute the accuracy of the statement, but it is in no way specifically Marxist. If, on the other hand, it means that 'we cannot know everything' or 'a judgement may be right in some circumstances but not in others', these again are ancient truisms. We did not, for example, need Marx's intellect to discover that rain is beneficial in time of drought but not in flood-time. This, of course, does not mean, as has often been pointed out, that the statement 'rain is beneficial' is true or false according to circumstances; it means that the statement is ambiguous. If it means 'rain is beneficial in all circumstances' it is clearly false; if it means 'in some circumstances', it is clearly true. If, however, we interpret the Marxist principle of the relativity of truth to signify that a statement, without changing its meaning, may be true or false according to circumstances, then this too belongs to the category of nonsense, assuming that, with Lenin, we take the traditional view of what constitutes truth. If, on the other hand, a 'truthful judgement' means the same as 'a judgement useful to the Communist party', then the principle of the relativity of truth once more becomes an obvious commonplace.

However, the question whether 'truth' should be understood genetically or in the traditional sense has never been clearly answered in the history of Marxism. As we saw, there are strong suggestions in Marx's works that truth should be understood as meaning 'validity' in relation to human needs. Lenin, however, was fairly explicit in his assertion of the traditional view that truth means 'conformity to reality'. Most manuals of 'diamat' follow him in this, but there are also frequent signs of the more pragmatic and political view that truth is that which 'expresses' social progress, in which case, of course, the criterion resides in pronouncements by the party authorities. The confusion is aided by the fact that Russian has two words for 'truth', *istina* and *pravda*, the former tending to express the traditional notion of that which *is*, while the latter, with moral overtones, suggests 'what is right and just' or 'what ought to be'. This ambiguity helps to blur the distinction between the traditional and the genetic concept of truth.

As to the principle of the 'unity of theory and practice', this too can be understood in different ways. Sometimes it is presented simply as a norm, signifying more or less that one should think only about matters of some practical use; in this case it does not fall into any of the above-mentioned categories, as they are not normative. Considered as a descriptive statement it may mean that people generally engage in theoretical reflection as a result of practical needs; this is true in a loose sense, but is not specifically Marxist. If, again, the unity of theory and practice means that practical success is a confirmation of the rightness of the thinking on which our actions are based, this is a criterion of truth which is acceptable as far as it goes, though it cannot be universal, since clearly in many fields of knowledge and science there is no such thing as practical verification. Finally, the principle can be understood in the specifically Marxian sense that thought is an 'aspect' of conduct and becomes 'true' by being aware of this fact. But this sense, which is examined in the chapters on Marx, Korsch, and Lukács, is practically absent from Soviet 'diamat'.

12. The roots and significance of Stalinism. The question of a 'new class'

The debate, involving both Communists and adversaries of Communism, on the social roots and 'historical necessity' of Stalinism began soon after Stalin's death and has continued ever since. We cannot go into all its details here, but will note the principal points.

The problem of the causes of Stalinism is not the same as that of its inevitability, a question whose meaning in any case requires elucidation. Anyone who holds that every detail of history is determined by foregoing events obviously need not trouble to analyse the specific background of Stalinism, but must accept its 'necessity' as an instance of that general principle. The principle, however, is a metaphysical postulate that there is no good reason to accept. From any analysis of the course of the Russian revolution it can be seen that there was no fatal necessity about the outcome. During the Civil War there were many occasions when the fate of Bolshevik power hung by a thread, as Lenin himself bore witness, and no 'laws of history' determined what the result would be. It may be assumed that if the bullet aimed at Lenin in 1918 had been deflected by an inch or two and had killed him, the Bolshevik regime would have fallen; so it would have done if he had failed to persuade the party leaders to agree to the Treaty of Brest-Litovsk, and other such instances can easily be quoted. Speculation as to what would have happened in these hypotheses is of no importance at the present day and is bound to be inconclusive. The turning-points in the evolution of Soviet Russia—War Communism, the N.E.P., collectivization, the purges—were not due to 'historical laws' but were all consciously willed by the rulers, and there is no reason to think that they 'had to' happen or that the rulers could not have decided otherwise.

The only meaningful form in which the question of historical necessity can be put in this case is: are there rational grounds for thinking that the Soviet system, whose distinguishing features were the nationalization of means of production and the Bolshevik party's monopoly of power, could not have maintained itself by any means essentially different from those used and established by the Stalinist system of government? It can reasonably be argued that the answer to this question is in the affirmative.

The Bolsheviks achieved power in Russia on a programme of peace and land for the peasants, two slogans which were in no way specifically socialist, let alone Marxist; and the support they received was mainly support for that programme. Their objective, however, was world revolution and, when that proved unattainable, the building of socialism in Russia on the basis of single-party authority. After the devastation of the Civil War there were no active social forces other than the party which were capable of any initiative, but there was by this time the established tradition of a political, military, and police apparatus responsible for the whole life of society and especially production and distribution. The N.E.P. was a compromise between ideology and reality, arising from a recognition of the fact that the state could not cope with the economic regeneration of Russia, that attempts to regulate the whole economy by coercion were a catastrophic failure, and that help could only come from the 'spontaneous' operation of the market. The economic compromise was not meant to involve any political concessions, but to keep the power monopoly intact. The peasantry was still unsocialized, but the only force capable of initiative was the state bureaucracy: this class was the bulwark of 'socialism', and the further development of the system reflected its interests and urge for expansion. The winding-up of N.E.P. and the enforcement of collectivization were certainly not part of the design of history, but were dictated by the system and the interests of its only active element: the continuation of N.E.P. would have meant that the state and bureaucracy were at the peasants' mercy and that economic policy, including export, import, and investment plants, must largely be subordinated to their demands. We do not know, of course, what would have happened if, instead of collectivization, the state had chosen the alternative of returning to complete freedom of exchange and a market economy. The fears of Trotsky and the 'left wing' that this would have aroused political forces intent on overthrowing Bolshevik power were by no means without foundation. At the very least the bureaucracy's position would have grown weaker rather than stronger, and there was ground for believing that the building of a strong military and industrial state would have been postponed indefinitely. The socialization of the economy, even at enormous cost to the population, was in the bureaucracy's interest and in the 'logic' of the system. Stalin, the embodiment of the ruling class and of a state which had made itself virtually independent of society, performed acts which had occurred at least twice before in Russian history: he called into being a new bureaucratic caste independent of the organic divisions of society, and freed it from all subservience to the people as a whole, the working class, or, finally, the party's inherited ideology. This caste very soon destroyed all the 'Westernizing' elements in the Bolshevik movement, and used Marxist phraseology as a means of restoring and enlarging the Russian Empire. The Soviet system waged constant war against its own people, not because the latter showed much resistance, but chiefly because the ruling class needed a state of war and aggression to maintain its position. The permanent threat to the state from enemies on the look-out for the slightest weakness, foreign agents, conspirators, saboteurs, and other bogies is an ideological means of justifying the bureaucratic monopoly of power; the state of war inflicts damage on the ruling group itself, but this is part of the price of government.

We have already discussed the reasons why Marxism was a suitable ideology for this system, which was unquestionably a new phenomenon in history despite all the Russian and Byzantine traditions that are often invoked by historians and critics of Communism—the state's high degree of autonomy *vis-à-vis* the civil population, the moral and mental traits of the *chinovnik*, etc. Stalinism came into being as a continuation of Leninism, based on the Russian tradition and a suitably adapted form of Marxism. The importance of the Russian and Byzantine heritage is discussed by such writers as Berdyayev, Kucharzewski, Arnold

Toynbee, Richard Pipes, Tibor Szamuely, and Gustav Wetter.

It does not follow from this that every attempt to socialize the means of production must necessarily result in a totalitarian society, i.e. one in which all organizational forms are imposed by the state and individuals are treated as state property. It is true, however, that the nationalization of all means of production and the complete subjection of economic life to state planning (however effective or ineffective that planning may be) practically amounts to a totalitarian society. If the basis of the system is that the central authority defines all the objectives and forms of the economy, and if the economy, including the work-force, is subjected to over-all planning by that authority, the bureaucracy must become the only active social force and acquire undivided control over other aspects of life as well. Many attempts have been made to devise a means of socializing property without nationalizing it, by leaving the economic initiative in the hands of producers. The idea has been partially applied in Yugoslavia, but the results so far are too slight and ambiguous to give a clear picture of its success. The essential point, however, is that two mutually restrictive principles are always in play: the more economic initiative is left in the hands of particular socialized units of production, and the more independence those units enjoy, the greater will be the role of 'spontaneous' market laws, competition, and the profit motive. A form of social ownership that allowed full autonomy to production units would be a return to free-for-all capitalism, the only difference being that individual factory owners would be replaced by collective ones, i.e. producers' co-operatives. The more elements of planning there are, the more limited are the functions and competence of producers' collectives. However, the idea of economic planning has been accepted, though in different degrees, in all developed industrial societies, and the increase of planning and state intervention has meant an increased bureaucracy. The problem is not how to get rid of bureaucracy, which would mean destroying modern industrial civilization, but how to control its activity by means of representative bodies.

As far as Marx's intention is concerned, despite all the reservations that can be culled from his writings he undoubtedly believed that a socialist society would be one of perfect unity, in which conflicts of interest would disappear with the elimination of their economic basis in private property. This society, he thought, would have no need of bourgeois institutions such as representative political bodies (which inevitably gave rise to bureaucracies alienated from the public) and rules of law safeguarding civil liberties. The Soviet despotism was an attempt to apply this doctrine in alliance with the belief that social unity can be produced by institutional means.

It would be absurd to say that Marxism was predestined to become the ideology of the self-glorifying Russian bureaucracy. Nevertheless, it contained essential features, as opposed to accidental or secondary ones, that made it adaptable to this purpose. In *Will the Soviet Union Survive Until 1984?* the Soviet historian Andrey Amalrik, who has been persecuted and imprisoned for his dissident views, compares the function of Marxism in Russia to that of Christianity in the Roman Empire. Just as the adoption of Christianity strengthened the imperial system and prolonged its life but could not save it from final destruction, so the assimilation of Marxist ideology has for a time preserved the Russian Empire but cannot avert its inevitable dissolution. One may accept Amalrik's theory in so far as it does not suggest that this was the point of Marxism from the beginning or that it was a conscious purpose of the Russian revolutionaries. Thanks to an unusual combination of circumstances, power in Russia was seized by a party professing Marxist doctrine. In order to stay in power the party was obliged successively to revoke all the promises contained in its ideology, which had no doubt been sincere in the mouths of its first leaders. The result was the creation of a new bureaucratic caste enjoying a monopoly of state power and devoted by nature to the tradition of Russian imperialism. Marxism became the prerogative of this caste and an effective instrument for the continuation of imperial policies.

In this connection many writers have discussed the question of a 'new class', i.e. whether 'class' is an appropriate designation for the governing circles of the U.S.S.R. and other socialist states. The point has been canvassed especially since the publication of Milovan Djilas's *The New Class* in 1957; but the discussion has a much longer history, some aspects of which have been noted in previous chapters. For example, Marx's anarchist critics, especially Bakunin, claimed that an attempt to organize society on the basis of his ideas must give rise to new privileged classes: the proletarians who were to replace the existing rulers would turn traitor to their own class and create a system of privileges that they would guard as jealously as their predecessors had done. This, Bakunin maintained, was inevitable because Marxism envisaged the continued existence of the state. Wacław Machajski, a Polish anarchist who wrote chiefly in Russian, drew far-reaching consequences from a modified version of this idea. He argued that Marx's idea of socialism specifically expressed the interests of intellectuals who hoped to attain a position of political privilege by means of the inherited social privilege of knowledge, which they already possessed. As long as the intelligentsia were able to give their children advantageous opportunities of acquiring knowledge there could be no question of equality, which was the essence of socialism. The working class, which was at present at the mercy of intellectuals, could only achieve its ends by depriving them of their chief capital, namely education. This argument, which to some extent recalled the syndicalism of Sorel, was based on the fairly obvious fact that in any society where there is both inequality of income and a strong correlation between education and social status, the children of the educated classes have a better chance than others of rising in the social hierarchy. This hereditary inequality could only be cured by destroying the continuity of culture and separating children from their parents in order to give them a completely uniform education: so that Machajski's Utopia would sacrifice both civilization and the family on the altar of equality. There were Russian anarchist groups who also detested education as a source of privilege. Machajski had followers in Russia, and for some years after the October Revolution the fight against his views was a recurrent propaganda theme: they were linked, not without cause, with 'syndicalist deviation' and the activities of the 'workers' opposition'.

The problem of the development of a new class under socialism was, however, also raised from another point of view. Some, like Plekhanov, argued that an attempt to build socialism before economic conditions were ripe for it must end in a new form of despotism. Others, like Edward Abramowski, spoke of the prior necessity of a moral transformation of society. They contended that the struggle for privilege of various kinds was bound to recur under a system of nationalized ownership, if Communism took over a society that had not been morally reformed and was still pervaded by the needs and ambitions inculcated by the old order. As Abramowski wrote in 1897, Communism in such conditions could only lead to a new class structure in which the old divisions were replaced by antagonism between society and a privileged bureaucracy, and which could only maintain itself by an extreme form of despotism and police rule.

Critics of the October Revolution pointed out from the beginning that a new system of privilege, inequality, and despotism was burgeoning in Russia; the term 'new class' was used by Kautsky as early as 1919. When Trotsky in exile developed his critique of the Stalinist regime he insisted, as did all orthodox Trotskyists after him, that there was no question of a 'new class' but only of a parasitical bureaucracy. He attached great importance to this distinction, even after coming to the conclusion that the regime could not be overthrown without a revolution. The economic basis of socialism, namely, public ownership of the means of production, was, he maintained, unaffected by the bureaucratic degeneration: consequently, there was no need for a social revolution, which had already taken place, but only for a political one which would sweep away the existing apparatus of government.

Trotsky, his orthodox followers, and other Communist critics of Stalinism denied the existence of a 'new class' on the ground that the privileges of the Soviet bureaucracy were not transmitted automatically from one generation to another, and that the bureaucrats did not personally own the means of production but only exercised collective control over them. This, however, turns the argument into a question of words. If 'class' is defined in such a way that one can only speak of a ruling and exploiting class when each of its members has a legal title, transmissible by inheritance, to the ownership of certain productive resources of society, then of course the Soviet bureaucracy is not a class. But it is not clear why the term should be restricted in this way. It was not so restricted by Marx. The Soviet bureaucracy has at its collective disposal all the productive resources of the state, though this fact is not embodied in any legal document but is simply a basic consequence of the system. Control over the means of production is essentially no different from ownership, if the collective possessor is irremovable under the existing system and cannot be legally challenged by any rival. Since the owner is collective there is no individual inheritance, and no one can bequeath to his children a particular position in the political hierarchy. In practice, however, as has often been described, privilege is systematically inherited in the Soviet state. The children of the ruling group are clearly privileged from the point of view of opportunities in life and access to restricted goods and advantages of various kinds, and the group itself is very well aware of its superior position. The political monopoly and the exclusive control of means of production support each other and could not exist separately. The high incomes of the ruling group are a natural consequence of its exploiting role, but are not the same as exploitation itself, which consists in the right to dispose freely, without any control by the public, of the whole mass of surplus value which that public creates. The public has no say as to how or in what proportion resources are divided between investment and consumption, or what is done with the goods that are produced. From this point of view the Soviet class division is much more rigid and less sensitive to social pressure than any capitalist system of ownership, since in Russia there is no way in which different sections of society can express and pursue their interests through administrative and legislative bodies. True, the position of individuals in the hierarchy depends on the will and caprice of their superiors, or, in the palmy days of Stalinism, on the pleasure of a single despot. In this respect their position is not wholly secure: the situation is more like an Oriental despotism, where people in the higher ranks were equally at the tyrant's mercy and might be dismissed or executed from one day to the next. But it is not clear why this state of affairs should preclude the observer from speaking of a 'class', still less why it should be considered typically 'socialist' and a proof of the immense superiority of socialism to 'bourgeois democracy', as Trotsky's adherents claim. Djilas in his book drew attention to the variety of privileges enjoyed by the socialist ruling class, emphasizing that the monopoly of power was the basis of these privileges and not a consequence of them.

With the above qualifications, there is no reason why the socialist bureaucracy should not be termed an 'exploiting class'. Indeed, the description appears to be used increasingly often, and Trotsky's distinctions are seen to be more and more artificial.

James Burnham, after breaking with Trotsky, wrote in 1940 his celebrated book *The Managerial Revolution*, in which he argued that the establishment of a new class in Russia was only a particular instance of a universal process that was occurring and would continue to develop in all industrial societies. Capitalism, he thought, was going through the same evolution: formal property rights meant less and less, and power was gradually passing into the hands of those who actually controlled production, i.e. the managing class. This was an inevitable consequence of the nature of modern industry. The new élite was simply the present-day form of the division of society into classes, and class divisions, privilege, and inequality were natural phenomena of social life. Throughout history the masses had been used, under various ideological banners, to overthrow the privileged classes of the day; the result, however, was only to replace them with new masters who at once set about oppressing the rest of society no less efficiently than their predecessors. The despotism of the new class in Russia was not an exception, but an illustration of this universal law.

Whether or not Burnham was right in saying that all social life entailed despotism in some form, his remarks are far from an adequate description of Soviet reality. The rulers of post-Revolutionary Russia were and are not the industrial managers but the political bureaucracy. The former, of course, are an important section of society, and groups of them may be strong enough to affect decisions by higher authority, especially in their own fields. But the key decisions, including those on industrial investment, imports, and exports, are political and are taken by the political oligarchy. It is very implausible to suggest that the October Revolution is a special case of the transference of power to managers as a result of progress in technology and work organization.

The Soviet exploiting class is a new social formation which in some ways resembles the bureaucracy of Oriental despotisms, in others the class of feudal barons, and in others again the capitalist colonizers of backward countries. Its position is determined by the absolute concentration of political, economic, and military power, to an extent never before seen in Europe, and by the need for an ideology to legitimize that power. The privileges its members enjoy in the field of consumption are a natural consequence of its role in society. Marxism is the charismatic aura with which it invests itself in order to justify its rule.

13. European Marxism during the last phase of Stalinism

The history of Marxism in the countries which fell under Soviet control as a result of the war can be roughly divided into four phases. In the first phase, from 1945 to 1949, the 'people's democracies' still exhibited elements of political and cultural pluralism, which were gradually subdued by Soviet pressure. The second phase, from 1949 to 1954, saw the complete or almost complete *Gleichschaltung* of the 'socialist camp' as regards politics and ideology, and the far-reaching Stalinization of all aspects of culture. In the third phase, beginning in 1955, the most striking feature as far as the history of Marxism is concerned was the emergence of various 'revisionist', anti-Stalinist trends, chiefly in Poland and Hungary but later also in Czechoslovakia and to some extent in East Germany. This period effectively came to an end in about 1968, when, in most of the bloc countries at least, Marxism took on a petrified and sterile form, while remaining the official ideology of the ruling party.

The 'Stalinization' and 'de-Stalinization' of Eastern Europe proceeded in a different fashion in each country, in accordance with varying circumstances. In the first place, some of them—Poland, Czechoslovakia, Yugoslavia—had been on the Allied side in the war, while others were officially tied to the Axis. Poland, Czechoslovakia, and Hungary, which belonged historically to Western Christianity, had different cultural traditions from Romania, Bulgaria, and Serbia. East Germany, Poland, and Czechoslovakia had a tradition of serious philosophical studies dating back to the Middle Ages, which was lacking in other bloc countries. Finally, in certain countries there had been an active underground and guerrilla movement during the war, while in others, likewise under German occupation, the resistance was feeble and did not take the form of an armed struggle. In the former category were Poland and Yugoslavia, with the important difference that in Yugoslavia the Communists were the most active fighters whereas in Poland they were a small fraction of the total resistance movement, the backbone of which consisted of forces owing allegiance to the London Government. All these differences had an important bearing on post-war events in Eastern Europe and the evolution of Marxism in the respective countries: they affected the speed and depth of the ideological invasion and the manner in which Stalinism was later rejected. The only country whose liberation from the German invader was due in large measure to its own, Communist-controlled forces was Yugoslavia, and it was only there that the Communists exercised undivided power from 1945 onwards. Elsewhere—in Poland, East Germany, Czechoslovakia, Romania, and Hungary—social democratic or peasant parties were allowed to function during the initial post-war years.

It is quite possible that many of the East European Communist leaders believed at first that their countries would be independent states, building up socialist institutions in alliance with Russia but not under its direct control. Such illusions, however, were short-lived. For the first two years international relations were marked by traces of the wartime alliance: the Communist parties maintained a show of fidelity to the Yalta and Potsdam agreements, which provided for democratic institutions, multi-party governments, and free elections in Eastern Europe. The onset of the cold war, however, put a stop to any hopes that the area might develop independently of the Soviet Union. In 1946–8 the non-Communist parties were destroyed or forcibly 'united' with the Communists, the first to suffer this fate being the East German social democrats. From the beginning, even when there were still genuine elements of a coalition government, the Communists entrenched themselves in key positions of power, especially the police and army. Ubiquitous Soviet 'advisers' had the final say in key questions of government, and directly organized the most savage and blatant forms of repression. In 1949, after the programmed suppression of the non-Communist parties, after elections marked by fraud and violence and after the *coup* in Czechoslovakia, the East European Communists under Stalin's close control enjoyed virtually exclusive power. Yet at the very time when Stalinism was thus establishing itself in the satellite countries it met with its first serious defeat in the form of the Yugoslav schism.

One of the instruments used by Stalin to exact obedience from the ruling Communist parties of Eastern Europe, and from Communists elsewhere, was a weakened version of the Comintern known as the Communist Information Bureau or 'Cominform'. Set up in September 1947 (the Comintern had been dissolved in 1943), this body comprised representatives of all the ruling Communist parties of Eastern Europe except the Albanian and East German—i.e. the Soviet, Polish, Czecho-slovak, Hungarian, Romanian, Bulgarian, and Yugoslav parties —as well as the French and Italians. Its orchestrator, under Stalin, was Zhdanov, and it was by his orders, for instance, that the Yugoslavs attacked the French and Italian Communists for not seizing power in their countries at the favourable juncture of 1944–5. (Their conduct had in fact been dictated by Stalin, but they nevertheless performed the appropriate self-criticism.) The Cominform's function was to transmit to Communists throughout the world the behests of Soviet policy disguised as unanimous resolutions of the principal parties. There were indeed signs that some East European parties really believed themselves entitled to act as sovereign governments: Czecho-slovakia and Poland displayed a rash interest in the Marshall Plan, and Bulgaria and Yugoslavia put forward a plan for Balkan federation. All such displays of independence were swiftly crushed and the offending parties called to order. At a time when a third world war was at least not unthinkable, Communists outside the Soviet Union must again be taught that there was only one authority determining 'correct' policy and that the slightest deviation from its orders would have unpleasant consequences.

At the first session of the Cominform Zhdanov described the division of the world into two political blocs as the key factor in the international situation. The Cominform also launched an international journal, of course dominated by the Soviet Communist party, as a vehicle for the latter's propaganda directives. This journal was indeed the Cominform's chief activity: it held only two more sessions, in June 1948 and November 1949, both for the purpose of condemning the Yugoslavs. Friction between the Soviet and Yugoslav parties began in the spring of 1948; its immediate cause was the annoyance of Tito and his colleagues at the crude and arrogant interference of Soviet 'advisers' in Yugoslav internal affairs, especially the army and police. Stalin, outraged by this lack of internationalism, attempted to bring Yugoslavia to heel and no doubt thought it would be an easy task. In propaganda activity the Yugoslavs had until then shown extreme subservience to Russia; but they were masters in their own house, and it turned out that the Soviet Union was very poorly represented there. (One of the main bones of contention was the recruitment of Yugoslavs to the Soviet police and espionage network.) Apart from some individuals who were directly on the Soviet payroll the Yugoslavs had no thought of yielding, and the only way to reconvert them to internationalism appeared to be by armed invasion, which Stalin, rightly or wrongly, considered too risky a course.

The Yugoslav party was officially condemned at the second session of the Cominform, from which Yugoslavia's delegates were absent. The Belgrade leaders were declared to be anti-Soviet nationalists (on grounds that were not explained), and Communist Yugoslavs were called on to overthrow the 'Titoist clique' if it did not immediately toe the line. The quarrel with Yugoslavia became the main theme of the Cominform journal, and at the third and last session of that body Gheorghiu Dej, the Romanian party secretary, made a speech on 'the Yugoslav Communist party in the grip of murderers and spies'. From this it appeared that all the Yugoslav leaders had from time immemorial been agents of various Western intelligence services, that they had established a Fascist regime, and that their main policy was and always had been to stir up trouble for the Soviet Union and serve the interests of American warmongers. Taking their cue from this, the Communist parties of the world unleashed a hysterical anti-Yugoslav campaign. A macabre result of the schism was that the 'people's democracies' staged a series of judicial murders, clearly patterned on the Moscow show trials, to purge the local Communist parties of 'Titoist' or suspect elements. Many leading Communists fell victim to these trials, which took place in Czechoslovakia, Hungary, Bulgaria, and Albania. In Czechoslovakia the main trial, that of Slánský and others, took place in November 1952, shortly before Stalin's death, and was distinguished by clear overtones of anti-Semitism. This theme also came to the fore in the Soviet Union during Stalin's last years, culminating in the arrest, in January 1953, of a group of doctors, nearly all Jews, who were accused of plotting to murder party leaders and others; those of them who survived the tortures personally ordered by Stalin were released immediately after his death. In Poland Gomulka, the party secretary, and other prominent figures were imprisoned but were not tried or executed; some lesser functionaries were shot or subsequently done to death in prison. In East Germany arrests and trials followed the general pattern, though their victims were less well known. In the remainder of the bloc 'Titoists', 'Zionists', other imperialist agents, and Fascists who had 'wormed their way' into the party secretaryship or the Politburo confessed to being hirelings of foreign intelligence and were for the most part executed after show trials. It should not be supposed that all the victims were really 'Titoists' in the sense of wanting a Communist regime less dependent on Russia. This was true of some, but others were cast as traitors for arbitrary reasons. The general purpose was to terrorize the East European ruling parties and teach them what Marxism, Leninism, and internationalism really meant: namely, that the Soviet Union was absolute master of the nominally independent bloc countries, and that the latter must obediently execute its commands.

Despite the ferocity with which all forms of pressure except armed invasion were brought to bear, the Yugoslavs maintained their independence and made the first substantial breach in Stalinist Communism since the war. Immediately after the schism the Yugoslav party ideology differed from the Soviet only in emphasizing that Communist parties must be independent and condemning Soviet imperialism; the general principles of Marxism–Leninism remained in force in Yugoslavia and were no different from those observed in the Soviet Union. Before long, however, the bases of political doctrine underwent revision also and the Yugoslavs set out to create their own model of a socialist society, differing in important ways from the Russian one.

The Cominform by this time was little more than an instrument of anti-Yugoslav propaganda, and its *raison d'être* disappeared when, in the spring of 1955, Khrushchev decided to make peace with Belgrade; it was not actually dissolved, however, until April 1956. Since then, as far as is known, the Soviet party has not tried to create any institutionalized forms of international Communism but has contented itself with exercising, as far as possible, direct control over individual parties and from time to time calling conferences to adopt resolutions on world topics. These, however, have had less success than formerly: despite all their efforts the Soviet leaders have not managed to secure international condemnation of the Chinese Communist party in the same way as they did in the case of Yugoslavia.

The last years of Stalin's rule were marked by the Sovietization of doctrine throughout the Communist world. The effects of this varied from one bloc country to another, but the pressures and trends were generally the same.

Polish Marxism, as we have seen in earlier chapters, had its own tradition, quite independent of the Russian one. There was no single orthodox form of this tradition and no precise party ideology; Marxism was only one feature, and not a very important one, in the Polish intellectual scene. However, there were historians, sociologists, and economists who, while not professing any cut-and-dried doctrine, made some use of Marxist categories in their work; among these were Ludwik Krzywicki and Stefan Czarnowski (1879–1937), an eminent sociologist and historian of religion, who in his last years gravitated towards Marxism to some extent. (In an essay on proletarian culture he analysed the origins of a new mentality and a new type of art specifically related to the situation of the working class.) In the first years after 1945 these traditions were revived: the new Marxist thought, like the old, was not confined to any precise channels but appeared rather as a background to rationalism and to the habit of analysing cultural phenomena in terms of social conflict. This loose, uncodified Marxism was voiced by journals including the monthly *Myśl współczesna* (*Contemporary Thought*) and the weekly *Kuźnica* (*The Forge*). In 1945–50 the universities were re-created on pre-war lines and mostly with the same teaching staff; there were as yet no ideological purges in the educational field; many scientific books and journals published at this time had nothing to do with Marxism. The regime did not yet call itself a 'dictatorship of the proletariat', and the party ideology did not stress Communist themes but patriotic, nationalist, or anti-German ones. Soviet-type Marxism was very much in the background at this period; its chief spokesman was Adam Schaff, who wrote books and manuals expounding the Leninist–Stalinist version of dialectical and historical materialism, though these were in a less primitive style than their Soviet counterparts. Even in the worst years, it may be said in general that Marxism in Poland did not descend to the Soviet level: despite the encroachment of Russian models it retained some degree of originality and a timid respect for the canons of rational thought.

In 1945–9 political and police repression became more intense. For about two years after the war there was armed conflict with survivors of the underground army who had fought the German invader and refused to surrender to the new regime imposed by Russia. Persecution and frequent bloodshed marked the struggle against armed underground units and wartime political organizations, as well as against the peasant party and other legal non-Communist groups. Nevertheless, cultural pressure at this time was confined to purely political questions; Marxism was not yet enjoined as a compulsory standard in philosophy or the social sciences, and 'socialist realism' in art or literature was unknown.

In 1948–9 the party purged itself of 'right-wing nationalists'; the leadership was changed, political life was adjusted to Soviet norms, rural collectivization was decided on (though never carried out to any extent), and the regime was officially declared to be a form of proletarian dictatorship. In 1949–50 the political house-cleaning was followed by the Sovietization of culture. Many academic and literary journals were closed down, and others were given new editors. In the early fifties some 'bourgeois' professors were dismissed: the number, however, was not large, and although prevented from teaching or publishing they still drew their salaries and wrote books which they were able to publish a few years later, when times were less severe. Some members of philosophical faculties were left in their jobs but ordered to confine themselves to teaching logic; others again were given posts under the Academy of Sciences, where they did not come into contact with students. The curriculum of social science departments was revised, and chairs of sociology were replaced by chairs of historical materialism. A special party institute was set up to train cadres to take the place of 'bourgeois' professors in the ideologically sensitive departments of philosophy, economics, and history. In philosophy the organ of the Marxist 'offensive' was the journal *Myśl Filozoficzna* (*Philosophical Thought*). For a time Marxist philosophers concentrated on combating the non-Marxist tradition, especially the Lwów–Warsaw school of analytical philosophy: Kotarbiński, Ajdukiewicz, Stanislaw Ossowski, Maria Ossowska, and others. Many books and articles criticized various aspects of the tenets of this school. Another target was Thomism, which had a lively tradition centred on the Catholic University of Lublin. (This university—a fact unparalleled in the history of socialist states— was never suppressed and functions to this day, despite various measures of pressure and interference.) Many Marxists of the older and younger generation—Adam Schaff, Bronislaw Baczko, Tadeusz Kroński, Helena Eilstein, Władysław Krajewski—took part in these battles; so did the present author, who does not regard the fact as a source of pride. Another subject of study was the Marxist contribution to Polish culture in past decades.

The time is not ripe for a full appraisal of the cultural developments of those years, but it can be said that the enforced 'Marxification' had some redeeming features. Intellectual life certainly became poor and sterile, but the dissemination of Marxism led to some advantages despite the coercion that accompanied it. Besides destructive and obscurantist elements it introduced other features that were of intrinsic value and are to a greater or lesser extent part of the world's intellectual patrimony: for example, the habit of envisaging cultural phenomena as aspects of social conflict, of emphasizing the economic and technical background of historical processes and generally studying phenomena in terms of broad historical trends. Some new directions in humanistic studies, though ideologically motivated, led to valuable results, for example, in regard to the history of Polish philosophy and social thought. Useful work was done in publishing translations of philosophical classics and republishing standard works of Polish social, philosophical, and religious thought.

In the Stalinist years the state was quite generous in subsidizing culture, so that a good deal of rubbish was produced but also much work of permanent value. The general standard of education and access to universities soon rose considerably as compared with before the war. What was destructive was not universal instruction in Marxism but its use as an instrument of coercion and political mendacity. Marxism, even in a primitive and stereotyped form, still served in some measure to implant fruitful and rational ideas that were part of its tradition; but the seeds could only thrive in proportion as the oppressive uses of the doctrine were relaxed.

On the whole Stalinism in the strict sense did less harm to Polish culture than to that of the other bloc countries, and the harm it did was less irrevocable. There were several reasons for this. In the first place there was a spontaneous though largely passive cultural resistance and a deep-rooted distrust or hostility towards everything that came from Russia. There was also a certain half-heartedness or inconsistency about the imposition of Stalinist culture: Marxism never enjoyed an absolute monopoly of humanistic studies, and attempts to exert pressure on the biological sciences in Soviet style were weak and ineffective. The campaign for 'socialist realism' produced some worthless apologetics but did not destroy literature and the arts; the purges in institutions of higher learning were on a comparatively small scale; the proportion of prohibited books in libraries was lower than elsewhere. Moreover, cultural Stalinism in Poland was comparatively short-lived: it began in earnest in 1949–50, and was already declining in 1954–5. It is possible, though hard to prove, that another moderating factor was at work, namely the ill will that many veteran Communists felt towards Stalin, who had destroyed the pre-war Polish Communist party and murdered its leaders.

In the other countries under Soviet suzerainty, cultural Stalinization was for various reasons more thorough and more destructive. East Germany was under direct Soviet occupation, and the combination of Stalinism with the Prussian tradition produced a rigidly obscurantist atmosphere (relieved by the activity of Ernst Bloch, whom we shall discuss separately). Moreover, until 1961 it was not difficult to flee to West Germany, and among the four million who did so were many intellectuals, the loss of whom increased the desolation of their native territory. Czechoslovakia too suffered a relentless ideological purge, the consequences of which can still be felt today. For several years the cultural dictator was Zdeněk Nejedlý, originally a musical historian, who censored the arts with a heavy hand, 'emending' Czech literary classics and banning performances of works by the 'cosmopolitan' Dvořák, etc. His counterpart in Bulgaria was Todor Pavlov, a typical Marxist dilettante and pretender to omniscience, who wrote on biology, literature, philosophy, and other subjects; his best-known work, published before the war and translated into Russian, was a treatise on Leninist epistemology entitled *The Theory of Reflection*. The term 'reflection' was used here in a global sense to denote every kind of influence that one thing can exert on another, from mechanical causation onwards; human acts of perception and abstract thought were merely a special case of this 'reflection' at the highest level of the organization of matter. It happened that Mikhalchev, a veteran professor of philosophy at Sofia, had been a pupil of Rehmke (d. 1930), a German empiriocriticist of the second rank; hence for many years the chief task of Bulgarian Marxist philosophers was to 'combat Rehmkianism'.

In Hungary Marxism was in a stronger position from the beginning, thanks to some eminent philosophers of the older generation: J. Révai, B. Fogarasi, and G. Lukács. Révai was for some time the party representative in charge of Stalinizing Hungarian culture. Lukács was in a doubtful position throughout this period, though his books and articles during the last years of Stalinism were of irreproachable orthodoxy except for his book on Hegel, written before the war and published in German in 1948: this was completely un-Soviet in style and by no means conformed to the Stalin–Zhdanov formula.

In Western Europe the position of Marxists was somewhat different. All the Communist parties, it is true, obediently supported Stalin's line at any given time, glorifying Soviet policy and preaching the cult of the Leader; but neither in France, Britain, nor Italy did the Soviet pattern completely dominate Marxist theoretical writing on philosophy and the historical sciences. The deviation, however, was less in respect of content than of style and the method of argument.

In France the Communist movement developed with great impetus in the first few years after 1945. From the outset of the cold war the party maintained a tough attitude in major

political and parliamentary affairs, sabotaging every government move irrespective of merits; in regional and municipal
affairs, however, their policy was skilful and flexible. At the same
time they developed elaborate and exclusive forms of cultural
life on rather similar lines to those of the German social
democrats before the First World War. The party ran many
periodicals, including the theoretical journal *Pensée*, and numbered in its ranks many eminent men and women of national
reputation: writers such as Aragon and Éluard, painters such
as Picasso and Léger, scientists such as the Joliot–Curies. All
this lent the Communist movement considerable prestige. A
fair amount of philosophical literature was produced, some of
it purely Stalinist, especially the party monthly *Nouvelle
Critique*. This journal, for instance, launched a campaign against
psychoanalysis, which was then a subject of increasing interest
in France. Most of the contributors, as was to be expected,
condemned it as a bourgeois doctrine, idealistic and mechanistic
to boot, reducing social phenomena to individual psychology,
and the human mind to biological impulses. Roger Garaudy,
who was to be noted in the sixties as a champion of 'liberal'
Communism, wrote books at this time that were purely Stalinist
in content, although certainly more learned and better written
than the Soviet output. One of these was *Grammaire de la liberté*
(1950), arguing that the way to have freedom was to nationalize
industry and abolish unemployment. In *Les Sources françaises du
socialisme scientifique* (1948) Garaudy sought to prove that Communism was deeply and specifically rooted in French culture.
He also wrote a book on Christianity, citing evidence of the
obscurantism of the Catholic Church and its opposition to the
advance of science.

A prolific writer of a somewhat different character, Henri
Lefebvre, was known before the war as an anthologist of Marx
and Hegel and author of books against nationalism and Fascism.
In 1947 he published *Logique formelle et logique dialectique* and
the interesting *Critique de la vie quotidienne*; later came a critique
of existentialism (something no French Marxist philosopher in
the fifties and sixties could avoid writing), then works on
Descartes, Diderot, Rabelais, Pascal, Musset, Marx, and Lenin,
also dissertations on painting and music. These works are all
sketches rather than profound studies, but they contain original

and useful observations. Lefebvre is a man of wide culture, especially in French terms; his writings are lively and ingenious, but he touches on too many themes to dwell for long on any of them. He had considerable influence on French Marxism because, among other things, he reverted frequently to Marx's early works, which Soviet Marxism practically ignored; he was particularly interested in the theme of 'total man'. It was largely thanks to Lefebvre that 'the young Marx' became a staple of French philosophy in the forties and early fifties. He also probably did most to popularize the Marxian term 'alienation', which (not that he intended this) became a favourite expression in French everyday language to designate a vaguely uncomfortable situation. Somewhat apart from the main stream of party philosophy at this time is the work of Auguste Cornu, an outstanding historian of Marxism.

The evolution of French Marxism in the years of the break-up of Stalinist ideology was affected by the wave of Hegelianism and existentialism in the 1940s. The chief introducer of Hegel, especially the *Phenomenology of Mind*, to French readers was Alexandre Kojève, who expounded and commented on his philosophy before the war, and Jean Hyppolite. Neither was a Marxist or a Communist, but they both took a sympathetic interest in Marx's ideas and analysed them seriously, emphasizing the elements in Hegel's schemata that influenced Marx's thought. Both Kojève and Hyppolite did much to divert French philosophy from its traditional channels and interests. In particular they gave currency to the idea of Reason embodied in the historical process—an anti-Cartesian concept, since Descartes regarded history as essentially the realm of chance, outside the reach of philosophy and incapable of being rationalized except by means of consciously fictitious and artificial constructions, the *fabula mundi* as Descartes called it. In lectures published in 1947 Kojève presented the *Phenomenology* as a history of man's self-creation by dint of labouring and struggling; in the dialectic of master and servant he perceived the source of Marx's theory of the proletariat and the idea of work as the demiurge of history. Kojève and Hyppolite showed Marx's philosophy of history to be a continuation of the Hegelian dialectic of negation—evil, slavery, and alienation being the necessary means whereby mankind achieves self-understanding and liberation. Hyppolite emphasized in particular that, for Hegel as for Marx, Reason was not a transcendental observer of the world with its own rules independent of the course of history, but was itself a factor, aspect, or expression of history; and that the progress of mankind towards 'rationality' was not a matter of gradually assimilating ready-made rules of thought, but of a growing sense of community and acknowledgement of rationality in others. For that purpose it was necessary that human beings should cease to function as commodities, and this was Marx's principal message.

Sartre's existentialist philosophy, which had enormous success in France for several years after the war, was in its then form quite irreconcilable with Marxism. Sartre maintained that human existence was a vacuum of absolute freedom in an alien, inert world governed by natural determinants. This freedom was an intolerable burden from which man sought to escape, but could not do so without a breach of good faith. The very fact that my freedom is absolute and unlimited deprives me of every alibi and makes me a hundred per cent responsible for everything I do. My constant self-anticipation, in which this freedom is displayed, is the generator of time, which is the true form of human existence and which, like freedom, is the separate property of every one of us. For Sartre there is no such thing as collective, communal time, nor is there any freedom other than the natural, hopeless, and oppressive necessity for the individual to create himself without ceasing—a process in which he is unaided by God or any transcendental values, by historical tradition or by his fellow men. Since I am defined as empty freedom and pure negativity, every being outside myself appears to me as an attempt to limit my freedom. It follows that by the very nature of existence, ontologically as it were, human relations can only take the antagonistic form of attempting to annex other human beings as if they were things —and this applies in all contexts, in love as in political domination.

Clearly there was no common ground between Marxism in any form and a doctrine which precluded any notion of human community or shared time and reduced the whole of life to an irrational pursuit of one's own vacuity. Accordingly, French Communist intellectuals raised a hue and cry against existentialism. On the other hand, Sartre from an early stage sought to identify with the working class and the oppressed in general, so that his relations with the Communist party were marked by hesitation and ambiguity. He oscillated, in fact, between identification with the Communists and violent hostility towards them, in a complicated evolution that we cannot go into here. At every stage, however, he endeavoured to preserve his own reputation as a 'Leftist', and even to represent himself and his philosophy as the embodiment of 'Leftism' *par excellence*. Consequently, even when attacking the Communists and reviled by them he made a point of directing far more vehement attacks against the forces of reaction, the bourgeoisie, or the United States Government. Believing as he did that the Communist party represented the aspirations of the proletariat, with which he identified himself, he not only allied himself for a time with political Communism but hailed the Soviet Union, in the last phase of Stalinism, as humanity's best hope of liberation. His whole political activity was vitiated by fear of being in the typical situation of an intellectual condemning events that he has no power to influence; in short, his ideology was that of a politician *manqué*, cherishing unfulfilled ambitions to be on the 'inside'.

Merleau-Ponty, who collaborated with Sartre for a time, was from the outset more sceptical of Marxism and Communism, although his theory of freedom—namely, that it is always co-determined by actual situations and exists only through the obstacles it overcomes—was closer to Marxism than Sartre's idea of freedom as a vacuum. In *Humanisme et terreur* (1947) he discussed Communist terror and its possible historical justifications and argued that we can never know the full meaning of our actions because we do not know all their consequences, which are part of that 'meaning' and for which we are responsible willy-nilly; hence the historical process and our part in it are inevitably ambiguous and uncertain. It followed that violence might be historically justified if its ultimate effect was to do away with violence; but he did not lay down any rules for recognizing violence of this beneficent kind. As time went on, Merleau-Ponty became increasingly critical of Communism.

The style and content of Marxist writing in the West European countries naturally reflected their different cultural traditions.

French Marxism was given to dramatic rhetoric, unctuous humanitarian phrases, and stirring revolutionary eloquence; it was impressionistic, logically untidy, but effective from the literary point of view. British Marxism preserved something of the empirical tradition: it was more down-to-earth and concerned with logical argument, better grounded in history and less fond of philosophical 'historicism'. Communism in Britain was very weak and never gained mass support among the working class; but it was not, as in some other countries, a purely intellectual movement, and always maintained links, tenuous though they might be, with the trade unions. Many intellectuals passed through the Communist party in the 1930s, and others did so after the war. Among Marxist philosophers of Communist persuasion were Maurice Cornforth and John Lewis. The former wrote a critique of logical empiricism and analytical philosophy entitled *Science versus Idealism* (1946), in which he defended the Engels–Lenin theory of knowledge and attacked 'logical atomism', the principle of the economy of thought and the reduction of philosophy to linguistic analysis. Lewis wrote, among other works, a critique of pragmatism. Benjamin Farrington made valuable contributions to history in the early post-war years, including a book on ancient Greek science in which he related philosophical doctrines to the contemporary state of technology.

While French Marxists laid stress on humanitarian phraseology and British ones on empirical and rationalist arguments, Italian Marxism, faithful to its own tradition, emphasized the note of 'historicism'. Even in the last years of Stalinism, Marxist philosophy in Italy was a long way from Leninist and Stalinist norms. In international affairs, however, the Italian Communist party, which, after the collapse of Fascism, recovered very quickly from twenty years of stagnation and inactivity, was no less submissive to the Soviet line than were comrades in other countries. Later, after 1956, Palmiro Togliatti (1893–1964) was to gain the reputation of being the most 'open-minded' of the Communist leaders and the most independent of Moscow, but there are no grounds for projecting this back into the Stalin era. At that time Togliatti faithfully conformed to every zigzag of Soviet policy; however, he had no difficulty in switching from rigid isolationism (described in party jargon as 'dogmatic', 'leftist', or 'sectarian') to the more flexible and effective 'popular front' policy. In cultural matters the Italians were generally less aggressive and abusive than Communists elsewhere, emphasizing the links between Marxism and native traditions and playing up 'positive' rather than reactionary elements in the latter. The publication in 1947–9 of Gramsci's *Notes from Prison* was a milestone in the history of Italian Communism, a source of inspiration enabling party intellectuals to accept a much more elastic version of Marxism than that permitted by the canons of Leninism. Prominent writers in the early fifties were Galvano della Volpe (1896–1968) and Antonio Banfi (1886–1957), who became Marxists and Communists fairly late in life and interpreted their new faith in the Italian spirit of universalist humanism. Della Volpe wrote a valuable book on Eckhart and a work on epistemology, *Logica come scienza positiva* (1950; 'logic' here means the theory of knowledge in general), in which he interpreted Marxism in anti-Hegelian and empiricist terms. Banfi emphasized the historical relativism of Marxism, as Labriola and Gramsci had done in Italy, or Sorel in France. On this interpretation Marxism was not so much a scientific account of the world, still less a system of metaphysics, but rather a historical expression of the current phase of man's self-creation, an articulation of the practical struggle for control over the conditions of human life.

To sum up, it may be said that the last years of Stalinism in Western Europe were not wholly fruitless as far as theoretical and historical works were concerned, but that the few books of any value (and even these would for the most part not be worth reading today for their own sake) were drowned in a flood of organized political mendacity, the blame for which rested on all Communist intellectuals of the world without exception. The French or Italian workers who joined the movement during those years generally took little interest in the Soviet system or the prospect of world revolution: they supported the party because it spoke out vigorously for their immediate claims and interests. The intellectuals, however, while they embraced Marxism and Communism as a universal doctrine, were well aware that the movement was wholly governed by Moscow and subordinated to Soviet political aims. They supported it nevertheless, and uncritically rejected all information (readily obtainable from books in the West, and from direct observation in the East European countries) that threw light on the true nature of the Soviet social system. They belauded this system whenever occasion offered, supporting it by word and deed and by their membership of the Communist parties. All of them took part in the farcical 'peace movement', which under its Orwellian title was a basic instrument of Soviet imperialism in the cold war years. All of them, without turning a hair, swallowed such fantastic inventions as the charge that the Americans were carrying on germ warfare in Korea. Any who entertained doubts of the perfection of the Soviet system told themselves that 'after all' Communism was the only, or the most effective, bulwark against Fascism, and must therefore be accepted a hundred per cent, without reservation. The psychological motives of this voluntary self-deception were various. Among them were a desperate need to believe that someone in the world embodied the age-old dreams of universal human brotherhood; the illusions of intellectuals concerning 'historical progress'; contempt for the democratic 'establishment', which in many West European countries had become thoroughly discredited between the wars; the longing for a master key to unlock all the secrets of the universe, including those of history and politics; the ambition to be on the crest of the wave of history, in other words on the winning side; the cult of force, to which intellectuals are especially prone. Desiring, as they believed, to be on the same side of the barricade as the deprived and persecuted of this world, the Communist intellectuals became the prophets of the most oppressive political system then existing, and willing agents of the huge and efficient apparatus of lies with which it sought to extend its power.

CHAPTER V

Trotsky

1. The years of exile

IN January 1929, after the Left Opposition in the Soviet Union had been almost entirely wiped out by repressive measures, its leader, Leon (Lev) Davidovich Trotsky, who had been in exile in Kazakhstan for a year, was deported to Turkey, where he took up his abode on Prinkipo Island in the Sea of Marmara. For a long time other countries were unwilling to admit to their territory a man reputed to be the most dangerous revolutionary in the world; during the four years he lived in Turkey Trotsky left it only once, to deliver a lecture in Copenhagen.

While in Turkey he wrote his vast *History of the Russian Revolution*, an analysis of the causes and development of the revolutionary process in which he sought to prove that history had confirmed the rightness of his predictions and especially the idea of 'permanent revolution': i.e. that the democratic revolution was bound to develop continuously into a dictatorship of the proletariat, and could only have been successful in that form. At this time he also wrote an autobiography and a huge number of articles, appeals, and letters for the purpose of supporting and developing the Left Opposition against Stalin, both in Russia and in the world at large. Within a few months of his deportation he founded a journal in Russian, the *Opposition Bulletin*, which continued to appear till the end of his life: it was published by his son, Leon Sedov, first in Germany and, after the Nazis came to power, in Paris. As with Trotsky's books in Russian, its main purpose was to promote the organization of an opposition movement in the Soviet Union; before long, however, police measures made it almost impossible to smuggle the journal into the country, and Trotsky's contacts with remnants of the Left in Russia were to all intents and purposes broken off.

At the same time Trotsky devoted a large part of his un-
tiring energy to enlisting adherents in other countries. Small
groups of dissident Communists existed here and there, and
through them he hoped eventually to regenerate the Comintern
and revive the spirit of true Bolshevism and Leninism in the
Communist movement. These groups, under the collective title
of the International Left Opposition, were active from 1930
onwards and regarded themselves as a fraction of the Comintern—an ideological fiction, since the Trotskyists had been
expelled from the Comintern once and for all, and those who
remained in Russia were mostly in camps and prisons. A meeting
of Trotskyists from several countries was held in Copenhagen
during their leader's stay there in November 1932, and a few
months later a similar meeting took place in Paris. For some
years Trotsky had firmly opposed the foundation of a Fourth
International, as he held that Stalinism, having no social base,
must collapse at any moment and that its only possible and
natural heirs would be the 'Bolshevik Leninists', who would
restore the Comintern to its true purpose. In 1933, however,
after Hitler's accession to power, he decided that a new international revolutionary organ was necessary, and set about
organizing his followers under a new banner. The Fourth International was officially set up at a congress in Paris in September
1938.

At the end of 1932 Trotsky formulated the strategy and
ideology of the International Left Opposition in eleven points:
(1) recognition of the independence of the proletarian party,
and hence condemnation of the Comintern's policy of the 1920s
in China (Communists joining the Kuomintang) and Britain
(the Anglo-Russian trade union committee); (2) the international and therefore permanent character of the revolution;
(3) the Soviet Union was still a workers' state despite its
'bureaucratic degeneration'; (4) condemnation of Stalin's
policy, both in its 'opportunist' phase in 1923–8 and in its
'adventurist' phase in 1928–32; (5) Communists must work in
mass organizations, especially trade unions; (6) rejection of the
formula of the 'democratic dictatorship of proletariat and
peasants' and of the possibility of its developing peacefully into
a dictatorship of the proletariat; (7) the necessity for interim
slogans during the struggle for the dictatorship of the prole-

tariat, in cases where it was necessary to fight against feudal institutions, national oppression, or Fascism; (8) a united front with mass organizations, including social democrats, but not in an 'opportunist' form; (9) rejection of Stalin's theory of 'social Fascism'; (10) a distinction within the Communist movement between Marxists, the centre, and the Right; alliance with the Right against the centre (the Stalinists) was ruled out, and the centre should be supported against class enemies; (11) there should be democracy within the party.

Trotsky held to these principles until the end, but their full meaning only became clear in his more detailed analyses of the nature of the Soviet state, the concept of party democracy, and the idea of political alliances.

During his first years of exile Trotsky deluded himself that the opposition in Russia was a tremendous political force, that the Stalinist bureaucracy was increasingly losing its grip, and that the Soviet Communist party was polarizing rapidly into true Bolsheviks on the one hand and 'Thermidorians', i.e. advocates of a capitalist restoration, on the other. When it came to a clash between these two forces the bureaucracy would once more have to seek help from the Left if the Soviet system was to survive. Accordingly, Trotsky addressed letters and declarations to the Soviet leaders assuring them that the Opposition was prepared to join in the struggle against restoration and foreign intervention; he promised that he would not take revenge on his opponents, proposed an 'honourable agreement', and offered the Stalinists his aid against class enemies in the hour of mortal danger. Clearly, he imagined that when a crisis eventually came Stalin would beg him for help, and he would then name his conditions. This, however, was fantasy; Stalin and his followers had no intention of coming to terms with the Trotskyists, and would not ask them for aid under any circumstances. The Left Opposition in Russia did not gain in strength, as Trotsky thought it must by virtue of the laws of history, but was ruthlessly exterminated. When Stalin proclaimed the 'new course' of forced industrialization and collectivization the majority of oppositionists fell into line, recognizing that Stalin had taken over their policy; this applied, for example, to Radek and Preobrazhensky. Rakovsky, the most prominent Leftist after Trotsky, resisted longer than the rest, but after a few years of persecution he too capitulated. None of these ever again occupied a political post of any importance, and none escaped destruction in the Great Purge. Trotsky continued to believe that the opposition stood for the authentic forces of the proletariat as against the ruling bureaucracy, which lacked any social base; the opposition must therefore prevail in the end, and temporary defeats and persecutions could not destroy it. Repressions, he wrote, might be effective against a class condemned by history, but never against a 'historically progressive' class. In actual fact the Left Opposition vanished completely within a few years of Trotsky's exile, as a result of repression, slaughter, demoralization, and capitulation. It is true, however, that Stalin could hardly have done more to keep alive Trotsky's hopes and his belief in the potential strength of the opposition. The series of campaigns against 'Trotskyism', the show trials, and judicial murders might indeed have convinced an outside observer that 'Trotskyism' was still a powerful enemy of the Soviet state. Stalin in fact had an obsessive hatred of Trotsky and used his name as a symbol of universal evil, a stigma with which he branded adversaries of all descriptions or anyone whom he wished to destroy for any reason. In this way he coined portmanteau expressions—such as 'the Trotskyist-Rightist bloc', 'Trotskyist-Fascist', 'Trotskyist-imperialist', 'Trotskyist-Zionist'—to suit the purposes of his successive campaigns; the prefix 'Trotskyist' served much the same purpose as 'Jewish' in the mouth of anti-Semites who talk of 'the Jewish-Communist conspiracy', 'Jewish-plutocratic reactionaries', 'Jewish-Liberal corruption', etc. From the beginning of the thirties 'Trotskyism' had no specific meaning in Stalin's propaganda, but was simply an abstract emblem of Satanism. As long as Stalin was opposed to Hitler, Trotsky was pilloried as Hitler's agent; when Stalin and Hitler made friends, Trotsky became an agent of Anglo-French imperialism. In the Moscow show trials his name recurred *ad nauseam* as the victims, one by one, related how the arch-fiend in exile had impelled them to conspiracy, sabotage, and murder. This paranoid mythology of Stalin's purges was a constant reassurance to Trotsky himself: since he was so incessantly denounced, it must be that Stalin was genuinely afraid of the 'Bolshevik Leninists' who stood ready to dislodge him from the throne he had usurped. More than once Trotsky expressed the view that the Moscow trials had been organized in the hope that he, Trotsky, would be handed back to the Soviet police: Stalin, according to some, regretted that he had expelled his enemy instead of murdering him without further ado. Trotsky believed, too, that the last Comintern congress in 1937 was called for the sole purpose of meeting the Left Opposition threat. In short, the exiled leader played the part for which Stalin had cast him, but the duel took place largely in his own imagination. The International Left Opposition, like the Fourth International after it, was a cipher in political terms. Trotsky himself, of course, was a celebrated figure, but the movement which, according to the great laws of history, was bound to shake the foundations of the world at any moment proved to be an unimportant sect with virtually no impact on Stalinist parties anywhere.

A few Communists who were disillusioned by Stalinism or had been associated with Trotsky in the Comintern came out on his side, including Chen Tu-hsiu, the former head of the Chinese party. Intellectuals in various countries supported Trotsky as the embodiment of the true revolutionary spirit, which the Soviet leaders no longer represented. But sooner or later his adherents fell away, especially the intellectuals; Trotsky himself was largely responsible for this fact, as he demanded absolute obedience and tolerated no deviation from his own opinion on any subject. Apart from personal issues, his dictatorial manner, and astonishing belief in his own omniscience, the chief disagreement was over relations with the Soviet Union. Trotsky's insistence that the U.S.S.R. was still a dictatorship of the proletariat, and that the bureaucracy was not a class but only an excrescence on the healthy body of socialism, was a prime cause of argument and schism, as his views seemed increasingly out of touch with obvious reality. He remained obdurate, however, on this matter throughout his life, with the result that all the important intellectuals abandoned his cause: Souvarine in France, Victor Serge, Eastman, and, later, Hook, Shachtman, and Burnham in the U.S.A. He also lost the support of Diego Rivera, the well-known painter, who was his host in Mexico. The doctrinaire rigidity of Trotskyist groups caused them to break up incessantly and was one reason, though doubtless not the chief one, why the movement never became a political force. Trotsky himself, whenever the complete fruit-lessness of his efforts was pointed out, had the same answer ready: Lenin in 1914 was almost completely isolated, and three years later he led the revolution to victory. What Lenin had done he, Trotsky, could do, as he too represented the profound tendencies of historical development. This belief inspired all his activity and political analyses, and was the source of his indomitable hope and energy.

As to the empirical evidence on which Trotsky based his hopes of an early victory of the Left in Russia, from today's viewpoint it appears amazingly slight. One or two minor Soviet diplomats quitted their posts and remained in the West; Trotsky cited this repeatedly as a proof that the Stalinist party was breaking up and that 'Thermidorian elements' and traitors to the revolution were coming to the fore, which must mean that the true Bolsheviks on the other side of the barricade were also gaining in strength. At the outbreak of war in 1939 he read in a newspaper that someone in Berlin had painted on a wall the slogan 'Down with Hitler and Stalin, long live Trotsky!' This filled him with encouragement, and he wrote that if there ever had to be a black-out in Moscow under Stalin, the whole city would be plastered with such notices. Later he read that a French diplomat had told Hitler that if France and Germany went to war, Trotsky would be the only victor; this too he quoted triumphantly in several articles as proof that even the bourgeoisie understood how right he was. He was unshakeably convinced that the war must end in a world revolution in which the true Bolsheviks, i.e. the Trotskyists, would be victorious. His article on the foundation of the Fourth International ended with the prophecy that 'During the next ten years the programme of the Fourth International will be the guide of millions, and these revolutionary millions will know how to storm earth and heaven' (*Writings of Leon Trotsky, 1938–1939*, ed. N. Allen and G. Breitman, 1974, p. 87).

In the summer of 1933, after long efforts, Trotsky finally secured permission to live in France, subject to various police restrictions. He stayed at different addresses for two years, his personal situation growing more and more dangerous: all the Stalinist parties were loudly hostile, and terrorist operations of the Soviet police were on the increase. In June 1935 he was granted asylum in Norway, where he wrote perhaps the best-known of his books, *The Revolution Betrayed*: a general analysis of the Soviet system, its degeneration and prospects, and an appeal for the overthrow of Stalin's bureaucracy by revolution. At the end of 1936 the Norwegian Government got rid of their awkward guest by sending him to Mexico, where he spent the rest of his life. Much of his energy during this period was devoted to unmasking the forgeries of the Mosocw trials, in which he was denounced as the master-mind behind all the conspiracies, sabotage, and acts of terrorism perpetrated by the accused. Through the efforts of Trotsky's friends an international commission of inquiry was set up under the chairmanship of John Dewey, the American philosopher and educationist; this body visited Mexico and took evidence from Trotsky himself, and in due course concluded that the trials were a complete fabrication.

Trotsky lived in Mexico for over three and a half years. The local Stalinists organized a campaign of persecution, and in May 1940, together with Soviet agents, made an armed attack on his house. Trotsky and his wife miraculously escaped alive, but not for long: an agent of the Soviet police, posing as a visitor, struck him down on 20 August. His son Leon, who acted as his father's representative in Europe, died in Paris in 1938, probably poisoned by Soviet agents. Another son, Sergey, who never left Russia or engaged in politics, disappeared in Stalin's prisons. Trotsky's daughter Zina committed suicide in Germany in 1933.

During his eleven years of exile Trotsky published innumerable articles, pamphlets, books, and manifestos; he issued instructions, advice, and appeals at every turn, either to the world proletariat as a whole or to the workers of Germany, Holland, Britain, China, India, and America. Inasmuch as all these documents were read only by a handful of true believers and had not the slightest influence on events, one might be inclined to dismiss Trotsky's activity as a game with toy soldiers. But the fact remains that the assassin's ice-pick was not a toy and that Stalin devoted much energy to destroying Trotskyism throughout the world—a purpose in which he was largely successful.

2. Trotsky's analysis of the Soviet system, the bureaucracy, and 'Thermidor'

All Trotsky's analyses are based on the conviction that his and Lenin's policies were unfailingly right, that the theory of permanent revolution was abundantly borne out by events, and that 'socialism in one country' was a pernicious error. In an article on 'Three Concepts of the Russian Revolution' (1939) he argued as follows. The Populists believed that Russia could bypass capitalism altogether; the Mensheviks thought the Russian revolution could only be of a bourgeois character, so that there could be no question at that stage of a dictatorship of the proletariat. Lenin then put forward the slogan of a democratic dictatorship of the proletariat and peasantry in the hope that a revolution conducted under this banner would give the impulse for a socialist victory in the West, which would make possible a rapid transition to socialism in Russia. Trotsky's own view was that the programme of the democratic revolution could only succeed in the form of a dictatorship of the proletariat, but that the latter could only maintain itself if the revolution spread to Western Europe. In 1917 Lenin took the same line, as a result of which the proletarian revolution was successful in Russia. As Trotsky shows at length in his *History of the Revolution*, none of the Bolsheviks doubted that the Russian proletariat could only conquer if it was supported by the Western proletariat, and the pernicious idea of 'socialism in one country' did not enter anyone's head until it was invented by Stalin at the end of 1924.

How did it happen, then, that Trotsky's unquestionably correct policy, which was also Lenin's from 1917 onwards, resulted in government by a 'parasitic bureaucracy', and that Trotsky himself was driven from power and branded as a traitor? The answer was to be found in an analysis of the degeneration of Soviet power and 'Thermidorianism'.

During the first years of his exile Trotsky took the view that Stalin and his group occupied the 'centre' of the Russian political spectrum and that the chief danger to the revolution came from the 'Right'—then represented by Bukharin and his followers—and counter-revolutionary elements which threatened a 'Thermidorian reaction', i.e. the restoration of capitalism. Accordingly, Trotsky offered to support Stalin against counter-revolution. Stalin, he thought, had made too many concessions to the Right, with the result, as seen in the successive trials of the 'Industrial party' and the Mensheviks, that saboteurs and enemies of the people had occupied the highest posts in the state planning organization and were deliberately slowing up industrialization. (Trotsky believed implicitly in the guilt of the accused, and it did not occur to him for a moment that these trials might be fabrications; he only began to wonder years afterwards, when his own misdeeds and those of his friends were proved by equally strong evidence in the great show trials.) In the early thirties Trotsky also spoke of 'Bonapartism' in the Stalinist regime. In 1935, however, he observed that in the French Revolution Thermidor had come first and Napoleon afterwards; the order should be the same in Russia, and, as there was already a Bonaparte, Thermidor must have come and gone. In an article entitled 'The Workers' State, Thermidor, and Bonapartism' he amended his theory somewhat. He stated that the Thermidorian reaction had taken place in Russia in 1924 (i.e. when he himself was finally removed from power); it was not, however, a capitalist counter-revolution but a seizure of power by the bureaucracy, which had begun to destroy the advance guard of the proletariat. The dictatorship of the proletariat had been preserved, as the state still owned the means of production, but political power had passed into the hands of the bureaucrats; the Bonapartist system must soon collapse, however, as it was contrary to the laws of history. A bourgeois counter-revolution was possible, but it could be avoided if the true Bolshevik elements were properly organized. Trotsky added, however, that he had in no way altered his view as to the working-class character of the Soviet state, but was merely expressing the historical analogy with more precision; in France, too, Thermidor was not a return to the *ancien régime*. The Soviet bureaucracy was not a social class, but a caste which had deprived the proletariat of its political rights and introduced a brutal despotism. Its existence in its present form, however, depended on the system of state ownership, the supreme achievement of the October Revolution, which the bureaucracy was obliged to defend and did defend in its own way. It was therefore the duty of the world proletariat to defend the Soviet Union unconditionally as the bastion of world revolution, while at the same time fighting against Stalinist degeneration (Trotsky did not explain in detail how these aims could be combined in practice). By 1936 he came to the conclusion that Stalinism could not be overthrown by reforms and internal pressures: there must be a revolution to remove the usurpers by force. That revolution would not alter the system of ownership, and would therefore not be a social revolution but a political one. It would be carried out by the advance guard of the proletariat, embodying the traditions of true Bolshevism which Stalin had destroyed.

The theory of 'socialism in one country' was responsible for all the bureaucracy's failures at home and abroad. It meant abandoning hope of world revolution and hence of Russia's main support in the world proletariat. Socialism in one country was impossible, i.e. it could be started but not completed: in a state closed within itself, socialism was bound to degenerate. The Comintern, which until 1924 had pursued a correct policy aimed at stirring up world revolution, had been transformed by Stalin into an instrument of Soviet policy and espionage, reducing the worldwide Communist movement to a state of degeneracy and impotence.

Trotsky made many attempts to explain how it was that the political power of the proletariat had been destroyed and the bureaucracy had gained control and introduced (as he later put it more than once) a totalitarian system of government. These attempts, contained in various books and articles, do not form a consistent argument. At times he maintained that the chief cause of degeneration was the delay in the outbreak of world revolution: the West European proletariat did not assume its historic mission in time. On the other hand, he maintained equally often that the defeat of revolution in Europe was the fault of the Soviet bureaucracy. It thus remained in doubt which phenomenon was the cause and which the effect—though later, as he pointed out, they aggravated each other. In *The Revolution Betrayed* we are told that the social basis of the growth of the bureaucracy was the faulty policy of the N.E.P. years, which favoured the kulaks. If so, one would expect that the liquidation of the kulaks and forced industrialization under the first five-year plan would at least have weakened the bureaucracy if not destroyed it; in fact precisely the opposite happened, and Trotsky nowhere explains why this was so. Later in the same book he says that the bureaucracy was originally an organ of the working class but that later, when it became involved in the distribution of goods, it began to place itself 'above the masses' and to claim privileges. This does not explain, however, whether and in what way the system of privilege could have been avoided, and why the working class, which was truly in charge, permitted such a thing to happen. Still in the same work, Trotsky says that the main cause of bureaucratic government was the slowness of the world proletariat to fulfil its historic mission. In an earlier pamphlet, *Problems of Development of the U.S.S.R.* (1931), he gives other reasons: the weariness of the Russian proletariat after the Civil War, the collapse of illusions fostered in the heroic days of the Revolution, the defeat of revolutionary outbreaks in Germany, Bulgaria, and Estonia, and the bureaucracy's betrayal of the Chinese and British proletariat. In an article in the following year he stated that the war-weary workers handed over power to the bureaucracy for the sake of order and reconstruction; but he did not explain why these tasks could not have been carried out by 'true Bolshevik–Leninists' under his own leadership.

From all these explanations one clear argument emerges, namely that Trotsky himself did not contribute in the smallest measure to the establishment of a bureaucratic regime, and that the bureaucracy had nothing in common with the dictatorship of the first six years after the Revolution, but was its exact contrary. The fact that the party apparatus exercised absolute power during those years had, it seems, nothing to do with the regime of Stalin and his clique, since the party in those days was the 'advance guard of the proletariat', while Stalin's subsequent apparatus represented nothing and no one. In that case, we may ask, why could not the proletariat shake off the clique of usurpers who lacked any social backing? Trotsky has an answer to this too: the proletariat does not rebel against Stalin's government (elsewhere, however, we read that it is in constant rebellion) because it fears that in the present situation a proletarian revolution might lead to the restoration of capitalism.

It is not clear from Trotsky's arguments whether there

was any means of avoiding such a disastrous outcome. It seems, on the whole, that there was not, since otherwise Trotsky and his group, who invariably pursued the right policy and 'expressed' the true interests of the proletariat, would surely have prevented the bureaucracy taking over. If they did not prevent it, it was because they could not; and if the bureaucracy continued to maintain itself without any visible social foundation, this must surely be due to the operation of historical laws.

3. Bolshevism and Stalinism. The idea of Soviet democracy

Trotsky thus took every opportunity to emphasize that there was no continuity between true Bolshevism or Leninism, that is to say Trotsky's own ideology and politics on the one hand, and Stalinism on the other. Stalinism was not only not the true heir of Leninism, but a glaring contradiction of it. In an article of 1937 he takes issue with Mensheviks and anarchists who were saying: 'We told you so from the beginning.' Not at all, replies Trotsky. The Mensheviks and anarchists predicted that despotism and the stifling of the Russian proletariat would come as a result of Bolshevik government; they have indeed come, but as a result of Stalin's bureaucracy, which has nothing to do with true Bolshevism. Again, Pannekoek and some German Spartacists say that the Bolsheviks set up a dictatorship of the party instead of a dictatorship of the proletariat, and that Stalin established a bureaucratic dictatorship on that basis. This is not the case either. The proletariat could not take over state power except through its own vanguard, in which the working masses' aspirations to freedom were crystallized.

In this article as in many others, Trotsky was obliged to answer the objections frequently raised by his adversaries and also by such supporters as Serge, Souvarine, and Burnham. Surely, they pointed out, the Bolsheviks had from the beginning, with Trotsky's active participation, liquidated all Russian political parties including the socialists; they had themselves forbidden the formation of groups within the party, had destroyed the freedom of the press, had bloodily suppressed the Kronstadt revolt, and so forth.

Trotsky answered these objections many times, and always in the same way: the actions complained of were right and necessary and in no way infringed the healthy foundations of proletarian

dcmocracy. In a letter to the workers of Zurich, published in
August 1932, he wrote that the Bolsheviks had certainly used
force to destroy the anarchists and Left S.R.s (other parties are
not even mentioned in this context), but they did so in defence
of the workers' state, and therefore their action was right; the
class struggle could not be carried on without violence, the
only question was which class the violence was exercised by.
In a pamphlet of 1938, *Their Morals and Ours*, he explained
that it was absurd to compare Communism with Fascism, as
the resemblance in their methods was 'superficial' and related
to secondary phenomena (for example, the abolition of general
elections); what mattered was the class in whose name such
methods were used. Trotsky, it was objected, had taken hostages,
including children, from the families of political opponents, and
was now indignant when Stalin did the same thing to
Trotskyists. But, he replied, there was no true analogy, for what
Trotsky did was necessary to fight the class enemy and bring
victory to the proletariat, whereas Stalin was acting in the
interests of the bureaucracy. In a letter of 1940 to Shachtman
he agrees that the Cheka originated and functioned when he was
in power—of course it did, but it was a necessary weapon against
the bourgeoisie, whereas now Stalin was using it to destroy
'true Bolsheviks', so there was no proper comparison. As to the
suppression of the Kronstadt revolt, how could a proletarian
government be expected to give up an important fortress to
reactionary peasant soldiers, among whom there might be a few
anarchists? As to the forbidding of party groups, this was
absolutely necessary, for when all non-Bolshevik parties were
liquidated the antagonistic interests that were still present in
society were bound to seek expression in different tendencies
within the one party.

It is clear from this that for Trotsky there was no question of
democracy as a form of government, or of civil liberties as a
cultural value: from this point of view he was faithful to Lenin
and did not differ from Stalin. If power was wielded by the
'historically progressive' class (through its vanguard, of course),
then by definition this was an authentic democracy, even if
oppression and coercion in every form were otherwise the order
of the day; for all this was in the cause of progress. But from the
moment that power was taken over by a bureaucracy that did

not represent the interests of the proletariat, the same forms of government automatically became reactionary and therefore 'anti-democratic'. In an article of 1931 entitled 'The Right–Left Bloc' Trotsky wrote: 'What we mean by the restoration of party democracy is that the real revolutionary proletarian core of the party win the right to curb the bureaucracy and to really purge the party: to purge the party of the Thermidorians in principle as well as their unprincipled and careerist cohorts who vote according to command from above, of the tendencies of tail-endism as well as the numerous factions of toadyism, whose title should not be derived from the Greek or Latin but from the real Russian word for toady in its contemporary, bureaucratized and Stalinized form. This is the reason we need democracy' (*Writings of Leon Trotsky, 1930–1931*, ed. G. Breitman and S. Lovell, 1973, p. 57). It is thus clear that by 'democracy' Trotsky means government by Trotskyists, expressing the historical aspirations of the proletariat.

In an article of December 1939 Trotsky again answers the question whether he himself was not responsible for the liquidation of all political parties except the Bolsheviks. Certainly, he replies, and it was quite right to do so. 'But,' he goes on, 'one cannot identify the laws of civil war with the laws of peaceful periods'—and then, it clearly having occurred to him that in that case the liquidated parties should have been re-legalized after the Civil War, he adds: '[or] the laws of dictatorship or the proletariat with the laws of bourgeois democracy' (*Writings of Leon Trotsky, 1939–1940*, ed. N. Allen and G. Breitman, 1973, p. 133).

In a statement dating from the end of 1932 we read: 'Every regime must be judged first and foremost according to its own rules. The regime of the proletarian dictatorship cannot and does not wish to hold back from infringing the principles and formal rules of democracy. It has to be judged from the standpoint of its capacity to ensure the transition to a new society. The democratic regime, on the other hand, must be judged from the standpoint of the extent to which it allows the class struggle to develop within the framework of democracy' (*Writings of Leon Trotsky, 1932–1933*, 1972, ed. G. Breitman and S. Lovell, p. 336).

In short, it is right to be indignant and to attack democratic states when they infringe the principles of democracy and freedom, but one must not treat a Communist dictatorship in this way, because it does not recognize democratic principles; its superiority lies in the promise to create a 'new society' in the future.

In *The Revolution Betrayed* we are even told that Stalin's constitution, by proclaiming universal suffrage, made it clear that there was no longer a dictatorship of the proletariat. (Trotsky also remarks that by introducing the secret ballot Stalin evidently wished to purge his regime of corruption to some extent. Incredible as it may seem, he evidently took Stalin's elections at face value.)

Thus, while Trotsky constantly attacked Stalin and his regime and demanded a return to 'Soviet democracy' and 'party democracy', it is clear in the light of his general principles that 'democracy' signifies the rule of those whose policy is 'right': it does not mean that the 'rightness' of a policy is determined as the result of different groups contending for popular support. In *The Revolution Betrayed* he writes of the need to regain freedom for 'Soviet parties', starting with the Bolsheviks (i.e. Trotsky and his followers); but it not clear which other parties qualify as 'Soviet'. Since only the genuine vanguard of the proletariat is to exercise power, that vanguard must also have the right to decide which parties are 'Soviet' and which are counter-revolutionary. In Trotsky's eyes, the upshot seems to be that socialist freedom means freedom for Trotskyists and no one else.

The same arguments apply to cultural freedom. Trotsky sometimes expressed indignation at the gagging of art and science by Stalin's regime. In *The Revolution Betrayed* he recalled that in 1924 he himself had formulated rules for the dictatorship of the proletariat in art and literature: the sole criterion was to be whether a work was for or against the Revolution, and beyond that there should be perfect freedom. In July 1932 he wrote that there should be freedom in art and philosophy, 'eliminating pitilessly only that which is directed against the revolutionary tasks of the proletariat' (*Writings, 1932–1933*, p. 279). This, however, is the same principle that prevailed under Stalin: the party authorities decide what is 'directed against the revolutionary tasks of the proletariat' and must therefore be 'pitilessly eliminated'. Freedom thus defined has never been

infringed in the Soviet state. Of course, under such a general
formula the degree of repression and regimentation of culture
may be greater or less according to various political circumstances, and in the twenties it was certainly less than in the
thirties. Since, however, the principle is that the rulers decide in
every case what manifestations of culture are in accordance with
their political needs, no degree of repression and enslavement
can possibly offend against the dictatorship of the proletariat.
The whole question reduces once again to the same pattern:
if Trotsky had been in charge he would not, of course, have
allowed freedoms that he thought dangerous to his authority;
Stalin behaved in the same way, and in both cases it was a
matter of self-interest. The whole difference comes down to this,
that Trotsky believed himself to 'represent the historical interests
of the proletariat', while Stalin believed that he, Stalin, did so.

In *Their Morals and Ours* Trotsky endeavoured to refute the
objection of those of his followers who claimed that his rule
of morality was simply 'What is good for me is right' and that
in his view the end justified the means. To this he replied that
if the means were to be justified by something other than the
aims evolved by history, that something could only be God.
In other words his questioners were falling into religiosity,
just as the Russian revisionists Struve, Bulgakov, and
Berdyayev had done; they tried to combine Marxism with some
kind of morality superior to class, and ended up in the bosom
of the Church. Morals in general, he declared, were a function
of the class struggle. At the present time morality could be in the
interest of the proletariat or in that of Fascism, and, obviously,
warring classes might sometimes use similar means; the only
important question was which side they benefited. 'A means
can be justified only by its end. But the end in its turn
needs to be justified. From the Marxist point of view, which
expresses the historical interests of the proletariat, the end is
justified if it leads to increasing the power of man over
nature and to the abolition of the power of man over man'
(*Their Morals and Ours*, 1942, p. 34). In other words, if a policy
is conducive to technical progress (the power of man over
nature), any means which furthers that policy is automatically
justified; it is not clear, however, why Stalin's policy should in
that case be condemned, since it certainly raised the country's

technical level. As to the abolition of the power of man over man, Trotsky himself enunciated the principle (which Stalin took over) that before this power can be abolished it must be increased to the highest degree; Trotsky reiterated this view in an article in June 1933. But in future things will be different. The 'historical aim' is embodied in the proletarian party, which therefore decides what is moral and what is immoral. As to Souvarine's remark that, as Trotsky's party does not exist, he must regard himself alone as the embodiment of morality, the prophet replies once again by pointing to Lenin's example— he too stood alone in 1914, and what happened after that?

In a sense the critics' objection was invalid: Trotsky did not maintain that what served his party's interests was morally good, and what injured them was morally bad. He held simply that there were no such things as moral criteria, but only criteria of political efficacy: 'Problems of revolutionary morality are fused with the problems of revolutionary strategy and tactics' (ibid., p. 35). To say that a thing was good or bad in itself, irrespective of political consequences, was tantamount to believing in God. It was meaningless to ask, for instance, whether it was right in itself to murder the children of one's political opponents. It had been right (as Trotsky says elsewhere) to kill the Tsar's children, because it was politically justified. Why then was it wrong for Stalin to murder Trotsky's children? Because Stalin did not represent the proletariat. All 'abstract' principles of good and bad, all universal rules of democracy, freedom, and cultural values were without significance in themselves: they were to be accepted or rejected as political expediency might dictate. The question of course then arises why anyone should side with the 'vanguard of the proletariat' rather than with its opponents, or identify himself with any aims whatever. Trotsky does not answer this question, but merely says that 'The end flows naturally from the historical movement' (ibid., p. 35). This presumably means, though he does not say so clearly, that we must first find out what is historically inevitable, and then support it for no other reason than that it is inevitable.

As for democracy within the party, Trotsky is quite categorical about this also. In Stalin's party, when his own group was in opposition, he naturally demanded free intra-party discussion and even freedom to form 'fractions'. On the other hand, he defended the prohibition of fractions enacted by himself and others at the Tenth Congress in 1921, on the ground that it was an 'extraordinary measure'. It is hard to interpret this otherwise than as meaning that it is right to prohibit fractions when they are wrong, but that Trotsky's group must not be prohibited because it expresses the interest of the proletariat. During his exile he also endeavoured to impose 'true Leninist' principles on the small groups of his adherents: he unceasingly condemned all variations from his own statements, ordered the exclusion of all who resisted his authority on any subject, and proclaimed the doctrine of Communist centralism at every turn. He denounced Souvarine's group of 'Communist democrats' in Paris, saying that their very name showed that they had broken with Marxism (on which point he may have been right). He reprimanded Naville's group when, in 1935, they proclaimed a programme of their own within the Left Opposition. He condemned Luciano Galicia, the leader of the Mexican Trotskyists, who forgot about centralism and demanded full freedom of opinion within the Fourth International. He lashed out furiously at the American Trotskyist Dwight Macdonald, who had said that all theory must be treated with scepticism: 'He who propagates theoretical scepticism is a traitor' (*Writings, 1939–1940*, p. 341). He pronounced irrevocable sentence on Burnham and Shachtman when they finally came to doubt that the Soviet Union was a workers' state, and talked of Soviet imperialism in invading Poland and in the war with Finland. On this occasion he refused to agree to a referendum within the American Trotskyist party (which, with about a thousand members according to Deutscher, seems to have been the biggest contingent in the Fourth International) on the ground that party policy was not 'simply an arithmetical total of local decisions' (*In Defence of Marxism*, 1942, p. 33). The fact that this absolutism caused his movement to shrink and to become more and more like a tiny religious sect, convinced that its members and they only were destined to salvation, did not worry Trotsky at all—once more, what about Lenin in 1914? He also shared Lenin's 'dialectical' view that the true or 'underlying' majority did not consist of those who happened to be in larger number but of those who were right or stood for historical progress. He seems to have genuinely believed that the working masses of the world were on his side in their inmost hearts, even though they did not yet know it; for the laws of history made clear that this must be so.

Trotsky's attitude to the problems of national oppression and self-determination was on similar lines. His writings contain a few references to Stalinist suppression of the national aspirations of the Ukrainians and other peoples; at the same time he emphasized that no concessions must be made to Ukrainian nationalists, and that true Bolsheviks in the Ukraine must not form a 'people's front' with them. He went so far as to say that the Ukrainians, divided as they were among four states, constituted an international problem no less crucial than, in Marx's opinion, the Polish question had been in the nineteenth century. But he saw nothing reprehensible in the socialist state bringing the 'proletarian revolution' to other countries by means of armed invasion. In 1939–40 he explained indignantly to Shachtman and Burnham that the Soviet invasion of Poland coincided with the revolutionary movement in that country, that the Stalinist bureaucracy had given a revolutionary impulse to the Polish proletariat and peasantry, and that in Finland too the war with the Soviet Union had awakened revolutionary feelings. True, this was a revolution of a 'special kind', since it was introduced at the point of the bayonet and did not spring from the depths of popular feeling, but it was a genuine revolution all the same. Trotsky's knowledge of what was happening in Eastern Poland and Finland was based, of course, not on any empirical data but on the 'laws of history': the Soviet state, degenerate though it was, represented the interests of the popular masses, and therefore the latter must support the invading Red Army. On this point Trotsky certainly cannot be accused of deviating from Leninism: as the 'true' national interest coincides with that of the vanguard of the proletariat, it follows that wherever the vanguard is in power (albeit in a state of 'bureaucratic degeneration') the right of national self-determination has been realized, and the masses must support this state of affairs, for so the theory requires.

4. *Criticism of Soviet economic and foreign policy*

Since, in theory at least, industrialization and the future

agricultural policy were a vital issue to the Left Opposition in the Soviet Union, Trotsky was in an awkward position when it turned out that Stalin had taken over all the opposition's policies, and had done so in an intensified form. He solved the difficulty by declaring that Stalin had indeed carried out the opposition's aims but had done so in a bureaucratic and ill-considered manner. 'The Left Opposition began with the struggle for the industrialization and agrarian collectivization of the Soviet Union. This fight is won in a certain sense, namely in that, beginning with 1928, the whole policy of the Soviet government represents a bureaucratically distorted application of the principles of the Left Opposition' (*Writings of Leon Trotsky, 1933–1934*, ed. G. Breitman and B. Scott, 1972, p. 274). The bureaucracy 'had been compelled' to carry out these measures in its own interest, by the logic of government, and although it had performed the historical tasks of the proletariat in a distorted manner, the changes in themselves were 'progressive'; moreover, it was leftist pressure that had forced Stalin to change his tune. 'Between the creative forces of the revolution and the bureaucracy there exists a profound antagonism. If the Stalinist apparatus constantly comes to a halt at certain limits, if it finds itself compelled even to turn sharply to the left, this occurs above all under the pressure of the amorphous, scattered, but still powerful elements of the revolutionary party' (*Writings, 1930–1931*, p. 224). As to collectivization, Trotsky criticized the haste and lack of economic preparation and emphasized that the Stalinists were wrong in regarding the kolkhozes as socialist institutions: they were no more than a transitional form. What was more, collectivization turned out to be a step towards the restoration of capitalism. In *The Revolution Betrayed* Trotsky wrote that Stalin had annulled the nationalization of the land by giving it to the kolkhozes, and by allowing the peasants to cultivate private plots on the side he had strengthened the element of 'individualism'. Thus, when Soviet agriculture lay in ruins and millions of peasants were starving to death, or were kept alive only by the permission they had at last received to maintain private plots, Trotsky's chief concern was the danger of 'individualism' that this represented. He even held that the fight against the kulaks was insufficiently thorough, as Stalin had given them a chance to organize in the kolkhozes and, after the first liquidation campaign, had made further substantial concessions which must lead to renewed class differentiation in the countryside. (This was Trotsky's line in 1935, when he perceived a 'swing to the right' in Stalin's foreign policy and therefore looked for symptoms of a similar turn in Soviet internal affairs.)

On several occasions, in *The Revolution Betrayed* and elsewhere, Trotsky condemned the 'barbarous' introduction of piece-work into Soviet industry. It was hard to tell from his arguments, however, whether he thought material incentives to productivity should be replaced by police compulsion or revolutionary zeal, and, in the latter case, how that zeal was to be evoked.

As to Stalin's foreign policy, Trotsky harped on the theme that international revolution was being abandoned for the sake of 'socialism in one country': hence the revolution had been successively betrayed in Germany, China, and Spain. (The Spanish Civil War, according to Trotsky, was 'essentially' a proletarian struggle for socialism.) He did not say whether the Red Army should have been sent to aid the German Communists in 1923 (as he himself had vainly tried to do in 1920), or to aid the Chinese in 1926. In general Trotsky opposed the policy of supporting the 'national bourgeoisie' in undeveloped countries. This policy was often quite successful in weakening the great capitalist Powers; Trotsky, however, thought it pernicious on the ground that in colonial territories, as elsewhere, the tasks of the 'bourgeois revolution' could only be performed under Communist leadership, which would bring the revolution continuously into a socialist stage. It was, for instance, absurd to suppose that India could gain its independence otherwise than by a proletarian revolution; this was absolutely ruled out by the laws of history. The example of Russia showed that the only possibility was a 'permanent revolution' led from the outset by the proletariat, i.e. the Communist party. Trotsky regarded Russian models as absolutely binding on all countries of the world, and he therefore had ready-made answers to all their problems whether or not he knew anything about their history or specific conditions.

Trotsky did not dispute that Communists in a revolutionary period must make use of transitional aims before they could control the situation completely. Thus in a letter of August

1931 to the Chinese Trotskyists he wrote that the idea of a national assembly must not be dropped from their programme, because when the support of the poor peasants was being canvassed 'the proletariat will have to convoke a national assembly in order not to arouse the mistrust of the peasantry and in order not to provide an opening for bourgeois demagogy' (*Writings, 1930–1931*, p. 128). On the other hand, we read elsewhere that it would be a fatal mistake to repeat Lenin's pre-1917 slogan of a 'dictatorship of the proletariat and peasantry'. At the outset of the Russian revolution the government was referred to as representing the proletariat and the poor peasantry. As to this, Trotsky writes: 'True, subsequently we called the Soviet government worker and peasant. But by this time the dictatorship of the proletariat was already a fact, the Communist Party was in power, and consequently the name Workers' and Peasants' Government could not give rise to any ambiguity or grounds for alarm' (ibid., p. 308). In short, once the Communists were in power there could be no harm in fictitious and deceptive names.

Trotsky's supporters and admirers, such as Deutscher, have often emphasized, as a fact greatly to his credit, that he opposed the slogan of 'social Fascism'. It is true that he criticized this slogan because it cut off the Communists from the working masses in the social democratic parties, but he does not seem to have had any real policy to suggest as far as the social democrats were concerned. He wrote that there could be no question of permanent co-operation with organizations which did not break radically with reformism and which sought to regenerate social democracy. At the same period, before Hitler's accession to power, he blamed the Stalinists simultaneously for talking of 'social Fascism' and for capitulating to the social democrats. In June 1933, just after the Nazi victory, he declared that there could be no thought of a united front with the German social democrats, who were Hitler's lackeys. But Trotsky's indignation was aroused in earnest by the change of Soviet policy in 1934–5. Stalinism had at last shown its Rightist countenance: the Stalinists were allying themselves with the renegades of the Second International and, worse still, were talking of peace and international arbitration and dividing states into democratic and Fascist as if that were the important difference. They spoke of Fascism threatening world war, yet as Marxists they must know that imperialist war had an 'economic foundation'. They even accepted at Geneva a formula defining the aggressor in terms which would apply equally to all wars, including those between capitalist states. This was a surrender to bourgeois pacifism: Marxists could not be opposed to all wars in principle, they left that sort of cant to Quakers and Tolstoyans. Marxists judged war from the class point of view and were not interested in bourgeois distinctions between the aggressor and his victim; their principle was that a war in the interests of the proletariat, be it aggressive or defensive, was a just war, while a war between imperialists was a crime.

In reality all Trotsky's earlier appeals for a change of attitude towards the social democrats were illusory and could have borne no fruit even if he had been in power: for he seems to have imagined that it was possible to maintain ideological 'purity' *vis-à-vis* the social democrats while at the same time soliciting their help in particular circumstances. When Stalin, to prevent France coming to terms with Nazi Germany, launched the policy of the 'popular front' and an anti-Fascist alliance with the socialists, he realized that he must pay a price, at all events in propaganda terms, if his policy was to be successful. Trotsky, on the other hand, thought it possible to form an anti-Nazi front with the socialists while denouncing them at every turn as impostors, agents of the bourgeoisie, traitors to the working class, and lackeys of imperialism—the only taboo epithet being 'social Fascists'. It is evident that if he had been in charge of the Comintern at that time, his policy would have been even less successful than Stalin's.

Trotsky was indeed a true adherent of Lenin's opinion that (as the latter repeated many times during the war and the Revolution) reliance on international treaties, arbitration, disarmament, and so on was idle reactionary chatter. It did not matter who was the aggressor, but which class was waging the war. The socialist state, representing the interests of the world proletariat, was 'right' in every war, regardless of who began it, and could not seriously consider itself bound by treaties with imperialist governments. Stalin was concerned with the security of the Soviet state, not with world revolution, and therefore had to present himself on various occasions as an advocate of peace and a champion of international law and democracy. Trotsky, however, believed that the main elements of the situation were still as he had seen them in 1918: on one side the imperialists, on the other the socialist state and the world proletariat waiting for the right slogans to unleash a revolution. Stalin, the exponent of Realpolitik, did not believe in the 'rising tide of revolution', and used the European Communist parties as instruments of Soviet policy. Trotsky was the advocate of incessant 'revolutionary war', and his whole doctrine was based on the conviction that the world proletariat was, in the nature of things and by the laws of history, tending towards revolution, and that only the erroneous policy of the Stalinist bureaucracy prevented this innate trend from taking effect.

5. Fascism, democracy, and war

How doctrinaire and unrealistic Trotsky's political thinking was in the 1930s may be judged from his remarks on the coming war and his recommendations for action in the face of the Fascist threat.

A few days after the outbreak of war he wrote: 'I do not see the slightest reason for changing those principles in relation to world war which were elaborated between 1914 and 1917 by the best representatives of the workers' movement under the leadership of Lenin. The present war has a reactionary character on both sides. Whichever camp is victorious, humanity will be thrown far behind' (*Writings, 1939–1940*, p. 85). These words— written after the German invasion of Poland and the Anglo-French declaration of war, but before the Soviet invasion of mid-September—were an epitome of Trotsky's views on the subject of a war among capitalist states such as Nazi Germany, Fascist Italy, Poland, France, Britain, and the U.S.A. For many years he repeated indefatigably that it was a fatal illusion and a capitalist trick to suggest that there was or could be a front of 'democratic' states against Fascism, or that it made any difference whether victory went to Hitler or to a coalition of the Western democracies, since neither side had nationalized its factories. The proletariat of the belligerent countries, instead of helping their reactionary governments to fight Hitler, should rise against them as Lenin had urged during the First World War. The cry of 'national defence' was in the highest degree reactionary and anti-Marxist; what was at issue was a proletarian revolution, not the defeat of one bourgeoisie by another.

In a pamphlet of July 1934 entitled *War and the Fourth International* Trotsky wrote:

The sham of national defence is covered up wherever possible by the additional sham of the defence of democracy. If even now, in the imperialist epoch, Marxists do not identify democracy with fascism and are ready at any moment to repel fascism's encroachment upon democracy, must not the proletariat in case of war support the democratic governments against the fascist governments? Flagrant sophism! We defend democracy against fascism by means of the organizations and methods of the proletariat. Contrary to Social Democracy we do not entrust this defence to the bourgeois state ... Under these conditions, the support by a workers' party of "its" national imperialism for the sake of a fragile democratic shell means the renunciation of an independent policy and the chauvinistic demoralization of the workers ... The revolutionary vanguard will seek a united front with the working-class organizations—against its own 'democratic' government—but in no case unity with its own government against the hostile country. (*Writings, 1933–1934*, pp. 306–7)

The Third International, Trotsky emphasized in an article in 1935, had always combated pacifism, not only social-patriotism, and had always condemned talk of disarmament, arbitration, the League of Nations, etc.; yet today it was endorsing all these bourgeois policies. When *L'Humanité* called for the defence of 'French civilization' it showed that it had betrayed the proletariat and was taking a nationalist stand, inviting workers to help their own government to fight German imperialism. Wars were the product of capitalism, and it was senseless to argue that the chief danger at present was from Nazism. 'On this road one quickly arrives at the idealization of French democracy as such, counterposed to Hitler Germany' (*Writings of Leon Trotsky, 1934–1935*, ed. G. Breitman and B. Scott, 1971, p. 293).

A year before the war Trotsky declared that democracy and Fascism were simply two alternative instruments of exploitation —the rest was all a deceit.

Really, what would a military bloc of imperialist democracies against Hitler mean? A new edition of the Versailles chains, even more heavy, bloody and intolerable ... The Czechoslovakian crisis revealed with remarkable clarity that fascism does not exist as an independent factor. It is only one of the tools of imperialism. 'Democracy' is another of its tools. Imperialism rises above them both. It sets them in motion according to needs, at times counterposing them to one another, at times amicably conciling [*sic*] them. To fight against fascism in an alliance with imperialism is the same as to fight in an alliance with the devil against his claws or horns. (*Writings, 1938–1939*, p. 21)

In short, there was no such thing as a fight between democracy and Fascism. International treaties took no account of such pseudo-antagonisms: the British might conclude a pact with Italy, the Poles with Germany. No matter who the contending parties were, the coming war would bring about an international proletarian revolution—such was the law of history. Humanity would not endure the war longer than a few months; rebellions against national governments, led by the Fourth international, would break out on every hand. In any case the war would at once wipe out all traces of democracy, so that it was absurd to talk about the defence of democratic values. In reply to a Trotskyist group in Palestine who suggested that Fascism was the chief threat to be resisted at that time and that it was wrong to preach defeatism in countries combating it, Trotsky wrote that their attitude was no better than social-patriotism. For all true revolutionaries, the chief enemy was always at home. In another letter, of July 1939, he declared: 'The victories of fascism are important, but the death agony of capitalism is more important. Fascism accelerates the new war, and the war will tremendously accelerate the revolutionary movement. In case of war every small revolutionary nucleus can and will become a decisive historic factor in a very short time' (*Writings, 1938–1939*, p. 349). The Fourth International would play the same part in the coming war as the Bolsheviks had in 1917, but this time the downfall of capitalism would be complete and final. 'Yes, I do not doubt that the new world war will provoke with absolute inevitability the world revolution and the collapse of the capitalist system' (ibid., p. 232).

When war actually came it did not alter Trotsky's opinion on these matters, but strengthened it. In the manifesto of the

Fourth International, published in June 1940, he declared that 'A socialist who comes out today for the defence of the "fatherland" is playing the same reactionary role as the peasants of the Vendée who rushed to the defence of the feudal regime, that is of their own chains' (*Writings, 1939–1940*, p. 190). It was pointless to talk of defending democracy against Fascism, for Fascism was a product of bourgeois democracy, and it was not any 'fatherland' that had to be defended, but the interests of the world proletariat. 'But the first to be vanquished in the war will be the thoroughly rotten democracy. In its definitive downfall it will drag down with it all the workers' organizations which served as its support. There will be no room for reformist unions. Capitalist reaction will destroy them ruthlessly' (ibid., p. 213). ' "But isn't the working class obliged in the present conditions to aid the democracies in their struggle against German fascism?" This is how the question is put by broad petty-bourgeois circles for whom the proletariat always remains only an auxiliary tool for this or that faction of the bourgeoisie. We reject this policy with indignation. Naturally there exists a difference between the political regimes in bourgeois society, just as there is a difference in comfort between various cars in a railway train. But when the whole train is plunging into an abyss, the distinction between decaying democracy and murderous fascism disappears in the face of the collapse of the entire capitalist system ... The victory of the imperialists of Great Britain and France would be no less frightful for the ultimate fate of mankind than that of Hitler and Mussolini. Bourgeois democracy cannot be saved. By helping their bourgeoisie against foreign fascism, the workers could only accelerate the victory of fascism in their own country' (ibid., p. 221).

Here, again, is Trotsky's advice to the Norwegian workers at the time of Hitler's invasion. 'Should the Norwegian workers have supported the "democratic" camp against the fascist? ... In reality this would be the crudest kind of blunder ... In the world arena we support neither the camp of the Allies nor the camp of Germany. Consequently we have not the slightest reason or justification for supporting either one of their temporary tools within Norway itself' (*In Defense of Marxism*, p. 172).

Accordingly, if the workers of Poland, France, or Norway had read Trotsky's proclamations and obeyed them they would have turned their arms against their own governments at the time of the Nazi invasion, as it made no difference whether they were ruled by Hitler or their own bourgeoisie; Fascism was an instrument of the bourgeoisie, and it was an absurdity to talk of all classes forming a common front against Fascism. Lenin, in the same way, had preached defeatism in the First World War, and lo, the revolution had broken out. Trotsky, it should be observed, thought it very likely that the war would be one of all capitalist states against the Soviet Union, as the former were united by class-interest. If, however, the Soviet Union were allied with one capitalist Power against another, the war could only be a very short one, as a proletarian revolution would at once break out in the defeated capitalist state, as in Russia in 1917, and the two hostile Powers would then unite against the fatherland of the proletariat.

Thus, for Trotsky, the general upshot of the war was a foregone conclusion. Capitalism would finally collapse, Stalinism and Stalin would be swept away, the world revolution would break out, the Fourth International would instantly gain ascendancy over the workers' minds and appear as the final victor. As he wrote in reply to the criticisms of Serge, Souvarine, and Thomas: 'All the parties of capitalist society, all its moralists and all its sycophants will perish beneath the debris of the impending catastrophe. The only party that will survive is the party of the world socialist revolution, even though it may seem non-existent today to the sightless rationalizers, just as during the last war the party of Lenin and Liebknecht seemed to them non-existent' (*Their Morals and Ours*, p. 47). In addition Trotsky made many detailed predictions with complete assurance. It was, for instance, absolutely impossible for Switzerland to avoid being dragged into the war; democracy could not survive in any country, but must by an 'iron law' develop into Fascism; if Italian democracy were restored it could only last a few months before being swept away by the proletarian revolution. As Hitler's army consisted of workers and peasants it was bound eventually to ally itself with the peoples of the occupied countries, for the laws of history taught that the bonds of class were stronger than any other.

As to the general nature of the Fascist danger, Trotsky put forward a very interesting analysis in August 1933. 'Theoretically, the victory of fascism is undoubtedly evidence of the fact that democracy has exhausted itself; but politically the fascist regime preserves democratic prejudices, recreates them, inculcates them into the youth and is even capable of imparting to them, for a short time, the greatest strength. Precisely in this consists one of the most important manifestations of the reactionary historic role of fascism' (*Writings, 1932–1933*, p. 294). 'Under the yoke of the "fascist" dictatorship the democratic illusions were not weakened, but became stronger' (ibid., p. 296). In other words, the threat of Fascism lies in the fact that people subjected to it long for democracy, and thus democratic prejudices are preserved instead of being dispelled; Hitler is dangerous because he makes it harder to destroy democracy.

Shortly before his death Trotsky reaffirmed his predictions as to the development of the war and at the same time put the question, in a rhetorical vein, as to what would happen if they were not fulfilled; he answered that it would signify the bankruptcy of Marxism.

If this war provokes, as we firmly believe, a proletarian revolution, it must inevitably lead to the overthrow of the bureaucracy in the USSR and the regeneration of Soviet democracy on a far higher economic and cultural basis than in 1918 ... If, however, it is conceded that the present war will provoke not revolution but a decline of the proletariat, there remains another alternative: the further decay of monopoly capitalism, its faster fusion with the state, and the replacement of democracy, wherever it still remains, by a totalitarian regime. The inability of the proletariat to take into its hands the leadership of society could actually lead under these conditions to the growth of a new exploiting class from the Bonapartist fascist bureaucracy. This would be, according to all indications, a regime of decline, signalizing the eclipse of civilization. An analogous result might occur in the event that the proletariat of advanced capitalist countries, having conquered power, should prove incapable of holding it and surrender it, as in the USSR, to a privileged bureaucracy. Then we would be compelled to acknowledge that the reason for the bureaucratic relapse is rooted not in the backwardness of the country and not in the imperialist environment, but in the congenital incapacity of the proletariat to become a ruling class. Then it would be necessary in retrospect to establish [*sic*] that in its fundamental traits the present

USSR was the precursor of a new exploiting regime on an international
scale ... However onerous the second perspective may be, if the world
proletariat should actually prove incapable of fulfilling the mission
placed upon it by the course of development, nothing else would
remain except only to recognize that the socialist programme, based
on the internal contradictions of capitalist society, ended as a Utopia.
(*In Defence of Marxism*, pp. 8–9)

This is an unusual argument to find in Trotsky's works.
Naturally he states with confidence that the pessimistic second
alternative is an unreal one, and he continues to believe that
world revolution is inevitable, not merely as a general proposition but as a result of the war in progress. But the mere fact
that he envisages another hypothesis seems to point to a certain
hesitation, if we compare the above passage with the absolute
confidence in victory that he expresses elsewhere.

Trotsky did not admit the idea that capitalism might be
capable of reforming itself. Roosevelt's 'New Deal' seemed to him
a desperate and reactionary attempt, foredoomed to failure. He
believed, moreover, that the United States, having reached the
highest stage of technical development, was already ripe for
Communism. (In an article of March 1935 he promised the
Americans that when they did go Communist their production
costs would be cut by eighty per cent, and in 'The U.S.S.R. in
Wartime', written shortly before his death, he declared that
with a planned economy they could soon raise their national
income to 200 billion dollars a year, and so ensure prosperity
for all.) In *The Revolution Betrayed* we read that if anyone
supposed that capitalism could thrive for more than a decade
or two he must, by the same token, believe that socialism in
the Soviet Union made no sense and that the Marxists had
misjudged their historical moment, for the Russian revolution
would in that case stand as a mere episodic experiment like the
Paris Commune.

6. Conclusions

From the perspective of today, Trotsky's literary and political
activity in the 1930s gives an impression of extreme wishful
thinking: it is an unhappy mixture of unfulfilled prophecies, fantastic illusions, false diagnoses, and unfounded hopes. Of course
it is not of the first importance that Trotsky failed to foresee

the course of the war: many people in those days made predictions, most of which were belied by events. What is important
and characteristic, however, is that he invariably presented his
speculations as scientifically exact prognoses, based on a profound dialectic and understanding of great historical processes.
In fact his prophecies were partly founded on hopes that history
would vindicate his judgement, and partly on doctrinaire
deductions from supposed historical laws which he believed must
come into play sooner rather than later. One wonders what
would have happened if Stalin had foreseen the outcome of the
war and had taken his revenge on Trotsky not by killing him but
by letting him live to see the collapse of all his hopes and
prophecies, not a single one of which came true. The war was
an anti-Fascist war; no proletarian revolution took place in
Europe or America, apart from the Soviet conquest of Eastern
Europe; the Stalinist bureaucracy was not swept away, but
became immeasurably stronger, as did Stalin himself; democracy survived, and was restored in West Germany and Italy;
most of the colonial territories gained their independence without a proletarian revolution; and the Fourth International
remained an impotent sect. If Trotsky had seen all this, would he
have admitted that his pessimistic hypothesis had proved to be
the right one and that Marxism was an illusion? We cannot tell,
of course, but his mentality would probably not have allowed
him to draw such an inference; he would no doubt simply
have noted that the operation of the laws of history had again
been somewhat delayed, but would have remained firm in his
belief that the great moment was at hand.

Trotsky, as a true doctrinaire, was insensitive to everything
that was happening around him. Of course he followed events
closely and commented on them, and did his best to obtain
accurate information about the Soviet Union and world politics.
But the essence of a doctrinaire is not that he does not read
newspapers or collect facts: it consists in adhering to a system
of interpretation that is impervious to empirical data, or is so
nebulous that any and every fact can be used to confirm it.
Trotsky had no need to fear that any event might cause him to
change his mind, as his basic premises were always in the
form 'on the one hand ... on the other hand', or 'admittedly
... but nevertheless'. If Communists suffered a set-back any-

where in the world, it confirmed his diagnosis that the Stalinist bureaucracy (as he had always said) was leading the movement to ruin. If there was a Communist success it also confirmed his diagnosis: the working class had shown, despite the Stalinist bureaucracy, that it was still full (as he had always said) of revolutionary spirit. If Stalin made a 'rightist' move it was a triumph for Trotsky's analysis: he had always predicted that the Soviet bureaucracy would degenerate into reaction. But if Stalin made a swing to the left it was also a triumph for Trotsky, who had always declared that the revolutionary vanguard in Russia was so strong that the bureaucracy must take account of its wishes. If a Trotskyist group in some country increased its membership, that was of course a good sign: the best elements were beginning to understand that true Leninism was the right policy. If, on the other hand, a group dwindled in size or underwent a split, this too confirmed the Marxist analysis: the Stalinist bureaucracy was stifling the consciousness of the masses, and in a revolutionary era unstable elements always desert the battlefield. If Soviet Russia scored economic success it confirmed Trotsky's argument: socialism, supported by the consciousness of the proletariat, was gaining ground in spite of the bureaucracy. If there were economic set-backs or disasters, Trotsky was right again: the bureaucracy, as he had always said, was incompetent and lacked the support of the masses. A mental system of this kind is watertight and immune from correction by the facts. Obviously, various forces and conflicting tendencies are at work in society, and different ones prevail at different times; if this commonplace truth is erected into a philosophy, there is no danger of its being empirically refuted. Trotsky, however, like many other Marxists, imagined that he was conducting scientific observations with the aid of an infallible dialectical method.

Trotsky's attitude to the Soviet state is psychologically understandable: it was to a large extent his own creation, and it is not surprising that he could not admit the idea that his offspring had degenerated beyond recall. Hence the extraordinary paradox which he repeated incessantly and which, in the end, even faithful Trotskyists found hard to swallow: the working class had been politically expropriated, robbed of all its rights, enslaved and trampled on, but the Soviet Union was still a working-class dictatorship, since the land and factories were the property of the state. As time went on, more and more of Trotsky's adherents left him on account of this dogma. Some, noting the obvious analogies between Soviet Communism and Nazism, had pessimistic forebodings as to the inevitability of totalitarian systems throughout the world. The German Trotsky-ist Hugo Urbahns concluded that state capitalism would become universal in one form or another. Bruno Rizzi, an Italian Trotskyist who in 1939 published a book in French on 'world bureaucratization', held that the world was moving towards a new form of class society, in which individual ownership was replaced by collective ownership vested in a bureaucracy, as exemplified by the Fascist states and the Soviet Union. Trotsky opposed such ideas furiously: it was nonsense to suggest that Fascism, the organ of the bourgeoisie, could expropriate its own class in favour of a political bureaucracy. Similarly, Trotsky broke with Burnham and Shachtman when they came to the conclusion that it no longer made any discernible sense to call the Soviet Union a 'workers' state'. Shachtman pointed out that under capitalism economic and political power could be separate, but that this was impossible in the Soviet Union, where property relations and the proletariat's participation in political power were dependent on each other; the proletariat could not lose political power and continue to exercise an economic dictatorship. The political expropriation of the prole-tariat meant the end of its rule in every other sense, and it was therefore absurd to maintain that Russia was still a workers' state; the ruling bureaucracy was a 'class' in the true meaning of the term. Trotsky to the end firmly opposed this conclusion, reiterating his single argument that the implements of pro-duction in the Soviet Union belonged to the state. This, of course, no one denied. The dispute was psychological rather than one of theory: to recognize that Russia had created a new form of class society and exploitation would have meant admitting that Trotsky's life-work had been in vain, and that he himself had helped to bring about the exact opposite of what he intended. This is a kind of inference that few are prepared to draw. For the same reason Trotsky maintained tooth and nail that when he was in power the Soviet Union and the Comin-tern had been above reproach in every way: it was a true dictatorship of the proletariat, a true proletarian democracy, with genuine support from the working masses. All repressions, cruelties, armed invasions, etc. were justified if they were in the interest of the working class, but this had nothing to do with Stalin's later measures. (In exile Trotsky maintained that there was no religious persecution in Russia—the Orthodox Church had simply been deprived of its monopoly power, which was right and proper. On this point he was obliged to defend the Stalinist regime, as it had not deviated in any way from Lenin's policy.) Trotsky never suggested that the armed incursions carried out by the new-born Soviet state in Lenin's day might have been wrongful. On the contrary, he repeated many times that the revolution could not alter geography; in other words, the Tsarist frontiers ought to be preserved or restored, and the Soviet regime had every right to 'liberate' Poland, Lithuania, Armenia, Georgia, and the other border states. He maintained that if it had not been for bureaucratic degeneration the Red Army in 1939 would have been welcomed as a liberator by the working masses of Finland; but he did not ask himself why in that case, when he was in power and there was no 'degeneration', the working masses of Finland, Poland, or Georgia had failed to greet their liberators with enthusiasm in accordance with the laws of history.

Trotsky did not concern himself with philosophical questions. (Towards the end of his life he did try to expound his views on dialectics and formal logic, but it was clear that all the logic he knew consisted of fragments recollected from high school and from youthful studies of Plekhanov, all of whose absurdities he repeated. Burnham advised Trotsky to drop the subject, pointing out that he knew nothing of modern logic.) Nor did he attempt any theoretical analysis of the foundations of Marxism. It was sufficient for him that Marx had shown that the decisive feature of the modern world was the struggle between the bourgeoisie and the proletariat, and that this was bound to end in the victory of the proletariat, a worldwide socialist state, and a classless society. He did not concern himself to discover on what these prophecies were based. Being convinced of their truth, however, and of the fact that he as a politician embodied the interests of the proletariat and the deep-seated trend of history, he maintained unswervingly his faith in the final outcome.

At this point we should answer an objection. It may be said that the complete inefficacy of Trotsky's efforts and of his International do not invalidate his analysis, since a man may be right even if most or all of his fellows disagree with him, and *force majeure* is not an argument. Here, however, we may recall Oscar Wilde's remark that whether force is an argument depends on what one wants to prove; and we may add, in the same line of thought, that force is an argument if the point at issue is whether one is strong or not. The fact that a theory is rejected by everyone or almost everyone, as has happened more than once in the history of science, does not prove that it is wrong. But it is a different matter with theories that have an inbuilt self-interpretation to the effect that they are an 'expression' of great historical tendencies (or of the will of Providence); that they embody the true consciousness of the class which is destined soon to triumph, or that they constitute a revelation of truth, and that therefore, simply as theories (or as 'theoretical consciousness'), they must inevitably prevail over all others. If a theory of this kind fails to secure recognition, its failure is an argument against it on its own premises. (On the other hand, success in practice is not necessarily an argument in its favour. The early victories of Islam were not a proof that the Koran was true, but a proof that the faith inspired by it was a powerful rallying-point because it corresponded to essential social needs; in the same way, Stalin's successes did not prove that he was 'right' as a theorist.) For this reason the failure of Trotskyism in practice, unlike the rejection of a scientific hypothesis, is also a theoretical failure, that is to say a proof that the theory as Trotsky conceived it was wrong.

Trotsky, with his dogmatic cast of mind, did not contribute to the theoretical elucidation of any point of Marxist doctrine. But he was an outstanding personality, endowed with immense courage, will-power, and endurance. Covered with obloquy by Stalin and his henchmen in all countries, persecuted by the most powerful police and propaganda machine in the world, he never faltered or gave up the fight. His children were murdered, he was driven out of his country and hunted down like an animal, and was finally done to death. His amazing resistance to every trial was the result of his faith and by no means conflicted—on the contrary—with his unshakeable dogmatism and inflexibility of mind. Unfortunately, the intensity of a faith and the willingness of its adherents to undergo persecution for it are no proof that it is intellectually or morally right.

Deutscher says in his monograph that Trotsky's life was 'the tragedy of the precursor'; but there is no good reason to maintain this, and it is not clear what he is supposed to have been the precursor of. He contributed, of course, to unmasking the forgeries of Stalinist historiography, and to refuting the lies of Soviet propaganda concerning conditions in the new society. But all his predictions as to the future of that society and of the world turned out to be wrong. Trotsky was not unique in criticizing Soviet despotism, nor was he the first to do so. On the contrary, he criticized it much more mildly than the democratic socialists, and he did not object to it *qua* despotism but only to its ultimate aims, which he diagnosed on ideological principles. The opposition that has found expression in Communist countries since Stalin's death has no connection with Trotsky's writings or thoughts, either factually or in the minds of the critics themselves. His ideas play no part at all in the 'dissident' movement in those countries, even among the dwindling band of those who attack the Soviet system from a Communist viewpoint. Trotsky did not offer any alternative form of Communism or any doctrine different from Stalin's. The main thrust of his attack, against 'socialism in one country', was merely an attempt to continue a certain tactical line which had become unfeasible for reasons that had nothing to do with Stalin. Trotsky was not a 'forerunner' but an offshoot of the revolution, thrown off at a tangent to the course which it followed in 1917–21, but which it subsequently had to abandon for both internal and external reasons. It would be more exact to call his life the tragedy of an epigone, rather than that of a forerunner; but this is not an adequate description either. The Russian revolution changed course in certain respects, but not in all. Trotsky advocated ceaseless revolutionary aggression and endeavoured to convince himself and others that if he had been running the Soviet state and the Comintern, the whole world would have been set ablaze without delay; his reason for so believing was that Marxist historiosophy taught him that such were the laws of history. However, the Soviet state was obliged by events to alter course on this point, and Trotsky did not cease to upbraid its leaders on that account. As far as the internal regime was concerned, however, Stalinism was the natural and obvious continuation of the system of government established by Lenin and Trotsky. Trotsky refused to recognize this fact and persuaded himself that Stalin's despotism bore no relation to Lenin's; that coercion, police repression, and the devastation of cultural life were due to a 'bureaucratic' *coup d'état* and that he himself bore no vestige of responsibility for them. This desperate self-delusion is psychologically explicable. What we have here is not merely the tragedy of an epigone, but that of a revolutionary despot entangled in a snare of his own making. There was never any such thing as a Trotskyist theory—only a deposed leader who tried desperately to recover his role, who could not realize that his efforts were vain, and who would not accept responsibility for a state of affairs which he regarded as a strange degeneration, but which was in fact the direct consequence of the principles that he, together with Lenin and the whole Bolshevik party, had established as the foundations of socialism.

CHAPTER VI

Antonio Gramsci:
Communist revisionism

GRAMSCI is probably the most original political writer among the post-Lenin generation of Communists. His relation to Leninism was and still is a subject of controversy. Italian Communists such as Togliatti generally represent him as a Marxist–Leninist *pur sang*, or at any rate claim that whatever is original in his doctrine is a complement to Leninism and never a denial of it. To some extent this interpretation is prompted by tactical motives: when Italian Communists invoke the authority of Gramsci to justify their deviations from the Soviet ideological model, it is convenient to emphasize that they are basically of one mind with the tutelary genius of the Communist movement. Gramsci himself never called Lenin's authority into question, and it is not clear how far he was aware that his own writings—which consist for the most part of unfinished essays and notes from prison, often fragmentary, elliptical, and ambiguous—could serve as the basis for an alternative type of Communism, differing from Lenin's in some essential points.

Although Gramsci's writings do not amount to a coherent theory but rather to a vague and embryonic sketch, some aspects of them are clear and original enough to justify the view that they constitute an independent attempt to formulate a Communist ideology, and not merely an adaptation of the Leninist schema. An indirect confirmation of this is the frequency with which seekers after a more democratic and 'open' version of socialism—especially Communists and ex-Communists—turn to Gramsci for inspiration, and also the acute difficulties and resistance that occur when attempts are made to introduce his ideas to Communist parties outside Italy, especially ruling parties.

Although Gramsci died in 1937 his writings really belong to the history of post-Stalinist Marxism, as it was only in the fifties and sixties, after the publication of a six-volume edition of his letters and notes from prison, that his ideas began gradually to be canvassed in ideological disputes. His position *vis-á-vis* Leninist–Stalinist orthodoxy is somewhat like that of Rosa Luxemburg: lip-service is paid to him as a martyr in the Communist cause, but his writings are more embarrassing than useful. As to the articles he published up to 1926, before his imprisonment, their significance is only apparent in the light of his prison writings. Without this completion, the articles in question would be chiefly material for a history of the Italian Communist movement, but could not be said to constitute an original body of theory. From the point of view of Marxist doctrine, the prison writings are the essential part of his work.

1. Life and works

Antonio Gramsci (1891–1937), who became the leader of the Italian Communist party, was born in the village of Ales in Sardinia, the son of a petty official. As the result of a child-hood accident he was hunchbacked and physically under-developed. Owing to political intrigues his father went to prison for some years, which reduced the family to destitution. The son had to work at various casual jobs while still a small boy, but he completed secondary school at Cagliari and in autumn 1911 won a scholarship to Turin University (as did Palmiro Togliatti in the same year).

As a freshman at University, Gramsci was not yet a socialist in the full sense. His horizon was to some extent limited by Sardinian regionalism: his fellow islanders, not without cause, regarded the neglect and poverty from which they suffered as owing, in some measure at least, to the privileges enjoyed by the expanding industry of northern Italy. The grievances of impoverished villagers and exploited miners found an outlet in separatist and regionalist tendencies rather than in socialism, which had scarcely taken root in Sardinia at that time.

Before long, however, Gramsci's studies and the industrial environment of Turin led him to take an interest in national politics. He took a humanistic course and was especially attracted by linguistics: throughout his life he took a lively interest in what is nowadays called socio-linguistics, the study of the effect of social situations on linguistic change. He no doubt joined the socialist party around the end of 1913, as did his Turin friends Angelo Tasca, Umberto Terracini, and Palmiro Togliatti, who were in due course to play a key part in the formation of the Communist party.

Gramsci broke off his university education in the spring of 1915, by which time he had acquired an extensive knowledge of history and philosophy. As for all Italian intellectuals of that generation, his philosophical teacher *par excellence* was Benedetto Croce. Gramsci was certainly not a Crocean in the literal sense, but the writings of the Italian Hegelianist introduced him to the realm of European philosophical problems. He admired Croce's critique of positivism and, for a time at least, hoped that Italian Marxism might be based on a critical assimilation of Croce, subjecting the latter to the same treatment as Marx performed on Hegel. In later years Gramsci became increasingly critical towards Croce, as the latter became more and more anti-Marxist; but he never ceased to recognize that Crocean philosophy had played a huge part in Italian intellectual life, even when he was chiefly concerned to point out its 'reactionary' effects.

In the same way, even when he had completely broken with Sardinian localism in favour of the orthodox Marxist class interpretation of Italian affairs, he never abandoned the theme of the Italian South and the peculiar importance of the opposition between it and the North in Italian history, past and present.

The 1913 elections and the European war turned Gramsci into a professional politician. From the end of 1914 he began to write for the Italian socialist press, and from 1916 he was a co-editor of the Piedmont edition of *Avanti*, for which he wrote political notes and reviewed books and plays, as well as helping to educate and organize the Turin workers. Although it is hard to ascribe to him a definite philosophical attitude at this time, it is clear from various occasional remarks that he did not share the faith, then popular among socialists, in the beneficent operation of 'historical laws' that would assure humanity of a socialist future; he did not believe in the natural inevitability of progress, but was inclined to place more reliance on human will-power and the force of ideas than was permitted by the orthodoxy of his day. No doubt he was already to some extent influenced by the activism of Sorel, with whose views he never identified himself but to whom his interpretation of Marxism owed a great deal.

By 1917, when revolutionary riots broke out in Turin, Gramsci was already one of the city's socialist leaders. His personal view of Marxism was expressed in an article of November 1917, often quoted today, on the October Revolution in Russia, entitled 'The Revolution against *Das Kapital*', In it he observed that the Bolsheviks had won victory in Russia despite Marx's belief that that country would first go through a phase of Western-type capitalism. The Bolsheviks' revolutionary will had overthrown Marx's schema, but it had drawn strength from what was alive in Marxism and from elements which, though sullied by the intrusion of positivism, were a continuation of German and Italian idealism.

In May 1919 there appeared the first number of *L'Ordine Nuovo*, a weekly edited by Gramsci, Togliatti, Tasca, and Terracini, which was to play an important part in the ideological training of the future Italian Communist party. On October of that year the Socialist Party held a congress at Bologna at which it decided by a large majority to join the Third International. The party was divided into hostile groups and was far from meeting Lenin's requirements from the Comintern point of view, but the Soviet leader regarded Gramsci and his friends as closest to the Bolshevik orientation. An extreme left faction led by Amadeo Bordiga held that the party should eschew all parliamentary activity, which only dulled the revolutionary will of the working class: Communists must have nothing to do with bourgeois institutions and must prepare for an immediate struggle for power, eliminating from their ranks any who did not share this view. Both the centre of the party and its right wing rejected this policy of 'abstentionism', and the Right disapproved of seizing power by violence. In these controversies the *Ordine Nuovo* group was chiefly distinguished by its advocacy of workers' councils: this became the dominant idea of the movement, and Gramsci its most eloquent exponent.

Workers' councils came into being during the big strikes in Turin in 1919 and 1920, in part spontaneously and in part as a result of *Ordine Nuovo* propaganda. Gramsci held that they were a completely new form of social organization and that their functions must not be confused either with those of the trade unions, which were to improve working conditions under capitalism, or with those of the Socialist party, which were parliamentary and ideological. The councils were the proper means of enabling all the workers of a factory, regardless of party allegiance, religion, etc., to shoulder the task of organizing production; they were the germ of the future workers' state, the main organ of the dictatorship of the proletariat. They should be elected by all the wage-earners of a given plant without exception, so as to take over the functions of capitalists in the factories and, in due course, the organization of the state.

Gramsci thought that workers' councils were the Italian counterpart of the Russian experience, and no doubt imagined (at any rate before his visit to Moscow) that the Soviet system embodied the same idea of a real transference of power to the workers. 'All power to the Soviets' was indeed in line with Lenin's doctrine in *State and Revolution*, but not with Russian reality. Gramsci's view, in addition, betrays the strong influence of Sorel's idea that it was the task of the real producers not only to manage production but to organize the whole of social life. The society of the future would, so to speak, take its pattern from the shop-floor; in addition to being autonomous organs of production, the councils would be the matrix of a new proletarian culture, and would bring about the spiritual transformation of the working class.

For different reasons, this doctrine was unacceptable to both the anti-parliamentary Communist Left and the centre and Right. The Left held that the true purpose of socialist revolution was to destroy the institutions of political power by force and to set up new central bodies operating in the name of the proletariat: from this point of view, though not in its avowed anti-parliamentarianism, it agreed with Lenin. The Right identified proletarian rule with domination by the Socialist party, backed by a majority of society and exercising authority by democratic means. Both factions considered that Marxist doctrine precluded the idea of a dictatorship of the proletariat in the sense of direct rule by the workers—whose proper place was the factory, not Parliament or party head-quarters. The reformists wanted representative democracy with a socialist majority, while the Left called for a dictatorship of the party; Gramsci, however, imagined a society in which every process of life was subject to control by the whole mass of producers, whose economic, political, and cultural liberation must advance simultaneously.

Despite Gramsci's hopes, the series of strikes accompanied by workers' occupation of the factories and the establishment of workers' councils did not develop into a nation-wide movement. In the spring of 1920 the Turin workers were forced to return to work on their employers' terms. Gramsci was almost alone in his stubborn defence of the councils as the basic weapon of the emancipation of the proletariat.

He was not alone, however, in fighting to create a Communist party in the true, Leninist sense of the term. *L'Ordine Nuovo* declaimed incessantly against reformism and the irresoluteness of the party leadership, complaining that despite the Bologna decisions the party had remained a purely parliamentary institution with no single will of its own, and had abandoned the idea of a proletarian revolution. After another, unsuccessful attempt by the Turin workers to occupy the factories in August–September 1920 the Communist group, in accordance with Lenin's wishes, decided to transform itself into a separate party. The anti-parliamentary faction reluctantly gave up the principle of 'abstentionism', which was in conflict with the formal directives of the Comintern. In November the Communists issued a separatist manifesto, and at the next congress of the Socialist party, at Livorno in January 1921, the split was effected: the Communists secured about one-third of the votes and set up the Italian Communist party. Gramsci (now chief editor of *L'Ordine Nuovo*, which had become a daily) was a member of the first Central Committee, which was dominated by Bordiga's followers. A controversy at once broke out within the party, the main issue being whether and how far the Communists should seek alliance with other Socialist parties: this question became increasingly critical as Fascism began manifestly to gain ground in Italy. Gramsci favoured a policy of broad alliances, and this fitted in with the change of

Comintern policy as the Bolsheviks realized that the 'tide of revolution had ebbed'. In May 1922 Gramsci went to Moscow as the Italian party's representative on the Executive Committee of the Comintern; he remained there a year and a half, and took part in the Fourth Comintern Congress in November 1923. Meanwhile Mussolini had carried out his 'march on Rome'. The Comintern withdrew its support from Bordiga, who, in accordance with his 'purely class' attitude, saw no essential difference between bourgeois democracy and Fascism and opposed the 'united front' policy. Numerous arrests deprived the Communist party of its leadership, and Gramsci was recognized as head of the party by the Comintern. At the end of 1923 he left Moscow for Vienna, from where he tried to revive the Italian party, at that time torn by fractional strife. He arrived back in Italy in May 1924, was elected to Parliament and thus enjoyed personal immunity for the time being. The party was in a state of extreme weakness and disorganization. After a long struggle Gramsci defeated Bordiga's faction (the latter was in prison, but was still able to dominate local groups) and, at a congress held at Lyons in January 1926, gained a majority for his policy of forming a united front to restore democracy in Italy. The Communists, together with other anti-Fascist groups, had seceded from Parliament in June 1924, but they now decided to return and use what was left of parliamentary institutions for propaganda purposes. These manoeuvres were of little avail against the increasingly repressive measures of the Fascist government. Gramsci was arrested in November 1926, and in the following June was sentenced to imprisonment for twenty years and four months. Confined successively in various towns, he was permitted after a time to write and to receive books. The rest of his life was spent, as far as his weak health and prison conditions allowed, in reading and writing notes which constitutes one of the most original contributions to twentieth-century Marxism.

It was undoubtedly thanks to his imprisonment that Gramsci was able to remain a member of the Communist party. He escaped being expelled from it or condemned by the International precisely because he was almost completely cut off from party contacts. He read newspapers and received belated accounts of political developments from relatives who visited

him, but he himself had no influence on events. Shortly before
his arrest he sent a letter to the Bolshevik leaders in which he
took the side of the then majority (Stalin and Bukharin) against
Trotsky but expressed disquiet at the ferocity of their intestine
conflicts accusing the Bolsheviks in scarcely veiled terms of
forgetting their duty to the international proletariat and
jeopardizing the whole of Lenin's work. At the same time, being
convinced that the wrong class could not fight unless it were
allied with the peasantry, he was against Trotsky's programme
of forced industrialization at the peasants' expense. Togliatti,
who had taken Gramsci's place as Italian representative in the
Comintern, had decided to support Stalin through thick and
thin, as he did for the next thirty years, and Gramsci was alone in
his criticism of Moscow. However, at the turn of the year 1928–9
Stalin switched the policy of the Comintern and the Bolshevik
party in a direction completely opposite to Gramsci's views. The
idea of a united front was abandoned, the attack was concentrated against social democracy ('social Fascism'), it was
announced that the world revolution was imminent and that
Communists must be prepared for a direct transition to the
dictatorship of the proletariat; Bukharin fell, and Stalin set about
the mass collectivization of Soviet agriculture. Togliatti
organized a purge of refractory elements in what was left of the
Italian party (one of the victims was Angelo Tasca). Gramsci
expressed opposition to the new Comintern policy and sympathy
with the expelled 'deviationists' in a conversation with his
brother, who visited him in prison; however, as Gramsci's
biographer Giuseppe Fiori has shown, the brother gave Togliatti
a false account of what was said, and thus saved Gramsci from
certain condemnation by the party authorities and the
Comintern.

Towards the end of 1933 Gramsci was allowed to move to a
private clinic under police supervision, and at the end of the
next year, when already in very poor health, he was temporarily
released. He worked until the middle of 1935 and was then
moved to a hospital in Rome, where he died in April 1937.

In addition to letters, Gramsci wrote nearly three thousand
pages in prison. All these writings were published after the
Second World War; the first edition of the letters, in 1947, was
abridged by the Italian Communists for political reasons. The

various notes written in 1929–35 were collected into six further volumes: *Il materialismo storico e la filosofia di Benedetto Croce* (1948), *Gli intellettuali e l'organizzazione della cultura* (1949), *Il risorgimento* (1949), *Note sul Machiavelli, sulla politica e sullo Stato moderno* (1949), *Letteratura e vita nazionale* (1950), *Passato e presente* (1951). Some of his earlier articles and pamphlets were also reprinted.

The prosecutor who declared at Gramsci's trial that 'this brain must be put out of action for twenty years' achieved the exact opposite of what he intended. If Gramsci had been allowed to pass the Fascist years in exile he would inevitably have become one of the many outcasts of Communism—unless he had gone to Moscow, when he would certainly have been done to death—and would have spent the rest of his days in a barren defence of his political actions for the benefit of a non-existent public. Thanks to the imprisonment which cut him off willy-nilly from current affairs, he was obliged to work on more theoretical and fundamental topics. As a result we have his interesting notes, containing among other things an attempt at a Marxist philosophy of culture whose originality and breadth of view cannot be denied.

2. The self-sufficiency of history; historical relativism

The main theme of Gramsci's reflections is that which dominated Marx's early writings: the question of the relation of human thoughts, feelings, and will to 'objective' social processes. Few other Marxists expressed so emphatically the viewpoint generally known as historicism (in one sense of that term) in contrast to transcendentalism. The essence of this view is that the meaning and 'rationality' of all human behaviour and every product of human activity, including works of the mind such as philosophy and science, is manifested only in relation to the 'global' historical processes of which they are part. In other words, the 'truth' of philosophy or science is 'truth' in a socially pragmatic sense: what is true is that which, in a particular historical situation, expresses the real developmental trend of that situation. Neither philosophies nor sciences can be judged by any other criteria than those we use to judge social institutions, religious beliefs, emotions, or political movements. This anti-positivist and anti-scientistic relativism of Gramsci's was no doubt rooted in his Crocean studies, but he believed it to be the quintessence of Marxism—or of 'the philosophy of praxis', a term which he generally used in his prison notes to elude the censor, but which was also an accurate description from his point of view. Marxism, in particular, was also 'true' in this historical sense, i.e. it expressed the 'truth' of its times better than any other theory. Ideas could not be understood outside their social and historical context, irrespective of function and origin; there was thus no such thing as 'scientific philosophy' in the sense in which most Marxists used this term, i.e. a philosophy that 'reflected' reality as it was, regardless of whether we knew it or not. But, in the same way, there was no such thing as 'scientific science', i.e. science that merely described the universe as it was, independent of man. 'If we are to escape solipsism and also the mechanistic conceptions implied in the idea of thought as a receptive and ordering activity, we must pose the question "historically" (*storicisticamente*), at the same time basing our philosophy on "will" (in the last analysis, practical or political activity)—but a rational, not an arbitrary will, realizing itself in so far as it corresponds to objective historical necessities: that is to say, in so far as it is identical with the progressive actualization of universal history. If that will is represented initially by a single individual only, its rationality is attested by the fact that it becomes accepted permanently by the bulk of mankind and is thenceforward a culture, a matter of "common sense", a conception of the world, with an ethic in conformity with its structure' (*Opere*, vol. 2, 1949, pp. 22–3). In other words, the rightness of an idea is confirmed by, or perhaps actually consists in, the fact that it prevails historically—a view irreconcilable with the usual one that truth is truth no matter whether or when it is known, or who regards it as true and in what way. 'Ideas are not born of other ideas, philosophies do not beget other philosophies, but these are the ever-new expression of real historical development ... Every truth, even though it may be universal and expressible in an abstract formula of the mathematical type ... owes its efficacy to being expressed in the language of particular, concrete situations; if it cannot be so expressed it is a Byzantine, scholastic abstraction, a pastime for phrase-mongers' (*Opere*, vol. 7, 1952, p. 63). Gramsci, it is true, disclaims the imputation of relativism, but it is not clear how he can be acquitted of being a historical relativist. Criticizing Bukharin, he says: 'To think of a philosophical statement as being true in a particular historical period, i.e. as the necessary, inseparable expression of a particular historical activity or praxis, but as being overtaken and "nullified" [*vanificata*] in a subsequent period—to think this without falling into scepticism or moral and ideological relativism, in other words to take an historicist view of philosophy, is a somewhat arduous and difficult mental enterprise' (*Il materialismo storico*, *Opere*, vol. 2, p. 133). It is hard to get more than this out of Gramsci as far as the epistemological sense of 'truth' is concerned. But the basic thought is clear: it amounts to reducing all products of the mind to a historical function, and refusing to distinguish sharply between science and 'non-scientific' forms of mental activity. 'According to the theory of praxis it is clear that human history is not explained by the atomistic theory, but that the reverse is the case: the atomistic theory, like all other scientific hypotheses and opinions, is part of the superstructure' (ibid., p. 162). What was thus 'clear' to Gramsci was not so to the majority of Marxists, who rather took the opposite view that the scientific explanation of the universe accumulates historically as the advance of 'truth' in the everyday sense, and that 'science', unlike religious belief, art, or political opinions, is thus not part of the 'superstructure': on this view Marxism itself, as a scientific theory, can be vindicated 'objectively', i.e. independently of the fact that it also performs political functions as the weapon of the working class.

By virtue of this 'absolute historicism' (Gramsci's phrase), all the concepts by which our knowledge of the world is organized are related primarily not to 'things' but to relations between the users of those concepts. 'Matter is thus not to be considered in itself [*come tale*] but as it is socially and historically organized for production; in the same way, natural science is to be regarded essentially as an historical category, a human relationship' (ibid., p. 160). The same applies to the idea of 'human nature': as Gramsci repeats many times, there is no such thing as unchanging human nature, but only historically variable social relationships. He appears to reject the common-sense view that all historical changes occur within the limits set by relatively permanent biological and physical circumstances, by which man finds the universe to be governed. In this respect Gramsci reverts to the idea of 'pure historicism' which is present in Marx but was almost completely discarded from evolutionist interpretations in the style of Engels. (Before Gramsci, only Brzozowski attempted to conceive Marxism in this radically anti-scientistic way, though such tendencies can be found in Labriola in a less radical form.) For Gramsci nothing exists but the changing form of human 'praxis': all meaning derives from praxis and is related to it. Questions and answers are meaningful only in so far as they can be integrated in the human process of self-creation. In this sense human history is indeed the absolute boundary of knowledge.

For the same reason Gramsci, more than any other Marxist, rejected the view that the whole realm of the 'superstructure' is an expression of the 'truly real' aspects of social life, i.e. relations of production. The very distinction between 'base' and 'superstructure' seemed to him inessential. He repeated more than once, especially in controversy with Croce, that it was absurd to tax Marxists with holding that the 'superstructure' was a world of mere appearances or a 'less real' side of life than production relations. In the various aspects of the 'superstructure' social classes became aware of their position and opportunities, and were able to change the social conditions of which they thus became conscious. This was a continuous process, and there was therefore no point in talking of a clear 'primacy' of the base or debating which came 'first', still less in postulating a one-way determinism whereby the 'base' created the 'superstructure' it required. If any form of 'superstructure' could be called a mere appearance, this only meant that it had outlived its historical function and was no longer capable of organizing social forces: this might apply to philosophical or religious doctrines or artistic trends as well as to scientific theories.

3. Critique of 'economism'. Prevision and will

Gramsci uses the terms 'fatalistic', 'deterministic', and 'mechanistic' almost without distinction and always with reference to views that he considers radically opposed to Marxist doctrine. He does not dispute that there is a strong strain of determinism in the history of Marxism, but he attributes this to the historical circumstances of the early phase of the workers' movement. As long as the oppressed class does not possess the initiative but is restricted mainly to defensive action, it is apt to develop the compensatory idea that it is bound to triumph sooner or later because of 'historical laws', and that history is 'objectively' on its side. This is a primitive, quasi-religious faith, necessary in the early stages and comparable to fatalistic theories of predestination in Christianity. It reached its height in German idealism in the proposition that freedom is the awareness of necessity (Gramsci appears to interpret Hegel's formula in a stoic sense); it is in fact nothing more than the cry 'It is God's will.' Throughout history fatalistic beliefs have functioned as the ideology of dependent groups, and so it was in the early days of the workers' movement. However, once the proletariat is no longer condemned to a defensive attitude but becomes aware of its social position and able to take the initiative, it no longer needs to believe in a historical providence watching over its fate: any such belief is henceforth a hindrance, to be jettisoned as quickly as possible.

The philosophy of praxis cannot, by its very nature, rely on the operation of 'historical laws' as the agents of social change, as hidden deities using human beings to bring about their ends. Certainly the working class, when it reaches the level of consciousness at which it is able to take the initiative, encounters historical circumstances which cannot be arbitrarily altered: the rejection of determinism does not mean that in any given situation human will-power can achieve whatever it likes and is subject to no limits at all. But the question which of several possible developments will take place is not prejudged by any laws of history, for history is nothing but human praxis and therefore includes will. 'It may be said', Gramsci writes, 'that the economic factor (understood in the immediate, Judaic sense of historical economism) is only one of several ways in which the basic historical process manifests itself (factors of race, religion etc.); but it is this basic historical process that the philosophy of praxis seeks to explain, and this is why it is a philosophy, an "anthropology" and not a mere canon of historical research' (*Passato e presente, Opere*, vol. 7, pp. 183–4). Gramsci does not explain what he means by the 'basic historical process' of which economic changes, like cultural ones, are no more than a particular manifestation. It is clear, however, that he regards evolutionist and determinist theories of history, and likewise the principle of the causal 'primacy' of production relations *vis-à-vis* cultural phenomena, as a complete misconception of Marxism.

Since the historical process is indivisible and merely 'expresses' itself in different aspects of social life, it is impossible to maintain the 'technological' conception of the relationship between theory and practice which is also current among Marxists, i.e. the view that it is the task of theoreticians to provide practical politicians with effective plans of action based on a 'scientific' and 'objective' analysis of social processes. Gramsci protests against the idea that theory is instrumental or ancillary to practice. Important social processes occur thanks to the development of class-consciousness, and this is impossible without organization and intellectuals. Political action and awareness of that action, its direction and purpose, are not two separate phenomena but aspects of a single one, and it is difficult to speak of any 'primacy'. Intellectuals as such are participants in social 'praxis', and politicians as such are theoreticians. Accordingly, Gramsci declares that Lenin rendered a service to philosophy by improving the theory and practice of politics. This is in line with Gramsci's view of the 'unity of theory and practice', but at the same time it appears to deny Lenin the title of a philosopher in the strict sense; Gramsci in fact makes no mention of Lenin's philosophical views.

For the same reason, in Gramsci's view, there is no point in separating historical prognoses from the acts by which they are fulfilled. The act of foreseeing coincides with the act of realizing what is foreseen. 'In reality we can predict "scientifically" only the struggle but not its concrete phases, which are bound to be the result of conflicting forces in constant movement: these can never be reducible to fixed quantities, because quantity in them is always transforming itself into quality. In fact we "foresee" to the extent that we are active, bringing a conscious effort to bear and thus contributing materially to the result "foreseen". Prevision is thus not an act of scientific cognition but the abstract expression of an effort, the practical way in which a collective will is created. How, indeed, could prevision be an act of cognition? We can only know what is or has been, not what will be—for this does not exist, and is therefore by definition unknowable. Thus prevision can only be a practical act' (*Il materialismo storico*, p. 135).

Thus, in Gramsci's view, we do not know social processes by 'observing' them from outside; there is in fact no such observation. Cognition is an 'aspect' or 'expression' of social development, on the same footing as economic changes. (Gramsci expressly denies that economic development can be 'reduced' to the improvement of productive forces: in his *Notes on Machiavelli* (*Opere*, vol. 5) he joins issue with Achille Loria as the spokesman of this pseudo-Marxist 'economism'.) In the same way he rejects the traditional distinction between Is and Ought, as it was found in Kant and the neo-Kantians but also among Marxists of 'positivist' tendency. Ought is the form in which men express their desires, hopes, and wishes: it is therefore a part of social reality, as good as any other. It is as real as that which is; it is in fact inchoate action, just as all cognition is a form of practical action. Indeed, from the point of view of a philosophy in which 'praxis' is the most general category, the distinction between Is and Ought does not arise, any more than it does in pragmatism.

It does not follow, however—and this is an important point in Gramsci's argument—that people's thoughts are simply a perfect, unblemished reflection of their social position and practical activity. If this were so, one could not speak of false consciousness, ideological mystification, or the gradual development of class awareness, for consciousness would always be absolutely transparent; but we know that matters are otherwise. Gramsci frequently points out that there is a contradiction between what people profess and what they implicitly acknowledge, as revealed in their behaviour; and this contradiction is the rule rather than the exception. People have, as it were, two conflicting attitudes or sets of standards, those they proclaim and those expressed in their acts. Which of these is the individual's 'true' attitude? Gramsci clearly inclines to think that what matters is what people do, even if their words belie it: as far as the 'unity of theory and practice' is concerned, real consciousness is expressed in deliberate social behaviour, whereas any utterances to the contrary are merely verbal and 'superficial'.

Gramsci does not discuss particular instances, but we can see what he is driving at: an outstanding example is the situation in which the dependent classes verbally acknowledge the principles inculcated by Church and education and tending to uphold class domination—in particular, the principle of the sanctity of property—but at the same time behave in practice as if they did not take these principles seriously, for instance when factories are occupied by the workers.

Gramsci did not develop or particularize these observations, however, and their exact purpose is not clear. That people say one thing and do another is a fairly commonplace truth, even in the form which accepts that they are not acting out of hypocrisy or bad faith but are really incapable of understanding their own motives, the reasons for their acts, and the extent to which they conflict with acknowledged principles. This kind of inconsistency is in no way a prerogative of the oppressed but is at least equally characteristic of the privileged classes, as seventeenth-century moralists pointed out. Nor does it follow from the divergence that the principles governing actual behaviour are 'more real' than those that are professed but not practised; indeed, it is not clear what this statement would mean. The most we can infer from the fact that the inconsistency is so prevalent is that moral rules are chiefly a means of compelling people to behave in ways contrary to their natural inclinations—a state of things which applies to all fields of moral behaviour and not only those related to the class struggle. The influence of verbally acknowledged standards on actual conduct varies along a continuous spectrum, and it is therefore of doubtful utility to speak of two kinds of *Weltanschauung*, the explicit and the implicit. Least of all, however, should we assume that in case of divergence it is the 'implicit' view expressed in action that deserves approval, and not the other. The sanctity of property is violated in practice not only by the oppressed but just as much by the privileged; not only in acts pertaining to the class struggle, but in individual cases of theft and extortion. No doubt Gramsci's real point was simply that social classes often pursue their interests in ways contrary to the accepted norms of the culture to which they belong: but to establish this undoubted fact there is no need to invoke a theory of 'two *Weltanschauungen*'.

As we have seen, in Gramsci's view Marxism was not a 'scientific' account of social reality from which practical rules can be deduced for effective political action, but was an expression of the class-consciousness of the proletariat and an aspect or component of its practical struggle. Accordingly, he argued, there was no point in dividing it into 'philosophical', 'sociological', and 'political' aspects. Philosophy, he frequently stated, might either be synonymous with history or the social process, or it might be the theoretical awareness of that process and thus an inseparable part of it. Sociology as such was a foredoomed attempt to apply characteristic modes of scientific thought to social phenomena, in the hope that these would prove amenable to law and would be as predictable as the revolutions of the planets. But this idea was no more than a relic of mechanism. There was no 'Marxist sociology' and there were no 'sociological laws'. What people thought about social phenomena was itself a social phenomenon, an expression of their initiative or passivity towards the world. The 'philosophy of praxis', in particular, was an act of self-knowledge of the proletariat as it assumed the role of an initiator of great historical processes: it was thus not a mere description of reality, but a practical act. In this respect, though not in all others, Gramsci's critique of 'mechanism' coincides with Lukács's.

Gramsci endeavoured by all possible means to minimize or obliterate the distinction between thought and behaviour. Since specifically human behaviour was always more or less conscious, and since, on the other hand, the most refined forms of philosophical, theoretical, and scientific thought were nothing but ways in which human beings became socially aware of their own practice, and were consequently themselves part of that practice, it followed that everything in human behaviour was in some way 'philosophical'; everyone had a philosophy of his own, though he could not necessarily express it properly.

These views of Gramsci's were called in question more than once, by Marxists and others. On the one hand, he emphasized the unique role of intellectuals in forming class-consciousness and organizing the class struggle; on the other hand, he often spoke as if the difference between implicit and theoretical consciousness was of no importance—everyone was a philosopher, because he acted consciously; philosophy was nothing but a name for the historical process, the sum of all human actions. It was easy to infer from this that it made no real difference whether a person simply performed an act or whether he could give a coherent account of why he did so: in other words, a working man who took some action to defend his interests was as much a 'theoretician' as Marx, who tried to evolve from such acts a universal theory of history. This view would lead to complete theoretical nihilism, which Gramsci in fact disavowed, thus showing himself to be inconsistent. His concern was to present theory as a mere 'aspect' of behaviour, with no special status. But it is impossible to argue from behaviour to theoretical consciousness: the fact that a snail's behaviour obeys biological laws does not mean that the snail is aware of them. Human behaviour, indeed, is always more or less conscious, but because human beings are very often unaware of their true motives or the causes of their actions, they are not essentially different from snails in this regard. The notion of 'theoretically implicit consciousness' turns out to be self-contradictory.

4. Critique of materialism

Total historicism and the view that collective praxis is the only absolute reality, determining whether any philosophical question or answer is meaningful or not, is a denial of materialism, since it is a denial of any metaphysic whatever. From this point of view Gramsci was consistent, and his aim was to restore the original Marxist intuition which had been obscured by the naïveties of Engels and Lenin. His anti-metaphysical standpoint is most clearly seen in an extended critique of Bukharin's *Theory of Historical Materialism*, first published in 1921 and later translated into French; but he repeated the same ideas many times on other occasions. If, indeed, everything we have to do with is manifested to us only in connection with our practical activities, there is no point in inquiring about the universe 'in itself'. According to Gramsci, Marxism teaches that 'there is no "reality" existing in and for itself [*per sè stante, in sè e per sè*] but only in historical relation to human beings who modify it' (*Opere*, vol. 2, p. 23). Elsewhere we read:

Is it supposed that there can be an objectivity outside history and outside humanity? But who is to judge of such objectivity? Who can

adopt the viewpoint of the 'universe in itself', and what would such
a viewpoint mean? It may very well be held that we have to do here
with a residue of the idea of God, particularly the mystical notion of
an unknown God ... 'Objective' always means 'humanly objective',
which may correspond exactly to 'historically subjective', i.e. 'objective'
would mean 'universal subjective'. Man possesses objective knowledge
in so far as knowledge is real for the whole human race *historically*
unfied in a unitary cultural system ... The concept of 'objectiveness'
in metaphysical materialism is apparently intended to mean an
objectivity that exists outside us as well as within us; but when we
say that a certain reality would exist even if man did not, we are
either using metaphor or falling into a kind of mysticism. We can
know reality only in relation to mankind, and since man is historical
development [*divenire*, 'becoming'], so the same is true of knowledge,
reality, objectivity, etc. (*Opere*, vol. 2, pp. 142–3).

There is no need to demonstrate that these ideas are the
precise contrary of the materialist metaphysics of Engels and
Lenin. Gramsci, however, occasionally appeals to Engels and
specifically to his statement that the materiality of the universe
is proved by the historical development of science and
philosophy. According to Gramsci this statement somehow in-
corporates the history of science into the very concept of materiality: that is to say, the development of knowledge did not so
much prove the 'materiality of the universe' as create it. This
view comes out most clearly in his critique of Lukács, who
rejected Engels's idea of the 'dialectic of nature' on the ground
that dialectic, being a process of the unification of subject and
object, could only apply to human history. Gramsci appears
to defend Engels, arguing that Lukács presupposes dualism as
between nature and man; if the history of nature is included
in the history of mankind, there is no reason why dialectic
should not apply to nature also. This reasoning not only does
not rehabilitate Engels's materialism but emphasizes Lukács's
'historical subjectivism', as it subsumes natural history into
human history and not the other way about. On this interpretation Marxism turns out to be collective solipsism, a world-picture
that is made wholly relative to human social practice.

In Gramsci's eyes materialism, far from being the contrary
of religion, is the direct outcome of religious superstition; it is
like primitive common sense, the apparent 'obviousness' of
which only conceals a lack of critical thought.

The broad public does not even believe that there can be such a problem as whether the outside world exists objectively: one has only to put the question thus to be greeted by an outburst of irrepressible, Gargantuan laughter. The public 'believes' that the outside world is objectively real, but the question arises: what is the origin of that 'belief', and what is the critical value of the term 'objectively'? It is in fact a belief of religious origin, even if the person in question has no religious feelings. Because all religions have always taught that the world, nature, the universe were created by God before he created man, so that man came upon the world ready-made, catalogued and defined once and for all, this belief has become a cast-iron tenet of 'common sense' and lives on as sturdily as ever, even though religious feelings have become dulled or extinguished. And consequently, to appeal to common-sense experience in order to laugh subjectivism out of court is a kind of 'reactionary' device, an implicit return to religious sentiment; as we see Catholic writers and speakers resort to the same means to bring about the same effect of corrosive ridicule. (*Opere*, vol. 2, p. 138)

Gramsci's allusions are clear. He grew up at a time when Catholic philosophy was dominated by the battle with modernism and its 'idealist' doctrines, when the easiest way to rout an adversary for the benefit of an uneducated audience was to claim that the idealists held that 'that table there' did not exist or was a mere appearance, whereas any child could see that they were wrong. Lenin's polemic against 'idealism' was on the same level, and it is not surprising that analogies presented themselves.

Gramsci was well aware of the crudeness of the forms in which Marxism was most commonly taught and preached. To some extent he regarded this as unavoidable or at any rate understandable: Marxism was, after all, a world-view for the proletariat, who were a socially dependent group, and in its everyday forms it could not rise far above the level of popular superstition and everyday common sense. But in this shape it could not effectively challenge the ideologies of the educated classes: it could only score cheap, illusory victories against its most primitive adversaries. If Marxists wanted to make real headway in the intellectual field they must tackle opponents of substance and make a genuine attempt to understand the latter's views.

Gramsci was one of the few Marxists who attempted to restore historical 'immanentism' or anti-metaphysical 'collective sub-jectivism' as the true philosophical content of Marxism, at a time when corroborative evidence was sparse. (Marx's early writings, above all the 1844 Paris Manuscripts, were published while Gramsci was in prison, and he cannot have read them; the *Theses on Feuerbach* were the chief available material for the philosophical interpretation of Marxism.) In this respect his ideas are completely incompatible with Leninist orthodoxy.

5. *Intellectuals and the class struggle. The concept of hegemony*

In the search for forms in which the new class, striving to dominate social life, might or should organize its own culture, Gramsci frequently addressed himself to the history of the Roman Church. He seems to have been impressed by the ideological strength of Christianity, and he laid particular stress on the care taken by the Church at all periods to prevent an excessive gap developing between the religion of the learned and that of simple folk, and to preserve the link between the teaching imparted to the faithful at all levels. Gramsci indeed maintained that the link was purely 'mechanical', but he recognized that the Church had had enormous success in the struggle for mastery over men's consciences. If the working class was to meet the demands of the situation which enabled it to create a new culture and a new system of power, it must also create new forms of intellectual work and a new interrelation between politics and economic production on the one hand and, on the other, the activity of those intellectuals who took the side of the proletariat.

The proletariat needed 'organic' intellectuals (one of Gramsci's favourite and most frequent adjectives): that is to say, intellectuals who did not simply describe social life from outside in accordance with scientific rules, but who used the language of culture to 'express' the real experiences and feelings which the masses could not express for themselves. In order to under-stand those experiences, they must feel the same passions as the masses. Gramsci used the term 'intellectuals' in a wide sense, practically equivalent to 'intelligentsia' or the whole educated class. On the one hand, each of the 'main' social classes developed its own intellectual stratum; on the other, intellectual work united people into a single stratum which preserved the continuity of culture through the ages and was bound by a certain solidarity. The fact that intellectuals appeared to form a separate *métier* of their own, as opposed to being the mouth-pieces of a particular class standpoint, inclined them towards idealistic philosophies which asserted the complete autonomy of intellectual activity. The victory of the working class was impossible without a cultural victory, and for this it needed to evolve an intellectual stratum which could express the actual experiences of the masses with conviction and in educated language. This applied to philosophy as well as literature, both of which could not really be explained by their own historical 'logic', but 'expressed' the distinctive social relationships of a given epoch. It did not follow that, for instance, literature could be reduced to political propaganda. On the contrary, a work of art was a work of art not because of its moral or political content but because of the form with which that content was identified; an extra-artistic intention governing the artist's work could not in itself produce a work of any value. Hence it was no use trying to produce an artificial culture without in-tellectuals who themselves truly shared the values of the working class.

Just because the historical process was a single whole, neither cultural activities nor intellectuals had any autonomous signifi-cance. It followed that the 'organic' character of intellectual and artistic work was also a condition of cultural achievement.

Gramsci believed that the working class was on the way to creating its own original culture, quite different from that of the bourgeoisie: it would destroy bourgeois myths and prejudices and set up for the first time truly universal spiritual values. It is not clear from Gramsci's arguments how far he expected cultural continuity to be broken by the proletarian revolution. He did not talk the language of the Russian radicals of Proletkult, but he insisted that the new culture must be 'quite different' from the old. Such language admits of any desired conclusion as regards the manner and extent to which the old culture is to be destroyed.

However, and this was an important point in Gramsci's argument, the workers could only win if they achieved cultural 'hegemony' before attaining political power. The concept of hegemony is important in Gramsci's writings, but it is used in varying senses. Occasionally he seems to identify it with political power exercised by coercion, but as a rule he distinguishes the two concepts, so that hegemony signifies the control of the intellectual life of society by purely cultural means. Every class tries to secure a governing position not only in public institutions but also in regard to the opinions, values, and standards acknowledged by the bulk of society. The privileged classes in their time secured a position of hegemony in the intellectual as well as the political sphere; they subjugated the others by this means, and intellectual supremacy was a precondition of political rule. The main task of the workers in modern times was to liberate themselves spiritually from the culture of the bourgeoisie and the Church and to establish their own cultural values in such a way as to attract the oppressed and intellectual strata to themselves. Cultural hegemony was a fundamental and prior condition of attaining political power. The working class could only conquer by first imparting its world-view and system of values to the other classes who might be its political allies: in this way it would become the intellectual leader of society, just as the bourgeoisie had done before seizing political control.

No oppressed class in history had yet succeeded in doing this. The typical situation was that of a gulf between mass culture and the intellectuals; a particularly striking example, with far-reaching consequences, was the divergence between Renaissance humanism and the Reformation. The latter was a mass movement, the former a purely intellectual critique. In the last analysis, Gramsci believed, humanism and the Renaissance were reactionary. Modern intellectual liberalism was analogous to the humanistic critique, and Marxism to the Reformation. Croce was the modern equivalent of Erasmus, with his vacillation, irresolution, and constant gravitation towards the political establishment. His critique of Catholic modernism, while ostensibly based on the same grounds as his opposition to Catholicism in general, had 'objectively' aided the Jesuits to combat modernism. (The Jesuits had conducted their campaign much more skilfully than the 'integralists' favoured by Pius X, who interpreted 'modernism' so widely as to estrange many intellectuals from the Church, while affording the real modernists greater room for manoeuvre.) Croce's conservative and liberal reformism was based on the Hegelian doctrine that every synthesis preserves elements of thesis and antithesis: he claimed to judge the conflict from the standpoint of an arbiter who could foresee the future synthesis and the contribution to it of each of the present contestants. But it was not in fact possible to know this, and the object of any conflict was to destroy the adversary and not to save him for a future synthesis. In practice Croce's philosophy amounted to constant attempts to moderate and assuage the conflict, which only helped to confirm the hegemony of the bourgeoisie. His critique of Catholicism had a most important effect, but a reactionary one: by detaching the intellectuals of southern Italy from the Church he estranged them from the peasant masses, associated them with national bourgeois and then with cosmopolitan culture, and finally made them spiritual vassals of the bourgeoisie. As the intellectual leader of Italian liberalism, Croce did much to deepen the gulf between the educated classes and the people and to prevent the development of a new proletarian culture. His anti-Catholicism and his anti-Marxism (or rather his pronounced revisionism) went hand in hand; the former cut the intelligentsia off from the peasantry, the latter from the working class.

Gramsci dreamed of a Marxism that would be a kind of synthesis of humanism and the Reformation, avoiding the natural crudity of a popular world-view but preserving its appeal to the masses while acquiring the ability to solve complex cultural problems. It would be 'a culture that, in Carducci's words, would synthesize Robespierre and Kant, politics and philosophy, into a dialectical unity within a social group, no longer merely French or German but European and world-wide' (*Opere*, vol. 2, p. 200). Croce was right in saying that one must not take away people's religion without giving them something that satisfied the same needs, but he admitted despite himself that idealistic philosophy could not fill the bill. Marxism must indeed take the place of previous world-views, but it could only do so if it met the same spiritual needs as they had—in other words, people must be able to recognize it as an expression of their own experience.

The question arises whether Gramsci's idea of a new proletarian culture differed from that of Lenin, who emphasized that culture was 'ancillary' to political objectives. On the one hand, Gramsci regarded cultural hegemony, achieved by purely ideological means, as a prior condition of attaining political power, whereas for Lenin that attainment of power was a purely technical question: power could and must be seized whenever circumstances allowed. On the other hand, we read in Gramsci's *Notes on Machiavelli*: 'If it is the case that every type of state must go through a phase of economic-corporative primitivism, we must infer that the content of the political hegemony of the new social group that has established the new type of state must be chiefly of an economic order: it is a matter of reorganizing the structure and the real relations between human beings and the economic world of production. The superstructural elements are bound to be exiguous, provisional and contentious, but with scattered elements of "planning". The cultural aspect, above all, will be negative, directed towards criticism of the past, obliterating it from memory and destroying it; the lines of construction will as yet be outlines only, rough sketches that can and must be revised at any moment to conform to the new structure that is being built' (*Opere*, vol. 5, pp. 132–3).

It is difficult to read these words in any but the obvious sense that, as far as culture is concerned, the new proletarian state will concentrate on destroying the heritage of the past, relegating the question of new values to an uncertain future. In this vital matter, as in several others, Gramsci's notes are lacking in order and consistency.

6. *Organization and mass movement. The society of the future*

There is no doubt that Gramsci, unlike Lenin, took a highly sensitive view of the difference between, on the one hand, the proletariat as the real subject of the political struggle and the subsequent building of socialism, and, on the other, the political organization which was to direct these processes. He never side-stepped such questions, as Lenin did, by saying that the masses were led by the party and the party by its leaders, that this was how things must be and that there was no problem about it. Gramsci wanted the political movement of the working class to be a movement of real workers, not of professional politicians seeking support from the working class. In this respect many of his arguments coincide with the criticisms of Rosa Luxemburg.

Gramsci's thoughts on the role of the party, and his critique of party bureaucracy, first appeared in his journalistic writings at the time of *L'Ordine Nuovo* and were aimed chiefly at the bureaucratic and 'inorganic' type of political leadership practised by the German and Italian social democrats. 'The Party', he wrote,

identifies itself with the historical consciousness of the popular masses and governs their spontaneous, irresistible movement; this government is disembodied, it operates through millions of spiritual ties, it is an irradiation of authority (*prestigio*) that can only become an effective government at certain supreme moments ... The Party is the upper hierarchy of that irresistible mass movement: it exercises the most effective of dictatorships, that which is born of prestige, the conscious and spontaneous acceptance of an authority that is acknowledged to be indispensable for the success of the work in hand. Woe betide us if, through a sectarian conception of the Party's function in the revolution, we should try to turn it into a material hierarchy, to fix in mechanical forms of immediate power the governing apparatus of the moving masses, to constrict the revolutionary process into Party forms. If that happens we may succeed in diverting part of mankind from its course and in 'dominating' history, but the true revolutionary process will escape from the control and influence of the Party, which will unconsciously become an organ of conservatism. (Article of 27 Dec. 1919, quoted in *2000 Pagine di Gramsci*, ed. Ferrata and Gallo, 1964, vol. 1, pp. 446–7)

'The Communist Party is the instrument and historical form of the process of inward liberation whereby the workman is changed from an executor to an initiator: instead of a mass he becomes a guide and leader, instead of an arm—a brain and a will' (article of 4 Sept. 1920, ibid., p. 491).

Gramsci's many references to the 'dialectical unity' in which the spontaneous movement from below combines with the planned, organized activity of the party are not specific enough to form an articulate theory. However, his main point is clearly that the political organization should be subordinate to the real aspirations of the working class and should not be allowed to claim that it expresses those aspirations by virtue of its own 'scientific' omniscience, regardless of what the empirical 'masses' actually think. A party for which the 'masses' are only an object of tactical manoeuvres and not a source of inspiration is doomed to degenerate into a clique of professionals and to become a reactionary force. This view is reflected in two important aspects of Gramsci's thought: his idea of the revolution, and the role he assigns to workers' councils.

As we have seen, Gramsci does not regard the revolution as a mere technical question of seizing power, an operation that the political machine can and should carry out whenever circumstances are favourable. The proletarian revolution is not only a question of political opportunity but also of cultural and technical conditions: the spiritual emancipation of the working masses and the attainment of a level of social development such that a socialist transformation can be effective. As he wrote in *L'Ordine Nuovo*, the revolution is not proletariat and Communist simply because it transfers power to people who call themselves Communists, or because it abolishes the institutions of the old regime. It is proletariat and Communist when it liberates existing productive forces, strengthens the initiative of the proletariat, and establishes a society the development of which is accompanied by the disappearance of class divisions and the withering away of state institutions. It must find on the scene forces that are capable of transforming the apparatus of production from an instrument of oppression into an instrument of liberation. In this context the Communist party must be a party of the masses spontaneously seeking to throw off their bonds, and not a Jacobin-type party using the masses for its own ends.

Gramsci's attitude in this matter was certainly that of a Communist and not a reformist social democrat. When he spoke of 'economic maturity' he did not mean, as did orthodox members of the Second International, that socialists must wait until the state of productive forces developed to a point at which the working class could attain power by parliamentary means. He was of course convinced, like all Marxists, that socialism grew out of the conflict between the level of technology and existing production relations which barred the way to further technical progress, so that socialist revolution could be effective only in a state of highly developed capitalism; but he did not try to define this situation more closely, and probably did not think it possible to do so in the abstract. He did not believe, however, in the attainment of power by parliamentary means. The political revolution must, he considered, be a movement of the masses, aware of their desire for liberation and intellectually mature enough to take charge of the whole machinery of production, not through a political apparatus but of their own accord.

For the same reason, the idea of workers' councils played a dominant role in his thoughts at the time of *L'Ordine Nuovo*. They could not, he argued, be replaced by the party or the trade unions, but were the true form of the organization of a communist society of producers and were the principal organ of liberation of the proletariat. They did not make the party superfluous, however: it would continue to have its place as an agent of organization and communist education. But the councils, besides looking after production, were the true organ of the dictatorship of the proletariat. Arising in a capitalist society, they were a model of the proletarian state of the future, and thus opened a new era of human history. The party was not to be their 'ready-made superstructure', nor was its function to supervise them: its task was to aid the liberation of the proletariat and bring the day of revolution closer.

In short, Gramsci believed literally in 'government by councils' as distinct from government by the party. He thus shared the view which Lenin set out in *State and Revolution* but repudiated immediately after seizing power, and which oppositionists in the Bolshevik party vainly tried to reassert for some years afterwards.

Like all Communists, Gramsci was convinced that the parliamentary system of government was done for and could not provide a model for the state of the future. However, he emphasized in his *Notes on Machiavelli* that this did not mean he favoured bureaucratic government. It remained a question whether a representative system could be devised which was neither parliamentary nor bureaucratic. In the *Notes on Machiavelli*, as opposed to his articles in *L'Ordine Nuovo*, Gramsci does not appear to think that workers' councils provide the answer. (They are not mentioned in his prison writings.)

While Gramsci's critique of bureaucratic centralism in 1919–20 was apparently chiefly directed against the parties of the Second International, his prison writings on the subject seem clearly to be aimed against Communism in its Leninist form. 'The predominance of bureaucratic centralism in the state is a sign that the governing group is saturated and is turning into a narrow clique whose object is to safeguard its own petty privileges, restraining or even stifling the development of opposing forces, even when those forces are in accord with the basic interests of the ruling elements ... The pathological manifestations of bureaucratic centralism are due to a lack of initiative and responsibility at the base, that is to say the political backwardness of peripheral forces, even when these are homogeneous with the dominant territorial group' (*Opere*, vol. 5, pp. 76–7). In his remarks about the 'latter-day Prince'—for the modern counterpart of the *Principe* is no other than the political party, the organization of a collective will—he repeatedly criticizes totalitarian parties that degenerate into a privileged caste to which mass movements and mass initiative are not a source of strength but a threat. It is hard to know exactly how far Gramsci was aware of the course of events in Russia which led to absolute control by the party bureaucracy and the destruction of all democratic elements, whether political or industrial. But his criticism is so general and fundamental that it is hard to doubt that he had in mind not only Fascism but Soviet Communism. Noting that the ruling party also exercises police power, he observes: 'A party's police function may be either progressive or regressive. It is progressive when it aims at keeping dispossessed reactionary forces within the bounds of legality and raising the backward masses to the level of the new legality. It is regressive when it aims at restraining the living forces of history and maintaining an outdated, anti-historical legality that has become a mere empty shell ... When the party is progressive it functions "democratically" (in the sense of democratic centralism); when it is regressive it functions "bureaucratically" (in the sense of bureaucratic centralism). In the latter case the party is merely an executive, not a deliberating body; accordingly it is technically a policing organ, and its title of a "political party" is no more than a mythological metaphor' (ibid., p. 26). The reference to 'dispossessed reactionary forces' clearly indicates that he is talking about the Communist party in power and not the Fascists; and it is hard to imagine that when he spoke of the degeneration of that party he had in mind only an abstract possibility and not the process that was actually going on, and of which he was more or less well informed. At the same time he certainly still believed that Communism could be realized in the form described (as he thought) by Marx, i.e. a system in which the mass of producers exercised direct control over production and political life, and which still paid honour to Marx's principle that the educator must likewise be educated.

Like Sorel, whom he criticized but from whom he learnt much, Gramsci believed that a socialist society meant extending to the whole of social life the principles that governed a democratically organized production plant: it should be a community of producers in which political rule and economic authority conditioned and supported each other. Like Marx, he believed that socialism would in time obliterate the difference between civil society and the state, or rather would cause the first to absorb the second, while the police functions of the state would wither away and become unnecessary. On this point he did not differ from Marxists of any other shade of opinion. He speculated concerning the schools of the future, which on the one hand would not be based on the 'Jesuit', 'mechanical' system of learning by rote, but on the other hand would not pretend that all learning was child's play. They would encourage pupils to show initiative and independence and would at the same time provide all-round education with emphasis on knowledge for its own sake, rather than prematurely forcing pupils into vocational specialization.

7. *Summary*

If we compare Gramsci's Communist doctrine with Lenin's we find certain basic differences which are logically intercon-nected.

In the first place, unlike either Lenin or the materialists and evolutionists of the Second International, Gramsci rejects Engels's brand of materialism, which interprets human history as a modified continuation of natural history, and he rejects the idea of knowledge as a copy or 'reflection' of some reality independent of man, and of praxis as a method of testing the truth of hypotheses. Gramsci's position is one of species subjectivism and historical relativism. All reality that can be meaningfully spoken of is a component of human history, including reality as observed by science. Consequently, human history is the impassable frontier of human knowledge. Not only are there no such things as universal natural laws of which history is a special case, but nature itself is part of human history, for it is known to us only in relation thereto. Thus human praxis determines the meaning of all components of knowledge, and (contrary to Lukács's view) there is no fundamental distinction between scientific and humanistic knowledge, for all knowledge is in fact humanistic.

Secondly, it follows that all cognition is an expression of the actual historical consciousness of social groups, and no distinction can be drawn between social consciousness on the one hand and the 'scientific' or 'objective' knowledge of scholars on the other, although one can distinguish more and less primitive forms of consciousness. Consequently—and this is a crucial difference—Gramsci rejects the idea of 'scientific socialism', i.e. the doctrine (accepted by both Kautsky and Lenin, and in a modified form by Lukács) that socialist theory must be evolved by intellectuals outside the workers' movement and then injected into that movement as its 'correct' and 'authentic' class-consciousness. True, socialist theory does not come into being without the aid of intellectuals, who are a necessary element in socialism; but it is no better than a doctrinaire pastime unless it expresses the actual experience of the working class.

Thirdly, it also follows that Gramsci takes a different view of the party. On pain of degenerating into a body of professional politicians fighting for jobs, it must not regard itself as the repository of a 'scientific world-view' elaborated outside the empirical consciousness of the proletariat. It must not be a party of manipulators, using tactical and demagogical means to achieve a temporary advantage and finally grasping the opportunity to exercise dictatorial power. The party can of course do these things, but if it does it will turn into a reactionary privileged clique. To be able to perform the tasks associated with the conquest of power by the proletariat, it must identify itself with the latter's real aspirations and organize them or 'express' them in its ideology.

Hence, fourthly, Gramsci's interpretation of the revolution. It is not, in his view, a mere technical act of seizing power, a *coup d'état* enabling the Communists to impose their will on society. Communist revolution is a mass process in which the toiling masses, backed by the 'democratic confidence' of all working classes, take over economic and political leadership, in their own name and not through a separate political entity. Workers' councils are the proper instrument of this process, the object of which is to transform society so as to render superfluous all forms of political rule, to prevent the recurrence of class divisions, and to bring about the withering-away of the state and the unification of society. A revolution in this sense cannot take place unless it is preceded by a large measure of spiritual emancipation of the working class, transforming it from an object of the political process into a subject and initiator.

On all these points, which are clearly linked together, Gramsci's idea of Communism conflicts with Lenin's—except the idea of government by workers' councils, which Lenin took up briefly and discarded almost at once, and which was contrary to his basic political doctrine of dictatorship by the party as the repository of 'scientific socialism'. The idea of 'scientific socialism' and the manipulative conception of the party's role were common to Lenin and the social democrats, with the important difference that the latter believed in representative democracy, whereas rule by naked force was one of Lenin's chief theoretical tenets. In addition, the social democrats, in the name of historical determinism, maintained that the revolution could not take place until such time as the forces of production had reached the proper stage of development, whereas Lenin was resolved to seize power the moment political circumstances enabled him to do so. Gramsci did not believe in historical determinism or in 'laws of history' using the human will as their instrument, but he also rejected the Blanquist or Jacobin notion of a political *coup* as a purely technical operation. He believed that the human will was not governed by any historical necessity, but he naturally did not regard it as completely unfettered. Socialist revolution was for him a matter of will—but it must be the will of the masses, who aspired to organize production themselves and had no desire to transfer their rights to self-appointed 'scientific' guardians.

Gramsci was a Communist and not a social democrat inasmuch as he excluded the possibility of attaining power by parliamentary means and also rejected parliamentarism in a socialist society (though, like Lenin, he accepted participation in the parliamentary struggle in certain situations). He also envisaged the radical expropriation of the bourgeoisie, the collectivization of all means of production, and the eventual abolition of the state, and looked forward to a society of perfect unity. Yet his idea of Communism was different from Lenin's both philosophically and politically, though he was probably not fully aware of this. One may say that Gramsci provided the ideological nucleus of an alternative form of Communism, which, however, has never existed as a political movement, still less as an actual regime.

It can thus be seen why the exponents of modern 'humanist' or 'democratic' trends in Communism, as well as various forms of revisionism, seek encouragement in Gramsci's writings. The main theme of internal criticism in the Communist movement is that of the socialist bureaucracies, which claim the right to rule by force on the ground that they embody the 'true' desires and aspirations of the working class, not because the workers have elected them democratically but because they are the holders of an infallible scientific theory. The criticism of 'scientific socialism', in the sense of that term which identifies it with the self-glorification of the ruling bureaucracies, comes very close to Gramsci's ideas and explains the popularity of his writings in revisionist circles. Whether his variant of Communism is as practicable as Lenin's (which has proved practicable beyond any shadow of doubt) is another question, which we shall consider later.

CHAPTER VII

György Lukács:
reason in the service of dogma

LUKÁCS's personality and his role in the history of Marxism are, and no doubt will be for a long time, a matter of lively controversy. It is agreed, however, that he was the most outstanding Marxist philosopher during the period of Stalinist orthodoxy. Indeed, we may go further and say that he was the only one: he alone expressed the fundamental tenets of Leninism in the language of the German philosophical tradition and, unlike the unsophisticated Marxists of his day, he wrote in a manner that enabled at least some Western intellectuals to digest his thoughts. But it is a matter of dispute whether he was a true philosopher of Stalinism, an intellectual exponent of that particular system, or rather, as some would have it and as he himself often suggested in later times, a kind of Trojan horse—an ostensibly orthodox disciple who, under the pretence of Stalinism, was in fact purveying a 'genuine', non-Stalinist form of Marxism.

The question is indeed extremely complicated. Lukács joined the Communist party unexpectedly, at a comparatively late stage of his intellectual life: he was thirty-three and had published a number of works unconnected with Marxism, although critics, as usual, have been at pains to show that his thought developed on consistent lines throughout. During the rest of his life (he lived to be eighty-six) he remained faithful to the Communist cause through various political upheavals and ideological changes. He was frequently condemned and attacked by orthodox Stalinists and frequently submitted to party discipline, recanting his previous opinions only to disavow or modify the recantation when times became easier. Thus his works are full of palinodes, retractions, withdrawals of retractions, and reinterpretations of earlier writings, particularly in forewords and epilogues to reprints of his books that appeared in the 1960s.

From the beginning of his Marxist career to the end of his life Lukács professed fidelity to Lenin and Leninism, and the question how far he was a 'Stalinist philosopher' depends in part on the more general question of the relationship between Leninism and Stalinism. The quotations from Stalin and flattering remarks about him that occur in Lukács's writings (though much less often than in the average ideological output of the time) are not a decisive argument, as for many years practically every work published in the Soviet Union or its dependencies was studded with references to Stalin and his glorious intellect. This applied even to manuals of physics, cookery books, and so on, though it was still possible to distinguish between ritual homage and genuinely Stalinist works: there was not really any such thing as 'Stalinist physics'. On the other hand, we cannot accept without reservation Lukács's later assurances that he was always critical of Stalinism but for tactical reasons conformed to the party line: for one who objects in private but joins in the public chorus of praise is not an objector, but a eulogist pure and simple. Thus the question can only be decided by examining the content of Lukács's writings and the political significance of his comments and actions at various times.

Lukács's voluminous works are devoted for the most part to questions of aesthetics and literary criticism; but it would be wrong to say that he was a critic first and foremost and a philosopher only in a lesser degree. In accordance with his conception of Marxism he always endeavoured to relate even the most detailed questions to the 'totality' of great social processes and the past and future history of mankind. This attitude, he believed, was as essential to Marxism as it was to Hegelianism, and accordingly he approached all questions from the standpoint of a philosopher.

Lukács's work has generally been considered in the context of international Marxism or German philosophy: most of his books were written in German and are concerned with the history of German culture. In recent years attention has also been drawn increasingly to the Hungarian 'background' of his philosophy and the important part played in his development by the Hungarian cultural tradition. However, the predominantly German strain in his work is clear when it is studied as an element in the history of Marxism; and he was certainly far better acquainted with the language, literature, and philosophy of Germany than with those of any other country besides his native Hungary, where he spent the beginning and end of his life.

1. Life and intellectual development. Early writings

György Lukács (1885–1971), the son of a banker, was born at Budapest, where he attended grammar school and university, graduating in 1906. From his schooldays onwards he belonged to socialist groups under the aegis of the left-wing social democrat Ervin Szabó (1877–1918). Szabó was not an orthodox Marxist but an exponent of anarcho-syndicalism, and it was mainly through him that Lukács for a time came under the influence of Sorel. From his earliest years Lukács was attracted by the modernist, anti-positivist outlook that prevailed at the turn of the century: he sought a 'global', all-embracing world-view, free from the inhibitions of positivism and empiricism but also capable of opposing the national, conservative, and Christian tradition. In short, he was in quest of a new metaphysic, like a great many of his contemporaries in all parts of Europe. In the same spirit he helped to found a theatrical group devoted to producing works by the new philosophical dramatists—Ibsen, Strindberg, and Gerhart Hauptmann. Despite difficulties and opposition this group maintained itself for four years, from 1904 to 1908. In 1906 and again in 1909–10 Lukács continued his studies in Berlin, where he attended the lectures of Simmel among others. Kantianism was then dominant in German universities, and young philosophers naturally fell under its influence. Lukács was attracted by versions of Kantianism which concentrated on the philosophy of history and the methodology of the social sciences and which sought to go beyond the 'critical' point of view (in Kant's sense of the term): i.e. they did not accept that the theory of knowledge must logically take precedence of all metaphysical questions, a view which meant in effect that the latter could not be framed correctly or would remain insoluble. Lukács returned to Germany in 1913 and studied at Heidelberg: he attended the lectures of Rickert, Windelband, and others, and made the acquaintance of Max Weber, Stefan George, Emil Lask, and Ernst Bloch.

From 1906 onwards he wrote articles for Hungarian literary

magazines: some of these were republished in his first book, which appeared in Hungarian in 1910 and in German in the following year, entitled *Die Seele und die Formen*. Like other early works by Lukács, this is a kind of philosophic essay on literary themes. Goldmann discerns in it a 'tragic Kantianism' with a phenomenological slant: Lukács's concept of 'form', he believes, corresponds to the 'significant structure' of the phenomenologists, but the approach is one of 'static structuralism', i.e. the quest for meaning independent of any consideration of genesis or historical change. Lukács, in fact, argues that every literary work should be regarded as an attempt to give form to the author's soul or sense of life. The attempt is natural and inevitable, but the form itself connotes an acceptance of the imperfect, a limitation of the content that it aims to express. It is as though the very process of artistic creativity, the attempt to subdue the spirit to forms, reveals our basic inability to achieve a true synthesis of the internal and the external, subjectivity and expression. Lukács opposes altogether the kind of artistic culture that only tries to depict the contingency of life and pays no heed to its 'essence': he thus rejects naturalism as firmly as impressionism. At the same time he appears to hold that the search for meaning and essence brings to light the inescapable tragedy of life, the individual's dependence on invisible and unintelligible powers that break out into insoluble conflicts. He is as far removed as possible from 'aestheticism', if by that is meant faith in the absolute autonomy of form *vis-à-vis* the genesis of a work: forms are a way of imparting unity to the world, but where spiritual life itself is impoverished and chaotic, the perfection of forms cannot restore its value. According to Lukács, modern artistic culture either seeks after 'abstract' form, i.e. it apes the perfection of past forms that will not accommodate a new content, or else it tries to reject form altogether; in either case the attempt does not signify a crisis of form as such, but only the weakness and spuriousness of the 'life' which seeks to express itself in art.

In *Die Theorie des Romans*, written at Heidelberg in 1914–15 and published in 1916 in the *Zeitschrift für Ästhetik und allgemeine Kunstwissenschaft* (and in book form in 1920), Lukács appeared to have reached a less pessimistic and fatalistic standpoint. Looking back in the 1950s he described this work as reactionary in all respects—idealistic, mystical, etc. Nevertheless, it is regarded today as one of his most important achievements. L. Congdon in his study points out the profound effect that Lukács's reading of Dostoevsky and Kierkegaard had on his development during the 1914–18 War. At that time he believed that the novel as a literary genre was an expression of the world in which relations between individuals were mediated by social forms and institutions, or 'reified' as he would have said at a later date. The very existence of the novel bore witness to a cultural disease, the inability of human beings to communicate directly. Dostoevsky's greatness lay in the fact that he had succeeded in portraying human relationships that were not determined by social or class conditions—so that in this sense, paradoxical as it might seem, his works were not novels at all. In the discussion of Dostoevsky's 'Utopia' there could certainly be discerned an anticipation of questions that were to occupy Lukács's attention in his subsequent Marxist works: questions as to the possibility of a society which, in accordance with Marx's romantic vision, would sweep away all social and institutional obstacles and enable human beings to meet one another as individuals, not representatives of anonymous forces. However, *Die Theorie des Romans* makes no mention of Marxism, though it shows the influence of Dilthey and Hegel: Lukács regards literary forms as the expression of changing historical totalities, each of which in turn seeks to achieve self-consciousness in artistic creation. In accordance with Hegel's philosophy of history, art is the realm of the objectivization of the 'spirit of the age', and its significance cannot be reduced to mere form; on the other hand, it has its own autonomy and is not simply a function of philosophy or science. The 'intellectualist' view of artistic creation is thus no less mistaken than romantic faith in the privileged position of art in creating a universal synthesis of human thought and activity.

Lukács's writings in his last pre-Marxist years show that, in his aesthetic studies as in other fields, he was absorbed by ethical problems: the contradiction between the decisions of individuals and the results of their acts, the conflict between the need for expression and the self-limiting function of expression, the conflict between the need for direct communication and the social forms that make it impossible. During the war, besides his unfinished essay on Dostoevsky, Lukács wrote a study (also unfinished) of Kierkegaard as a critic of Hegel. As Congdon points out, Lukács's conversion to Communism may itself have been the result of his seeing the situation in terms of Kierkegaard's 'either–or': a state of conflict in which there is no possibility of synthesis between two sets of values, and in which the individual must therefore choose between them.

After returning to Budapest in 1915 Lukács was among the leaders of an intellectual circle, and subsequently an independent study centre, where young intellectuals seeking philosophical and moral answers to the problems of war-torn Europe attempted to give expression to their feelings of despair and hope. Several of Lukács's comrades in this endeavour were to become eminent in different cultural spheres: Karl Mannheim, Zoltán Kodály, Arnold Hauser, Béla Bartók, and Michael Polanyi. The general atmosphere was left-wing, but not such as to encourage Bolshevik sympathies. Consequently, Lukács's friends were surprised when he joined the Communist party immediately after its foundation, at the end of 1918, especially as he had published an article a few days earlier asserting that the Bolsheviks had no rational ground for maintaining that the conflict-free society of the future could be brought about by dictatorship and terror. Apparently, however, he believed—as did many of those who became Communists as a result of the war and the collapse of the Second International—that Bolshevism was the only practical alternative for those who refused to accept, actively or passively, the system which was responsible for the horrors of war and the threat to civilization itself.

In any case, from then on Lukács accepted Communism whole-heartedly as a moral, intellectual, and political solution. Despite various philosophical adventures, he completely identified himself with the Communist movement for the rest of his life. He believed that Marxism was the final answer to the problem of history, that Communism guaranteed the final reconciliation of all human forces and the free play on all human possibilities; that the conflict between the individual and society, between one person and another, between contingent existence and 'essence', morality, and law, had 'in principle' been resolved, and that it remained only to unite oneself in practice with the historical movement which promised that the synthesis would without fail be realized.

For some time it looked as though the hope of a European Communist revolution would come true at an early date. A few months after the overthrow of the Dual Monarchy a Soviet republic was set up in Hungary under Béla Kun (who subsequently lost his life in a Russian gaol, a victim of Stalin's terror); it lasted from the end of March to the end of July 1919. Lukács joined the government as deputy to the Commissar for Education (Zsigmond Kunfi, a social democrat and theoretician close to the Austrian Marxists). The brief Communist dictatorship was followed by savage mass repression, but most of the leaders escaped abroad. Lukács, after a few weeks of clandestine activity in Budapest, reached Vienna, where he was arrested for a short time; he was saved from extradition, partly owing to a protest by a group of writers including Thomas and Heinrich Mann.

Thereafter he led the life of a political *émigré*, carrying on theoretical and propaganda work and involved in the incessant quarrels of his Hungarian fellow exiles. These disputes had no practical effect on the situation in Hungary but, as is usually the case, aroused bitter passions among the *émigrés* with their rival plans for revolution. Lukács belonged at this time to the so-called Communist Left; in 1920–1 he edited a journal *Kommunismus*, of similar tendency, which was once criticized by Lenin for its anti-parliamentary standpoint.

In 1919–22 Lukács wrote a number of theoretical essays, published in book form in 1923 as *Geschichte und Klassenbewusstsein* (*History and Class-Consciousness*: English trans. 1971). This is considered his *magnum opus*, although he declared more than once that in some respects at least it no longer represented his views. At all events, among all his works it is this one which gave rise to most controversy and left the deepest traces on the Marxist movement. In it he emphasized the importance of the Hegelian sources of Marxism and also put forward an original interpretation of the whole of Marx's philosophy, in which the category of 'totality' was presented as the foundation of Marxist dialectic. He set out to show that the chief philosophical disputes among the Marxists of the Second International had been conducted from positions alien to Marx's ideas, and in particular that the orthodox line had continued to ignore the essential feature of dialectical materialism, namely the interaction of the object and subject of history in the movement towards unity. His work was largely directed against the evolutionist or positivist interpretations of Marxism that dominated the Second International, and was designed to supply a philosophical basis for the revolutionary, Leninist theory of socialism and the party. On two points, however, Lukács parted company with Leninism: he criticized Engels's idea of the dialectic of nature as basically contrary to the theory of the dialectic itself, and he disputed the theory of 'reflection' which Lenin had declared to be the essence of Marxist epistemology.

It was not surprising, therefore, at a period when Communist ideology was hardening into dogmatic form, that Lukács's book was sharply attacked in the most official manner possible, namely at a session of the Third International. At the Fifth Comintern Congress in Moscow in July 1924 Zinovyev, then chairman of its Executive Committee, denounced Lukács's work as a harmful revisionist attack on Marxism; this view was endorsed by Bukharin. At the same time Zinovyev attacked Antonio Graziadei, who had recently published a book criticizing Marx's theory of value, and also Karl Korsch. His condemnation of Lukács was expressed in general terms, without any specific charges, and it may be doubted whether he had in fact read the offending work. Soon, however, more reasoned attacks were delivered by philosophers such as A. M. Deborin, N. Luppol, and L. Rudas. Lukács is not known to have performed any self-criticism at the time, but he did so in 1933; he also repeated in several later works that he regarded *History and Class-Consciousness* as erroneous and reactionary, at least on the two points mentioned above. The book disappeared without trace from Communist annals and was only rediscovered after Stalin's death. It had its effect, however, on non-Communist German Marxists, and today it is regarded as one of the most important theoretical documents in the history of Marxism.

Other theoretical works by Lukács in the early post-war years include an article 'Tactics and Ethics', published in Hungarian in 1919, and essays on Lassalle (1925) and Moses Hess (1926) in *Archiv für die Geschichte des Sozialismus und der Arbeiterbewegung*: the former was occasioned by an edition of Lassalle's letters, the latter by the republication of Hess's writings and the appearance of a life of him by Theodor Zlocisti. In 1924

Lukács published a short book on Lenin, written immediately after the latter's death (*Lenin. Studie über den Zusammenhang seiner Gedanken*). All these works were concerned with the same broad theme as *History and Class-Consciousness*: the Marxist conception of history as an integral whole, and the resolution of the traditional dilemmas of freedom and necessity, what is and what ought to be. In 1925 Lukács published a critical review of Bukharin's manual of historical materialism.

Up to 1928 Lukács was actively involved in controversies among Hungarian Communist groups, and in that year he drew up a fractional programme to be presented at the next party congress. This document, known after Lukács's pseudonym as the 'Blum theses', was severely criticized by the majority group under Béla Kun, and afterwards by the Comintern Executive in an open letter to the Hungarian Communists.

The 'Blum theses' (first published, in an abridged form, in 1956) are sometimes quoted today as a proof that in the Stalin era Lukács consistently opposed what was later euphemistically called 'sectarianism', and that he advocated a 'popular front' of the kind proposed by the Comintern at its last congress in 1935, after the set-backs of the early 1930s. In actual fact, Lukács's opposition to Béla Kun's policy in the twenties was of a very limited kind. Far from proposing joint action with the social democrats against Horthy's regime in Hungary, Lukács maintained that social democracy was 'on the road to Fascism' and could not be regarded as a democratic opposition: he subscribed, in fact, to the designation 'social Fascism' which was one of the more fantastic symptoms of Communist paranoia in the late twenties and early thirties. He also declared, in accordance with the slogans of the new era, that the battle was not between democracy and Fascism but between class and class. On the other hand, he put forward the controversial formula of a 'democratic dictatorship' of the proletariat and peasantry as a transitional stage leading to the dictatorship of the proletariat, while making it clear that there was no question of co-operating with the bourgeoisie or the social democrats to build up democracy. In this way he sought to apply certain of Lenin's pre-revolutionary maxims to Hungary. The Comintern, on the other hand, envisaged an immediate transition to the dictatorship of the proletariat, i.e. to a Communist monopoly of power, and it condemned the 'Blum theses' as advocating a policy of 'liquidation'. The whole dispute had no effect whatever on events in Hungary, then or later, and from this point of view it did not matter what ideas were worked out by a handful of powerless *émigrés*. However, the result of the condemnation was that Lukács hastily recanted in order to avoid expulsion from the party, and from then on withdrew from political activity and confined himself to theoretical work.

In the thirties and during the Second World War Lukács published very little. In 1930–1 he spent some time in Moscow, where he worked in the Marx-Engels-Lenin Institute and became acquainted with Marx's early manuscripts, which had still not appeared in print. After returning to Berlin he wrote a few articles for *Die Linkskurve*, including an important essay on literature and politics entitled 'Tendenz oder Parteilichkeit?' (1932). When Hitler came to power he returned to the Soviet Union and stayed in Moscow till the end of the war, working at the Institute of Philosophy of the Academy of Sciences. The intensive studies of those years bore fruit in numerous publications after 1945. Among these were *Der junge Hegel*, finished before the war but published only in 1948; *Goethe und seine Zeit* (1947); *Essays über Realismus* (1948: on realism in literature); studies of Russian literature (*Der russische Realismus in der Weltliteratur*, 1949); *Thomas Mann* (1949); *Deutsche Realisten des neunzehnten Jahrhunderts* (1951); *Balzac und der französische Realismus* (1952); *Existentialisme ou marxisme?* (1948); a history of irrationalist German philosophy as a source of Nazism (*Die Zerstörung der Vernunft*, 1954); and a study of the historical novel (*Der historische Roman*, 1955).

Throughout this period Lukács's position as a Communist ideologist and Marxist was ambiguous. He remained a party member and did his best to conform scrupulously to each new phase of the 'ideological struggle'. Nevertheless, when the Stalin line hardened from 1949 onwards and repression intensified in the 'peoples' democracies', Lukács again came under fire, the attacks being led by J. Révai, then cultural dictator of Hungary. Once more Lukács bowed to the party's judgement and performed self-criticism. His books continued to appear—mostly in the G.D.R., in German—but in party circles they were considered rather suspect, unduly 'liberal' and not a hundred per cent Marxist.

A new turn of events came with the upheavals of 'de-Stalinization' in 1956, triggered off by the Twentieth Congress of the Soviet Communist party and Khrushchev's famous speech about Stalin's 'mistakes'. Lukács was one of those in Hungary who criticized the 'distortions' of the Stalin era; he belonged to the 'Petőfi Circle', which played an important part in the ideological ferment that preceded the Hungarian uprising. Lukács directed his main attack against ideological 'dogmatism' and the primitive attitude towards literary and philosophical questions in the Stalin era. When the Hungarian anti-Stalinist movement reached its height with the formation of Imre Nagy's government in October 1956, Lukács was co-opted on to the party's Central Committee and for a few days held the post of Minister of Culture. After the Soviet invasion he was deported to Romania with the rest of Nagy's government, most of whom were murdered by the Soviets; Lukács, one of the few survivors, returned to Budapest in the spring of 1957. He soon became the target of fresh attacks, in which his former pupil J. Szigeti played a prominent part. He sought to resume party membership, but was not allowed to as he refused to perform self-criticism on this occasion; apparently, however, he was readmitted in 1967, the condition being waived. In any case, to the end of his life he maintained the belief that socialism, begun in Russia and continued in Eastern Europe, would liberate itself from the aftermath of Stalinist 'distortions' and return to the path of 'true' Marxism. He stated in an interview that the worst socialism was better than the best capitalism. In the political field he whole-heartedly endorsed the Soviet policy of 'coexistence' and opposed Chinese 'dogmatism'. His scholarly activity after the uprising was mainly devoted to problems of Marxist aesthetics. In 1957 he published an essay 'Über die Besonderheit als Kategorie der Ästhetik', and in 1963 a two-volume work *Die Eigenart des Ästhetischen*. As the cultural pressure eased in Hungary in the sixties he enjoyed more reasonable conditions of work and publication facilities. A volume celebrating his eightieth birthday appeared in West Germany in 1965.

In addition to his aesthetic studies he embarked on a basic

handbook of Marxist doctrine: this work, nearly completed, appeared posthumously under the title *Zur Ontologie des gesellschaftlichen Seins*, as part of a fourteen-volume edition of his works published by the firm of Luchterhand.

Lukács died at Budapest in 1971. In the previous decade interest in his ideas increased rapidly, as is shown by the number of books, articles, and discussions concerning them, and also by numerous translations and new editions of his works themselves. Attacks from the Stalinist angle practically ceased; on the other hand, he was criticized by some (Deutscher, Adorno, Lichtheim) as a Stalinist writer and ideologist. Discussion has centred mainly on his literary and aesthetic views and his conception of the dialectic, especially in *History and Class-Consciousness*. His posthumous work did not arouse great interest and must have disappointed those who looked for new ideas on the interpretation of Marxism: it is a conventional exposé of historical materialism, with Lukács's customary attacks on empiricism and positivism. On the other hand, he broke fresh ground in 1964 and 1969 in articles on Solzhenitsyn, whom he hailed as the harbinger of a great renewal of socialist realism.

Lukács left a number of disciples in Hungary who have tried, with greater or less fidelity, to continue his work and range of interests. In Western Europe perhaps the most zealous advocate of his philosophy was Lucien Goldmann, whose work requires special notice.

2. *The whole and the part: critique of empiricism*

Both in 'Tactics and Ethics' and in *History and Class-Consciousness* Lukács puts the question 'What is orthodox Marxism?' and replies that this concept does not involve the acceptance of any particular tenet. An orthodox Marxist does not, as such, owe allegiance to any specific view and may criticize Marx's ideas so long as he remains faithful to the essence of Marxism, namely the dialectical method. 'Method' does not mean here a set of rules for intellectual operations, as it does in logic, but a particular way of thinking which includes awareness that in thinking about the world it is also helping to change it, being at the same time a practical commitment. The Marxian dialectic is not merely a way of perceiving or describing social reality, or even indicating how it should be described: it is the mainspring of social revolution and does not exist outside the revolutionary process, of which, as method, it forms an integral part.

This conception of method, Lukács argues, involves regarding the social universe as a single whole of 'totality'. His vew that this is the key to Marxist theory did not alter from 1919 to 1971. The text that he quotes most often is probably the introduction to the *Grundrisse*, in which Marx expounds his view of the primacy of the abstract over the concrete. Marxism, according to Lukács, would be impossible if it did not involve the principle that the social 'totality' cannot be reconstructed by accumulating facts. Facts do not interpret themselves: their meaning is only revealed in relation to the whole, which must be known in advance and is thus logically prior to the facts. In this respect Marx follows Hegel. 'We thus understand the fundamental assertion of the dialectical method, the Hegelian theory of the concrete concept. This theory states, in brief, that the whole is prior to its parts: the part must be interpreted in the light of the whole and not vice versa' ('Tactics and Ethics', p. 25). The concrete must not be contrasted with phenomena that can only be apprehended by the mind, since for both Marx and Hegel the concrete itself can only be so apprehended, as a single aspect of the whole. 'This absolute primacy of the whole, its unity over and above the abstract isolation of its parts—such is the essence of Marx's conception of society and of the dialectical method' (ibid., p. 27).

Thus Marx's theory of revolution and socialism can be based only on a global understanding of society that cannot be achieved by any detailed, factual analysis. This is why opportunists and revisionists always appeal to facts, knowing that there is no logical transition from facts to the revolutionary transformation of society. Empiricism is the ideological foundation of revisionism and reformism in the workers' movement. 'And every orthodox Marxist who realizes that the moment has come when capital is only an obstacle to production, and that it is time to expropriate the exploiters, will reply in the words of Fichte, one of the greatest of the classical German philosophers, when vulgar Marxists adduce "facts" that appear to contradict the process: "So much the worse for the facts!"' (ibid., p. 30).

Lukács does not appear to have used this phrase elsewhere

in his attacks on empiricism, but his attitude on the point remained unchanged. In *History and Class-Consciousness* he emphasizes that a theory which simply takes account of facts as they are directly given is, by the same token, locating itself within capitalist society. But to understand the meaning of facts is to situate them in a 'concrete whole' and to discover the 'mediation' between them and the whole, which of course is not directly given. The truth of the part resides in the whole, and if each part is properly examined the whole can be discerned in it. The whole is the vehicle of the 'revolutionary principle', in social practice as well as in theory. There is only one single science, embracing the whole of human history—politics, economics, ideology, law, etc.—and it is that whole which gives meaning to every separate phenomenon. Did not Marx say that a spinning-jenny in itself is only a spinning-jenny, and that it becomes capital only in particular social conditions? No direct perception of a machine can reveal its function as capital: that can only be seen by considering the whole social process of which it forms a part. Facts are not the final reality but are artificially isolated aspects (*Momente*) of the whole: the over-all trend of historical evolution is more real than the data of experience.

But—and this is the next fundamental point—the 'whole' is not simply a state of affairs comprising all the particulars of reality at a given moment. It must be understood as a dynamic reality, involving a certain trend, its direction, and its results. It is in fact identical with present, past, and future history—but a future which is not simply 'foreseen' like a fact in nature, but which is created by the act of foreseeing it. Thus the 'whole' is anticipatory, and present facts can only be understood in relation to the future.

This is particularly important in distinguishing the revolutionary from the reformist viewpoint in the socialist movement. In the eyes of reformists the significance of the current social and political struggle of the working class is exhausted in its immediate consequences. For Marx, on the other hand, each fragment of the actual struggle, including the workers' fight for economic betterment, only derives meaning from the prospect of revolution. Such was the dialectic and revolutionary attitude of those leaders, like Lenin and Rosa Luxemburg, who combated opportunism and revisionism and always kept in view the 'final goal'. In his essay on Rosa Luxemburg Lukács especially praises her power of 'global' analysis. She saw the phenomenon of accumulation not as an isolated occurrence but as part of the process leading unavoidably to the proletarian revolution, and was thus able to show that it could not continue indefinitely but must bring about the collapse of capitalism. Opportunists like Otto Bauer were unable to think in terms of an integral historical process, and as a result they surrendered to capitalism, seeking only to cure its 'bad aspects' by ethical means. Once the integral viewpoint is abandoned, capitalism does indeed seem invincible, as the peculiar laws governing its economy appear to be 'given' as unalterable facts and laws of nature, which may be turned to use but cannot be nullified. A global view, on the other hand, shows capitalism to be a historical and transient phenomenon, and is therefore the vehicle of revolutionary consciousness.

In his book on Lenin, Lukács again uses the notion of *Totalität* to describe the core of Lenin's doctrine and the secret of its greatness. Lenin was the one genius who discerned the revolutionary trend of the age independently of particular facts and events, or rather in the facts themselves, and united all current issues, even the smallest, in a single great socialist perspective. He knew that the global process was more real than any of its details, and despite all appearances he saw that the hour for revolution had already struck. From the economic point of view he added nothing to the theory of imperialism, but he surpassed Hilferding by his brilliant success in integrating economic theory with current political developments.

The interrelated concepts of the 'whole' and of 'mediation' apply to all spheres of social inquiry, and play a prominent part in Lukács's view on literature. By 'mediation' he means any kind of subordinate totality into which observed facts and phenomenon must be fitted before they are integrated into the universal whole, the global historical process of past, present, and future. Frequently, however, he also uses 'mediation' to mean the intellectual process which relates the concrete to the whole. Whereas inability to think globally enslaves us to given situations and prevents our transcending the existing order of society, so that in terms of socialism we end up as reformists and revisionists, on the other hand those who overlook the need for 'mediation' are in danger of succumbing to the primitive error of lumping all phenomena together in a single undifferentiated whole, ignoring the specific character of various aspects of life and culture. An example of an ideology taking account of totality but not of mediation can be found in Nazism as it later revealed itself. In addition, almost all the artistic trends condemned by Lukács can be described as deficient either in 'mediation' or in a sense of totality. Naturalism confines itself to direct description and fails to reach the level of integral social criticism; symbolism creates only 'subjective' wholes, while the various forms of decadence exalt partial experience into eternal metaphysical truth, and thus likewise fall short of an integral view. In socialism the lack of a sense of 'mediation' results in sectarianism, i.e. inability to grasp the particular functions of subordinate interrelations: for instance, the claim that the tasks of art in socialist society should be determined solely by its propaganda value overlooks the mediating role of specifically aesthetic criteria. The main burden of Lukács's later criticism of Stalinism was that it lacked 'mediation' by failing to appreciate the diversity of means involved in the building of socialism, and by reducing art and science to a purely political role.

A special case, within Marxism, of failure to understand the nature of 'totality' and 'mediation' is afforded by all reductionist interpretations which take for granted the one-way determination of certain factors in history by other such factors. As the whole is always prior to its parts, so the determination of parts by the whole is more fundamental than that of some parts by others. In his last work Lukács contends that the maxim 'social being determines consciousness' has nothing to do with what is called economism. This maxim 'does not link the world of forms and the content of consciousness with the economic structure in a directly productive relationship, but links it with the whole of social being. The determination of consciousness by social being is thus of a purely general kind. Only vulgar Marxism, from the Second International to the age of Stalin and after, claimed to establish a direct, unqualified causal link between the economy, or even particular aspects of it, on the one hand and ideology on the other' (*Zur Ontologie des gesellschaften Seins*, 'Die ontologischen Grundprinzipien von Marx', p. 39). In other words, the basic dependence in social life is not between the base and the superstructure but between social being (or 'the whole', i.e. everything) and particular elements of the whole.

3. The subject and object of history. Theory and practice. What is and what ought to be. Critique of neo-Kantianism and evolutionism

Nevertheless—and this is the next fundamental quality of dialectical thinking emphasized by Lukács in his *magnum opus*— the dialectic is not simply a scientific method that can be transferred at will from one object to another, nor is it independent of the subject who applies it. For in both Hegel's and Marx's theory it is, as already explained, an active constituent of the social reality to which it is applied as a method, and not simply a way of apprehending that reality. It is the expression of history ripening towards the final transformation, and is also the theoretical consciousness of the social agent, namely the proletariat, by which that transformation is to be brought about. In other words, it is not the case that anyone, independent of his political status and social commitment, can adopt the dialectical method and successfully apply it to any object that he may choose. For the dialectic does not exist outside the revolutionary struggle of the proletariat: it is the self-awareness of that struggle and a component of it.

The dialectic presupposes the conception of society as a whole; and only the social agent which is itself a 'whole'—i.e. Marx's 'universal class', the proletariat—can perceive the 'whole' in isolated phenomena. In accordance with Hegel's principle, 'the truth is the subject'; i.e., in the present case, the truth concerning the historical process can be revealed only from the viewpoint of the class whose revolutionary initiative is destined radically to transform the whole of social life and to abolish the class society.

Marxism is not, as the theoreticians of the Second International would have it, a scientific description of historical reality that anyone can accept if he applies logical rules correctly. It is nothing else than the theoretical consciousness of the working class as it matures towards revolution; and the class-consciousness of the proletariat is not a mere reflection of an independent historical process, but is the indispensable driving force of that process. Unlike all previous revolutions, the agents of which did not understand what they were doing and fell victim to illusions, the proletarian revolution, as a matter of principle, cannot be brought about without the complete, un-mystified self-awareness of the proletariat in regard to its position in society and the destiny it is called on to fulfil.

The proletariat is thus privileged by history, not only in the sense that it is called on to achieve the radical upheaval that will once and for all abolish class divisions, exploitation, and social conflict, the separation of individual from social being, alienation, false consciousness, and the dependence of humanity on impersonal historical powers. In addition to all this the proletariat is privileged from the epistemological point of view, inasmuch as its historical role entails the complete understanding of society: only it can apprehend history as a whole, for only in its actions is the totality truly realized as a revolutionary movement. The proletariat's self-awareness coincides with its awareness of history as a whole; theory and practice coincide, as the proletariat transforms the world in the process by which it arrives at a mature understanding of the world. In this particular case the understanding and transformation of reality are not two separate processes, but one and the same phenomenon.

For this reason both the neo-Kantians in the Marxist movement and their evolutionist adversaries were at fault in distinguishing between the 'pure science' of history and the 'socialist ideal' deriving, as a kind of moral imperative, from arbitrarily established values. Since subject and object coincide in the knowledge of society; since, in this case, science is the self-knowledge of society and, by the same token, a factor in determining its situation at any stage of history; and since, in the case of the proletariat, this self-knowledge is at the same time a revolutionary movement, it follows that the proletariat cannot at any point disjoin its 'ideal' from the actual process of realizing it. Socialism is not a state of affairs waiting for humanity and guaranteed by the impersonal laws of history, nor is it a moral 'imperative': it is the self-knowledge of the proletariat, an aspect of its actual struggle.

In this way Marxism resolves the dilemma that perplexed the theoreticians of the Second International. Both the evolutionists and the neo-Kantians supposed that Marx's theory was an account of 'inevitable' historical laws and that, as a scientific doctrine, it contained no normative element. The neo-Kantians inferred that the necessary normative factors or ideals must be imported from Kantian moral philosophy. To this the orthodox replied that Marxism must be content with historical description, and that it was both impossible and unnecessary to demonstrate that socialism was desirable as well as inevitable. According to Lukács, however, both parties were arguing from essentially un-Marxist positions, as they followed Kant in taking for granted the dualism of 'what is' and 'what ought to be', whereas Hegel and Marx after him had overcome that dualism. Marxism is not a mere description of the world but the expression and self-knowledge of a social process by which the world is revolutionized, and thus the subject of that self-knowledge, i.e. the proletariat, comprehends reality in the very act of transforming it. The division of social life into 'objective' processes outside human control, and the impotent awareness that merely observes or moralizes, is a characteristic and inevitable attitude of classes which, even if in their own day they may have represented over-all progress, were not and are not universal classes in the same sense as the proletariat—that is to say, they cannot rise to an understanding of history as a whole, being fettered to their own particular interests. The proletariat, however, as its particular interest coincides with that of humanity as a matter of principle and not merely by a temporary accident, truly embodies the unity of the subject and object of history. In the revolutionary activity of this class history achieves self-knowledge: historical necessity appears, and must appear, as free action, free because fully conscious. The 'objective' process and awareness of it are one and the same: there is no difference between social 'being', that which actually is, and the theoretical or moral consciousness of the class which is the agent of that process. Subject and object, freedom and necessity, the fact and the norm are no longer opposed but are aspects of a single reality. This puts an end to the Kantian dilemma of how obligation can be deduced from empirical facts, and likewise to the dilemma of 'scientism'.

In the same way there is no longer a conflict between voluntarism and determinism, or human will and scientific prediction. Since awareness of society as a whole is not simply information that anyone can acquire but is the self-knowledge of actual revolutionary praxis, it follows that there is no such thing in Marxism as 'objective' prediction based on historical laws and independent of the will that governs future changes. The act of foreseeing coincides with the act of effecting what is foreseen: the proletariat knows the future in the act of creating it, not after the fashion of a weather forecast where the changes that actually happen are unaffected by anything the forecaster can do.

This unity of the object and subject of history, of the cognitive and normative aspects of consciousness, is, Lukács argues, the most precious legacy of Hegelianism to Marxism. This does not mean, of course, that it was taken over in a directly Hegelian form. Hegel could not have discovered the identity of the object and subject in history itself, as in his time there was no real historical basis for it. Consequently, he transferred the identity into the extra-historical sphere of reason, and ascribed to Mind the role of a demiurge in the evolution of history. Thus he could not, although it was his aim to do so, overcome finally the dualism of object and subject: it was left to Marx to achieve this.

In the same line of thought it is clear that there cannot in principle be anyone who is a mere 'theoretical Marxist', i.e. who recognizes the validity of Marx's social theory and historical predictions but takes no part in making them come true. To be precise, such an attitude is possible, but it is not a Marxist attitude. A Marxist must be someone who plays a practical part in the movement that gives effect to the theory, for the theory is itself nothing but the self-awareness of the movement.

This viewpoint is a basis for the criticism of many different trends within Marxism and also in non-Marxist socialism. Lukács, as we have seen, used it to refute the theoreticians of the Second International, both orthodox and neo-Kantian, but also Marx's predecessors and contemporaries. Lassalle, for instance, was not a Marxist, as he revised Hegel from a Fichtean standpoint, modifying the contemplative theory of history by an 'activist' element introduced from outside in the guise of will or moral consciousness. Thus, instead of rebutting Hegelianism, he reverted to a pre-Hegelian position. In the same way Lukács argues in his study of Hess that Cieszkowski's or Hess's philosophy of action did not surmount the dualism of theory versus practice, but eternalized it in the dualism of the socialist movement and its philosophical consciousness: philosophy, in Hess's system, was not the product and self-awareness of the class movement, but a kind of wisdom, independent of party, which it behoved the movement to acquire. Finally, Hess preached a moral Utopia which, while ostensibly criticizing Hegel's 'contemplative' attitude, rejected that part of his thinking which came close to Marxism, namely the conviction that philosophy is an expression of its own time and cannot transcend the limits of the age. Hegel's refusal to look into the future was 'reactionary', but 'from the methodological point of view' it was extremely realistic in rejecting utopianism and in regarding philosophy as the expression of an era and not as Mind entering history from outside it. Marx rebutted the contemplative viewpoint, not by supplementing historical knowledge with arbitrary norms or utopian constructions, but by discerning the future as a real trend already active in the present.

*4. Critique of the 'dialectic of nature' and the theory of reflection.
The concept of reification*

As the dialectic consists of the interaction of the historical subject and object in the movement towards unity, it follows that Engels's idea of the 'dialectic of nature' is untenable; indeed, on this point Lukács accuses Engels of culpable misapprehension of the spirit of Marxian dialectic. If the dialectic denotes a mere system of ready-made natural laws ascertained by man, we are still in the realm of 'predestined' reality and the idea of knowledge as purely contemplative. The 'laws of dialectic' turn out to be an unalterable property of nature: we can discover them and use them, but this 'external' knowledge of nature and its exploitation by human technology have nothing to do with dialectic as understood by Marx and Hegel. The dialectic loses its revolutionary character, and the unity of theory and practice can be conceived only in a contemplative bourgeois, reified sense—the technical exploitation of the world as it exists, not the collective subject taking possession of the world by revolutionary action. Historical materialism, on the other hand, shows us the world as a product of human activity, but one which men have so far treated as something alien, failing to realize that they themselves are its creators. Pre-Marxist philosophy with its dichotomy between knowledge and praxis was obliged to see the world as a collection of crystallized 'data', and praxis as a set of arbitrary ethical precepts and technical devices. By contrast, when, as in the class-consciousness of the proletariat, the subject's self-awareness coincides with knowledge of the whole—when social being is recognized as man-made and subject to conscious regulation by the organized community—then the dichotomy ceases to exist and the dilemma of empiricism versus utopianism is resolved. What Engels called 'practice' (experimentation, technology) does not transform man into a conscious creator of reality, but only increases his mastery of the environment; technical progress does not itself break the bounds of the bourgeois system. Man, exploiting the laws of nature that he has discovered, does not cease to be an 'object' of history. He only becomes a 'subject' when he assimilates and identifies with the external world, abolishing the state of affairs in which that world is a mere datum and knowledge is no more than perception or contemplation. The idea of the unity of subject and object cannot survive if the dialectic relates to external nature.

For the same reason, knowledge cannot be regarded as the mere 'reflection' of a pre-existing reality. In criticizing this idea Lukács does not expressly join issue with Lenin, but he clearly attacks his philosophy. From the point of view of the dialectic as Lukács understands it, to treat cognition as the 'reflection' of the external world in mental experience is to perpetuate the dualism of thought and being and to assume that they are fundamentally alien to each other. If, however, cognition signifies taking possession of the world in a process of revolutionary change, and if understanding and changing the world are a single indivisible act of the liberated consciousness of the proletariat, it no longer makes sense to speak of knowledge as a process whereby an already existing world duplicates itself in the passive human consciousness. The process of thought is not dialectic unless it is part of the historical process of transforming its object.

The 'contemplative' notion of reality, which leaves no room for the unity of theory and practice or the subject's creative role, is linked by Lukács—a point on which he lays special weight in *History and Class-Consciousness*—with 'reification' as a typical feature of the mystified consciousness of capitalist society. The term 'reification' was not used by Marx and in fact owes its currency to Lukács himself, but the idea is thoroughly Marxian: the analysis of 'commodity fetishism' in Volume I of *Capital* is really an analysis of the reified consciousness. The bourgeoisie, by virtue of its social situation, must have a false consciousness: it is contrary to its interests to understand the nature of economic crises and the transient historical character of the system in which it plays the dominant role. In a society which subordinates production entirely to the increase of exchange-value, and in which relations between human beings are crystallized in object-values and themselves take on the character of objects, individuals themselves turn into things. A man is no longer a specific individual but part of a huge system of production and exchange; his personal qualities are merely an obstacle to the complete uniformity and rationalization of the productive mechanism. He is a mere unit of labour force, an article to be bought and sold according to the laws of the market. One result of the omnipotence of exchange-value is the rationalization of legal systems, disregard for tradition, and the tendency to reduce individuals to juridical units. Rationalization is applied to technology and the organization of labour, leading to increasing specialization and the particularization of productive activity; the individual is more and more spiritually crippled and confined to a narrow range of skills by the division of labour. Everything is specialized, activities become partial and fragmented, the unity of society becomes unintelligible and unattainable. Bourgeois philosophy endorses this tyranny of reification and has neither the power nor the desire to rise to an understanding of the whole. All it understands is either empirical reality, from which no 'whole' is capable of emerging, or, on the other hand, normative ethics or arbitrary Utopias which, by definition, have nothing to do with 'facts'. Bourgeois rationalism, which extols mathematics as the most perfect form of knowledge, has no interest in phenomena beyond what is calculable and predictable and can therefore be exploited technically. Anything that might symbolize the 'whole' is banned from the domain of scientific knowledge and labelled an unknowable 'thing in itself'. The contradiction between the irrationality of 'facts' and the desire to apprehend the whole led to the idealist dialectic, which sought to restore the unity of subject and object by denying objectivity altogether; it ascribed creativity to the subject, but, being unable to conceive this creativity as revolutionary practice, endowed it with a moral and internal form.

Reification, in short, cannot be overcome within the terms of bourgeois consciousness. Only when the proletariat, which is a mere commodity in bourgeois society, becomes aware of its own situation will it be able to understand the social mechanism as a whole. The consciousness of the proletariat may be thought of as the acquisition of self-knowledge by a commodity. In the proletariat's situation the process of reification, the transformation of men and women into things, takes on an acute form. When the proletariat becomes aware of itself as a commodity it will at the same time understand, and rebel against the reification of all forms of social life. Its awakened subjectivity will liberate the whole of humanity from the thraldom of objects; its self-knowledge is not a mere perception of the world as it is, but a historical movement of emancipation, and for consciousness of this kind there can be no question of a mere 'reflection' of reality.

Does this argument mean that from the point of view of liberated consciousness the problem of 'truth' in the traditional sense, i.e. the correspondence of judgement with reality, no longer arises, or that truth is relative to social class or to the human species? Lukács's answer to this question is vague and ambiguous. He disclaims an 'anthropological' or pragmatist conception of truth, since, as he says, pragmatism makes man the measure of things but cannot dialectically transform man himself: instead of considering the subject in his interaction with the object, it raises him to the status of a deity. Marxism, on the other hand, does not declare truth to be relative to the individual or the species, but claims that the meaning of different truths is apparent only in the social process. Thought is a factor in the progress of history, and history is the development of forms of objectivity.

This explanation is by no means clear. If, as Lukács says, truth is attainable only from a particular (class) point of view, we may still ask: is it nevertheless inherently true, i.e. the description of a given state of affairs independently of whether it is perceived or not? Lukács, however, appears to consider this a wrongly framed question, as it presupposes a 'contemplative' and 'reified' consciousness outside the object. It is not clear how we can avoid the conclusion that in his view not only is truth revealed solely from a particular class angle, but that nothing is true at all except in the class-consciousness that is identical with the practical revolutionary movement—in other words, participation in the movement equals possession of the truth, which is of course more than saying that it is a condition of possessing the truth. If we accept Lukács's premises, how can we avoid concluding that truth is relative to class, or that nothing is true at all without the qualification 'for the working class'? If for this phrase we substitute 'for future humanity, freed from false consciousness', we are still involved in a species-based relativism which excludes 'truth' in the traditional sense. There are good reasons for holding that this position is in accordance with the doctrine of the early Marx, but it cannot be described as anything but species relativism.

When Lukács speaks of the 'unity of subject and object' in the cognitive process, or the 'unity of theory and practice', he generally uses terms applicable to all knowledge and all objects, but it would seem that he has in mind the object of human and social sciences, namely human history and man as a social being. As a disciple not only of Hegel but also of Dilthey and Windelband, he no doubt wished to maintain the principle of the fundamentally different character of humanistic knowledge ('the humanistic coefficient', as Znaniecki called it) and to emphasize that in awareness of human realities the subject is present in a different way than in the natural sciences, as the act of knowing is a component of the known reality and alters its character. The subject in question is always a collective subject, more precisely a social class. Sometimes, however, owing to his vagueness and disregard of logic, Lukács used expressions suggesting that the 'object' that tends towards unity with the 'subject' is the whole universe, including non-human nature. Yet his real purpose was to distinguish between man and nature and not 'unify' them. To treat the world of human behaviour and historical processes as a reality no less 'given' and 'objective' than stones and stars is to permit one's consciousness to become 'reified'. For the proletarian consciousness there is no such thing as a social universe that exists in itself and whose nature must first be learnt like that of any other object, so that we may then apply technical devices to it for a purpose that must then be irrationally prescribed by moral imperatives. A technological attitude to social phenomena, which treats them as a mere object of political engineering and in which the human agent is purely subjective and inspired by moral laws alone, is a bourgeois delusion—though Engels did not escape it when he extended the dialectic to nature and described social laws as no less objective than the laws governing the formation of geological deposits. Once the proletariat comes on the scene, conscious of its role in production and in the dynamic unity of history, 'historical laws' are identified with human will, and freedom becomes identical with historical necessity.

For the same reason Lukács makes no distinction between bourgeois and Marxist sociology, maintaining that sociology as such is inevitably part of bourgeois ideology. Its task is to study social phenomena 'objectively', i.e. as objects accessible to the observer irrespective of his participation in them. This presumed separation of subject and object is the *raison d'être* of sociology, and therefore Lukács regards 'Marxist sociology' as a contradiction in terms. His criticism of Bukharin in 1925 was based on the same ground. Bukharin had reverted to mechanistic materialism, which sought to interpret social processes in the same way as natural ones, regarding natural science as the model of all knowledge instead of criticizing it as a product of bourgeois consciousness. In this way Bukharin rejected historical materialism in favour of a 'contemplative' epistemology and sought to find in technology the 'objective' forces governing history, as though technology was an independent motive force and not a factor in social conditions.

Lukács's criticism, aimed directly at Engels and implicitly at Lenin, naturally aroused the wrath of orthodox Russian Marxists. Deborin wrote an article branding Lukács as an idealist in his views of nature and society. As to the alleged contradiction between Marx and Engels, Deborin and all others who took up the question pointed triumphantly to the preface to the second edition of the *Anti-Dühring* (1885), in which Engels said that Marx had read and approved his work before it went to press. The idea of the identity of subject and object, Deborin argued, was the purest idealism, as Lenin had himself shown. Consciousness 'reflected' reality, and in denying this Lukács was repeating the absurdities of Mach. All in all, Deborin's rebuttal was primitive and unskilful, and Lukács did not hasten to recant his errors. In 1933, in an article 'Mein Weg zu Marx', he withdrew his criticism of the theory of reflection and the dialectic of nature, but only in general terms and without going into the substance of the dispute. In the following year, however, in an article in *Pod znamenem Marksizma* (*Under the Banner of Marxism*) entitled 'The Significance of [Lenin's] *Materialism and Empiriocriticism* for the Bolshevization of Communist Parties', he made an act of abject self-criticism ascribing his deviation to residual influences of syndicalism and idealism. *History and Class-Consciousness*, he declared, was an idealistic work, and as idealism was the ally of Fascism and of its social democratic hangers-on, his error was dangerous in practice as well as in theory. Fortunately, the Bolshevik party under the leadership of Comrade Stalin was fighting indomitably for the purity of Marxism–Leninism, steering a steady course with Lenin's work as its infallible compass. Lukács repeated his recantation several times in similar terms, blaming his mistake either on 'revolutionary impatience' (though it is hard to see how this would lead to denying the dialectic of nature) or on his Hegelian and syndicalist background. After Stalin's death he tempered his self-criticism to a great extent. In the preface to a new edition of his book in 1967 he admitted to having neglected Marx's distinction between objectivization and alienation and, in consequence, pushed too far his own theory of the identity of subject and object (i.e. presumably by suggesting that all 'objectivity' ceased to exist in the proletarian consciousness, and not only the 'alienated' object). As, however, labour itself was necessarily a process of 'objectivization', it could not be said that all objectivity disappeared in the revolutionary process, and therefore it was wrong completely to exclude 'reflection' from the act of cognition.

In short, Lukács did not deliver a clear judgement on his early work. He certainly did not abandon his theory of totality and mediation, or (with the qualification explained above) his critique of reification; and he held to his view of the basic distinction between humanistic and natural science. He apparently continued to regard it as a merit of his book that it had drawn attention to the Hegelian sources and aspects of Marx's dialectic. The upshot of his revised theory seems to be that in the revolutionary movement object and subject coincide, but only to a certain degree; it remains true that the cognition of social reality is itself a part of that reality, and that the proletarian consciousness revolutionizes the world in the very act of understanding it. It can also still be maintained that Marxism has overcome the dilemma of freedom versus necessity, facts versus values, will versus foreknowledge; but it is not the case that this does away with objectivity altogether. This being Lukács's final position, are we to take it simply as meaning that he wished to exclude the idea that all reality, including external nature and the objectified material products of human labour, was subsumed into conscious revolutionary praxis—in other words, that he desired to limit the identity of subject and object to the sphere of social processes (of course only in the liberated consciousness of the proletariat) and not extend it to the extra-human world? If so, this would not mean a significant departure from his original thesis but rather a restatement of it; the book, as we saw, could be read as meaning that he had in mind 'objectivity' in general and not merely that of historical processes, but this would seem to be due to a want of logical discipline rather than to a considered theory.

5. *Class-consciousness and organization*

It might seem that the glorification of the class-consciousness of the proletariat as a force which not only transforms social institutions but also, in so doing, resolves all problems of philosophy, art, and the social sciences, was related in Lukács's mind to the real proletariat and not its 'organized' expresssion, i.e. the party: that is to say, his view of the revolution would be that of Rosa Luxemburg rather than Lenin. In fact, however, his works from 1919 onwards leave no doubt that he held firmly to Lenin's conception of the party and that his whole theory of class-consciousness formed a logical basis for that conception.

The 'proletarian consciousness' is not to be understood as that of the empirical working class, nor as a sum or average of individual consciousnesses. There must always be a gap between the empirical consciousness of actual workers and the 'true' class-consciousness of the proletariat. The former will never quite catch up with the latter, yet it is this 'true' consciousness that is the motive power of history, and its vehicle is the party—a special form of social existence, a necessary mediator between the spontaneous workers' movement and the totality of history. What individual workers think, either unanimously or in the main, is simply of no significance as to the content of the proletarian consciousness. The latter is embodied in the party, and it is only in and through the party that the spontaneous movement can apprehend its own meaning, since it is powerless of itself to rise to a conception of the whole. Thus the unity of theory and practice, of necessity and freedom, are truly realized only in the party's revolutionary will.

Expounding this view in *History and Class-Consciousness*, Lukács showed (without saying so explicitly) that Lenin's theory of the party was not a logical concomitant of Lenin's philosophy but was fully in accord with Marx's humanistic relativism and the theory of all-absorbing 'praxis', whereby epistemological and metaphysical problems are deprived of content. Lukács reiterated this view in his book on Lenin and several later works. The party is the visible embodiment of class-consciousness, the sole guarantor of the correct political orientation of the proletariat and the sole exponent of its 'real' will. Lukács does not, of course, infer from this, any more than Lenin did, that the party can do everything in practice without the proletariat, or that the latter's aid is not important to it. The point is merely that the proletariat's 'real' interest, its will, desires, and aspirations and also its theoretical consciousness, are quite independent of the desires, feelings, thoughts, and awareness of the empirical working class.

We thus see the political importance for Lukács of the critique of empiricism. As long as we remain on an empirical footing all our knowledge of the proletariat comes from observing actual workers: we cannot comprehend the totality of history, as the empirical state of human consciousness is merely an index of its immaturity. It can be seen that Lukács's theory of the unity of theory and practice is logically better suited to Lenin's idea of the party than is Lenin's own philosophy. For it is hard, on the basis of the theory of 'reflection', to defend the assertion that the party, embodying the 'true' consciousness of the proletariat, is right notwithstanding any empirical evidence which might refute its doctrine. This proposition, on the other hand, follows smoothly from the idea of 'totality' and its corollary, 'so much the worse for the facts'. The all-embracing totality brings into 'dialectical unity' facts and values, knowledge and will, freedom and necessity. The proletariat therefore, embodied in the party, is *theoretically* right on the strength of its social position and historical mission; or rather its theoretical rightness is the same as its progressive function, and no other criteria are to the purpose. Politically, this is a more convenient philosophy than Lenin's, for, once granted that the party is in possession of the practico-theoretical 'whole', there is no need to seek any further justification. As the proletariat is privileged in the cognitive sense thanks to its social role, and as the genesis of its consciousness guarantees that that consciousness is right, true, and unmystified, so, assuming further that the proletarian consciousness is embodied in the party, we arrive at the desired conclusion: the party is always right. Lukács, of course, does not formulate it in so many words—neither did Lenin or even Stalin—but it is the ideological foundation of Communist training and has been accepted in practice by all Communist intellectuals.

By the end of the Stalin era the epistemologically privileged position of the proletariat was reduced for practical purposes to the view that Comrade Stalin was always right. Lukács provided a better theoretical foundation for belief in the infallibility of the party than anyone before him, Lenin included. In 'Tactics and Ethics' he had already stated that 'it is the great achievement of Russian Bolshevism to incorporate, for the first time since the Paris Commune, the consciousness of the proletariat and its self-knowledge in terms of world history' (p. 36). In the nature of things, Bolshevism was the truth of the present age—a belief that Lukács never renounced. Even if it turned out in after days that the party or its leader had made mistakes, it was still true that the party was 'dialectically' right and that it was a moral and intellectual duty to stand by it, mistakes or no. Thus, when Lukács followed the new leaders in noticing Stalin's 'mistakes', he still maintained that he had been right to defend those mistakes at the time. This was indeed the typical, classical standpoint of Communist ideologists, backed up by Lukács's philosophy: the party might be 'formally' wrong but not 'dialectically' so. To oppose its politics and ideology was in all circumstances a political mistake and therefore a cognitive error, since the party embodied the historical consciousness in which the movement of history and awareness of that movement were merged into one.

Lukács also had no doubt that the dictatorship of the proletariat was and ought to be realized as the dictatorship of the party. Thus in his book on Lenin he condemned the ultra-Leftists (or 'workers' opposition' in the Bolshevik party) who regarded the Soviets (workers' councils) as the permanent forms of class organization and sought to establish them in place of the party and trade unions. The Soviets, Lukács argued, were naturally designated organs of the struggle against the bourgeois government in the revolutionary period, but those who wished to endow them with state power after the revolution simply did not understand the difference between a revolutionary and a non-revolutionary situation, in short they were thinking 'un-dialectically'. The party's role after a successful revolution was greater and not less than before, one reason being that in the post-revolutionary period the class struggle, far from abating, became inevitably more and more acute. This doctrine as to the role of the Soviets differs to some extent from that expressed in Lukács's main work, where he said that it was their function to liquidate the bourgeois distinction between executive, legislative, and judicial powers and to be an instrument of 'mediation' between the immediate and ultimate interests of the proletariat. This might suggest that Lukács ascribed to the Soviets functions which, according to Lenin, belonged exclusively to the party (although other references to the party in *History and Class-Consciousness* do not support this view). However, in his work on Lenin he corrects any such ultra-leftist errors and makes it clear that after a victorious revolution the Soviets can be dispensed with. From that time on, it would appear, the task of abolishing the bourgeois separation of powers devolves on the party—in other words, the latter makes the laws, carries them out, and judges offenders without aid or supervision from any quarter. In this way, in 1924, Lukács proclaimed a world-view purged of any remnants of syndicalism.

6. Critique of irrationalism

Lukács's chief work was devoted, in effect, to providing Leninism with a better philosophical basis than Lenin himself had offered. In this sense Lukács could be called an inconsistent Leninist, encumbered to some extent by the typical shortcomings of the intellectual. While accepting Bolshevik policy without question he imagined that, as a philosopher, he could be a better Bolshevik than the party leaders, expounding their theoretical position in a more coherent and convincing manner.

His later philosophical works show, however, that he understood the true nature of fidelity to Leninism–Stalinism: what was required was not to devise justifications of one's own for the party's decisions and doctrines at any given time, but to support them and act upon them in practice. The few works of pure philosophy which he published in the thirties and forties evince an almost complete assimilation to Stalinism. It is true that Lukács's erudition distinguished him at all times from run-of-the-mill ideologists of Stalinism, who were all ignoramuses. Whether he wrote about Goethe, Dilthey, or Hegel, he obviously knew what he was talking about and had the subject at his fingers' ends. It was this, rather than what he actually wrote, that infuriated his orthodox critics. To some extent, moreover, he preserved an individual style of writing. This was suspect in the Stalin era, when everybody wrote in the same way and no two philosophers could be distinguished on stylistic grounds. Monotonous clichés and an impoverished vocabulary were the order of the day, and to have a style of one's own was practically an ideological deviation. In this respect Lukács was an imperfect Stalinist, but he made up for it in many others.

An important document of this period is *Die Zerstörung der Vernunft* (*The Destruction of Reason*), a work which Adorno called 'The Destruction of Lukács's Reason'. This is a history of irrationalist philosophy, chiefly in Germany, from Schelling and the Romantics to Heidegger ('the Ash Wednesday of parasitic subjectivism') and the existentialists, with the primary purpose of revealing the ideological sources of Nazism. Schelling, who substitutes incommunicable intuition for rational dialectic; Schopenhauer, who proclaims the incurable absurdity of mankind and history and sees the world as governed by irrational will; and Kierkegaard, who glorifies irrational faith and places it above reason—these are the prophets of the first period, ending in 1848. Nietzsche is the chief ideologist of the second period, in which the class struggle of the proletariat becomes the dominant feature of social life: his negation of history, contempt for the common people, and unabashed pragmatism are devoted to the service of the bourgeoisie, which he extols as the 'master race'. Philosophic irrationalism reaches its height in the imperialist age from 1890 onwards: neo-Kantian formalism and agnosticism are replaced by attempts to create a new all-embracing world-view, but one based on intuition and impervious to rational analysis. The objective validity of science itself is questioned, as it is regarded as the product of irrational historical or instinctive forces. This period is ushered in by Dilthey's 'philosophy of life' (*Lebensphilosophie*), which leads directly to Nazi ideology. It opposes positivism, but does so from the point of view of the irrationality of history and the subjectivity of culture. It also criticizes capitalism, but from the outdated standpoint of reactionary Romanticism; it attacks democracy and sets out in quest of a new organic unity that eventually found its embodiment in the Fascist state.

What makes *The Destruction of Reason* an essentially Stalinist work is not, of course, the fact that it seeks the origins of Nazism in German philosophy. There is nothing specifically Marxist, let alone Stalinist, in such a line of thought, which has been pursued by many historians and writers, including Thomas Mann. The typically Stalinist feature of Lukács's work is the contention that since Marxism came on the scene, all non-Marxist philosophy has been reactionary and irrationalistic. In this way the whole of German philosophical culture outside Marxism is condemned as an intellectual apparatus preparing the way for Hitler's assumption of power in 1933. Everybody was a herald of Nazism in one way or another. Clearly, Lukács's conception of irrationalism is not only vague, indefinite, and absurdly wide, but in many respects it is almost directly contrary to the usual conception of the term. In epistemology the word 'irrationalist' is generally applied to doctrines which hold that the most perfect forms of cognition cannot be expressed in language but are achieved only in particular incommunicable acts. Some of the thinkers listed by Lukács were certainly irrationalists in the true sense, but it does not follow that they paved the way for Nazism. Lukács, however, calls everyone an irrationalist who was not an orthodox Marxist. If Max Weber, as a sociologist, analysed the character of the charismatic leader, it proves that this was required of him by the age which produced the charismatic Führer. If the analytical philosophers deny that the world can be apprehended as a whole and confine themselves to observing isolated fragments, they are by the same token falling into irrationalism, as is Mannheim when he emphasizes the part played by extra-cognitive factors in the formation of social theories. Irrationalists are all those who hold that any elements or aspects of being are outside the range of discursive knowledge; all who discover irrational forces in human behaviour; all who do not believe in historical laws; all who profess subjective idealism; and all who do not accept that the meaning of the 'totality' of history can be scientifically ascertained. In other words, the irrationalists and (consequently) allies of Nazism are all who do not believe in the 'dialectical reason' that Lukács took over from Hegel—reason being regarded as capable of comprehending the whole of history and human society, including its Communist future, and thus giving significance to the present. Or, to put it in yet another way, all philosophers who do not profess Communism in its current orthodox form, i.e. Stalinism, are irrationalists and therefore Nazis 'objectively' if not by actual conviction. The whole history of German and indeed European culture, including Croce, Windelband, Bergson, and the analytic philosophers, is seen as imbued with the immanent purpose of ensuring Hitler's triumph. All non-Marxist philosophers of the nineteenth and twentieth centuries were engaged in the destruction of 'reason', that is to say of the belief that there is a historic 'totality' which includes the future and to which Marxism provides the key by predicting the expropriation of the bourgeoisie and a worldwide Communist dictatorship. It would be hard indeed to find a more striking example of anti-rationalism than that afforded by Lukács's own philosophy of blind faith, in which nothing is proved but everything asserted *ex cathedra*, and whatever does not fit the Marxian schemata is dismissed as reactionary rubbish.

Lukács's polemic against existentialism, published in 1948, is another outstanding specimen of Stalinist philosophy, embodying all the main points of the Lenin–Stalin–Zhdanov catechism. Philosophy must be either idealistic or materialistic, there is no third way; subjective idealism leads to solipsism, the philosophy of madmen, while objective idealism invents imaginary ideas or spirits governing the world. Either spirit or matter must be primary: those who claim to stand above the opposition between the two are deceivers or self-deceived. Lenin's *Materialism and Empiriocriticism* provides unanswerable arguments to refute all idealists, whether his immediate opponents or those, like the existentialists, who have come on the scene later. The latter seek to reconstruct the whole of being on the basis of pure consciousness, although science has long since exploded such nonsense—even though natural scientists, for lack of Marxist education, have not yet grasped the fact that all the achievements of science point to the triumph of dialectical materialism.

Existentialism or Marxism? is perhaps the most flagrant example of Lukács's intellectual degradation: it is indistinguishable in style and content from the standard products of Soviet philosophy under Stalin, including the ritual advice to physicists, of whose subject Lukács knew nothing.

There is no indication that Lukács ever disavowed his works of this period; *The Destruction of Reason* was republished unchanged after Stalin's death, in 1954.

7. *The whole, mediation, and mimesis as aesthetic categories*

Lukács's main ambition was to lay the foundations of a Marxist aesthetic. His many works in this field are concerned variously with literary theory and criticism and with general aesthetics. However, even when he tries to establish categories relating to all forms of art his information is chiefly drawn from the history of literature, especially drama and the novel, and it is not always clear how his doctrine is to be applied outside this sphere. His works on aesthetics—apart, of course, from those written before he was a Marxist—can be treated as a single whole, as his views on theory, and even on particular writers and artistic trends, do not seem to have undergone any change from the 1920s to his last years.

Certain general observations by Lukács on the 'nature' of art have no specifically Marxist content. He states that art, unlike science, is anthropomorphic in character, being concerned with social conditions. For this reason art is essentially hostile to religion, even if its immediate purpose is to serve as an adjunct to faith or worship: for, whatever the artist's intention, art iself is a thing of this world. Historically, art is rooted in magic practices, but it differs from them in that its purpose is to arouse particular feelings and attitudes, which in magic is only a secondary or subordinate aim. Art offers images of reality, but these are charged from the outset with an emotional content and imply an active attitude towards the world they describe. All art conveys cognitive values: it increased man's knowledge of himself and therefore of the world. It enables people to step outside immediate practical reality and rise to an understanding of the sense of the universe. It should not therefore be treated as a mere entertainment or distraction: it plays a major part in man's spiritual evolution, being a means by which he creates himself and becomes aware of his own species-nature.

Hence, although art cannot be reduced to purely cognitive functions—since, unlike science, it presents the world in the form of images and in such a way that their transmission entails an act of evaluation—it is nevertheless a 'reflection' of reality, based on a particular form of imitation or mimesis. This is not a mere passive copying of the world, but involves selection and a certain degree of universalization. By means of individual images, art presents a view of the world that lays claim to universality: in this sense the 'individual' and the 'universal' are presented, in the work of art, as a single unity.

It has often been objected to Lukács—as to all others who speak of art in terms of 'reflection' or 'mimesis'—that, even if we know roughly what these expressions mean in relation to a play, a novel, or a figurative painting, it is not at all clear how a piece of music or architecture, or an ornament, can be said to 'reflect' reality. Lukács maintains, however, that mimesis is a category applicable to all artistic phenomena. Music, for instance, conveys emotions that are aroused by social conditions, and thus 'reflects', albeit indirectly, the historical links between human beings. Architecture likewise expresses human attitudes and needs by organizing space in a particular way. Ornaments imitate natural figures and present them in a form that expresses human attitudes towards them. Such explanations as these have often struck Lukács's critics as artificial, and they also call in question the real meaning of the idea of reflection or mimesis. If a piece of music reflects the world by expressing emotions, and if these emotions must in some way be connected with social life, then to say that art 'reflects' reality would seem to mean simply that it is influenced by the various phenomena and interconnections of social life; but this is so general and obvious a statement as not to be of much use. In any case, it is clear that when Lukács is talking about works of literature he uses the term 'reflection' in a much stronger sense. Not only do social conditions affect artistic production, which nobody would deny, but works of art present an image of reality from which the reader or spectator can learn something about that reality and recognize its 'structure' or its internal conflicts.

Lukács is in fact seeking to define art in such a way as to justify the conclusion that only 'realistic' works truly deserve the name of art; his condemnation of artistic 'decadence' is likewise based on this conclusion. But again, it is not at all clear how music, architecture, or even lyric poetry can be judged from the point of view of 'realism'. If the term 'mimesis' denotes any kind of dependence of a work of art on social phenomena, then certainly all art must be imitative and also 'realistic'; but in that case the notions of mimesis and realism have lost their meaning. Lukács's main concern is with drama and the novel, to which they are undoubtedly more applicable; but here again he seems to use 'mimesis' in two different senses, a descriptive and a normative. In the former sense any novel or play in some measure reflects the world, social conditions, and conflicts, and every work of art is socially committed: it takes one side or the other in regard to the basic issues of the day, irrespective of how far the author is aware of his involvement or the real significance of his work (often he does not understand it). In the normative sense, however, 'mimesis' is the quality of a work that imitates reality 'correctly', presenting the problems of its time as they 'truly' are; the author of such a work, of course, is on the 'right' or progressive side. This seems to be the sense in which Lukács uses the term 'mimesis' most frequently.

The same is true of the notion of 'totality' as applied to literature. Every literary work reflects in some way the totality of social life, since when we adopt an attitude towards the world, even a reactionary one, it is necessarily related to the world as a whole—not because we so intend, but because all human affairs are linked together and by engaging in a particular conflict we are also engaged, willy-nilly, in a universal one. But, more often than not, Lukács also uses 'totality' in a normative sense. 'Genuine' works of literature are those which seek to mirror the world as a whole, and it is for the critic or ideologist to ensure, as far as he may, that the work embodies a true reference system giving significance to its component parts and subordinating them to an over-all artistic purpose. In this sense 'totality' is not simply an attribute of all literature but an ideal to be aimed at in socialist art. Lukács, however, does not clearly formulate the distinction.

The demand that art should reflect 'totality' is aimed primarily against naturalism—the idea that it suffices to describe reality in terms of direct observation, simply recording what happens or what meets the eye. Literature, thus limited, cannot convey the meaning of events, which only reveals itself in relation to the whole: it requires conceptual understanding and not mere observation. But—and this is the nub of the argument, as Lukács urged in his dispute with Bloch on the subject of expressionism and realism—the totality of our society, or capitalism as an integrated system, is the true though invisible reality governing every single individual phenomenon. He who is able to make sense of the smallest details of human life by relating them to the whole can alone be said to depict social reality as it truly is, and to practice 'mimesis' in the normative sense of the term. Since this universality and sense of the whole requires a prior understanding of the nature of society such as only Marxism can provide, it follows that in the present age only a Marxist, in the sense in which Lukács understands this term, can possess the qualifications of a good writer.

This, of course, does not mean that to be a good writer it suffices to master the conceptual understanding of the principle of totality. To create a work of art he must be able not only to relate the parts to the whole but also to present the whole in terms of individual images. Art is subject not only to the principle of wholeness but also to that of speciality (*Besonderheit*). This is the artistic counterpart of 'mediation' and is, in Lukács's view, the basic category of aesthetic analysis. Taking experience as its point of departure, art endeavours to find the type in the individual, the universal in particular phenomena. Lukács's 'speciality' may be defined, it seems, as this process whereby a writer transforms individual experiences into types or images of universal validity, so that they become the medium through which the reader apprehends the social whole. To say that art is subject to the category of 'speciality' does not mean that its place is 'in between' the universality of science and the immediacy of day-to-day experience, but that it reflects universality in particular images. In these images the universal and the individual do not appear separately but in a state of unity, and it may thus be said that art subsumes the two elements (in Hegel's sense of *aufheben*), or synthesizes them into aspects of a single phenomenon.

The relative prominence of the individual and the universal varies in different types of literature and different schools of art. Drama is, by its nature, more universal than the novel. Naturalism tends towards the individual, while allegory emphasizes the universal.

As several critics have pointed out, the view that an artist, at least in some forms of art, makes use of images to present 'typical' phenomena (i.e. not necessarily frequent or everyday ones, but such as reveal the salient features of their age or of this or that social milieu) is not specifically Marxist, and was often advanced by pre-Marxist or non-Marxist thinkers. Indeed, it seems to be a common-sense viewpoint as long as it is not applied to all kinds of art and is not erected into an arbitrary rule, so that art which does not 'typify' in this way is stigmatized as not being art in the 'good' sense. Lukács, however, violates both these provisos. As to the specifically Marxist element in his theory, it consists in relating everything to the 'totality' considered as a social system defined by Marxist categories, i.e. capitalism or socialism as the case may be.

However, the category of 'totality' figures in Lukács's aesthetics in other contexts also. Not only is art supposed to reveal the totality of society, but it is a means whereby man himself strives to achieve 'totality' as his mode of being—i.e. to become a complete and harmonious personality, not impaired by any one-sided preoccupations. The kind of art which favours this aspiration or helps men to become conscious of it is truly humanistic art, but it can only be such if it aims to be in advance of its time. In other words, it is the business of art not only to describe reality but to foresee it. In an article 'Es geht um Realismus' Lukács says that Marx considered Balzac a prophetic writer, as he created characters of a type that existed only in embryo in his time but developed later, under the Second Empire. In the same way, Lukács says, Gorky anticipated types that did not exist when he wrote his first novels. Writers have this faculty because they are able to perceive trends and foresee their outcome. It is not clear on this basis, however, in what way the Stalinist literature of socialist realism was at fault when it set out to describe not what was but what ought to be, as correctly anticipated by 'Marxist–Leninist science'; for that literature presumably conformed to Lukács's ideal pattern in that it used scientific analysis to discern the shape of future events.

8. Realism, socialist realism, and the avant-garde

From several of Lukács's arguments it may be inferred that the only literature that deserves to be called realistic is that which relates human life to the 'whole' as understood by Marxism. However, Lukács distinguishes two forms of realism: critical and socialist. To the former category belong practically all the great writers of the past; and, at least as far as the nineteenth century is concerned, it makes no difference what their conscious world-outlook was. Balzac, Scott, and Tolstoy were reactionary in their political views, but they created great works owing to their skill in painting a realistic picture of the world they lived in. There was, according to Lukács, a 'contradiction' between their literary performance and their political attitudes. It is not clear, however, in what this 'contradiction' lay. On the contrary, it would seem that Balzac's legitimist and aristocratic outlook was fully in harmony with his critique of post-Revolutionary society, just as Tolstoy's emphasis on the virtues of country life and undogmatic religion were fully consonant with his attack on the Church and the privileged classes. The only 'contradiction', in fact, seems to be between these writers' world-outlook and Marxist doctrine.

Critical realism, in Lukács's view, is an attribute of writers who, while they did not manage to achieve a Communist outlook, strove to record accurately the conflicts of their time and did not confine themselves to particular events, but described great historical movements through the medium of individual destinies. They were not mere naturalists, but neither were they allegorists or metaphysicians: they did not retreat from the world into the isolation of the individual psyche, nor did they elevate particular mental or spiritual events to the status of a timeless, eternal, unalterable human condition. Such realists were Balzac, Tolstoy, and the other great Russians of his day and, in more recent times, Anatole France, Bernard Shaw, Romain Rolland, Feuchtwanger, and, above all, Thomas Mann.

Lukács observes more than once that realistic art generally comes to the fore in advanced countries or those that are going through a period of social and economic growth. In cases where this does not apply, he explains that backward countries may sometimes produce great literature as an attempt to break out of their very backwardness. These arguments are not peculiar to Lukács but are often found in Marxist writing. If 'advanced' countries like eighteenth-century France produce 'advanced' literature, this is a clear confirmation of historical materialism; if backward countries like nineteenth-century Russia produce 'advanced' literature it is again a confirmation of historical materialism, as in such cases ideology makes up for the deficiencies of the 'base'.

Contrasted with realism is the whole of modernist and *avant-garde* literature: naturalism, expressionism, surrealism, etc. Examples of this decadent form of art are the works of Kafka, Joyce, Musil, Montherlant, Samuel Beckett, and others. The decisive shortcoming of all modernist literature is its inability to grasp the 'totality' and to perform the act of mediation. A writer is not to blame for depicting loneliness, for example, but he must show it to be a fatal consequence of capitalism; Kafka, however, presents us with 'ontological loneliness' as though it were a permanent human condition of universal validity. He paints what is immediately before his eyes and fails to penetrate to the 'whole' which alone gives it meaning, and in this he resembles the naturalists. In the same way, the world may be realistically described as being in a state of chaos and panic, but only if this is shown to be due to the horrors of capitalism. If, as in Joyce, the hero's spiritual life and perception of time disintegrate without cause and without hope of remedy, the universe so depicted must be false, and the work of art a bad one.

Lacking a historical perspective, *avant-garde* art presents situations as permanent when they are in fact conditioned by history and social forms, and endows them with a 'transcendental' quality. (It may be remarked that Lukács uses terms like 'transcendental' and 'mystic' in an arbitrary and vaguely pejorative way, regardless of their meaning in philosophical tradition: all we can gather is that they denote something bad.) The great characters of literature, from Achilles and Oedipus to Werther and Anna Karenina, are all social beings—for man himself is a social being, as Lukács reminds us with a reference to Aristotle; but the heroes of modernist literature are wrenched from their social and historical background. The narrative becomes purely 'subjective', or else, as with Beckett and Montherlant, animal man is contrasted with social man: this corresponds to Heidegger's condemnation of society (*das Man*) and leads to Nazi racism of the Rosenberg type. (All these examples are in *The Meaning of Contemporary Realism*, first published in 1958; English trans. 1963.) Modernist literature, in short, is not an enrichment of art but a negation of it.

The acme of literature, however, consists in socialist realism. 'The perspective of socialist realism is, of course, the struggle for socialism ... Socialist realism differs from critical realism, not only in being based on a concrete socialist perspective, but also in using this perspective to describe the forces working towards socialism *from the inside*' (*The Meaning of Contemporary Realism*, p. 93). Critical realists have from time to time depicted contemporary political struggles and created socialist heroes; but socialist realists portray these from within and identify with the forces of progress. The greatness of socialist realism lies in the fact that the historical totality of the movement towards socialism is evident in every facet of the work. To this category belong some at least of Gorky's novels, Sholokhov's *And Quiet Flows the Don*, and the works of Aleksey Tolstoy, Makarenko, and Arnold Zweig.

To avoid misjudgement it should be pointed out that Lukács had a thorough knowledge of European literature and was perfectly well aware of the difference between great and mediocre works. His aversion to modernist writers such as Proust, Kafka, and Musil—in fact almost everyone later than Thomas Mann—does not have to be explained by ideology: most people find it hard to come to terms with literature radically different from what they were used to in their youth. His dislike of the *avant-garde* was certainly genuine, though it was sometimes based on amazingly primitive arguments. As to socialist realism, the examples he cited were all outstanding or at least meritorious: he did not refer to hack writers of the Stalinist period whose works have long since been pulped. The result is that it is not easy to find citations by him of works of socialist realism dating from the 1930s and after, though he frequently speaks in general terms of the flourishing state of Soviet literature under Stalin. At a period when literature was in fact completely crushed, when many prominent writers died in concentration camps and when almost the only works published were servile panegyrics in honour of the Great Leader, written by mediocrities and devoid of literary merit, Lukács accounted as follows for the absence of modernist art in Russia: 'As proletarian rule became stronger, as socialism penetrated the Soviet economy more deeply and universally, and as the cultural revolution affected the toiling masses on a broader and deeper front, so avant-garde art has been driven out by an increasingly conscious realism. The decline of expressionism is due in the last analysis to the maturity of the revolutionary masses' ('Es geht um den Realismus'). In other words, Lukács ascribed to revolutionary maturity what he well knew to be the work of police repression. It is worth noting that although Lukács does not quote much from Stalin as a rule, he indulges in many interpretations of this kind. Typical examples can be found in the article 'Tendenz oder Parteilichkeit?', in which he objects to the description of socialist art as 'tendentious'. Literature should not be 'tendentious', but it should be 'true to the party'. By 'tendentious' literature we mean a kind which eclectically mingles 'pure art' with alien political elements introduced from without. This procedure (to be observed in Mehring) signifies the 'primacy of form over content'; it is a Trotskyist view of art, which opposes the purely aesthetic components of a work to political ones which are essentially non-aesthetic. True revolutionary writers, however, refuse to distinguish between art and its political message. Their works are imbued with party spirit, which means that they convey a correct Marxist understanding of the movement of reality towards socialism and present a harmonious integration of individual description and historical perspective.

Lukács continued to be involved with socialist realism till the end of his career as a critic. During the 'thaw' after Stalin's death he wrote a few essays touching on the literature of the previous period. He observed that Stalinism suffered from a lack of 'mediation' in culture as in other fields; Stalinist literature had become abstract and schematic instead of describing the real conflicts of socialist society; it attempted to portray general theoretical truths directly instead of through the medium of images based on reality. It had overlooked the specific nature and claims of art and had subordinated it to propaganda. Optimism had become schematic instead of historical. The heroes of Stalinist fiction displayed no qualities typical of the new society. Lenin's article of 1905 on party literature, which —as Krupskaya had testified—was concerned only with political writings, had been applied to all literature and turned into a general code of conduct for artists. Critical realism had been buried prematurely, and the notion of decadence had been so widened as to condemn all the more recent products of that school.

Despite these criticisms, however, Lukács never renounced the view that socialist realism was 'basically' and 'historically' a higher form of art than any of its predecessors, nor did he revise the criteria for defining it: relationship to the 'whole', optimism, 'partyism' (*Parteilichkeit*), Marxist orthodoxy, and identification with the forces of revolution. There is no reason to suppose that his book on realism, a purely Stalinist work, did not reflect his later views with equal accuracy.

The most astonishing expression of Lukács's ideas on socialist realism, however, is contained in his articles on Solzhenitsyn. He greeted the latter's novels as the first signs of a renaissance of socialist realism because, he said, the accounts of life in the camps presented day-to-day events as symbols of a whole era. Solzhenitsyn was not a mere naturalist, but related phenomena to the social 'whole'—and, Lukács adds for good measure, he could not be accused of intending to restore capitalism in Russia. His weakness was, however, that he criticized Stalinism from a plebeian and not a Communist viewpoint, and his art would suffer if he did not overcome this. In short, Lukács advised Solzhenitsyn to become a Communist for the sake of his literary development; but he failed to cite any example of a good writer who had become still better as a result of embracing Communism.

It seems a pathetic end to Lukács's aesthetic doctrine that in his closing years, after Russian culture had been devastated by two decades of Stalinism, of which he had been an eminent spokesman, he should have discovered 'socialist realism' in the work of a convinced and passionate adversary of Communism— for there could be no doubt that this was Solhenitsyn's position from the beginning: it is irrelevant that Lukács did not live to read *The Gulag Archipelago*. Lukács's verdict on Solzhenitsyn is a symbol of the nullity of his whole theory of literature.

9. The exposition of Marxist mythology. Commentary

Lukács was, beyond doubt, an outstanding interpreter of Marx's doctrine, and rendered great service by reconstructing it in a completely different way from that followed by the previous generation of Marxists. Besides emphasizing Marx's profound debt to the Hegelian dialectic as the interplay of subject and object seeking identity, he was the first to show clearly that, in the dispute among Marxists between neo-Kantians and evolutionists, both sides were arguing from non-Marxian posi- tions; and that Marx believed in a dialectic in which the understanding and transformation of the world were one and the same process, so that the dilemmas of freedom versus necessity, facts versus values, and will versus prediction lost their meaning. The questions that the theorists of the Second International put to Marx missed the point of his philosophy, as they presupposed an 'objective' historical process governed by its own laws; whereas, as Lukács showed, in the historically privileged case of the working class the 'objective' process coincided with the development of awareness of that process, so that free action and historical inevitability became one and the same thing. Lukács certainly formulated a radically new and, I believe, correct interpretation of Marx's philosophy, and from this point of view his achievement seems unquestionable.

However, the fact that Lukács interpreted Marx afresh and more accurately than anyone before him does not mean that he was right to adopt Marx's belief in the unity of theory and practice, freedom and necessity. Despite his intention, his work had the effect of revealing the mythological, prophetic, and utopian sense of Marxism which had eluded Marx's more scientistic followers. The blurring of the distinction between descriptive and normative elements is in fact characteristic of the way in which a myth is apprehended by believers: narration and precept are not distinguished, but are accepted as a single reality. That which the myth commands, or holds up to be worshipped and imitated, is not presented as a separate conclusion but is directly perceived as part of the story. To understand a myth rightly is not only to understand its factual content but to accept the values implied in it. In this sense a disciple understands the myth differently from an outside observer—a historian, anthropologist or sociologist—he understands the myth in the act of self-commitment and, in this sense, it is right to say that it can be understood only 'from within', by an act of practical affirmation. Such, in Lukács's view, is the position with Marxism. A non-Marxist cannot understand it properly, as to do so requires actual participation in the revolutionary movement. Marxism is not simply a theory *about* the world, which can be accepted by anyone whether or not he approves the values of the political Marxist movement; it is an understanding of the world that can only be enjoyed within that movement and in political commitment to it. Marxism in this sense is invulnerable to rational argument: outsiders cannot understand it correctly, and therefore cannot criticize it effectively. Thus, as Lukács showed, the Marxist consciousness obeys the epistemological rules appropriate to a myth.

At the same time Lukács pointed out the prophetic character of that consciousness, in that it does away with the distinction between will and prediction. A prophet does not speak with his own voice but with the voice of God or History; and neither God nor History 'foresees' anything in the way that human beings foresee events over which they have no influence. With God, the act of foreseeing is identical with the act of creating the thing foreseen, and the same is true of the ultimate History in which the subject and object of action are identified with each other. (God never acts from without, but always immanently.) The historical subject that has identified its own consciousness with the historical process no longer distinguishes between the future it foresees and the future it creates.

The historical subject, as understood by Lukács, embodies the utopian consciousness *par excellence*. This consciousness appears in that very part of the doctrine that is directed against utopian socialism, particularly in Marx's belief, elucidated and emphasized by Lukács, that socialism must not be treated either as an ordinary moral command, the result of an evaluative process, or as a matter of 'historical necessity'. If the distinction between facts and values, between an act of pure cognition and one of moral affirmation, is not present in the proletarian consciousness, it is because socialism is not simply desirable or simply necessary, nor even both at once: it is a 'unity' of the two, a state of things that realizes the essence of humanity—but an essence that already exists, not the arbitrary precept of a moralist. The socialist future of the world is not something that we desire as a matter of preference or that we foresee on the basis of a rational analysis of historical tendencies: it is something which already exists as a Hegelian reality of a higher order, which cannot be empirically perceived but is more real than all empirical facts. In the same way Lukács's 'totality' is real but non-empirical. Thus when speaking of the socialism of the future we need not use either normative language or the language of scientific prediction. Socialism is the meaning of history and is therefore already present in today's events. The typical utopian ontology presents the future not as something desired or expected but as the *modus* of being of the present day. It is Lukács's undoubted merit to have revealed this ontology, of Hegelian and Platonic origin, as a basic feature of Marxism.

In so doing, however, Lukács gave Marxism an irrational and anti-scientific form. His conception of 'totality' protects it in advance from any rational or empirical criticism: for the totality cannot be deduced from any accumulation of facts or empirical arguments, and if the facts appear to be contrary to it, it is they that are wrong. This being so, it may be asked how we can possibly know the totality, or know that we know it. Lukács replies that we can know it by means of a correct dialectical 'method'; but on investigation it proves that this method consists precisely in relating all phenomena to the whole, so that we must know the latter before we can start. The method, and knowledge of the whole, presuppose each other; we are in an elementary vicious circle, the only way out of which is to assert that the proletariat possesses the whole truth by virtue of its privileged historical position. But this is only an apparent escape, for how do we know that the proletariat is thus privileged? We know it from Marxist theory, which must be right because it alone comprehends the whole: so we are back in the vicious circle again.

The only recourse is to say that the whole is not to be discovered by pure scientific observation but only by active participation in the revolutionary movement. This, however, involves a genetic criterion of truth: Marxism is true because it 'expresses' the proletarian consciousness, and not the other way about. But this is merely a criterion of authority: the truth must be recognized as such not because it is supported by ordinary scientific arguments but because it emanates from a historically privileged class, and we know that class to be so privileged because we are told so by the theory of which it is the exponent. Moreover, the mythology of the proletariat as an infallible class is reduced in Lukács's theory to pure party dogmatism. The content of class-consciousness is decided not by the class itself but by the party in which its historical interest is embodied: so the party is the source and criterion of all truth. Q.E.D.

On this basis the unity of theory and practice, of facts and values turns out to be simply the primacy of political commitment over intellectual values: an assurance given by the Communist movement to its members that they possess the truth by virtue of belonging to the movement. Lukács's Marxism implies the abandonment of intellectual, logical, and empirical criteria of knowledge, and as such it is anti-rational and anti-scientific.

10. Lukács as a Stalinist, and his critique of Stalinism

As already mentioned, Lukács always considered himself a true disciple of Lenin, and his criticisms of Stalinism after 1956 were made on the basis that Stalin had distorted Lenin's principles. His speeches, interviews, and articles on the subject give a fairly exact idea of his opinions on the Stalinist past. In a postscript of 1957 to 'Mein Weg zu Marx' he wrote: 'At the beginning of the imperialist era Lenin developed the question of the significance of the subjective factor and in so doing extended the bounds of classical theory. Stalin turned this into a system of subjectivist dogmas. It was a tragedy that with his great talent, rich experience, and unusual quickness of mind he did not break out of the vicious circle or even perceive clearly the error of subjectivism. It also seems to me tragic that his last work begins with a well-founded criticism of economic subjectivism, while at the same time it does not occur to him that he himself was the spiritual father and patron of that subjectivism' (*Schriften zur Ideologie und Politik*, ed. Ludz, 1967, pp. 652–3).

Stalin, then, was a tragic subjectivist; and, as we have seen, Lukács elsewhere states that the Stalin era suffered from a lack of 'mediation' in cultural policy. It was wrong to lump together all non-Communist forces (the theory of 'social Fascism'), and to say that there was no longer any place in literature for critical realism. It was wrong, too, to stifle all discussion *within the party*, and to subject oppositionists to police repression. However, as Lukács stated in a letter to Alberto Carocci published in 1962, it did not follow that the victims of Stalin's purges, such as Trotsky and his followers, should be rehabilitated politically. In principle, Stalin was right as against Trotsky, but Stalin himself subsequently pursued a Trotskyist policy instead of a Leninist one. It was a mistake to subordinate the whole of culture to propaganda aims, regardless of its intrinsic values. An especially pernicious effect of Stalinism was the degradation of Marxist theory. The task now was to restore confidence in Marxism, to reconstruct its intellectual values, to overcome dogmatism and subjectivism, and to re-establish Leninist principles of socialist organization and Marxist thought.

As to the causes of Stalinism, Lukács confines himself to generalities about the backwardness of Russia and the havoc wrought by the years of war, revolution, and civil war.

Lukács at no time questioned the Leninist foundations on which the whole edifice of Stalinism was reared. He did not question the principle of one-party dictatorship and the abolition of the 'bourgeois' division of authority into legislative, executive, and judicial: in other words, he accepted that the governing party should be subject to no form of public control and that socialism ruled out competition between independent political forces. In short, he accepted despotism in principle, although he later criticized some of its extreme manifestations. He was one of those Communists, numerous in the late 1950s, who believed that democracy could exist within the ruling Communist party although it had been abolished for the rest of the community. This delusion, however, did not last long, and the experience of Stalinism showed clearly that the liquidation of democracy in the state was bound to lead, in a short time, to the liquidation of democracy within the ruling party: the process, indeed, began under Lenin and with his encouragement. The reason is that when state democracy is abolished it is inevitable, whatever anyone's intentions, that groups within the party will, if they are allowed, become advocates of other, non-party forces and reflect various social pressures. In other words, intra-party democracy, in which sects are permitted to exist, is essentially the same as a multi-party system, with the revival under one name or another of the political organisms that the party has just destroyed. Thus, if the party bureaucracy is to remain all-powerful within the state, democracy within the party can be no more than a pious wish.

The same holds good in the field of culture. In an interview published in *Szabad Nép* on 14 October 1956, a few days before the Hungarian uprising, Lukács stated that different artistic trends should be allowed to exist in a socialist state, but that there could be no question of ideologies freely competing, and that, for example, the teaching of philosophy in universities must be exclusively carried on by Marxists (*Schriften*, p. 634). But this is precisely the Stalinist principle of government: for if it is laid down that only Marxists have the right to teach, there must be an authority to decide who is and who is not a Marxist; and this authority can only be the ruling party, i.e. the party bureaucracy. If the party says somebody is not a Marxist, then by definition he is not. Hence the principle of a Marxist monopoly is identical with the Stalinist system, and from this point of view it is not clear how that system was at fault in its cultural policy.

In the late 1950s, when the political and ideological ferment in Eastern Europe was at its height, Lukács was one of the most timid and cautious critics of Stalinism, never questioning its basic principles but only certain manifestations. However, phenomena such as mass terror and the extermination of political adversaries are not a necessary feature of totalitarian Communism: it may resort to such means in case of need, but it may also do without them. Nor is it incompatible with the system for ideological discussions to take place 'within Marxism': as a matter of fact such discussions took place even in the worst years, and Stalin often called for 'a frank discussion'. All that the Stalinist system requires is acceptance of the principle that the limits of discussion and of cultural freedom are fixed at any given time by the party (i.e. the party bureaucracy), which cannot be subject to any higher authority. Lukács accepted this principle, and at no time called it in question.

During the war, when Stalin played on anti-German nationalism and, among other things, described Hegel as the philosopher of the aristocratic reaction against the French Revolution, Lukács, we may believe, was unable to swallow such nonsense, and the publication of his book on Hegel was consequently held up for some years. There is no reason to doubt that he rejected Stalin's views on Hegel, but here again what counted with him was the political justification. In the postscript, already quoted, to 'Mein Weg zu Marx' he declared that although he thought Stalin wrong on many points he did not engage in opposition, not only because it was physically impossible to do so but because any opposition could easily have degenerated into support for Fascism. In short, Stalin might have made mistakes, but he, Lukács, had been right not to oppose Stalinism. But this avowal, dating from 1957, is a clearer proof of Lukács's actual Stalinism than any glorification of Stalin during his lifetime. The argument is that it was right to support Stalin and Stalinism without reservation, even while harbouring, internally and invisibly, objections to the party's current policy. But Stalinism demanded no loyalty other than that expressed in outward obedience, and the burden of Lukács's argument is precisely to justify such obedience. As long as the world is torn by the struggle between capitalism and socialism, and if socialism is assumed on philosophical grounds to be an essentially superior system irrespective of any empirical facts, then clearly any internal opposition to socialism as it exists at a given time is a blow struck in favour of the enemy. Any public criticism, however mild, of the system and its leaders is exploited in some way by the adversary—a fact which, ever since Soviet Russia came into existence, has been effectively used to silence real, imaginary, or potential critics by branding them as allies of imperialism. What is notable in Lukács's case is not that he submitted to this form of blackmail but that he provided a theoretical justification for it, in full accord with his rule of thinking in terms of the 'whole' and of comprehensive systems.

This rule of Lukács's, in fact, is tantamount to a general justification of the typical Communist contempt for facts. Communism is defined in theoretical terms as a higher form of society which will do away with the division of labour, introduce 'true' freedom and equality, abolish exploitation, lead to a blossoming of culture, and so on. All these truths are valid *a priori*, whatever the actual face of Communism may be. The most repellent forms of totalitarian despotism, oppression, and exploitation cannot detract from its superiority: at most it may be conceded in after years, when the party allows a measure of criticism, that there have been occasional mistakes or that 'survivals of capitalism' were at work. The superiority of socialism is absolute and is not susceptible to empirical proof or disproof. Lukács's achievement is to have elevated the practice of contempt for facts as compared with 'systems' to the dignity of a great theoretical principle, of which Marxism can be justly proud.

In Stalin's day Lukács glorified the Soviet system as the supreme embodiment of freedom, maintaining that, with the exploiters overthrown, work had become identical with pleasure, as Marx had promised; that socialism had replaced 'apparent and superficial freedom' by the genuine variety, and that only under the new system did writers enjoy true contact with the people. All this is in no way surprising: these are the regular clichés of Stalinist propaganda. (A good example is the article 'Frei oder gelenkte Kunst?', published in 1947, which abounds in stock phrases contrasting Soviet freedom with capitalist corruption.) But even in Lukács's later writings there is no suggestion that his views on these matters had changed. In *The Meaning of Contemporary Realism* he wrote: 'In socialist society the individual will enjoy greater freedom to choose a place for himself in society than under capitalism ("freedom" being understood here, of course, as conscious acceptance of historical necessity—

a necessity which subsumes much that is apparently arbitrary)'
(p. 112). Thus true, superior socialist freedom is still made to
consist in accepting historical necessity. On this definition it
may be wondered whether the mind of men could conceive a
system (under Communist party rule, of course) so despotic that
it did not qualify to be regarded as an embodiment of the
highest freedom.

In the same way Lukács's aesthetic doctrine, at least in its
specifically Marxist features and especially in regard to socialist
and critical realism and *avant-garde* literature, is a perfect
theoretical justification of Stalin's cultural policy. Lukács, in fact,
forged the conceptual instruments of cultural despotism. If
socialist realism is 'basically' the highest form of art for historiosophical reasons, and if its characteristic feature is that the author
relates particulars to the 'whole', i.e. the battle for socialism,
and identifies with those who are fighting that battle, then clearly
the socialist state must foster and encourage the type of art in
which its own interests are expressed. Literature and painting
whose main function was to glorify Stalin are really in terms
of Lukács's doctrine, true examples of socialist realism; in general
he was well aware of the difference between good and bad art,
but in the last resort what mattered was the content, i.e. in this
case ideological values or the relation to the 'whole'.

Lukács also helped to popularize the deplorable misuse of the
term 'dialectical' either to express a commonplace (as that two
phenomena interact on each other, or that in observing an
object various circumstances should be taken into account, or
that a certain judgement may be right in some conditions and
wrong in others), or as a knock-down argument enabling the
user to dismiss empirical facts and maintain that 'superficially'
things may appear thus and so, but 'dialectically' the case
is the exact opposite. In his book on Lenin, for example, he
accuses the reformists of having an 'un-dialectic conception of
the nature of a majority', from which it would appear that the
'dialectical' sense of this term is the opposite of what common
sense or common arithmetic understands by it. (Since Communism has never, in any situation, had a majority of the people
on its side, it is certainly convenient to maintain that it nevertheless commanded a majority in the deeper, dialectical sense—an
irrefutable statement in the light of the theory that Com-

munism necessarily stands for the true interests of humanity.) In this and similar cases the term 'dialectical' is designed to convey that its user is in possession of a special, profound, infallible method of observing and understanding the world. In an interview given in October 1969 (English text in the *Cambridge Review*, 28 January 1972) Lukács even stated that 'in Lenin there existed a dialectical unity of patience and impatience'.

Lukács was an extremely important figure in the history of Marxism not only by virtue of his contribution to the interpretation of Marx's thought, or because he showed how the latter's philosophy could be used to justify the self-glorification of Communist bureaucracies, or again because he originated or revived certain concepts which have had a strong influence on the shape of Marxism at the present day. Besides all this he is important as an outstanding representative of those intellectuals who identified with the totalitarian system, denied their own intellectual values for the purpose, and evolved a theoretical justification of that denial. Lukács is depicted in literature as the Jesuit Naphta in Thomas Mann's *The Magic Mountain*: a highly intelligent character who needs authority, finds it, and renounces his own personality for its sake. Lukács in fact was a true intellectual, a man of immense culture (unlike the vast majority of Stalinist ideologists), but one who craved intellectual security and could not endure the uncertainties of a sceptical or empirical outlook. In the Communist party he found what many intellectuals need: absolute certainty in defiance of facts, an opportunity of total commitment that supersedes criticism and stills every anxiety. In his case, too, the commitment was such as to afford its own assurance of truth and invalidate all other intellectual criteria.

From the time of his identification with Communism and Marxism Lukács *knew* that all problems of philosophy and the social sciences had been solved in principle and that the only remaining task was to ascertain and proclaim the true content of Marx's and Lenin's ideas, so as to bring about a correct understanding of the received canon. He gave no further thought to the question whether the Marxian 'totality' was itself a true one and how its truth could be proved. Consequently, his works, as we have pointed out, are a collection of dogmatic statements and not of arguments. Having once and for all found a standard of truth and accuracy, he applied it to one object after another: the philosophy of Hegel or Fichte, Goethe's poetry, or Kafka's novels. His dogmatism was absolute, and almost sublime in its perfection. In his critique of Stalinism he did not step outside its fundamental bases.

Lukács is perhaps the most striking example in the twentieth century of what may be called the betrayal of reason by those whose profession is to use and defend it.

CHAPTER VIII

Karl Korsch

In the early 1920s Karl Korsch was a well-known figure in the Marxist movement. After his expulsion from the Communist party in 1926, however, his name almost completely disappeared from circulation, though he remained active in politics and as a writer for over a quarter of a century. Posthumously, in the sixties, he was again officially mentioned, and some translations and new editions of his works were published. At present he enjoys the deserved reputation of having made some of the most interesting contributions to the interpretation of Marxism.

Together with Lukács he was the most eminent of those who tried to reconstruct Marx's original philosophy, or rather anti-philosophy, in opposition both to the evolutionism and scientism of the Marxists of Kautsky's generation and also to the neo-Kantian revisionists, and by so doing to furnish a correct basis, which in time became an anti-Leninist one, for the revolutionary strategy of the class struggle. Korsch's reconstruction is important for several reasons. In the first place, it made clear the Hegelian origin of Marxist dialectic. Secondly, it revived the almost forgotten early Marxist conception of the unity of theory and practice. Thirdly, it emphasized the purely negative aspect of Marxism as the consciousness of the proletariat, making a complete break with all traditional forms of life in bourgeois society including the state, law, ethics, philosophy, and science. In some respects the utopian radicalism of this reconstruction is reminiscent of Sorel. Whether or not Korsch identified with Marxism as reinterpreted by him, his version is certainly one of the most fruitful attempts to consider Marx from the point of view of *The German Ideology* rather than the *Critique of the Gotha Programme*.

1. Biographical data

Karl Korsch (1886–1961) was born near Hamburg, the son of a civil servant. He studied law and philosophy at different universities, received his doctorate in law at Jena in 1910, and in 1912 went to London for further studies. He joined the Fabian Society, and, as his biographers observe, the ideas of British socialism made a permanent impression on his mind, even during his later ultra-revolutionary phase. While fundamentally opposed to all reformism he nevertheless maintained that both revolutionaries and British reformists were truly devoted to socialism and that they recognized the importance of subjective factors, unlike the orthodox leaders of the Second International, who relied on the beneficent effects of historical determinism.

In the First World War Korsch served for a time as an officer, but was reduced to the ranks for expressing anti-war sentiments. He joined the anti-war group of German socialists (the USPD) and was among the left-wing members of the social democratic party who formed the German Communist party (KPD) in 1920. He took an active part in the revolution of November 1918, and in 1923 was Minister of Justice in the short-lived revolutionary government of Thuringia. In the same year he became a professor at Jena University, a post he occupied until Hitler's accession to power. From 1924 he was a Communist member of the Reichstag, and for a year he also edited the party's theoretical journal, *Die Internationale*. At that time he published theoretical articles and reviews, including two short essays on the dialectic, and also what is perhaps his most important work, *Marxismus und Philosophie*, published in 1923 in *Archiv für Geschichte des Sozialismus und der Arbeiterbewegung* (English trans., *Marxism and Philosophy*, 1970). These writings caused him to be regarded within the party as an 'ultra-Leftist', a revisionist and an idealist, for which errors he and Lukács were condemned by Zinovyev at the Fifth Comintern Congress in July 1924. (Later, in July 1926, he received a mention from Stalin himself, who described him at a plenum of the Central Committee as an 'ultra-Leftist' theoretician who believed that the Soviet state had reverted to capitalism and that Russia needed a new revolution.)

While identifying with Communism, Korsch from the first had

reservations as to the principles of the Third International, especially the organizational forms which placed the whole Communist movement in the hands of a professional apparatus and also subordinated the worldwide structure to the dictates of Moscow. Like other 'left-wing' deviationists he held that the party was no substitute for the revolutionary potential of the true proletariat. He finally came to believe that the Comintern was an instrument of counter-revolution and that the Soviet system was a proletarian dictatorship exercised not by the proletariat, but over it. He was expelled from the party in the spring of 1926, after which time he wrote and spoke as an independent Marxist. In 1930 he republished *Marxismus und Philosophie* with an extensive commentary; earlier, in 1929, he wrote a long and violent attack on Kautsky, whose *magnum opus*, *Die materialistische Geschichtsauffassung*, appeared in 1927. In 1932 he published an edition of *Das Kapital* with an introduction, and in 1931 he wrote an essay, not published at the time, on the crisis of Marxism. In the 1930s he still considered himself a Marxist, but continued to criticize Kautsky and Lenin, whose philosophies, he believed, had much in common despite their political differences. He also insisted more and more strongly that Marxism in the form inherited from the nineteenth century did not adequately express the consciousness of the modern proletariat, and that there was need for a new theory which would be a continuation but also a revision of Marxist doctrine. He put forward these views in *Karl Marx* (1938) and in articles entitled 'Why I am a Marxist' (1935) and 'Leading Principles of Marxism: a Restatement' (1937).

When Hitler came to power in 1935 Korsch emigrated to Denmark, where he lived for two years, and then to England. In 1936 he moved to the U.S.A., where he spent the rest of his life. The first political writer to draw attention to his importance as an interpreter of Marx was no doubt Iring Fetscher in the late fifties; in the next two decades he was the subject of a fairly large body of literature.

2. *Theory and practice. Movement and ideology. Historical relativism*

The essence of Marxism, Korsch repeatedly emphasized, was the practical interpretation of human consciousness; but this had been completely eliminated from the positivist version of

Marxism which dominated the Second International.

All Marxists, to be sure, subscribed to the doctrine of the 'unity of theory and practice'; but they usually meant by it—and Engels's writings tended to confirm this interpretation—that practice was 'the basis of knowledge and the touchstone of truth'. It followed, in the first place, that practical considerations for the most part determined the range of the cognitive interests of human beings, that technical needs and material interests were the strongest incentive in the advance of science, and that people were deluded if they supposed that a disinterested thirst for information played any part in the extension of knowledge. (This last might be taken either as a historical judgement or as a normative precept.) In the second place, the current view meant that practical efficacy was the best confirmation of the hypotheses on which action is based. These two opinions, which were logically independent of each other, were applied both to the natural and to the social sciences. It might be observed that irrespective of whether or to what extent the 'unity of theory and practice', thus understood, was a reality, it was quite compatible with the traditional or transcendental conception of truth as consisting in the conformity of our judgement with a state of affairs completely independent of our cognitive activity. In other words, the unity of theory and practice, thus understood, did not conflict with what Marx called the 'contemplative' conception of knowledge. The cognitive act—irrespective of the stimuli that provoked it, or of how the accuracy of its content was determined—was still the 'passive' assimilation of a ready-made universe.

In Korsch's view, however, the point of Marxism was not to supplement the traditional interpretation of cognition with observations regarding the motivation of cognitive acts and the verification of judgements, but to subject that interpretation to a radical change. Marxism was concerned particularly—though, as will appear, not exclusively—with knowledge of the social universe. Theoretical knowledge was not a mere 'reflection' of the social movement but a part, aspect, or expression of it; it must be interpreted as an essential component of the movement itself, and thus it was 'good' or 'true' in so far as it expressed the movement adequately and was aware that it did so. This applied above all to Marxism itself, which was an 'expression' of the class struggle of the proletariat and not a 'science' as understood by the positivists. This interpretation derived from Hegelian sources, for had not Hegel said that philosophy must be the intellectual expression of its own age?

It was the essence of Marxism to have drawn the fullest possible conclusions from this point of view. Above all, as Korsch argued at length in *Marxism and Philosophy*, Marxism was not a new philosophical doctrine but the abolition (*Aufhebung*) of philosophy. To abolish philosophy, however, does not simply mean to despise or abandon it or dismiss it as an illusion, as Mehring would have us do. For the very reason that philosophy was an 'expression' of the historical process, it could not be done away with by ignoring it or by the exercise of philosophy itself, but only by means of a revolutionary and practical critique of society, whose existing philosophy dwelt in a 'mystified' consciousness. Bourgeois society was an indissoluble whole (*Totalität*) and could only be attacked as such. The forms of consciousness of bourgeois society 'can only be abolished in thought and consciousness by a simultaneous practico-objective overthrow of the material relations of production themselves, which have hitherto been comprehended through these forms' (*Marxism and Philosophy*, p. 81). The fact that society is a *Totalität* means, in particular, that capitalist relations of production are what they are, only in conjunction with their ideological superstructure. In so far as Marxism is a theoretical and practical attack on that society, an expression of the movement that is to destroy it, it is also a philosophical critique. 'Eventually, it aims at the concrete abolition of philosophy as part of the abolition of bourgeois social reality as a whole, of which it is an ideal component' (ibid., p. 68). This is the correct understanding of Marx's important concept of a 'Critique of Political Economy'—the sub-title of *Das Kapital* in the original: not merely an academic criticism of economic doctrines, but a practical attack on society through one of its main components, namely the economic ideologies which serve to perpetuate capitalist exploitation.

If we consider social realities as a whole, we perceive the concurrence (*Zusammenfallen*) of reality and the theoretical forms that express it. They cannot exist separately, although the mystified bourgeois consciousness falsely imagines itself to be an external analysis of the social scene and not a part of it. Marxism, while unmasking this illusion, sees itself as a practical phenomenon, the expression and component of a social movement revolutionizing the present system.

Although Korsch regards ideologies as a necessary element in the social whole, he emphasizes that they are by no means 'on a level' with economic phenomena. On the contrary, he says, there are three degrees of reality: firstly, economics, which are the 'one true reality', secondly, the state and law, which are reality in an ideological disguise, and thirdly, 'pure ideology (pure nonsense), which is unreal and without an object' (ibid., p. 12).

In social affairs, the act of investigation coincides with its object—such is the Hegelian interpretation adopted by Marxism. From this point of view Korsch likens the Marxist theory of society to the view of Clausewitz (also a Hegelian) that the theory of war is not a matter of external observation but is part of war itself. If we lose sight of this identity, we cannot grasp the Hegelian-Marxist sense of the dialectic. The dialectic is not simply a 'method' applicable at will to any object. It would seem that in Korsch's view it is altogether impossible to expound the materialistic dialectic as a collection of statements or precepts of investigation. As an expression of the revolutionary movement of the working class it is part of that movement and not a mere theory or 'system'. 'The materialist dialectic of the proletariat cannot be learnt in the abstract, or from so-called examples, as a separate "science" with its own "subject-matter". It can only be *concretely* applied in proletarian revolutionary practice and in the theory which is a real, immanent part of that revolutionary practice' ('Über materialistische Dialektik', in *Marxismus und Philosophie*, p. 177).

This approach, it may be noted, involves a radical epistemological relativism. If philosophy and theories of society are 'nothing more than' the intellectual expression of practical social movements and interests, it must be inferred that they cannot be evaluated except from the point of view of whether they reflect those movements adequately, and whether the movements themselves are 'progressive' or not. In other words, no theory is true in itself in the sense of giving a correct description of the world, i.e. 'reflecting' it accurately; the question of 'truth' in the ordinary sense is meaningless, and theories are 'good' or 'valid' in so far as they are 'progressive' and conscious of their own origins. It follows that Marxism is 'true' only in the sense that at the present stage of history it articulates the consciousness of the 'progressive' movement and is aware of that fact, and furthermore that a theory which is true at one time may be false at another by reason of a change in its social function. For instance, the doctrines of the 'progressive bourgeoisie' were true as long as the bourgeoisie was progressive, but subsequently became reactionary and therefore false; and the same might one day be true of Marxism. Korsch in fact accepts all these conclusions, though he does not state them clearly enough. He states that it is the essence of dialectical materialism to regard *all* theoretical truths as strictly *diesseitig* (this-worldly), a term which is to be understood as the opposite of 'transcendental'. 'All truths with which we as human, this-worldly beings are or have ever been concerned are likewise human, this-worldly, and transient (*vergänglich*)' (article of 1922, 'Der Standpunkt der materialistischen Geschichtsauffassung', in *Marxismus und Philosophie*, p. 153). No truths are immutable in themselves; what we call truths are the instruments of practical action by social classes. Korsch's theory is thus a kind of collective pragmatism which completely alters the nature of Marxism as a 'science'. On several occasions he joins issue with both Hilferding and Kautsky, who asserted that Marxism was only a theory of the laws of social development and did not, as such, involve any social commitment or value-judgements, but could be accepted even by those who did not share the objectives of the socialist movement. In Korsch's view this separation of theory from practice, of doctrinal truth from the revolutionary movement, was a complete distortion of Marxism. Since Marxism is simply the class-consciousness of the revolutionary proletariat, it can only be recognized in the act of practical commitment to that movement; there can in principle be no such thing as 'purely theoretical' Marxism.

What is more, the doctrine of relativism, historicism, and the rejection of the idea of 'truth' in the ordinary sense applies not only to the social sciences but also to natural science. There is no basic difference in this respect between our knowledge of nature and of society. Historical and natural reality are 'one and the same universe': both are part of the process of human life, and they are linked on the economic plane and specifically in material production. All natural circumstances—biological, physical, geographical—affect our lives not directly but through the intermediary of productive forces, and thus present themselves to us as social and historical phenomena. The whole universe as known to us is a social universe: as far as we are concerned, there is no such thing as nature independent of history and wholly external to us.

Thus not only the social but the natural sciences are historical and practical 'expressions' of a particular social 'totality' and of class-interests. The revolutionary movement, in abolishing society as we know it, abolishes not only its philosophy but all other sciences. Korsch maintains that when the present order is overthrown even mathematics will have to be transformed; though he adds that it would be foolish for a Marxist to claim that a new, Marxist mathematics can be put into operation at the present time. In general, he contends, the function of Marxism is chiefly negative: it is a component of the movement to destroy bourgeois society, not a collection of new sciences to replace the existing ones.

While Korsch extends the 'class viewpoint' to cover natural science, he does not share Lukács's view of the dialectic of nature. Since knowledge of nature, no less than knowledge of society, is part of a social, practical attitude, there is no ground for asserting that nature as we know it is not 'dialectical', for it too is a human creation. On this point Korsch's view appears to be the same as Gramsci's.

The proletarian revolutionary movement ends by 'abolishing' all the economic, social, and ideological forms of bourgeois society. It does not create a new philosophy or sociology, but abolishes both these things along with all other sciences, the state, law, money, the family, ethics, and religion. Korsch, for instance, criticizes Pashukanis for writing about 'socialist ethics': Communism has no ethics of its own, but does away with ethics as a form of consciousness. He does not, however, explain exactly how the 'abolition' of ethics or science is to come about, but confines himself to vague generalities for which he finds some support in equally general observations by Marx. Marx believed that in time to come there would be 'a single science' embracing all aspects of reality, and that people would be so integrated as to express the whole of their social being equally in all forms of activity and thought; as in the utopias of Cieszkowski and Hess, thought and action would in some mysterious way coincide. One can imagine that in such a society there would indeed be no room for ethics as a collection of general norms regulating communal life, since every individual would experience himself immediately as a 'social being': that is to say, he would identify spontaneously with the 'whole', and would need no 'abstract' norms or rules for this purpose. This, it would seem, is what both Korsch and Lukács meant by the 'abolition' of all bourgeois institutions: the elimination of all 'reified' forms of life, i.e. all instruments or agencies which in any way mediate between individuals. The society of the future would consist of individuals with a permanent, indestructible awareness of their identity with the community; they would also themselves be perfectly integrated, having overcome the division of labour and recognizing no difference between thought, feeling, and conduct. As we have shown earlier, this Messianic era of the perfect integration of all human powers is the essence of Marx's Utopia, and Korsch deserves credit for reviving awareness of it.

3. Three phases of Marxism

The question arises, however: how is it that this essential feature of Marx's interpretation of the world was overlooked for decades and replaced by evolutionist, determinist, and positivist scientism? Korsch seeks to explain this aberration in terms of historical materialism, that is to say he tries to explain the history of Marxism itself on Marxist principles.

His view is that Marxism has gone through three clearly differentiated stages, corresponding to three phases of the development of the workers' movement. He defines this chronology in similar terms in several essays, and most fully in the introduction to the second edition of *Marxismus und Philosophie*. The first phase corresponds to the first few years of the formation of Marx's thought, from 1843 to 1848, when revolutionary theory was taking shape as the consciousness of the proletariat directly based on an actual class struggle: the unity of theory and practice was not a mere slogan but a reality. After June 1848, however, the situation changed as capitalism entered upon a new phase of development and expansion. For the rest of the nineteenth century Marxism could only develop as a theory, and, despite the theoretical achievements of Marx and Engels, scientific socialism did not and could not exist in the sense of class-consciousness actually assimilated and created by the proletariat. Theory became independent of the revolutionary movement, and this altered its content. Especially after Marx's death, his ideas increasingly took on the character of a 'system', supposedly based on purely scientific values. This form of Marxism divorced from revolution became the dogmatic ideology of the orthodoxy of the Second International. Marx himself was not free from guilt in the matter of stripping Marxism of its revolutionary content, especially in the *Critique of the Gotha Programme*; but the main cause lay in objective political conditions, which simply did not permit the theory to function as 'only the expression' of an actual movement. More and more, Marxists treated scientific socialism as the sum of different sciences—economics, sociology, history, philosophy—with no 'direct relation' to the class struggle: that is to say, these sciences theorized about the class struggle but were not themselves part of it. Only around the turn of the century came the third phase, with attempts to revive the 'subjective aspect' of Marxism as a proletarian theory of the class struggle. This change was due to three main developments: trade union reformism, revolutionary syndicalism, and Bolshevism. The tendency of all these was to shift the attention of theorists from the economic laws of capitalism to the 'subjective activity of the working class', and thus to restore Marxism to its proper function as the intellectual superstructure of the actual class movement. Leninist Communism, however, did not radically overcome the dogmatism of the Second International. Theory was still regarded as a 'reflection' of the external world, not an expression of the activity of the proletariat; thus both Lenin and Kautsky took the view that theory came into existence independently of the workers' movement and was then instilled into it from outside. Lenin, moreover, treated theory simply as a practical tool in the technical sense, a statement being 'true' or 'false' according as it served the party's interest. Korsch repeated this last objection several times, though it is not clear at first sight in what way Lenin's utilitarian attitude towards theory differed from his own opinion that Marxism was defined by its function in the class struggle and not by its content alone. It appears, however, that Korsch took the view that a revolutionary theory must be the 'expression' of a movement, and not an instrument forged outside the movement by leaders or theoreticians. Although he does not use these terms, it may be said that in his view the historical meaning of a theory is determined by its origin and not by its actual function.

However, as Korsch observed in 1931, none of the main forms of theoretical activity in which the 'subjective aspect' of Marxism was revived was appropriate to the needs of the class struggle of the proletariat in its current phase. There was a clear divergence between Russian Communism and the position of Western theoreticians of the revolution such as Lukács, Pannekoek, and Korsch himself. Leninism had proved to be an adequate theoretical form for the anti-imperialist struggle in countries on the periphery of the capitalist world, but the working class in the developed capitalist countries needed a new basis of theory which Marxism in its inherited form could not provide. Korsch therefore abandoned his original hope that it was sufficient to return to authentic Marxism to restore the revolutionary consciousness of the modern proletariat. He did not, however, formulate a theory of his own as a substitute, supplement, or revision of Marxism; it cannot be inferred from his writings what such a theory would have been like, or how it would have differed from traditional Marxism.

4. Critique of Kautsky

It is quite understandable that from the point of view of Korsch's interpretation of Marxism the whole of Kautsky's theoretical work must have seemed a perfect and classical specimen of the aberration into which Marxism fell when it lost touch with the revolutionary movement. Korsch's violent attack on Kautsky's *magnum opus* is thus essentially a reaffirmation of his own position. He objected to Kautsky not so much as a reformist (reformism based on the actual struggle of the trade unions was in Korsch's view a higher form of Marxism than 'orthodox' evolutionism) but rather as a naturalist and Darwinist who regarded historical materialism as the application to human history of the general principles of organic evolution. The main points of his attack are as follows.

Firstly, he observes, Kautsky treats Marxism as a purely scientific theory, the truth of which has nothing to do with its class function and can be established by universally recognized criteria of scientific accuracy. This, however, amounts to emptying Marxism of its revolutionary content and reverting to 'mystified' bourgeois objectivism.

Secondly, Kautsky replaces the dialectic by a general epistemology borrowed from Mach and based on the principle that thoughts must correspond to facts and to one another. As for the dialectic of nature, which was of importance to Marx and Engels only in so far as it figured in the dialectic of history, Kautsky presented it as a collection of universal laws of development, of which human history is a particular example. His standpoint is that of nineteenth-century scientific materialism or popular Darwinism, summed up in the view that man is an animal and is subject to all the laws of species evolution; all history is explained by adaptation to the environment, and all human behaviour by biological instincts. Kautsky, seeking to deduce eternal laws of history from biology, is really trying to perpetuate the specific features of bourgeois society, and is incapable of perceiving that society as a historical interrelated whole which can only be, and must be, abolished as the totality of its component parts. It is not surprising that in treating society as an objective process subject to natural laws, and constructing his theory in isolation from its 'subjective' base, Kautsky is obliged, like the neo-Kantians, to reassert the distinction, which Marx resolved, between what is and what ought to be—thus resorting to idealistic normativism as a complement to the materialism of natural science.

Thirdly, Kautsky's theory of the state is absolutely contrary to Marxism. He regards the state as the permanent and highest form of social existence, and democracy as the supreme achievement of history. The state, in his view, accounts for existing relations of production, and not vice versa. As to the origin of the state, Kautsky, in opposition to Engels, invokes the hypotheses of violence and conquest. States, he says, were usually formed by warlike nomads raiding peaceful settlements; today, however, democratic state forms are gradually prevailing

everywhere. Thus Kautsky abandons the whole theory of the
state as an instrument of oppression and exploitation, in favour
of a bourgeois theory of democratic progress. Instead of the
revolutionary abolition of the state he thinks only of its further
democratization, and he is thus an advocate of bourgeois state-
hood. The abolition of the state, of money, and of the division
of labour—all these ideas, which belong to the essence of
Marxism, he treats as an anachronistic Utopia. He believes that
the class struggle of the proletariat can henceforth be carried
on within the framework of the bourgeois state and its democratic institutions, and he rejects on principle the idea of
revolutionary violence.

All in all, Kautsky is an example of a degenerate form of
Marxism, perverted in such a way as to impose a brake on the
class struggle.

Korsch's analysis is itself typical of Communist criticism: one
can see from it why Korsch is outraged by Kautsky, but it
does not give reasons why we should agree with the former rather
than the latter on any particular point. When, for instance,
Kautsky argues that as a matter of history states were generally
created by conquest, and by a particular form of conquest,
Korsch does not dispute the statement or advance new historical
facts, since facts do not interest him: he only remarks indignantly
that Kautsky is in disagreement with Engels (which Kautsky
was well aware of, and himself emphasized). Similarly, Kautsky
tried to give practical reasons why prophecies about the abolition
of the state, law, money, and the division of labour were unreal;
Korsch does not try to refute these arguments, but only repeats
that Kautsky's critique empties Marxism of its revolutionary
content. The whole of his attack is devoid of argumentative
force or theoretical substance, and is merely a restatement of
his own interpretation of Marxism.

Korsch's indifference to empirical argument is indeed admirably suited to his whole doctrine. Since a theory, as he
constantly repeats, can only be the intellectual expression of a
social movement, whether or not it is conscious of performing
this function, it is pointless to judge it by any universal criteria
of scientific accuracy: one either sides with the bourgeoisie or
with the proletariat, and everything else follows automatically
from that commitment. Rational cognitive criteria cease to exist,

and the act of political identification takes the place of theoretical reflection. By professing Marxism in this form, Korsch perhaps expressed more clearly than anyone else the latent anti-intellectualism of Marxism and Communism.

5. Critique of Leninism

In the first half of the 1920s Korsch was an avowed Leninist, as may be seen from his article 'Lenin und die Komintern' (1924), from his reviews of Lukács's book on Lenin and of articles by Stalin. In particular he took Lenin's side against Rosa Luxemburg on the question of the party and 'spontaneity'. His support was stated in general terms, however, and it is clear that from the beginning he was opposed to the substitution of party control for the Soviets, and believed in the direct dictatorship of the working class as a whole. It is also clear, though he did not say so at that time, that his whole reconstruction of Marxism as an expression of proletarian consciousness was incompatible with Lenin's 'theory of reflection'.

Soon after breaking with the Communist party Korsch made a clear statement of his disagreement with Leninism. He repeated several times that from the theoretical point of view there was little or no difference between the Leninists and the orthodox of the Second International. Both believed in Marxism as a 'science' and as the true reflection of reality, whereas it was in fact the class self-awareness of the revolutionary movement and, as such, was an aspect of that movement and not merely an objective account of empirical facts. The separation of subject and object, theory and practice, was exactly the same in Lenin's case as in Kautsky's. Lenin had also abandoned the Marxist idea of the abolition of philosophy and had tried to create a new doctrine which preserved Hegel's cognitive absolutism while substituting 'matter' for 'spirit'. This was no more than a terminological device; true Marxism knew nothing of any absolute, or of any transcendental epistemology. Lenin had failed to understand the dialectic; he had situated the dialectical movement in the external world—nature or society— ignoring the fact that knowledge is not a mere copy or reflection of the objective process, but an active element in it. Hence pure theory and pure practice were as much divorced in his thinking as in any positivism, and so were the method and content of knowledge. As a result, the Leninists had created a system in which the doctrine invented by them independently of the class struggle was used as an instrument of ideological dictatorship over science and art.

There was a close link between Lenin's philosophical positivism and Soviet despotism: for, once it was accepted that the theory was not an expression of the actual workers' movement but a 'scientific' doctrine claiming to possess 'objective truth' on grounds independent of the movement, this doctrine became a despotic ideology enabling the party apparatus to exercise a dictatorship over the proletariat.

Korsch finally reached the conclusion that the Soviet state was a totalitarian counter-revolutionary system, a form of monopoly state capitalism which had no more than verbal links with Marxism and was closer to Fascist totalitarianism than to a proletarian dictatorship as understood by Marx.

6. A new definition of Marxism

In a brief essay or declaration of 1935 entitled 'Why I am a Marxist' Korsch re-formulated the main features of Marxist doctrine in four points, as follows.

Firstly, all the tenets of Marxism are particular, not general (as official Soviet doctrine would have it). Marxism does not comprise any general theory of the relation between the 'base' and the 'superstructure'; Engels's statements about 'mutual influence' are valueless, as we cannot establish any quantitative criterion of measurement. The only statements that are valid are particular descriptions of particular phenomena at a given stage of history.

Secondly, Marxism is critical and not positive. It is neither a science nor a philosophy, but a theoretical and practical critique of existing society, and is therefore itself a kind of praxis. However, the proletariat must be able to distinguish between true and false scientific claims, and therefore Marxism consists of 'exact, empirically verifiable knowledge', no less precise than that of natural science.

Thirdly, the subject of Marxism is capitalist society in the period of its decline, including everything that throws light on the historical character of existing relations of production. Fourthly, its purpose is not to contemplate the world but to change it, and theory is 'subordinated' to revolutionary aims.

The first of these points, it will be seen, is a drastic limitation of the scope of Marxism: it would be very hard to show that Marx never made general statements about the interdependence of various aspects of social life, but was content to observe particular historical phenomena. As to the second point, it is not clear how the general rule of empiricism can be reconciled with the notion of a theory which (as Korsch apparently continued to maintain) is only the expression of an actual social movement. If Marxism is subject to criteria of empirical verification in the same way as any other science, its validity must depend on whether it satisfies those criteria and not on how adequately it expresses a particular class-interest. In that case, the fact that Marxism serves as a political instrument is logically irrelevant to its value or content; it can be professed by anyone who thinks it meets the requirements of scientific accuracy, whether or not he accepts the values of socialism and the workers' movement. But in this same statement Korsch explicitly rejects that viewpoint, which was characteristic of the theoreticians of the Second International. Thus his revised version of Marxism still appears to contain an incurable contradiction.

CHAPTER IX

Lucien Goldmann

1. Life and writings

GOLDMANN, as we have mentioned, was the most active exponent of Lukács's ideas in France, and he endeavoured to reduce the latter's doctrine to methodical rules and even to a codified system. He also showed, in studies on Jansenism, how these rules might be applied to historical research. His chief interest was the methodology of the humanistic sciences, and his work on the history of philosophy and literature was conceived from the outset as a demonstration of method rather than as a description.

Lucian Goldmann (1913–70), a Romanian Jew, was born in Bucharest, where he initially studied law. Afterwards he studied philosophy, Germanic philology, and economics, at Vienna and Lwów in 1933, and in Paris from 1934 onwards. During the Nazi occupation he moved to Switzerland, where he worked for a time as assistant to the psychologist Jean Piaget, an association that had a marked effect on his later work and habits of thought. He attempted on many occasions to show that Piaget's 'genetic epistemology' agreed in the main, as to its theoretical basis and results, with his own theory of 'genetic structuralism', and that the latter, properly understood, was nothing but the dialectical method evolved by Hegel, Marx, and the young Lukács, although Piaget's results were achieved experimentally and were not due to any philosophical inspiration. Goldmann prepared a doctoral thesis on Kant at Zurich; after the war he returned to Paris and lived there till his death, working in the Centre national de recherche scientifique and later in the École pratique des hautes études. In 1952 he published a short book on humanistic methodology entitled *Sciences humaines et philosophie*, and in 1955 his principal work, *Le Dieu caché. Étude sur la vision tragique dans les 'Pensées' de Pascal et dans le théâtre de Racine* (English trans., *The Hidden God*,

1964). The purpose of this book was to show how the observation of significant 'structures of consciousness', related to the
specific situations of social classes, could be of use in understanding cultural phenomena and bringing to light aspects that
would otherwise remain unexplored.

In subsequent years Goldmann did not publish any large
work, but he produced numerous essays and addresses which
were collected in the volumes *Recherches dialectiques* (1959), *Pour
une sociologie du roman* (1964), and *Marxisme et sciences humaines*
(1970). He also wrote *Racine* (1956) and *Situation de la critique
racinienne* (published posthumously in 1971). For many years he
was a zealous expounder of the dialectic. His flowing white locks
and bear-like silhouette were familiar to participants in innumerable congresses and humanistic symposia, at which, in a
bass voice and passionate, somewhat aggressive tones, he would
expatiate time and again on the principles of genetic structuralism as exemplified particularly in Pascal and Racine.

Unlike Lukács, whose disciple he considered himself to be,
Goldmann was not politically active; he was never a Stalinist
and at no time belonged to any party, except for a Trotskyist
group which he joined for a few months in early youth. He was,
however, a convinced socialist, and in his last years took a lively
interest in workers' councils as a new form of socialist development in Western society.

2. *Genetic structuralism,* Weltanschauung, *and class-consciousness*

As mentioned above, Goldmann regarded the names of Hegel,
Marx, Lukács, and Piaget as four milestones in the history of
the dialectical method and the interpretation of social
phenomena. Thanks to the methods they had worked out,
humanistic science was able to overcome the traditional opposition, emphasized by the neo-Kantians, between explanation
and understanding, to free itself from the dichotomy of facts and
values, and finally to combine the historical and genetic viewpoint with the structural one. The main ideas of genetic
structuralism are as follows.

The first task of humanistic science is to identify its object
correctly. It is not obvious, nor a matter of simple common sense,
how the subjects of study are to be defined or singled out:
whether they should consist, for instance, of an individual person,

a work of art or philosophy, a whole cultural era, philosophy in the technical sense, or painting considered as a distinct activity. According to dialectical thought, no empirical facts are significant in themselves: their meaning only comes to light when they are combined into a whole or structure of some kind. For the student of civilization these structures consist of human behaviour patterns involving an interdependence of intellectual activity and its products, of moral and aesthetic values and the actions intended to give effect to them. The observer is not bound by the limitations that restrict people's understanding of their own behaviour; on the contrary, it is his business to understand them better and more consistently than they do themselves, and this applies also to the interpretation of artistic and philosophical works. His task is to discover the 'significant structures' that alone give meaning to particular facts, ideas, and values. 'Facts concerning man always form themselves into significant global structures, which are at one and the same time practical, theoretical and emotive, and these structures can be studied in a scientific manner, that is to say they can be both explained and understood, only within a practical perspective based upon the acceptance of a certain set of values' (*The Hidden God*, p. ix).

The dialectic is based on the principle that cultural activities are not the work of individuals but of social groups, and particularly of classes as historically privileged communities. Cultural achievements are to be considered as the response of these groups to 'global' situations, which they are designed to affect in a way favourable to the group interest. Thus the genetic interpretation of a work of art or philosophy must not be related to the personal qualities of its creator, for this would leave out of account the community, which is the true begetter of civilization. Nor is it correct to study the 'influence' of tradition on the individual thinker, writer, or artist, for it is he who, as it were, selects the influence he will undergo in order to express the aspirations of his class. In short, genetic explanation means explanation in the light of a social situation, not of some immanent cultural 'logic' or individual psychology.

So far, Goldmann does not go beyond the standard rules of historical materialism. He goes on to argue, however, that by formulating these rules more specifically it is possible to resolve all the traditional dilemmas of humanistic methodology. He attaches particular importance to the distinction, scarcely noticed by Marx but developed by Lukács, between actual and potential class-consciousness: the latter is called by Lukács *zugerechnetes Bewusstsein*, and by Goldmann *conscience possible*. Lukács states in *History and Class-Consciousness* that by relating the empirical consciousness of a social class to the 'totality' of the historical process we can discover not only what that class actually thinks, feels, and desires, but also what it would think, feel, and desire if it had a clear, unmystified understanding of its position and interests. The dialectic, in other words, enables us to discover the full extent of the potential consciousness of a particular class in particular historical conditions; and this conception according to Goldmann, provides the key to the study of civilization. Potential consciousness is not a fact, but a theoretical construction. It can and does happen, however, that outstandingly gifted members of a class transcend the average and express that class's aspirations or interests in a more perfect form, thus converting potential into actual consciousness.

Thus an observer sufficiently skilled in dialectic can discover what form of consciousness is perfectly appropriate to a particular group, or what this archetypal consciousness might be or ought to have been. Goldmann claimed specifically to have analysed the Jansenist consciousness in this way.

However, the explanation of cultural phenomena by class origin does not mean 'reducing' culture to economic behaviour. On this point, too, Goldmann agrees with Lukács. Human communities are integral wholes, and only by abstraction do we distinguish different 'factors' and spheres of life. There is not really any separate history of economics, politics, religion, philosophy, or literature: there is a single concrete historical process, manifesting itself in various forms of behaviour. The true subject of humanistic study is not a cause-and-effect relation between economics and culture. The 'primacy' of economics in Marx's theory is not a law of history; it merely reflects the fact that human beings through the ages have had to devote most of their time to satisfying elementary material needs. Under socialism they will no longer have to. Hence cultural activities are neither mere 'effects' or by-products of economic history, nor are they simply means of pursuing other interests and aspirations which, supposedly, are the only real ones. On the contrary, class structures may be studied through their expression in literature or philosophy.

If we accept that all human behaviour has a meaning, but that it is revealed not in the motives of individuals but only in the more or less conscious endeavours of large social groups, then, according to Goldmann, we no longer need distinguish between explanation and understanding as two separate, independent modes of investigation. 'Understanding' is not, as Dilthey would have it, a matter of imitative experience (*Nacherlebnis*) or empathy. 'Understanding presents itself to us as a purely intellectual approach based on a description, as exact as possible, of the significant structure', while 'explanation is simply the integration of that structure, as a constitutive and functional element, in a structure that directly comprises it' (*Marxisme et sciences humaines*, pp. 65–6). There is a hierarchy of structures; when we describe an inferior structure we 'understand' it, i.e. we grasp its meaning; when we include it in a larger structure we understand that structure, and at the same time we explain the lesser by the greater. There is thus no difference between the two methods, but only in the scope of the object: the act of explaining a particular structure, and understanding one superior to it in the hierarchy, is one and the same.

A 'structure' is not necessarily a harmonious whole. On the contrary, it usually presents internal contradictions owing to the fact that the values pursued by a given class are mutually incompatible, or unattainable in the historical circumstances of the time, or that attempts to realize them bring about opposite results to those intended. A structure is thus not only an orderly system, but a complex of tensions as well.

While non-genetic structuralism (especially that of Lévi-Strauss) confines itself to constructing internally connected wholes, and while genetic structuralism of the Freudian type considers only the psychological genesis of the meanings under observation, genetic structuralism as developed by Marx, Lukács, and Piaget (and of course Goldmann himself) regards individuality only as a manifestation of collective tensions, struggles, and aspirations.

In addition to surmounting the distinction between explanation and comprehension, genetic structuralism makes it possible to resolve the dichotomy of facts and values. The 'wholes' or structures that are the object of our study are an indissoluble complex of practical and mental activities, moral and aesthetic attitudes. Intellectual activity presupposes such evaluative acts, which cannot in fact be separated from purely cognitive ones. Reality always presents itself as a field for practical activity; perception at every level selects its object in accordance with human values and desires, and is always, as it were, incipient action. There is simply no such thing as pure, disinterested contemplation. Acts of cognition must and can only be understood as a particular 'aspect' of man as a practical being. Thus humanist studies, conscious of this 'integrality' of all human behaviour, cannot without distortion distinguish between purely intellectual activity and evaluative attitudes.

Piaget helped to illustrate this practical character of mental activity by showing that all cognitive structures—for instance, the concepts and rules of logic, arithmetic, and geometry—arise, on both the ontogenetic and the phylogenetic level, from the convergence of various circumstances, including human communications, language, and practical habits formed in early childhood. Piaget showed experimentally, as it were, that our intellectual 'structuralization' of the world cannot be explained by transcendental norms of rationality, but derives from social and practical circumstances. Cognitive norms are instruments of communal life and practice; they therefore comprise evaluative and practical elements, and could not be framed without them.

For the genetic structuralist the object of study *par excellence* is the world-view (*vision du monde, Weltanschauung*) or pattern of aspirations, feelings, and ideas that unites the members of a group (generally a social class) and opposes them to other groups. This unitary principle is so important that, Goldmann argues, it is wrong for the humanist to study art or literature, philosophical or theological ideas as separate subjects. The world-view must be studied through all forms of expression and not only, for instance, in its discursive philosophical aspect. Hence, too, the history of philosophy, art, or literature is not a proper object of study in itself. The historian of Jansenism must investigate that phenomenon or world-view as a whole, so as to reveal the common ideological inspiration behind the writings of Pascal and Racine and the painting of Philippe de Champaigne. Thus Goldmann seeks to reorganize humanistic studies so as to subordinate them in their entirety to the study of large communities and the cultural monuments created by them.

All these rules are not so unambiguous that a mere statement of them suffices to indicate how they should be applied. It may be useful, therefore, to show how this is done in *Le Dieu caché*, although the subject of that work is somewhat too particular as far as our own argument is concerned.

3. The tragic world-view

Although Goldmann considered himself a Marxist, he never adopted the simplistic division of the history of philosophy into two trends labelled 'materialism' and 'idealism'. He saw the units of historical meaning quite differently, and attached particular importance to the 'tragic world-view', as he perceived it in Jansenism and to some extent in the works of Kant.

The tragic world-view in the seventeenth century was, he believed, an attempt to rediscover a global picture of the world that had been shattered by the inroads of rationalism and empiricism. These doctrines, which reflected the ambitions of the *tiers état*, had destroyed the idea of human fellowship and the ordered conception of the universe, replacing them by the notion of the rational individual and the concept of unlimited space. The new world-view called in question the traditional hierarchy and sought to transform society into a collection of free, equal, autonomous, and isolated units. In philosophy and literature its champions were Descartes and Corneille. Cartesianism eliminated all sources of morality outside the individual; there was no room for God in its world, or for the universe considered as a beneficent order. The tragic world-view had to take account of these effects of rationalism, which already dominated the intellectual life of Europe. It attempted to counter the new spirit, as it were, from within: it accepted reason, but disputed its monopoly; and it insisted that there was a God, while admitting that he was not directly present in nature. Science having concealed God from human eyes, the tragic world-view produced the idea of a *deus absconditus*. Pascal's God is at the same time always present and always absent. He is a spectator of human life, but his presence cannot be confirmed by reason. He is no longer man's helper nor even (as for Descartes) a guarantor of the validity of knowledge; he is a judge and nothing more.

Rationalism had shaken the foundations of order in the world. The tragic view expressed the consciousness of those who could not efface the results of rationalism but were ill at ease in an ambiguous world, deserted by Providence and deprived of clear moral laws. The tragic view admits no gradation between perfection and nothingness. The eye of the hidden God deprives the world of all its value, but precisely since he is hidden, the empirical world is the only one we can perceive directly, and it is therefore everything to us as well as nothing. Those who hold this view are the victims of a constant inner conflict: they can neither flee from the world nor live in it so as to realize transcendent values. The only consistent attitude they can adopt is to live in the world while constantly refusing allegiance to it. This was the attitude of Pascal when he wrote the *Pensées*, and of Racine at the time of *Phèdre*.

Jansenism was not a single unified movement, though its adherents shared certain characteristics and values: the doctrine of efficacious grace, anti-Molinism, rejection of the *dieu des philosophes*, aversion to mysticism, defence of Jansen, and the anti-historical rejection of the world. Goldmann distinguished four main variants of the Jansenist attitude. The first (Martin de Barcos, Pavillon, the Racine of *Andromaque* and *Britannicus*) stood for complete rejection of the world, from which it took refuge in contemplation. The second sought to reform the world by remaining in it and discriminating between good and evil (Arnauld, Nicole, Pascal in the *Provinciales*). The third attempted to compromise with the world (Choiseul, Arnauld d'Audilly). The fourth, and the most consistent, accepted the tragic situation: it remained in the world while denying the world, and expressed man's uncertainty and helplessness in the extreme form of the *pari*, the wager that applied not only to salvation but to the very existence of God (Pascal's *Pensées*, Racine's *Phèdre*).

In the tragic predicament in which God deprives the world of all value and yet, by his absence, obliges man to regard it as his only good, the human outlook is reduced to a permanent paradox, constantly denying and affirming the same proposition: for man's life is lived among antagonistic values, none of which can eliminate the others. It is part of the tragic consciousness to feel that one lives for the realization of values that cannot be realized completely—and therefore not at all, for those who believe in 'all or nothing'. Man can turn only to God, but God does not answer him. Thus the true utterance of the tragic consciousness is a monologue, a voice crying in the wilderness. The *Pensées* are a monologue of this kind, not an apologetic treatise.

Pascal and Racine represent Jansenism in a consummate form, expressing fully what others say by halves, and thus they exemplify the maximum 'potential consciousness' of the community to which they belong. It is a class-consciousness, that of the *noblesse de robe* during the transition to absolute monarchy, when the former was being more and more displaced from its social fastnesses by the new royal bureaucracy. While depriving it of its *raison d'être*, however, the monarchy was still its economic mainstay, and hence the consciousness of the *noblesse de robe* took on a tragic and paradoxical form; the new political trends were strange and hostile to it, but it could not aspire to alter them radically. This confusion and perplexity found its literary and philosophical expression in Jansenism—the ideology of a class driven into less and less favourable positions, and bound up with a system that maintained it on the one hand and destroyed it on the other.

In the tragic consciousness there is no place for mysticism. On the contrary, God appears as an infinitely remote being. He cannot be reached in mystic unity but only in prayer, which stresses the distance that mysticism seeks to annihilate.

Pascal reached the zenith of tragic consciousness in 1657, immediately after the date of the *Provincial Letters*. He denied the value of all worldly knowledge, yet went on with scientific research; he refused to compromise with authority, yet declared his obedience to the Church. He did not believe that truth and righteousness could triumph in this world, but he proclaimed that the whole of life should be devoted to fighting for them. This attitude also conditioned his literary style: in the world of tragedy no statement is true and no action is right unless accompanied by another which contradicts it. To this extent Pascal is also an exponent of dialectical thought, although his dialectic is static and tragic: there is no synthesis, no escape from the clash of opposites. In Pascal's world man lives between two extremes, but he does not feel this as a natural position (as in Thomist philosophy), because both extremes attract him equally and seem equally right, so that he lives in a state of constant tension. He cannot accept finitude, and he sees infinity as unattainable; he affirms himself only through his own weakness and incapacity for synthesis. He yearns for 'wholeness', but perceives that his yearning is in vain. In the last resort Pascal cannot recognize any basic principles of cognition, either the *cogito* or the rules of empiricism, but falls back on the *raisons du cœur*, on a practical faculty as the only trustworthy guide. In this respect too he anticipates dialectical thought; his dialectic reaches its acme in the *pari*, where a question fundamental to human destiny, the existence of God, is decided not by theoretical reasoning but by a gambler's throw. Pascal knows that reason left to itself is helpless, and he thus knows, as it were, that cognitive activity is only an 'aspect' of the complete man. Since not only God's will but his very existence are hidden from us we are forced to take the risk of wagering on this cardinal question, and the situation that makes this necessary does not depend on our own will. The *pari* is an act of hope, a practical act to decide a theoretical question. It is similar in this to Kant's practical reason, which decides metaphysical questions in reliance on the possibility of a supreme good, and also to Marx's invocation of the classless society: it is by no means scientifically proved that there is bound to be such a society, but by believing in it we commit ourselves actively to its cause.

Neither the past nor the future play a part in Pascal's dialectic: only the present, which is constantly passing away, and the nostalgic sense of eternity. Society is full of evil, and no rules of justice can be discerned in it, but we are condemned to live in the world of men although we have no hope that it will change radically for the better. Pascal's social conservatism and his paradoxical contempt for all the values of law, custom, and social hierarchy are both consequences of the tragic world-view.

In this analysis of Goldmann's we have an example of the construction of historical categories which explain structures of consciousness in relation to the class situation. Such categories, if properly devised, make it possible to give a uniform sense to phenomena without isolating them from their historical sources, and thus they satisfy the demands of both structuralist thought and genetic interpretation. By constructing such conceptual aids we provide ourselves with the means of interpreting a wide range of phenomena. Having seen Jansenism to be the ideology of the *noblesse de robe*, we can also see libertinism as the ideology of the *noblesse de cour*, expressed for example in Molière's plays. *Le Misanthrope* is an attack on Jansenism; *Dom Juan*, while accepting libertinism in principle, is also a partial critique of it and a reassertion of *la mesure*.

4. Goldmann and Lukács. Comment on genetic structuralism

Goldmann, as already mentioned, regarded himself as a disciple and continuer of Lukács's work, especially the early Lukács of *Die Seele und die Formen* and *History and Class-Consciousness*. (In Goldmann's view the basic elements of the dialectic as Lukács subsequently developed them can already be found in his pre-Marxist work.) In fact, however, Goldmann adopted only part of Lukács's theory, omitting other features which Lukács himself regarded as fundamental. Goldmann attempted to put into effect the concept of historical 'totality'; he believed that scientific observation must lead to the discovery of class-consciousness as it ought to be, were it fully consistent; that the dialectical method made it possible to resolve the dichotomy of facts and values, understanding and explanation; that cognitive acts were always involved in practical attitudes, so that it was impossible to isolate an element of pure theoretical contemplation in human behaviour; and, accordingly, that there were no absolute criteria of knowledge, no basic judgements. In all these ideas he was faithful to Lukács. But he was not interested in what Lukács regarded as an essential point, namely the mythology of the proletariat as the repository of the liberated absolute consciousness, nor did he hold that that perfect consciousness was embodied in the Communist party. All these questions were quite alien to him, and consequently in all specific matters he was much less dogmatic than Lukács. His general view, which he repeated many times, was that the Marxist critique of 'reification' in capitalist society was fully applicable at the present day. The transformation of all human products and individuals into goods comparable in quantitative terms; the disappearance of qualitative links between people; the gap between private and public life; the loss of personal responsibility and the reduction of human beings to executors of tasks imposed by a rationalized system; the resulting deformation of personality, the impoverishment of human contacts, the loss of solidarity, the absence of generally recognized criteria of artistic work, 'experimentation' as a universal creative principle; the loss of authentic culture owing to the segregation of the different spheres of life, in particular the domination of productive processes treated as an element independent of all others—these were all features of the consumption-oriented society. On the other hand, Goldmann believed that historical development had invalidated another part of Marx's analysis, namely the pauperization of the proletariat and the growth of revolutionary consciousness. Capitalism had managed to provide the workers with a relatively secure and satisfactory life, and there was therefore no reason to expect that their revolutionary mood and aspirations would reach an explosive pitch as forecast by the early Marxists. On this point Goldmann disagreed with Lukács, and it is an essential one: Lukács would not have been Lukács without his faith in the revolutionary consciousness of the proletariat.

For similar reasons Goldmann did not fully accept Lukács's aesthetic theory. He did not believe in 'socialist realism' as the 'highest phase' of culture. Unlike Lukács he was keenly alive to new trends in literature and art, and was a sympathetic critic of such authors as Gombrowicz, Robbe-Grillet, Jean Genet, and Nathalie Sarraute, whose work is diametrically opposed to anything that could be called 'socialist realism'. In these writers too he looked for a 'structure' which corresponded to particular social phenomena, whether or not they themselves intended or even perceived the correspondence: for instance, Robbe-Grillet's *Les Gommes* revealed the self-regulating mechanism of capitalist society, while the same author's *La Jalousie* was about reification.

In this sense Goldmann can be called a moderate Lukácsist, which is as much as to say that he was not a Lukácsist at all: he only adopted certain categories of Lukács's which he thought useful in studying the history of the dialectic and of civilization generally.

Goldmann's political views also had little in common with Communist dogmatism. As we have seen, he did not believe in a proletarian revolution taking place as the classical doctrine had predicted. He believed, however, that the most important need was for a new social order which would free the world from 'reified' structures and restore a sense of authenticity and human solidarity. He was particularly interested in the movement for workers' self-government (*autogestion ouvrière*), which Serge Mallet sought to place on a theoretical basis, and in Yugoslav experiments in this sphere. He thought this movement might lead in time, without violent revolutionary shocks, to a reunification of economic and cultural life; that it might give the workers a new sense of responsibility and of belonging to the community, and re-forge the links which capitalism had broken by quantifying all human values. But he did not define socialism in institutional terms, nor in terms of increased consumption. To him, the main features of the socialist ideal were spiritual values, the directness of social ties, and the responsibility of the individual. He did not believe in any laws of history guaranteeing that the ideal would be realized; it was a duty to wager on it, but there was no certainty of a pay-off.

As Goldmann was much less burdened with the dogmatic heritage of Marxism than was Lukács, his historical studies are a good deal less schematic. *Le Dieu caché* is certainly an interesting investigation; many points in it may be criticized by historians of the seventeenth century, but it nevertheless draws attention to aspects of Jansenism that may well repay further study. This does not mean, however, that we can accept Goldmann's methodological rules without reservation, or that their meaning is absolutely clear.

In particular, the doctrine of 'potential consciousness' seems extremely doubtful. To accept it as a tool of historical research implies that we can deduce from the situation of a particular class what its consciousness would have been if it had corresponded perfectly to that situation. This, however, is a fantasy. Even if we suppose with Goldmann—contrary to the evidence of history, to common sense, and even to Marx—that every world-view stands in a one-to-one correspondence with the class situation in which it arises, the deduction would still be impossible, for we should also have to know the general laws according to which particular class situations always produce particular forms of ideology, art, philosophy, or religion. We do not know any such laws and we never shall, for the possibility of doing so is excluded by the nature of the subject under examination, which is the whole process of history, unique and unrepeatable. There can be no law which says that 'Whenever conditions are exactly as they were in France in the middle of the seventeenth century they will produce the doctrines of Gassendi, Descartes, Pascal, etc.' To formulate the idea of seeking such 'laws' suffices to demonstrate its absurdity.

Goldmann believed, however, that it was possible in this way to argue from the historical situation of a class to its intellectual and artistic production, and that he had done so in one instance at least. To believe that such a feat is possible does not necessarily mean that the class situation 'produces' corresponding cultural phenomena; a more modest postulate will suffice, namely that the two spheres are not causally related but that there is a one-to-one correspondence between them. If we believe this, however, we must also believe that the deduction can be made in the opposite direction, for example that from Pascal's *Pensées* we could reconstruct the economic and political history of France in his day. But in any case it is easy to see that the one-to-one correspondence is pure fantasy. If it were fully ascertainable it would mean that we could reconstruct the works of art and philosophy *ex nihilo*, from a mere knowledge of the class situation in the society which produced them: thus from what we knew of the position of the *noblesse de robe* in Mazarin's time we should be able to write the *Pensées* even if we had never read or heard of them. No less than this is required for a confirmation of the theory of 'potential consciousness'. (Goldmann did indeed maintain that he had deduced the existence of Martin de Barcos from a general analysis of Jansenism: he had inferred that there must have been such a person, and had discovered afterwards that he was right.) Goldmann endeavoured to interpret all Pascal's ideas without exception, and even his forms of expression, as the reflection of a specific class-consciousness: this, he maintained, accounted for the fact that the *Pensées* were unfinished (though it is also true that Pascal died while writing them), that they are a collection of fragments and not a coherent treatise, that Pascal was a Catholic and not a Protestant (though in any case he was born and brought up a Catholic), and so on. Explanations of this kind are ingenious, but they do not add up to more than an intellectual *tour de force*.

Goldmann says, it is true, that in investigating the phenomena of consciousness we must distinguish 'essential' from accidental features. This seems to imply that only the former can be explained by the class situation or correlated with it; but it is not clear how we are supposed to make the distinction. We must either, it would seen, decide *a priori* what the world-view of a particular class must be, or else beg the question by classifying as 'essential' the features that can in fact be explained by the class situation.

Since, however, Goldmann believes that almost everything to do with a given *Weltanschauung* can be correlated with the class situation of its 'collective subject', his analyses ignore all the other social and psychological circumstances that in fact play a part in the creation of a philosophy. In holding that Jansenism is directly related to the class whose aspirations it somehow 'expresses', he leaves out of account such antecedent facts as the existence of the Church and the relatively autono-mous way in which conflicts within it were fought out, either in matters of dogma or, for example, the organizational differences between the secular and regular clergy. In the same way he completely ignores the immanent logic of the develop-ment of philosophy and theology, as well as individual, bio-graphical, and psychological factors.

In the last resort Goldmann falls a victim to a highly simplified and selective interpretation of Marxism. His object is to discover 'significant structures', which may be described as units of historical 'meaning'; this latter term, as many of his remarks indicate, is to be taken as signifying an unconscious or semi-conscious purposiveness, a kind of lower-grade purposive action such as that we attribute to animals. But he lays down quite arbitrarily that a 'unit of meaning' can only consist of a social class with a particular set of values and aspirations which are due to its position, and that these values and aspirations are the only possible frame of reference for studying the history of civilization. To justify this method it must be assumed that all human behaviour of importance, especially intellectual and artistic creation, is 'in the last resort' an expression of class-interests, anything else being mere chance or secondary rationalization. This may be in accordance with some of Marx's more simplistic formulas, but it is not borne out by the facts. We know that in practice all kinds of circumstances contribute to the formation of a world-view, and that all phenomena are due to an inexhaustible multiplicity of causes. To interpret Pascal in terms of individual psychology is certainly possible, and no less certainly inadequate; the same could be said of an interpretation relating his ideas purely to theological controversies, and it is equally inadequate to interpret him in terms of social class. To say this is not to hold out the hope that a complete, all-round synthesis of the truth could ever be formulated; doubtless it could not. But, while the attempt to interpret Pascal in class terms may be interesting and instructive, it does not require to be supported by a methodology which asserts dogmatically and gratuitously that there is no other way to interpret Pascal (or any other cultural figure), and that this method explains everything that is worth explaining. 'Genetic structuralism' of this kind cannot account for the continuity and permanence of any cultural achievements: if the meaning of Pascal's work is exhausted by the fact that it reflects the position of the *noblesse de robe* in seventeenth-century France, how is it that anyone at the present day, including Lucien Goldmann, can be interested in Pascal or find his work relevant to themselves? This continuity and permanence require us to suppose that, irrespective of the changing circumstances and class struggles that contribute to the creation of cultural values, there is a universal history of culture that is beyond class. The same spiritual needs, the same uncertainties and anxieties recur time and again in history, though their expression is affected by historical and psychological factors of all kinds.

Again, it does not seem that we are any closer to resolving the dichotomy of facts and values, despite Goldmann's assurances that, following Marx and Lukács, he has provided a key to this awkward problem. His writings contain no logical analysis of the difficulty, and no attempt to answer the questions raised by traditional positivism or by Max Weber. A clear distinction must, however, be made between values as studied by the sociologist and psychologist, and values as a concealed assumption of investigative method. If we accept Goldmann's view that in studying philosophies we always find practical motives embedded in intellectual processes, this does not imply anything as to the prospect of 'surmounting' the dichotomy of value-judgements and descriptive judgements. What is more, to suppose that all our descriptions are concealed value-judgements and that they regularly reflect class-aspirations is a dangerous habit of mind and may lead to intellectual nihilism, since it means that we cannot judge human thought by any purely intellectual criteria of empiricism or logic: all cultural achievements will seem equally permeated by class-interest, from the crudest political propaganda to the sublimest products of the intellect. Nor will there be any universal rules enabling us to discuss philosophical or scientific questions independently of class attitudes. Even if we agree with Marx that man is a practical being and that his mind is at the service of practical needs, we must still make some further distinctions. For, granted that we select phenomena on practical grounds at the level of elementary perception, and that the increase of knowledge is also largely governed by practical circumstances, it does not follow that there are no universal logical and empirical criteria (universal to the human species, not necessarily in a transcendental sense) for the evaluation of human knowledge and intellectual activity; and such criteria can be well enough distinguished from those by which we make moral or aesthetic judgements. To maintain that in all fields of culture, including scientific work, we have to do only with 'global' complexes of values, emotions, and practical behaviour, and that these complexes are only intelligible when correlated with social class, is to preclude the application of logic and the verifiability of scientific results, and to reduce everything to a single undifferentiated 'class-interest'.

Goldmann certainly did much to revive Marxism in France, and gave an example of ingenuity in applying Marxist rules of interpretation to Jansenism. His historical analyses were less schematic than his general methodological principles; but these principles do not remove the doubt as to the value of the Marxist understanding of the history of civilization.

CHAPTER X

The Frankfurt school
and 'critical theory'

THE term 'Frankfurt school' has been used since the 1950s to denote an important German para-Marxist movement, the history of which goes back to the early twenties and is associated with that of the Institut für Sozialforschung. One may speak here of a 'school' in a rather stricter sense than in the case of other trends within Marxism, though as usual there are doubts as to whether and how far particular individuals belong to it. There is, at all events, a clearly continuous mode of thought spanning two intellectual generations; the pioneers are no longer alive, but they have left successors in the field.

The abundant academic and publicistic output of the Frankfurt school covers multifarious domains of humanistic science: philosophy, empirical sociology, musicology, social psychology, the history of the Far East, the Soviet economy, psychoanalysis, the theory of literature and of law. In the present short account there can of course be no question of commenting on this output as a whole. The school is characterized, in the first place, by the fact that it treats Marxism not as a norm to which fidelity must be maintained, but as a starting-point and an aid to the analysis and criticism of existing culture; hence it has made free use of many non-Marxist sources of inspiration such as Hegel, Kant, Nietzsche, and Freud. Secondly, the school's programme was expressly non-party: it did not identify with any political movement, in particular Communism or social democracy, towards both of which it has often expressed a critical attitude. Thirdly, the school was clearly influenced by the interpretation of Marxism evolved by Lukács and Korsch in the 1920s, especially the concept of 'reification' as an epitome of the problems of the modern world. However, it can in no way be regarded as a school of Lukács's disciples; for its members—

and this is the fourth important point— have always emphasized the independence and autonomy of theory and have opposed its absorption by all-embracing 'praxis', even though they were also engaged in criticizing society with a view to transforming it. Fifthly—and here again the Frankfurt school differs basically from Lukács—while accepting Marx's position as to the exploitation and 'alienation' of the proletariat, it did not identify with the latter in the sense of regarding its existing class-consciousness, let alone the dictates of the Communist party, as an *a priori* norm. It emphasized the universality of 'reification' as a process affecting all strata of society, and came to be more and more doubtful of the proletariat's revolutionary and liberating role, so that in the end it jettisoned this part of Marx's doctrine altogether. Sixthly, although profoundly 'revisionist' *vis-à-vis* orthodox versions of Marxism, the school regarded itself as a revolutionary intellectual movement; it rejected the reformist position and maintained the need for a complete transcendence of society, while admitting that it had no positive Utopia to offer, and even that in present conditions a Utopia could not be created.

The period of the school's development was also that of the rise, victory, and fall of Nazism, and much of its output was concerned with relevant social and cultural problems such as racial prejudice, the need for authority, and the economic and ideological source of totalitarianism. Almost all the chief members of the school were middle-class German Jews; only a few had any real cultural links with the Jewish community, but their origin no doubt had some influence on the range of topics in which the school was interested.

In philosophy the Frankfurt school took issue with logical empiricism and positivist trends in the theory of knowledge and the methodology of science; also with pragmatism, utilitarianism, and, later, German existentialism. Its members attacked the 'mass society' and the degradation of culture, especially art, through the increasing influence of the mass media. They were pioneers in the analysis and aggressive criticism of mass culture and in this respect were successors of Nietzsche, defenders of élite values. They combined these attacks with criticism of a society in which the means whereby a professional bureaucracy could manipulate the masses were becoming more and more

effective: this applied both to Fascist and Communist totalitarianism and to the Western democracies.

1. Historical and biographical notes

The Institut für Sozialforschung (Institute for Social Research)
was founded by a group of young intellectuals at Frankfurt
at the beginning of 1923. The funds were provided by the family
of one of their number, Felix Weil, but the Institute was
officially a department of Frankfurt University. The principal
founders and early members were as follows.

Friedrich Pollock (1894–1970), an economist, later known
for the first serious analysis of planned economy in Soviet Russia
(*Die planwirtschaftlichen Versuche in der Sowjetunion 1917–1927*,
1929).

Carl Grünberg (1861–1940), the Institute's first director, was
of a different intellectual background from most of its members.
An orthodox Marxist of the older generation, he specialized
in the history of the workers' movement and from 1910 edited
the *Archiv für die Geschichte des Sozialismus und der Arbeiterbewegung*.

A central figure in the Institute, and its director from 1930,
was Max Horkheimer (1895–1973), a psychologist and philosopher by training, a pupil of Hans Cornelius and author of
works on Kant.

Another of the earliest members was Karl Wittfogel (b. 1896),
then a member of the Communist party and afterwards known
as the author of works on Chinese history (*Wirtschaft und
Gesellschaft Chinas*, 1931; *Oriental Despotism*, 1957). He worked
with the Institute for a few years only; his importance in the
history of Marxism is that he explored the question, on which
Marx had barely touched, of the 'Asiatic mode of production'.
He cannot, however, be regarded as a typical representative of
the Frankfurt school.

Another scholar who, besides Horkheimer, made a decisive
contribution to the formation of an individual school of philosophy at Frankfurt was Theodor Wiesengrund-Adorno (1903–
1970), who, however, did not join the Institute until the late
twenties. A philosopher, musicologist, and composer, he obtained
his doctorate with a study of Husserl and then wrote a thesis on
Kierkegaard's aesthetics; after 1925 he studied composition and
musicology at Vienna. Horkheimer and Adorno between them

may be regarded as the embodiment of the Frankfurt school.

Leo Lowenthal (b. 1900), who also joined the Institute rather late, made a significant contribution to its ideology with works on the history and theory of literature.

In the 1930s, after the Institute left Germany, it was joined by Walter Benjamin (1892–1940), one of the most eminent German literary critics between the wars. His work, however, is not important as a contribution to the development of Marxism: of all the well-known writers of the Frankfurt school, he was least connected with the Marxist movement.

Other Communists besides Wittfogel were Karl Korsch, of whom we have written separately, and Franz Borkenau, who is known chiefly for works attacking Communism after his break with the party. His book on the rise of capitalism (*Der Übergang vom feudalen zum bürgerlichen Weltbild*, 1934) may, however, be regarded as a product of the Frankfurt school, as it analyses the connection between the spread of the market economy and rationalist philosophy, a theme typical of those studied by the Institute.

Henryk Grossman (1881–1950), a Polish Jew, worked with the Institute from the late 1920s but was not a typical member: he belonged to traditional Marxist orthodoxy, and devoted himself to economic analyses for the purpose of confirming Marx's predictions of the falling profit rate and the collapse of capitalism.

In the early thirties the Institute was joined by Herbert Marcuse, to whom we devote a separate chapter on account of his later activity, and Erich Fromm, afterwards one of the best-known heretics among erstwhile Freudians.

From 1932 the Institute published the *Zeitschrift für Sozialforschung* (*Journal for Social Research*), which was its principal organ and in which many of its basic theoretical documents first appeared. After the move to the United States the *Journal* was continued for two years (1939–41) under the title *Studies in Philosophy and Social Sciences*.

When the Nazis came to power at the beginning of 1933 the Institute was, of course, unable to continue functioning in Germany. A branch had previously been founded in Geneva, to which some of the German members now moved. Another branch was set up in Paris, where the *Journal* continued to appear. Adorno spent the first few years of emigration at Oxford, and in 1938 moved to the United States, where almost all the Institute's members arrived sooner or later (Fromm being the first). Wittfogel was in a concentration camp for some months, but was finally released. The *émigrés* set up the International Institute for Social Research at Columbia University, which continued the Frankfurt projects and started new ones on similar lines. Walter Benjamin, who lived in Paris from 1935, fled from the Nazis in September 1940 and committed suicide on the Franco-Spanish border. Horkheimer and Adorno spent the war years in New York and Los Angeles; they returned to Frankfurt in 1950 and 1949 respectively, and took up professorships at the University there. Fromm, Marcuse, Lowenthal, and Wittfogel remained in America.

The fundamental principles of the Frankfurt school, applying both to epistemology and to the critique of civilization, were formulated by Horkheimer in a series of articles in the *Journal*, most of which were republished in 1968 under the title of *Kritische Theorie* (two volumes, edited by A. Schmidt). The most general and programmatic of these articles, written in 1937, was entitled 'Traditionelle und kritische Theorie'. Others discussed various philosophical questions, for example the relation of critical theory to rationalism, materialism, scepticism, and religion; we also find critiques of Bergson, Dilthey, and Nietzsche, and essays on the role of philosophy, the concept of truth, and the specific nature of the social sciences. Horkheimer's use of the term 'critical theory' was apparently meant to emphasize three aspects of his philosophical approach. Firstly, independence *vis-à-vis* existing doctrines, including Marxism; secondly, the conviction that civilization was irremediably diseased and needed a radical transformation, not merely partial reform; and thirdly, the belief that the analysis of existing society was itself an element of that society, a form of its self-awareness. Horkheimer's thought was permeated by the Marxist principle that philosophical, religious, and sociological ideas can only be understood in relation to the interests of different social groups (but not that everything 'in the last resort' comes down to class-interest), so that theory is a function of social life; on the other hand, he defended the autonomy of theory, and there is an unresolved tension between these two viewpoints. Horkheimer defends Hegelian Reason against the empiricists, positivists, and pragmatists; he is convinced that we can ascertain truths which cannot be expressed either as empirical hypotheses or as analytical judgements; but, it would seem, he does not accept any theory of a transcendental subject. He opposes scientism, i.e. the view that the methods actually used in natural science constitute all the intellectual equipment we need in order to achieve cognitive results of any value. To this view he has at least two objections: firstly, that in social matters, unlike natural science, observation is itself an element in what is observed, and secondly, that in all fields of knowledge the operation of Reason is required in addition to empirical and logical rules; yet the principles governing Reason are not sufficiently elucidated and it is not clear whence we are to derive them.

These thoughts of Horkheimer's essentially foreshadow such later works of the Frankfurt school as Adorno's *Negative Dialectics*: he is clearly at pains to avoid all 'reductionist' formulas in dealing with either traditionally Hegelian or traditionally Marxist questions. The subjectivity of the individual cannot be fully described in social categories and resolved into its social causes, nor can society be described in psychological terms; the subject is not absolutely prior, nor is it a mere derivative of the object; neither the 'base' nor the 'super-structure' is manifestly primary; 'phenomenon' and 'essence' are not presented independently of each other; praxis cannot absorb theory, nor vice versa; in all these cases we have to do with mutual interaction. These thoughts are not so precise, however, as to provide a basis for methodological rules that would preserve us at once from all the temptations of 'reductionism', dogmatism, idealism, and vulgar materialism. In all cases of interaction we have to do with the partial autonomy of factors affecting one another, but the boundaries of this autonomy are not clearly drawn. By emphasizing the need for constant 'mediation' Horkheimer apparently seeks to guard his position against all 'reductionist' traditions.

It is also clear, both from Horkheimer and from other writings of the Frankfurt school, that the critical theory associated empiricist and positivist doctrines with the cult of technology and technocratic tendencies in social life. One of the school's main themes is that the world is threatened by the progress of technology served by a science which is essentially indifferent to the world of values. If scientistic rules and restrictions are to govern all cognitive activity in such a way that it cannot generate value-judgements, then the progress of science and technology is bound to lead to a totalitarian society, the increasingly successful manipulation of human beings, the destruction of culture and of personality. Hence the importance of Hegelian Reason (*Vernunft*), which, as opposed to understanding (*Verstand*), can formulate 'global' judgements, prescribing the ends to be followed and not only the means of achieving ends that are themselves determined irrationally. A scientistic culture cannot and will not do this, as it presupposes that ends cannot be determined scientifically and must therefore be a matter of caprice. It does not appear, however, that Horkheimer or any other member of the Frankfurt school can explain how the same cognitive faculty can determine both ends and means, or how we proceed from observing phenomena to understanding the hidden 'essence' which teaches us not only what man empirically is but also what he would be if he fully realized his own nature.

In combating the phenomenalistic standpoint of the positivists, the Frankfurt school followed in the footsteps of the young Marx and were animated by the same interest. Their object was to ascertain what man really was and what were the requirements of true humanity—its essential aims, which could not be empirically observed nor yet arbitrarily determined, but must be discovered. The members of the school seem to have held that something is 'objectively' due to man by reason of his very humanity, and in particular that he is entitled to happiness and freedom. However, they tended to reject the young Marx's view that humanity is realized in the process of work, or that work in itself, in the present or in the future, could reveal the 'essence of humanity' and bring it to full perfection. It is nowhere clear in these arguments how faith in the paradigm of humanity is to be reconciled with the belief that man is determined by his self-creation in history. Nor is it clear how the statement that intellectual activity cannot exceed the bounds of historical praxis is to be squared with the demand for a 'global' criticism in which the totality of that praxis is opposed by theory or Reason.

All these elements of the critical theory are already present in the 1930s, in Horkheimer as in Marcuse or Adorno. The last-named studied the question of subjectivity and the object, and the problem of 'reification', chiefly in the context of Kierke-gaard's philosophy and of musical criticism. The commercializa-tion of art under monopoly capitalism was a recurrent theme of his; jazz music as a whole appeared to him a symptom of this degradation. His main point was that in a mass culture art loses its 'negative' function, i.e. that of representing a Utopia above and beyond existing society. It was not so much the 'politicization' of art that he objected to as, on the contrary, the replacement of its political function by passive, mindless enjoyment.

As to the work of Walter Benjamin, this cannot be wholly summed up in terms of the history of Marxism. Among his many writings on philosophy and literary criticism few can be described as showing a Marxist background. Nevertheless, he was for a long time an adherent of historical materialism in his own sense of the term, and went through a period of attraction towards Communism, though he never joined the party. He seems to have tried to graft historical materialism on to his own theory of culture, which had nothing to do with Marxism and which he had worked out beforehand. Gershom Scholem, his close friend and one of the greatest present-day authorities on the history of Judaism, emphasizes that Benjamin had at all times a strong mystical streak, and also that he had read very little Marx. Benjamin had a lifelong interest in the hidden meanings of words, which led him to study the language of magic, the cabbala, and the origins and functions of speech in general. He seems to have regarded historical materialism as a possible clue to the secret meaning of history, but his own speculations led to the view that it was a special case or application of a more general theory connecting human behaviour with a general 'mimetic' impulse in nature. In any case his thoughts on history had nothing to do with a theory of universal progress or determinism. He was impressed, on the other hand, by the dialectic of uniqueness and recurrence in history, mythology, and art. What seems to have attracted him in Communism was not the idea of regularity in history but rather that of discontinuity (hence his interest in Sorel). In *Theses on the Idea of History* (*Thesen über den Begriff der Geschichte*), written a few months before his death, he remarked that nothing had been so disastrous to the German workers' movement as the belief that it was swimming with the stream of history. Especially harmful and suspect, in his opinion, were versions of Marxism that regarded history as the progressive conquest of nature, seen as an object of exploitation—a view which he thought redolent of technocratic ideology. History, he wrote in the same *Theses*, was a construction, the scene of which was not empty, un-differentiated time but time filled by the *Jetztzeit*—the existence of bygone events, constantly revived in the present. This idea of unfading 'presentness' recurs in several places in his work. Benjamin had a strong, conservative sense of the permanence of the past, which he endeavoured to reconcile with a revolu-tionary faith in the discontinuity of history. He connected this latter idea with the Jewish Messianic tradition, holding, contrary to Marxist doctrine, that purely immanent eschatology was impossible; the *eschaton* could not manifest itself as a natural continuation of the course of events up to the present but, like the advent of the Messiah, presupposed a hiatus in time. But the discontinuous and catastrophic nature of history could not deprive the past of its meaning-generating significance. From Benjamin's various reflections, vague and ambiguous as they are, on the disappearance of the ancient links between art on the one hand and myth and ritual on the other it can be seen that he did not by any means consider this rift to be a source of pure gain: he seems to have believed that something essential must be salvaged from the mythical heritage of mankind if culture was to survive. He also apparently believed that there was a pre-existing treasury of the senses which human language and art did not create, but revealed; language, he held, conveys meaning not by virtue of convention and chance, but by a kind of alchemic affinity with objects and experience. (In this connection he was interested in Marr's speculations on the origin of language.) The purely instrumental view of language, charac-teristic of positivism, seemed to him of a piece with the general breakdown of inherited meaning in a civilization heading towards technocracy.

It does not seem that Benjamin had much in common with Marxism, despite his occasional professions. He was certainly linked with the Frankfurt school by his interest in various forms of cultural decadence resulting from the commercialization of art. He may for a time have believed more than other members of the school in the liberating potential of the proletariat, but the latter was in his view not so much the organizer of new relations of production, as the standard-bearer of a new culture which might one day restore the values that were perishing as the influence of myths declined.

The triumph of Nazism, with its catastrophic effect on German culture, naturally turned the attention of the Frankfurt school to investigating the psychological and social causes of the astonishing success of totalitarianism. Both in Germany and later in the United States the Institute carried out empirical studies for the purpose of investigating attitudes that found expression in the desire for authority and readiness to submit to it. In 1936 a collective work, *Studien über Autorität und Familie*, was published in Paris, based on theoretical argument as well as empirical observation; its main authors were Horkheimer and Fromm. Horkheimer sought to explain the growth of authoritarian institutions in terms of the decline and transference of family authority and the correspondingly increased importance of political institutions in the 'socialization' of the individual. Fromm interpreted the need for authority in psychoanalytical terms (the sado-masochistic character); he did not, however, share Freud's pessimism as to the inevitable conflict between instincts and the demands of communal life, or the permanently repressive role of culture. The Frankfurt writers sought to illuminate the phenomenon of Nazism from many sides and to discover its psychological, economic, and cultural roots. Pollock discussed Nazism in terms of state capitalism, of which he saw another example in the Soviet regime: both systems presaged a new era of domination and oppression based on state direction of the economy, autarkic tendencies, and the elimination of unemployment by coercion. Nazism was not a continuation of the old capitalism but a new formation in which the economy was deprived of its independence and subordinated to politics. Most writers of the school thought that the prospects of individual freedom and authentic culture were poor in view of contemporary trends, the growth of state control over the individual, and the bureaucratization of social relationships. Nazi and Soviet totalitarianism were not, they believed, historical aberrations but symptoms of a universal trend. Franz Neumann, however, in a book of 1944, took a more traditionally Marxist view: he held that Nazism was a form of monopoly capitalism and could not cope with the typical 'contradictions' of that system, so that its duration was bound to be limited.

In the United States the school continued to produce studies of social psychology designed to elucidate the causes that brought about and maintained attitudes, beliefs, and myths characteristic of totalitarian systems. These included a volume on anti-Semitism and a collective work, by Adorno and others, *The Authoritarian Personality* (1950), based on the results of projective tests and questionnaires. This was a study of the correlation between different personality traits of those inclined to welcome and revere authority, and the link between the existence and strength of these traits and such social variables as class, upbringing, and religion.

Adorno and Horkheimer remained extremely active to the end of their lives, publishing works in post-war America and Germany which are regarded as classic documents of the Frankfurt school. Among these are a joint work, *Dialektik der Aufklärung* (1947), Horkheimer's *Eclipse of Reason* (1947) and his *Zur Kritik der instrumentellen Vernunft* (1967). Adorno, besides numerous works on musicology (*Philosophie der neuen Musik*, 1949; *Dissonanzen: Musik in der verwalteten Welt*, 1956; *Moments Musicaux*, 1966), published *Negative Dialektik* (1966), the philosophical summa of the school, also a critique of existentialism (*Jargon der Eigentlichkeit: zur deutschen Ideologie*, 1964) and essays on the theory of culture, some of which were collected in *Prismen* (1955). He also edited, with Scholem, a two-volume edition of Benjamin's writings (1955). His unfinished *Ästhetische Theorie* was published posthumously in 1973. English translations of three of the above works (*Dialectic of Enlightenment*; *Negative Dialectics*; *The Jargon of Authenticity*) also appeared in 1973.

In the following sections I shall try to describe more fully some of the main points of the 'critical theory', without keeping to chronological order. I shall leave Adorno's musicology out of account, not because it is unimportant but because of my own incompetence in this sphere.

2. Principles of critical theory

The rules of 'critical' as opposed to 'traditional' theory were formulated in Horkheimer's programmatic essay of 1937, the main ideas of which are as follows.

In studies of social phenomena up to the present it has normally been assumed either that these should be based on the ordinary rules of induction and should aim at formulating general concepts and laws, expressed quantitatively as far as possible, or else that, as phenomenologists believe, it is possible to discover 'essential' laws independent of empirical results. In both cases the state of things under observation was separate from our knowledge about it, just as the subject-matter of natural science was furnished to it 'from outside'. It was also believed that the development of knowledge was governed by its own immanent logic, and that if some theories were discarded in favour of others this was because the former involved logical difficulties or proved incompatible with new data of experience. In reality, however, social changes were the most powerful agent of alterations in theory; science was part of the social process of production, and underwent change accordingly. Bourgeois philosophy had expressed its misguided faith in the independence of science in various transcendentalist doctrines which prevented people realizing the social genesis and social functions of knowledge; they also maintained a picture of knowledge as an activity that consisted of describing the world as it was but not of going beyond it or criticizing it, since this required evaluative judgements which science could not supply. The world of science was a world of ready-made facts which the observer sought to reduce to order, as though perception of them was quite independent of the social framework within which it took place.

For critical theory, however, there is no such thing as 'facts' in this sense. Perception cannot be isolated from its social genesis; both it and its object are a social and historical product. The individual observer is passive *vis-à-vis* the object, but society as a whole is an active element in the process, although unconsciously so. The facts ascertained are in part determined by the collective praxis of human beings who have devised the conceptual instruments used by the investigator. Objects as we know them are partly the product of concepts and of collective praxis, which philosophers, unaware of its origin, mistakenly petrify into a pre-individual transcendental consciousness.

Critical theory regards itself as a form of social behaviour and is aware of its own functions and genesis, but this does not mean that it is not a theory in the true sense. Its specific function is that it refuses to accept implicitly, as traditional theory does, that the rules of existing society—including the division of labour, the place assigned to intellectual activity, the distinction between the individual and society—are natural and inevitable. It seeks to understand society as a whole, and for that purpose it must in some sense take up a position outside it, although on the other hand it regards itself as a product of society. It criticizes society by analysing its categories. Existing society behaves as a 'natural' creation independent of the will of its members, and to understand this is to realize the 'alienation' to which they are subject. 'Critical thought is motivated today by the endeavour genuinely to transcend the situation of tension, to remove the opposition between the purposiveness, spontaneity, and rationality of the individual and the labour conditions on which society is based. It implies the conception that man is in conflict with himself until he recovers this identity' (*Kritische Theorie*, ed. A. Schmidt, vol. ii, p. 159).

Critical theory recognizes that there is no absolute subject of knowledge, and that subject and object do not yet coincide in the process of thinking about society, although that process is in fact society's self-knowledge. Their coincidence lies in the future; it cannot, however, be the result of mere intellectual progress, but only of the social process which will make humanity master of its fate again by stripping social life of its quasi-natural, 'external' character. This process involves a change in the nature of theory, the function of thought and its relation to the object.

Horkheimer's view, it will be seen, is here close to Lukács's: thought about society is itself a social fact, theory is inevitably part of the process it describes. But the essential difference is that Lukács believed that the complete unity of the subject and object of history, and thus the unity of social praxis and the theory that 'expresses' it, was realized in the class-consciousness of the proletariat; whence it followed that the observer's self-identification with the class outlook of the proletariat (sc. the Communist party line) was a guarantee of theoretical correctness. Horkheimer explicitly rejects this, declaring that the situation of the proletariat offers no guarantee in the matter of knowledge. Critical theory is in favour of the liberation of the proletariat, but it also wishes to preserve its independence, and refuses to commit itself to passive acceptance of the proletarian viewpoint; otherwise it would turn into social psychology, a mere record of what the workers thought and felt at any given moment. Precisely because it is 'critical', theory must remain autonomous *vis-à-vis* every existing form of social consciousness. Theory conceives itself as an aspect of praxis devoted to creating a better society; it retains a militant character, but it is not simply activated by the existing struggle. Its critical attitude to the 'totality' of the social system is not a matter of value-judgements superimposed on theoretical findings, but is implicit in the conceptual apparatus inherited from Marx: such categories as class, exploitation, surplus value, profit, impoverishment, and crises 'are elements of a conceptual whole, the purpose of which is not to reproduce society as it is but to change it in the right direction' (ibid., p. 167). Theory thus has an active and destructive character in its own conceptual framework, but has to take account of the fact that it might be in opposition to the actual consciousness of the proletariat. Critical theory, following Marx, analyses society in the light of abstract categories, but it does not forget at any stage that, *qua* theory, it is a criticism of the world it describes, that its intellectual act is at the same time a social act, that it is thus a 'critique' in the Marxian sense. Its subject is a single, particular historical society: the capitalist world in its present form, which impedes human development and threatens the world with a return to barbarism. Critical theory looks forward to another society in which men and women will decide their own fate and not be subject to external necessity; in so doing it increases the likelihood of such a society coming about, and it is aware of this fact. In the future society there will be no difference between necessity and freedom. The theory is in the service of human emancipation and happiness and the creation of a world fitted to human powers and needs, and it declares that mankind has potentialities other than those manifested in the existing world.

As can be seen, the main principles of 'critical theory' are those of Lukács's Marxism, but without the proletariat. This difference makes the theory more flexible and less dogmatic, but also obscure and inconsistent. Lukács, by identifying theory with the class-consciousness of the proletariat, and this in turn with the wisdom of the Communist party, clearly defined his criteria of truth: namely, in the observation of society, truth does not proceed from the application of general scientific rules that are valid also in natural science, but is defined by its origin; the Communist party is infallible. This epistemology at least has the merit of being consistent and perfectly clear. But in 'critical theory' we do not know how genetic criteria are to be combined with the intellectual autonomy of the theory and whence the rules governing its correctness are to be derived, since it rejects 'positivist' criteria but also refuses to identify with the proletariat. On the one hand, Horkheimer repeats (in 'Der Rationalismusstreit in der gegenwärtigen Philosophie', 1934) Feuerbach's statement that it is man who thinks, and not the Ego or Reason; in so doing he emphasizes that both the rules of scientific procedures and the stock of concepts used in science are a creation of history, the outcome of practical needs, and that the content of knowledge cannot be divorced from its social genesis—in other words, there is no transcendental subject. On this basis it might seem that the theory is 'good' or correct because it stands for 'social progress', or that intellectual value is defined by social function. But, on the other hand, the theory is supposed to retain its autonomy *vis-à-vis* reality; its content must not be derived from any identification with an existing movement, and it must not be pragmatistic in terms even of the human species, let alone a social class. It is not clear, therefore, in which sense it claims to be true: because it describes reality as it is, or because it 'serves the interests of the liberation of humanity'? The clearest answer that Horkheimer offers is perhaps the following: 'The open dialectic does not, however, lose the imprint of truth. The discovery of limitations and one-sidedness in one's own thought and that of others is an important aspect of the intellectual process. Both Hegel and his materialist successors rightly emphasized that this critical, relativist approach is part of knowledge. But certainty and the affirmation of one's own conviction do not require us to imagine that the unity of concept and object has been achieved and that thought can come to a stop. The results obtained from observation and inference, methodical research and historical events, everyday work and the political struggle, are true if they stand up to the cognitive means at our disposal (*den verfügbaren Erkenntnismitteln standhalten*)' ('Zum Problem der Wahrheit', ibid., vol. i, p. 246). This explanation is far from being unambiguous. If it means that critical theory, whatever the social circumstances in which it is evolved, is in the last resort subject to the rules of empirical verification and is judged as true or false accordingly, then it is no different epistemologically from the theories it condemns as 'traditional'. If, however, something more is meant, namely that in order to be true a theory must stand the empirical test and be 'socially progressive' as well, then Horkheimer fails to tell us what to do if these two criteria conflict. He merely repeats generalities about truth not being 'supra-historical' and about the social conditioning of knowledge, or what he calls the necessary 'social mediation' between a concept and its object; he assures us that the theory is not 'static', that it does not 'absolutize' either the subject or the object, and so on. All that is clear is that 'critical theory' refuses to accept Lukács's party dogmatism and seeks to maintain its status as theory while also refusing to acknowledge empirical criteria of verification. In other words, it exists by virtue of its own ambiguity.

Critical theory, thus understood, also comprises no specific Utopia. Horkheimer's predictions are confined to trite generalities: universal happiness and freedom, man becoming his own master, the abolition of profit and exploitation, etc. We are told that 'everything' must be changed, that it is not a matter of reforming society but of transforming it, but we are not told how this is to be done or what will be put in its place. The proletariat no longer ranks as the infallible subject of history, though its liberation is still an objective of the theory. Since, however, the latter does not claim to be the effective lever of general liberation, there is nothing clearly left of it except the conviction that it constitutes a higher mode of thought and will contribute to the emancipation of mankind.

Horkheimer's remarks on the social preferences and interests involved in the conceptual apparatus used by various theories of society are certainly true, though they were not new even in his day. But the fact that the social sciences reflect different interests and values does not mean, as Horkheimer seems to think (following Lukács, Korsch, and Marx), that the difference between empirical and evaluative judgements has been 'transcended'.

In this sense the 'critical theory' is an inconsistent attempt to preserve Marxism without accepting its identification with the proletariat and without recognizing the class or party criteria of truth, but also without seeking a solution of the difficulties that arise when Marxism is truncated in this manner. It is a partial form of Marxism, offering no replacement for what it leaves out.

3. Negative dialectics

There is, as far as I am aware, no summarized version of what is regarded, no doubt rightly, as the most complete and general exposition of Adorno's thought, namely *Negative Dialectics*. Probably it would be impossible to compile such a summary, and probably Adorno was well aware of this and deliberately made it so. The book may be called an embodied antinomy: a philosophical work that sets out to prove, by example or argument, that the writing of philosophical works is impossible. The difficulty of explaining its content is not only due to its extremely intricate syntax, which is evidently intentional, or the fact that the author uses Hegelian and neo-Hegelian jargon without any attempt to explain it, as though it were the clearest language in the world. The pretentious obscurity of style and the contempt that it shows for the reader might be endurable if the book were not also totally devoid of literary form. It is in this respect a philosophical counterpart to the formlessness that manifested itself some time earlier in the plastic arts, and later in music and literature. It is no more possible to summarize Adorno's work than to describe the plot of an 'anti-novel' or the theme of an action painting. It can no doubt be said that the abandonment of form in painting did not lead to the destruction of art, but actually liberated pure painting from 'anecdotic' work; and, similarly, the novel and drama, although they consist of words, have survived the loss of form (which can never be complete) to the extent that we are able to read Joyce, Musil, and Gombrowicz with understanding. But in philosophical writing, the dissolution of form is destructive in the highest degree. It may be tolerable if it is due to the author's attempt to catch fleeting 'experience' in words and to make his work directly 'expressive', like Gabriel Marcel; but it is hard to endure a philosopher who continues to deal in abstractions while at the same time contending that they are a meaningless form of discourse.

With this reservation we may try to give an idea of Adorno's argument. The main theme that pervades his book and is expressed, for example in his critique of Kant, Hegel, and the existentialists appears to be as follows. Philosophy has always been dominated by the search for an absolute starting-point, both metaphysical and epistemological, and in consequence, despite the intentions of philosophers themselves, it has drifted into a search for 'identity', i.e. some kind of primordial being to which all others were ultimately reducible: this was alike the trend of German idealism and positivism, of existentialists and transcendental phenomenologists. In considering the typical traditional 'pairs' of opposites—object versus subject, the general versus the particular, empirical data versus ideas, continuity versus discontinuity, theory versus practice—philosophers have sought to interpret them in such a way as to give primacy to one concept or the other and so create a uniform language by means of which everything can be described: to identify aspects of the universe in respect of which all others are derivative. But this cannot be done. There is no absolute 'primacy': everything philosophy is concerned with presents itself as interdependent with its opposite. (This, of course, is Hegel's idea, but Adorno claims that Hegel was afterwards untrue to it.) A philosophy which continues in traditional fashion to strive to discover the 'primal' thing or concept is on the wrong track, and, moreover, in our civilization it tends to strengthen totalitarian and conformist tendencies, by seeking order and invariability at any cost. Philosophy in fact is impossible; all that is possible is constant negation, purely destructive resistance to any attempt to confine the world within a single principle that purports to endow it with 'identity'.

Thus summarized, Adorno's thought may seem desperate or sterile, but it does not seem that we have done it an injustice. It is not a dialectic of negativity (which would be a metaphysical theory), but an express negation of metaphysics and epistemology. His intention is anti-totalitarian: he is opposed to all ideas that serve to perpetuate a particular form of domination and reduce the human subject to 'reified' forms. Such attempts, he argues, take on a paradoxical 'subjectivist' form, especially in existentialist philosophy, where the petrification of the absolute individual subject as the irreducible reality involves indifference to all social relationships that increase the enslavement of man. One cannot proclaim the primacy of this monadic existence without tacitly accepting everything that lies outside it.

But Marxism too—especially in Lukács's interpretation, though he is not expressly mentioned in this context—serves the same totalitarian tendency under colour of criticizing 'reification'. 'The remaining theoretical inadequacy in Hegel and Marx became part of historical practice and can thus be newly reflected upon in theory, instead of thought bowing irrationally to the primacy of practice. Practice itself was an eminently theoretical concept' (*Negative Dialectics*, p. 144). Adorno thus attacks the Marxist–Lukácsist 'primacy of practice', in which theory is dissolved and loses its autonomy. In so far as his opposition to the 'philosophy of identity' is turned against the anti-intellectualism of Marxism and its all-absorbing 'practice', he defends the right of philosophy to exist; he even begins his book with the statement that 'Philosophy, which once seemed obsolete, lives on because the moment to realize it was missed' (p. 3). At this point Adorno clearly departs from Marxism: there may, he argues, have been a time when Marx's hopes for the liberation of humanity by the proletariat and the abolition of philosophy by its identification with 'life' were realistic, but that time has passed. Theory must abide in its autonomy, which of course does not mean that theory in its turn has any absolute 'primacy'; nothing whatever has 'primacy', everything depends on everything else and, by the same token, has its own measure of 'substantiality'. 'Practice' cannot fulfil the tasks of theory, and if it claims to do so it is simply the enemy of thought.

If there is no absolute primacy it is also the case, in Adorno's opinion, that all attempts to embrace the 'whole' by means of reason are bootless and serve the cause of mystification. This does not mean that theory must resolve itself wholly into particular sciences as the positivists would have it: theory is indispensable, but for the present it cannot be anything but negation. Attempts to grasp the 'whole' are based on the same faith in the ultimate identity of everything; even when philosophy maintains that the whole is 'contradictory' it retains its prejudices concerning 'identity', which are so strong that even 'contradiction' can be made their instrument if it is proclaimed to be the ultimate foundation of the universe. Dialectic in the true sense is thus not merely the investigation of 'contradiction', but refusal to accept it as a schema that explains everything. Strictly speaking, the dialectic is neither a method nor a description of the world, but an act of repeated opposition to all existing descriptive schemata, and all methods pretending to universality. 'Total contradiction is nothing but the manifested untruth of total identification' (p. 6).

In the same way there is no epistemological absolute, no single unchallengeable source of wisdom; the 'pure immediacy' of the cognitive act, if it exists, cannot be expressed except in words, and words inevitably give it an abstract, rationalized form. But Husserl's transcendental ego is also a false construction, for there are no acts of intuition free from the social genesis of knowledge. All concepts are ultimately rooted in the non-conceptual, in human efforts to control nature; no concepts can express the whole content of the object or be identified with it; Hegel's pure 'being' proves in the end to be nothingness.

The negative dialectic can, as Adorno says, be called an anti-system, and in that sense it appears to coincide with Nietzsche's position. However, Adorno goes on to say that thought itself is negation, just as the processing of any substance is a 'negation' of its form as presented to us. Even the statement that something is of a certain kind is negative inasmuch as it implies that that something is not of another kind. This, however, reduces 'negativity' to a truism; it is not clear how there could be any philosophy that is not 'negative' in this sense, or whom Adorno is arguing against. His main intention, however, appears to be a less truistic one, namely to put forward no definite answers to the traditional problems of philosophy but to confine himself to exploding philosophy as it is today, since by its urge towards 'positiveness' it inevitably degenerates into acceptance of the *status quo,* namely the domination of man by man. The bourgeois consciousness at the time of its emancipation combated 'feudal' modes of thought but could not bring itself to break with 'systems' of all kinds, since it felt that it did not represent 'complete freedom'—from this observation of Adorno's we gather that he stand for 'complete freedom' as against 'systems'.

In his critique of 'identity' and 'positiveness' Adorno continues a traditional motif taken over by the Frankfurt school from Marx: the critique of a society which, being subject to the domination of 'exchange-value', reduces individuals and things to a common level and a homogeneous anonymity. A philosophy which expresses and affirms that society cannot do justice to the variety of phenomena or the interdependence of different aspects of life; on the one hand it homogenizes society, on the other it reduces people and things to 'atoms'—a process in which, Adorno observes, logic plays its part also: on this point he is faithful to the tradition of recent Marxist philosophy, which inveighs against logic while ignoring its modern developments.

Science, too, it appears, is a party to the general conspiracy of civilization against man, as it identifies rationality with measurability, reduces everything to 'quantities', and excludes qualitative differences from the scope of knowledge; Adorno does not suggest, however, that a new 'qualitative' science is ready and waiting to take over.

The upshot of his critique is not to defend relativism, for that too is part of 'bourgeois consciousness'; it is anti-intellectual (*geistesfeindlich*), abstract, and wrong, because what it treats as relative is itself rooted in the conditions of capitalist society: 'the alleged social relativity of views obeys the objective law of social production under private ownership of the means of production' (p. 37). Adorno does not say what 'law' he refers to, and, true to his contempt for bourgeois logic, does not reflect on the logical validity of his criticism.

Philosophy in the sense of a 'system' is impossible, he argues, because everything changes—a statement he enlarges on as follows. 'The invariants, whose own invariance has been produced (*ein Produziertes ist*), cannot be peeled out of the variables as if all truth were then in our possession. Truth has coalesced with substance, which will change; immutability of truth is the delusion of *prima philosophia*' (p. 40).

On the one hand, concepts have a certain autonomy and do not emerge simply as copies of things; on the other, they do not enjoy 'primacy' as compared with things—to agree that they do would mean accepting bureaucratic or capitalist government. 'The principle of dominion, which antagonistically rends human society, is the same principle which, spiritualized, causes the difference between the concept and its subject matter (*dem ihm Unterworfenen*)' (p. 48). Hence nominalism is wrong ('The concept of a capitalist society is not a *flatus vocis*'—p. 50 n.), and so is conceptual realism: concepts and their objects subsist in a constant 'dialectical' association, in which primacy is obliterated. In the same way positivist attempts to reduce knowledge to that which is simply 'given' are misguided, as they seek to 'dehistoricize the contents of thought' (p. 53).

Anti-positivist attempts to reconstruct an ontology are no less suspect; for ontology as such—not any particular ontological doctrine—is an apologia for the *status quo*, an instrument of 'order'. The need for an ontology is genuine enough, since the bourgeois consciousness has replaced 'substantial' by 'functional' concepts, treating society as a complex of functions in which everything is relative to something else and nothing has a consistency of its own. Nevertheless, ontology cannot be reconstructed.

At this point, as at many others, the reader may well wonder how Adorno intends his propositions to be applied. What are we to do if ontology and the lack of it are both bad and are both likely to involve us in the defence of exchange-value? Perhaps we should not think of these questions at all, but declare ourselves neutral in philosophical matters? But Adorno will not have this either: it would be a surrender of another kind, an abandonment of reason. Science, just because it puts faith in itself and refuses to seek self-knowledge by any methods other than its own, condemns itself to being an apologia for the existing world. 'Its self-exegesis makes a *causa sui* of science. It accepts itself as given and thereby sanctions also its currently existing form, its division of labour, although in the long run the insufficiency of that form cannot be concealed' (p. 73). The humanistic sciences, dispersed in particular inquiries, lose interest in cognition and are stripped of their armour of concepts. Ontology, which comes to science 'from outside', appears with the abruptness of a pistol-shot (in Hegel's phrase) and does not help them to acquire self-knowledge. In the end we do not know how to escape from the vicious circle.

Heidegger's ontology not only does not cure this state of affairs, but proposes something even worse. Having eliminated from philosophy both empiricism and Husserl's concept of the *eidos*, he seeks to apprehend Being—which, after this reduction, is pure nothingness; he also 'isolates' phenomena and cannot conceive them as aspects (*Momente*) of the process of manifestation; in this way phenomena are 'reified'. Heidegger, like Husserl, believes that it is possible to proceed from the individual to the universal without 'mediation', or to apprehend Being in a form unaffected by the act of reflection. This, however, is impossible: Being, however conceived, is 'mediated' by the subject. Heidegger's 'Being' is constituted, not simply 'given': 'We cannot, by thinking, assume any position in which that separation of subject and object will directly vanish, for the separation is inherent in each thought; it is inherent in thinking itself' (p. 85). Freedom can be sought only by observing the tensions that arise between opposite poles of life, but Heidegger treats these poles as absolute realities and leaves them to their fate. On the one hand he accepts that social life must be 'reified', i.e. he sanctions the *status quo*, while on the other he ascribes freedom to man as something already gained, thus sanctioning slavery. He attempts to rescue metaphysics, but wrongly supposes that what he is trying to rescue is 'immediately present'. All in all, Heidegger's philosophy is an example of *Herrschaftswissen* in the service of a repressive society. It calls on us to abandon concepts for the sake of a promised communion with Being—but this Being has no content, precisely because it is supposed to be apprehended without the 'mediation' of concepts; basically it is no more than a substantivization of the copula 'is'.

It would seem that, speaking in as general terms as possible, the main thrust of Adorno's attack on Heidegger's ontology lies in the Hegelian contention that the subject can never be wholly eliminated from the results of metaphysical inquiry, and that if we forget this and attempt to place subject and object 'on opposite sides' we shall fail to comprehend either one or the other. Both are inseparable parts of reflection, and neither has epistemological priority; each is 'mediated' by the other. Similarly, there is no way of apprehending by cognition that which is absolutely individual—what Heidegger calls *Dasein* or *Jemeinigkeit*. Without the 'mediation' of general concepts, the pure 'this thing here' becomes an abstraction; it cannot be 'isolated' from reflection. 'But truth, the constellation of subject and object in which both penetrate each other, can no more be reduced to subjectivity than to that Being whose dialectical relation to subjectivity Heidegger tends to blur' (p. 127).

The passage in which Adorno comes closest to explaining what he means by 'negative dialectics' is as follows: 'In a sense, dialectical logic is more positivistic than the positivism that outlaws it. As thinking, dialectical logic respects that which is to be thought—the object—even where the object does not heed the rules of thinking. The analysis of the object is tangential to the rules of thinking. Thought need not be content with its own legality; without abandoning it, we can think against our thought, and if it were possible to define dialectics, this would be a definition worth suggesting' (p. 141). It does not appear that we can infer more from this definition than that the dialectic need not be cramped by the rules of logic. In another passage we are indeed told that it is freer still: for 'Philosophy consists neither in *vérités de raison* nor in *vérités de fait*. Nothing it says will bow to tangible criteria of any "being the case"': its theses on conceptualities are no more subject to the criteria of a logical state of facts than its theses on factualities are to the criteria of empirical science' (p. 109). It would be hard indeed to imagine a more convenient position. The negative dialectician declares, firstly, that he cannot be criticized from either the logical or the factual point of view, as he has laid down that such criteria do not concern him; secondly, that his intellectual and moral superiority is based on his very disregard of these criteria; and thirdly, that that disregard is in fact the essence of the 'negative dialectic'. The 'negative dialectic' is simply a blank cheque, signed and endorsed by history, Being, Subject, and Object, in favour of Adorno and his followers; any sum can be written in, anything will be valid, there is absolute liberation from the 'positivist fetishes' of logic and empiricism. Thought has transformed itself dialectically into its opposite. Anyone who denies this is enslaved to the 'identity principle', which implies acceptance of a society dominated by exchange-value and therefore ignorant of 'qualitative differences'.

The reason why the 'identity principle' is so dangerous, according to Adorno, is that it implies, firstly, that each separate thing is what it is empirically, and secondly, that an individual object can be identified by means of general concepts, i.e. analysed into abstractions (an idea of Bergson's, whom Adorno, however, does not mention). The task of the dialectic, on the other hand, is firstly to ascertain what a thing is in reality, not merely to what category it belongs (Adorno does not give examples of an analysis of this kind), and secondly to explain what it ought to be according to its own concept, although it is not yet (an idea of Bloch's, to whom Adorno also does not refer in this context). A man knows how to define himself, while society defines him differently in accordance with the function it assigns to him; between the two modes of definition there is an 'objective contradiction' (again no examples given). The object of the dialectic is to oppose the immobilization of things by concepts; it takes the position that things are never identical with themselves; it seeks out negations, without assuming that the negation of a negation signifies a return to the positive; it recognizes individuality, but only as 'mediated' by generality, and generality only as an aspect (*Moment*) of individuality; it sees the subject in the object and vice versa, practice in theory and theory in practice, the essence in the phenomenon and the phenomenon in the essence; it must apprehend differences but not 'absolutize' them, and it must not regard any particular thing as a starting-point *par excellence*. There cannot be a point of view that presupposes nothing, such as Husserl's transcendental subject; the delusion that there can be such a subject is due to the fact that society precedes the individual. The idea that there can be a spirit which comprises everything and is identical with the whole is as nonsensical as that of a single party in a totalitarian regime. The dispute as to the primacy of mind or matter is meaningless in dialectical thinking, for the concepts of mind and matter are themselves abstracted from experience, and the 'radical difference' between them is no more than a convention.

All these precepts concerning the dialectic should, in Adorno's opinion, serve definite social or political ends. It even appears that criteria of practical action can be deduced from them. 'For the right practice, and for the good itself, there really is no other authority than the most advanced state of theory. When an idea of goodness is supposed to guide the will without fully absorbing the concrete rational definitions, it will unwittingly take orders from the reified consciousness, from that which society has approved' (p. 242). We thus have a clear practical rule: firstly there must be an advanced (*fortgeschritten*) theory, and secondly, the will must be influenced by 'concrete rational definitions'. The object of practice, thus enlightened, is to do away with reification which is due to exchange-value; for in bourgeois society, as Marx taught, the 'autonomy of the individual' was only apparent, an expression of the contingency of life and the dependence of human beings on market forces. It is hard to gather from Adorno's writings, however, what non-reified freedom is to consist of. In describing this 'complete freedom' we must not, in any case, use the concept of self-alienation, as it suggests that the state of freedom from alienation, or the perfect unity of man with himself, has already existed at some former time, so that freedom can be achieved by going back to the starting-point—an idea which is reactionary by definition. Nor is it the case that we know of some historical design that guarantees us a joyful future of freedom and the end of 'reification'; up to now there has been no such thing as a single process of universal history: 'history is the unity of continuity and discontinuity' (p. 320).

There can be few works of philosophy that give such an overpowering impression of sterility as *Negative Dialectics*. This is not because it seeks to deprive human knowledge of an 'ultimate basis', i.e. because it is a doctrine of scepticism; in the history of philosophy there have been admirable works of scepticism, full of penetration as well as destructive passion. But Adorno is not a sceptic. He does not say that there is no criterion of truth, that no theory is possible, or that reason is powerless; on the contrary, he says that theory is possible and indispensable and that we must be guided by reason. All his arguments go to show, however, that reason can never take the first step without falling into 'reification', and it is thus not clear how it can take the second or any further steps; there is simply no starting-point, and the recognition of this fact is proclaimed as the supreme achievement of the dialectic. But even this crucial statement is not clearly formulated by Adorno, nor does he support it by any analysis of his concepts and maxims. As with many other Marxists, his work contains no arguments but only *ex cathedra* statements using concepts that are nowhere explained; indeed, he condemns conceptual analysis as a manifestation of positivist prejudices to the effect that some ultimate 'data', empirical or logical, can provide philosophy with a starting-point.

In the last resort Adorno's argument boils down to an assortment of ideas borrowed uncritically from Marx, Hegel, Nietzsche, Lukács, Bergson, and Bloch. From Marx he takes the statement that the whole mechanism of bourgeois society is based on the domination of exchange-value, reducing all qualitative differences to the common denominator of money (this is Marx's form of romantic anti-capitalism). From Marx also comes the attack on Hegelian philosophy for subjecting history to an extra-historical *Weltgeist* and asserting the primacy of 'that which is general' over human individuals, substituting abstractions for realities and thus perpetuating human enslavement. Again from Marx comes the attack on Hegel's theory of subject and object, in which the subject is defined as a manifestation of the object, and the object as a subjective construction, thus producing a vicious circle (but it is not clear how Adorno avoids this vicious circle, as he denies absolute 'priority' to either subject or object). Adorno departs from Marx, on the other hand, in rejecting the theory of progress and historical necessity and the idea of the proletariat as the standard-bearer of the Great Utopia. From Lukács comes the view that all that is evil in the world can be summed up in the term 'reification' and that perfected human beings will cast off the ontological status of 'things' (but Adorno does not say what the 'de-reified' state will be like, still less how it will be attained). Both the Promethean and the scientific motif of

Marxism are discarded, and there remains only a vague romantic Utopia in which man is himself and does not depend on 'mechanical' social forces. From Bloch, Adorno derives the view that we possess the idea of a Utopia 'transcending' the actual world, but that the especial virtue of this 'transcendence' is that it cannot, in principle, have any definite content at the present time. From Nietzsche comes the general hostility to the 'spirit of the system' and the convenient belief that a true sage is not afraid of contradictions but rather expresses his wisdom in them, so that he is forearmed against logical criticism. From Bergson comes the idea that abstract concepts petrify changeable things (or, as Adorno would say, 'reify' them); Adorno himself, on the other hand, contributes the hope that we can create 'fluid' concepts that do not petrify anything. From Hegel, Adorno takes the general idea that in the cognitive process there is a constant 'mediation' between subject and object, concepts and perception, the particular and the general. To all these ingredients Adorno adds an almost unparalleled vagueness of exposition: he shows no desire whatever to elucidate his ideas, and clothes them in pretentious generalities. As a philosophical text, *Negative Dialectics* is a model of professorial bombast concealing poverty of thought.

The view that there is no absolute basis for human reasoning can certainly be defended, as is shown by sceptics and relativists who have propounded it in various forms. But Adorno not only adds nothing to this traditional idea but obscures it by his own phraseology (neither subject nor object can be 'absolutized'; perceptions cannot be 'abstracted' from concepts; there is no absolute 'primacy' of practice, etc.), while at the same time imagining that this 'negative dialectic' can lead to some practical consequences for social behaviour. If we do try to extract intellectual or practical rules from his philosophy, they reduce to the precepts: 'We must think more intensively, but also remember that there is no starting-point for thought' and 'We must oppose reification and exchange-value'. The fact that we can say nothing positive is not our fault and not Adorno's, but is due to the domination of exchange-value. For the present, therefore, we can only negatively 'transcend' existing civilization as a whole. In this way the 'negative dialectic' has provided a convenient ideological slogan for left-wing groups who sought a pretext for root-and-branch destruction as a political programme, and who extolled intellectual primitivism as the supreme form of dialectical initiation. It would be unjust, however, to accuse Adorno of intending to encourage such attitudes. His philosophy is not an expression of universal revolt, but of helplessness and despair.

4. Critique of existential 'authenticism'

Existentialism was clearly the main competitor of the Frankfurt school as regards the critique of 'reification', and was far more influential as a philosophy. German thinkers rarely used the term, but on the face of it the intention of their anthropological theories was the same: to express in philosophical language the contrast between the self-determining consciousness of the individual and the anonymous world of social ties conforming to rules of their own. Thus, in the same way as the attacks on Hegel by Marx, Kierkegaard, and Stirner contained a common element, namely their critique of the primacy of impersonal 'generality' over real subjectivity, so the Marxists and existentialists were on common ground in criticizing the social system which confined human beings to socially determined roles and made them dependent on quasi-natural forces. The Marxists, following Lukács, called this state of things 'reification' and ascribed it, as did Marx, to the all-powerful effect of money as a leveller in capitalist conditions. Existentialism did not concern itself with explanations such as the class struggle or property relationships, but it too was fundamentally a protest against the culture of developed industrial societies, reducing the human individual to the sum of his social functions. The category of 'authenticity' or 'authentic being' (*Eigentlichkeit*), which plays an essential part in Heidegger's early writings, was an attempt to vindicate the irreducible identity of the individual subject as against the anonymous social forces summed up in the term 'the impersonal' (*das Man*).

Adorno's attack on German existentialism was thus perfectly understandable: he wished to assert the claim of the Frankfurt school to be the sole fighter against 'reification', and to prove that existentialism, while appearing to criticize reification, in reality endorsed it. This is the purpose of *Jargon der Eigentlichkeit: zur deutschen Ideologie* (1964), in which he joins issue principally with Heidegger but also with Jaspers and occasionally Buber, Bollnow, and others. Adorno accepts the idea of 'reification' and the Marxist view that it results from the subjection of human beings to exchange-value, but he rejects the idea of the proletariat as the saviour of humanity and does not believe that 'reification' can be done away with simply by nationalizing means of production.

The main points of Adorno's attack on existentialism are as follows.

Firstly, the existentialists have created a deceptive language, the elements of which are intended, by some peculiar 'aura', to arouse a magic faith in the independent power of words. This is a rhetorical technique which precedes any content and is merely designed to make it appear profound. The magic of words is supposed to take the place of an analysis of the true sources of 'reification' and to suggest that it can be cured simply by incantations. In reality, however, words cannot directly express irreducible subjectivity, nor can they generate 'authentic being': it is quite possible to adopt the watchword of 'authenticism' and believe that one has escaped from reification, while in fact remaining subject to it. Moreover—and this seems to be the essential point—'authenticism' is a purely formal catchword or incantation. The existentialists do not tell us in what way we are to be 'authentic': if it suffices simply to be what we are, then an oppressor and murderer is doing his duty by being just that. In short (though Adorno does not put the point in these words), 'authenticism' does not imply any specific values and can be expressed in any behaviour whatsoever. Another deceptive concept is that of 'authentic communication' as opposed to the mechanical exchange of verbal stereotypes. By talking of authentic communication the existentialists seek to persuade people that they can cure social oppression simply by expressing thoughts to one another, and conversation is thus turned into a substitute for what should come after it (Adorno does not explain what this is).

Secondly, 'authenticism' cannot in any case be a cure for reification because it is not interested in its sources, namely the rule of commodity fetishism and exchange-value; it suggests that anyone can make his own life authentic, while society as a whole continues to be under the spell of reification. This is a classic case of distracting people's attention from the real causes of their slavery, by conjuring up the illusion that freedom can be realized in the individual consciousness without any change in the conditions of communal life.

Thirdly, the effect of existentialism is to petrify the whole area of 'non-authentic' life as a metaphysical entity which cannot be done away with but can only be resisted by an effort confined to one's own existence. Heidegger, for instance, speaks of empty, everyday chatter as a manifestation of the reified world, but he regards it as a permanent feature, not realizing that it would not exist in a rational economy that did not squander money on advertising.

Fourthly, existentialism tends to perpetuate reification not only by distracting attention from social conditions but by the way in which it defines existence. According to Heidegger, individual human existence (*Dasein*) is a matter of self-possession and self-reference. All social content is excluded from the idea of authenticity, which consists of willing to possess oneself. In this way Heidegger actually reifies human subjectivity, reducing it to a tautological state of 'being oneself', unrelated to the world outside.

Adorno also attacks Heidegger's attempts to investigate the roots of language, which he regards as part of a general tendency to glorify bygone times, Arcadian rusticity, etc., and consequently as related to the Nazi ideology of 'blood and soil'.

Adorno's criticism follows the main lines of conventional Marxist attacks on 'bourgeois philosophy': existentialism makes a pretence of fighting reification but in fact aggravates it by leaving social problems out of account and promising the individual that he can have 'true life' by simply deciding to 'be himself'. In other words, the objection is that the 'jargon of authenticity' contains no political programme. This is true, but the same could be said of Adorno's own jargon of reification and negation. The proposition that we must constantly set our faces against a civilization subject to the levelling pressures of exchange-value does not itself imply any specific rule of social behaviour. The case is different with orthodox Marxists, who maintain that reification with all its baneful consequences will cease when all factories are taken over by the state; but Adorno specifically rejects this conclusion. He condemns society based on exchange-value without giving any indication of what an alternative society would be like; and there is something hypo-critical in his indignation at the existentialists' failure to provide a blueprint for the future.

Adorno is certainly right in saying that 'authenticism' is a purely formal value from which no conclusions or moral rules can be deduced. It is dangerous, moreover, to set it up as the supreme virtue, since it affords no moral protection against the idea that, for example, the commander of a concentration camp can, by behaving as such, achieve perfect fulfilment as a human being. In other words, Heidegger's anthropology is amoral inasmuch as it contains no definition of values; but is 'critical theory' in any better case? True, it includes 'reason' and 'freedom' among its basic concepts. But we are told little of 'reason' in its higher dialectical form except that it is not bound by the trivialities of logic or the cult of empirical data, and as regards 'freedom' we are chiefly told what it is not. It is neither bourgeois freedom, which enhances reification instead of curing it, nor is it freedom as promised and realized by Marxism–Leninism, for that is slavery. Clearly, it must be something better than these, but it is hard to say what. We cannot anticipate Utopia in positive terms; the most we can do is negatively to transcend the existing world. Thus the precepts of critical theory are no more than a call to unspecified action, and are just as formal as Heidegger's 'authenticism'.

5. *Critique of 'enlightenment'*

Although Horkheimer's and Adorno's *Dialectic of Enlightenment* consists of loose and uncoordinated reflections, it contains some basic ideas which can be reduced to a kind of system. Written towards the end of the Second World War, the book is dominated by the question of Nazism, which, in the authors' view, was not simply a monstrous freak but rather a drastic manifestation of the universal barbarism into which humanity was falling. They attributed this decline to the con-sistent operation of the very same values, ideals, and rules that had once lifted mankind out of barbarism, and that were summed up in the concept of 'enlightenment'. By this they did not mean the specific eighteenth-century movement to which the term is usually applied, but the 'most general sense of progressive thought ... aimed at liberating men from fear and establishing their sovereignty' (*Dialectic of Enlightenment*, p. 3). The 'dialectic' consisted in the fact that the movement which aimed to conquer nature and emancipate reason from the shackles of mythology had, by its own inner logic, turned into its opposite. It had created a positivist, pragmatist, utilitarian ideology and, by reducing the world to its purely quantitative aspects, had annihilated meaning, barbarized the arts and sciences, and increasingly subjected mankind to 'commodity fetishism'. The *Dialectic of Enlightenment* is not a historical treatise but a collection of haphazardly chosen and unexplained examples to illustrate various forms of the debasement of 'enlightened' ideals; after some introductory remarks on the concept of enlightenment it includes chapters on Odysseus, the marquis de Sade, the entertainment industry, and anti-Semitism.

Enlightenment, seeking to liberate men from the oppressive sense of mystery in the world, simply declared that what was mysterious did not exist. It aspired to a form of knowledge that would enable man to rule over nature, and it therefore deprived knowledge of significance, jettisoning such notions as substance, quality, and causality and preserving only what might serve the purpose of manipulating things. It aimed to give unity to the whole of knowledge and culture and to reduce all qualities to a common measure; thus it was responsible for the imposition of mathematical standards on science and for creating an economy based on exchange-value, i.e. transforming goods of every kind into so many units of abstract labour-time. Increased dominion over nature meant alienation from nature, and likewise increased domination over human beings; the theory of knowledge produced by enlightenment implied that we know things in so far as we have power over them, and this was true in both the physical and the social world. It also signified that reality had no meaning in itself but only took its meaning from the subject, while at the same time subject and object were completely separate from each other. Science ascribed reality only to what might occur more than once—as if in imitation of the 'repetition principle' that governs mythological thinking. It sought to contain the world within a system of categories, turning individual things and human beings into abstractions and thus creating the ideological foundations of totalitarianism. The abstractness of thought went hand in hand with the domination of man by man: 'The universality of ideas as developed by discursive logic, domination in the conceptual sphere, is raised up on the basis of actual domination' (p. 14). Enlightenment in its developed form regards every object as self-identical; the idea that a thing may be what it is not yet is rejected as a relic of mythology.

The urge to enclose the world in a single conceptual system, and the propensity to deductive thinking, are especially pernicious aspects of enlightenment and are a menace to freedom.

For enlightenment is as totalitarian as any system. Its untruth does not consist in what its romantic enemies have always reproached it for: analytical method, return to elements, dissolution through reflective thought; but instead in the fact that for enlightenment the process (*Prozess*) is always decided from the start. When in mathematical procedure the unknown becomes the unknown quantity of an equation, this marks it as the well-known even before any value is inserted. Nature, before and after the quantum theory, is that which is to be comprehended mathematically ... In the anticipated identification of the wholly conceived and mathematized world with truth, enlightenment intends to secure itself against the return of the mythic. It confounds thought and mathematics ... Thinking objectifies itself to become an automatic, self-activating process ... Mathematical procedure becomes, so to speak, the ritual of thinking ... it turns thought into a thing, an instrument (*Dialectic of Enlightenment*, pp. 24–5).

Enlightenment, in short, will not and cannot grasp what is new; it is only interested in what is recurrent, what is already known. But, contrary to the rules of enlightenment, thought is not a matter of perception, classification, and counting; it consists in 'the determinate negation of each successive immediacy' (*bestimmende Negation des je Unmittelbaren*) (ibid., p. 27)—i.e., presumably, in advancing beyond what is to what may be. Enlightenment turns the world into a tautology, and thus reverts to the myth which it sought to destroy. By restricting thought to 'facts' which must then be arranged in an abstract 'system', enlightenment sanctifies what is, that is to say social injustice; industrialism 'reifies' human subjectivity, and commodity fetishism prevails in every sphere of life.

The rationalism of enlightenment, while enhancing man's power over nature, also increased the power of some human beings over others, and by this token it has outlived its usefulness. The root of the evil was the division of labour and, along with it, the alienation of man from nature; domination became the one purpose of thought, and thought itself was thereby destroyed. Socialism adopted the bourgeois style of thinking, which regarded nature as completely alien and thus made it totalitarian. In this way enlightenment embarked on a suicidal course, and the only hope of salvation seems to consist in theory: 'true revolutionary practice (*umwälzende Praxis*) depends on the intransigence of theory in the face of the insensibility (*Bewusstlosigkeit*) with which society allows thought to ossify' (p. 41).

According to the *Dialectic of Enlightenment* the legend of Odysseus is a prototype or symbol of the isolation of the individual precisely because he is fully socialized. The hero escapes from the Cyclops by calling himself 'Noman': to preserve his existence, he destroys it. As the authors put it, 'This linguistic adaptation to death contains the schema of modern mathematics' (p. 60). In general the legend shows that a civilization in which men seek to affirm themselves is only possible through self-denial and repression; thus, in enlightenment, the dialectic takes on a Freudian aspect.

The perfect epitome of eighteenth-century enlightenment was the marquis de Sade, who carried the ideology of domination to its utmost logical consequence. Enlightenment treats human beings as repeatable and replaceable (hence 'reified') elements of an abstract 'system', and this too is the meaning of de Sade's way of life. The totalitarian idea latent in enlightenment philosophy assimilates human characteristics to interchangeable commodities. Reason and feeling are reduced to an impersonal level; rationalist planning degenerates into totalitarian terror; morality is derided and despised as a manœuvre by the weak to protect themselves against the strong (an anticipation of Nietzsche); and all traditional virtues are declared inimical to reason and illusory, a view already implicit in Descartes's division of man into an extended and a thinking substance.

The destruction of reason, feeling, subjectivity, quality, and nature itself by the unholy combination of mathematics, logic, and exchange-value is especially seen in the degradation of culture, a crying example of which is the modern entertainment industry. A single system dominated by commercial values has taken over every aspect of mass culture. Everything serves to perpetuate the power of capital—even the fact that the workers have attained a fairly high standard of living and that people can find clean homes to live in. Mass-produced culture kills creativity; it is not justified by the demand for it, since that demand is itself part of the system. In Germany at one time the state at least protected the higher forms of culture against the operation of the market, but this is now over and artists are the slaves of their customers. Novelty is anathema; both the output and the enjoyment of art are planned in advance, as they must be if art is to survive market competition. In this way art itself, contrary to its primal function, helps to destroy individuality and turn human beings into stereotypes. The authors lament that art has become so cheap and accessible, for this inevitably means its degradation.

In general their concept of 'enlightenment' is a fanciful, unhistorical hybrid composed of everything they dislike: positivism, logic, deductive and empirical science, capitalism, the money power, mass culture, liberalism, and Fascism. Their critique of culture—apart from some true observations, which have since become commonplace, on the harmfulness of commercialized art—is imbued with nostalgia for the days when the enjoyment of culture was reserved to the élite: it is an attack on the 'age of the common man' in a spirit of feudal contempt for the masses. Mass society was attacked from various quarters even in the last century, by Tocqueville, Renan, Burckhardt, and Nietzsche among others; what is new in Horkheimer and Adorno is that they combine this attack with an onslaught on positivism and science, and that, following Marx, they discern the root of the evil in the division of labour, 'reification', and the domination of exchange-value. They go much further than Marx, however: the original sin of enlightenment, according to them, was to cut man off from nature and treat the latter as a mere object of exploitation, with the result that man was assimilated to the natural order and was exploited likewise. This process found its ideological reflection in science, which is not interested in qualities but only in what can be expressed quantitatively and made to serve technical purposes.

The attack, it can be seen, is essentially in line with the romantic tradition. But the authors do not offer any way out of the state of decadence: they do not say how man can become friends with nature again, or how to get rid of exchange-value and live without money or calculation. The only remedy they have to offer is theoretical reasoning, and we may suspect that its chief merit in their eyes is to be free from the despotism of logic and mathematics (logic, they tell us, signifies contempt for the individual).

It is noteworthy that whereas socialists formerly denounced capitalism for producing poverty, the main grievance of the Frankfurt school is that it engenders abundance and satisfies a multiplicity of needs, and is thus injurious to the higher forms of culture.

The *Dialectic of Enlightenment* contains all the elements of Marcuse's later attack on modern philosophy, which allegedly favours totalitarianism by maintaining a positivist 'neutralism' in regard to the world of values and by insisting that human knowledge should be controlled by 'facts'. This strange paralogism, equating the observance of empirical and logical rules with fidelity to the *status quo* and rejection of all change, recurs again and again in the writings of the Frankfurt school. If the supposed link between positivism and social conservatism or totalitarianism (the authors treat these as one and the same!) is studied in the light of history, the evidence is all the other way: positivist, from Hume onwards, were wedded to the liberal tradition. Clearly, there is no logical connection either. If the fact that scientific observation is 'neutral' towards its object and abstains from evaluation implies that it favours the *status quo*, we should have to maintain that physio-pathological observation implies approval of disease and a belief that it should not be combated. Admittedly, there is an essential difference between medicine and social science (though the remarks of the Frankfurt philosophers in this context purport to apply to all human knowledge). In the social sciences, observation itself is part of the subject-matter, if that is taken to include the entire social picture. But it does not follow that a scientist who abstains as far as he can from value-judgements is an agent of social stability or conformism; he may or may not be, but nothing can be inferred in this respect from the fact that his observation is 'external' and uncommitted. If, on the other hand, the observer is 'committed' not only in the sense of having some practical interest in view but also in regarding his cognitive activity as part of a certain social practice, he is more or less obliged to regard as true whatever seems conducive to the particular interest with which he identifies, i.e. apply genetic, pragmatic criteria of truth. If this principle were adopted, science as we know it would disappear and be replaced by political propaganda. Undoubtedly, various political interests and preferences are reflected in various ways in social science; but a rule which sought to generalize such influences instead of minimizing them would turn science into a tool of politics, as has happened with social science in totalitarian states. Theoretical observation and discussion would completely forfeit their autonomy, which is the reverse of what the Frankfurt writers would wish, as they indicate elsewhere.

It is also true that scientific observation does not of itself produce aims; this is the case even if some value-judgements are implicit in the rules prescribing the conditions under which certain statements or hypotheses become part of science. The canons of scientific procedures are not, of course, infringed by the fact that the investigator wants to discover something that will serve practical ends, or that his interest is inspired by some practical concern. But they are infringed if, on the pretext of 'overcoming' the dichotomy of facts and values (and the Frankfurt writers, like many other Marxists, are constantly boasting of having done this), the truth of science is subordinated to the criteria of any interest whatsoever; this simply means that anything is right which suits the interests with which the scientist identifies himself.

The rules of empirical observation have evolved for centuries in the European mind, from the late Middle Ages onwards. That their development was somehow connected with the spread of a market economy is possible, though certainly not proved; on this as on most other subjects, the proponents of 'critical theory' offer only bare assertions, devoid of historical analysis. If there actually is a historical link, it still by no means follows that these rules are an instrument of 'commodity fetishism' and a mainstay of capitalism; any such assumption is in fact pure nonsense. The writers we are discussing seem to believe that there is, at any rate potentially, some alternative science which would satisfy the demands of human nature, but they cannot tell us anything about it. Their 'critical theory' is in fact not so much a theory as a general statement that theory is of great importance, which few would deny, and a plea for a critical attitude towards existing society, which we are invited to 'transcend' in thought. This injunction, however, makes no sense as long as they cannot tell us in what direction the existing order is to be transcended. From this point of view, as we have already noted, orthodox Marxism is more specific, as it does at least claim that once the means of production are publicly owned and the Communist party installed in power, only a few minor technical problems will stand in the way of universal freedom and happiness. These assurances are completely refuted by experience, but at least we know what they mean.

The *Dialectic of Enlightenment* and other works of the Frankfurt school contain many sound remarks on the commercialization of art in industrial society and the inferiority of cultural products dependent on the market. But the authors are on very doubtful ground when they say that this has led to the degradation of art as a whole and of the artistic enjoyment open to people in general. If this were so it would mean that, for instance, country folk in the eighteenth century enjoyed some higher forms of culture, but that capitalism gradually deprived them of these and substituted crude, mass-produced objects and entertainments. It is not obvious, however, that eighteenth-century rustics enjoyed higher artistic values, in the form of church ceremonies, popular sports and dances, than television offers to present-day workers. So-called 'higher' culture has not disappeared, but has become incomparably more accessible than ever before, and is undoubtedly enjoyed by more people: while it is highly unconvincing to argue that its dramatic formal changes in the twentieth century are all explicable by the domination of exchange-value.

Adorno, who refers to the degradation of art in many of his writings, seems to think that the present situation is hopeless, i.e. that there is no source of strength which would enable art to revive and perform its proper function. On the one hand, there is 'affirmative' art, which accepts the present situation and pretends to find harmony where there is only chaos (for example, Stravinsky); on the other, there are attempts at resistance, but, as they have no roots in the real world, even geniuses (for example, Schönberg) are forced into escapism, shutting themselves up in self-sufficient realms of their own artistic material. The *avant-garde* movement is a negation, but for the present at least it can be nothing more; as far as it goes it is true for our time, unlike mass culture and bogus 'affirmative' art, but it is a feeble and depressing truth, expressive of cultural bankruptcy. The last word of Adorno's theory of culture is apparently that we must protest, but that protest will be unavailing. We cannot recapture the values of the past, those of the present are debased and barbarous, and the future offers none; all that is left to us is a gesture of total negation, deprived of content by its very totality.

If the foregoing is a true account of Adorno's work, not only can we not regard it as a continuation of Marx's thought, but it is diametrically opposed to the latter by reason of its pessimism: failing a positive Utopia, its final response to the human condition can only be an inarticulate cry.

6. Erich Fromm

Erich Fromm (b. 1900), who has lived in the U.S.A. since 1932, began as an orthodox Freudian but is primarily known as a co-founder of the 'culturalist' school of psychoanalysis, together with Karen Horney and Harry Sullivan. This school departed so radically from the Freudian tradition (except for sharing the same general field of interest) as to leave little of the original bases of psychoanalytical anthropology, the theory of culture, and even the theory of neuroses. Fromm may be regarded as a cousin of the Frankfurt school, not only because he belonged to the Institut für Sozialforschung and published articles in the *Journal*, but also in view of the content of his work. He shared the conviction of his Frankfurt colleagues that the Marxian analyses of reification and alienation were still valid and were vital to the solution of the basic problems of modern civilization. Like the others, he did not agree with Marx as to the liberating role of the proletariat; alienation, in which he was specially interested, was a phenomenon affecting all social classes. He did not, however, share Adorno's negativism and pessimism. Although he had no faith in historical determinism and did not expect the laws of history to bring about a better social order, he was convinced that human beings had an immense creative potential which could be brought into play to overcome their alienation from nature and one another and to establish an order based on brotherly love. Unlike Adorno, he believed it possible to define in broad lines the character of a social life in harmony with human nature. Again, unlike Adorno, whose books are full of pride and arrogance, Fromm's writings are imbued with goodwill and faith in the human capacity for friendship and co-operation; it was for this reason, perhaps, that he found Freudianism unacceptable. He may be called the Feuerbach of our time. His books are simple and readable; their didactic and moralistic intention is not concealed, but is expressed plainly and straightforwardly. Whatever their immediate subject—the theory of character, Zen Buddhism, Marx, or Freud—all are inspired by critical and constructive thought. Among the titles are *Escape from Freedom* (1941), *Man for Himself* (1947), *The Sane Society* (1955), *Zen Buddhism* and *Psychoanalysis* (with D. T. Suzuki and R. de Martino, 1960), and *Marx's Concept of Man* (1961).

Fromm believes that Freud's theory of the unconscious opened up an extremely fertile field of inquiry, but he rejects almost completely the theory of anthropology based on the libido and the purely repressive functions of culture. Freud held that the human individual can be defined by the instinctual energies that inevitably oppose him to others; the individual is antisocial by nature, but society exists to give him a measure of security in return for the limitation and repression of his instinctive desires. Unsatisfied desires are channelled into other, socially permitted areas and are sublimated into cultural activity; however, culture and social life continue to police the impulses that cannot be destroyed, and the cultural products that are created as a substitute for unfulfilled desires help to curb those impulses still further. Man's position in the world is hopeless inasmuch as the satisfaction of his natural cravings would mean the ruin of civilization and the destruction of the human race. The conflict between the demands of instinct and the communal life which is necessary to human beings can never be resolved, nor can the complex of causes which incessantly drive them into neurotic solutions. Sublimation in the form of creative activity is only a substitute, and moreover it is only available to the few.

To this Fromm replies that Freud's doctrine is an illegitimate universalization of a particular limited historical experience, and, moreover, is based on a false theory of human nature. It is not the case that an individual can be defined by the sum of his instinctive desires, directed exclusively towards his own satisfaction and consequently hostile to others. Freud talks as if, by giving something of himself to others, a man parts with a piece of wealth that he might have kept; but love and friendship are an enrichment and not a sacrifice. Freud's view is a reflection of particular social conditions causing the interests of individuals to conflict with one another; but this is a historical phase, not a necessary effect of human nature. Egoism and egocentricity are not protective but destructive of the individual's interests, and they spring from self-hatred rather than self-love.

Fromm concedes that man is equipped with certain permanent instincts, and that in this sense one can speak of unchanging human nature. He even holds that the contrary view, that there are no anthropological constants, is a dangerous one, as it suggests that human beings are infinitely malleable and can adapt to any conditions, so that slavery, if properly organized, could last for ever. The fact that people do rebel against existing conditions shows that they are not infinitely adaptable, and this is a ground for optimism. But the main thing is to ascertain which human traits are really constant and which are a matter of history; and here Freud went badly wrong, mistaking the effects of capitalist civilization for unalterable characteristics of the human race.

In general, Fromm continues, human needs are not confined to individual satisfaction. People need links with nature and with one another—not just any links, but such as to give them a sense of purpose and belonging to a community; they need love and understanding, and they suffer when isolated and deprived of contact. A human being also needs conditions in which he can make full use of his abilities: he is not born simply to cope with conditions and dangers, but to engage in creative work.

For this reason the development of the human species, or the self-creation of man, has been a history of conflicting tendencies. Ever since man freed himself from the natural order and thus became truly human, the need for security and the creative urge have often been opposed to each other. We want freedom, but we are also afraid of it, for freedom signifies responsibility and the absence of security. Consequently, men take refuge from the burden of freedom in submission to authority and in closed systems; this is an inborn tendency, though a destructive one, a false escape from isolation into self-renunciation. Another form of escape is hatred, in which man tries to overcome his isolation by blind destruction.

On the basis of these views, Fromm distinguishes psychological types or orientations which differ from Freud's in that they are explained in terms of social conditions and family relationships and not merely by the distribution of the libido; moreover, unlike Freud, he expressly labels them good or bad. Characters are formed from infancy by the child's surroundings and the system of punishments and rewards that it encounters. The 'receptive' type is characterized by compliance, optimism, and passive benevolence; people of this kind are adaptable but lack creative power. The 'exploitative' type, on the contrary, is aggressive, envious, and inclined to treat others purely as a source of profit to itself. The 'hoarding' type expresses itself less in active aggression and more in hostile suspicion; it is stingy, self-centred, and inclined to sterile fastidiousness. Another unproductive type is the 'marketing' orientation, which derives satisfaction from adapting itself to prevailing fashions and customs. Creative characters, on the other hand, are neither aggressive nor conformist, but seek contact with others in a spirit of kindness combined with initiative and a measure of non-conformity. This is the best combination of all, as their non-conformity does not degenerate into aggression, while their desire for co-operation and capacity for love does not sink into passive adaptation. These various characters correspond to the typology previously worked out by Freudians, especially Abraham, but Fromm's explanation of their origin emphasizes not the infant's successive sexual fixations but the part played by the family circle and the values current in society.

Capitalist society as developed in Europe in the last few hundred years has liberated huge creative possibilities in human beings, but also powerful destructive elements. Men have become aware of their individual dignity and responsibility, but have found themselves in a situation dominated by universal competition and conflict of interests. Personal initiative has become a decisive factor in life, but increased importance also attaches to aggression and exploitation. The sum total of loneliness and isolation has grown beyond measure, while social conditions cause people to treat one another as things and not as persons. One of the delusive and dangerous remedies against isolation is to seek protection in irrational authoritarian systems such as Fascism.

In Fromm's view his radical revision of Freudianism has a Marxist complexion, both because it explains human relationships in terms of history and not of defence mechanisms and instinctual energy, and because it is based on value-judgements in harmony with Marx's thought. Fromm regards the Manuscripts of 1844 as the fundamental exposition of Marx's doctrine; he insists that there is no essential change between that work and *Capital* (on which point he joins issue with Daniel Bell), but he considers that the *élan* of the early texts is somewhat lost in the later works. The central issue, he contends, is that of alienation, representing the sum of human bondage, isolation, unhappiness, and misfortune. Totalitarian doctrines and Communist regimes have in his view nothing in common with Marx's humanistic vision, the chief values of which are voluntary solidarity, the expansion of man's creative powers, freedom from constraint and from irrational authority.

Marx's ideas are a revolt against conditions in which men and women lose their humanity and are turned into commodities, but also an optimistic profession of faith in their ability to become human once again, to achieve not only freedom from poverty but freedom to develop their creative powers as well. It is absurd to interpret Marx's historical materialism to signify that people are always actuated by material interests. On the contrary, Marx believed that they forfeited their true nature when circumstances compelled them to care for nothing but such interests. To Marx, the main problem was how to free the individual from the shackles of dependence and enable human beings to live together in amity once more. Marx did not hold that man must be eternally the plaything of irrational forces beyond his control; on the contrary, he maintained that man could be the master of his fate. If, in practice, the alienated products of human labour turned into anti-human forces, if people were enthralled by false consciousness and false needs and if (as both Freud and Marx held) they did not understand their own true motives, all this was not because nature had so ruled forever. On the contrary, a society dominated by competition, isolation, exploitation, and enmity was a contradiction of human nature, which—as Marx believed no less than Hegel or Goethe—found its true satisfaction in creative work and fellowship, not in aggression or passive adaptation. Marx wanted men to return to unity with nature and among themselves, thus bridging the gulf between subject and object; Fromm, who especially stresses this motif from the 1844 Manuscripts, observes that Marx is in agreement here with the whole tradition of German humanism and also with Zen Buddhism. Of course Marx wanted to see an end to poverty, but he did not want consumption to increase indefinitely. He was concerned with human dignity and freedom; his socialism was not a matter of satisfying material needs but of creating conditions in which men could realize their own personalities and be reconciled with nature and one another. Marx's themes were the alienation of labour, the loss of meaning in the labour process, the transformation of human beings into commodities; the basic evil of capitalism, in his view, was not the unjust distribution of goods but the degradation of mankind, the destruction of the 'essence' of humanity. This degradation affected everyone, not only the workers, and accordingly Marx's message of emancipation was universal and did not only apply to the proletariat. Marx believed that human beings could understand their own nature rationally and, by so doing, free themselves from false needs that conflicted with it; this they could do for themselves, within the historical process, without any help from extra-historical sources. In maintaining this, Fromm believes, Marx was in line not only with utopian thinkers of the Renaissance and Enlightenment but also with chiliastic sects, the Hebrew prophets, and even Thomism.

In Fromm's view the whole question of human liberation is summed up in the word 'love', which implies treating others as an end and not a means; it also signifies that the individual does not give up his own creativity or lose himself in the other's personality. Aggressivity and passivity are two sides of the same phenomenon of degradation, and must both be replaced by a system of relations based on fellow-feeling without conformism and creativity without aggression.

As this summary indicates, Fromm's endorsement of Marx rests on a true interpretation of his humanistic outlook, but is nevertheless highly selective. Fromm does not consider the positive functions of alienation or the role of evil in history; to him as to Feuerbach, alienation is simply bad. Moreover, Fromm adopted from Marx only the ultimate idea of the 'whole human being', the Utopia of reunion with nature and perfect solidarity among mankind, helped and not hindered by individual creativity. He endorses this Utopia, but ignores all that part of Marx's doctrine which tells us how to bring it about—his theory of the state, the proletariat, and revolution. In so doing he has chosen the most acceptable and least controversial aspects of Marxism: for anyone would agree that people should live on good terms and not cut one another's throats, and that it is better to be free and creative than stifled and oppressed. In short, Fromm's Marxism is little more than a series of trite aspirations. Nor is it clear from his analysis how men came to be dominated by evil and alienation, or what ground there is for hoping that healthy tendencies will in the end prevail over destructive ones. Fromm's ambiguity is typical of utopian thought in general. On the one hand, he professes to derive his ideal from human nature as it actually is, although it is not at present realized—in other words, it is man's true destiny to develop his personality while living in harmony with others; but, on the other hand, he is aware that 'human nature' is also a normative concept. Clearly, the concept of alienation (or the de-humanization of man) and also the distinction between false and true needs must, if they are to be more than mere arbitrary norms, be based on some theory of human nature as we know it from experience, albeit in an 'undeveloped' state. But Fromm does not explain how we know that human nature requires, for instance, more solidarity and less aggression. It is true that people are in fact capable of solidarity, love, friendship, and self-sacrifice, but it does not follow that those who display these qualities are more 'human' than their opposites. Fromm's account of human nature thus presents an ambiguous mixture of descriptive and normative ideas, which is likewise characteristic of Marx and many of his followers.

Fromm did much to popularize the idea of Marx as a humanist, and was undoubtedly right to combat the crude and primitive interpretation of Marxism as a 'materialistic' theory of human motives and short cut to despotism. But he did not discuss the relationship between Marxism and modern Communism, saying merely that Communist totalitarianism was contrary to the ideals of the 1844 Manuscripts. His picture of Marx is thus almost as one-sided and simplistic as the one he criticizes, which presents Marxism as a blueprint for Stalinism. As for the pre-established harmony between Marxism and Zen Buddhism, it is based on a few sentences in the Manuscripts about a return to union with nature. These are no doubt consonant with the young Marx's apocalyptic idea of a total and absolute reconciliation of everything with everything else, but it is an exaggeration to regard them as part of the hard core of Marxist doctrine. Fromm in fact retains only that part of Marx's doctrine which he held in common with Rousseau.

7. Critical theory (continued). Jürgen Habermas

Habermas (b. 1929) ranks as one of the chief living German philosophers. The titles of his principal books—*Theorie und Praxis* (1963), *Erkenntnis und Interesse* (1968), *Technik und Wissenschaft als 'Ideologie'* (1970)—indicate his main philosophical interests. His work comprises an anti-positivist analysis of all kinds of links between theoretical reasoning—not only in the historical and social sciences, but also in natural history—and the practical needs, interests, and behaviour of human beings. It is not, however, a sociology of knowledge, but rather a epistemo-logical critique designed to show that no theory can be properly based on the criteria propounded by the positivist and analytical schools, that positivism always contains assumptions dictated by non-theoretical interests, but that it is possible to find a viewpoint from which practical interest and the theoretical approach coincide. These are topics that certainly fall within the sphere of interest of the Frankfurt school; but Habermas displays more analytical precision than his mentors of the previous generation.

Habermas takes up Horkheimer's and Adorno's theme of the 'dialectic of the Enlightenment'— the process whereby Reason, striving to emancipate mankind from prejudice, by its own inner logic turns against itself and serves to maintain prejudice and authority. In the classic period of the Enlightenment, represented by Holbach, Reason saw itself as a weapon in the social and intellectual battle against the existing order, and it upheld the essential virtue of boldness in attack. Evil and falsity were one and the same in its eyes, and so were liberation and truth. It did not seek to dispense with evaluation, but declared openly the values by which it was guided. Fichte's Reason, which based itself on the Kantian critique and therefore could not invoke the oracle of empiricism, was nevertheless also conscious of its own practical character. The acts of understanding and of constituting the world coincided in it, as did Reason and Will; the practical interest of the self-liberating ego was no longer separate from the theoretical activity of Reason. For Marx too, Reason was a critical power, but, in contrast to Fichte's view, its strength was not rooted in moral consciousness but in the fact that its emancipating activity coincided with the process of social emancipation; the critique of false consciousness was at the same time a practical act of abolishing the social conditions to which false consciousness was due. Thus the Enlightenment in Marx's version expressly maintained the link between Reason and interest. However, with the progress of science, technology, and organization that link was broken; Reason gradually lost its emancipating function, while rationality was more and more restricted to technical efficiency, no longer proposing aims but merely organizing means. Reason took on an instrumental character, abandoning its meaning-generating function to serve the ends of material or social technology; the Enlightenment turned against itself. The delusion that Reason was independent of human interests was sanctioned as the epistemology of positivism, as a scientific programme free from value-judgements and thus incapable of performing emancipative functions.

Habermas, however, like the rest of the Frankfurt school, is not concerned with the 'primacy of practice' in Lukács's sense or in that of pragmatism. He is concerned with a return to the idea of praxis as distinct from technique, i.e. restoring the concept of Reason aware of its practical functions, not subject to any aims imposed 'from outside' but somehow comprising social aims by virtue of its own rationality. He therefore seeks an intellectual faculty which can synthesize practical and theoretical reason, as it is capable of identifying the sense of objects and thus neither can nor will be neutral as regards aims.

The essence of Habermas's critique, however, lies in his contention that such neutrality has not been, and never could be, actually attained, and that positivist programmes and the idea of theory liberated from value are therefore an illusion of the Enlightenment in its stage of self-destruction. Husserl rightly argued that the so-called facts or objects posited by natural science as ready-made reality, unconstructed things-in-themselves, are in fact organized in a primal, spontaneously created *Lebenswelt*, and that every science takes over from pre-reflective reason a repertoire of forms dictated by various practical human interests. He was wrong, however, in supposing that his own idea of a theory purged of these practical residua might later be used for practical ends; for phenomenology cannot propose any cosmology, any idea of universal order, and such an idea is indispensable if theory is to have a practical purpose. The natural sciences, Habermas goes on, are constituted on the basis of technical interest. They are not neutral in the sense that their content is uninfluenced by practical considerations; the material they are prepared to admit to their store is not a reflection of facts as they exist in the world, but an expression of the effectiveness of practical technical operations. The historico-hermeneutic sciences are also in part determined by practical interests, though in another way: in their case the 'interest' consists in preserving and enlarging the possible area of understanding among human beings, so as to improve communication. Theoretical activity cannot escape from practical interest: the subject–object relationship must itself involve some degree of interest, and no part of human knowledge is intelligible except in relation to the history of the human race, in which these practical interests are crystallized; all cognitive criteria owe their validity to the interest by which cognition is governed. Interest operates in three spheres or 'media'—work, language, and authority—and to these types of interest correspond respectively the natural, the historico-hermeneutic, and the social sciences. In self-reflection, however, or 'reflection on reflection', interest and cognition coincide, and it is in this realm that 'emancipative reason' takes shape. If we cannot discover the point at which reason and will, or the determination of ends and the analysis of means, coincide, we are condemned to a situation in which, on the one hand, we have an apparently neutral science and, on the other, fundamentally irrational decisions as to ends: the latter cannot then be rationally criticized, each is as good as any other.

Habermas does not go so far as Marcuse in criticizing science: he does not claim that the very content of modern science, as opposed to its technical application, serves anti-human ends, or that modern technology is inherently destructive and cannot be used for the good of humanity, but must be replaced by technology of a different kind. To say this would only make sense if we could propose alternatives to existing science and technology, which Marcuse is unable to do. All the same, science and technology are not wholly innocent in respect of their applications, when these take the form of weapons of mass destruction and the organization of tyranny. The point is that modern productive forces and science have become elements of the political legitimation of modern industrial societies. 'Traditional societies' based on the legality of their institutions on mythical, religious, or metaphysical interpretations of the world. Capitalism, by setting in motion the self-propelling mechanism of the development of productive forces, has institutionalized the phenomenon of change and novelty, overthrown the traditional principles of the legitimation of authority, and replaced them by norms corresponding to those of equivalent commercial exchange—the rule of mutuality as the basis of social organization. In this way property relations have lost their directly political significance and become production relations governed by the laws of the market. The natural sciences began to define their scope in terms of technical application. At the same time, as capitalism evolved, state intervention in the field of production and exchange became more and more important, with the result that politics ceased to be only part of the 'superstructure'. The political activity of the state—represented as a purely technical means of improving the organization of public life—tended to merge with science and technology, which were supposed to serve the same purpose; the dividing line between productive forces and the legitimation of power became obscured, in contrast to the capitalism of Marx's day when productive and political functions were clearly separate. Thus Marx's theory of the base and superstructure began to be out of date, as did his theory of value (having regard to the enormous importance of science as a productive force). Science and technology took on 'ideological' functions in the sense that they produced an image of society based on a technical model, and technocratic ideologies which deprive people of political consciousness (i.e. awareness of social aims), by implying that all human problems are of a technical and organizational character and can be solved by scientific means. The technocratic mentality makes it easier to manipulate people without violence and is a further step towards 'reification', blurring the distinction between technical activity, which in itself has nothing to say about aims, and specifically human relationships. In a situation where state institutions have a powerful influence on the economy, social conflicts too have changed their character and bear less and less resemblance to class antagonism as Marx understood it. The new ideology is no longer merely an ideology but is merged with the very process of technical progress; it is harder to identify, with the result that ideology and real social conditions can no longer be contrasted as they were by Marx.

The increase of productive forces does not itself have an emancipating effect; on the contrary, in its 'ideologized' form it tends to make people apprehend themselves as things, and to obliterate the distinction between technology and praxis—the latter term signifying the spontaneous activity in which the acting subject determines his own goals.

The purpose of Marx's critique was that people should become truly subjects, i.e. that they should rationally and consciously control the processes of their own lives. But the critique was ambiguous inasmuch as the self-regulation of social life could be understood as either a practical or a technical problem, and in the latter case it could be thought of as a manipulative process similar to the technical handling of inanimate objects—which is what happens under both capitalist planning and bureaucratic socialism. In this way reification is not cured but aggravated. True emancipation, on the other hand, is the return to 'praxis' as a category involving the active participation of everyone in the control of social phenomena; in other words, people must be subjects and not objects. For this purpose, as Habermas observes, there must be an improvement of human communication, free discussion of existing power systems, and a fight against the de-politicization of life.

The critique of Marx in *Knowledge and Interest* goes perhaps even further. Habermas says there that Marx finally reduced the self-creation of the human species to the process of productive work, and in so doing prevented himself from fully understanding his own critical activity: for reflection itself appears in his theory as an element of scientific work in the same sense in which it is related to natural science, that is to say it is modelled on patterns of material production. Thus critique as a praxis, as subjective activity based on self-reflection, did not fully take shape in Marx's work as a separate form of social activity. In the same book Habermas criticizes scientism, Mach, Peirce, and Dilthey, and argues that the forms of methodological self-knowledge of the natural or historical sciences also reflect an understanding of their cognitive status and of the interest behind them. He points out, however, the 'emancipative' potential of psychoanalysis, which in his opinion makes it possible to attain a viewpoint in which the operation of reason and the interest and emancipation coincide in self-reflection, or, to put it otherwise, the cognitive and the practical interest become identical. Marx's schema cannot provide a ground for such unity, as he reduced the specific characteristic of the human species to the capacity for instrumental (as distinct from purely adaptive) action, which meant that he could not interpret the relations between ideology and authority in terms of distorted communication, but reduced them to relations stemming from human labour and the battle with nature. (Habermas's thought is not quite clear on this point, but he apparently has in mind that in psychoanalysis, auscultation is also therapy—the patient's understanding of his own situation is at the same time a cure for it. This is not correct, however, if it suggests that the act of understanding is the whole cure, for according to Freud the essence of the therapeutic process consists in transference, which is an existential and not an intellectual act.) In Marx's theory the coincidence does not take place: the interests of reason and emancipation do not combine to form a single practico-intellectual faculty. If this is

Habermas's argument, his interpretation of Marx is at variance with Lukács's judgement (which I believe to be correct) that the essential feature of Marxism consists in the doctrine that the act of understanding the world and the act of transforming it achieve identity in the privileged situation of the proletariat.

Habermas does not clearly define his key concept of 'emancipation'. It is evident that, in the spirit of the whole tradition of German idealism, he is seeking for a focal point at which practical and theoretical reason, cognition and will, knowledge of the world and the movement to change it, all become identical. But it does not appear that he has actually found such a point or shown us how to arrive at it. He is right in saying that the criteria of epistemological evaluation must be understood as an element in the history of the human species, in which the processes of technical progress and the forms of communication both appear as independent variables; that none of the rules by which we determine what is cognitively valid is grounded transcendentally (in Husserl's sense); and that positivist criteria of the validity of knowledge are based on evaluation related to human technical abilities. But it does not follow that there is or can be a vantage-point from which the distinction between knowledge and will can be seen as eliminated. It may be that, in some cases, acts of self-understanding by individuals or societies are themselves part of the practical behaviour leading to 'emancipation', whatever this term means. But the question will always remain: by what criteria are we to judge the accuracy of that self-understanding, and on what principle do we decide that 'emancipation' consists in one state of affairs rather than another? On the second point we cannot avoid making a decision that goes beyond our knowledge of the world. If we believe that we can become endowed with some higher spiritual power which distinguishes between good and bad and, in the same act, determines what is true and what is false, we are not effecting any synthesis but are simply replacing the criteria of truth by criteria of an arbitrarily established good: i.e. we are returning to individual or collective pragmatism. 'Emancipation' in the sense of a union between analytical and practical reason is, as we have seen, only possible in instances of religious illumination, where knowledge and the existential act of 'commitment' do indeed become one. But there is nothing more dangerous to civilization than to suppose that the operation of reason can be wholly founded on such acts. It is indeed true that analytical reason, or the whole body of rules by which science functions, cannot provide its own basis; the rules are accepted because they are instrumentally effective, and if there are any transcendental norms of rationality they are not known to us. Science can function without concerning itself with the existence of such norms, for science is not to be confused with scientistic philosophy. Decisions as to good and evil and the meaning of the universe cannot have any scientific foundation; we are bound to make such decisions, but we cannot turn them into acts of intellectual understanding. The idea of a higher reason synthesizing these two aspects of life can only be realized in the realm of myth, or remain a pious aspiration of German metaphysics.

Another member of the younger generation of the Frankfurt school is Alfred Schmidt, whose book on Marx's concept of nature (1964) is an interesting and valuable contribution to the study of this complicated question. Schmidt argues that Marx's concept contains ambiguities thanks to which it has been interpreted in conflicting ways (nature as a continuation of man, the return to unity, etc.; contrariwise, man as a creation of nature, defined by his attempts to cope with its alien forces). Schmidt contends that Marx's doctrine cannot in the last resort be interpreted as an unequivocally monistic 'system', but that Engels's materialism was in line with an essential aspect of Marx's thought.

Iring Fetscher, undoubtedly one of the most eminent historians of Marxism, can only be regarded as a member of the Frankfurt school in the very broad sense that his works show him to be receptive to those aspects of Marxism in which the writers of the school are interested. His great achievement is to have expounded lucidly the different versions and possible interpretations of the Marxian inheritance, but his own philosophical position does not appear to be based on the typical ideas of the Frankfurt school such as the negative dialectic and emancipating reason. Apart from their welcome clarity, his works are characterized by the restraint and open-mindedness of the historian.

8. Conclusion

When we consider the place of the Frankfurt school in the evolution of Marxism, we find that its strong point was philosophical anti-dogmatism and the defence of the autonomy of theoretical reasoning. It freed itself from the mythology of the infallible proletariat and the belief that Marx's categories were adequate to the situation and problems of the modern world. It also endeavoured to reject all elements or varieties of Marxism that postulated an absolute, primary basis of knowledge and practice. It contributed to the analysis of 'mass culture' as a phenomenon that cannot be interpreted in class categories as Marx understood them. It also contributed to the critique of scientistic philosophy, by drawing attention (though in fairly general and unmethodical terms) to the latent normative assumptions of scientistic programmes.

The Frankfurt philosophers were on weak ground, on the other hand, in their constant proclamation of an ideal 'emancipation' which was never properly explained. This created the illusion that while condemning 'reification', exchange-value, commercialized culture, and scientism they were offering something else instead, whereas the most they were actually offering was nostalgia for the pre-capitalist culture of an élite. By harping on the vague prospect of a universal escape from present-day civilization, they unwittingly encouraged an attitude of mindless and destructive protest.

In short, the strength of the Frankfurt school consisted in pure negation, and its dangerous ambiguity lay in the fact that it would not openly admit this fact, but frequently suggested the opposite. It was not so much a continuation of Marxism in any direction, as an example of its dissolution and paralysis.

CHAPTER XI

Herbert Marcuse: Marxism as a totalitarian Utopia of the New Left

MARCUSE did not become a well-known figure outside academic circles until the late 1960s, when he was acclaimed as an ideological leader by rebellious student movements in the U.S.A., Germany, and France. There is no reason to suppose that he sought the spiritual leadership of the 'student revolution', but when the role devolved upon him he did not object. His Marxism, if that is the right name for it, is a curious ideological mixture. Originating in the interpretation of Hegel and Marx as prophets of a rationalist Utopia, it evolved into a popular ideology of 'global revolution' in which sexual liberation played a prominent part, and in which the working class was rudely displaced from the centre of attention to make way for students, racial minorities, and the lumpenproletariat. In the seventies Marcuse's importance has faded considerably, but his philosophy is still worth discussing, less on account of its intrinsic merits than because it coincided with an important, though perhaps ephemeral, tendency in the ideological changes of our time. It also serves to illustrate the amazing variety of uses that can be made of Marxist doctrine.

As far as his interpretation of Marxism goes, Marcuse is generally considered as a member of the Frankfurt school, to which he is linked by his negative dialectic and faith in the transcendental norms of rationality. Born in Berlin in 1898, he belonged in 1917–18 to the Social Democratic party, but left it, as he afterwards wrote, following the murder of Liebknecht and Rosa Luxemburg; since then he has not belonged to any political party. He studied at Berlin and Freiburg im Breisgau, where he took his doctor's degree (under Heidegger's supervision) with a dissertation on Hegel. His *Hegels Ontologie und Grundzüge einer Theorie der Geschichtlichkeit* was published in 1931. Before emigrating from Germany he also wrote a number of articles clearly indicating the future course of his thought; he was one of the first to draw attention to the importance of Marx's Paris Manuscripts, immediately after their publication. He emigrated after Hitler's accession to power, spent a year in Switzerland, and then moved permanently to the United States. He worked until 1940 in the Institute for Social Research set up by German *émigrés* in New York, and during the war served in the Office of Strategic Services—a fact which, when it became known in later years, helped to destroy his popularity with the student movement. He taught in various American universities (Columbia, Harvard, Brandeis, and from 1965 San Diego), and retired in 1970. In 1941 he published *Reason and Revolution*, an interpretation of Hegel and Marx with particular reference to the critique of positivism. *Eros and Civilization* (1955) was an attempt to erect a new Utopia on the basis of Freud's theory of civilization, and also to refute psychoanalysis 'from within'. *Soviet Marxism* appeared in 1958, and in 1964 he published perhaps the most widely read of his books, a general critique of technological civilization entitled *One-Dimensional Man*. Some minor writings also attracted much attention, especially 'Repressive Tolerance' in 1965 and a series of essays dating from the fifties and sixties and published in 1970 under the title *Five Lectures: Psychoanalysis, Politics and Utopia*.

1. Hegel and Marx versus positivism

Marcuse has a range of perennial targets comprising 'positivism' (defined in a highly personal way), technological civilization based on the cult of work and production (but not of consumption and luxury), American middle-class values, 'totalitarianism' (so defined as to make the United States a signal example of it), and all the values and institutions associated with liberal democracy and toleration. According to Marcuse, all these objects of attack constitute an integral whole, and he is at pains to demonstrate their fundamental unity.

Marcuse follows Lukács in attacking positivism for its 'worship of facts' (an expression not defined more closely), which prevents us from discerning the 'negativity' of history. But, unlike Lukács, whose Marxism concentrates on the dialectic between subject and object and the 'unity of theory and practice', Marcuse lays most stress on the negative, critical function of reason, providing standards whereby any given social reality can be judged. He agrees with Lukács in emphasizing the link between Marxism and the Hegelian tradition, but differs completely from him as to its nature: the essential basis of Hegelian and Marxian dialectic, according the Marcuse, is not the movement towards the identity of subject and object, but towards the realization of reason, which is at the same time the realization of freedom and happiness.

In his articles published in the 1930s Marcuse already took the view that reason is the fundamental category providing a link between philosophy and human destiny. This idea of reason developed on the basis of the conviction that reality is not 'directly' reasonable but can be reduced to rationality. German idealist philosophy made reason the supreme court of appeal, judging empirical reality by non-empirical criteria. Reason in this sense presupposes freedom, as its pronouncements would be meaningless if men were not completely free to judge the world they live in. Kant, however, transferred reality to the internal sphere, making it a moral imperative, while Hegel in his turn confined it within the bounds of necessity. But Hegel's freedom is only possible thanks to the operation of reason whereby man is aware of his real identity. Thus Hegel appears in the history of philosophy as a champion of the rights of reason revealing to human beings their own truth, i.e. the imperative demands of authentic humanity. The self-transforming operation of reason creates the dialectic of negativity which opens up new horizons at every stage of history, advancing beyond the empirically known possibilities of that stage. In this way Hegel's work is a summons to perpetual nonconformity and a vindication of revolution.

However—and this is one of the main contentions of *Reason and Revolution*—the demand that reason should rule the world is not a prerogative of idealism. German idealism rendered a service to civilization by combating British empiricism, which forbade men to go beyond 'facts' or appeal to *a priori* rational concepts, and which *consequently* supported conformism and social conservatism. But critical idealism regarded reason as located only in the thinking subject, and did not succeed in relating its demands to the sphere of material social conditions:

it was left to Marx to achieve this. Thanks to him, the postulate of the realization of reason became a postulate of the rationalization of social conditions in accordance with the 'true' concept or true essence of humanity. The realization of reason is at the same time the transcendence of philosophy, its critical function being thus fully discharged.

Positivism, which is not so much a denial of critico-dialectical philosophy as of philosophy altogether (for philosophy in the true sense has always been anti-positivist), is based on accepting the facts of experience and thus affirming the validity of every situation that actually occurs. In positivist terms it is impossible rationally to designate any objectives: these can only be the result of arbitrary decisions, with no foundation in reason. But philosophy, whose business it is to seek the truth, is not afraid of utopias, for truth is a Utopia as long as it cannot be realized in the existing social order. Critical philosophy must appeal to the future and therefore cannot base itself on facts but only on the demands of reason: it is concerned with what man can be and with his essential being, not his empirical state. Positivism, by contrast, sanctifies every compromise with the existing order and abdicates the right to judge social conditions.

The spirit of positivism is exemplified in sociology—not of any particular school, but sociology itself, as a branch of knowledge governed by Comtean rules. Sociology of this kind deliberately confines itself to noting and describing social phenomena, and if it does go so far as to investigate the laws of communal life, it refuses to go beyond such laws as it finds actually in operation. Hence sociology is an instrument of passive adaptation, whereas critical rationalism derives from reason itself the strength with which it demands that the world be subject to reason.

What is more, positivism is not only equivalent to conformism but is the ally of all totalitarian doctrines and social movements; its main principle is that of order, and it is ready at all times to sacrifice freedom to the order which authoritative systems provide.

It is clear that Marcuse's whole argument rests on the belief that we can know, independently of empirical data, the transcendental demands of rationality according to which the world must be judged; and also that we know what constitutes the essence of humanity, or that a 'true' human being would be like as opposed to an empirical one. Marcuse's philosophy can only be understood on the basis of the transcendality of reason, with the proviso that reason 'manifests itself' only in the historical process. This doctrine, however, is based on both historical and logical fallacies.

Marcuse's interpretation of Hegel is almost exactly the same as that of the Young Hegelians attacked by Marx. Hegel is presented simply as the advocate of supra-historical reason, evaluating facts by its own criteria. We have seen more than once how ambiguous Hegel's thought is in this respect; but it is a parody of his ideas to ignore the anti-utopian strain completely and reduce his doctrine to a belief in transcendental reason telling men how to achieve 'happiness'. In addition, it is more than misleading to depict Marx as a philosopher who transferred the categories of Hegelian logic into the realm of politics. Marcuse's argument ignores all the essential features of Marx's critique of Hegel and of the Hegelian Left. In his zeal to present Hegel as a champion of freedom against any kind of authoritarian regime, he makes no mention of Marx's criticism of Hegel's 'reversal of subject and predicate', whereby the values of individual life are made to depend on the requirements of universal reason. Yet this criticism, regardless of how far it was based on a true interpretation, was the point of departure for Marx's Utopia, and it is flouting history to ignore it for the sake of depicting a harmonious transition from Hegel to Marx. The picture is further distorted by the suppression of Marx's critique of the Young Hegelians and their Fichtean interpretation of Hegel. Marx's account of his own philosophical position was based first and foremost, on his emancipation from the Young Hegelian faith in the sovereignty of supra-historical reason—the very faith which Marcuse seeks to ascribe to Marx.

These distortions enable Marcuse to assert that modern totalitarian doctrines have nothing to do with the Hegelian tradition but are the embodiment of positivism. In what, however, does positivism consist? Marcuse is content with the label of 'fact-worship', and lists as its chief proponents Comte, Friedrich Stahl, Lorenz von Stein, and even Schelling. This, however, is a confusion of ideas for the sake of an arbitrary, unhistorical exposition. Schelling's 'positive philosophy' has nothing but the name in common with historical positivism.

Stahl and von Stein were in fact conservatives, and so was Comte in a sense. But Marcuse sets out to depict as 'positivists' all supporters of a given social order, and then to proclaim, in the teeth of obvious facts, that all empiricists, i.e. all who wished to subject theory to the test of facts, were automatically conservatives. Positivism in the historical sense—as opposed to the sense in which Schelling and Hume can scarcely be distinguished —embodies the principle, among others, that the cognitive value of knowledge depends on its empirical background: so that science cannot draw a line between the essential and the phenomenal, in the manner of Plato or Hegel, nor can it enable us to say that a given empirical state of things is inconsistent with a true concept of those things. Positivism, it is true, does not provide us with a method for determining the norm of a 'true' human being or a 'true' society. But empiricism by no means obliges us to conclude that existing 'facts' or social institutions must be supported simply because they exist: on the contrary, it expressly denies such a conclusion, regarding it as logically nonsensical on the same ground as that which forbids us to deduce normative judgements from descriptive ones.

Not only is Marcuse wrong in proclaiming a logical link between positivism and totalitarian politics, but his assertion of a historical link is directly contrary to the facts. The positivist outlook which developed and flourished in Britain from the late Middle Ages onwards, and without which we would not have modern science, democratic legislation, or the idea of the rights of man, was from the beginning inseparable linked with the idea of negative freedom and the values of democratic institutions. It was Locke and his successors, not Hegel, who founded and disseminated the doctrine of human equality, based on the principles of empiricism, and the value of individual freedom under the law. The twentieth-century positivists and empiricists, especially the analytical school and the so-called logical empiricists, not only had nothing to do with Fascist trends but, without exception, opposed them in no uncertain terms. Thus there is no logical or historical link whatever between positivism and totalitarian politics—unless, as some of Marcuse's remarks suggest, the word 'totalitarian' is to be understood in a sense as remote from the usual one as the word 'positivism'.

On the other hand, both logical and historical arguments

speak with much greater force in favour of a connection between Hegelianism and totalitarian ideas. It would, of course, be absurd to say that Hegel's doctrine leads to the commendation of modern totalitarian states, but it would be less absurd than to say the same thing of positivism. A deduction of this kind could be made from Hegelianism by stripping it of many important features, but from positivism no such deduction could be made at all: all that can be done is to assert without proof, as Marcuse does, that positivism means fact-worship, therefore it is conservative, therefore totalitarian. It is true that the Hegelian tradition played no essential part as a philosophic basis of non-Communist totalitarianism (Marcuse says nothing of the Communist variety in this context); but, when he comes to the instance of Giovanni Gentile, Marcuse simply declares that although Gentile used Hegel's name he actually had nothing in common with him, but was close to being a positivist. Here we have a confusion of the 'question of right' and the 'question of fact', as Marcuse seeks to rebut the possible objection that Hegelianism was, as a matter of fact, used as a justification of Fascism. It is no answer to this objection to say that it was used improperly.

In short, the whole of Marcuse's critique of positivism, and most of his interpretation of Hegel and Marx, are a farrago of arbitrary statements, both logical and historical. These statements, moreover, are integrally bound up with his positive views on the global liberation of mankind and his ideas on happiness, freedom, and revolution

2. *Critique of contemporary civilization*

Being in possession of transcendental norms, or the normative concept of 'humanity' as opposed to empirical human destiny, Marcuse examines the question why and in what respects our present civilization fails to correspond with this model. The basic determinant of the authentic concept of mankind is 'happiness', a notion which includes freedom and which Marcuse claims to find in Marx—although Marx does not actually use it and it is not clear how it can be deduced from his writings. In addition to the empirical fact that human beings seek 'happiness', we must begin by acknowledging that happiness is their due. To discover why they fail to assert this claim,

Marcuse takes as his starting-point Freud's philosophy of civilization. He accepts this to a large extent as far as the interpretation of past history is concerned, but calls it in question as regards the future; Freud, in fact, observed that there is no law which says that human beings are entitled to happiness or certain to obtain it. Freud's theory of instinct and the three levels of the psyche—the id, the ego, and super-ego—explains the conflict between the 'pleasure principle' and the 'reality principle' which has governed the whole development of civilization. In *Eros and Civilization* and in three lectures analysing and criticizing Freud's theory of history, Marcuse considers whether and how far that conflict is necessary. His arguments may be summarized as follows.

According to Freud there is an eternal, inevitable clash between civilized values and the demands of human instincts. All civilization has developed as a result of society's efforts to repress the instinctive desires of individuals. Eros, or the life-instinct, was not originally limited to sexuality in the reproductive sense: sexuality was a universal characteristic of the human organism as a whole. But, in order to engage in productive work, which in itself gives no pleasure, the human race found it necessary to confine the range of sexual experience to the genital sphere and to restrict even this narrowly conceived sexuality to the minimum. The store of energy thus released was devoted not to pleasure but to the struggle with man's surroundings. In the same way the other basic determinant of life, Thanatos or the death-instinct, was transformed in such a way that its energy, directed outwards in the form of aggression, could be used to overcome physical nature and increase the efficiency of labour. As a result, however, civilization necessarily took on a repressive character, as instincts were harnessed to tasks that were not 'natural' to them. Repression and sublimation were conditions of the development of culture, but at the same time, according to Freud, repression gave rise to a vicious circle. As labour came to be regarded as good in itself and the 'pleasure principle' was wholly subordinated to increasing its efficiency, human beings had to fight down their instincts unremittingly for the sake of these values, and the sum total of repression increased with the advance of civilization. Repression was a self-propelling mechanism, and the instruments produced by civilization to lessen the suffering arising from repression themselves became organs of repression in a still higher degree. In this way the advantages and freedoms procured by civilization are paid for by increasing the loss of freedom, especially by the growing volume of alienated labour—the only kind of labour that our civilization permits.

Marcuse takes note of this theory but modifies it in an essential respect, thus rebutting Freud's pessimistic predictions. Civilization, he says, has as a matter of fact developed by repressing instincts, but there is no law of biology or history which requires this to be so forever. The process of repression was 'rational' in the sense that, as long as basic commodities were scarce, men could only live and improve their condition by diverting their instinctual energies into 'unnatural' channels so as to further material production. But, once technology made it possible to satisfy human needs without repression, this became an irrational anachronism. Since unpleasant work can be reduced to a minimum and there is no threat of a scarcity of goods, civilization no longer requires us to thwart our instincts: we can allow them to revert to their proper function, which is a condition of human happiness. 'Free time can become the content of life and work can become the free play of human capacities. In this way the repressive structure of the instincts would be explosively transformed: the instinctual energies that would no longer be caught up in ungratifying work would become free and, as Eros, would strive to universalize libidinous relationships and develop a libidinous civilization' (*Five Lectures*, p. 22). Production will cease to be regarded as a value in itself; the vicious circle of increasing production and increasing repression will be broken; the pleasure principle and the intrinsic value of pleasure will come into their own, and alienated labour will cease to exist.

Marcuse makes it clear, however, that in speaking of 'libidinous civilization' and the return of instinctual energy to its proper functions he does not have in mind 'pansexualism' or the abolition of sublimation, whereby, according to Freud, men have found an illusory satisfaction of their frustrated desires in cultural creativity. The liberated energy will not manifest itself in a purely sexual form but will eroticize all human activities; these will all be pleasurable, and pleasure will be recognized as an end in itself. 'Incentive to work are no longer necessary. For if work itself becomes the free play of human abilities, then no suffering is needed to compel men to work' (ibid., p. 41). In general there will be no need for social control of the individual, whether through institutions or in an internalized manner—and these, according to Marcuse, are both features of totalitarianism. There will thus no longer be any 'collectivization' of the ego: life will be rational and the individual will once more be fully autonomous.

This 'Freudian' aspect of Marcuse's Utopia presents obscurities at all its vital points. Freud's theory was that the repression of instincts was necessary not only to liberate the energy needed for production but also to make possible the existence of any social life at all in the specifically human sense. Instincts are directed towards the satisfaction of purely individual desires; the death-instinct, according to Freud, can either work towards self-destruction or be transformed into external aggression; man ceases to be an enemy to himself, only in so far as he becomes an enemy to others. The only way to prevent the death-instinct becoming a permanent source of enmity between each human being and all his fellow humans is to force its energies into other channels. The libido is likewise asocial, as its treats other human beings only as possible objects of sexual satisfaction. In short, the instincts not only have no power, left to themselves, to create human society or form the basis of a community, but their natural effect is to make such a community impossible. Leaving aside the difficult question how, in that case, societies can ever have come into existence, the situation is, in Freud's view, that the society which does exist can only maintain itself by numerous taboos, commands, and prohibitions, which keep the instincts under control at the price of unavoidable suffering.

Marcuse does not address himself to this question. He seems to agree with Freud that the suppression of instincts has been necessary 'up to now', but holds that it has been an anachronism since the abolition of scarcity. But, while disputing Freud's theory of the eternal conflict between instincts and civilization, he accepts the view that instincts are essentially devoted to satisfying the individual's 'pleasure principle'. It is not clear, in view of this, how the 'libidinous civilization' can maintain itself and what forces will keep human society in being. Does Marcuse hold, in opposition to Freud, that man is naturally good and inclined to live in harmony with others, and that aggression is an accidental aberration of history which will disappear along with alienated labour? He does not say so, and inasmuch as he accepts the Freudian concept and classification of instincts, he expressly suggests the contrary. Even if he were right in asserting that 'in principle' mankind has plenty of everything and that there is no essential problem about the satisfaction of material needs, it is still not at all clear what forces are to maintain the new civilization in which all instincts have been liberated and allowed to revert to their native channels. Marcuse seems to be unconcerned with these problems, as he is interested in society chiefly in so far as it constitutes a barrier to instinct, i.e. to individual satisfaction. He seems to believe that as all questions of material existence have been solved, moral commands and prohibitions are no longer relevant. Thus when Jerry Rubin, the American hippie ideologist, says in his book that machines will henceforth do all the work and leave people free to copulate whenever and wherever they like, he is expressing, albeit in a primitive and juvenile way, the true essence of Marcuse's Utopia. As to Marcuse's qualifications of the notion of eroticism, they are too vague to convey any tangible meaning. What could the eroticization of the whole man signify, except his complete absorption in sensual pleasures? The utopian slogan is void of content; nor can we see how Marcuse imagines that the Freudian sublimation would remain in force after all the factors that brought it about had ceased to operate. According to Freud sublimation, expressed in cultural creativity, is only an illusory, ersatz satisfaction of instinctual appetites that civilization does not permit us to gratify. This theory can be and has been criticized, but Marcuse does not attempt to do so. He seems to assume that cultural creativity has in the past been an ersatz as described by Freud, but that it will nevertheless go on in the future although there will be no need for such sublimation.

Marcuse's whole inversion of Freud's theory seems to have no intelligible purpose other than a return to pre-social existence. Marcuse, of course, does not spell out this conclusion, but it is not clear how he can avoid it without contradiction. His reliance on Marx at this point is extremely dubious. Marx thought that the perfect society of the future would be so constituted that each individual would treat his own powers and abilities as direct social forces, thus removing the conflict between individual aspirations and communal needs. But Marx, on the other hand, did not hold Freud's view as to the nature of instincts. One cannot without contradiction maintain that men are instinctively and inevitably enemies of one another, and yet that their instincts must be liberated so that they can live together in peace and harmony.

3. 'One-dimensional man'

Marcuse, however, also criticizes modern civilization, especially that of America, in terms that do not necessarily involve Freud's philosophy of history but revert to the theme of his Hegelian studies, i.e. the transcendental norms of rationality as they affect the problem of human liberation. *One-Dimensional Man* is a study of this kind.

The prevailing civilization, he argues, is one-dimensional in all its aspects: science, art, philosophy, everyday thinking, political systems, economics, and technology. The lost 'second dimension' is the negative and critical principle—the habit of contrasting the world as it is with the true world revealed by the normative concepts of philosophy, which enable us to understand the true nature of freedom, beauty, reason, the joy of living, and so on.

The philosophical conflict between dialectical and 'formal' thinking goes back to Plato and Aristotle: the former extolled the importance of normative concepts with which to compare the objects of experience, while the latter developed 'sterile' formal logic and thus 'separated truth from reality'. What we need now, according to Marcuse, is to return to the ontological concept of truth as being not merely a characteristic of propositions, but reality itself: not empirical, directly accessible reality, but of a higher order, that which we perceive in universals. The intuition of universals leads us into a world which, though non-empirical, exists in its own way and ought to exist. 'In the equation Reason = Truth = Reality ... Reason is the subversive power, the "power of the negative" that establishes, as theoretical and practical Reason, the truth for men and things—that is, the conditions in which men and things become what they really are' (*One-Dimensional Man*, p. 123). The truth of concepts is grasped by 'intuition', which is 'the result of methodic intellectual mediation' (p. 126). This truth is normative in character, and in it Logos and Eros coincide. This is beyond the scope of formal logic, which tells us nothing about the 'essence of things' and restricts the sense of the word 'is' to purely empirical statements. But when we make statements like 'virtue is knowledge' or 'man is free', 'if these propositions are to be true, then the copula "is" states an "ought", a desideratum. It judges conditions in which virtue is *not* knowledge', etc. (p. 133). Thus the word 'is' has a twofold meaning, an empirical and a normative, and this duality is the subject of all genuine philosophy. Or again, one may speak of 'essential' and 'apparent' truths: dialectic consists in maintaining the tension between what is essential, or what ought to be, and what appears (i.e. facts); accordingly, dialectic is a critique of actual conditions and a lever of social liberation. In formal logic this tension is banished and 'thought is indifferent towards its objects' (p. 136), and this is why true philosophy developed beyond it. Dialectic cannot in principle be formalized, as it is thought determined by reality itself. It is a critique of direct experience, which perceives things in their accidental shape and does not penetrate to the deeper reality.

The Aristotelian mode of thought, which confines knowledge to direct experience and to the formal rules of reasoning, is the basis of all modern science, which deliberately ignores the normative 'essence' of things and relegates the question of 'what ought to be' to the realm of subjective preference. This science and the technology based on it have created a world in which man's rule over nature goes hand in hand with enslavement to society. Science and technology of this kind have indeed raised living standards, but they have brought oppression and destruction in their wake.

Scientific-technical rationality and manipulation are welded together into new forms of social control. Can one rest content with the assumption that this unscientific outcome is the result of a specific societal *application* of science? I think that the general direction in which it came to be applied was inherent in pure science even where no practical purposes were intended ... The quantification of nature, which led to its explication in terms of mathematical structures, separated reality from all inherent ends and, consequently, separated the true from the good, science from ethics ... The precarious ontological link between Logos and Eros is broken, and scientific rationality emerges as essentially neutral ... Outside this rationality, one lives in a world of values, and values separated out from the objective reality becomes subjective. (*One-Dimensional Man*, pp. 146–7.)

Thus, Marcuse continues, the ideas of goodness, beauty, and justice are deprived of universal validity and relegated to the sphere of personal taste. Science tries to concern itself only with what is measurable and can be put to technical use; it no longer asks what things are, only how they work, and proclaims itself indifferent to the purpose they are used for. In the scientific world-picture things have lost all ontological consistency, and even matter has somehow disappeared. Socially, the function of science is basically conservative, as it affords no ground for social protest. 'Science, *by virtue of its own method* and concepts, has projected and promoted a universe in which the domination of nature has remained linked to the domination of man' (ibid., p. 166). What is required is a new, qualitative, normative science which 'would arrive at essentially different concepts of nature and establish essentially different facts' (ibid.).

This deformed science, leading to the enslavement of man, finds its philosophical expression in positivism, and particularly analytical philosophy and operationalism. These doctrines reject all concepts that do not bear a 'functional' sense or make it possible to foresee and influence events. Yet such concepts are the most important of all, as they enable us to transcend the world as it is. Worse still, positivism preaches tolerance of all values and thus displays its own reactionary character, as it countenances no restrictions of any kind in regard to social practice and value-judgements.

Given the predominance of this functional attitude to thought, it follows that society must be composed of one-dimensional beings. It becomes a victim of false consciousness, and the fact that most people accept the system does not make it any more rational. A society of this kind (by which Marcuse means chiefly America) can absorb all forms of opposition without injury to itself, as it has emptied the opposition of its critical content. It is capable of satisfying a host of human needs, but these needs are themselves bogus: they are foisted on individuals by interested exploiters, and they serve to perpetuate injustice, poverty, and aggression. 'Most of the prevailing needs to relax, to have fun, to behave and consume in accordance with the advertisements, to love and hate what others love and hate, belong to this category of false needs' (p. 5). As to which needs are 'true' and which are false, no one can decide this except the individuals concerned, and that only when they are rescued from manipulation and external pressure. But the modern economic system is devised to multiply artificial needs in a condition of freedom which is itself an instrument of domination. 'The range of choice open to the individual is not the decisive factor in determining the degree of human freedom, but *what* can be chosen and what *is* chosen by the individual' (p. 7).

In this world people and things are reduced, without exception, to a functional role, deprived of 'substance' and autonomy. Art is likewise involved in the universal degradation of conformism, not because it abandons cultural values but because it includes them in the existing order. Higher European culture was once basically feudal and non-technical, moving in spheres independent of commerce and industry. The civilization of the future must recover that independence by creating a second dimension of thoughts and feelings, upholding the spirit of negation, and restoring universal Eros to its throne. (At this point Marcuse for once gives a practical instance of what he means by 'libidinous civilization', pointing out that it is much more comfortable to make love in a meadow than in an automobile on a Manhattan street.) The new civilization must also be opposed to liberty as we know it, for 'inasmuch as the greater liberty involves a contraction rather than extension and development of instinctual needs, it works *for* rather than *against* the status quo of general repression' (p. 74).

4. *The revolution against freedom*

Is there a way out of the system which multiplies bogus needs and offers the means of satisfying them, and which binds the multitude under a spell of false consciousness? Yes, says Marcuse, there is. We must completely 'transcend' existing society and strive for a 'qualitative change'; we must destroy the very 'structure' of reality so that people can develop their needs in freedom; we must have a new technology (not simply a new application of the present one) and recapture the unity of art and science, science and ethics; we must set free our imaginations and harness science to the liberation of mankind.

But who is to do all this when a majority of the people, and especially of the working class, are absorbed by the system and are not interested in the 'global transcendence' of the existing order? The answer, according to *One-Dimensional Man*, is that 'underneath the conservative popular base is the substratum of the outcasts and outsiders, the exploited and persecuted of other races and other colours, the unemployed and the unemployable. They exist outside the democratic process ... The fact that they start refusing to play the game may be the fact which marks the beginning of the end of a period' (pp. 256–7).

It appears, then, that the lumpenproletariat of the racial minorities of the United States is the section of humanity ordained above all others to restore the unity of Eros and Logos, to create the new qualitative science and technology, and to free mankind from the tyranny of formal logic, positivism, and empiricism. However, Marcuse explains elsewhere that we can also count on other forces, namely students and the peoples of economically and technically backward countries. The alliance of these three groups is the chief hope for the liberation of humanity. Student movements of revolt are 'a decisive factor of transformation', though in themselves insufficient to bring it about (see 'The Problems of Violence and the Radical Opposition', in *Five Lectures*). Revolutionary forces must use violence, because they represent a higher justice and because the present system is itself one of institutionalized violence. It is absurd to talk of confining resistance within legal limits, for no system, not even the freest, can sanction the use of violence against itself. Violence is justified, however, when the aim is liberation. It is, moreover, an important and encouraging sign that the students' political revolt is combined with a movement towards sexual liberation.

Violence is inevitable because the present system afflicts the majority with a false consciousness from which only a few can liberate themselves. Capitalism has devised such means of assimilating all forms of culture and thought that it can disarm its critics by turning their criticism into an element of the system: what is needed, therefore, is criticism by violence, which cannot be thus digested. Freedom of speech and assembly, tolerance, and democratic institutions, are all means of perpetuating the spiritual dominance of capitalist values. It follows that those endowed with a true and unmystified consciousness must strive for liberation from democratic freedoms and tolerance.

Marcuse has no hesitation in drawing this conclusion, which he expresses perhaps with most clarity in his essay on 'Repressive Tolerance' (in *A Critique of Pure Tolerance* by Robert Paul Wolff and others, 1969). In the past, he argues, tolerance was a liberating ideal, but today it is an instrument of oppression, as it strengthens a society which, with the assent of the majority, builds nuclear arsenals, pursues imperialist policies, and so on. Tolerance of this kind is a tyranny of the majority against liberationist ideals; moreover, it tolerates doctrines and movements that ought not to be tolerated, as they are wrong and evil. Every particular fact and institution must be judged from the point of view of the 'whole' to which they belong, and since in this case the 'whole' is the capitalist system, which is inherently evil, freedom and tolerance within the system are likewise evil in themselves. Therefore a true, deeper tolerance must involve intolerance towards false ideas and movements. 'The tolerance which enlarged the range and content of freedom was always partisan—intolerant toward the protagonists of the repressive status quo' (p. 99). When it is a question of establishing a new society (which, as it belongs to the future, cannot be described or defined except as the contrary of the present one), indiscriminate tolerance cannot be permitted. True tolerance 'cannot protect false words and wrong deeds which demonstrate that they contradict and counteract the possibilities of liberation' (p. 102). 'Society cannot be indiscriminate where the pacification of existence, where freedom and happiness themselves are at stake: here, certain things cannot be said, certain ideas cannot be expressed, certain policies cannot be proposed, certain behaviour cannot be permitted without making tolerance an instrument for the continuation of servitude' (ibid.). Freedom of speech is good, not because there is no such thing as objective truth, but because such truth exists and can be discovered; hence freedom of speech cannot be justified if it is shown to be perpetuating untruth. Such freedom assumes that all desirable changes can be effected through rational discussion within the 'system'; but in fact everything that can be achieved in this way serves to corroborate the system. 'A free society is indeed unrealistically and undefinably different from the existing ones. Under these circumstances, whatever improvement may occur "in the normal course of events" and without subversion is likely to be an improvement in the direction determined by the particular interests which control the whole' (p. 107). Freedom to express various opinions is bound to mean that the opinions expressed will reflect establishment interests, because of the establishment's power to form opinion. True, the mass media describe the atrocities of the modern world, but they do so in an impassive, impartial manner. 'If objectivity has anything to do with truth, and if truth is more than a matter of logic and science, then this kind of objectivity is false, and this kind of tolerance inhuman' (p. 112). To combat indoctrination and develop the forces of liberation 'may require apparently undemocratic means. They would include the withdrawal of toleration of speech and assembly from groups and movements which promote aggressive policies, armament, chauvinism, discrimination on the grounds of race and religion, or which oppose the extension of public services, social security, medical care, etc. Moreover, the restoration of freedom of thought may necessitate new and rigid restrictions on teachings and practices in the educational institutions' (p. 114), as those enclosed within these institutions have no real freedom of choice. If it is asked who is entitled to decide when intolerance and violence are justified, the answer depends on which cause is to be served thereby. 'Liberating tolerance ... would mean intolerance against movements from the Right and toleration of movements from the Left' (pp. 122–3). This simple formula epitomizes the kind of 'tolerance' that Marcuse advocates. His object, he declares, is not to set up a dictatorship but to achieve 'true democracy' by combating the idea of tolerance, on the ground that the vast majority cannot form right judgements when their minds are deformed by democratic sources of information.

Marcuse did not write from a Communist standpoint but

rather from that of the 'New Left', which broadly shared his ideas. His attitude to existing forms of Communism was one of mixed criticism and approbation, expressed in highly vague and ambiguous terms. He uses the words 'totalitarian' and 'totalitarianism' in such a way that they would fit the U.S.S.R. as well as the U.S.A., but generally disparages the latter as compared with the former. He recognizes that one system is pluralistic and the other based on terror, but does not regard this as an essential distinction: '"totalitarian" here is redefined to mean not only terroristic but also pluralistic absorption of all effective opposition by the established society' (*Five Lectures*, p. 48). '"Totalitarian" is not only a terroristic political co-ordination of society, but also a non-terroristic economic-technical coordination which operates through the manipulation of needs by vested interests' (*One-Dimensional Man*, p. 3). 'In the realm of culture, the new totalitarianism manifests itself precisely in a harmonizing pluralism, where the most contradictory works and truths peacefully coexist in indifference' (ibid., p. 61). '... is there today, in the orbit of advanced industrial civilization, a society which is not under an authoritarian regime?' (ibid., p. 102).

Terror, in short, can either be exerted by terror or by democracy, pluralism, and tolerance. But when terror is exercised for the purpose of liberation there is a promise that it will come to an end, whereas terror in the form of freedom lasts forever. On the other hand, Marcuse repeatedly expresses the view that the Soviet and capitalist systems are growing more alike, as types of the same process of industrialization. In *Soviet Marxism* he sharply criticizes Marxist state doctrine and claims that the system based upon it is not a dictatorship of the proletariat but a method of speeding up industrialization by means of a dictatorship over the proletariat and peasantry, the Marxist ideology being skewed for this purpose. He realizes the primitive intellectual level of the Soviet version of Marxism and the fact that it serves purely pragmatic aims. On the one hand, he believes that Western capitalism and the Soviet system show marked signs of converging in the direction of increased centralization, bureaucracy, economic rationalization, regimented education and information services, the work ethos, production, etc. On the other hand, however, he sees more hope for the Soviet system than for capitalism because, in the former, bureaucracy cannot become completely entrenched or perpetuate its interests: 'in the last resort' it must take second place to over-all technical, economic, and political aims which are incompatible with a system of government by repression. In a state based on class, rational technical and economic development conflicts with the interests of the exploiters. The same situation occurs in Soviet society, as the bureaucracy tries to exploit progress for its own ends, but there is a possibility of the conflict being resolved in the future, which is not the case with capitalism.

5. *Commentary*

While Marcuse's early works may be regarded as expressing a version of Marxism (based, it is true, on a false Young Hegelian interpretation of Hegel), his later writings, though they frequently invoke the Marxist tradition, have little in common with it. What he offers is Marxism without the proletariat (irrevocably corrupted by the welfare society), without history (as the vision of the future is not derived from a study of historical changes but from an intuition of true human nature), and without the cult of science; a Marxism, furthermore, in which the value of liberated society resides in pleasure and not in creative work. All this is a pale and distorted reflection of the original Marxist message. Marcuse, in fact, is a prophet of semi-romantic anarchism in its most irrational form. Marxism, it is true, contains a romantic strain—a yearning for the lost values of pre-industrial society, for unity between man and nature and direct communication among human beings, and also the belief that man's empirical life can and should be reconciled with this true essence. But Marxism is not itself if it is stripped of all other elements than these, including its theory of the class struggle and all its scientific and scientistic aspects.

However, the main point about Marcuse's writing is not that he professes to be a Marxist despite clear evidence to the contrary, but that he seeks to provide a philosophical basis for a tendency already present in our civilization, which aims at destroying that civilization from within for the sake of an apocalypse of the New World of Happiness of which, in the nature of things, no description can be given. Worse still, the only feature of the millennium that we can deduce from Marcuse's work is that society is to be ruled despotically by an enlightened group whose chief title to do so is that its members will have realized in themselves the unity of Logos and Eros, and thrown off the vexatious authority of logic, mathematics, and the empirical sciences. This may seem a caricature of Marcuse's doctrine, but it is hard to extract anything more from an analysis of his writings.

Marcuse's thought is a curious mixture of feudal contempt for technology, the exact sciences, and democratic values, plus a nebulous revolutionism devoid of positive content. He bemoans the existence of a civilization which (1) divorces science from ethics, empirical and mathematical knowledge from values, facts from norms, the description of the universe from insight into its normative essence; (2) has created 'sterile' logic and mathematics; (3) has destroyed the unity of Eros and Logos and does not understand that reality contains its own unrealized 'standard', so that by intuition we can compare it with an objective norm of itself; and (4) has staked everything on technological progress. The destructive effects of science are inherent in its content and are not simply due to its social misapplication. This perverted civilization must be opposed by a dialectic which upholds the 'unity' of knowledge and values and transcends reality by invoking its normative essence. Those who have achieved this higher wisdom, untainted by logic and the rigours of empiricism, are entitled for that reason to use violence, intolerance, and repressive measures against the majority who form the rest of the community. The élite in question consists of revolutionary students, the illiterate peasantry of economically backward countries, and the lumpen-proletariat of the U.S.A.

On basic points Marcuse gives no indication of what his actual claims are. How do we tell, for instance, that the true essence of humanity is revealed by one particular intuition and not another? or how do we know which models and normative concepts are the right ones? There is and can be no answer to these questions: we are at the mercy of arbitrary decisions by Marcuse and his followers. In the same way, we do not know what the liberated world is going to look like, and Marcuse expressly says that it cannot be described in advance. All we are told is that we must completely 'transcend' existing society and civilization, carry out a 'global revolution', create 'qualitatively new' social conditions, and so on. The only positive conclusion to be drawn is that whatever tends to destroy existing civilization is praiseworthy: there is no reason to suppose, for instance, that the burning of books, which happened in various university centres in the U.S.A., was not a good way to start the revolutionary process of 'transcending' the corrupt world of capitalism in the name of a higher reason *à la* Plato or Hegel.

Marcuse's attacks on science and logic go hand in hand with attacks on democratic institutions and 'repressive tolerance' (the opposite of 'true' tolerance, i.e. of repressive intolerance). The principles of modern science, which clearly distinguishes normative acts and evaluations from logical thought and empirical method, are in fact closely linked with the principles of tolerance and free speech. Scientific rules, whether formal or empirical, define an area of knowledge within which disputants can appeal to shared principles and, in due course, agree on this basis which theories or hypotheses are acceptable. In other words, science has evolved a code of thought, consisting of deductive and probabilistic logic, which imposes itself coercively on the human mind and creates a sphere of mutual understanding among all who are prepared to recognize it. Beyond this sphere lies the realm of value, where discussion is also possible, but only in so far as certain specific values, unprovable by the laws of scientific thought, are recognized by those concerned; yet basic values cannot be validated with the help of rules governing scientific thought. These simple principles enable us to distinguish between the fields to which compelling laws apply and those in which there are no such laws and mutual tolerance is therefore necessary. But if it is required that our thought be subject to the intuition of normative 'essences', and if it is declared that only on this condition can it be truly called thought and conform to the demands of higher reason, this amounts to a proclamation of intolerance and thought control, as the exponents of a particular idea are not obliged to defend their opinion by invoking the common stock of logical and empirical rules. To inveigh against 'sterile' formal logic (and all Marcuse tells us about logic is that it is sterile) and against the natural sciences with their quantitative orientation (sciences of which Marcuse certainly knows nothing, any more than he does of economics and technology) is simply to exalt ignorance. Human thought developed and produced science by enlarging the area of knowledge that was not subject to arbitrary judgement, thanks to the Platonic distinction between knowledge and opinion, *episteme* and *doxa*. This distinction, of course, leaves no room for an ultimate, all-embracing synthesis in which thoughts, feelings, and desires are merged in a higher 'unity'. Such an aspiration is only possible when a totalitarian myth claims supremacy over thought—a myth based on 'deeper' intuition, so that it does not have to justify itself, but assumes command over the whole of spiritual and intellectual life. For this to be possible, of course, all logical and empirical rules have to be declared irrelevant, and this is what Marcuse purports to do. The object he strives after is a unified body of knowledge which despises such trivial aims as technological progress, and whose merit is to be one and all-embracing. But there can only be such knowledge if thought is allowed to shake off the external compulsions of logic; moreover, since each person's 'essential' intuition may be different from that of others, the spiritual unity of society must be based on other foundations than logic and facts. There must be some compulsion other than the rules of thought, and that must take the form of social repression. In other words, Marcuse's system depends on replacing the tyranny of logic by a police tyranny. This is corroborated by all historical experience: there is only one way of making a whole society accept a particular world-view, whereas there are different ways of imposing the authority of rational thought, provided the rules of its operation are known and acknowledged. The Marcusian union of Eros and Logos can only be realized in the form of a totalitarian state, established and governed by force; the freedom he advocates is non-freedom. If 'true' freedom does not mean freedom of choice but consists in choosing a particular object; if freedom of speech does not mean that people can say what they like, but that they must say the right thing; and if Marcuse and his followers have the sole right to decide what people must choose and what they must say, then 'freedom' has simply taken on the contrary of its normal sense. In these terms a 'free' society is one that deprives people of freedom to choose either objects or ideas except at the behest of those who know better.

It should be noted that Marcuse's demands go much further than Soviet totalitarian Communism has ever done, either in theory or in practice. Even in the worst days of Stalinism, despite universal indoctrination and the enslavement of knowledge to ideology, it was recognized that some fields were neutral in themselves and subject only to logical and empirical laws: this was true of mathematics, physics, and also technology except for one or two brief periods. Marcuse, on the other hand, insists that normative essences must prevail in every domain, that there must be a new technology and a new qualitative science of which we know nothing whatever except that they *are* new; they must be freed from the prejudices of experience and 'mathematization'—i.e. attainable without any knowledge of mathematics, physics, or any other science—and must absolutely transcend our present knowledge.

The kind of unity that Marcuse craves for and which he imagines to have been destroyed by industrial civilization has in fact never existed: even primitive societies, as we know, for example, from Malinowski's work, distinguished the mythical from the technical order. Magic and mythology have never taken the place of technique and rational effort, but only complemented them in spheres over which mankind has no technical control. The only possible forerunners of Marcuse are the theocrats of the Middle Ages and early Reformation who sought to eliminate science or deprive it of independence.

Neither science nor technology, of course, offers any basis for a hierarchy of aims and values. Aims-in-themselves, as opposed to means, cannot be identified by scientific methods; science can only tell us how to attain our ends and what will happen when we do attain them, or when a certain course of action is followed. The gap here cannot be bridged by any 'essential' intuition.

Marcuse combines contempt for science and technology with the belief that we must strive for higher values because all the problems of material welfare have been solved and commodities exist in plenty: to increase the amount can only serve the interests of capitalism, which lives by creating false needs and instilling a false consciousness. In this respect Marcuse is typical of the mentality of those who have never had to trouble themselves to obtain food, clothing, housing, electricity, and so on, as all these necessities of life were available ready-made. This accounts for the popularity of his philosophy among those who have never had anything to do with material and economic production. Students from comfortable middle-class bacgrounds have in common with the lumpenproletariat that the technique and organization of production are beyond their mental horizon: consumer goods, whether plentiful or in short supply, are simply there for the taking. Contempt for technique and organization goes hand in hand with a distaste for all forms of learning that are subject to regular rules of operation or that require vigorous effort, intellectual discipline, and a humble attitude towards facts and the rules of logic. It is much easier to shirk the laborious task and to utter slogans about global revolution transcending our present civilization and uniting knowledge and feeling.

Marcuse of course repeats all the usual complaints about the destructive effect of modern technology and the spiritual impoverishment that results from a utilitarian approach to life in which the individual amounts to no more than the function he performs. These are not his own invention, but are long-standing truisms. The important point, however, is that the destructive effects of technology can only be combated by the further development of technology itself. The human race must work out scientifically, with the aid of 'sterile' logic, methods of social planning to neutralize the adverse consequences of technological advance. For this purpose it must foster and establish values that make life more endurable and facilitate the rational consideration of social reforms, namely the values of tolerance, democracy, and free speech. Marcuse's programme is the exact opposite: to destroy democratic institutions and tolerance in the name of a totalitarian myth, subjecting science and technology (not only in practical application, but in their theoretical aspects as well) to a nebulous 'essential' intuition which is the exclusive property of philosophers hostile to empiricism and positivism.

There could hardly be a clearer instance of the replacement of Marx's slogan 'either socialism or barbarism' by the version 'socialism equals barbarism'. And there is probably no other philosopher in our day who deserves as completely as Marcuse to be called the ideologist of obscurantism.

CHAPTER XII

Ernst Bloch:
Marxism as a futuristic gnosis

In the realm of philosophy, Bloch's writings are certainly the most extravagant of the peripheral manifestations of Marxism. He stands alone in his attempt to graft on to the inherited doctrine a complete metaphysic, cosmology, and speculative cosmogony in a gnostic and apocalyptic style, inspired by the most varied sources. Although we use the word 'graft' as an interpretation of Bloch's intent, he himself believed that he was piecing together the fragments of Marx's thought so as to reveal its hidden metaphysical meaning: a picture of the world tending towards a universal synthesis of all forces and factors, not only social phenomena but the cosmos as a whole. According to this philosophy the significance of being is revealed only in acts directed towards the future. Such acts, of which 'hope' is the most general description, are both cognitive and affective, but they are also the actual creation of the hoped-for reality, a movement of the universe towards its own entelechy. Bloch's works are in fact prophetic appeals, couched in an aphoristic and poetic prose which derives from the literary tradition of German expressionism. His style, involved and bristling with neologisms, is indigestible reading for anyone not familiar with the oddities of German philosophical language, which have flourished exuberantly from the days of Meister Eckhart to those of Heidegger, not forgetting Böhme and Hegel. Besides a fondness for unusual words and linguistic combinations, Bloch took over Heidegger's device of turning adverbs, conjunctions, etc. into nouns: *das Wohin, das Wozu, das Woher, das Nicht, das Noch-nicht, das Dass,* and so forth. Some critics regard him as a master of German prose; others consider his style artificial and pretentious, concealing poverty of thought beneath a welter of baroque ornamentation. Certainly at times the reader feels as though he were amid the fumes of an alchemist's laboratory, and when he reduces the poetic verbiage to everyday terms he may find it sterile and commonplace. Nevertheless, Bloch's metaphysical constructions should not be ignored. Interest in his philosophy has tended to increase of late; some theologians, even, have found inspiration in it, and, what is relevant to our own purpose, for most of his life he considered himself to be a full-blown Marxist.

1. Life and writings

Ernst Bloch (1885–1977), the son of assimilated Jewish parents, was born at Ludwigshafen. His intellectual development coincided with the modernist or neo-Romantic revolt against positivism and evolutionism. This revolt took the form of both unorthodox variants of Kantianism and *Lebensphilosophie*, allied with Bergsonian trends and with an interest, fostered by Oriental lore, in the hermetic, occult, and gnostic tradition and in non-dogmatic, uncodified expressions of the religious instinct. From 1905 onwards Bloch studied under Lipps at Munich and Külpe at Würzburg. His doctoral thesis on Rickert's philosophy, published in 1909 as *Kritische Erörterungen über Rickert und das Problem der modernen Erkenntnistheorie*, contained the germ of important later themes. In particular it called for a new utopian theory of knowledge (and even, according to Bloch, a new logic) which would apply to things not as they actually are but only as they may become. This theory would not be based on the principle of identity and the formula 'S is P', but would address itself to the latent potentialities and future destiny of objects, allowing room for the operations of fancy and dealing in propositions of the type 'S is not yet P'. It would thus provide for elements that are as yet wholly or partially latent, in the human mind, and thus for the expression of the unconscious.

Bloch continued his studies at Berlin, where his philosophical mentor was Simmel. He also studied physics and was interested in a wide range of humanistic subjects: poetry, painting, music, and drama. He absorbed socialist ideas, though as far as is known he did not join any political party. During the 1914–18 War he became a Marxist, but in a restricted sense. His utopian ideas on metaphysics and the theory of knowledge were not expressed at this time as a reconstruction of Marx's thought; instead, he added Marxism to them as a separate political ideology. This is especially clear in the first important book on which he worked during the war, published in 1918 as *Geist der Utopie* (a second, revised edition appeared in 1923). By this time, in Bloch's usage, the word 'Utopia' had lost the pejorative sense which it bore for Marx and the whole Marxist tradition. Bloch, on the contrary, held that Marxism was insufficiently utopian, and that it was not bold enough in anticipating a world that was inherently possible although not immediately so. This utopian boldness was present, on the other hand, in the tradition of chiliastic popular movements and especially German revolutionary anabaptism, the subject of Bloch's next book (*Thomas Münzer als Theologe der Revolution*, 1921). Mot of the ideas that he was to develop throughout his life are contained in *Geist der Utopie*: like his subsequent works, it does not itself define a Utopia except in very general terms, but is a summons to utopian thought. Its argument is that man is a utopian subject, a focus of unrealized possibilities which it is the task of philosophy to awaken into life. The primacy of practical reason is thus valid in philosophy, not in Kant's sense but in the sense that philosophy's task is not merely to describe what is, but to contribute to the emergence of a world that is still latent and cannot be born without human initiative. Our souls contain strata of the not-yet-conscious, of our own hidden future and that of all being: we are not yet what we really and essentially are, and the universe itself has not yet attained its own essence and its own calling. What that essence and destiny are cannot be ascertained by empirical observation and scientific rules, but our imagination is capable of encompassing the world which may be, though it is not yet.

Bloch thus follows the Platonists in believing that things have a 'truth' of their own which does not coincide with their actual empirical existence but which can be discovered. In his view, however, this 'truth' is not actually in being anywhere, but can be made actual by the human will and human activity. We are able to discover this form within us: Utopia is contained in our actual experience, but it consists in a complete transformation of the universe, a grand apocalypse, the descent of the Messiah, a new heaven, and a new earth. Utopian philosophy is not eschatology in the sense of merely awaiting the *eschaton*, but is a way of attaining it; it is not a contemplation but an action, an act of the will rather than of reason. Everything we were promised by the Messianism of past ages, there is a possibility of actuating by our own power. There is no God to guarantee that we shall succeed: God himself is part of the Utopia, a finality that is still unrealized.

In *Geist der Utopie* Bloch followed the tradition of Jewish apocalyptic literature, which he combined with vague ideas of socialism and anarchism: it is not clear what the world which has attained salvation is to be like, except that it will be a realm of freedom with no need for mediating institutions such as the state and politics. Here Bloch conformed to Marx's ideas, but in so general a form as to preserve no more of Marxism than can be found in Thomas Münzer's sermons. The comparison, moreover, seems to be to Marx's disadvantage: he is reproached for putting too much faith in the impersonal mechanism of history, whereas the Utopia can only be brought about by human will. Thus the early Bloch's respect for Marx's views is similar to that we have seen in Sorel, and is basically different from any of the standard versions of Marxism.

In the twenties and until Hitler's accession to power Bloch lived in Germany as an independent writer, occupying no academic post. He was a friend of Walter Benjamin and also of Lukács, though he criticized the latter for the schematic and purely 'sociological' interpretation of the world in *History and Class-Consciousness*, and also for his dogmatic condemnation of expressionist literature. In these years Bloch also published a collection of essays entitled *Durch die Wüste* (1923), attacking the utilitarianism, nihilism, and pragmatism of bourgeois civilization, and *Spuren* (1930), a rambling work inspired by various anecdotes and legends. Forced to emigrate in 1933, he spent some time in Switzerland, Paris, and Prague. In 1935 he published *Erbschaft dieser Zeit*, a critique of Nazism and an analysis of its cultural sources. In this work he identified himself wholly with Marxism and also with political Communism, though he never joined any Communist party or accepted the Stalinist version of Marxism which was then in force. He supported Stalin, however, at the critical period of the great purges and the Moscow trials.

In 1938 Bloch emigrated to the United States, where he spent the war years, writing for *émigré* German periodicals and preparing his *magnum opus, Das Prinzip Hoffnung*. Returning to Europe in 1949, he affirmed his solidarity with Stalinist socialism by accepting an appointment as Professor of Philosophy at Leipzig. He spent the next twelve years in East Germany and, especially in the early part of this period, repeatedly professed his absolute political loyalty to the regime. At this time he published a book on Hegel (*Subjekt–Objekt. Erläuterungen zu Hegel*, 1951); a short essay on Avicenna, whose thousandth anniversary according to the Muslim calendar was then being celebrated ('Avicenna und die Aristotelische Linke', 1952); an essay on Thomasius ('Christian Thomasius. Ein deutscher Gelehrter onhe Misere', 1953); and three volumes of *Das Prinzip Hoffnung* (1954, 1955, 1959), a revision and enlargement of the text as originally written. As a non-party Marxist whose political loyalty was unquestioned, Bloch received rewards and tokens of respect from the authorities; his idiosyncratic interpretation of Marxism was tolerated despite the strict Stalinist orthodoxy of philosophical teaching and literature in East Germany at that time. Every now and then, however, articles attacking him were published by official party philosophers, and the attacks were intensified after the Twentieth Congress of the Soviet Communist party in 1956: this event gave rise to passionate discussions throughout Eastern Europe, and Bloch, albeit in cautious and fairly abstract terms, evinced a definite sympathy for 'liberal' or 'revisionist' ideas. Thus it was that, two years after a Festschrift in honour of his seventieth birthday, a collective work was published denouncing him for 'revisionism', 'idealism', 'mysticism', flirting with religion, and voicing anti-Marxist demands for greater cultural freedom in the G.D.R. In 1956 a group of his pupils and collaborators were imprisoned for 'revisionist' plans of party and political reform, and Bloch himself was forbidden to teach, though publication of the third volume of *Das Prinzip Hoffnung* was finally allowed. Bloch had become increasingly disillusioned with East European socialism, and, happening to be in West Berlin in the summer of 1961, when the Berlin wall was erected, he resolved to join the millions who were fleeing from the G.D.R. to West Germany. Although seventy-six years old he was offered a university chair at

Tübingen, where he lived till his death. Having broken politically with the Soviet system, he became the advocate of a renewal of Communism. Besides republishing several earlier works he published in these years *Naturrecht und menschliche Würde* (1961), an attempt to salvage the concept of natural law in Marxist terms, also *Tübinger Einleitung in die Philosophie* (two vols., 1963–4), *Atheismus im Christentum* (1968), and numerous articles and essays. He received many honours and awards, and the firm of Suhrkamp embarked on a sixteen-volume edition of his works from 1959 onwards.

Throughout his life Bloch was a typical example of what may be called an academic thinker, whose knowledge of political reality was mainly derived from books. He had a vast knowledge of literature and philosophy, but his powers of analysis were extremely poor. His frequent political statements, both during his Stalinist and anti-Stalinist days, were naïve, vague, and stereotyped, mere echoes of current slogans and clichés. It is clear that he had no conception of economics. Throughout his life he remained a literary man deeply versed in books, dreaming of a perfect world yet unable to explain how it was to be created, or even what form its perfection was to take.

2. Basic ideas

Bloch's writings consist to a large extent of self-contained aphorisms expressed in one or a few sentences, and conveying in a concise form the essence of his philosophy. Here are some examples:

Der Mensch ist dasjenige, was noch vieles vor sich hat. Er wird in seiner Arbeit und durch sie immer wieder umgebildet. Er steht immer wieder vorn an Grenzen, die keine mehr sind, indem er sie wahrnimmt, er überschreitet sie. Das Eigentliche ist im Menschen wie in der Welt ausstehend, wartend, steht in der Furcht, vereitelt zu werden, steht in der Hoffnung, zu gelingen. (*Das Prinzip Hoffnung*, Suhrkamp ed., pp. 284–5)

(Man is he who has much before him. He is constantly transformed in and through his work. He is always reaching boundaries that are boundaries no longer: as he perceives them, so he passes beyond them. That which is genuine in man and in the world waits and endures, in the fear of frustration and the hope of success.)

Von früh auf will man zu sich. Aber wir wissen nicht, wer wir sind.

Nur dass keiner ist, was er sein möchte, scheint klar. Von daher der gemeine Neid, nämlich auf diejenigen, die zu haben, ja zu sein scheinen, was einem zukommt. Von daher aber auch die Lust, Neues zu beginnen, das mit uns selbst anfängt. Stets wurde versucht, uns gemäss zu leben. (Ibid., p. 1089)
(From our earliest days we try to find ourselves. But we do not know who we are. All that seems clear is that no one is what he would like to be. Hence our usual envy of others who seem to have, or even to be, what is rightly ours. But hence also the joy of starting something new that begins with us. We have always tried to live in accordance with our own being.)
Ich bin. Aber ich habe mich nicht. Darum werden wir erst. Das Bin ist innen. Alles Innen ist an sich dunkel. Um sich zu sehen und gar was um es ist, muss es aus sich heraus. (*Tübinger Einleitung*, i, 11)
(I am, but I do not possess myself. Thus we are still in course of becoming. The 'am' is within us, and whatever is within is in darkness. In order to perceive itself and what is around it, it must come out of itself.)

This is a typical sample of Bloch's ideas, and of his characteristic lack of precision. Most of his imposing volumes consist of variations on the same theme; their repetitiveness is almost without parallel. From the aphorisms quoted above, an outline of his doctrine may be constructed.

The universe, and man in particular, are not finite but contain many possibilities. No objective laws, operating independently of man, decide which possibilities will be finally realized. The eventualities are either total destruction or perfection. Perfection consists in the identity of empirical existence with the hidden 'essence' of man and the universe. We must not, however, speak of this as a 'return', since that would suggest that perfection was realized in some golden age of the past, so that the subsequent history of the cosmos and mankind has been a decline and not an ascent. The truth is that our essence, with which we may or may not succeed in identifying, awaits its own fulfilment. This depends on human will and on our ability to surmount the successive barriers that life places in our way; and the condition of our success is to maintain a positive attitude towards the future, in other words a state of hope. Hope is an affective quality but it is also something more: it embodies a particular kind of knowledge, revealing to us the world as it is capable of being. Moreover, it is an attribute of the whole of being, as the urge towards goodness and perfection which pervades the universe is expressed in the orientation of the human mind. Cosmic destiny is fulfilled by human activity. The future, which does not yet exist, is not mere nothingness but has its own peculiar ontological status as a real possibility latent in things and human attitudes. The task of philosophy is to arouse this slumbering utopian potential of mankind.

To indicate how Bloch develops this thought we shall take *Das Prinzip Hoffnung* as a basis, since this work appears to include all his important ideas and concepts.

3. Greater and lesser day-dreams

From the dawn of history, Bloch observes, in all cultures and at all stages of individual and social development, men have dreamt of a better and brighter life, of superhuman powers and a world without care, suffering, and struggle: in short they have, more or less skilfully, constructed various kinds of Utopia. We find the germ of such utopias in children's dreams, fairy-tales, and popular legend—in such archetypes as Aladdin's lamp, seven-league boots, magic carpets, Fortunatus's cap, or the ring of Gyges. At the lowest level these day-dreams relate simply to immediate private ends such as wealth, glory, or sexual satisfaction: we do not seek to change the world, but only to get more out of it for ourselves. At the higher level, in revolutionary utopias, our attitude is the reverse. We refuse to allow that one man's happiness should be bought at the cost of another's misfortune or enslavement; we want not only a better world than the present, but a paradisal state in which there is no longer any evil, misfortune, or suffering. 'Whereas the negative emotions of expectation (*die negativen Affekte der Erwartung*) and their utopian images are oriented towards hell as their ultimate end (*ihr Unbedingtes*), the positive emotions of expectation [i.e. hope] —are oriented no less absolutely towards paradise' (*Das Prinzip Hoffnung*, p. 127).

In other words, the positive or what Bloch calls the 'concrete' Utopia is the expectation of absolute perfection, the Hegelian consummation of history: it is the will having as its object the Totum, Ultimum, or *eschaton*. Bloch insists that there are only two possibilities, all or nothing, absolute destruction and nothingness or absolute perfection; there is no middle term.

'Nothingness too is a utopian category, though an extremely anti-utopian one ... nothingness, in the same way as a positive Utopicum: one's native home (*Heimat*) or the All are present only as an objective possibility' (p. 11). 'Since the historical process is undetermined inasmuch as its trend and outcome are as yet unrealized, its final upshot (*Mündung*) may be either Nothing or All, total failure (*das Umsonst*) or total success' (p. 222).

The expressions Totum, Ultimum, Optimum, *summum bonum*, *eschaton*, the All, being (*das Sein*), and *Heimat* all mean the same thing. *Heimat* represents being-in-oneself, man's complete reconciliation with himself and the universe, the elimination of all that is negative, the final state (*Endzustand*) in which all alienation is overcome. The utopian will, according to Bloch, is not a matter of endless endeavour or endless progress: it aspires to actual fulfilment within a finite time.

The history of civilization is one of innumerable utopias, not only great all-embracing ones but partial ones as well; all of them, however, have reflected the human desire for absolute goodness. Utopian dreams can be found in poetry and drama, music and painting. There are architectural utopias, geographical ones such as Eldorado or Eden, medical ones such as the dream of eternal youth or the final abolition of disease and physical disability. Sport is a kind of Utopia, in which people try to overcome the natural limitations of the human frame. Dancing, fairs, circuses—even these are expressions of man's constant yearning for perfection, unconscious though it often is. Finally there are the elaborate blueprints of a perfect world in utopian literature, in the chiliastic visions of the Middle Ages and the sixteenth century, in the whole history of religion with its Messianic expectations and ideas of salvation, the Saviour, and heaven.

Man, according to Bloch, is essentially Utopia-minded, believing in a perfect world and anticipating the future with undying hope. There is scarcely any aspect of culture that is not pervaded by this irresistible utopian energy, and we would therefore expect it to have left a strong mark on the history of philosophy. In fact, however, almost the whole of European philosophy before Marx turned away from the future and culpably fixed its eyes on the past; it was content to interpret the existing world instead of planning a better one and teaching men how to create it. It is not clear why philosophy distinguished itself thus negatively from other branches of culture. 'Plato's theory that all knowledge is nothing but *anamnesis*, the recollection of something once seen—this version of knowledge centred on the past (*Ge-wesenheit*) has since been repeated incessantly' (p. 158). Even doctrines which contained projections of a final state of perfection did not really envisage the future: their Ultimum was a false one, as it was always realized initially in the Absolute. Such philosophies, including Hegel's, did not recognize the Novum: they had no notion of real change and orientation towards the future. 'Throughout Judaeo-Christian philosophy, from Philo and Augustine to Hegel, the Ultimum is related only to the Primum and not to the Novum, so that what finally comes about is only a repetition of what was in the beginning—something already fulfilled, which has meanwhile become lost or alienated' (p. 233). Thus pre-Marxian philosophy recognized an Ultimum but knew of no true novelty in the world, as it assumed an initially realized Absolute. Perfection or salvation was represented as the return to a lost paradise, not the conquest of a possible one.

It might seem that Bloch would at least approve of twentieth-century attempts to describe a real Novum, such as we find in the metaphysics of Bergson or Whitehead. This is not so, however. In Bergson, it appears, the 'new' is an abstraction, a mere negation of repetition; moreover, his whole philosophy is not one of anticipation, but is impressionistic and liberal-anarchic. From some of Bloch's remarks it would seem that not only philosophy but the whole of human knowledge before Marx was fettered to the past, capable only of describing it and not of looking to the future. Capitalism intensified this attitude by turning all objects into commodities and thus bringing about the 'reification' of thought: reified thought, reduced to the form of commodities, expresses itself as fact-worship or 'crawling empiricism'. On this point Bloch more or less follows Lukács and the Frankfurt school. 'The fetishism of facts' and 'shallow empiricism', devoid of imagination and fettered to 'isolated' phenomena, are incapable of apprehending the 'whole' or of grasping the 'essential' in the course of history (*was wesentlich geschieht*) (p. 256).

All these comments on philosophy, past and present, add up to casual condemnation with no attempt at analysis. Bloch devotes somewhat more attention to psychoanalysis, which from his point of view is the negation of the future *par excellence*. Bloch, as we have seen, is concerned to replace the category of the unconscious by the 'not yet conscious', that which is latent within us in the form of anticipation but is not yet articulate. But in all versions of psychoanalysis, whether Freud's or those of his more or less faithful disciples, the unconscious derives from accumulations of the past and contains nothing new. This backward orientation is even more evident in Jung, the 'psycho-analytical Fascist', who interprets the whole human psyche in terms of collective prehistory and proclaims 'hatred of intelligence' as the only remedy for the ills of modern life. Freud, being a liberal, sought to bring the unconscious into the light of day, whereas Jung wants to thrust our consciousness back beneath the surface. As for Adler, he in a simply capitalist way considers the will to power as the fundamental human impulse (p. 63). In any case, all forms of psychoanalysis are backward-looking, which is accounted for by the fact that they express the consciousness of the bourgeoisie, a class without a future.

The revolutionary utopias of past ages reflected humanity's desire for perfection and even the knowledge that it was possible; post-Marxian utopias are, without exception, reactionary. Wells's 'bourgeois democratic Utopia', for instance, 'is coated with a moral veneer, a simulacrum of human rights, as if the capitalist whore could once more become a virgin'; but 'freedom as the Utopia of Western capitalism is chloroform, nothing else' (p. 682).

4. Marxism as a 'concrete Utopia'

Marxism, and it alone, has given humanity a full and consistent perception of the future. What is more, Marxism is wholly future-oriented: it recognizes the past only in so far as it is still alive and is therefore part of the future. Marxism has achieved the 'discovery that concrete theory-practice is strictly bound up with the observed mode of objective-real possibility' (p. 236). Marxism is a science, but one that has overcome the dualism of being and thought, of what is and what ought to be; it is both a theory of the future paradise and a praxis which brings it about.

Marxism is an all-embracing Utopia, but, unlike the dreams of previous ages, it is a concrete and not an abstract one. The phalansteries or the New Harmony were types of an abstract Utopia; Marx's concrete Utopia contains no exact predictions concerning the society of the future, but it opposes to the old fantasies 'an actively conscious participation in the immanent historical process of the revolutionary transformation of society' (p. 725). 'The point of a concrete Utopia is to understand precisely the dream concerning it, a dream rooted in the historical process itself' (p. 727). In short, what makes a Utopia concrete is that we can give no exact account of it—a truly classic instance of *lucus a non lucendo*.

Although Bloch declares that the supreme good, or the Totum, has been scientifically analysed, all we learn of it in his works is contained in a few phrases borrowed from Marx: it will be a classless society, a realm of freedom in which there will be no alienation, and so on. It will also mean the reconciliation of man with nature: Bloch mentions several times, as of key importance, the sentences about the 'humanization of nature' from Marx's Paris Manuscripts of 1844. For a Utopia cannot be 'concrete' unless it embraces the 'whole', i.e. the universe; as long as our imagination restricts itself to the organization of society and ignores nature, it is no better than 'abstract'.

Marxism is an act of hope, embodying knowledge of the anticipated world and the will to create it. This will and this knowledge have their counterpart, not in empirical reality but in the higher and more real 'essential' order. Unlike empiricist philosophy, Marxism, rightly understood, includes the ontology of that which is not yet (*Ontologie des Noch-Nicht*). 'Expectation, hope, intention towards possibilities that have not yet materialized—all this is not only a mark of human consciousness but, when rightly understood and regulated, is a fundamental determinant within objective reality as a whole. Since Marx there has been no possible inquiry into truth and no realism of decision that did not take account of the subjective and objective content of hope in the universe' (p. 5). 'The not-yet-conscious in man thus belongs wholly to that part of the external world that has not yet happened, not yet emerged or manifested itself. The not-yet-conscious communicates and interacts with what has not yet happened' (p. 12). 'Until reality has been completely determined, as long as it still embodies open possibilities in the form of new beginnings and new areas of development, we cannot absolutely reject a Utopia on the basis of purely factual reality ... A concrete Utopia finds its counterpart in emergent reality (*Prozesswirklichkeit*), the counterpart of the mediated Novum ... The anticipating elements are themselves a component of reality' (pp. 226–7).

We thus find in Bloch the typical neo-Platonic and Hegelian concept of non-empirical reality, which, however, in this case is not a perfection already actualized somewhere, like the Platonic ideas, nor a mere arbitrary normative construction, but which, as an anticipation, is invisibly present in the empirical world. Bloch himself does not invoke Hegel or the neo-Platonists in this content, but rather the Aristotelian concept of entelechy and the 'creative matter' of Aristotle's followers. The world, he believes, has a kind of immanent purposiveness whereby it evolves, out of incomplete forms, complete ones. These forms are both natural and normative. However, Bloch does not seem to be aware that his use of the concepts of energy, potentiality, and entelechy differs from Aristotle's in one major respect. These concepts are more or less intelligible when applied to particular objects and processes—a plant evolving a complete form hidden in a seed, for instance—but they cease to be intelligible when applied to being as a whole. Aristotle used them, in fact, to describe the empirical processes of development in the organic world and in purposive human activity. Bloch's concepts, however, relating to the entelechy of the whole universe, owe nothing to empirical observation: they merely express a speculative belief in the tendency of the universe towards a perfection about which we can predicate nothing. We do know, however, according to Bloch, that any objections to the hope of absolute perfection that may be raised on the basis of existing scientific knowledge are invalid *a priori*, because 'facts' have no ontological meaning and may be ignored without hesitation: what matters are the premonitions of the anticipating fancy. Thus Marxism, as Bloch understands it, need not be constrained in any way by our present state of knowledge. That a barley corn will grow into an ear of barley is something we

can rationally expect on the basis of experience; that the present
not very perfect universe is destined, by virtue of an immanent
natural purpose, to turn into a perfect one is clearly not only
unprovable, but hard to imagine with any degree of plausibility.
Bloch is aware of this and of the fact that the existing rules of
scientific thought give no support to his idea of the Ultimum;
instead, he invokes the aid of imagination, artistic inspiration,
and enthusiasm. This would not be out of the way if he considered himself a poet, but he contends that the anticipating
fancy is a science in its own right—not an ordinary one, but
a science of a superior kind, free from the irksome constraints
of logic and observation.

It is not sufficient to say, however, that the 'essence of the
universe' is in a 'not yet manifested state' (p. 149), so that the
possibilities inherent in it are, as it were, a task to be
accomplished, a latent desire, an 'objective fantasy' of Being as
a whole. It is also important that this task can be accomplished
only through the will and consciousness of mankind, and not
simply by the force of cosmic laws. The human race, in fact,
is not merely an executant of the universe's intentions, the
instrument of a blind mysterious providence; it also wields a
power of decision. Man can choose whether to bring the
universe to perfection or destruction—there is, as already stated,
no middle way—and which the outcome will be is not determined in advance. Thus man is in a sense the guide of the
universe, bearing on his shoulders not only the weight of human
history but that of Being as a whole. This idea is typical of
neo-Platonism, but Bloch, with enviable self-assurance, ascribes
it to Marx. In the *Tübinger Einleitung* (p. 231) he quotes Marx
as saying that 'man is the root of all things'; what Marx actually
wrote, at the age of twenty-five, was that 'man himself is the
root of man', which is obviously quite different.

Since Bloch's Ultimum, or paradise, is not simply the final
state of the world as it must be, but has to be realized by human
will, it is never clear in what sense the present really 'contains'
the future—in what sense our 'knowledge' of the future world
relates to that world, and how far it is merely an act of will.
From this point of view his concept of a higher or 'essential'
reality is no less ambiguous than the similar concept of the
surrealists. In surrealist philosophy it is not clear whether the

world to which we have access through special hallucinatory experiences is a ready-made reality to which they provide the key, or something we create even as we become aware of it. However, this ambiguity does not matter in the case of the surrealists, since their philosophy is only an offshoot of their art. Bloch, on the other hand, purports to be using the language of discursive philosophy, in which the ambiguity of basic concepts is suicidal.

Bloch is excusable on this point to the extent that his ambiguities are those of the Hegel–Marx tradition in general. As we saw in the case of Lukács, it is characteristic of this tradition to blur the distinction between foreseeing the future and creating it. It is here that prophets and scientists part company. When a scientist foretells occurrences, accurately or otherwise, he relies on observation of the past and on the belief that he understands the interrelations of events; he does not claim to know the future, since such knowledge is impossible, but only to foresee it with greater or less probability. A prophet, on the other hand, does not 'foresee' anything: the source of his knowledge of the future is not the past but the future itself, which in a mysterious way is already present to him, with an ontological status of its own. Bloch speaks of a reality which 'is not yet', but which he emphatically distinguishes from nothingness or pure negation. The 'not' certainly implies a lack, but it is a lack of *something* and therefore represents a striving towards that something, a creative desire by which the world is pervaded; it must be opposed to nothingness and not to the All (*Das Prinzip Hoffnung*, pp. 356–7). The subjective counterpart of the 'not yet', namely 'not-yet-awareness', is not to be regarded as pure negation but rather as an urge of the mind to become conscious of a certain object. Bloch refers to Leibniz's 'little perceptions' to explain what he has in mind: a kind of inarticulate knowledge which is none the less knowledge, a paradoxical state in which we know something that we do not know, or that we know potentially but not actually.

In this way the prophet is in an extremely convenient position. On the one hand, he does not have to give reasons for his predictions, as he makes it clear in advance that they are not based on pedestrian empiricism, that he scorns the tyranny of facts and logic. On the other hand, he delivers his prophecies with the utmost assurance, based on his special power of perceiving what is somehow already present although it has not yet occurred. His knowledge is higher and far more certain than the scientist's, and he does not have to explain its source or the reasons for it: anyone who demands explanations is a self-confessed exponent of 'reified consciousness' and a slave to 'crawling empiricism'.

Clearly, the self-styled prophet, enjoying this freedom of intellectual manœuvre, can promise whatever comes into his head, while assuring us that his promises are based on a superior type of knowledge. Bloch, while making the proviso that the social organization of the future Utopia cannot be described in advance, speaks of an entirely new kind of technology effecting a radical change in our lives. Capitalism, he explains, has created a technology based on a purely quantitative and mechanistic conception of nature as opposed to a qualitative approach. In the future we shall enjoy a miraculous technology which he calls 'non-Euclidean' (ibid., pp. 775 ff.). Leaving the details of the technical revolution to be worked out by others, he nevertheless assures us that if it were not for imperialism we should already be able to irrigate the Sahara and the Gobi desert, and turn Siberia and the Antarctic into pleasure resorts, at the cost of 'a few hundredweight of uranium and thorium'. 'Non-Euclidean technology' will restore man's intimacy with nature and make possible a 'qualitative' attitude towards it which 'abstract capitalism' (Bloch's own phrase) is incapable of achieving. Nor should we bother about the law of increasing entropy, as the techniques of the future will take care of that also.

5. Death as an anti-Utopia. God does not yet exist, but he will

Bloch's anticipations become even bolder when he deals with the problem of death and the 'subject of nature'. The third volume of *Das Prinzip Hoffnung* gives an extended account of ancient Egyptian, Greek, Jewish, Buddhist, Hindu, and Christian ideas on immortality, after which Bloch puts forward the following conclusions. The belief of traditional religions in immortality or the transmigration of souls is pure fantasy, but it is a manifestation of the utopian will and of human dignity. In the materialist dialectic, on the other hand, 'the universe is not bounded by Newton's mechanics' (p. 1303).

Dialectical as opposed to mechanistic materialism acknowledges no boundaries, no negations prescribed by an alleged 'natural order' ... The utopian final aim of its practice is the humanization of nature ... Here as everywhere else, Communist cosmology [*sic*] is the realm of problems related to the dialectical mediation between man and his labour on the one hand and a possible subject of nature on the other ... The word 'No' can never be pronounced from the outset: if nature contains no positive answer to the problems of our destiny, it also contains none that are, once and for all, negative ... No one knows what is in the universe outside the range of human labour, that is to say in unmediated nature; we do not know whether any subject or agency is at work there, and if so, of what kind it is ... All this depends on the development and prospects of human power, and hence, more precisely, on the development and unfolding horizons of Communism. (*Das Prinzip Hoffnung*, pp. 1382–3)

The kernel of human existence (*der Kern des Existierens*) has not yet fully displayed itself, and therefore it is 'exterritorial vis à vis the process of becoming and transformation' (ibid., p. 1390); if the world developed to a state of complete frustration (*zu einem absoluten Umsonst*), then and only then would death penetrate to the core of nature which lies in the human heart.

In so far as this argument can be understood, it may be summarized by saying that all the promises of traditional religion as to immortality are vain, but when we have built Communism we shall somehow overcome the problem of death. To put it as kindly as possible, this must be the most frivolous promise that has ever been uttered in the name of a political movement. It is paralleled only by the last of Bloch's utopian hopes—the eventual creation of God, as to which he argues as follows.

The kernel of all religion is the attainment of the kingdom of absolute human perfection. Hence, if the aim of religion is pushed to its furthest extent, it is seen to require the elimination of God as an entity limiting human powers, the removal of such limitation being implicit in all religious Utopias. Here, it would seem, Bloch is simply following Feuerbach, who held that the truth of religion is atheism: if we try to express exactly what people want from religion, it turns out to be the non-existence of God.

The intention of religion concerning the Kingdom conceived in its fullest sense, presupposes atheism ... Atheism excludes the *Ens perfectissimum* (which is what was meant by 'God') from the creation and evolution of the world, defining it not as a fact but as the only thing it can be, viz. the supreme utopian problem, the problem of finality. The place assigned in particular religions to what was called 'God' was ostensibly filled by the hypostasis of God, and when this is discarded the vacant place continues to exist, as the ultimate projection of a radical utopian intention ... The place corresponding to the God of olden times is not itself nothing ... Authentic, i.e. dialectical materialism does away with the transcendence and reality of any hypostasis of God, but it does not exclude what was meant by the *Ens perfectissimum* from the real Utopia of the kingdom of freedom, the final content of the qualitative process ... The Utopia of the kingdom destroys the fiction of God the Creator and the hypostasis of God in heaven, but it does not destroy the ultimate dwelling-place where the *Ens perfectissimum* preserves the abyss of its latent unfrustrated possibility. (*Dans Prinzip Hoffnung*, pp. 1412–13)

Thus religion, according to Bloch, does not simply terminate in the absence of religion but leaves a legacy in the shape of the final problem of perfected being. Instead of a ready-made heaven in the 'next world', we have the command to create a new heaven and a new earth. However, mindful of Lenin's scornful attitude to the 'God-builders' in the Russian social-democratic movement, Bloch makes it clear that he does not regard the world as a machine for the production of a supreme being, but that when God is removed we shall still possess the 'total content of the hope' to which the name 'God' was formerly given. This vague language seems to mean only that the perfect Being will emerge under Communism. Elsewhere this perfect Being is called the 'possible subject of nature' or the *Dass-Antrieb* (urge towards 'thatness'). To understand this last expression it should be realized that in Bloch's vocabulary 'thatness' represents either a state of things or a purpose ('in order that...'); he makes full use of this ambiguity, but it is probably simplest to read *das Dass* as signifying a purposive process or the awareness of an aim. In this way Communism will achieve the creation of God, which is more than all the religions of the world have done. Bloch's philosophy is in the last resort a theogony, a fantastic projection of the God that is to be: 'the true Genesis is not in the beginning but at the end' (p. 1628).

6. *Matter and materialism*

The picture of a world whose 'essence' embodies a Utopia or fantasy, and which is imbued with the purpose of attaining divine perfection, is on the face of it very different from traditional materialism, and it is understandable that it should be attacked by orthodox Leninists. Bloch himself maintains, however, that his philosophy is nothing but a continuation of dialectical materialism and in particular that it is based on materialism in Engels's sense—i.e. that it 'explains the universe in terms of itself' and presupposes no other reality than what is material.

In 'Avicenna and the Aristotelian Left' and in other works Bloch invokes the concept of creative matter which was present in the Aristotelian tradition and was taken over, he claims, by Marxism. Strato, Alexander of Aphrodysias, Avicenna, Averroës, Avicebron, David of Dinant, and finally Giordano Bruno evolved the concept of matter as a process, containing a diversity of forms and a permanent possibility of further development: any new thing that happens is not due to a force outside the universe, but is the manifestation of a potentiality residing in matter itself. There is no distinction between matter and form: forms are latent or manifest attributes of the single substratum, *natura naturans*.

In his lecture 'Zur Ontologie des Noch-Nicht-Seins' Bloch gives the following explanation purporting to be the definition of matter.

It is not a mere mechanical lump but—in accordance with the implicit sense of Aristotle's definition—it is both being-according-to-possibility (*kata to dynaton*, i.e. that which determines every possible historical phenomenon in accordance with conditions and with historical materialism), and also being-in-possibility (*dynamei on*, i.e. the correlative of that which is objectively and really possible or, ontically speaking, the possibility-substrate of the dialectical process). ('Sie ist nicht der mechanische Klotz, sondern—gemäss dem implizierten Sinn der Aristotelischen Materie-Definition—sowohl das Nach-Möglichkeit-Seiende (*kata to dynaton*), also das, was das jeweils geschichtlich Erscheinenkönnende bedingungsmässig, historischmaterialistisch bestimmt, wie das in-Möglichkeit-Seiende (Sein) (*dynamei on*), also das Korrelat des objektiv-real-Möglichen oder rein seinshaft: das Möglichkeits-Substrat des dialektischen Prozesses'.)

He goes on to say that 'inorganic nature, no less than human history, has its Utopia. This so-called inanimate nature is not a corpse but a centre of radiation, the abode of forms whose substance has not yet come into being.'

Thus, according to Bloch, matter is not characterized by any physical properties but simply by the fact of 'creativity' or immanent purpose. It is easy to point out that in that case 'materialism' means no more than that the world is subject to change and may develop in many unexpected ways. Matter is merely used as a term denoting 'all that is', and has all the divine attributes except complete actuality. In these nebulous arguments we do indeed hear echoes of Giordano Bruno, as well as of Böhme and Paracelsus. Matter is the *Urgrund*, an indeterminate *universum* out of which anything may come; thus conceived, it is indistinguishable from the God of pantheism. To say that 'all is matter' is a tautology, since matter is a synonym for 'all'—not only all that is actual, but all that is possible as well. It is not surprising, therefore, when Bloch tells us that 'matter' includes dreams, subjective images, aesthetic experiences, and the aesthetic qualities of the external world (which, it appears, are contained in nature but become actual through aesthetic perception). If God is possible his coming into existence involves no threat to materialism, since by definition he will be 'material' also.

What we have here is really not an assertion of materalism but of monism: the doctrine that there is one single substratum of all possible phenomena, including human subjectivity and all its products. Since the substratum in question has no qualities of its own and all we know of it is that it is 'creative' and contains all possibilities within itself, Bloch's monistic theory is likewise devoid of content. All that can exist, we are told, is material, and matter equals all that can exist.

Nevertheless, on two points at least Bloch's cosmology and metaphysics are regarded by him as supporting Marxism and, more precisely, the Leninist version thereof.

In the first place, not only does the universe embody an immanent purpose but, at least in the higher stages of evolution, it requires the participation of human subjectivity to realize its utopian potentialities or actualize its self-anticipations. Man is a product of matter, but since he appeared on the scene he has been, as it were, in charge of its further development: he is the head of creation, as in the theogony of Plotinus and Eriugena or the old neo-Platonist philosophy. That which is 'not yet conscious' in us is correlated, in an undefined way, with the 'not yet' of nature itself; the subjective 'not yet' is to become explicit through our efforts, thus making manifest the essence of the universe. Consequently, man cannot assume that the laws of evolution, whether consciously perceived or not, will ensure that the world becomes a better place. In terms of politics this means that the perfect world of the future can only be brought about by the conscious will of man. This is the metaphysical justification for Bloch's criticism of the 'fatalism' or determinism of the Second International, and for his allegiance to Leninist Marxism, which insists that revolutionary will plays a decisive part in the revolutionary process.

Secondly, the same metaphysic provides a bulwark against revisionism. As the future of the world is summed up in the dilemma 'all or nothing', if we do not want man and the universe to be destroyed we must go for the first alternative. Not only must the world be seen in terms of a movement evolving higher and higher forms, but it is intelligible only from the standpoint of final perfection. Metaphysics and social activity must alike be aimed at the *eschaton*, the complete and irreversible fulfilment of cosmic destiny, a synthesis of all the forces of being. Hence Bernstein is an enemy to Marxism when he preaches a revisionist programme of gradual or incomplete reforms lacking the horizon of ultimate perfection: the inspiration of the final goal is an inseparable part of Marxist philosophy, which on this fundamental point inherits the apocalyptic outlook of radical Anabaptism (*Das Prinzip Hoffnung*, pp. 676–9). Accordingly, one of Bloch's main criticisms of East European socialism in later years was that the party leaders promised various short-term advantages and improvements in lieu of the great utopian prospects offered by socialism.

7. *Natural law*

A special feature of Bloch's philosophy is his attempt to combine

Marxism with a theory of natural law. His ideas on this subject are set out in several works, particularly *Naturrecht und menschliche Würde*. The idea that man has certain rights by nature, and that no positive law can deprive him of these without ceasing to be law in the true sense, has played a large part in utopian thought from ancient times to the present. It gave rise to the theory of the social contract, the principle of popular sovereignty, and the doctrine that tyranny may be lawfully resisted. Unlike utopias in the classical sense, theories of natural law were inspired by the notion of human dignity rather than happiness or economic efficiency. In Bloch's view, while they paved the way to bourgeois democracy they contained elements of universal validity, not confined to that or any other political system. Marxism is in a sense the heir of Locke, Grotius, Thomasius, and Rousseau, not only of the utopians: for Communism is concerned not only with abolishing poverty but also with putting an end to the humiliation of man. The theories of natural law also partook of utopianism, as they contained anticipations of the notion of a supreme good. We also read in *Naturrecht und menschliche Würde* that the socialist Utopia comprises 'bourgeois' freedoms such as those of the press, assembly, and free speech. However, Bloch emphasizes that 'true' freedom involves the abolition of the state, and that ideals can only be fully realized in the stateless socialist society. When that comes there will be no more conflict between the individual and the community; freedom and happiness will not limit each other, compulsion will no longer be needed, and there will be universal brotherhood. It is not clear, however, why such a perfect society should need laws at all, and what would be the point of 'natural rights' which there was no occasion to assert against anyone, as all would be living in a state of spontaneous solidarity.

8. Bloch's political orientation

It was already clear in the 1930s, long before he took up his abode in the G.D.R., that although Bloch was not a member of any party, his political sympathies were wholly on the side of Stalinism. Not only did he proclaim the socialist Utopia, but he maintained that although the *summum bonum* was not fully in existence anywhere, it was already taking shape in the Soviet Union. *Das Prinzip Hoffnung* is full of passages that bear unambiguous testimony to its author's politics, as he loses no opportunity of praising the superiority of the new order: his expressions of this kind are mostly clichés without any probative force, but they are embedded in his philosophy in such a way as to seem organically linked with it. In particular he lays stress on the class interpretation of Utopia. We are told, for instance, that the petty-bourgeois idea of Utopia is egoistic, while the proletarian one is disinterested (pp. 33–4); concerning utopias of longevity, Bloch does not fail to point out that they are impossible under capitalism but will be realized under socialism. Monopolistic capitalism has degraded man's utopian aspirations by exploiting them in order to popularize record achievements out of which it derives profit (p. 54). Heidegger, it appears, is a propagandist for death at the behest of imperialism (p. 1365), and when he talks about fear and boredom 'he reflects, from the petty-bourgeois standpoint, society under monopoly capitalism, the normal state of which is perpetual crisis' (p. 124). Psychoanalysis, as we have seen, explains the human psyche by reference to the past because it arose in a society that has no future. Apropos of the utopian role of dancing, Bloch does not omit to mention that under capitalism it has a stultifying effect, as it is intended to dull people's senses and make them forget oppression, whereas the new 'socialist love of the fatherland' has revived the beauty of folk-dancing (pp. 456–8). Some of his remarks in this line sound like a downright parody of Stalinist propaganda. The book is full of ideological clichés such as: 'Socialism, as the ideology of the revolutionary proletariat, is nothing but true consciousness applied conceptually to the movement of events and the rightly understood trend of reality' (p. 177). Capitalist art and literature, we are told elsewhere, use the 'happy ending' to make up for the hopelessness of life in conditions of exploitation, whereas socialism 'has and maintains its own kind of happy ending' (p. 516). In the context of sport we hear about the degeneration of the human physique in an 'alienated society based on the division of labour' (p. 525); as to the prolongation of life and combating the effects of age, the Soviet Union has made progress in this direction for reasons which capitalism cannot afford to acknowledge (p. 535). Bloch cannot mention Malthus without adding that his spiritual descendants are

'American murderers' and that present-day Malthusianism is due to the imperialists' desire to practise genocide and exterminate the unemployed (p. 543). Capitalist freedom means freedom for the worker to starve, while in the 'land where socialism is being built' every effort is directed towards the abolition of violence (p. 1061). Under capitalism, moreover, there can be no such thing as true friendship, since the whole of life is dominated by buying and selling, whereas socialism is paving the way for universal friendship among all peoples (pp. 1132–3).

It is quite possible that Bloch inserted these nonsensical and servile propaganda phrases when revising *Das Prinzip Hoffnung* in the G.D.R. in the 1950s, and that they were a *sine qua non* of publication at the time. None the less, we must suppose that he believed them then and later, as they also figure in reprints published after he settled in West Germany.

In political speeches and articles written after 1961 (some of which are collected in a small volume entitled *Widerstand und Friede. Aufsätze zur Politik*, 1968) Bloch took up a position in favour of democratic socialism, though in very vague and general terms; he also condemned Stalinism in vague language, declaring that Marxism needs to be renewed, adapted to changing circumstances, and so on. Expressions of this sort had some meaning in Eastern Europe in 1955–6, but by the early sixties they had already become sterile clichés.

It would be unfair to say, however, that Bloch's identification with Leninism as a political doctrine and Stalinism as a political system is an organic and integral part of his metaphysical theory. That theory does not entail any specific political consequences or directives for self-commitment, and nothing of the kind could be deduced from *Das Prinzip Hoffnung* if the Stalinist trimmings were simply removed from its text. In this respect Bloch's case is on a par with that of Heidegger and his temporary identification with Nazism, though Heidegger was less outspoken and his philosophical works are not decked out with political moralizing in the same way. In their political utterances both men used their own characteristic concepts to buttress their loyalty to a totalitarian dictatorship, but the concepts themselves did not point in one direction more than another. The identification might equally have been the other

way round: Bloch's category of 'hope' might have been used
to glorify Nazism, and Heidegger's 'authenticity' (*Eigentlichkeit*)
might have served the cause of Communist propaganda. Both
concepts were vague and formal enough to be used in this way;
neither theory contains any inbuilt moral restriction to inhibit
such use, or prescribes any specific course of political action.
It may be urged that this is not a valid objection to any
metaphysic, since the latter has no duty to provide political
directives, nor does its value depend on the political use made
of it; such conclusions are not the necessary business of
philosophy. But neither Bloch nor Heidegger can be defended
on these lines, since they themselves claimed that their metaphysical doctrine, or philosophic anthropology, had and ought
to have the practical purpose, not only of explaining the world
but of showing how men must behave, and with what forces
they must ally themselves in order to live worthily. The objection
that a philosophical doctrine does not clearly suggest any
particular way of life or social commitment is valid if the
doctrine in question makes practical claims and purports to be
normative, not merely descriptive. Heidegger's aggressive and
arrogant phenomenology of existence has been of incomparably
greater importance to twentieth-century philosophy, and has
provided infinitely more stimulus to culture, than Bloch with
his obscure and convoluted style; but they have this in common,
that they both sought to erect a metaphysical foundation for
practical life in the world and not merely for contemplation.
For this purpose they devised respectively the obscure and purely
formal categories of *Eigentlichkeit* and *Hoffnung*, which turn out
to be applicable in any way one chooses.

9. Conclusion and comments

The present writer cannot claim to assess the merits or defects
of Bloch's German prose. As a philosopher, Bloch must be termed
a preacher of intellectual irresponsibility. He cannot be credited
with inventing a Utopia, still less a 'concrete' one: we turn with
relief from his works to Fourier's 'abstract' Utopia with its
quaint particularities. Bloch does no more than urge us to have
utopian thoughts, and to speculate on a future that he himself
makes no attempt to delineate.

Like many other Marxists, Bloch does not trouble to substantiate his assertions but merely proclaims them. On the rare occasions when he puts forward an argument, it usually reveals his logical helplessness. For instance, he says there is no such thing as unchanging human nature, because even such a universal phenomenon as hunger has taken different forms in the course of history, in that people at different times have preferred different foods (*Das Prinzip Hoffnung*, pp. 75–6). The reader who endeavours to follow his arguments generally finds that they consist of truisms and tautologies, disguised in verbiage of intolerable complexity. Here are some examples:

'Wir leben nicht, um zu leben, sondern weil wir leben, doch gerade in diesem Weil oder besser: diesem leeren Dass, worin wir sind, ist nichts beruhigt, steckt das nun erst fragende, bohrende Wozu' ('Zur Ontologie des Noch-Nicht-Seins'). ('We do not live in order to live but because we live. But in this "because", or rather in the empty "that" in which we live, there is no reassurance, but rather the full challenge of the tormenting "why?"') In other words, people often wonder what life is about.

Again: 'Es gäbe kein Heraufkommen in Zukunft, wenn das Latente schon erschienen wäre, und es gäbe ebenso kein Vergehen in Vergangenheit, wenn das in ihr Erschienene, bereits zur Erscheinung Gelöste dem Überhaupt in der Tendenz entspräche' (ibid.). ('There would be no ascent into the future if that which is latent had already appeared, and no lapse into the past if that which appeared and was released in it corresponded to the "altogetherness" of the trend'.) This seems to mean that if nothing changed, nothing would change.

Or again: 'Das Wirkliche ist Prozess; dieser ist die weitverzweigte Vermittlung zwischen Gegenwart, unerledigter Vergangenheit und vor allem: möglicher Zukunft' (*Das Prinzip Hoffnung*, p. 225). ('The real is a process; this process is the widely ramified mediation between the present, the undisposed-of past and, above all, the possible future'.) It is hard to detect in this any meaning beyond the commonplace statement that the world is subject to change.

Bloch's incapacity for analysis is raised to the rank of a theoretical virtue in his frequent wholesale condemnations of 'positivism', the 'fetishism of facts', and 'positivist logic'. Like Lukács, he adopts the slogan 'so much the worse for the facts' (*Tübinger Einleitung*, p. 114), declaring that it signifies the 'primacy of practical reason' and the need for 'humanization' of the world and of the 'logic of philosophy'.

It should perhaps be pointed out that I am not criticizing Bloch for his attack on positivism in general or for refusing to accept the concept of a 'fact' as something self-evident, requiring no argument. Bloch, however, is not a philosophical critic. It suffices to compare his contemptuous phrases about the 'fetishism of facts' with the rational discussions among positivists themselves concerning the concept of a 'fact', or to compare the penetrating critique of positivism in Volume I of Jaspers's *Philosophy*, or in the works of the phenomenologists Husserl and Ingarden, with Bloch's invective against 'crawling empiricism'.

What disqualifies Bloch's philosophy is not that it is wrong but that it lacks content. There is certainly no harm in fantasies about a better future or dreams of invincible technology used to promote human happiness. The trouble with his fantastic projections is not that we cannot tell how to bring them about, but that we are not told in what they consist. Roger Bacon, Leonardo, and Cyrano de Bergerac dreamt of flying-machines, which were impossible with the technology of those days, but if men had not dreamed of them at a time when they could not be constructed, very likely they would never have evolved the technology to make their dreams come true. In this sense utopian projections are a necessary part of life. Unlike those 'concrete' visions, however, Bloch's Utopia is the dream of a perfect world, the nature of whose perfection is a closed book to us. He tells us that the technology of the future will be 'non-Euclidean', but he does not explain what this means, except that it will be 'qualitative' and will restore the harmony between man and nature (capitalism, according to Bloch, is incapable of producing 'true technology').

What is peculiar to Bloch is not that he fantasizes about a better future but that, firstly, his fantasy lacks content; secondly, he believes that it can and must include final perfection within its scope (philosophy has to embrace the whole of future time); and thirdly, he claims that his generalities are a higher form of scientific thought, beyond the grasp of those who worship facts or practise formal logic.

Bloch's thought is a medley of the most varied traditions: neo-Platonic gnosis, the naturalism of the Renaissance and after, modernistic occultism, Marxism, romantic anti-capitalism, cosmic evolutionism, and the theory of the unconscious. Traces of romantic anti-capitalism can certainly be found in Marx and are very strong among the German Marxists or para-Marxists of Bloch's generation, including the Frankfurt school and Marcuse (not Lukács). Bloch maintains that his attacks on capitalism have nothing to do with romantic conservatism, but in fact they are closely linked. He laments that capitalism has killed the beauty of life, mechanized personal relationships, and replaced the aesthetic values of everyday life by purely utilitarian ones. He calls aeroplanes 'mock birds' and believes that nature contains altogether new forms of technology, about which, however, he can only tell us that they will be quite different and will have no harmful consequences.

The core of Bloch's philosophical writing is the idea of transforming 'hope' into a metaphysical category, so that hope becomes a quality of being. This is a kind of inversion of Gabriel Marcel's 'metaphysic of hope', where hope is not an emotional state but a form of existence touched by the grace of God. Bloch, on the other hand, believes that although hope is part of being, it is actualized by human activity. Man does not receive it from nature, still less from God; he activates the hope that is latent in being, and awakens the God asleep in nature. From the point of view of Christian philosophy, Bloch's idea must represent the acme of the sin of pride.

Although his ontologizing of hope cannot be deduced from any Marxist source, Bloch helped in one way to throw light on Marxism by revealing its neo-Platonic roots, which were hidden to Marx himself. He pointed out the link between Marx's belief in the prospect of man's complete reconciliation with himself, and the neo-Platonic gnostic tradition that found its way into Marxism through Hegel. He emphasized the soteriological strain which was blurred in Marx and could therefore be neglected and overlooked, but which set the whole Marxian idea in motion: namely the belief in the future identification of man's authentic essence with empirical existence, or, more simply, the promise *eritis sicut dei*. In this sense Bloch was right to connect Marxism with the gnostic sect that worshipped the serpent in Genesis, maintaining that it and not Jehovah was the true guarantor of the Great Promise. Bloch helped to reveal an essential facet of Marxism which had previously been noticed only in criticisms, for the most part ineffectual, by Christian writers. To this extent his work has not been in vain.

Bloch's philosophy may also be more favourably viewed if we consider not its intrinsic merits but its relation to intellectual conditions in the G.D.R. and Eastern Europe as a whole under the destructive pressure of Stalinism with its levelling influence. Bloch's thought is not only richer, more varied, and many-sided than the cardboard schemata of Soviet dialectical materialism: it also has the virtue that one cannot imagine it being transformed into a party dogma or a 'world-view' imposed by the state. Its very vagueness preserves it from being used as a rigid catechism. In some essential points it diverges so far from Marxist–Leninist schemata as to be irreconcilable with official doctrine. Above all it implies a certain rehabilitation of religion, and this not only in the historical sense that certain forms of religion may in past ages have 'played a progressive role for their time'. This formula is acceptable to Marxism–Leninism, but Bloch goes further: in his view religion has a permanent indestructible root, which in some undefined way must be preserved in futuristic Marxism. Religion therefore must not be treated as a mere collection of superstitions, arising from the ignorance of former times or the search of oppressed peoples for illusory consolation. Although Bloch, like all orthodox Leninist–Stalinists, condemned all non-Marxist philosophy of Marx's day and after, he sought to include in the Marxist tradition certain aspects of the intellectual culture of past ages which stood in very low repute with his orthodox fellow Marxists: among these were several elements of Christianity and also Leibnizian philosophy, the doctrine of natural law and various strands of neo-Platonism. Philosophers in the G.D.R. who had undergone Bloch's influence could no longer swallow Marxist–Leninist schemata without question. In this respect, too, his ideas played a part in combating the dogmatic state ideology of East European socialism.

CHAPTER XIII

Developments in Marxism
since Stalin's death

1. 'De-Stalinization'

JOSEPH VISSARIONOVICH STALIN died of an apoplectic stroke on 5 March 1953. The world had scarcely assimilated the news when his successors, jockeying for power among themselves, inaugurated the process misleadingly known as 'de-Stalinization'. This reached its peak almost three years later, when Nikita Khrushchev announced to the Soviet Communist party, and soon to the whole world, that he who had been the leader of progressive humanity, the inspiration of the world, the father of the Soviet people, the master of science and learning, the supreme military genius, and altogether the greatest genius in history was in reality a paranoiac torturer, a mass murderer, and a military ignoramus who had brought the Soviet state to the verge of disaster.

The three years that had elapsed since Stalin's death had been full of dramatic moments, of which we may briefly mention a few. In June 1953 a revolt of East German workers was crushed by Soviet troops. Soon afterwards it was officially announced that Lavrenty Beriya, one of the key men in the Kremlin and head of State Security, had been arrested for various crimes (news of his trial and execution did not come until December). Around the same time (though the West heard of this much later and unofficially) the inmates of several Siberian concentration camps rebelled; although brutally suppressed, these revolts probably helped to bring about a change in the repressive system. The cult of Stalin was much abated within a few months of his death; in the 'theses' proclaimed by the party to celebrate its fiftieth anniversary in July 1953 his name was mentioned only a few times and was not accompanied by the usual dithyrambs. In 1954 there was some relaxation in cultural policy, and in the autumn it became clear that the Soviet Union was preparing for a reconciliation with Yugoslavia, which meant recanting the charges of 'Titoist conspiracy' that had been the pretext for executing Communist leaders throughout Eastern Europe.

Since the cult of Stalin and his irrefragable authority had for many years been the linchpin of Communist ideology throughout the world, it was not surprising that its reversal led to confusion and uncertainty in all Communist parties and stimulated increasingly sharp and frequent criticism of the socialist system in all its aspects—economic absurdities, police repression, and the enslavement of culture. This criticism spread throughout the 'socialist camp' from the end of 1954 onwards; it was most vehement in Poland and Hungary, where the revisionist movement, as it was called, developed into a wholesale attack on all aspects of Communist dogma without exception.

At the Twentieth Congress of the Communist Party of the Soviet Union in February 1956 Khrushchev made his famous speech on the 'cult of personality'. This took place at a closed session, but in the presence of foreign delegates; the speech was never printed in the Soviet Union, but its text was made known to some party activists and was published shortly afterwards by the U.S. State Department. (Among the Communist countries Poland seems to have been the only one where the text was distributed in print 'for internal use' by trusted party members; the Western Communist parties for a long time refused to acknowledge its authenticity.) In it Khrushchev gave a detailed account of Stalin's crimes and paranoiac delusions, the torture, persecution, and murder of party officials, but he did not rehabilitate any members of the opposition movements: the victims whose names he cited were irreproachable Stalinists like Postyshev, Gamarnik, and Rudzutak, not the dictator's former opponents like Bukharin and Kamenev. Nor did Khrushchev make any attempt at a historical or sociological analysis of the Stalinist system. Stalin had simply been a criminal and a maniac, personally to blame for all the nation's defeats and misfortunes. As to how, and in what social conditions, a bloodthirsty paranoiac could for twenty-five years exercise unlimited despotic power over a country of two hundred million inhabitants, which throughout that period had been blessed with the most progressive and democratic system of government in human history—to this enigma the speech offered no clue whatever. All that was certain was that the Soviet system and the party itself remained impeccably pure and bore no responsibility for the tyrant's atrocities.

The bombshell effect of Khrushchev's speech in the Communist world was not due to the amount of new information it contained. In the Western countries a good deal of literature was already available, both of an academic kind and in the form of first-hand accounts, describing the horrors of the Stalin system in fairly convincing terms, and the details cited by Khrushchev did not alter the general picture or add a great deal to it; while in the Soviet Union and its dependent countries both Communists and non-Communists knew the truth from personal experience. The disruptive effect of the Twentieth Congress on the Communist movement was due to two important peculiarities of that movement: the Communist mentality, and the party's function in the system of government.

Not only in the 'socialist bloc', where the authorities used every means to prevent information seeping in from the outside world, but also in the democratic countries, the Communist parties had created a mentality that was completely immune to all facts and arguments 'from outside', i.e. from 'bourgeois' sources. For the most part Communists were victims of magic thinking, according to which an impure source contaminates the information that comes from it. Anyone who was a political enemy on fundamental issues must automatically be wrong on particular or factual questions. The Communist mind was well armed against the incursions of fact and rational argument. As in mythological systems, truth was defined in practice (though not, of course, in ideological manuals) by the source from which it emanated. Reports which had caused no tremor as long as they appeared in 'bourgeois' books or newspapers had the effect of a thunderclap when confirmed by the Kremlin oracle. What were yesterday the 'despicable lies of imperialist propaganda' suddenly became the appalling truth. Moreover, the fallen idol did not simply leave a pedestal to be occupied by someone else. Stalin's dethronement meant not only the collapse of one authority, but that of a whole institution. Party members could not pin their hopes on a second Stalin coming to repair the errors of the first; they could no longer take seriously the official assurances that although Stalin had been bad, the party and the system were immaculate.

Secondly, the moral ruin of Communism momentarily shook the entire system of power. The Stalinist regime could not exist without the cement of ideology to legitimize party rule, and the party apparatus at this time was sensitive to ideological shocks. Since, in Leninist–Stalinist socialism, the stability of the whole power system depends on that of the governing apparatus, the confusion, uncertainty, and demoralization of the bureaucracy threatened the whole structure of the regime. De-Stalinization proved to be a virus from which Communism never recovered, though it made shift to adapt itself, at all events in temporary fashion.

In Poland, although social criticism and 'revisionist' tendencies were already far advanced at the time of the Twentieth Congress, that Congress and Khrushchev's speech greatly accelerated the dissolution of the party; it emboldened critics to attack the system more openly, and so far weakened the governing apparatus that social discontent, which had accumulated for years and was kept down by intimidation, came more and more clearly to the surface. In June 1956 there was a workers' rising at Poznań; though touched off by immediate economic hardship it reflected the pent-up hatred of the whole working class for the Soviet Union and the Polish Government alike. The revolt was quelled, but the party was demoralized and disoriented, rent by faction and undermined by 'revisionism'. In Hungary the situation reached a point where the party collapsed completely, the population went into open rebellion, and the government announced that it was withdrawing from the Soviet military camp (the Warsaw Pact); the Red Army intervened to crush the revolt, its leaders were mercilessly dealt with, and almost all the government team of October 1956 were put to death. Poland escaped invasion at the last moment, owing in part to the fact that the former party leader Władysław Gomułka, who had escaped with his life during the Stalin purges, came forward as a providential figure to avert the explosion, his background of political imprisonment serving to gain the confidence of the population. The Russian leaders, at first highly mistrustful, decided in the end—quite rightly, as it turned out—

that although Gomulka had taken over without Kremlin sanction
he would not prove too disobedient, and that invasion would
be a greater risk. The 'Polish October', as it was called, far from
ushering in a period of social and cultural renewal or 'liberalization', stood for the gradual extinction of all such attempts. In
1956 Poland was, relatively speaking, a country of free speech
and free criticism, not because the government had planned it
so but because they had lost control of the situation. The
October events started a process of reversal, and the margin of
freedom which still remained grew less year by year. Of the
rural co-operatives that had been compulsorily set up, the great
majority were soon disbanded; but from October 1956 onwards
the party machine regained its lost positions step by step. It
repaired the dislocation of government, imposed restrictions on
cultural freedom, put a brake on economic reform, and reduced
to a purely decorative role the workers' councils that had formed
spontaneously in 1956. Meanwhile the invasion of Hungary
and the wave of persecution that followed there struck terror
into the other 'people's democracies'. In East Germany a few
of the more active 'revisionists' were locked up. De-Stalinization
led in the end to brutal repressions, but the devastation throughout the bloc was such that the Soviet system could never be
the same as before.

The term 'de-Stalinization' (like the term 'Stalinism') was
never officially used by the Communist parties themselves, which
spoke instead of 'correcting errors and distortions', 'overcoming
the cult of personality', and 'returning to Leninist norms of
party life'. These euphemisms were meant to convey the impression that Stalinism had been a series of regrettable errors
committed by the irresponsible Generalissimo but had nothing
to do with the system itself, and that it sufficed to condemn
his ways in order to restore the pre-eminently democratic
character of the regime. But the terms 'de-Stalinization' and
'Stalinism' are misleading for other reasons than those which
precluded their use in the official vocabulary of Communist
countries. The Communists eschewed them because 'Stalinism'
gave the impression of a system and not of accidental deviations
arising from the ruler's faults of character. But, on the other
hand, the term 'Stalinism' also suggests that the 'system' was
bound up with Stalin's personality, and that his condemnation

was the signal for a radical change in the direction of 'democratization' or 'liberalization'.

Although the background to the Twentieth Congress is not known in detail, it is clear in retrospect that certain features of the system that had prevailed for twenty-five years could not be maintained without Stalin and the inviolable authority he had wielded. Since the great purges Russia had lived under a regime in which none of the most privileged members of the party and government, even the Politburo, could be sure from one day to the next whether they would be suffered to live or be destroyed at the tyrant's whim, by the mere lifting of his infallible finger. It is not surprising that after Stalin's death they were anxious that no successor of his should get into the same position. The condemnation of 'errors and distortions' was a necessary part of the unwritten mutual security pact among the party leaders; and in the Soviet Union, as in the other socialist countries, intra-party conflicts were henceforth settled without the deposed oligarchs losing their lives. The system of periodic massacre had certainly had its merits from the point of view of political stability, making faction impossible and ensuring the unity of the apparatus of power; but the price of that unity was one-man despotism and the reduction of all members of the apparatus to the conditions of slaves whose very tenure of life was uncertain, though they enjoyed privileges as the custodians of other slaves whose condition was more abject still. The first effect of de-Stalinization was the replacement of mass terror by selective terror which, though still of considerable scope, was not completely arbitrary as it had been under Stalin. Soviet citizens henceforth knew more or less how to avoid prison and the concentration camp, whereas previously there had been no rules at all. One of the important events of Khrushchev's era was the liberation of millions from the camps.

Another effect of the change was that various moves were made towards decentralization, and it became easier for rival political groups to form in secret. There were also attempts at economic reform, which improved efficiency to some extent; however, the dogma of the primacy of heavy industry was upheld (except for a brief interlude under Malenkov), and no steps were taken to make production more responsive to mass demand by releasing market mechanisms. Nor was there any substantial

improvement in agriculture, which despite frequent 'reorgan-
izations' remained in the miserable state to which it had been
reduced by collectivization.

All the changes, however, did not amount to 'democratization'
but left unimpaired the foundations of Communist despotism.
The abandonment of mass terror was important for human
security, but it did not affect the state's absolute power over
the individual; it did not confer on citizens any institutional
rights, or infringe the state and party monopoly of initiative and
control in all spheres of life. The principle of totalitarian
government was upheld, whereby human beings are the property
of the state and all their aims and actions must conform to its
purposes and needs. Although various departments of life resisted
absorption, so that the process was never complete, the whole
system operated, as it still does, to enforce state control to the
utmost degree possible. Indiscriminate terror on a vast scale is
not a necessary and permanent condition of totalitarianism; the
nature and intensity of repressive measures may be affected by
various circumstances; but under Communism there can be no
such thing as the rule of law, in which law acts as an
autonomous mediator between the citizen and the state, and
deprives the latter of its absolute power *vis-à-vis* the individual.
The present repressive system in the Soviet Union and other
Communist countries is not simply a 'survival of Stalinism' or
a regrettable blemish that may be cured in time without a
fundamental change in the system.

The only Communist regimes in the world are of the Leninist–
Stalinist pattern. On Stalin's death the Soviet system changed
from a personal tyranny to that of an oligarchy. From the point
of view of state omnipotence this is a less effective system; it
does not, however, amount to de-Stalinization, but only to an
ailing form of Stalinism.

2. *Revisionism in Eastern Europe*

From the second half of the 1950s the term 'revisionism' was
used by the party authorities and official ideologists in Communist countries to stigmatize those who, while remaining party
members or Marxists, attacked various Communist dogmas. No
precise meaning was attached to it, or indeed to the label of
'dogmatism' affixed to party 'conservatives' who opposed the

post-Stalin reforms, but as a rule the term 'revisionism' connoted democratic and rationalist tendencies. As in former times it had been applied to Bernstein's critique of Marxism, party functionaries took to linking the new 'revisionism' with Bernstein's views, but the connection was remote and insubstantial. Few of the active 'revisionists' were especially interested in Bernstein; many problems that had been at the centre of ideological debate around 1900 were no longer topical; some of Bernstein's ideas that had aroused furious indignation at the time were now accepted by orthodox Communists, such as the doctrine that socialism might be achieved by legal means—a purely tactical change, but none the less important ideologically. 'Revisionism' did not come from reading Bernstein but from living under Stalin. However vaguely the term was used by party leaders, however, there was in the fifties and sixties a genuine, active political and intellectual movement which, operating for a time within Marxism or at least using Marxist language, had a highly disruptive effect on Communist doctrine.

In 1955–7, as Communist ideology disintegrated, attacks on the system were widespread. The typical feature of this period was that Communists, while not the only critics of existing conditions, were the most active and conspicuous ones, and on the whole the most effective. There were several reasons for this predominance. In the first place, as the revisionists belonged to the 'establishment' they had much easier access to the mass media and to unpublished information. Secondly, in the nature of things they knew more than other groups about Communist ideology and Marxism, and about the state and party machine. Thirdly, Communists were used to the idea that they should take the lead in everything, and the party did, after all, include a number of members endowed with energy and initiative. Fourthly, and this was the chief reason, the revisionists, at least for a considerable time, used Marxist language: they appealed to Communist ideological stereotypes and Marxist authorities, and made a devastating comparison between socialist reality and the values and promises to be found in the 'classics'. In this way the revisionists, unlike others who opposed the system from a nationalist or religious point of view, not only addressed themselves to party opinion but awakened an echo in party circles; they were listened to by the party apparatus and thereby contributed to its ideological disarray, which was the principal condition of political change. They used party language to some extent because they still believed in Communist stereotypes, and to some extent because they knew it would be more effective; the proportion as between faith and deliberate camouflage is hard to estimate at this distance of time.

In the wave of criticism which affected all aspects of life and gradually undermined all the sanctities of Communism, some demands and viewpoints were peculiar to the revisionists while others were common to them and non-party or non-Marxist opponents of the regime. The principal demands put forward were as follows.

In the first place, all the critics called for a general democratization of public life, the abolition of the system of repression and the secret police, or at least the subordination of the police to a judiciary acting in accordance with law and independence of political pressure; they demanded freedom of the Press, sciences, and arts, and the abolition of preventive censorship. The revisionists also called for intra-party democracy, and some of them demanded the right to form 'fractions' within the party. From the beginning there were differences among the revisionists on these points. Some demanded democracy for party members without advancing any more general claims, appearing to believe that the party could be a democratic island in a non-democratic society; they thus accepted, expressly or by implication, the principle of the 'dictatorship of the proletariat', i.e. of the party, and imagined that the ruling party could afford the luxury of internal democracy. In time, however, most of the revisionists came to see that there could be no democracy for the élite only; if intra-party groups were allowed to exist they would become the mouthpieces of social forces which were otherwise denied utterance, so that a system of 'fractions' within the party would become a substitute for a multi-party system. It was necessary to choose therefore between the free formation of political parties, with all its consequences, and dictatorship by one party, which involved dictatorship within that party.

Important among democratic objectives was the independence of trade unions and workers' councils. The cry 'All power to the councils' was even heard—not very loudly, it is true, but the idea of workers' councils independent of the party, which could not only bargain with the state over questions of pay and working conditions but also play an effective part in industrial management, was frequently advanced in both Poland and Hungary; later on, the example of Yugoslavia was quoted. Workers' self-government went naturally with the decentralization of economic planning.

An important reform desired by non-party critics was freedom of religion and an end to persecution of the Church. The revisionists, who were for the most part anti-religious, stood aside from this question; they believed in the separation of Church and State and did not support the demand, which was widespread in those years, for the reintroduction of religious education into schools.

The second category of demands universally put forward related to state sovereignty and equality among members of the 'socialist bloc'. In all the bloc countries Soviet supervision was extremely thorough in many spheres; the army and police in particular were under specific and direct control, and the duty to follow the elder brother's example in everything was the foundation of state ideology. The whole population felt keenly the humiliation of their country, its dependence on the Soviet Union, and the latter's unscrupulous economic exploitation of its neighbours. While, however, the Polish population as a whole was strongly anti-Russian, the revisionists generally invoked traditional socialist principles and avoided the language of nationalism. A frequent demand by both revisionists and others was for the abolition of the privileges enjoyed by the bureaucracy, not so much in matters of pay but in the extra-legal arrangements that freed them from the hardships of everyday life—special shops and medical facilities, housing priorities, and so on.

The third main area of criticism was economic management. There was, it should be noted, scarcely any call for the restoration of industry to private hands; most people were used to the idea that it should be publicly owned. They demanded, however, the cessation of compulsory agricultural collectivization; a reduction in the extremely burdensome investment programme; an enlargement of the role of market conditions in the economy; profit-sharing by workers; rationalized planning and the abandonment of unrealistic all-embracing plans; a reduction in the norms and directives that hampered enterprise; and concessions to private and co-operative activity in the field of services and small-scale production.

In all these matters revisionist demands coincided with those of the population in general; the revisionists, however, used socialist and Marxist arguments instead of nationalist and religious ones, and they also put forward aspirations relating to party life and Marxist studies. In this respect, like other heretics in history, they appealed for a 'return to the sources', i.e. they based their criticism of the system on Marxist tradition. More than once, especially in the early stages, they invoked Lenin's authority, searching his writings for texts in support of intra-party democracy, the participation of the 'broad masses' in government, and so on. In short, the revisionists for a time opposed Lenin to Stalinism, as survivors of the movement still do from time to time. They did not have much intellectual success, as the discussions made it increasingly clear that Stalinism was the natural and legitimate continuation of Lenin's ideas; but politically their arguments were of some importance, as we have seen, in helping to disrupt Communist ideology by appealing to its own stereotypes. The peculiarity of the situation was that both Marxism and Leninism spoke a language full of humane and democratic slogans which, while they were empty rhetoric as far as the system of power was concerned, could be and were invoked against that system. By pointing out the grotesque contrast between Marxist–Leninist phraseology and the realities of life, the revisionists laid bare the contradictions of the doctrine itself. The ideology became detached, as it were, from the political movement of which it had been a mere façade, and began to live a life of its own.

While, however, attempts to hold fast to Leninism were soon abandoned by most of the revisionists, the hope of a return to 'authentic' Marxism lasted much longer.

The main issue that divided the revisionists from their party colleagues was not the fact that they criticized Stalinism; at that time, especially after the Twentieth Congress, hardly any party members defended it with all its aberrations. Nor did the difference even lie chiefly in the extent of their criticism, but rather in their rejection of the official view that Stalinism was a 'mistake' or a 'distortion' or a series of 'mistakes and distortions'. Most of them held that the Stalinist system had made few mistakes from the point of view of its social functions, that it was a fairly coherent political system in itself, and that the roots of the evil must therefore be sought not in Stalin's personal faults or 'mistakes' but in the nature of Communist power. They believed for some time, however, that Stalinism was curable in the sense that Communism could be restored or 'democratized' without questioning its foundations (though it was far from clear what exactly were basic features and what were accidental ones). But, as time went on, the revisionists saw more and more clearly that this position too was untenable: if the one-party system was a necessary condition of Communism, then Communism was unreformable.

It appeared, however, for some time yet that Marxist socialism was possible without Leninist political forms, and that Communism might be attacked 'within the framework of Marxism'. Hence many attempts were made to reinterpret the Marxist tradition in an anti-Leninist sense.

The revisionists began by requiring that Marxism should subject itself to the normal rules of scientific rationality, instead of relying on the monopolistic power of censorship, police, and privilege. They argued that such privilege inevitably led to the degeneration of Marxism and deprived it of vitality; that Marxism must be able to defend its existence by the empirical and logical methods universally accepted by science; and that Marxist studies were withering away because Marxism had been institutionalized into a state ideology immune from criticism. It could only be regenerated by free discussion in which Marxists would have to defend their positions by rational argument. The critics attacked the primitiveness and sterility of Marxist writings, their inadequacy to the main problems of the present age, their schematic and ossified character, and the ignorance of those who were regarded as the chief exponents of the doctrine. They attacked the poverty of the conceptual categories of Leninist–Stalinist Marxism and the simplistic attempts to explain all culture in terms of the class struggle, to reduce all philosophy to 'the conflict between materialism and idealism', to turn all morality into an instrument for the 'building of socialism', and so on.

As far as philosophy is concerned, the revisionists' main

objective may be defined as the vindication of human subjectivity in opposition to Leninist doctrine. The main points of their attack were as follows.

In the first place, they criticized Lenin's 'theory of reflection', arguing that the sense of Marx's epistemology was entirely different. Cognition did not consist of the object being reflected in the mind, but was an interaction of subject and object, and the effect of this interaction, co-determined by social and biological factors, could not be regarded as a copy of the world. The human mind could not transcend the manner in which it was associated with being; the world as we know it is partially man-made.

Secondly, the revisionists criticized determinism. Neither Marx's theory nor any factual considerations justified a determinist metaphysic, especially as far as history was concerned. The idea that there were unalterable 'laws of history' and that socialism was historically inevitable was a mythological superstition which might have played a part in stirring up enthusiasm for Communism but was none the more rational for that. Chance and uncertainty could not be excluded from past history, still less from predictions of the future.

Thirdly, they criticized attempts to deduce moral values from speculative historiographical schemata. Even if it were supposed, wrongly, that the socialist future was guaranteed by this or that historical necessity, it would not follow that it was our duty to support such necessities. What is necessary is not for that reason valuable; socialism still needs a moral foundation, over and above its being allegedly the result of 'historical laws'. For the idea of socialism to be restored, a system of values must first be re-created independently of historiosophical doctrine.

All these criticisms had the common aim of restoring the role of the subject in the historical and cognitive process. They were combined with a criticism of the bureaucratic regime and the absurd pretentions of the party apparatus to superior wisdom and knowledge of 'historical laws' and, on the strength of this, to unrestricted power and privilege. From the philosophical point of view, revisionism soon broke completely with Leninism.

In the course of their criticism the revisionists naturally appealed to various sources, some Marxist and some not. In Eastern Europe some part was played by existentialism, especially the works of Sartre, as many revisionists were attracted by his theory of freedom and the subject's irreducibility to the status of a thing. Many others found inspiration in Hegel, while those who were interested in Engels's philosophy of science brought analytical philosophy to bear on his and Lenin's 'dialectic of nature'. The revisionists read Western critical and philosophical literature about Marxism and Communism: Camus, Merleau-Ponty, Koestler, Orwell. Marxist authorities of the past played only a secondary role in their discussions and criticisms. Trotsky was scarcely mentioned; some interest was taken in Rosa Luxemburg for her attacks on Lenin and the Russian revolution (but an attempt to publish her book on that subject in Poland was unsuccessful); among philosophers Lukács was popular for a while, chiefly on account of his theory of the historical process in which subject and object tend towards identity. Somewhat later, Gramsci became an object of interest: his works contained the outline of a theory of knowledge completely opposed to Lenin's, together with critical reflections on Communist bureaucracy, the theory of the party as an advance guard, historical determinism, and the 'manipulative' approach to socialist revolution.

Further reinforcement came at this time from the Italian Communists. Palmiro Togliatti, who had till then enjoyed the deserved reputation of a dyed-in-the-wool Stalinist, went on record after the Twentieth Congress with a criticism of the Soviet leaders, moderate as to language but important in its consequences. He accused them of casting the whole responsibility for Stalinism on to Stalin and failing to analyse the causes of bureaucratic degeneration, and ended with an appeal for 'polycentrism' in the world Communist movement, i.e. an end to Moscow's hegemony over the other parties.

Revisionism in Poland, where the critical movement in the 1950s went much further than in the rest of Eastern Europe, was the work of a numerous group of party intellectuals— philosophers, sociologists, journalists, men of letters, historians, and economists. It found expression in the specialized Press and in literary and political weeklies (especially *Po prostu* and *Nowa Kultura*), which played an important part until they were suppressed by the authorities. Among the philosophers and sociologists who were frequently attacked as revisionists were

B. Baczko, K. Pomian, R. Zimand, Z. Bauman, M. Bielińska, and the present writer, who was singled out as the chief culprit. Economists who advanced revisionist theories were M. Kalecki, O. Lange, W. Brus, E. Lipiński, and T. Kowalik.

In Hungary the chief centre of revisionism was the 'Petőfi Circle' in Budapest, which included some of Lukács's disciples. Lukács himself took a prominent part in its discussions, but both he and his followers emphasized their fidelity to Marxism much more strongly than the Polish revisionists; Lukács called for freedom 'within the framework of Marxism' and did not question the principle of single-party rule. It may be—this is only a supposition—that the much more orthodox character of Hungarian revisionism was the reason why it became so detached from the movement of popular discontent that the revisionists were unable to keep the attack on the party within bounds; the result was a mass protest, expressly anti-Communist in character, leading to the collapse of the party and to Soviet invasion. This caused a shock not only in Poland, where it became obvious at once that ideas of a 'democratized' Communist system were fairy-tales, but also among Western Communists: some of the smaller parties split up, while others lost the support of many intellectuals. Among Communists throughout the world the invasion of Hungary provoked various dissident movements and attempts to reconstruct the movement and its doctrine on non-Soviet lines. In Britain, France, and Italy many works were published on the possibility or otherwise of democratic Communism; the 'New Left' of the sixties was largely inspired by these sources.

The revisionist movement in Hungary was destroyed by the Soviet invasion. In Poland it was combated over a period of years by various, relatively mild forms of repression: the closure of periodicals or enforced dismissal of contributors who refused to toe the line, the temporary banning of publication by individual writers, intensified censorship in all branches of culture. The main reason, however, why Polish revisionism gradually declined was not the use of such measures but the disintegration of party ideology, undermined by revisionist criticism.

As an attempt to renew Marxism by returning to its 'sources' —chiefly the young Marx and his idea of the self-creation of humanity—and to reform Communism by curing its repressive and bureaucratic character, revisionism could be effective only as long as the party took the traditional ideology seriously and the apparatus was in some degree sensitive to ideological questions. But revisionism itself was a major cause of the fact that the party lost its respect for official doctrine and that ideology increasingly became a sterile though indispensable ritual. In this way revisionist criticism, especially in Poland, cut the ground from under its own feet. Writers and intellectuals continued their manifestations, protests, and attempts to put political pressure on the authorities, but there were less and less inspired by truly revisionist, i.e. Marxist, ideas. In the party and bureaucracy the importance of Communist ideology was manifestly declining. Instead of people who, even if they had taken part in the atrocities of Stalinism, were in their way loyal Communists and attached to Communist ideals, the reins of power were now held by cynical, disillusioned careerists who were perfectly aware of the emptiness of the Communist slogans they made use of. A bureaucracy of this kind was immune to ideological shocks.

Revisionism itself, on the other hand, had a certain inner logic which, before long, carried it beyond the frontiers of Marxism. Anyone who took seriously the rules of rationalism could not be interested any longer in the degree of his own 'loyalty' to Marxist tradition, or feel any inhibition about using other sources and theoretical stimuli; Marxism in its Leninist–Stalinist form was such a poor and primitive structure that on close analysis it practically disappeared. Marx's own doctrine certainly afforded more food for the mind, but in the nature of things it could not provide answers to questions that philosophy and the social sciences had raised since Marx's day, nor could it assimilate various important conceptual categories evolved by twentieth-century humanistic culture. Attempts to combine Marxism with trends originating elsewhere soon deprived it of its clear-cut doctrinal form: it became merely one of several contributions to intellectual history, instead of an all-embracing system of authoritative truths among which, if one looked hard enough, one could find the answer to everything. Marxism had functioned for decades almost entirely as the political ideology of a powerful but self-contained sect, with the result that it was almost completely cut off from the external world of ideas; when attempts were made to overcome this isolation it generally proved too late—the doctrine collapsed, like mummified remains suddenly exposed to the air. From this point of view, orthodox party members were quite right to fear the consequences of trying to breathe fresh life into Marxism. Revisionist appeals which seemed to be the merest common sense—Marxism must be defended in free discussion by the intellectual methods universally applied in science, its ability to solve modern problems must be analysed without fear, its conceptual apparatus must be enriched, historical documents must not be falsified, and so on—all proved to have catastrophic results: instead of Marxism being enriched or supplemented, it dissolved in a welter of alien ideas.

In Poland revisionism lived on for a time but became less and less important ideologically as compared with other forms of opposition. It was represented in the early sixties by Kuroń and Modzelewski, who put forward a Marxist and Communist political programme. Their analysis of Polish society and government, which led them to the conclusion that a new exploiting class had come into existence in the Communist countries and could only be overthrown by a proletarian revolution, was arrived at on traditional Marxist lines. It cost them several years' imprisonment, but their resistance helped to form a students' opposition movement leading to fairly widespread riots in March 1968. This, however, had little to do with Communist ideology: most of the students protested in the name of civic and academic liberties, but did not interpret these in any specifically Communist or even socialist sense. After the riots were crushed the government launched an attack in the cultural field (closely linked with the struggle between rival party cliques at that time), and in so doing revealed that its main ideological principle was anti-Semitism.

The year 1968, which was also that of the Soviet invasion of Czechoslovakia, virtually marked the end of revisionism as a separate intellectual trend in Poland. At present the opposition which articulates itself in various forms makes scarcely any use of Marxist or Communist phraseology, but finds fully adequate expression in terms of national conservatism, religion, and traditional democratic or social-democratic formulas. Communism has ceased in general to be an intellectual problem, remaining simply a matter of government power and repression. The situation is a paradoxical one. The ruling party still officially professes Marxism and the Communist doctrine of 'proletarian internationalism'; Marxism is a compulsory subject in all places of higher learning, manuals of it are published and books are written about its problems; yet this state ideology has never been in such a lifeless condition as now. No one in practice believes in it, neither the rulers nor the ruled, and both are aware of this fact; yet it is indispensable, since it constitutes the main foundation of the legitimacy of the regime, as the dictatorship of the party is based on the claim that it 'expresses' the historical interests of the working class and the people. Everyone knows that 'proletarian internationalism' is nothing but a phrase to cover the fact that the East European countries are not masters of their own affairs, and that the 'leading role of the working class' simply means dictatorship by the party bureaucracy. Consequently, the rulers themselves, when they wish to arouse at least some degree of response from the population, appeal less and less to the ideology that exists only on paper, and instead use the language of *raison d'état* and national interest. Not only is the official ideology lifeless, but it is no longer clearly formulated as it was in Stalin's day, since there is no authority competent to do so. Intellectual life continues, though harassed by censorship and various police restrictions, but Marxism plays next to no part in it, although state support maintains it artificially in being and immune from criticism. In the field of ideology and the humanistic sciences the party can only act negatively, by means of repression and prohibitions of all kinds. Even so, the official ideology has had to forfeit a large part of its former universalist claims. Marxism, of course, may not be criticized directly, but even in philosophy works appear which completely ignore it and are written as if it had never existed. In sociology a certain number of orthodox treatises are regularly published, mainly to secure an attestation of their authors' political reliability, while at the same time many other works fall into the category of ordinary empirical sociology, using the same methods as in the West. The scope permitted to such works is of course limited: they may deal with changes in family life or working conditions in industry, but not the sociology of power or of party life. Severe restrictions are imposed, for purely political rather than Marxist reasons, on the historical sciences, especially where recent history is concerned. The Soviet rulers seem to be firmly convinced that they represent the continuation of Tsarist policy, and hence the study of Polish history, which for two centuries was dominated by relations with Russia, the Partitions, and national oppression, is subject to a multitude of taboos.

To a certain extent one may still speak of revisionism in the context of Polish economic studies, where it takes the form of practical recommendations for increased efficiency. The best-known authors in this field are W. Brus and E. Lipiński, who both invoke the Marxist tradition but in a form closer to social democracy. They argue that the faults and inefficiency of the socialist economy cannot be cured by purely economic means, as they are tied up with the repressive political system. Economic rationalization therefore cannot succeed without political pluralism, i.e. in practice without abolishing the specifically Communist regime. Nationalization of the means of production, Brus contends, is not the same as public ownership, since the political bureaucracy has a monopoly of economic decision; a truly socialized economy is incompatible with political dictatorship.

To a somewhat lesser degree Władysław Bieńkowski may be classed as a revisionist: in works published outside Poland he analyses the causes of social and economic deterioration under bureaucratic governments. He appeals to the Marxist tradition, but goes beyond it in examining the autonomized mechanisms of political power independent of the class system (in Marx's sense of 'class').

Similar tendencies connected with the decline of Communist faith, the reduced vitality of Marxism and its transformation into a political rite can be observed, though in varying degrees, in all the Communist countries.

In Czechoslovakia 1956 was a much less important year than in Poland and Hungary, and the revisionist movement was late in developing, but the general trend was the same as else-where. The best-known revisionist among Czech economists is Ota Šik, who in the early sixties advanced a typical programme of reform: increased influence of the market on production, greater autonomy of enterprises, decentralized planning, an analysis of political bureaucracy as the cause of socialist economic inefficiency. Although political conditions were more difficult than in Poland, a revisionist group of philosophers also came into being. Its best-known member was Karel Kosik, who in *Dialectics of the Concrete* (1963) put forward a number of typically revisionist issues: a return to the idea of praxis as the most general category in the interpretation of history; the relativity of ontological questions *vis-à-vis* anthropological ones, the abandonment of materialist metaphysics and of the primacy of the 'base' over the 'superstructure'; philosophy and art as co-determinants of social life and not merely its products.

The economic crisis in Czechoslovakia at the beginning of 1968 precipitated political change and the replacement of the party leadership. This at once let loose an avalanche of political and ideological criticism, dominated by revisionist ideas. The proclaimed objectives were the same as they had been in Poland and Hungary: abolition of the repressive police system, legal guarantees of civic freedom, the independence of culture, democratic economic management. The demand for a multi-party system, or at least the right to form different socialist parties, was not directly put forward by those of the revisionists who were party members, but figured constantly in the discussions.

The Soviet occupation in August 1968 and the mass repressions that followed had the effect of almost completely stifling Czechoslovak intellectual and cultural life, which still presents a highly depressing picture even in comparison with the other bloc countries. On the other hand, precisely because the reform movement in Czechoslovakia did not disintegrate of itself but was suppressed by force of arms, the country offers a more fertile soil for revisionist ideas. It may be imagined that, if the invasion had not taken place, the reform movement begun under Dubček and supported by the great majority of the population might eventually have brought about 'socialism with a human face' without shaking the foundations of the system. This of course is a matter of speculation, and depends on what exactly is regarded as fundamental. What does seem clear, however, is that if the reform movement had continued and had neither been suppressed by invasion nor, as in Poland, had disintegrated from fear of invasion, it must soon have led to a multi-party system, thus destroying the Communist party dictatorship and therefore destroying Communism as that doctrine conceives itself.

East Germany, where the system of repression was generally more thorough than elsewhere, did not witness any widespread revisionist movement, but was none the less shaken by the events of 1956. The philosopher and literary critic Wolfgang Harich put forward a democratic programme of German socialism, which earned him several years' imprisonment. Some well-known Marxist intellectuals left the country (Ernst Bloch, Hans Mayer, Alfred Kantorowicz). The strict regimentation of ideas made any attempt at revisionism extremely difficult, as it still does, but occasionally a reformist voice was heard. In philosophy the most important name in this connection is that of Robert Havemann, a professor of physical chemistry with an interest in philosophical questions, who, unlike many other revisionists, remained a convinced Marxist throughout. In essays and lectures, published of course in West Germany, he sharply criticized the party dictatorship in science and philosophy and the custom of deciding theoretical questions by bureaucratic decree; in addition he attacked the doctrine of dialectical materialism and the official norms of Communist morality. He did not, however, criticize Marxism from a positivist standpoint but, on the contrary, wished to return to a more 'Hegelianized' version of the dialectic. He maintained that the chief enemy of Marxism was mechanistic materialism, which was generally taught under the name Marxism. He attacked the Leninist version of determinism as morally dangerous and incompatible with modern physics. Following Hegel and Engels he postulated a dialectic that was not merely a description but an aspect of reality, including logical relations; in this way, like Bloch, he tried to justify a finalistic attitude within the terms of dialectical materialism. He condemned the Stalinist enslavement of culture, and declared that the philosophical negation of freedom in the mechanistic doctrine that usually passed for Marxism went hand in hand with the destruction of cultural freedom under Communism. He called for the rehabilitation of 'spontaneity' as a philosophic category and as a political value, but at the same time emphasized his fidelity to dialectical materialism and Communism. Havemann's philosophical writings are less precise than one might expect from a chemist.

In the U.S.S.R. there was no revisionism to speak of in philosophy, but some economists proposed reforms aimed at the rationalization of management and distribution. Official Soviet philosophy was little affected by de-Stalinization, while the unofficial variety soon lost all contact with Marxism. In official philosophy the principal change was that the schemata of dialectical materialism were no longer taught after the exact pattern of Stalin's booklet. The textbook published in 1958 followed Engels in distinguishing three laws of the dialectic (including the negation of the negation), not four; materialism was expounded first and the dialectic second, a reversal of Stalin's order. The dozen or so 'categories' of the dialectic enumerated in Lenin's *Philosophical Notes* provided the basis of a newly arranged schema. Soviet philosophers held several discussions on the time-honoured theme of the 'relation of the dialectic to formal logic', the majority view being that there was no conflict between the two, as their subject-matter was different; some also challenged the theory that 'contradictions' might occur in reality itself. Hegel ceased to personify the 'aristocratic reaction to the French Revolution'; henceforth it was correct to speak of his 'limitations' and also his 'merits'.

All these inessential and superficial changes made no breach in the structure of the Leninist–Stalinist 'diamat'. None the less, Soviet philosophy enjoyed some benefit from de-Stalinization, though less than other disciplines. A younger generation came on the scene and, of its own accord—since there were hardly any qualified teachers except a few chance survivors from Stalin's purges—began to look into Western philosophy and logic, to study foreign languages, and finally even to explore non-Marxist Russian traditions. In the first years after Stalin's death it was clear that the young philosophers were most attracted by Anglo-Saxon positivism and the analytical school. The treatment of logic became more rational and less subject to political control. The five-volume *Philosophical Encyclopedia* published in the 1960s is on the whole better than the output of Stalin's day: the main ideological articles, especially those relating to Marxism, are on the same level as before, but there are also many concerned with logic and the history of philosophy which are written on sensible lines and are not merely dictated by state propaganda. Thanks to the younger philosophers' efforts to renew contact with European and American thought, a few modern works have been translated from Western languages. Timid and cautious attempts to 'modernize' Marxism were perceptible for a time in *Philosophical Science (Filosofskie Nauki)*, which began to appear in 1958. On the whole, however, publications did not reflect the mental changes that were taking place. The backwoodsmen trained in Stalin's day continued to decide which of the younger men should be allowed to publish or teach in universities, and naturally favoured their own kind. However, some of the younger and better educated philosophers found ways of expressing themselves in other fields that were less strictly controlled.

On the whole, however, philosophy, the first discipline to be destroyed by Communism, was also the slowest to revive, and the results so far are extremely meagre. Other branches of learning recovered in more or less the opposite order to that in which they were originally 'Stalinized'. Within a few years of the dictator's death the natural sciences virtually ceased to be ideologically regulated, though the choice of research subjects continued to be strictly controlled, as it still is. In physics, chemistry, medical, and biological research the state provides material resources and lays down the purposes for which they are used, but it no longer insists that the results shall be orthodox from the Marxist point of view. The historical sciences are still closely controlled, but here too areas of less political sensitivity are less subject to regulation. For some years theoretical linguistics were relatively free and revived the tradition of the Russian formalistic school, but eventually the state intervened here also by closing some institutions, having noticed that they were being used as an outlet for various unorthodox ideas. On the whole, however, the period from 1955 to 1965 was one of considerable and often successful efforts to revive Russian culture after years of devastation; this applies to literature, painting, drama, and films as well as historiography and philosophy. In the second half of the sixties increasing pressure was again brought to bear on suspect individuals and institutions. Unlike the situation in Eastern Europe, Marxism in the Soviet Union showed hardly any signs of reanimation. Among the clandestine or semi-clandestine ideological developments which were especially lively from about 1965 onwards, Marxist trends were scarcely noticeable: instead we find the most varying tendencies, including Great Russian chauvinism (often in a form that might be called 'Bolshevism without Marxism'), the national aspirations of the oppressed non-Russian peoples, religion (specifically Orthodox or broadly Christian or Buddhist), and traditional democratic ideas. Marxism or Leninism accounts for only a small fraction of the general opposition, but it does exist, its best-known Soviet spokesmen being the brothers Roy and Zhores Medvedyev. The former, a historian, is the author of some valuable works, including a general analysis of Stalinism on a large scale. This contains much information not known from elsewhere and certainly cannot be regarded as an attempt to palliate the horrors of the Stalinist system; nevertheless, like the author's other works, it is based on the view that there is a clear break between Leninism and Stalinism and that Lenin's plan for the socialist society was completely distorted and deformed by Stalin's tyranny. (The present writer, as will be clear from previous chapters of this work, takes exactly the opposite view.)

In the last two decades the ideological situation in the Soviet Union has gone through changes in many ways similar to those that have occurred in the other socialist countries. Marxism is practically extinct as a doctrine, though it performs a useful service in justifying Soviet imperialism and the whole internal policy of oppression, exploitation, and privilege. As in Eastern Europe, the rulers have to resort to other ideological values than Communism if they wish to find common ground with their subjects. As far as the Russian people itself is concerned the values in question are those of chauvinism and imperial glory, while all the peoples of the Soviet Union are susceptible to xenophobia, especially anti-Chinese nationalism and anti-Semitism. This is all that remains of Marxism in the first state in the world to be constituted on allegedly Marxist principles. This nationalist and to some extent racist outlook is the true, unavowed ideology of the Soviet state, not only protected but inculcated by means of allusions and unprinted texts; and, unlike Marxism, it awakens a real echo in popular feeling.

There is probably no part of the civilized world in which Marxism has declined so completely and socialist ideas have been so discredited and turned to ridicule as in the countries of victorious socialism. It can be said with little fear of contradiction that if freedom of thought were allowed in the Soviet bloc, Marxism would prove to be the least attractive form of intellectual life throughout the area.

3. *Yugoslav revisionism*

Yugoslavia's special role in the evolution of Marxism lies in the fact that we have to do here not only with individual philosophers or economists professing revisionist ideas, but with what may be called the first revisionist Communist party and even the first revisionist state.

After her excommunication by Stalin Yugoslavia was in a difficult situation, both economically and ideologically. At first her official ideology did not depart from the Marxist–Leninist model except for one important point: by asserting their sovereignty in the face of Soviet imperialism the Yugoslavs rejected Soviet claims to ideological supremacy and attacked the elder brother's Great Power chauvinism. Before long, however, the Yugoslav party began to devise its own model of socialism and its own ideology, loyally Marxist in intent but concentrating on workers' self-government and socialism without bureaucracy. The formation of this ideology and the corresponding economic and political changes extended over many years. In the early 1950s the party leaders were already talking of the danger of bureaucratization and criticizing the Soviet system as a degenerate type of state in which the extreme centralization of power had killed what was most valuable in the socialist ideal, namely the self-determination of the working people and the principle of public ownership as distinct from nationalization. The party leaders and theoreticians drew an increasingly sharp distinction between state socialism on Soviet lines and an economy based on workers' self-government, in which the collectives did not simply fulfil production norms imposed by the authorities but themselves decided all questions of production and distribution. By successive measures of reform industrial management was more and more entrusted to bodies representing the workers themselves. The state's economic functions were curtailed, and party doctrine pointed to this as a sign of the withering-away of the state in accordance with Marxist theory.

At the same time state control of cultural life was relaxed, and 'socialist realism' ceased to be a canon of artistic merit.

The programme approved by the party at its Sixth Congress in April 1958 set out the official version of socialism based on self-government. It is an unusual type of party document for those years, being concerned with theory as well as propaganda. It distinguished the nationalization of the means of production from their socialization, and emphasized that the concentration of economic management in the hands of the bureaucracy led to social degeneration and was a brake on socialist development. It also led to a fusion between the state and the party apparatus, and instead of the state withering away it would become increasingly powerful and bureaucratic. In order to build socialism and put an end to social alienation it was necessary to transfer production to the producers, i.e. into the hands of workers' associations.

It was evident from the beginning that if workers' councils were to have unlimited authority in each individual production unit the result would be a system of free competition differing from the nineteenth-century model only in the ascription of ownership to particular concerns; no economic planning would be possible. Accordingly, the state reserved to itself various basic functions concerning the investment rate and the distribution of the accumulation fund. The reforms of 1964–5 further reduced the powers of the state without abandoning the idea of planning; the state was to regulate the economy chiefly through the nationalized banking system.

The economic and social effects of the Yugoslav model of workers' self-government were and still are the subject of much discussion and lively disagreement, both in Yugoslavia and among economists and sociologists throughout the world. If the system is not to be a bureaucratic fiction it requires a considerable extension of market relations and increased influence of the market on production, and this predictably soon led to certain undesirable consequences as the normal laws of accumulation took effect once more. The gap between more and less economically developed parts of the country tended to grow wider instead of narrowing; pressure on wages threatened to push down the investment rate below what was socially desirable; competitive conditions led to the appearance of a class of rich industrial managers whose privileges excited popular discontent; the market and competition caused an increase in inflation and unemployment. The Yugoslav leaders and economists are aware that self-government and planning tend to limit each other and can only be reconciled by compromise, but the terms of the compromise are a matter of constant dispute.

It is true, on the other hand, that the Yugoslav economic reforms were accompanied by an expansion of cultural and even political freedom well beyond anything that occurred in the rest of Eastern Europe, let alone the Soviet Union. To call this a sign of the 'withering-away of the state', however, was at no time anything but an ideological fiction. The state voluntarily restricted its own economic power—an unusual event—but it did not give up its monopoly of political initiative or the use of police methods to deal with opposition. The situation is a curious one: Yugoslavia still enjoys more freedom of the spoken and written word than other socialist countries, but it is also subject to harsh police measures. It is easier than elsewhere to publish a text attacking the official ideology, but it is also easier to be put in prison for doing so; there are many more political prisoners in Yugoslavia than in Poland or Hungary, yet in those countries the police control of cultural matters is more severe. Single-party rule has not been infringed in any way, and to call it in question is a punishable offence. In short, the elements of pluralism in social life extend as far as the ruling party thinks proper. Yugoslavia has gained much from its reforms and from being excluded from the Soviet camp, but it has not become a democratic country. As to workers' self-government, its pros and cons are still a matter of controversy; at all events it is a new phenomenon in the history of Communism.

The question of self-government and de-bureaucratization also has a philosophical aspect. From the early 1950s there has been in Yugoslavia a large and dynamic group of Marxist theoreticians, discussing questions of epistemology, ethics, and aesthetics and also the political problems connected with changes in Yugoslav socialism. From 1964 onwards this group published a philosophical journal, *Praxis* (closed down by the authorities in 1975) and organized annual philosophical debates on the island of Korčula, attended by many scholars from different countries. The group has concentrated on typically revisionist themes such as alienation, reification, and bureaucracy; its philosophical orientation is anti-Leninist. Most of these philosophers, whose literary output is very large, were partisan fighters in the Second World War; some of the principal names are G. Petrović, M. Marković, S. Stojanović, R. Supek, L. Tadić, P. Vranicki, D. Grlić, M. Kangrga, V. Korać, and Z. Pesić-Golubović.

The main object of this group, who are perhaps the most active circle of Marxist philosophers in the world today, is to restore Marx's humanistic anthropology in its radical opposition to Leninist–Marxist 'diamat'. Most or all of them reject the 'theory of reflection' and seek, following Lukács and Gramsci to some extent, to establish 'praxis' as a fundamental category in relation to which not only other anthropological concepts but also ontological questions are secondary. Their starting-point is thus the early Marxian idea that man's practical contact with nature determines the meaning of metaphysical problems and that cognition is the effect of eternal interaction between subject and object. From this point of view historical determinism cannot hold its ground if it posits that anonymous 'laws of history' in the last resort determine the whole of human behaviour; we must take seriously Marx's saying that people make their own history, and not transform it, on evolutionist lines, into the statement that history makes people. The *Praxis* philosophers criticized Engels's definition of freedom as 'understood necessity', pointing out that it does not leave room for the active, spontaneous human subject. They thus took up the revisionist idea of the 'vindication of subjectivity', linking their analysis with the critique of Soviet state socialism and support for workers' self-government as the true path of socialist development in accordance with Marx's doctrine. At the same time, however, while emphasizing that socialism requires the active management of the economy by producers and not by a party bureaucracy calling itself the 'advance guard of the working class', they were aware that economic self-government, if carried too far, produces inequalities which are contrary to the idea of socialism. Orthodox Yugoslav Communists accused the *Praxis* group of wanting to have it both ways, by instituting full self-government but abolishing the market so as to avoid inequality. The Yugoslav revisionists seem to be divided on this matter, but their writings often strike a utopian note, expressing the conviction that it is possible to do away with 'alienation', to assure everyone of full control over the results of their actions, and to remove the conflict between the need for planning and the autonomy of small groups, between individual interests and long-term social tasks, between security and technical progress.

The *Praxis* group played an important part in disseminating a humanistic version of Marxism not only in Yugoslavia but in the international philosophical world; they also contributed to reviving philosophical thought in Yugoslavia, and were an important centre of intellectual resistance to autocratic and bureaucratic forms of government in that country. As time went on they came increasingly into conflict with the state authorities; nearly all their active members were finally expelled or resigned from the Communist party, and in 1975 eight of them were removed from their posts at Belgrade University. Their writings appear to reflect increasing scepticism as to the Marxian Utopia.

Milovan Djilas, one of the leading Yugoslav Communists in the forties and fifties, cannot be regarded as a revisionist. His ideas on the democratization of socialism were condemned by the party as far back as 1954, and his later works (including the famous *New Class*, which we have already discussed) cannot be considered Marxist even in the loosest sense. Djilas completely gave up utopian ways of thought, and has many times pointed out the links between the original Marxist doctrine and its political realization in the form of bureaucratic despotism.

4. Revisionism and orthodoxy in France

From the second half of the 1950s lively discussions went on among French Marxists, with revisionist tendencies partly drawing support from existentialism and partly in conflict with it. Existentialism as expounded by both Heidegger and Sartre had one essential feature in common with Marxist revisionism, namely its emphasis on the opposition between irreducible human subjectivity and thing-like forms of existence; at the same time, it pointed out that human beings had a constant tendency to flee from subjective, i.e. free and independent, existence into a 'reified' state. Heidegger developed an elaborate system of categories wherewith to express the drift into 'unauthenticity' and anonymity, the urge to identify with impersonal reality.

In the same way Sartre's analyses of the opposition between 'being-in-itself' and 'being-for-itself', and his passionate denunciation of the *mauvaise foi* which hides our freedom from us and causes us to shun responsibility for ourselves and for the world, were in full accord with revisionist attempts to restore Marxism as a philosophy of subjectivity and freedom. Marx, and Kierkegaard in his own way, had both protested against what they saw as Hegel's attempt to merge human subjectivity into impersonal historical being; from this point of view the existentialist tradition coincided with what the revisionists regarded as Marx's fundamental doctrine.

At a later stage Sartre ceased to identify Marxism with the Soviet Union and French Communism, but at the same time he came decidedly closer to identifying himself with Marxism. In *Critique de la raison dialectique* (1960) he put forward a revision of existentialism and also his own interpretation of Marxism. This long and amorphous work contains some points which clearly indicate that hardly a shadow remained of Sartre's former existentialist philosophy. In it he stated that Marxism was a contemporary philosophy *par excellence* and that for purely historical reasons it could be criticized only from a pre-Marxist, i.e. reactionary, standpoint, just as in the seventeenth century Locke and Descartes could be criticized only from a scholastic point of view. For this reason Marxism was invincible, and particular manifestations of it could only be validly criticized 'from the inside'.

Leaving aside the absurd contention as to the historical 'invincibility' of Marxism (according to Sartre's argument, Leibniz's criticism of Locke and Hobbes's of Descartes must have been based on scholastic positions!), the *Critique* is interesting as an attempt to find room within Marxism for 'creativity' and spontaneity, abandoning the 'dialectic of nature' and historical determinism but preserving the social significance of human behaviour. Conscious human acts are not presented simply as projections of freedom producing human 'temporality', but as movements towards a 'totalization', their sense being co-determined by existing social conditions. In other words, the individual is not absolutely free to determine the meaning of his acts, but neither is he a slave to circumstances. There is a possibility of the free fusion of many human projects constituting a Communist society, but it is not guaranteed by any 'objective' laws. Social life does not only consist of individual acts rooted in freedom, but is also a sedimentation of history by which we are limited. It is, in addition, a fight with nature, which imposes its own obstacles and causes social relationships to be dominated by scarcity (*rareté*), so that every satisfaction of a need can be a source of antagonism and makes it more difficult for human beings to accept one another as such. People are free, but scarcity deprives them of particular choices and to that extent diminishes their humanity; Communism, by abolishing scarcity, restores the freedom of the individual and his ability to recognize the freedom of others. (Sartre does not explain how Communism abolishes scarcity; on this point he takes Marxist assurances on trust.) The possibility of Communism lies in the possibility of the voluntary combination of many individual projects in a single revolutionary purpose. The *Critique* gives a description of groups engaged in common action without infringing the freedom of any of the individuals concerned—a vision of revolutionary organization intended to replace the discipline and hierarchy of the Communist party and to harmonize individual freedom with effective political action. The account, however, is so generalized as to ignore the real problems of such harmonization. All that can be seen is that Sartre envisaged the objective of devising a form of Communism free from bureaucracy and institutionalization, the latter in all its forms being contrary to spontaneity and a cause of 'alienation'.

Apart from many superfluous neologisms it does not appear that the *Critique* contains any new interpretation of Marxism; as regards the historical character of perception and knowledge, and the negation of the dialectic of nature, Sartre follows in Lukács's footsteps. As to reconciling spontaneity with the pressure of historical conditions, the work seems to tell us little except that freedom must be safeguarded in revolutionary organization and that there will be perfect freedom when Communism has done away with shortages. Neither of these ideas is especially new in the Marxist context; what would have been new is an explanation of how these effects are to be achieved.

Revisionism in the strict sense, i.e. as expressed by philosophers deriving from the Communist tradition, did not coincide with

'Sartrism', but in some ways it showed existentialist inspiration.

This brand of revisionism took several forms. In the late forties some dissident Trotskyists including C. Lefort and C. Castoriadis formed a group called Socialisme ou barbarie, with a periodical of the same name. This group rejected Trotsky's view that the Soviet Union was a workers' state that had degenerated, but argued that it was ruled by a new class of exploiters who collectively owned the means of production. They traced this new form of exploitation to Lenin's theory of the party, and wished to revive the idea of workers' self-government as the true form of socialist rule; the party was not only superfluous, but ruinous to socialism. This group introduced French thinkers to ideas which became crucial from the late fifties onwards: workers' self-government, non-party socialism, and industrial democracy.

A more philosophic type of revisionism was represented by the journal *Arguments*, published from 1956 by a group of philosophers and sociologists who had mostly resigned or been expelled from the Communist party: Kostas Axelos, Edgar Morin, Pierre Fourgeyrollas, François Châtelet, and Jean Duvignaud, also Henri Lefebvre, who was expelled from the party in 1958. This group did not use the typical language of Communist philosophy but sought to combine the Marxist themes of alienation and reification with categories drawn from psychoanalysis, biology, and modern sociology; none of them claimed to be true Marxists. Axelos, who was a kind of Heideggerist with Marxist tendencies, criticized Marx for interpreting human existence in terms of technology; Joseph Gabel, in a book on false consciousness, pointed out similarities between the social and psychiatric symptoms of 'reification'; Châtelet, in a book on early Greek historiography, discussed the connection between the urge to write history and awareness of making it; Fougeyrollas criticized Marx's reduction of 'alienation' to class and economic conditions. In general this group took the view that Marx's categories were inadequate for the analysis of society at its present technological level, and that they failed to reflect man's 'planetary' situation, the biological conditions of existence, and non-economic sources of alienation. Lefebvre, without disavowing the Marxian Utopia of the 'complete man', about which he had written much when a Communist, turned his attention to the specific forms of 'reification' which arise in a consumer society in conditions of relative welfare, increasing leisure, and increasing urbanization. Like many other neo-Marxists he maintained that if 'emancipation' has a meaning it relates primarily to shaking off the oppressive rules of capitalist society as they are internalized in consciousness. He appears, however, to have ceased to believe that alienation could be completely overcome. He resumed, in a new version, his 'critique of everyday life', declaring that this, as opposed to productive activity, was the sphere in which human isolation, mechanization, and mutual incomprehension were most acute, and which was therefore the proper scene for a true revolution that would expand human potentialities.

Most of the French revisionists abandoned the belief that the working class, thanks to its special historical mission, would become the liberator of humanity; their scepticism on this point, coinciding with the critique of the Frankfurt school, removed from their philosophy what is certainly the corner-stone of Marxism. For this reason, when the word 'revolution' occurs in their writings it is not to be taken in the Marxist sense; it denotes a revolution in people's feelings, their way of life, or their mutual relations, rather than the seizure of political power by this or that 'advance guard'. After a few years it became clear that none of the revisionists of this group except perhaps Lefebvre could be called a Marxist in any tangible sense, although concepts or themes from the Marxist tradition appear from time to time in their writings.

As to Roger Garaudy, who for many years was the party's chief philosophical spokesman, in the late 1950s he began by following the general course of de-Stalinization. In *Perspectives de l'homme* (1959) he offered a humanistic interpretation of Marx and made friendly gestures towards existentialists, phenomenologists, and even Christians. In *D'un réalisme sans rivages* (1963) he interpreted literary realism on broad enough lines to afford a welcome to Proust and Kafka. The tactical purpose of these books was fairly clear; they were in line with the Communist party's efforts to emerge from the intellectual isolation it had imposed upon itself. But Garaudy pushed his humanistic interpretation to the point of criticizing the Soviet system and denouncing the invasion of Czechoslovakia. Expelled from the party in 1970 after a series of quarrels and accusations, he published the relevant documents in the same year under the ambitious title *Toute la vérité*; in this book he presents himself as a Communist anxious to renew the party and cure it, for efficiency's sake, of ideological sclerosis.

In the second half of the 1960s, when the fashion in Paris changed from existentialism to structuralism, attention turned to a completely different interpretation of Marxism put forward by the French Communist Althusser. One reason for the popularity of structuralism was that it originated as a method of linguistics, which was regarded as the only humanistic discipline capable of evolving more or less exact 'laws'; the hope was now entertained that a 'scientific' status could be conferred on other humanistic studies, which had hitherto been sadly deficient in this respect. Lévi-Strauss was the first French advocate of a structural, non-historical approach to humanistic studies, paying little attention to the individual but concentrating on the analysis of a system of signs as they operated in the myths of primitive societies; the 'structure' of that system was not consciously devised by anyone and was not present to the minds of its users, but could be discovered by the scientific observer. In two successive works—*Pour Marx* (1965) and *Lire le Capital* (1966, with E. Balibar)—Althusser endeavoured to show that Marxism could provide a structuralist method of investigation from which human subjectivity and historical continuity were consciously excluded. He directed his attack against 'humanism', 'historicism', and 'empiricism', and claimed that Marx's intellectual development had undergone a distinct break in 1845, at the time of *The German Ideology*. Before that date Marx was still enslaved to Hegel and Feuerbach and described the world in 'humanistic' and 'historicist' categories (such as alienation), having in mind concrete human individuals; afterwards, however, he discarded this ideological approach and evolved a strictly scientific theory, which alone is genuine Marxism (why the later Marx is more genuine than the earlier, Althusser does not explain). This Marxism, which is most fully expounded in *Capital* and whose methodology is set out in the Introduction to the *Grundrisse*, rejects the idea that the historical process can be described in terms of the actions of human subjects. As with all scientific works, according to Althusser, the subject of *Capital* is not actual reality but a theoretical construct, all elements of which are dependent on the whole. The essence of historical materialism is not that it makes certain aspects of historical reality dependent on others (the superstructure and the base respectively), but that each of them depends on the whole (an idea of Lukács's, to whom Althusser does not refer in this context). Every sphere has its own rhythm of change, however; they do not all develop evenly, and at any given moment they are at different stages of evolution. Althusser does not define 'ideology' and 'science', merely stating that science cannot be bounded by any 'external' criteria of truth, as the positivists would have it, but creates its own 'scientificity' in its own 'theoretical practice'. Having thus disposed of the problem of what constitutes a science, he declares that Marx's analysis of capitalist society is not concerned with human subjects but with production relations, which determine the functions of the people involved in them. (It is true, we may observe, that *Capital* treats individuals as mere embodiments of functions determined by capital movements, but this is merely a repetition of Marx's earlier observation that capital in fact reduces them to units of wealth or labour-power, this being the 'dehumanizing' effect that Communism promises to abolish. Thus we have to do not with a universal methodical rule but with a critique of the anti-humanist nature of exchange-value.)

The subject of observation, then, is 'structure' (a term used incessantly in these books, but nowhere explained) and not its individual human elements. By 'humanism' Althusser seems to mean a theory which reduces the historical process to individual acts, or which sees in human individuals the same species-nature multiplied through many examples, or which explains historical change in terms of human needs and not impersonal 'laws'. 'Historicism' (though Althusser does not explain this term either) apparently consists in treating all forms of culture, and science in particular, as relative to changing historical conditions, in Gramsci's manner, and thus belittling the special dignity and 'objectivity' of science. In true Marxism, however, science does not belong to the 'superstructure'; it has its own rules and its own evolution, it constructs objective conceptual wholes and is not an 'expression' of class-consciousness; thus Lenin was right in saying that it must be brought into the working-class movement from outside and cannot come into existence as a mere element or product of the class struggle. For it is an essential fact that the different aspects of social life develop unevenly (a point which Althusser claims to find in Mao Tse-tung) and do not all express the same *Zeitgeist* in the same way. Each of them is relatively autonomous, and the social 'contradictions' that culminate in revolution are always the product of conflicts arising from these 'inequalities'. To this last phenomenon Althusser gives the name 'super-determination', meaning apparently that particular phenomena are determined not only by an existing complex of conditions (for example, capitalism) but also by the developmental rhythm of the aspect of life in questions; thus, for example, the state of science depends on the previous history of science as well as on the entire social situation, and the same is true of painting, etc. This seems a highly innocuous conclusion, a repetition of Engels's remarks about the 'relative independence of the superstructure'. Althusser observes on occasion, again following Engels, that in spite of 'super-determination' the situation is always governed by production relations 'in the last resort', but he does not add anything to make Engels's vague statement more precise. The upshot is simply that particular cultural phenomena are generally due to a variety of circumstances, including the history of the aspect of life they belong to and the present state of social relations. We are not told what is so 'scientific' about this obvious truth, why it is a revolutionary discovery of Marxism, or how it helps us to account for any particular fact, let alone predict the future. Nor does Althusser explain how we can compare two different fields, for example sculpture and political theory, in order to show that they are or are not at the same stage of development. This could only be done on the assumption that we can deduce from historical laws what conditions in the realm of sculpture would correspond to a given state of 'production relations'; but Althusser does not suggest any way of making such a deduction. (The idea that party leaders were capable of making it has always been highly convenient in Communist countries, where ideological persecution was held to be justified because the existing state of social consciousness 'lagged behind' production relations; the rulers, it was implied, knew what form that consciousness should take so as to be in conformity with the 'base'.)

Later Althusser came to believe that the epistemological turning-point in Marx's views around 1845 was not so clearly defined as he had thought, since regrettable traces of humanism, historicism, and Hegelianism were still to be found in *Capital*. Only two of Marx's writings, the letter known as the *Critique of the Gotha Programme* and some notes in the margin of Adolph Wagner's book on political economy, were completely free from the ideological taint. At this point we begin to wonder if Marxism existed at all in Marx's day, or whether it was left to Althusser to invent it.

The popularity of Althusser's view especially in the later sixties was not a matter of politics, as his books do not lead to any specific political conclusion. A more important point was that he opposed the tendency among Marxists to make advances to existentialists, phenomenologists, or Christians, thus diluting their own philosophy and depriving it of its uniqueness. Althusser stood for ideological 'integralism' and the assurance that Marxism was a self-sufficient doctrine, a hundred per cent scientific and needing no assistance from outside. (The mythology of 'science' has always played a tremendous part in Marxist propaganda. Althusser is constantly proclaiming how scientific he is, and many other Marxist writers do likewise. It is not a habit of real scientists, or of humanistic scholars.) Apart from a few neologisms, Althusser did not make any fresh contribution to theory. His work is merely an attempt to revert to ideological austerity and doctrinal exclusivism, a belief that Marxism can be preserved from the contamination of other ways of thought. From this point of view it is a return to old-fashioned Communist bigotry, but at the same time it bears witness to the directly opposite process which set in as a result of the post-Stalinist 'thaw'. Just as, before the First World War, the 'infection' of Marxism by current intellectual fashions led to such phenomena as neo-Kantian Marxism, anarcho-Marxism, Marxist Darwinism, empiriocritical Marxism, and so on, in the same way Marxists of the past two decades, desperately trying to make up for their long isolation, have resorted to various ready-made or popular philosophies, so that we have Marxism tempered by Hegelianism, existentialism, Christianity, or, as in Althusser's case, structuralism. Other causes of the vogue for structuralism which made itself felt in the humanistic sciences in the late fifties are a separate subject, which we shall not discuss here.

Revisionism as we have described it was only one of several manifestations of the post-Stalinist disintegration of Marxism. Its importance was that by its critical attitude it contributed much to the decline of ideological faith in the Communist countries and to showing up the intellectual as well as the moral destitution of official Communism. At the same time it drew attention to neglected aspects of Marxist tradition, and gave an impulse to historical studies. The values and aspirations to which it gave currency are by no means extinct and are still prominent in the democratic opposition in Communist countries, but are not usually expressed in a specifically revisionist context; that is to say, the criticism of Communist despotism is conducted more and more seldom, and with less and less effect, in terms of 'purging Communism of abuses', 'reforming Marxism', or 'going back to the sources'. To fight against despotic regimes it is not, after all, necessary to prove that they are contrary to Marx's or Lenin's ideas (and in the case of Lenin the contradiction is especially hard to prove anyway); such arguments were appropriate to the particular situation of the 1950s, but they have now lost much of their importance. Similarly, in philosophy the vindication of human subjectivity against 'historical laws' or the 'theory of reflection' does not need to be based on Marxist authorities and can get on better without them. In this sense revisionism has largely ceased to be a live issue; but this does not affect the continuing value of some of its ideas and critical analyses.

5. *Marxism and the 'New Left'*

The so-called New Left is also a complex of phenomena witnessing, on the one hand, to the universalization of Marxist phraseology and, on the other, to the disintegration of the doctrine and its inadequacy to modern social problems. It is hard to define the common ideological features of all groups and sects which claim to belong to the New Left or are considered by others to form part of it. A group of this name with revolutionary aspirations arose in France in the later fifties (the Parti Socialiste Unifié grew out of it to some extent), and similar groups were formed in Britain and other countries. The movement was catalysed by the Soviet Twentieth Congress and, perhaps to a still greater degree, by the invasion of Hungary and the Suez crisis of 1956; its literary organs in Britain were the *New Reasoner* and the *University and Left Review*, which later merged into the *New Left Review*. The New Left condemned Stalinism in general and the invasion of Hungary in particular, but its members differed among themselves as to how far the 'degeneration' of the Soviet system was inevitable and whether there was any prospect of the political, moral, and intellectual renewal of the existing Communist parties. At the same time they emphasized their fidelity to Marxism as the ideology of the working class, and some even professed allegiance to Leninism. They also took care to differentiate their criticism of Stalinism from that of the social democrats or the Right, and to avoid being classed as 'anti-Communist'; they were at pains to preserve a revolutionary and Marxist ethos and to match their criticism of Stalinism with renewed attacks on Western imperialism, colonialism, and the arms race.

The New Leftists contributed to the ferment in the Communist parties and to the general revival of ideological discussion, but they do not appear to have worked out any alternative model of socialism except in very general terms. The designation 'New Left' was claimed by various dissidents who sought to revive 'true Communism' outside the existing parties, as well as bigger and smaller Maoist, Trotskyist, and other groups. In France the name *gauchiste* is generally used by groups who emphasize their opposition to all forms of authority, including Leninist 'advance guard' parties. The post-Stalinist years saw a certain revival of Trotskyism, and this led to the formation of numerous splinter groups, separate 'internationals', etc. In the sixties the term 'New Left' was generally used in Europe and North America as a collective label for student ideologies which, while not identifying with Soviet Communism and often expressly disavowing it, used the phraseology of worldwide anti-capitalist revolution and looked chiefly to the Third World for models and heroes. So far these ideologies have not produced any intellectual results worth the name. Their characteristic tendencies may be described as follows.

Firstly, they maintain that the concept of a society's 'ripeness' for revolution is a bourgeois deceit; a properly organized group can make a revolution in any country and bring about a radical change of social conditions ('revolution here and now'). There is no reason to wait; existing states and governing élites must be destroyed by force, without arguing about the political and economic organization of the future—the revolution will decide these in its own good time.

Secondly, the existing order deserves destruction in all its aspects without exception: the revolution must be worldwide, total, absolute, unlimited, all-embracing. As the idea of total revolution began in the universities, its first blows were naturally directed against 'fraudulent' academic institutions, against knowledge and logical skills. Periodicals, pamphlets, and leaflets declared that revolutionaries must not get into discussion with teachers who asked them to explain their demands or terminology. There was much talk of 'liberation' from the inhuman oppression that required students to pass exams or to learn one subject rather than another. It was also a revolutionary duty to oppose all reforms in the universities or in society: the revolution must be universal, and all partial reforms were a conspiracy of the establishment. Either everything or nothing must be changed, for, as Lukács, Marcuse, and the Frankfurt school had taught, capitalist society was an indivisible whole and could only be transformed as such.

Thirdly, the working class could not be relied on, as it had been irredeemably depraved by the bourgeoisie. At the present time students were the most oppressed members of society, and therefore the most revolutionary. All were oppressed, however: the bourgeoisie had introduced the cult of labour, and the first duty was therefore to stop work—the necessities of life would be forthcoming in some way or another. One disgraceful form of oppression was the prohibition of drugs, and this too must be fought against. Sexual liberation, freedom from work, from academic discipline and restrictions of all kinds, universal and total liberation—all this was the essence of Communism.

Fourthly, the patterns of total revolution were to be found in the Third World. The heroes of the New Left were African, Latin American, and Asian political leaders. The United States must be transformed into the likeness of China, Vietnam, or Cuba. Apart from leaders of the Third World and Western ideologists interested in its problems, like Frantz Fanon and Régis Debray, the student New Left especially admired negro leaders in the United States who advocated violence and black racialism.

While the ideological fantasies of this movement, which reached its climax around 1968–9, were no more than a nonsensical expression of the whims of spoilt middle-class children, and while the extremists among them were virtually indistinguishable from Fascist thugs, the movement did without doubt express a profound crisis of faith in the values that had inspired democratic societies for many decades. In this sense it was a 'genuine' movement despite its grotesque phraseology; the same, of course, could be said of Nazism and Fascism. The sixties brought into the public view acute problems which humanity can only solve, if it can at all, on a worldwide basis: overpopulation, environmental pollution, the poverty, backwardness, and economic failures of the Third World; at the same time it has become clear that owing to predatory and contagious nationalism the likelihood of effective global action is very small. All this, together with political and military tension and fears of a world war, not to mention various symptoms of crisis in the educational field, has brought about a general atmosphere of insecurity and a feeling that present remedies are ineffectual. The situation is one of a kind frequently met with in history, where people feel they have got into a blind alley; they long desperately for a miracle, they believe that a single magic key will open the door to paradise, they indulge chiliastic and apocalyptic hopes. The sense of universal crisis is intensified by the speed of communication, whereby all local problems and disasters are at once known all over the world and merge into a general sense of defeat. The New Left explosion of academic youth was an aggressive movement born of frustration, which easily created a vocabulary for itself out of Marxist slogans, or rather some expressions from the Marxist store: liberation, revolution, alienation, etc. Apart from this, its ideology really has little in common with Marxism. It consists of 'revolution' without the working class; hatred of modern technology as such (Marx glorified technical progress and believed that one reason for the impending breakdown of capitalism was its inability to sustain such progress—a prophecy that could not be repeated today with absurdity); the cult of primitive societies (in which Marx took scarcely any interest) as the source of progress; hatred of education and specialized knowledge; and the belief in the American lumpenproletariat as a great revolutionary force. Marxism, however, did have an apocalyptic side which has come to the fore in many of its later versions, and a handful of words and phrases from its vocabulary sufficed to convince the New Left that it was possible at a stroke to transform the world into a miraculous paradise, the only obstacles to this consummation being the big monopolies and university professors. The chief complaint of the New Left against official Communist parties was and is that they are not revolutionary enough.

In general we have a situation today in which Marxism provides ideological pabulum for a wide range of interests and aspirations, many of them unconnected with one another. This is a long way, of course, from the medieval type of universalism in which all conflicting human interests and ideas clothed themselves in the garb of Christianity and spoke its language. The intellectual panoply of Marxism is only used by certain schools of thought, but they are quite numerous. Marxist slogans are invoked by various political movements in Africa and Asia and by countries striving to emerge from backwardness by methods of state coercion. The Marxist label adopted by such movements or applied to them by the Western Press often means no more than that they receive war material from the Soviet Union or China, and 'socialism' sometimes means little more than that a country is ruled despotically and that no political opposition is allowed. Scraps of Marxist phraseology are used by various feminist groups and even so-called sexual minorities. Marxist language is least frequently met with in the context of defending democratic freedoms, though this does sometimes occur. Altogether Marxism has achieved a high degree of universality as an ideological weapon. Russia's interests as a world Power, Chinese nationalism, the economic claims of French workers, the industrialization of Tanzania, the activities of Palestine terrorists, black racialism in the United States—all express themselves in Marxist terms. One cannot seriously judge the Marxist 'orthodoxy' of every one of these movements and interests: the name of Marx is often invoked by leaders who have heard that Marxism means having a revolution and taking power in the people's name, this being the sum total of their theoretical knowledge.

There is no doubt that this universalization of Marxist ideology is due first and foremost to Leninism, which showed itself able to direct every existing social claim and grievance into a single channel and use the impetus thus provided to secure dictatorial power for the Communist party. Leninism raised political opportunism to the dignity of a theory. The Bolsheviks rose to victory in circumstances irrelevant to any Marxist schema of 'proletarian revolution'; they prevailed because they used as a lever the aspirations and desires that were actually present in society, i.e. chiefly national and peasant interests, although from the point of view of classical Marxism these were 'reactionary'. Lenin showed that those who wish to seize power must take advantage of every crisis and every manifestation of discontent, regardless of doctrinal considerations. In a world situation in which, despite all Marxist prophecies, nationalist feelings and aspirations are the most powerful and active forms of ideology, it is natural for 'Marxists' to identify with them whenever nationalist movements are strong enough to disrupt the existing power structure.

Since, however, the various interests throughout the world which use Marxist language are often opposed to one another, the universality of Marxism, looked at in another way, amounts to its disintegration. In the holy war between the Russian and Chinese empires, both sides can invoke Marxist slogans with equal right. In this situation schisms are bound to occur, such as those which rent the international Communist movement in the years after Stalin's death. It is noticeable, moreover, that the various schisms express tendencies which were already present in embryonic form in the twenties, but disappeared under the pressure of Stalinism or survived only in marginal forms. These included elements of what later became Maoism (Sultan-Galiyev, Roy), Communist reformism (represented today by various West European parties, especially those of Italy and Spain), the idea of workers' councils exercising the dictatorship of the proletariat, and the ideology of 'left-wing' Communism (Korsch, Pannekoek). All these ideas, in somewhat altered forms, have reappeared at the present day.

An important manifestation of Marxism in the last fifteen years or so is the ideology of industrial self-government. This is not genetically derived from Marxism, however, but rather from anarchist and syndicalist traditions represented by Proudhon and Bakunin. The idea of factory management by the workers was canvassed by British guild socialists in the nineteenth century without any impetus from Marxism. Socialists, like anarchists, already realized at that time that the nationalization of industry would not in itself do away with exploitation, and, on the other hand, that the complete economic autonomy of individual firms would mean the restoration of capitalist competition with all its consequences; they therefore proposed a mixed system of parliamentary democracy and representative industrial democracy. Bernstein also concerned himself with the question, and after the October Revolution the cry for industrial democracy was raised by the Communist Left Opposition both in the Soviet Union and in the West. After Stalin's death the issue was revived, partly on account of the Yugoslav experiment. One of the first to take it up in France was the ex-Communist Serge Mallet, author of *La Nouvelle Classe ouvrière* (1963). Mallet analysed some social consequences of the automation of industry, pointing out that skilled technicians were increasingly important as an 'advance guard' of the working class, but in a new sense of this phrase, namely that of carrying on the struggle for democratic control of production. In that struggle the old distinction between economics and politics disappeared; the prospects of socialism were not connected with the hope of a worldwide political revolution preluded by the economic claims of the proletariat, but with the extension of democratic methods of organizing production, in which skilled wage-earners could play an essential part.

The question of the possibility and prospects of industrial democracy has come to be of key importance in discussions on democratic socialism; it has in itself nothing in common with the apocalyptic dreams of the New Left as inspired by Marcuse or Wilhelm Reich, and is historically and logically independent of Marxism.

A by-product of the revival of ideological discussion since Stalin's death has been the increased interest in the history and theory of Marxism, expressed in a profusion of academic literature. The fifties and sixties saw the production of many valuable works of this kind, by a wide variety of authors. These include declared adversaries of Marxism (Bertram Wolfe, Zbigniew Jordan, Gustav Wetter, Jean Calvez, Eugene Kamenka, Inocenty Bocheński, John Plamenatz, Robert Tucker) and others whose attitude to it is critical but favourable (Iring Fetscher, Shlomo Avineri, M. Rubel, Lucio Coletti, George Lichtheim, David McLellan), as well as a smaller number of orthodox Marxists of one school or another (Auguste Cornu, Ernst Mandel). Many studies were devoted to the origins of Marxism and particular aspects of its doctrine; there is a wealth of literature on Lenin and Leninism, Rosa Luxemburg, Trotsky, and Stalin. Some Marxists of an earlier generation, like Korsch, were rescued from oblivion. All the old interpretive problems were revived, and some new ones made their appearance. There was discussion of Marx's relationship to Hegel, that of Marxism to Leninism, the 'dialectic of nature', the possibility of a 'Marxist ethic', historical determinism and the theory of value. Themes related to Marx's early views—alienation, reification, praxis—continue to be the object of debate. The profusion of works directly or indirectly related to Marxism is such that of recent years a degree of satiety has become noticeable.

6. The peasant Marxism of Mao Tse-tung

The Chinese revolution is indisputably one of the most important events of twentieth-century history, and its doctrine, known as Maoism, has accordingly become one of the chief elements in the contemporary war of ideas, irrespective of its intellectual value. Measured by European standards the ideological documents of Maoism, and especially the theoretical writings of Mao himself, appear in fact extremely primitive and clumsy, sometimes even childish; in comparison, even Stalin gives the impression of a powerful theorist. However, judgements of this kind must be made with some caution. Those who, like the present writer, do not know Chinese and have only a scanty and superficial knowledge of China's history and culture doubtless cannot grasp the full meaning of these texts, the various associations and allusions perceptible to a reader acquainted with Chinese thought; in this respect one must rely on the views of experts, who, however, do not always agree.

More than elsewhere in this book, the remarks that follow are based on second-hand information. It may, however, be stated at the outset that despite the theoretical and philosophical claims of Maoism it is first and foremost a collection of practical precepts, which in some ways have proved highly effective in the Chinese situation.

What is nowadays called Maoism, or in China 'the Thought of Mao Tse-tung', is an ideological system whose origins date back several decades. Some characteristic features of Chinese as opposed to Russian Communism were already visible in the late 1920s. It was only after the Chinese Communists' victory in 1949, however, that their ideology, including in particular Mao's utopian vision, began to take on a definite form, and some very important aspects developed only in or after the late fifties.

Maoism in its final shape is a radical peasant Utopia in which Marxist phraseology is much in evidence but whose dominant values seem completely alien to Marxism. Not surprisingly, this Utopia owes little to European experience and ideas. Mao never left China except for two visits to Moscow when he was already head of the new state; as he himself declared, he knew next to nothing of any foreign language, and his knowledge of Marx was probably also fairly limited. For instance, while laying claim to Marxist orthodoxy he was in the habit of saying that everything had two sides, a good and a bad; he would presumably not have done so if he had known that Marx derided this form of dialectic as petty-bourgeois nonsense. Again, if he had known that Marx referred to the 'Asiatic mode of production' he would probably have discussed it too, whereas there is no mention of it in his works. His two philosophical essays—'On Practice' and 'On Contradiction'— are a popular and simplified exposition of what he had read in the works of Stalin and Lenin, plus some political conclusions adapted to the needs of the moment; to put it mildly, much good will is needed to perceive any deep theoretical significance in these texts.

This, however, is not the essential point. The importance of Chinese Communism does not depend on the intellectual level of its dogmas. Mao was one of the greatest, if not the very greatest, manipulator of large masses of human beings in the twentieth century, and the ideology he used for the purpose is significant by reason of its effectiveness, not only in China but in other parts of the Third World.

Communism in China was a continuation of the revolutionary events that began with the overthrow of the Empire in 1912 and were the outcome of developments going back several decades, particularly the Taiping rebellion of 1850–64 (one of the bloodiest civil wars in history). Mao was the main architect of the second phase of the revolution, which, as in Russia, did not orginate under Communist auspices but what Lenin would have called 'bourgeois democratic' ones: the sharing-out of large estates to the peasants, the liberation of China from foreign imperialists, and the abolition of feudal institutions.

Mao Tse-tung (1893–1976) was the son of a well-to-do farmer in Hunan Province. He attended a village school, where he learnt the elements of the Chinese literary tradition and acquired a taste for learning that carried him on to secondary school. At an early age he joined Sun Yat-sen's revolutionary republican party, the Kuomintang. After fighting for a time in the republican army he resumed his studies until 1917; during these years he also wrote poetry. Later he worked in the University library at Peking. At this time he was a nationalist and a democrat with socialist leanings, but not a Marxist.

The Kuomintang's objectives were to free China from Japanese, Russian, and British imperialism, to set up a constitutional republic, and to improve the peasants' lot by economic reforms. After a fresh outbreak of unrest in 1919 the first Marxist group was formed in Peking, and in June 1921, under the aegis of a Comintern agent, this group of a dozen members, including Mao, founded the Chinese Communist party. On the Comintern's instructions the party at first co-operated closely with the Kuomintang and tried to gain support from China's embryonic proletariat (in 1926 urban workers represented one in 200 of the population). After Chiang Kai-shek's massacre of Communists in 1927, after unsuccessful attempts to stage an insurrection and to reach an *entente* with the breakaway left wing of the Kuomintang, the Communists changed their policy and branded their ex-leader Chen Tu-hsiu as a 'right-wing opportunist'. Though decimated, the party continued to concentrate its efforts on reaching the workers, but Mao at an early stage advocated switching to the peasants and organizing a peasant army. Both groups within the party, however, emphasized anti-imperialist and anti-feudal objectives; there was scarcely any sign of a specifically Communist outlook. Mao set about organizing an armed peasant movement in his native province of Hunan, and in the areas it conquered this force expropriated big landowners, liquidated traditional institutions, and set up schools and co-operatives.

For the next two decades Mao lived in the countryside, away from urban centres. He soon became not only an outstanding organizer of peasant guerrillas but also the unchallenged leader of the Chinese Communist party and the only such leader in the world who did not owe his position to Moscow's endorsement. For twenty years, a period full of remarkable victories and dramatic defeats, he fought in extremely difficult conditions against the Kuomintang and the Japanese invader, siding for a time with the former against the latter. The Communists organized the bases of their future state in the territory they occupied, but continued to emphasize the 'bourgeois democratic' character of their revolution and to call for a 'popular front' including not only all the peasants and workers but also the lower middle-class and the 'national' bourgeoisie, i.e. those who were not in league with the imperialists. The party continued to take this line for the first few years after its victory in 1949.

In 1937, during the period of guerrilla warfare, Mao delivered two philosophical lectures to the party's military school at Yenan, which at the present day constitute almost the whole of the philosophical education available to the Chinese people. In the lecture 'On Practice' he states that human knowledge springs from productive practice and social conflict, that in a class society all forms of thought without exception are class-determined, and that practice is the yardstick of truth. Theory is based on practice and is its servant; human beings perceive things with their senses and then form concepts by means of which they comprehend the essence of things they cannot see. In order to know an object one must bring practical action to bear on it: we know the taste of a pear by eating it, and we understand society only by taking part in the class struggle. The Chinese began by fighting imperialism on the basis of 'superficial, perceptual knowledge', and only afterwards reached the stage of rational knowledge of the internal contradictions of imperialism and were thus able to fight it effectively. 'Marxism emphasizes the importance of theory precisely and only because it can guide action' (*Four Essays on Philosophy,* 1966, p. 14). Marxists must adapt their knowledge to changing conditions or they will fall into right-wing opportunism; while, if their thinking outstrips the stages of development and they mistake their imagination for reality, they will fall victims to pseudo-Leftist phrase-mongering.

The lecture 'On Contradiction' is an attempt to explain the 'law of the unity of opposites' with the aid of quotations from Lenin and Engels. The 'metaphysical' outlook 'sees things as isolated, static and one-sided' (ibid., p. 25) and regards movement or change as something imposed from without. Marxism, however, lays down that every object contains internal contradictions and that these are the cause of all change, including mechanical motion. External causes are only the 'condition' of change, while internal causes are its 'basis'. 'Each and every difference already contains contradiction, and difference itself is contradiction' (p. 33). Different spheres of reality have their characteristic contradictions, and these are the subject-matter of the different sciences. We must always observe the particular features of every contradiction, so as also to perceive the 'whole'. A thing turns into its opposite: for instance, the Kuomintang was revolutionary at first but then became reactionary. The world is full of contradictions, but some are more important than others, and in every situation we must discern the main contradiction from which the other, secondary ones derive— for example, in capitalist society, that between the bourgeoisie and the proletariat. We must understand how to unravel and overcome contradictions. Thus 'at the beginning of our study of Marxism, our ignorance of or scanty acquaintance with Marxism stands in contradiction to knowledge of Marxism. But by assiduous study, ignorance can be transformed into knowledge, scanty knowledge into substantial knowledge' (pp. 57–8). Things turn into their opposites: landowners are dispossessed and turn into paupers, while landless peasants become landowners. War gives way to peace, and peace again to war. 'Without life there would be no death; without death there would be no life. Without "above" there would be no

"below"; without "below" there would be no "above" ...
Without facility there would be no difficulty; without difficulty
there would be no facility' (p. 61). A distinction must also be
drawn between antagonistic contradictions such as those
between hostile classes, and non-antagonistic ones such as that
between a right and a wrong party line. The latter can be
resolved by correcting errors, but if this is not done they may
turn into antagonistic contradictions.

A few years later, in 1942, Mao delivered an address to his
followers on 'Art and Literature'. Its main points are that art
and literature are in the service of social classes; that all art
is class-determined; that revolutionaries must practise forms of
art that serve the cause of revolution and the masses; and that
artists and writers must transform themselves spiritually so as
to help the masses in their struggle. Art must not only be good
artistically but also politically right. 'All dark forces which
endanger the masses of the people must be exposed, while all
revolutionary struggles of the masses must be praised—this is
the basic task of all revolutionary artists and writers' (*Mao
Tse-tung, An Anthology of his Writings*, ed. Anne Fremantle, 1962,
pp. 260–1). Writers are warned not to be led astray by so-called
love of humanity, for there can be no such thing in a society
divided into hostile classes: 'love of humanity' is a slogan
invented by the possessing class.

Such is the gist of Mao's philosophy. It is, as may be seen,
a naïve repetition of a few commonplaces of Leninist–Stalinist
Marxism. Mao's originality, however, lay in his revision of
Lenin's strategic precepts. This, and the peasant orientation of
Chinese Communism, were the essential causes of its victory.
The 'leading role of the proletariat' remained in force as an
ideological slogan, but throughout the revolutionary period it
meant little more than the leading role of the Communist party
in organizing peasant guerrillas. Mao not only emphasized that
in China, unlike Russia, the revolution came from the country
to the town, but he saw the poor peasantry as a natural
revolutionary force and—in opposition to both Marx and Lenin
—expressly stated that social strata were revolutionary in
proportion to their poverty. He firmly believed in the revolutionary potential of the peasantry, not only because the proletariat
in China was such a small class, but for reasons of principle.

His slogan of 'encirclement of the city by the country' was opposed as far back as 1930 by the then party leader, Li Li-san. The 'orthodox' revolutionaries at that time, obedient to Comintern directives, pressed for the strategy followed in Russia, with the main emphasis on strikes and revolts by workers in big industrial centres, peasant warfare being regarded as a sideline. It was Mao's tactics that proved effective, however, and in after years he emphasized that the Chinese revolution had been victorious in spite of Stalin's advice. Soviet material aid to the Chinese Communists in the thirties and forties seems to have been of no more than a token character. Possibly—this is merely a speculation, not based on direct evidence—Stalin realized that if Communism were victorious in China he could not hope in the long run to keep five hundred million people in subjection to the Soviet Union, and therefore quite rationally preferred to see China weak, divided, and ruled by quarrelling military cliques. The Chinese Communists, however, continued to profess loyalty to the Soviet Union in all their official statements, and in 1949 Stalin had no choice but to proclaim his delight at the new Communist victory and do his best to turn his formidable neighbour into a satellite.

The Sino–Soviet conflict was not due to any ideological heresy but to the independence of the Chinese Communists and the fact that, as we may suppose, the Chinese revolution was contrary to the interests of Russian imperialism. In an article of 1940, 'On New Democracy', Mao wrote that the Chinese revolution was 'essentially' a peasant revolution based on peasant demands and that it would give power to the peasantry; at the same time he emphasized the need for a united front against Japan comprising the peasants, workers, lower middle class, and patriotic bourgeoisie. The culture of the new democracy, he declared, would develop under the leadership of the proletariat, i.e. the Communist. In short, Mao's programme at that time was similar to 'first-stage' Leninism: a revolutionary dictatorship of the proletariat and peasantry, led by the Communist party. He repeated the same thing in a speech of June 1949, 'On the People's Democratic Dictatorship', though he laid more emphasis then on the 'next stage', in which the land would be socialized, classes would disappear, and 'universal brotherhood' ensue.

The first few years after the Communist victory seemed to be a period of unruffled Sino–Soviet friendship, with the Chinese leaders paying deferential homage to their elder brother, although, as became known afterwards, serious friction developed at the very first inter-state negotiations. At that time it was hard to speak of a clearly differentiated Maoist doctrine. As Mao himself was to point out on several occasions, the Chinese had no experience of economic organization and therefore copied Soviet models. Only with time did it come to light that these models were, in some important respects, contrary to the ideology which was perhaps already latent in the Chinese revolution but had not yet expressed itself in an articulate form.

After 1949 the Chinese traversed at high speed several stages of development, each accompanied by a further advance towards the crystallization of Maoism. In the fifties it appeared that the country was retracing the course of Soviet evolution at an accelerated rate. Large holdings of land were divided among needy peasants; private industry was tolerated within limits for a few years, but in 1952 it was subjected to strict control, and in 1956 it was completely nationalized. Agriculture was collectivized from 1955, first by means of co-operatives but soon in a 'highly developed' form of public ownership, though peasants were allowed to keep private plots. At this time the Chinese, following the Russians, maintained the absolute priority of heavy industry. The first economic plan (1953–7), which was intended to enforce strictly centralized planning and give a powerful stimulus to industrialization at the expense of the countryside, introduced several features of Soviet Communism: an expanded bureaucracy, a deepening of the cleavage between town and countryside, and a highly repressive system of labour laws. Inevitably, it became clear that rigorous central planning was an impossibility in a country of small peasant holdings. The change of administrative methods which followed, however, was not confined to various forms of planning decentralization but found expression in a new Communist ideology in which production targets and modernization took second place, while the main stress was on breeding a 'new type of man' embodying the real or supposed virtues of rural life.

For a time it even seemed that this stage would involve some relaxation of cultural despotism. This delusion was connected with the short-lived 'hundred flowers' campaign launched by the party in May 1956—i.e. after the Soviet Union's Twentieth Congress—and endorsed by Mao himself. Artists and scholars were encouraged to exchange their ideas freely; all schools of thought and artistic styles were to compete with one another; the natural sciences, in particular, were declared to have no 'class character', and in other fields progress was to be the result of unfettered discussion. The 'hundred flowers' doctrine aroused the enthusiasm of East European intellectuals, who were experiencing the ferment of de-Stalinization in their own countries. Many people thought for a brief period that the most backward country of the socialist bloc from the economic and technical point of view had become the champion of a liberal cultural policy. These illusions lasted barely a few weeks, however, as the Chinese intellectuals were emboldened to criticize the regime in no uncertain terms, and the party at once reverted to its normal policy of repression and intimidation. The inner history of the whole episode is not clear. From some articles in the Chinese Press, and from a speech by Teng Hsiao-ping, the party's Secretary-General, to the Central Committee in September 1957 it might be thought that the 'hundred flowers' slogan was a ruse to induce 'anti-party elements' to come forward so that they might be more easily destroyed. (Teng declared that the party allowed weeds to grow as a deterrent example to the masses; they would then be pulled up by the roots and used to fertilize Chinese soil.) It may be, however, that Mao really believed for a time that the Communist ideology could hold its own in a free discussion among Chinese intellectuals. If so, his illusion was clearly dispelled almost at once.

China's failure to industrialize after the Soviet pattern probably caused or precipitated the political and ideological changes of the next decade, which the world observed with some bewilderment. At the beginning of 1958 the party under Mao's leadership announced a 'great leap forward' which was to work miracles of productivity in the ensuing five years. The targets for industrial and agricultural production, which were to multiply by factors of 6 and 2·5 respectively, put even Stalin's first five-year plan in the shade. These fantastic results were to be achieved, however, not by Soviet methods but by inspiring the population with creative enthusiasm, on the principle that the masses could do anything they set their minds to and must not be hampered by 'objective' obstacles invented by the bourgeoisie. All sectors of the economy without exception were to undergo dynamic expansion, and the perfect Communist society was just round the corner. Farms organized on the lines of Soviet kolkhozes were to be replaced by communes on a hundred per cent collective basis: private plots were abolished, communal meals and housing were introduced wherever possible; the Press carried reports of special establishments where married couples attended at regular intervals and in due order of priority to carry out their patriotic duty of begetting the next generation. One celebrated feature of the 'great leap' was the smelting of steel in a multiplicity of small village furnaces.

For a short time the party leaders basked in a statistical paradise (a false one, as was later admitted), but soon the whole project proved a complete fiasco, as had been predicted both by Western economists and by Soviet advisers in China. The 'great leap' resulted in a catastrophic fall in the standard of living because of the high accumulation rate; it involved enormous waste and filled the towns with workers from the countryside who soon proved redundant and had to go back to their fields amid general chaos and famine. The years from 1959 to 1962 were a period of set-backs and misery, owing not only to the failure of the 'great leap' but to disastrous harvests and the virtual breaking-off of economic relations with the Soviet Union; the sudden withdrawal of Soviet technicians brought many major projects to an abrupt standstill.

The 'great leap' reflected the development of the new Maoist tenet that the peasant masses could do anything by the power of ideology, that there must be no 'individualism' or 'economism' (i.e. material incentives to production) and that enthusiasm could take the place of 'bourgeois' knowledge and skills. The Maoist ideology began at this time to take on a more definite form. It was formulated in public statements by Mao and also, more explicitly, in utterances that were divulged only later in the turmoil of the 'cultural revolution'; some of these have been published in English by the eminent Sinologist Stuart Schram (*Mao Tse-tung Unrehearsed*, 1974, cited hereafter as Schram).

At the Lushan party conference in July–August 1959 Mao made a speech of self-criticism (of course not published at the time) in which he admitted that the 'great leap' had been a defeat for the party. He confessed that he had no idea of economic planning, and that it had not occurred to him that coal and iron do not move of their own accord but have to be transported. He took responsibility for the policy of rural steel smelting, declaring that the country was heading for catastrophe and that he now saw it would take at least a century to build Communism. The 'great leap', however, had not been entirely a defeat, as the leaders had learnt from their errors; everybody made mistakes, even Marx, and in such matters it was not only economics that counted.

The Sino–Soviet dispute, which became public knowledge in 1960, was due above all to Soviet imperialism and not to differences, though these did exist, as to Communist ideals and methods. The Chinese, while ardent in their professions of loyalty to Stalin, were not disposed to accept the status of an East European 'people's democracy'. An immediate cause of contention arose over nuclear weapons, which the Russians were prepared to make available to the Chinese only on condition that they retained control over their use; other issues that need not to be enumerated here included Soviet policy towards the U.S.A. and the doctrine of 'coexistence'. The extent to which the conflict was one of two empires and not merely two versions of Communism is shown by the fact that the Chinese un-reservedly approved the Soviet invasion of Hungary in 1956 and —twelve years later, after the breach—violently condemned the invasion of Czechoslovakia, although from the Maoist point of view Dubček's policy must have seemed arrant 'revisionism' and the 'Prague spring' with its liberal ideas was manifestly more 'bourgeois' than the Soviet system. Later, when the quarrel between two factions in China brought the country to the verge of civil war, it was clear that both of them were equally anti-Soviet in the basic sense, i.e. from the point of view of Chinese interests and sovereignty.

At the first stage of the conflict with Moscow, however, the Chinese showed that they attached importance to ideological differences and hoped, by creating a new doctrinal model, to supplant the Russians as leaders of world Communism or at least to gain a considerable following at Moscow's expense. As time went on they seem to have decided that instead of urging the world to follow China's example they could achieve better results by directly attacking Soviet imperialism. The 'ideological battle', i.e. the public exchange of insults between the Chinese and Soviet leaders, has continued since 1960, its intensity varying according to the international situation; but it has plainly become a conflict between rival empires for influence in the Third World, with each adversary resorting to *ad hoc* alliances with this or that democratic state. Chinese Marxism in its adapted form has become the ideological mainstay of Chinese nationalism, in the same way as happened previously with Soviet Marxism and Russian imperialism. Thus two powerful empires face each other, each laying claim to Marxist orthodoxy and each more hostile to the other than to the 'Western imperialists'; the development of 'Marxism' has led to a situation in which the Chinese Communists attack the United States Government chiefly on the ground that it is not sufficiently anti-Soviet.

The struggle within the Chinese Communist party went on in secret from 1958 onwards. The main issue was between those who favoured a Soviet type of Communism and those who endorsed Mao's formula for a new, perfect society; the former, however, were not 'pro-Soviet' in the sense of wanting to subject China to the dictates of Moscow. The specific points at issue may be summed up as follows.

Firstly, the 'conservatives' and 'radicals' had different ideas as to the army: the former wanted a modern army based on discipline and up-to-date technology, while the latter held to the tradition of guerrilla warfare. This was the cause of the first purge in 1959, among whose victims was the army chief P'eng Te-huai.

Secondly, the 'conservatives' believed in pay differentials and incentives more or less on the Soviet pattern, with the emphasis on cities and big heavy-industry plants, while the 'radicals' preached egalitarianism and relied on mass enthusiasm for the development of industry and agriculture.

Thirdly, the 'conservatives' believed in technical specialization at all levels of the educational system, so as to train doctors and engineers who could in time rival those of the developed countries. The 'radicals', on the other hand, emphasized

ideological indoctrination and believed that if this were successful, technical skills would somehow come of themselves.

The 'conservatives', logically enough, were prepared to seek
scientific knowledge and technology either from the Russians
or from Europe and America, while the 'radicals' contended
that scientific and technical problems could be solved by reading
the aphorisms of Mao Tse-tung.

The 'conservatives' were, in general, party bureaucrats of the
Soviet type, concerned for the technical and military modernization and economic development of China, and believing in
the strict hierarchical control of the party apparatus in every
sphere of life. The 'radicals' seemed to place considerable
faith in utopian fantasies of an impending Communist millennium; they believed in the omnipotence of ideology and direct
coercion by the 'masses' (under party leadership, however)
rather than by a professional apparatus of repression. As regards
their geographical base, the 'conservatives' were apparently
centred in Peking and the 'radicals' in Shanghai.

Both groups, of course, appealed to Mao's ideological
authority, which was unshakeable from 1949 onwards; in the
same way, all factions in the Soviet Union in the 1920s had
invoked the authority of Lenin. The difference was, however,
that in China the father of the revolution was still alive and
not only favoured the 'radical' group but had in effect created it,
so that its members were better off ideologically than their rivals.

They did not, however, enjoy the advantage in all respects.
As a result of the set-backs of 1959–62 Mao had to cope with
strong opposition among the party leaders, and his power seems
to have been appreciably limited. Some, indeed, believe that
he exercised no real authority from 1964 onwards; but the
secrecy of Chinese politics is such that all assessments of this
kind are uncertain.

The principal 'conservative' was Liu Shao-ch'i, who took over
the state presidency from Mao at the end of 1958 and who,
in the 'cultural revolution' of 1965–6, was denounced and
execrated as an arch-fiend of capitalism. He was the author of
a work on Communist education which, with two other booklets
of his, was staple party reading from 1939 onwards. A quarter
of a century later this faultless exposition of Marxist–Leninist–
Stalinist–Maoist doctrine suddenly turned out to be a poisonous

well of Confucianism and capitalism. The malign influence of Confucius, according to a host of critics, was visible in two main points. Liu had stressed the ideal of Communist self-perfection instead of a merciless class struggle, and he had depicted the Communist future as one of harmony and concord, whereas according to Mao's teaching tension and conflict were the eternal law of nature.

The struggle for power which broke out within the party at the end of 1965 and brought China close to civil war was thus not only one between rival cliques but between two versions of Communism. The 'cultural revolution' is generally reckoned as beginning with an article inspired by Mao and published in Shanghai in November 1965, which condemned a play by Wu Han, the vice-mayor of Peking, on the ground that under the guise of an historical allegory it attacked Mao for dismissing P'eng Te-huai from the post of Minister of Defence. This unleashed a campaign against 'bourgeois' influences in culture, art, and education and a call for a 'cultural revolution' to restore the country's revolutionary purity and prevent a return to capitalism. The 'conservatives', of course, echoed this objective, but tried to interpret it so as not to disturb the established order and their own positions. The 'radicals', however, managed to secure the dismissal of P'eng Chen, the party secretary and mayor of Peking, and to gain control of the chief newspapers.

In the spring of 1966 Mao and his 'radical' group launched a massive attack on the most vulnerable seats of 'bourgeois ideology', namely, the universities. Students were urged to rise against the 'reactionary academic authorities' who, entrenched in bourgeois knowledge, were opposing Maoist education. Mao, it was pointed out, had long proclaimed that in places of education half the time should be devoted to learning and half to productive work, that staff appointments and the admission of students should depend on ideological qualifications or 'links with the masses', not academic attainments, and that Communist propaganda was the most important feature of the curriculum. The Central Committee now called for the elimination of all who 'took the capitalist road'. As the bureaucracy paid lip-service to his ideas but sabotaged them in practice, Mao took a step which no Communist leader anywhere had ventured on before him, by appealing to the mass of unorganized youth to destroy his adversaries. The universities and schools began to form Red Guard detachments, storm troops of the revolution which were to restore power to the 'masses' and sweep aside the degenerate party and state bureaucracy. Mass meetings, processions, and street fighting became a feature of life in all the bigger cities (the countryside was largely spared). Mao's partisans skilfully exploited the discontent and frustration caused by the 'great leap' and directed it against bureaucrats who were blamed for economic failure and accused of wanting to restore capitalism. For several years the schools and universities ceased functioning altogether, as the Maoist groups assured pupils and students that by virtue of their social origin and fidelity to the Leader they were the possessors of a great truth unknown to 'bourgeois' scholars. Thus encouraged, bands of young people bullied professors whose only crime was their learning, ransacked homes in search of proofs of bourgeois ideology, and destroyed historical monuments as 'relics of feudalism'. Books were burnt wholesale; the authorities, however, had prudently closed the museums. The battle-cry was equality, popular sovereignty, and liquidation of the privileges of the 'new class'. After some months the Maoists also directed their propaganda to the workers. This proved a more difficult target, as the better paid and more stable section of the working class were not anxious to fight for wage equality or to make further sacrifices for the Communist ideal; however, some of the poorer workers were mobilized for the 'cultural revolution'. The result of the campaign was social chaos and a collapse in production; different factions among the Red Guard and the workers soon began to fight one another in the name of 'true' Maoism. Many violent clashes took place, with the army intervening to restore order.

It is clear that Mao could not have taken such a dangerous step as to call in non-party forces to destroy the party establishment if it were not for the fact that he himself, as the infallible source of wisdom, stood above all criticism, so that his opponents could not attack him directly. Like Stalin in former years, Mao was himself the embodiment of the party and could therefore destroy the party bureaucracy in the name of party interests.

For this reason, no doubt, the cultural revolution was a period in which the cult of Mao, already inflated to an extraordinary degree, took on such grotesque and monstrous forms as even to surpass—impossible though this might have seemed—the cult of Stalin in the years just before his death. There was no field of activity in which Mao was not the supreme authority. Sick people were cured by reading his articles, surgeons carried out operations with the aid of the 'little red book', public meetings recited in chorus the aphorisms of the greatest genius that humanity had ever produced. The adulation reached such a point that extracts from Chinese newspapers glorifying Mao were reprinted without comment in the Soviet Press for the amusement of its readers. Mao's most faithful aide and successor-designate, the army chief Lin Piao (who, however, soon 'proved' to be a traitor and a capitalist agent) laid down that ninety-nine per cent of the material used in Marxist–Leninist studies must be taken from the Leader's works; in other words, the Chinese were not to learn even about Marxism from any other source.

The purpose of the orgy of praise was, of course, to prevent critics at any time from undermining Mao's power and authority. In conversation with Edgar Snow (as the latter relates in *The Long Revolution*, 1973, pp. 70, 205) he remarked that Khrushchev probably fell 'because he had no cult of personality at all'. Later, after Lin Piao's disgrace and death, Mao sought to lay the blame on him for the degeneration of the cult. In April 1969, however, at the party congress which marked the end of the cultural revolution, Mao's position as leader and that of Lin Piao as his successor were officially written into the party statutes—an event without precedent in the history of Communism.

The 'little red book' of *Quotations from Chairman Mao Tse-tung* also came into prominence at this time. Prepared initially for army use, and with a preface by Lin Piao, it soon became universal reading and the basic intellectual diet of all Chinese. It is a kind of popular catechism containing everything the citizen ought to know about the party, the masses, the army, socialism, imperialism, class, etc., together with a good deal of moral and practical advice: thus it lays down that one should be brave and modest and not daunted by adversity, that an officer should not strike a soldier, that soldiers should not take goods without paying for them, and so on. Here is a selection of its precepts: 'The world is progressing, the future is bright, and no one can change this general trend of history' (*Quotations* . . . , 1976, p. 70). 'Imperialism will not last long because it always does evil things' (p. 77). 'Factories can only be built one by one. The peasants can only plough the land plot by plot. The same is even true of eating a meal . . . It is impossible to swallow an entire banquet in one gulp. This is known as a piecemeal solution' (p. 80). 'Attack is the chief means of destroying the enemy, but defence cannot be dispensed with' (p. 92). 'The principle of preserving oneself and destroying the enemy is the basis of all military principles' (p. 94). 'We should never pretend to know what we don't know' (p. 109). 'Some play the piano well and some badly, and there is a great difference in the melodies they produce' (p. 110). 'Every quality manifests itself in a certain quantity, and without quantity there can be no quality' (p. 112). 'Within the revolutionary ranks it is necessary to make a clear distinction between right and wrong, between achievements and shortcomings' (p. 115). 'What is work? Work is struggle' (p. 200). 'It is not true that everything is good; there are still shortcomings and mistakes. But neither is it true that everything is bad, and that too is at variance with the facts' (p. 220). 'It is not hard for one to do a bit of good. What is hard is to do good all one's life and never do anything bad' (p. 250).

The convulsions of the cultural revolution went on until 1969, and at a certain stage the situation was clearly out of control: various factions and groups emerged from the ranks of the Red Guards, each with its own infallible interpretation of Mao. Ch'en Po-ta, one of the chief ideologists of the revolution, often invoked the example of the Paris Commune. The only stabilizing factor was the army, which Mao prudently did not encourage to hold mass discussions or to attack its own bureaucratized leaders. The army restored order when local clashes became too violent, and it was noticeable that the provincial commanders were not over-eager to assist the revolutionaries. As the party apparatus had disintegrated to a large extent, the army's role naturally increased greatly. After the removal and political liquidation of several prominent figures including Liu

Shao-chi, Mao used the army to curb the revolutionary extremists, many of whom were sent to farm labour by way of re-education. The altered composition of the party leadership as a result of the struggle seemed to most observers to be a compromise solution which did not give a clear victory to any one faction. The 'radicals' were defeated only after Mao's death.

As we have seen, the years between 1955 and 1970 witnessed the development of a Maoist ideology which constitutes a new variant of Communist doctrine and practice, differing from the Soviet version in several important respects.

The theory of permanent revolution is basic in Mao's thought, as he declared in January 1958 (Schram, p. 94). In 1967, when the cultural revolution was in progress, he stated that this was only the first revolution in a series of indefinite length, and that it should not be thought that after two, three, or four of them everything would be well. Mao seems to have believed that stabilization always leads inevitably to privilege and the emergence of a 'new class'; this calls for periodical shock treatment in which the revolutionary masses destroy the germs of bureaucracy. Thus apparently there can never be a definitive social order without classes or conflicts. Mao often repeated that 'contradictions' were eternal and must eternally be surmounted; one of his charges against the Soviet revisionists was that they did not speak of contradictions between the leaders and the masses. One of Liu Shao-chi's errors was to believe in the future harmony and unity of society.

Mao's disbelief in a harmonious Communist social order is clearly at variance with the traditional Marxist Utopia. He went further still, however, in his speculations about the distant future: as everything changed and must perish in the long run, Communism was not eternal and neither was humanity itself. 'Capitalism leads to socialism, socialism leads to communism, and communist society must still be transformed, it will also have a beginning and an end ... There is nothing in the world that does not arise, develop and disappear. Monkeys turned into men, mankind arose; in the end, the whole human race will disappear, it may turn into something else, the earth itself will also cease to exist' (Schram, p. 110). 'In the future, animals will continue to develop. I don't believe that men alone are capable of having two hands. Can't horses, cows, sheep evolve? Can only monkeys evolve? ... Water has its history too. Earlier still, even hydrogen and oxygen did not exist' (pp. 220–1).

In the same way, Mao did not think that China's Communist future was guaranteed. A generation in time to come might choose to restore capitalism; but if so, its posterity would over-throw capitalism once again.

Another essential departure from orthodox Marxism was the cult of the peasantry as the mainstay of Communism, whereas to European Communists they were a mere auxiliary force in the revolutionary struggle and were otherwise despised. At the Ninth Party Congress in 1969 Mao declared that when the people's army conquered cities it was a 'good thing' because otherwise Chiang Kai-shek would have continued to hold them, but a 'bad thing' because it led to corruption in the party.

The cult of the peasantry and of rural life explains most of the characteristic features of Maoism, including the cult of physical labour as such. The Marxist tradition regards manual labour as a necessary evil from which men will be gradually freed by technological progress, but for Mao it has a nobility of its own and is of irreplaceable educational value. The idea of pupils and students spending half their time in physical labour is not motivated so much by economic needs as by its function in the forming of character. 'Education through work' is a universal value, closely connected with the egalitarian ideal of Maoism. Marx believed that the difference between physical and mental labour would eventually disappear, and that there ought not to be one set of people working exclusively with their brains while others used muscle only. The Chinese version of Marx's ideal of the 'complete man' is that intellectuals must be made to fell trees and dig ditches, while university teachers are recruited from the ranks of barely literate workers; for, Mao declared, even illiterate peasants understand economic matters better than intellectuals can do.

But Mao's theory goes further still. Not only must scholars, writers, and artists be deported to work in the villages or to educative labour in special institutions (i.e. concentration camps), but it must be realized that intellectual work can easily lead to moral degeneration and that people must at all costs be prevented from reading too many books. This thought recurs in various forms in many of Mao's speeches and conversations.

In general he seems to have held that the more people knew, the worse they were. At a conference at Chengtu in March 1958 he stated that throughout history young people with little knowledge had had the better of learned men. Confucius, Jesus, Buddha, Marx, and Sun Yat-sen had been very young and had not known much when they began to form their ideas; Gorky had only two years' schooling; Franklin sold newspapers in the streets; the inventor of penicillin had worked in a laundry. According to a speech of Mao's in 1959, in the reign of Emperor Wu-ti the Premier, Che Fa-chih, was illiterate, but he produced poetry; however, Mao added that he himself was not opposed to combating illiteracy. In another speech in February 1964 he recalled that there had only been two good emperors of the Ming dynasty, both illiterate, and that when the intellectuals took over the country it had gone to rack and ruin. 'It is evident that to read too many books is harmful' (Schram, p. 204). 'We shouldn't read too many books. We should read Marxist books, but not too many of them either. It will be enough to read a dozen or so. If we read too many, we can move towards our opposites, become bookworms, dogmatists, revisionists' (p. 210). 'Emperor Wu of the Liang dynasty did pretty well in his early years, but afterwards he read many books, and didn't make out so well any more. He died of hunger in T'ai Ch'eng' (p. 211).

The moral of these historical reflections is clear: intellectuals must be sent to work in the villages, teaching hours in schools and universities must be cut (Mao declared several times that they were too long at all stages of education), and admissions must be subject to political critieria. The last point was and is a matter of violent dispute within the party. The 'conservatives' argue that at least certain minimum academic criteria should apply to admissions and the conferring of degrees, while the 'radicals' hold that nothing ought to count except social origin and political consciousness. The latter view is clearly in line with the ideas of Mao, who in 1958 twice remarked with satisfaction that the Chinese were like a blank sheet of paper on which one could draw any picture one liked.

This deep mistrust of learning, professionalism, and the whole culture created by the privileged classes illustrates clearly the peasant origins of Chinese Communism. It is as far as can be from Marx's doctrine and the tradition of European Marxism, including Leninism, although at the outset of the Russian revolution there were symptoms of a similar hatred of education, especially in the Proletkult movement. In China, where the gulf between the educated élite and the masses seems formerly to have been deeper than in Russia, the idea that illiterates are naturally superior to scholars seems a perfectly natural outcome of the revolution from below. In Russia, however, hostility to education and professionalism was never a feature of the party programme. The party, of course, wiped out the old intelligentsia and set itself to turn humanistic studies, art, and literature into tools of political propaganda; but at the same time it proclaimed a cult of expertise and developed an educational system based on a high degree of specialization. The technical, military, and economic modernization of Russia would have been utterly impossible if the state ideology had exalted ignorance for its own sake and warned against reading too many books. Mao, however, seems to have taken it for granted that China would not and could not modernize itself in the Soviet manner. He often warned against 'blind' imitation of other countries. 'Everything we copied from abroad was adopted rigidly, and this ended in a great defeat, with the party organizations in the White areas losing one hundred per cent of their strength and the revolutionary bases and the Red Army losing ninety per cent of their strength, and the victory of the revolution being delayed for many years' (Schram, p. 87). On another occasion he observed that the copying of Soviet models had had fatal effects: he himself had for three years been unable to eat eggs and chicken soup, because some Soviet journal had said that it was bad for one's health.

Thus Maoism expresses not only the traditional hatred of peasants for an élite culture (a familiar feature, for example, in the history of the sixteenth-century Reformation), but also the traditional xenophobia of the Chinese and their mistrust of everything that came from abroad and from the white man, who had generally stood for imperialist encroachment. China's relations with the Soviet Union could only reinforce this general attitude.

For the same reason the Chinese sought for a new method of industrialization; this ended in the fiasco of the 'great leap forward', but the ideology behind it was not abandoned. Mao and his followers believed that the building of socialism must begin with the 'superstructure', i.e. the creation of a 'new man'; that ideology and politics must have priority as far as the rate of accumulation is concerned; and that socialism is not a matter of technical progress and welfare but of the collectivization of institutions and human relationships, from which it follows that ideal Communist institutions can be created in technically primitive conditions. For this, however, it is necessary to abolish all the old social links and the conditions that produce inequality: hence the Chinese Communists' zeal to destroy family ties, which are especially resistant to nationalization, as well as their campaign against private motivation and material incentives ('economism'). Rewards are still, of course, to some extent differentiated on grounds of skill and the type of work performed, but considerably less so, it would appear, than in the Soviet Union. Mao held that if people were properly educated they would work hard without special inducement, and that 'individualism' and a desire for one's own satisfaction were a pernicious survival of the bourgeois mentality and must be eradicated. Maoism is a typical instance of the totalitarian Utopia in which everything must be subordinated to the 'general good' as opposed to that of the individual, though it is not clear how the former can be defined except by the latter. Mao's philosophy made no use of the concept of the 'good of the individual', which plays an important part in Soviet ideology, and it also eschewed humanistic language in all its forms. Mao expressly condemned the notion of the 'natural rights of man' (Schram, p. 235): society consists of hostile classes and there can be no community or understanding between them, nor are there any forms of culture independent of class. The 'little red book' tells us (p. 15) that 'We should support whatever the enemy opposes and oppose whatever the enemy supports'—a sentence that probably no European Marxist would have written. There must be a complete break with the past, with traditional culture, and with anything that might bridge the gap between the classes.

Maoism, according to the Leader's repeated pronouncements, is the 'application' of Marxism to specifically Chinese conditions. As may be seen from the foregoing analysis, it is more accurately described as the use of Lenin's technique of seizing power, with Marxist slogans serving as a disguise for ideas and purposes that are alien or contrary to Marxism. The 'primacy of practice' is, of course, a principle rooted in Marxism, but it would be hard indeed to defend in Marxist terms the deduction that it is harmful to read books and that the illiterate are naturally wiser than the learned. The substitution of the peasantry for the proletariat as the most revolutionary class is flagrantly at variance with the whole Marxist tradition. So is the idea of 'permanent revolution' in the sense that class conflicts are bound to recur unceasingly and must therefore be resolved by periodical revolutions. The idea of abolishing the 'opposition' between mental and physical work is Marxist, but the cult of manual labour as the noblest human occupation is a grotesque interpretation of Marx's Utopia. As to the peasant being the supreme representative of the 'complete man' unspoilt by the division of labour, this idea may sometimes be met with among the Russian populists of the last century, but is again dia-metrically opposed to the Marxist tradition. The general principle of equality is undoubtedly Marxist, but it is hard to suppose that Marx would have seen it as embodied in the policy of packing off intellectuals to the rice-fields. To make a some-what anachronistic comparison, from the point of view of Marxian doctrine we may regard Maoism as belonging to the type of primitive Communism which, as Marx put it, has not only not overcome private ownership but has not even reached it.

In a certain limited sense Chinese Communism is more egalitarian than the Soviet variety; not, however, because it is less totalitarian, but because it is more so. It is more egalitarian inasmuch as wages and salaries are less differentiated; certain symbols of hierarchy, such as army badges of rank, have been abolished, and in general the regime is more 'populist' than in the Soviet Union. In keeping the population under control a more important part is played by institutions organized on a territorial or place-of-work basis, and the role of the pro-fessional police is correspondingly less. The system of universal espionage and mutual denunciation seems to work through local committees of various kinds and is openly treated as a civic duty. It is true, on the one hand, that Mao enjoyed far more popular support than the Bolsheviks ever have done, and therefore trusted more in his own strength than they: this is seen not so much in his repeated injunctions to let people speak out (for Stalin also took this line on occasion) as in the risk he took during the cultural revolution in inciting young people to overthrow the existing party apparatus. But, on the other hand, it is clear that during the whole chaotic period he kept in his hands the instruments of power and coercion which enabled him to restrain the excesses of those who followed his advice. On many occasions Mao preached the gospel of 'democratic centralism', and it is not clear that his interpretation differed in any way from Lenin's. The proletariat governs the country through the party, the party's operations are based on discipline, the minority obeys the majority, and the whole party obeys the central leadership. When Mao declares that centralism is 'First of all ... a centralization of correct ideas' (Schram, p. 163), there can be no doubt that it is the party which decides whether an idea is correct or not.

In February 1957 Mao delivered an address 'On the Correct Handling of Contradictions among the People', which is another of the main texts on which his reputation as a theorist is based. In it he declares that we must distinguish carefully between contradictions among the people and contradictions between the people and its enemies. The latter are resolved by dictatorship, the former by democratic centralism. Among 'the people' freedom and democracy prevail, 'But this freedom is freedom with leadership and this democracy is democracy under centralized guidance, not anarchy ... Those who demand freedom and democracy in the abstract regard democracy as an end and not a means. Democracy sometimes seems to be an end, but it is in fact only a means. Marxism teaches us that democracy is part of the superstructure and belongs to the category of politics. That is to say, in the last analysis it serves the economic base. The same is true of freedom' (*Four Essays on Philosophy*, pp. 84–6). The chief practical conclusion drawn from this is that contradictions among the people must be handled by a skilful combination of education and administrative measures, whereas a conflict between the people and its enemies has to be solved by dictatorship, i.e. by force. However, as Mao indicates elsewhere, 'non-antagonistic' contradictions among the people may in time turn into antagonistic ones if the proponents of incorrect views refuse to admit their error. This can hardly be read otherwise than as a warning to Mao's party opponents that if they acknowledge the truth promptly they will be pardoned, but if not, they will be declared class enemies and treated as such. As regards conflicting views among the people, Mao enumerates six criteria (ibid., pp. 119–20) for distinguishing right from wrong. Views and actions are right if they unite the people instead of dividing it; if they are beneficial and not harmful to socialist construction; if they help to consolidate and not weaken the people's democratic dictatorship; if they help to strengthen democratic centralism; if they help to support the leading role of the Communist party; and if they are beneficial to international socialist unity and the unity of the peace-loving peoples of the world.

In all these precepts concerning democracy, freedom, central-ism, and the leading role of the party there is nothing contrary to Leninist–Stalinist orthodoxy. There does, however, seem to be a difference in practice: not in the sense imagined by many Western enthusiasts for Maoism, that in China the 'masses' rule, but in the sense that government has a more consultative air because the party has more methods of ideological manipulation at its command than have the Soviet leaders. This has been due to the long-continued presence of the father of the revolution, whose authority was unquestioned, and to the fact that China is a pre-eminently rural society, confirming as it were Marx's saying that the peasants' leader must also be their lord. In a situation in which the classes representing the old culture have been practically destroyed and the channels of information are even more strictly controlled than in the Soviet Union (the 'centralization of correct ideas', as Mao put it), it is possible, without infringing the powers of the central government, for many questions of local politics or production to be settled by local committees instead of by the official government apparatus.

'Egalitarianism' is certainly one of the most important features of Maoist ideology; it is based, as we have seen, on a tendency to eliminate pay differentials and on the principle that all must perform a certain amount of manual work (though the leaders and chief ideologists seem to be exempt from this requirement). This does not, however, signify any trend towards equality in the political sense. In modern times, access to information is a basic asset and a *sine qua non* of real participation in government; and in this respect the Chinese population is more deprived even than that of the Soviet Union. In China everything is secret. Practically no statistics are publicly available; meetings of the Central Committee and organs of state administration are often held in complete secrecy. The idea that the 'masses' control the economy, in a country where no one outside the top hierarchy even knows what the economic plans are, is one of the most extravagant fantasies of Western Maoists. The information about foreign countries that the citizen can glean from official sources is minimal, and his cultural isolation is almost complete. Edgar Snow, one of the most enthusiastic observers of Chinese Communism, reported after a visit in 1970 that the only books available to the public were textbooks and the works of Mao; Chinese citizens could go to the theatre in groups (practically no individual tickets were sold), or they could read newspapers which told them next to nothing about the outside world. On the other hand, as Snow remarked, they were spared the stories of murders, drugs, and sexual perversion on which Western readers are nourished.

Religious life has been practically destroyed; the sale of objects used in religious worship is officially forbidden. The Chinese have done away with many aspects of the democratic façade that have survived in the Soviet Union, such as general elections or a public prosecutor's department independent of the police authorities: the latter, in practice, administer both 'justice' and repression. The extent of direct coercion is not known; nobody can even make a rough guess at the number of inmates of concentration camps. (In the Soviet Union much more is known about these matters, which is one effect of a certain relaxation since Stalin's death.) The difficulties with which experts contend are illustrated by the fact that estimates of China's population vary by some forty to fifty million.

The ideological influence of Maoism outside China derives from two main sources. In the first place, since the breach with the Soviet Union the Chinese leaders have divided the world not into the 'socialist' and 'capitalist' camps but rather into rich and poor countries; the Soviet Union is placed in the former category and is, moreover, according to Mao, the scene of a bourgeois restoration. Lin Piao sought to apply on an international scale the old slogan of the Red Chinese army concerning the 'encirclement of the cities by the countryside'. China's example certainly has a definite attraction for Third World countries. The achievements of Communism are manifest: it has freed China from foreign influence and, at a huge cost, set it on the path of technical and social modernization. The nationalization of the whole of social life has, as in other totalitarian countries, brought with it the abolition or alleviation of some of the chief plagues that afflict mankind, especially in backward agrarian countries: unemployment, regional starvation, and beggary on a vast scale. Whether the Chinese pattern can in fact be imitated successfully, for example, in the countries of black Africa, is a question beyond the scope of this work.

The other source of the ideological influence of Maoism, especially in the sixties, was the acceptance by some Western intellectuals and students of the utopian fantasies that constituted the façade of Chinese Communism. At that time Maoism endeavoured to project itself as the universal solution of all human problems. Various leftist sects and individuals seem to have seriously believed that it was the perfect cure for the ills of industrial society, and that the United States and Western Europe could and should be revolutionized on Maoist principles. At a time when the ideological prestige of Soviet Russia had collapsed, utopian longings fixed themselves on the exotic East, the more easily because of the general ignorance of Chinese affairs. For those in search of a perfect world and a sublime, all-embracing revolution, China became the Mecca of a new dispensation and the last great hope of revolutionary war—for had not the Chinese rejected the Soviet formula of 'peaceful coexistence'? Many Maoist groups were sadly disappointed when the Chinese to a large extent dropped their revolutionary proselytizing and turned to more 'normal' forms of political rivalry, having evidently ceased to hope that Maoism could become a real force in Europe or North America. It is indeed the case that Maoism in the Western countries had no significant effect on the position of the existing Communist parties: it caused no schism of any consequence and remained the property of small splinter groups. Nor did it have any noteworthy success in Eastern Europe, except for the special case of Albania.

Accordingly, the Chinese changed tactics and, instead of offering Maoism as a sovereign remedy of equal value to Britain, the United States, Poland, and the Congo, concentrated on unmasking Russian imperialism and seeking alliances, or at all events a measure of influence, on the basis of a common interest in checking Soviet expansion. It seems, indeed, that this is a much more promising course, though it is a straightforward political one and not a matter of Maoist ideology; as far as Marxist language is still used in prosecuting this policy, it is decorative rather than essential.

From the point of view of the history of Marxism, Maoist ideology is noteworthy not because Mao 'developed' anything but because it illustrates the unlimited flexibility of any doctrine once it becomes historically influential. On the one hand, Marxism has become the instrument of Russian imperialism; on the other, it is the ideological cement or superstructure of a huge country striving to overcome its technical and economic backwardness by other means than the ordinary operation of the market (of which, in many cases, it is virtually impossible for backward countries to take advantage). Marxism has become the motive force of a strong, highly militarized state, using force and ideological manipulation to mobilize its subjects in the cause of modernization. Certainly, as we have seen, there were important elements in the Marxist tradition which served to justify the establishment of totalitarian governments. But one thing is beyond doubt: Communism as Marx understood it was an ideal for highly developed industrial societies, not a method of organizing peasants to create the rudiments of industrialization. Yet it has turned out that this aim can be achieved by means of an ideology in which vestiges of Marxism are blended with a peasant Utopia and the traditions of Oriental despotism—a mixture that describes itself as Marxism *par excellence* and that works with a certain efficiency.

The obfuscation of Western admirers of Chinese Communism is scarcely believable. Intellectuals who cannot find words strong enough to condemn U.S. militarism go into ecstasies over a society in which the military training of infants begins in their third year and all male citizens are obliged to do four or five years' military service. Hippies are enamoured of a state which enforces severe labour discipline without holidays and upholds a puritanical code of sexual morals, not to speak of drug-taking. Even some Christian writers speak highly of the system, although religion in China has been ruthlessly stamped out. (It is of little importance here that Mao seems to have believed in an after life. In 1965 he mentioned twice to Edgar Snow that he was 'soon going to see God' (Snow, op. cit., pp. 89 and 219–20); he said the same thing in a speech in 1966 (Schram, p. 270), and also in 1959 (ibid., p. 154), when he referred humorously to his future meeting with Marx.)

The Chinese People's Republic is obviously a factor of enormous importance in the modern world, not least from the point of view of containing Soviet expansionism. This, however, is a matter which has little to do with the history of Marxism.

Epilogue

MARXISM has been the greatest fantasy of our century. It was a dream offering the prospect of a society of perfect unity, in which all human aspirations would be fulfilled and all values reconciled. It took over Hegel's theory of the 'contradictions of progress', but also the liberal-evolutionist belief that 'in the last resort' the course of history was inevitably for the better, and that man's increasing command over nature would, after an interval, be matched by increasing freedom. It owed much of its success to the combination of Messianic fantasies with a specific and genuine social cause, the struggle of the European working class against poverty and exploitation. This combination was expressed in a coherent doctrine with the absurd name (derived from Proudhon) of 'scientific socialism'—absurd because the means of attaining an end may be scientific, but not the choice of the end itself. The name, however, reflected more than the mere cult of science which Marx shared with the rest of his generation. It expressed the belief, discussed critically more than once in the course of the present work, that human knowledge and human practice, directed by the will, must ultimately coincide and become inseparable in a perfect unity: so that the choice of ends would indeed become identical with the cognitive and practical means of attaining them. The natural consequence of this confusion was the idea that the success of a particular social movement was a proof that it was scientifically 'true', or, in effect, that whoever proved to be stronger must have 'science' on his side. This idea is largely responsible for all the anti-scientific and anti-intellectual features of Marxism in its particular guise as the ideology of Communism.

To say that Marxism is a fantasy does not mean that it is

nothing else. Marxism as an interpretation of past history must
be distinguished from Marxism as a political ideology. No
reasonable person would deny that the doctrine of historical
materialism has been a valuable addition to our intellectual
equipment and has enriched our understanding of the past. True,
it has been argued that in a strict form the doctrine is nonsense
and in a loose form it is a commonplace; but, if it has become
a commonplace, this is largely thanks to Marx's originality.
Moreover, if Marxism has led towards a better understanding
of the economics and civilization of past ages, this is no doubt
connected with the fact that Marx at times enunciated his
theory in extreme, dogmatic, and unacceptable forms. If his
views had been hedged round with all the restrictions and
reservations that are usual in rational thought, they would have
had less influence and might have gone unnoticed altogether.
As it was, and as often happens with humanistic theories, the
element of absurdity was effective in transmitting their rational
content. From this point of view the role of Marxism may be
compared to that of psychoanalysis or behaviourism in the social
sciences. By expressing their theories in extreme forms, Freud
and Watson succeeded in bringing real problems to general
notice and opening up valuable fields of exploration; this they
could probably not have done if they had qualified their views
with scrupulous reservations and so deprived them of clear-cut
outlines and polemical force. The sociological approach to the
study of civilization was expounded by writers before Marx,
such as Vico, Herder, and Montesquieu, or contemporary but
independent of him, such as Michelet, Renan, and Taine; but
none of these expressed his ideas in the extreme, one-sided,
dogmatic form which constituted the strength of Marxism.

As a result, Marx's intellectual legacy underwent something
of the same fate as Freud's was to do. Orthodox believers still
exist, but are negligible as a cultural force, while the contribution of Marxism to humanistic knowledge, especially the
historical sciences, has become a general underlying theme, no
longer connected with any 'system' purporting to explain everything. One need not nowadays consider oneself or be considered
a Marxist in order, for instance, to study the history of literature
or painting in the light of the social conflicts of a given period;
and one may do so without believing that the whole of human

history is the history of class conflict, or that different aspects of civilization have no history of their own because 'true' history is the history of technology and 'production relations', because the 'superstructure' grows out of the 'base', and so forth.

To recognize, within limits, the validity of historical materialism is not tantamount to acknowledging the truth of Marxism. This is so because, among other reasons, it was a fundamental doctrine of Marxism from the outset that the meaning of a historical process can be grasped only if the past is interpreted in the light of the future: that is to say, we can only understand what was and is if we have some knowledge of what will be. Marxism, it can hardly be disputed, would not be Marxism without its claim to 'scientific knowledge' of the future, and the question is how far such knowledge is possible. Prediction is, of course, not only a component of many sciences but an inseparable aspect of even the most trivial actions, although we cannot 'know' the future in the same way as the past, since all prediction has an element of uncertainty. The 'future' is either what will happen in the next moment or what will happen in a million years; the difficulty of prediction increases, of course, with distance and with the complication of the subject. In social matters, as we know, predictions are especially deceptive, even if they relate to the short term and to a single quantifiable factor, as in demographic prognoses. In general we forecast the future by extrapolating existing tendencies, while realizing that such extrapolations are, always and everywhere, of extremely limited value, and that no developmental curves in any field of inquiry extend indefinitely in accordance with the same equation. As to prognoses on a global scale and without any limitation of time, these are no more than fantasies, whether the prospect they offer is good or evil. There are no rational means of predicting 'the future of humanity' over a long period or foretelling the nature of 'social formations' in ages to come. The idea that we can make such forecasts 'scientifically', and that without doing so we cannot even understand the past, is inherent in the Marxist theory of 'social formations'; it is one reason why that theory is a fantasy, and also why it is politically effective. The influence that Marxism has achieved, far from being the result or proof of its scientific character, is almost entirely due to its prophetic, fantastic, and irrational elements.

Marxism is a doctrine of blind confidence that a paradise of
universal satisfaction is awaiting us just round the corner. Almost
all the prophecies of Marx and his followers have already
proved to be false, but this does not disturb the spiritual
certainty of the faithful, any more than it did in the case of
chiliastic sects: for it is a certainty not based on any empirical
premisses or supposed 'historical laws', but simply on the
psychological need for certainty. In this sense Marxism performs
the function of a religion, and its efficacy is of a religious
character. But it is a caricature and a bogus form of religion,
since it presents its temporal eschatology as a scientific system,
which religious mythologies do not purport to be.

We have discussed the question of continuity between Marxism
and its embodiment in Communism, i.e. Leninist–Stalinist
ideology and practice. It would be absurd to maintain that
Marxism was, so to speak, the efficient cause of present-day
Communism; on the other hand, Communism is not a mere
'degeneration' of Marxism but a possible interpretation of it,
and even a well-founded one, though primitive and partial in
some respects. Marxism was a combination of values which
proved incompatible for empirical though not for logical reasons,
so that some could be realized only at the expense of others.
But it was Marx who declared that the whole idea of Communism could be summed up in a single formula—the abolition
of private property; that the state of the future must take over
the centralized management of the means of production, and
that the abolition of capital meant the abolition of wage-labour.
There was nothing flagrantly illogical in deducing from this that
the expropriation of the bourgeoisie and the nationalization of
industry and agriculture would bring about the general emancipation of mankind. In the event it turned out that, having
nationalized the means of production, it was possible to erect
on this foundation a monstrous edifice of lies, exploitation, and
oppression. This was not itself a consequence of Marxism; rather,
Communism was a bastard version of the socialist ideal, owing
its origin to many historical circumstances and chances, of which
Marxist ideology was one. But it cannot be said that Marxism
was 'falsified' in any essential sense. Arguments adduced at the
present day to show that 'that is not what Marx meant' are
intellectually and practically sterile. Marx's intentions are not

the deciding factor in a historical assessment of Marxism, and there are more important arguments for freedom and democratic values than the fact that Marx, if one looks closely, was not so hostile to those values as might at first sight appear.

Marx took over the romantic ideal of social unity, and Communism realized it in the only way feasible in an industrial society, namely, by a despotic system of government. The origin of this dream is to be found in the idealized image of the Greek city-state popularized by Winckelmann and others in the eighteenth century and subsequently taken up by German philosophers. Marx seems to have imagined that once capitalists were done away with the whole world could become a kind of Athenian *agora*: one had only to forbid private ownership of machines or land and, as if by magic, human beings would cease to be selfish and their interests would coincide in perfect harmony. Marxism affords no explanation of how this prophecy is founded, or what reason there is to think that human interests will cease to conflict as soon as the means of production are nationalized.

Marx, moreover, combined his romantic dreams with the socialist expectation that all needs would be fully satisfied in the earthly paradise. The early socialists seem to have understood the slogan 'To each according to his needs' in a limited sense: they meant that people should not have to suffer cold and hunger or spend their lives staving off destitution. Marx, however, and many Marxists after him, imagined that under socialism all scarcity would come to an end. It was possible to entertain this hope in the ultra-sanguine form that all wants would be satisfied, as though every human being had a magic ring or obedient jinn at his disposal. But, since this could hardly be taken seriously, Marxists who considered the question decided, with a fair degree of support from Marx's works, that Communism would ensure the satisfaction of 'true' or 'genuine' needs consonant with human nature, but not whims or desires of all kinds. This, however, gave rise to a problem which no one answered clearly: who is to decide what needs are 'genuine', and by what criteria? If every man is to judge this for himself, then all needs are equally genuine provided they are actually, subjectively felt, and there is no room for any distinction. If, on the other hand, it is the state which decides, then the greatest emancipation in history consists in a system of universal rationing.

At the present time it is obvious to all except a handful of New Left adolescents that socialism cannot literally 'satisfy all needs' but can only aim at a just distribution of insufficient resources—which leaves us with the problem of defining 'just' and of deciding by what social mechanisms the aim is to be effected in each particular case. The idea of perfect equality, i.e. an equal share of all goods for everybody, is not only unfeasible economically but is contradictory in itself: for perfect equality can only be imagined under a system of extreme despotism, but despotism itself presupposes inequality at least in such basic advantages as participation in power and access to information. (For the same reason, contemporary *gauchistes* are in an untenable position when they demand more equality and less government: in real life more equality means more government, and absolute equality means absolute government.)

If socialism is to be anything more than a totalitarian prison, it can only be a system of compromises between different values that limit one another. All-embracing economic planning, even if it were possible to achieve—and there is almost universal agreement that it is not—is incompatible with the autonomy of small producers and regional units, and this autonomy is a traditional value of socialism, though not of Marxist socialism. Technical progress cannot coexist with absolute security of living conditions for everyone. Conflicts inevitably arise between freedom and equality, planning and the autonomy of small groups, economic democracy and efficient management, and these conflicts can only be mitigated by compromise and partial solutions.

In the developed industrial countries, all social institutions for the purpose of evening out inequalities and ensuring a minimum of security (progressive taxation, health services, unemployment relief, price controls, etc.) have been created and extended at the price of a vastly expanded state bureaucracy, and no one can suggest how to avoid paying this price.

Questions such as these have little to do with Marxism, and Marx's doctrine provides virtually no help in solving them. The apocalyptic belief in the consummation of history, the inevitability of socialism, and the natural sequence of 'social formations'; the 'dictatorship of the proletariat', the exaltation of violence, faith in the automatic efficacy of nationalizing industry, fantasies concerning a society without conflict and an economy without money—all these have nothing in common with the idea of democratic socialism. The latter's purpose is to create institutions which can gradually reduce the subordination of production to profit, do away with poverty, diminish inequality, remove social barriers to educational opportunity, and minimize the threat to democratic liberties from state bureaucracy and the seductions of totalitarianism. All these efforts and attempts are doomed to failure unless they are firmly rooted in the value of freedom—what Marxists stigmatize as 'negative' freedom, i.e. the area of decision which society allows to the individual. This is so not only because freedom is an intrinsic value requiring no justification beyond itself, but also because without it societies are unable to reform themselves: despotic systems, lacking this self-regulating mechanism, can only correct their mistakes when these have led to disaster.

Marxism has been frozen and immobilized for decades as the ideological superstructure of a totalitarian political movement, and in consequence has lost touch with intellectual developments and social realities. The hope that it could be revived and made fruitful once again soon proved to be an illusion. As an explanatory 'system' it is dead, nor does it offer any 'method' that can be effectively used to interpret modern life, to foresee the future, or cultivate utopian projections. Contemporary Marxist literature, although plentiful in quantity, has a depressing air of sterility and helplessness, in so far as it is not purely historical.

The effectiveness of Marxism as an instrument of political mobilization is quite another matter. As we have seen, its terminology is used in support of the most variegated political interests. In the Communist countries of Europe, where Marxism is the official legitimation of the existing regimes, it has virtually lost all conviction, while in China it has been deformed out of recognition. Wherever Communism is in power, the ruling class transforms it into an ideology whose real sources are nationalism, racism, or imperialism. Communism has done much to strengthen nationalist ideologies by using them to seize power or hold on to it, and in this way it has produced its own gravediggers. Nationalism lives only as an ideology of hate, envy, and thirst for power; as such it is a disruptive element in the Communist world, the coherence of which is based on force. If the whole world were Communist it would either have to be dominated by a single imperialism, or there would be an unending series of wars between the 'Marxist' rulers of different countries.

We are witnesses and participators in momentous and complicated intellectual and moral processes, the combined effects of which cannot be foreseen. On the one hand, many optimistic assumptions of nineteenth-century humanism have broken down, and in many fields of culture there is a sense of bankruptcy. On the other hand, thanks to the unprecedented speed and diffusion of information, human aspirations throughout the world are increasing faster than the means of satisfying them; this leads to rapidly growing frustration and consequent aggressiveness. Communists have shown great skill in exploiting this state of mind and channelling aggressive feelings in various directions according to circumstances, using fragments of Marxist language to suit their purpose. Messianic hopes are the counterpart of the sense of despair and impotence that overcomes mankind at the sight of its own failures. The optimistic belief that there is a ready-made, immediate answer to all problems and misfortunes, and that only the malevolence of enemies (defined according to choice) stands in the way of its being instantly applied, is a frequent ingredient in ideological systems passing under the name of Marxism—which is to say that Marxism changes content from one situation to another and is cross-bred with other ideological traditions. At present Marxism neither interprets the world nor changes it: it is merely a repertoire of slogans serving to organize various interests, most of them completely remote from those with which Marxism originally identified itself. A century after the collapse of the First International, the prospect of a new International capable of defending the interests of oppressed humanity throughout the world is less likely than it has ever been.

The self-deification of mankind, to which Marxism gave philosophical expression, has ended in the same way as all such attempts, whether individual or collective: it has revealed itself as the farcical aspect of human bondage.

SELECTIVE BIBLIOGRAPHY

ADORNO, T. W. (with M. Horkheimer), *Dialektik der Aufklärung*, Amsterdam, 1947 (Eng. trans. J. Cumming, London, 1973).
— — *Prismen*, Frankfurt, 1955 (Eng. trans. S. and S. Weber, London, n.d.).
— — *Einleitung in die Musiksoziologie*, Frankfurt, 1962.
— — *Jargon der Eigentlichkeit*, Frankfurt, 1964 (Eng. trans. K. Tarnowski and F. Will, London, 1973).
— — *Negative Dialektik*, Frankfurt, 1966 (Eng. trans. E. B. Ashton, London, 1973).
AHLBERG, R., *'Dialektische Philosophie' und Gesellschaft in der Sowjetunion*, Berlin, 1960 (good bibliography).
ALEKSANDROV, G. F., *Istoria zapadnoevropeyskoy filosofii* (*History of West European Philosophy*), Moscow, 1946.
— — (ed.), *Dialektichesky materializm* (*Dialectical Materialism*), Moscow, 1954.
ALTHUSSER, L., *Pour Marx*, Paris, 1965 (Eng. trans. B. Brewster, London, 1969).
— — *Lire le Capital*, 2 vols., Paris, 1965 (Eng. trans. B. Brewster, London, 1970).
— — *Lénine et la philosophie*, 2nd edn. Paris, 1972 (Eng. trans. B. Brewster, London, 1971).
ARENDT, H., *The Origins of Totalitarianism*, Cleveland, 1958.
ARON, R., *L'Opium des intellectuels*, Paris (Eng. trans. T. Kilmartin, New York, 1962).
— — *D'une sainte famille à l'autre: essais sur les marxismes imaginaires*, Paris, 1969.
AVTORKHANOV, A., *Tekhnologia vlasti* (*The Technology of Power*), 2nd ed., Frankfurt, 1973.
AXELOS, K., *Marx, penseur de la technique*, Paris, 1961.

BACZKE, B., *Weltanschauung, Metaphysik, Entfremdung. Philosophische Versuche*, Frankfurt, 1969.
BAHR, E., *Ernst Bloch*, Berlin, 1964.

BAUER, R. A., *The New Man in Soviet Psychology*, Cambridge, Mass., 1952.

BAUMAN, Z., *Towards a Critical Sociology*, London and Boston, 1976.

BAUMANN, G., 'Die Schlüssel-Gewalt der Erkenntnis. Ernst Blochs philosophische Haltung der "konkreten Utopie"', thesis, Louvain, 1974.

BENJAMIN, W., *Schriften*, ed. Th. W. Adorno and G. Scholem, 2 vols., Frankfurt, 1955.

—— *Illuminations: Essays and Reflections*, ed. H. Arendt, New York, 1968.

BENSELER, F. (ed.), *Festchrift zum achtzigsten Geburtstag von Georg Lukacs*, Neuwied, 1965 (comprehensive bibliography).

BERDIAEV, N., *Wahrheit und Lüge des Kommunismus*, Darmstadt, 1953.

—— *Les Sources et le sens du communisme russe*, Paris, 1938.

BESANÇON, A., *Court traité de soviétologie à l'usage des autorités civiles, militaires et religieuses*, Paris, 1976.

BIENKOWSKI, Wl., *Motory i hamulce socjalizmu* (*Driving Forces and Brakes of Socialism*), Paris, 1969.

BLAKELEY, T. J., *Soviet Philosophy*, Dordrecht, 1964.

BLOCH, E., *Gesamtausgabe*, 16 vols., Frankfurt, 1959 ff.

—— *Man on his Own*, trans. E. B. Ashton, New York, 1970 (an anthology).

—— *On Karl Marx*, trans. J. Maxwell, New York, 1971 (a selection from *Das Prinzip Hoffnung*).

—— *Atheism in Christianity*, trans. J. T. Swann, New York, 1972.

BOCHENSKI, I. M., *Der sowjetrussische dialektische Materialismus*, 2nd edn. Berne, 1956 (Eng. trans. Dordrecht, 1953).

BOCIURKIW, B. R. and J. W. STRONG (eds.), *Religion and Atheism in the USSR and Eastern Europe*, Toronto, 1975.

BORKENAU, F., *European Communism*, London, 1953.

BRUS, W., *The Market in a Socialist Economy*, London, 1972.

—— *The Economics and Politics of Socialism*, London, 1973.

BRZEZINSKI, Z., *The Permanent Purge: Politics in Soviet Totalitarianism*, Cambridge, Mass., 1956.

—— *The Soviet Bloc: Unity and Conflict*, Cambridge, Mass., 1967.

BUKHARIN, N., *Teoria istoricheskogo materializma*, Moscow, 1921 (Eng. trans. *Historical Materialism*, New York, 1928; Ann Arbor, 1969).

—— (with E. Preobrazhensky), *The ABC of Communism*, London, 1924 and 1969.

—— *Imperialism and World Economy*, New York, 1929.

BÜTOW, H. G., *Philosophie und Gesellschaft im Denken Ernst Blochs*, Berlin, 1963.

BURNHAM, J., *The Managerial Revolution*, New York, 1941.

CARMICHAEL, J., *Trotsky: An Appreciation of his Life*, New York, 1975.

CAUTE, D., *Communism and the French Intellectuals*, New York, 1964.

CHAMBRE, H., *Le Marxisme en Union Soviétique*, Paris, 1955.

CHANG, P. H., *Radicals and Radical Ideology in China's Cultural Revolution*, New York, 1973.

CHATELET, F., *Logos et praxis. Recherches sur la signification théorique du marxisme*, Paris, 1962.

CH'EN, J., *Mao and the Chinese Revolution*, London and New York, 1965.

COHEN, S. F., *Bukharin and the Bolshevik Revolution: A Political Biography 1888–1938*, New York, 1973 (copious bibliography).

CONGDON, L., 'Lukács's Road to Marx', *Survey*, no. 2/3, 1974.

CONQUEST, R., *The Great Terror: Stalin's Purge of the Thirties*, London, 1968.

CRANSTON, M., *The Mask of Politics*, London, 1973.

DAHM, H., *Die Dialektik im Wandel der Sowjetphilosophie*, Cologne, 1963.

DANIELS, R. V. (ed.), *A Documentary History of Communism*, 2 vols., New York, 1960.

— — *The Conscience of the Revolution. Communist Opposition in Soviet Russia*, Cambridge, Mass., 1960.

DAUBIER, J., *Histoire de la révolution culturelle prolétarienne en Chine*, 2 vols., Paris, 1971.

DEBORIN, A. M., *Vvedenie v filosofiyu dialekticheskogo materializma (Introduction to the Philosophy of Dialectical Materialism)*, Petrograd, 1916; 4th edn. 1925.

— — *Lenin kak myslitel (Lenin as Thinker)*, Moscow, 1924.

— — and N. BUCHARIN, *Kontroversen über dialektischen und mechanistischen Materialismus*, Einl. von Oskar Negt, Frankfurt, 1969.

DE GEORGE, R. T., *Patterns of Soviet Thought*, Ann Arbor, 1966.

— — *The New Marxism*, New York, 1968.

DESAN, W., *The Marxism of J.-P. Sartre*, New York, 1965.

DESANTI, J., *Phénoménologie et praxis*, Paris, 1963.

DEUTSCHER, I., *Stalin. A Political Biography*, rev. edn., Harmondsworth, 1966.

— — *Marxism in Our Time*, London, 1972.

— — *The Prophet Armed. Trotsky 1879–1921*, London, 1954.

— — *The Prophet Unarmed. Trotsky 1921–1929*, London, 1959.

— — *The Prophet Outcast. Trotsky 1929–1940*, London, 1963.

DJILAS, M., *The New Class. An Analysis of the Communist System*, New York, 1957.

— — *The Unperfect Society. Beyond the New Class*, New York, 1969.

DOBB, M., *Soviet Economic Development since 1917*, New York, 1966.

DRAPER, T., 'The Strange Case of the Comintern', *Survey*, summer 1972.

ERHLICH, A., *The Soviet Industrialization Debate 1924–1928*, Cambridge, Mass., 1960.

FEDOSEEV, P. N. *et al.* (eds.), *Filosofskie problemy sovremennogo estestvoznania* (*Philosophical Problems of Contemporary Natural Sciences*), Moscow, 1959.

FETSCHER, I., *Von Marx zur Sowjetideologie*, Frankfurt, 1957.

FIORI, G., *Vita di Antonio Gramsci*, Bari, 1965 (Eng. trans. New York, 1971).

FISCHER, E., *Kunst und Koexistenz. Beitrag zu einer modernen marxistischen Aesthetik*, Hamburg, 1970.

FISCHER, L., *The Life of Stalin*, London, 1953.

FISCHER, R., *Stalin and German Communism*, Oxford, 1948.

FITZPATRICK, S., *The Commissariat of Enlightenment. Soviet Organization of Education and the Arts under Lunacharsky*, Cambridge, 1970.

FLECHTHEIM, O. K., *Bolschewismus 1917–1967*, Vienna–Frankfurt–Zurich, 1967.

— — *Weltkommunismus im Wandel*, Cologne, 1965.

FOUGEYROLLAS, P., *Le Marxisme en question*, Paris, 1959.

FRANK, P., *La Quatrième Internationale*, Paris, 1969.

FROMM, E., *Fear of Freedom*, London, 1942.

— — *Man for Himself*, New York, 1947.

— — *The Sane Society*, New York, 1955.

— — *Marx's Concept of Man*, New York, 1961.

GABEL, J., *La Fausse Conscience*, Paris, 1962.

GARAUDY, R., *Le Communisme et la morale*, Paris, 1945.

— — *Une Littérature des fossoyeurs*, Paris, 1948.

— — *L'Église, le communisme et les chrétiens*, Paris, 1949.

— — *Perspectives de l'homme: Existentialisme, pensée catholique, marxisme*, Paris, 1961.

— — *Dieu est mort: Étude sur Hegel*, Paris, 1962.

GIUSTI, V., *Il pensiero di Trotzky*, Firenze, 1949.

GOLDMANN, L., *Le Dieu caché*, Paris, 1954.

— — *Recherches dialectiques*, Paris, 1959.

— — *Marxisme et sciences humaines*, Paris, 1970.

GRAHAM, L. R., *Science and Philosophy in the Soviet Union*, London, 1971 (copious bibliography).

GRAMSCI, A., *Il materialismo storico e la filosofia di Benedetto Croce*, Turin, 1948.

— — *Gli intellettuali e l'organizzazione della cultura*, Turin, 1949.

— — *Il Risorgimento*, Turin, 1949.

— — *Note sul Machavelli, sulla politica e sullo stato moderno*, Turin, 1949.

— — *Litteratura e vita nazionale*, Turin, 1950.
— — *Passato e presente*, Turin, 1951.
— — *The Modern Prince and Other Writings*, London, 1957.
— — *Scritti giovanili*, Turin, 1958.
— — *2000 pagine di Gramsci*, ed. G. Ferrate and N. Gallo, Milan, 1964.
GROSSMANN, H., *Das Akkumulations- und Zusammenbruchgesetz des kapitalistischen Systems*, Leipzig, 1929.

HABERMAS, J., *Theorie und Praxis*, Neuwied and Berlin, 1963.
— — *Erkenntnis und Interesse*, Frankfurt, 1968.
— — *Technik und Wissenschaft als 'Ideologie'*, Frankfurt, 1968.
— — (ed.), *Antworten auf Herbert Marcuse*, Frankfurt, 1968.
HALDANE, J. S. B., *The Marxist Philosophy and the Sciences*, New York, 1939.
HARRINGTON, M., *Socialism*, New York, 1971.
HAVEMANN, R., *Dialektik ohne Dogma?*, Hamburg, 1964.
— — *Antworten, Fragen, Antworten*, Munich, 1970.
— — *Rückantworten an die Hauptverwaltung 'Ewige Wahrheiten'*, Munich, 1971.
HELLER, A., 'Lukács Esthetics', *New Hungarian Quarterly*, no. 24, 1966.
— — 'Jenseits der Pflicht. Das Paradigmatische der Ethik der deutschen Klassik im Oeuvre von G. Lukács', *Revue Internationale de Philosophie*, no. 106, 1973.
HIRSZOWICZ, M., *Komunistyczny Lewiatan (The Communist Leviathan)*, Paris, 1973.
HOBSBAWM, E. J., *Revolutionaries: Contemporary Essays*, London, 1973.
HORKHEIMER, M., *Kritische Theorie*, ed. Alfred Schmidt, 2 vols., Frankfurt, 1968.
— — *Eclipse of Reason*, New York, 1947.
— — *Zur Kritik der instrumentellen Vernunft*, Frankfurt, 1967.
HUDSON, W., 'The Utopian Marxism of Ernst Bloch', thesis, Oxford, 1975.
HYPPOLITE, J., *Studies on Marx and Hegel*, New York, 1969.

ISTITUTO GIANGIACOMO FELTRINELLI, *Storia del Marxismo contemporaneo*, Milan, 1974.

JAFFE, P. J., 'The Varga Controversy and the American CP', *Survey*, summer 1972.
JAGER, A., *Reich ohne Gott. Zur Eschatologie Ernst Blochs*, Zurich, 1969.
JAY, M., *The Dialectical Imagination. A History of the Frankfurt School and the Institute of Social Research 1923–50*, London, 1953 (copious bibliography).

JOHNSON, C. (ed.), *Change in Communist System*, Stanford, 1970.

JORAVSKY, D., *Soviet Marxism and Natural Science 1917–1932*, London, 1932.

JORDAN, Z. A., *Philosophy and Ideology. The Development of Philosophy and Marxism–Leninism in Poland since the Second World War*, Dordrecht, 1963 (excellent bibliography).

KAMENEV, L., E. PREOBRAJENSKY, N. BOUKHARINE, and L. TROTSKY, *La Question paysanne en URSS de 1924 à 1929*, présentation par M. Fichelson et A. Derischenbourg, Paris, 1973.

KAREV, N., *Za materialisticheskuyu dialektiku* (*For the Materialist Dialectics*), Moscow, 1930.

KARSCH, S., *Théorie et politique: Louis Althusser*, Paris, 1974.

KEDROV, B. M., *O kolichestvennykh i kachestvennykh izmeneniakh v prirode* (*On the Qualitative and Quantitative Chances in Nature*) Moscow, 1946.

— — *O proizvedenii Engelsa 'Dialektika prirody'* (*On Engels's Work 'Dialectics of Nature'*), Moscow, 1954.

KHASKHACHIKH, F. I., *O poznavaemosti mira* (*On The Knowability of the World*), Moscow, 1952.

KLINE, G. L. (ed.), *Soviet Education*, New York, 1957.

KOŁAKOWSKI, L., *Marxism and Beyond*, 2nd edn. London, 1971.

— — *Der revolutionäre Geist*, Stuttgart, 1972.

— — *Marxismus—Utopie und Anti-Utopie*, Stuttgart, 1974.

— — and S. HAMPSHIRE (eds.), *The Socialist Idea: A Reappraisal*, London, 1974.

KOLBANOVSKY, V. N., *Dialektichesky materializm i sovremennoe estestvoznanie* (*Dialectical Materialism and Contemporary Natural Science*), Moscow, 1964.

KONSTANTINOV, F. V. (ed.), *Istorichesky materializm* (*Historical Materialism*), Moscow, 1951.

KOREY, W., *Zinoviev on the Problem of World Revolution 1919–1922*, Colorado Univ. Press, 1960.

KORSCH, K., *Marxismus und Philosophie*, hg. und eingel. von E. Gerlach, 5th edn., Vienna, 1972 (Eng. trans. London, 1970).

— — *Die materialistische Geschichtsauffassung und andere Schriften*, hg. E. Gerlach, Frankfurt, 1971.

— — *Three Essays on Marxism*, Introduction by P. Breines, New York and London, 1972.

KOSIK, K., *Die Dialektik des Konkreten*, Frankfurt, 1967.

KRASSO, N. (ed.), *Trotsky: The Great Debate Renewed*, St. Louis, 1972.

KRUCZEK, A., 'Sultan-Galijew po 50 latach' ('Sultan-Galiev after 50 years'), *Kultura*, no. 9, 1973.

KUSIN, V. V. (ed.), *The Czechoslovak Reform Movement 1968*, London, 1973.

LABEDZ, L. (ed.), *Revisionism. Essays on the History of Marxist Ideas*, London, 1961.

LACROIX, J., *Marxisme, existentialisme, personnalisme*, Paris, 1949.

LAZITCH, B., *Les Partis communistes d'Europe 1919–1955*, Paris, 1956.

— — (ed.), *The Comintern—Historical Highlights*, London, 1966.

— — *Lénine et la IIIème Internationale*, Neuchâtel, 1951.

LEFEBVRE, H., *A la lumière du materialisme dialectique*, i: *Logique formelle, logique dialectique*, Paris, 1947.

— — *La Pensée de Karl Marx*, Paris, 1947.

— — *Problèmes actuels du marxisme*, Paris, 1957.

— — *La Somme et le reste*, Paris, 1959.

— — *Critique de la vie quotidienne*, 2 vols., Paris, 1962.

LEMBERG, E., *Ideologie und Gesellschaft. Eine Theorie der ideologischen Systeme*, Stuttgart, 1971.

LEONHARD, W., *The Three Faces of Marxism*, New York, 1974.

LEONOV, A. M., *Ocherk dialekticheskogo materializma* (*An Outline of Dialectical Materialism*), Moscow, 1948.

LEWIN, M., *Russian Peasants and Soviet Power: A Study of Collectivisation*, Evanston, Ill., 1958.

— — *Political Undercurrents in Soviet Economic Debates: From Bukharin to the Modern Reformers*, Princeton, 1974.

LEWYTZKYJ, B., *Politische Opposition in der Sowjetunion 1960–1972*, Munich, 1972.

LICHTHEIM, G., *Marxism in Modern France*, New York and London, 1966.

— — 'From Marx to Hegel. Reflections on Georg Lukacs, T. W. Adorno and Herbert Marcuse', *TriQuarterly*, no. 12, 1968.

— — *Lukács*, London, 1970.

LIEBER, H. J., *Die Philosophie des Bolschewismus in den Grundzügen ihrer Entwicklung*, Frankfurt, 1957.

LIFTEN, R. J., *Revolutionary Immortality: Mao Tse-tung and the Chinese Cultural Revolution*, London, 1969.

LOBKOWICZ, N., *Das Widerspruchsprinzip in der neueren sowjetischen Philosophie*, Dordrecht, 1960.

— — *Marxismus–Leninismus in der CSR*, Dordrecht, 1962.

LOSKY, N. O., *Dialektichesky materializm v SSSR* (*Dialectical Materialism in the USSR*), Paris, 1934.

LOWENTHAL, R., *World Communism. The Disintegration of a Secular Faith*, New York, 1966.

LUDZ, P. C., *Ideologiebegriff und marxistische Theorie. Ansätze zu einer immanenten Kritik*, Opladen, 1976.

LUKÁCS, G., *Schriften zur Literatursoziologie*, ausgew. und eingel. von Peter Ludz, 2nd edn. Neuwied, 1963.

—— *The Meaning of Contemporary Realism*, London, 1963.

—— *The Historical Novel*, Boston, 1963.

—— *Werke*, 14 vols., Neuwied, 1964–73.

—— *Schriften zur Ideologie und Politik*, ausgew. und eingel. von Peter Ludz, Neuwied, 1967.

—— *Solzhenitsyn*, London, 1970.

—— *History and Class-Consciousness*, London, 1971.

LUNACHARSKY, A. V., *Sobranie sochinenii (Collected Works)*, 8 vols., Moscow, 1963–7.

MACINTYRE, A., *Marcuse*, London, 1970.

MCKENZIE, K. E., *Comintern and the World Revolution 1928–1943*, New York, 1964.

MAKSIMOV, A. A. *et al.* (eds.), *Filosofskie voprosy sovremennoy fiziki (Philosophical Problems of Contemporary Physics)*, Moscow, 1952.

MALLET, S., *La Nouvelle Classe ouvrière*, Paris, 1963.

MANDEL, E., *Traité d'économie marxiste*, 2 vols., Paris, 1962.

MAO TSE-TUNG, *An Anthology of his Writings*, ed. A. Fremantle, New York, 1962.

—— *Four Essays on Philosophy*, Peking, 1966.

—— *Mao Tse-tung Unrehearsed: Talks and Letters 1956–71*, ed. and introduced by Stuart Schram, London, 1974.

MARCUSE, H., *Reason and Revolution*, New York, 1941; 2nd edn. 1954.

—— *Eros and Civilization*, Boston, 1955.

—— *Soviet Marxism*, New York, 1958.

—— *One-dimensional Man*, Boston, 1964.

—— (with P. Wolff and Barrington Moore, Jr.), *A Critique of Pure Tolerance*, Boston, 1967.

—— *Negations*, Boston, 1968.

—— *Five Lectures*, Boston, 1970.

MARIE, J.-J., *Staline*, Paris, 1967.

MARKOVIC, M., *Dialektik der Praxis*, Frankfurt, 1971.

—— *From Affluence to Praxis*, Ann Arbor, 1974.

MARTINET, G., *Les Cinq Communismes*, Paris, 1971.

MASCOLO, D., *Le Communisme: Révolution et communication ou la dialectique des valeurs et des besoins*, Paris, 1953.

MATTEUCI, A. G., *Antonio Gramsci e la filosofia della prassi*, Milan, 1951.

MEDVEDEV, R., *Let History Judge: The Origins and Consequences of Stalinism*, New York, 1973.

MEHNERT, K., *Der Sowjetmensch*, Stuttgart, 1958.
— — *Moscow and the New Left*, Berkeley, 1975.
MERLEAU-PONTY, M., *Humanisme et terreur. Essai sur le problème communiste*, Paris, 1947 (Eng. trans. Boston, 1969).
— — *Les Aventures de la dialectique*, Paris, 1955 (Eng. trans. Evanston, 1973).
MESZAROS, I., *Lukács' Concept of Dialectic*, London, 1972.
MEYER, A. G., *The Soviet Political System. An Interpretation*, New York, 1965.
MICAUD, C. A., *Communism and the French Left*, London, 1963.
MILLS, C. W., *The Marxists*, London, 1969.
MITIN, M. and I. RAZUMOVSKY (eds.), *Dialektichesky i istorichesky materializm (Dialectical and Historial Materialism)*, 2 vols., Moscow, 1932–3.
MOLTMANN, J., *Theologie der Hoffnung*, Munich, 1964.
MORAWSKI, S., 'Mimesis—Lukács' Universal Principle', *Science and Society*, winter 1968.
MORIN, E., *Autocritique*, Paris, 1959.

NAVILLE, P., *Psychologie, marxisme, matérialisme*, Paris, 1948.
— — *L'Intellectuel communiste*, Paris, 1956.
NOLLAU, G., *International Communism and World Revolution*, New York, 1961.
NOVE, A., *An Economic History of the USSR*, London, 1969.
— — *Stalinism and After*, London, 1975.

OGLESBY, C. (ed.), *The New Left Reader*, New York, 1969.
O polozhenii v biologicheskoy nauke. Stenografichesky otchet sessii Vsesoyznoy Akademii selskokhozyaistvennykh nauk im. V. I. Lenina 31 yulya–7 augusta 1947 (On the Situation in Biological Science. Stenographic report of the session of the Soviet Academy of Agricultural Science). Moscow, 1958.

PAPAIOANNOU, K., *L'Idéologie froide. Essai sur le dépérissement du marxisme*, Paris, 1967.
PARKINSON, G. H. R. (ed.), *Georg Lukács: The Man, his Work and his Ideas*, New York, 1970.
PETROVIC, G., *Philosophie und Revolution*, Hamburg, 1971.
— — *Marx in the Mid-twentieth Century*, New York, 1967.
POLITZER, G., *Principes fondamentaux de philosophie*, Paris, 1954.
POLLOCK, F., *Die planwirtschaftlichen Versuche in der Sowjetunion 1917–1927*, Leipzig, 1929.
POSTER, M., *Existential Marxism in Postwar France*, Princeton, 1975 (good bibliography).

POZZOLINI, A., *Che cosa ha veramente detto Gramsci*, Rome, 1968 (Eng. trans. London, 1970).

PREOBRAZHENSKY, E., *The New Economics*, London, 1965.

RATSCHOW, C. H., *Atheismus im Christentum? Eine Auseinandersetzung mit Ernst Bloch*, Gütersloh, 1971.

ROBERTS, P. C., *Alienation and Soviet Economy*, Albuquerque, 1971.

ROSENBERG, A., *A History of Bolshevism from Marx to the First Five-Year Plan*, London, 1934.

ROTHBERG, A., *The Heirs of Stalin: Dissidence and the Soviet Regime*, Ithaca, 1972.

ROZENTAL, M. M., *Voprosy dialektiki v 'Kapitale' Marksa (Problems of Dialectics in Marx's 'Capital')*, Moscow, 1955.

— — and P. YUDIN, *Kratky filosofsky slovar (Short Philosophical Dictionary)*, Moscow, 1939; 5th edn. 1963.

RUBINSHTEIN, S. L., *O myshlenii i putyakh ego issledovania (On Thinking and the Ways of Investigating it)*, Moscow, 1958.

— — *Bytie i soznanie (Existence and Consciousness)*, Moscow, 1957.

SAKHAROV, A. D., *Thoughts on Progress, Peaceful Coexistence and Intellectual Freedom*, New York, 1968.

SARTRE, J.-P., *Critique de la raison dialectique*, Paris, 1960.

— — 'Problème du marxisme', *Situations VI*, Paris, 1964.

SCHAPIRO, L., *The Communist Party of the Soviet Union*, London, 1960.

SCHMIDT, A., *Der Begriff der Natur in der Lehre von Marx*, Frankfurt, 1962.

SCHRAM, S. R., *Mao Tse-tung*, Harmondsworth, 1967.

SCHWARTZ, B. I., *Chinese Communism and the Rise of Mao*, Cambridge, Mass., 1951.

SHACHTMAN, M., *The Bureaucratic Revolution: The Rise of the Stalinist State*, New York, 1962.

SINCLAIR, L., *Leon Trotsky: A Bibliography*, Hoover Institute Press, 1972.

SKILLING, H. G., *Czechoslovakia's Interrupted Revolution*, Princeton, 1976.

SKOLIMOWSKI, H., *Polski marksizm (Polish Marxism)*, London, 1969.

SNOW, E., *China's Long Revolution*, London, 1974.

SOUBISE, L., *Le Marxisme après Marx*, Paris, 1967.

SOUVARINE, B., *Staline. Aperçu historique du bolchevisme*, Paris, 1935.

STALIN, I. V., *Sochinenia (Works)*, vols. 1–13, Moscow, 1946 ff. (not completed); Eng. trans. 1954 ff.

— — *Marksizm i voprosy yazykoznania*, Moscow, 1950 (*Marxism and Problems of Linguistics*), Eng. trans. New York, 1951.

— — *Ekonomicheskie problemy sotsializma v SSSR (Economic Problems of Socialism in the USSR)*, Moscow, 1952.

STOJANOVIC, S., *Critique et avenir du socialisme*, Paris, 1971.

TAMBURANO, G., *Antonio Gramsci: La vita, il pensiero, l'azione*, Manduria, 1963.

TIGRID, P., *Amère révolution*, Paris, 1977.

TODD, E., *La Chute finale. Essai sur la décomposition de la sphère soviétique*, Paris, 1976.

TÖKES, R. (ed.), *Dissent in USSR: Politics, Ideology and People*, Baltimore and London, 1975.

TREADGOLD, D. W. (ed.), *The Development of the USSR*, Seattle, 1964.

TROTSKY, L., *The History of the Russian Revolution*, 3 vols., New York, 1932.

— — *In Defense of Marxism* (Against the Petty-bourgeois Opposition), New York, 1942.

— — *Their Morals and Ours*, New York, 1942.

— — *Writings, 1929–1940*, ed. G. Breitman, B. Scott, N. Allen, S. Lovell, New York, 1971 ff (contains the articles and speeches written in exile, no major works).

— — *The Revolution Betrayed*, New York, 1972.

TUCKER, R. C., *Stalin as Revolutionary, 1879–1929. A Study in History and Personality*, New York, 1973.

— — (ed.), *Stalinism. Essays in Historical Interpretation*, New York, 1977.

— — *The Soviet Political Mind*, rev. edn. New York, 1971.

ULAM, A. B., *Stalin: The Man and His Era*, New York, 1973.

UNSELD, S. (ed.), *Ernst Bloch zu Ehren*, Frankfurt, 1965.

VACCA, G., *Lukács o Korsch?*, Bari, 1969.

VRANICKI, P., *Mensch und Geschichte*, Frankfurt, 1968.

WEINBERG, E. A., *The Development of Sociology in the Soviet Union*, London and Boston, 1974.

WETTER, G. A., *Der dialektische Materialismus. Seine Geschichte und sein System in der Sowjetunion*, 5th edn. Freiburg, 1960; Eng. trans. New York, 1958 (copious bibliography).

— — *Soviet Ideology Today*, New York, 1966.

WILSON, D., (ed.), *Mao Tse-tung in the Scales of History*, Cambridge, 1977.

WOLFE, B. D., *An Ideology in Power*, London, 1969.

WOLFF, K. H. and BARRINGTON MOORE, JR. (eds.), *The Critical Spirit: Essays in Honor of Herbert Marcuse*, Boston, 1967.

ZHDANOV, A. A., *On Literature, Music and Philosophy*, London, 1950.

ZITTA, V., *Georg Lukacs' Marxism: Alienation, Dialectics, Revolution*, The Hague, 1964.

Index